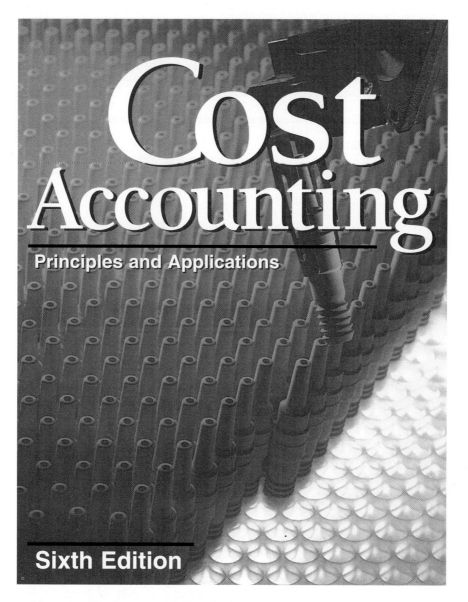

Cost Accounting
Principles and Applications

Sixth Edition

Horace R. Brock, PhD., C.P.A.
Distinguished Professor of Accounting Emeritus
College of Business Administration
University of North Texas
Denton, Texas

Linda A. Herrington, M.B.A., C.P.A.
Professor of Accounting
Community College of Allegheny County
Pittsburgh, Pennsylvania

 **Glencoe McGraw-Hill**

New York, New York   Columbus, Ohio   Woodland Hills, California   Peoria, Illinois

Photo Credits: Cover John Madere/The Stock Market; Part 1 Tom McHugh/Photo Researchers; Part 2 David A. Barnes/FPG; Part 3 Mark Joseph/Tony Stone Images.

Library Of Congress Cataloging-in-Publication Data

Brock, Horace R.
    Cost accounting: principles and applications/Horace R. Brock,
Linda A. Herrington.—6th ed.
      p. cm.
    Includes index.
    ISBN 0-02-803428-7
    1. Cost accounting. I. Herrington, Linda A. II. Title.
HF5686.C8B76 1998
657'.42—dc21

97-50268
CIP

Glencoe/McGraw-Hill
*A Division of The **McGraw·Hill** Companies*

Cost Accounting: Principles and Applications, Sixth Edition

Send all inquiries to:
Glencoe/McGraw-Hill
936 Eastwind Drive
Westerville, Ohio 43081

1 2 3 4 5 6 7 8 9 027 06 05 04 03 02 01 00 99 98

ISBN 0-02-803428-7

Contents

Cost and Analysis and Planning

Preface

A TOTAL INSTRUCTIONAL SYSTEM

A cost accounting instructional system should serve the career objectives of all students who require an understanding of accounting. Its components should satisfy the learning needs of students who are preparing for a wide range of business and professional pursuits. Moreover, instructors should be able to customize their cost accounting courses by matching instructional components with the abilities of individual students and with the levels of accomplishment that are required for different career objectives. A cost accounting instructional system should, therefore, contain performance objectives, reading resources, student application materials, comprehensive projects, student self-checks, and instructor's materials.

In preparing the sixth edition of *Cost Accounting: Principles and Applications,* the authors have created an instructional system that meets all of these criteria.

TEXTBOOK

This student resource text is designed for use in postsecondary cost accounting courses. The sixth edition provides a practical knowledge of cost accounting systems and procedures, and will prepare students for many of the career opportunities available in cost accounting. It will also enable them to understand and use cost accounting data in other types of business careers.

The book begins by giving students an overview of the nature and purpose of cost accounting. Then students learn the basic concept that cost flow matches work flow. After that, they are led throughout the major areas of cost accounting: job order cost accounting, process cost accounting, budgeting, standard costs, direct costing, and non-manufacturing costs.

Managerial considerations, especially as related to cost control, are indicated at every opportunity in Parts 1 and 2. Part 3 is devoted exclusively to cost accounting as a management tool. Also, the uses of computers in cost accounting are discussed throughout the text.

Each new segment of instruction is carefully explained and illustrated. Review questions and managerial discussion questions, along with application activities in the form of exercises, problems, and alternate problems, help students to integrate their learning while everything is fresh in their minds. Each chapter ends with a summary of the basic principles and procedures covered in the chapter.

SPECIAL NEW FEATURES OF THE TEXT

- Special vocabulary is emphasized by including a list of new terms on the chapter opener page, use of bold type where the term is defined, and a glossary of terms at the end of the textbook.
- Many new flow charts that capstone cost accounting concepts.
- Student Self-Review activities in each chapter include questions and answers to help students reinforce chapter concepts. These activities modularize each chapter into effective learning segments.
- Business Horizons bring real-world applications into the cost accounting course.
- A short, concise summary appears at the end of each chapter.
- A managerial emphasis in this edition is supported with Managerial Implications, Managerial Discussion Questions and Managerial Decision Cases.
- Each chapter contains Exercises and Problems A and B.
- Three Mini-Practice Sets support job order, process cost and budget, and standard cost accounting.
- Extensive reorganization of Capital Investment Decisions.
- Master problems have been added to emphasize key concepts in the Process Cost Accounting Section.

LEARNING AIDS

A number of learning aids are available for use with the sixth edition of *Cost Accounting: Principles and Applications*. These materials are designed to enhance the effectiveness of the course for the student.

Study Guide and Working Papers

The *Study Guide and Working Papers* manual permits each student to study at his or her own pace. Performance Objectives inform students what they should know and be able to do after completing each chapter. Reading assignments direct students to the appropriate section in the textbook reading assignment. (A self-check key is provided at the end of the *Study Guide and Working Papers.*) All the working papers needed to solve the problems or the alternate problems and the three Mini-Practice Sets in the textbook are provided in the *Study Guide and Working Papers.*

Spreadsheet Template Disk

The disks contain template files for Microsoft Excel, Version 5.0. The files are designed for students who have a basic understanding of spreadsheet construction and are able to build formulas for computations. The student disk contains one problem each for 24 of the chapters. The problems are identified in the textbook by a computer symbol. The instructor's disk contains the solutions for each problem.

Practice Sets

Two short practice sets are available for use with this textbook: *Robotor Manufacturing, Inc.—A Job Order Practice Set* and *Comptech Manufacturing Corporation—A Standard Costs and Budgeting Practice Set.* These practice sets will enhance the course by allowing students to apply their knowledge of cost accounting to realistic on-the-job situations.

TEACHING AIDS

A variety of helpful teaching aids are available for use with *Cost Accounting: Principles and Applications, Sixth Edition.*

Solutions Transparencies

An *Instructor Transparency Package* containing solutions for each of the regular problems in the text is available.

Course Management and Solutions Manual

This teaching aid contains chapter teaching pointers and answers to all the review questions, managerial discussion questions, exercises, and cases found in the textbook. A facsimile key for the problems and Mini-Practice Sets is included. Check figures are provided for the problems and Mini-Practice Sets, and these may be duplicated for the students.

This manual also contains teaching suggestions, model schedules, transparency masters of accounting forms, and instructions for using the spreadsheet template.

Glencoe Student Assessment System (GSAS)

The test generator component of the Glencoe Student Assessment system contains one test for each of the 27 chapters. The tests may be generated in printed or on-line form. The program allows the instructor to modify the tests.

ACKNOWLEDGMENTS

The authors would like to thank the following educators for their thoughtful reviews and careful checking, which provided a solid base for this revision:

Andy Anderson
Wichita State University
Wichita, KS

Michael J. Choma
Newport Business Institute
Lower Burrell, PA

Jarvis Dean
Chattanooga State Technical Community College
Chattanooga, TN

George L. DeOrio
Sawyer School
Pittsburgh, PA

Judith E. Kizzie
Clinton Community College
Clinton, IA

Tom Land
Bessemer State Technical College
Bessemer, AL

Leonard T. Long
Fisher College
Boston, MA

Jeffrey A. Trevas
Chaparral College
Tucson, AZ

Frank Walker
Lee University
Cleveland, TN

Horace R. Brock
Linda A. Herrington

26

P A R T
O N E

Job Order
Cost Accounting

Monitoring Costs

Every business is run to make a profit for its owners. *Profit* is the amount of income left after the various costs of operation have been deducted. In general, higher costs mean smaller profits, and lower costs mean larger profits. No wonder the successful manager keeps a close watch on costs; it is necessary for survival. Accounting provides the tools that management needs to monitor costs.

OBJECTIVES

1. Classify manufacturing costs as being direct materials, direct labor, or manufacturing overhead.
2. Explain the meaning of *prime costs* and *conversion costs.*
3. Explain the role of the three inventory accounts used in a manufacturing business.
4. State the purpose of cost accounting.
5. Determine the type of cost accounting system to be used in various types of manufacturing operations.
6. Prepare a statement of cost of goods manufactured.
7. Prepare an income statement for a manufacturing business.

NEW TERMS

Budget (p. 10)
Conversion cost (p. 8)
Cost accountant (p. 12)
Direct labor (p. 7)
Direct materials (Raw materials) (p. 5)
Finished Goods Inventory account (p. 9)
Indirect labor (p. 7)
Indirect materials (p. 7)
Job order cost system (p. 11)
Manufacturing (p. 4)
Manufacturing overhead (p. 7)
Prime cost (p. 8)
Process cost system (p. 11)
Raw Materials Inventory account (p. 8)
Statement of cost of goods manufactured (p. 3)
Work in Process Inventory account (p. 8)

MANAGEMENT'S NEED FOR COST INFORMATION

For cost information, management relies heavily on the income statement. The information in this statement helps the company operate on a sound basis. As a business enterprise becomes larger, managers are no longer able to depend solely upon personal observations and involvement in daily operations and must place greater reliance on production reports and cost statements. As a result, the financial statements for the firm become much more elaborate and the costs receive much more detailed treatment.

A wholesale or retail business acquires merchandise to resell to customers. Its income statement shows the details of the cost of goods sold. Computing the cost of goods sold for a merchandising business is a relatively straightforward process. The beginning inventory of merchandise is added to current net purchases to obtain the cost of goods available for sale; then the ending inventory of merchandise is subtracted to obtain the cost of goods sold.

Computing the cost of goods sold for a manufacturing business is much more complex and involves many more cost elements. For a manufacturer, the cost of goods sold in one period does not necessarily equal the cost of goods manufactured. For this reason, the Cost of Goods Sold section of the income statement of a manufacturing business shows the beginning inventory of goods finished in prior periods added to the cost of goods manufactured during the current period to obtain the cost of goods available for sale. The inventory of finished goods on hand at the end of the period is then subtracted from the total available to obtain the cost of goods sold.

A manufacturer must purchase raw materials and then incur many types of costs in converting the raw materials into products to be sold to customers. In a furniture factory, for example, raw materials in the form of lumber must be purchased and then processed by mechanical equipment to achieve the desired dimensions. Workers assemble the individual pieces and paint and finish them to specifications. Overhead expenses such as the consumption of supplies, utilities, building and equipment maintenance, and janitorial services are incurred as part of the process. With so many operations going on, management must maintain a close watch to see that work on the product is done carefully and efficiently and at a reasonable cost. Because of the many elements that comprise the cost of goods manufactured, the income statement of a manufacturing business is supported by a separate report known as a **statement of cost of goods manufactured.**

In a manufacturing business, the cost of goods manufactured appears in the Cost of Goods Sold section of the income statement. (The function of cost of goods manufactured is similar to that of merchandise purchases in a merchandising business.) The income statement for the year ended December 31, 19X9, for the Kramer Manufacturing Corporation is shown on page 4. The accompanying statement of cost of goods manufactured is shown on page 5.

KRAMER MANUFACTURING CORPORATION
Income Statement
Year Ended December 31, 19X9

Revenue			
Sales			$570,854
Cost of Goods Sold			
Finished Goods Inventory, Jan. 1		$ 38,700	
Add Cost of Goods Manufactured		**320,834**	
Total Goods Available for Sale		$359,534	
Less Finished Goods Inventory, Dec. 31		38,500	
Cost of Goods Sold			321,034
Gross Profit on Sales			$249,820
Operating Expenses			
Selling Expenses			
Sales Salaries Expense	$36,588		
Payroll Taxes Expense—Sales	2,345		
Delivery Expense	22,490		
Sales Supplies Expense	27,498		
Advertising Expense	16,710		
Total Selling Expenses		$105,631	
Administrative Expenses			
Officers' Salaries Expense	$65,000		
Office Salaries Expense	18,366		
Payroll Taxes Expense—Administrative	3,784		
Office Supplies Expense	6,412		
Bad Debts Expense	1,083		
Total Administrative Expenses		94,645	
Total Operating Expenses			200,276
Net Income From Operations			$ 49,544
Add Other Income			
Interest Earned			1,300
			$ 50,844
Less Other Expense			
Amortization of Organization Costs			500
Net Income Before Income Taxes			$ 50,344
Provision for Income Taxes			9,470
Net Income After Income Taxes			$ 40,874

MANUFACTURING COSTS CLASSIFIED

Manufacturing is the process of converting materials into finished goods by using labor and incurring other costs, generally called *manufacturing overhead*. Overhead costs include utilities, supplies, taxes, insurance, and depreciation. One of the functions of a cost accounting system is to classify and record all costs according to category. The three major manufacturing cost classifications—*direct materials, direct labor,* and *manufacturing overhead*—are the basis for all cost accounting procedures. (See the chart of typical costs on page 6.)

```
┌─────────────────────────────────────────────────────────────────────┐
│                 KRAMER MANUFACTURING CORPORATION                      │
│                 Statement of Cost of Goods Manufactured               │
│                    Year Ended December 31, 19X9                       │
│  Direct Materials                                                     │
│     Raw Materials Inventory, Jan. 1          $ 36,000                 │
│     Materials Purchases                       155,068                 │
│     Total Materials Available                 191,068                 │
│     Less Raw Materials Inventory, Dec. 31      35,000                 │
│  Direct Materials Used                                      $156,068  │
│  Direct Labor                                                 90,450  │
│  Manufacturing Overhead                                               │
│     Indirect Materials and Supplies          $  7,652                 │
│     Indirect Labor                             19,861                 │
│     Payroll Taxes Expense—Factory               7,522                 │
│     Depreciation—Factory Building               2,300                 │
│     Depreciation—Equipment                      1,500                 │
│     Repairs and Maintenance                    11,855                 │
│     Utilities                                   9,745                 │
│     Insurance                                   4,530                 │
│     Property Taxes—Factory Building             8,218                 │
│        Total Manufacturing Overhead                           73,183  │
│  Total Current Manufacturing Costs                          $319,701  │
│  Add Work in Process Inventory, Jan. 1                        15,489  │
│                                                             $335,190  │
│  Less Work in Process Inventory, Dec. 31                      14,356  │
│  Cost of Goods Manufactured                                 $320,834  │
└─────────────────────────────────────────────────────────────────────┘
```

Direct Materials

Direct materials, also called *raw materials,* are those materials used in the manufacturing process that become a significant part of the finished goods. For example, the metal frame and the lumber used in manufacturing a chair and the cloth and buttons used in manufacturing clothing are direct materials.

It is important to note that what is raw material to one manufacturer is considered finished goods by the supplier of those materials. For example, to the foundry that makes metal chair frames, these frames are finished goods. They are raw materials, however, to the manufacturer who purchases the frames to make the chairs.

The statement of cost of goods manufactured for the Kramer Manufacturing Corporation (above) shows that on January 1, 19X9, the corporation had an inventory of raw materials on hand of $36,000. During the year, purchases of raw materials amounted to $156,068. The addition of the purchases amount to the beginning inventory amount makes the total for materials available $191,068. On December 31, 19X9, the raw materials inventory was $35,000. This amount is subtracted from the amount of total materials available to get the cost of raw materials used. Therefore, the cost of raw materials used

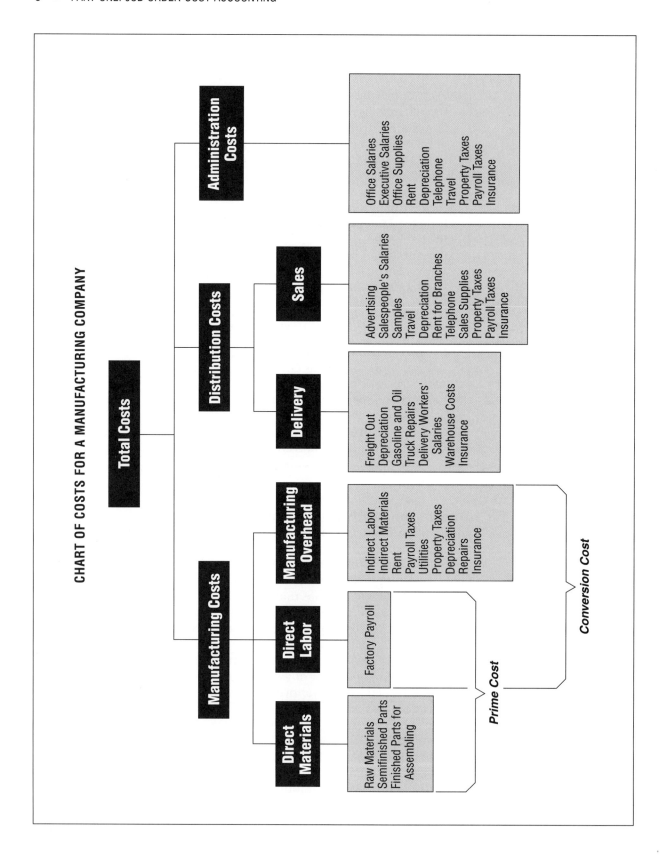

CHART OF COSTS FOR A MANUFACTURING COMPANY

Total Costs

Manufacturing Costs

Direct Materials

Raw Materials
Semifinished Parts
Finished Parts for Assembling

Direct Labor

Factory Payroll

Manufacturing Overhead

Indirect Labor
Indirect Materials
Rent
Payroll Taxes
Utilities
Property Taxes
Depreciation
Repairs
Insurance

Prime Cost

Conversion Cost

Distribution Costs

Delivery

Freight Out
Depreciation
Gasoline and Oil
Truck Repairs
Delivery Workers' Salaries
Warehouse Costs
Insurance

Sales

Advertising
Salespeople's Salaries
Samples
Travel
Depreciation
Rent for Branches
Telephone
Sales Supplies
Property Taxes
Payroll Taxes
Insurance

Administration Costs

Office Salaries
Executive Salaries
Office Supplies
Rent
Depreciation
Telephone
Travel
Property Taxes
Payroll Taxes
Insurance

by the Kramer Manufacturing Corporation for the year ended December 31, 19X9, is $156,068.

Direct Labor

The personnel who work directly with the raw materials in converting them to finished goods represent **direct labor.** In a factory that makes chairs, for example, the wages of workers who cut and sand lumber and of those who assemble the parts into finished chairs are considered direct labor costs. In the manufacturing of clothing, the earnings of cutters and sewing machine operators are direct labor costs. The statement of cost of goods manufactured for the Kramer Manufacturing Corporation shows a total direct labor cost of $90,450 for 19X9.

Manufacturing Overhead

All costs incurred in the factory that cannot be considered direct materials or direct labor are classified as **manufacturing overhead** (sometimes called *factory overhead, manufacturing expenses,* or *factory burden*). Manufacturing overhead is usually subdivided into three categories: indirect materials, indirect labor, and other manufacturing overhead. The manufacturing overhead items of the Kramer Manufacturing Corporation for 19X9, totaling $73,183, are shown in the statement of cost of goods manufactured on page 5.

Indirect Materials. Materials that are used in small amounts in the manufacturing process or that cannot easily be allocated to specific products are called **indirect materials.** The glue used in manufacturing armchairs and the thread used in sewing a suit are indirect materials. This is because only small amounts of glue and thread are used, even though they clearly become part of the finished goods. Records must be kept to show the exact amount of materials used in completing each specific job or group of products. Keeping detailed records for minor materials, however, would require a great deal more time and cost than the results would justify. It is more practical to group all such material together without charging them to specific products.

Another type of indirect material, sometimes called *factory supplies* or *operating supplies,* consists of items that are used in the manufacturing process but do not become a part of the finished goods. Examples of these are cleaning supplies used in the factory, oil used for lubricating the factory machinery, and minor repair parts. The Kramer Manufacturing Corporation shows a total of $7,652 for indirect materials for 19X9.

Indirect Labor. The wages of factory personnel who do not work directly on raw materials are called **indirect labor.** For example, the wages and salaries of such factory workers as the storeroom clerks, janitors, superintendent, maintenance crew, and factory supervisors are indirect labor costs. The Kramer Manufacturing Corporation's indirect labor cost for 19X9 is $19,861.

Other Manufacturing Overhead. Other manufacturing overhead includes such costs as payroll taxes on factory wages; rent, depreciation, taxes, and insurance on factory buildings and machinery; heat, light, and power; repairs and maintenance of machinery and equipment; and amortization of patents. Many of these relate to the physical plant (building, machinery, and equipment). Other manufacturing overhead is a growing part of the total cost of production because of the increasing use of expensive labor-saving equipment in many manufacturing processes. Sophisticated pieces of equipment such as computers and robots result in more costly maintenance, greater insurance and depreciation charges, and increased utility costs.

Prime and Conversion Costs

At this point you should be able to work Exercises 1–1 to 1–5 and Problems 1–1A to 1–3B.

In cost accounting, the term for the sum of direct materials and direct labor is **prime cost.** Prime cost reflects the primary sources of costs for units in production. The Kramer Manufacturing Corporation's prime cost for 19X9 is $246,518 ($156,068 + $90,450). The total of direct labor and manufacturing overhead is often called the **conversion cost.** Conversion cost indicates the costs required to convert the raw materials into finished products. The Kramer Manufacturing Corporation's conversion cost for 19X9 is $163,633 ($90,450 + $73,183). (See the chart of costs on page 5.)

INVENTORIES FOR A MANUFACTURING CONCERN

A manufacturing business has three distinct inventory accounts: Raw Materials Inventory, Work In Process Inventory, and Finished Goods Inventory. At the end of the fiscal period, the balance of each of the three accounts will appear in the Current Assets section of the balance sheet.

Raw Materials Inventory

The **Raw Materials Inventory account** reflects the cost of raw materials and factory supplies that will be used in the manufacturing process. Once direct materials are removed from the storeroom for use in the manufacturing process, their costs are no longer part of the raw materials inventory. Instead, these costs are then classified as part of work in process. In the same way, the costs of factory supplies that have been removed from the storeroom and applied in the manufacturing process are charged to manufacturing overhead. Some manufacturing firms may use a separate Supplies Inventory account if the quantities or value of supplies normally kept on hand are significant enough to justify the additional account.

Work in Process Inventory

The **Work in Process Inventory account** reflects the cost of raw materials, direct labor, and manufacturing overhead of goods on which manufacturing has begun but has not been completed at the end of the fiscal period. The statement of cost of goods manufactured for the Kramer Manufacturing Corporation shows that on January 1, 19X9, the cost of work in process was $15,489. This figure is added to the total manufacturing cost incurred in the current year, $319,701, to determine the total costs to be accounted for, $335,190. Finally, the ending work in process inventory of $14,356 is subtracted to arrive at the cost of goods manufactured of $320,834.

Finished Goods Inventory

The **Finished Goods Inventory account** reflects the costs of goods that have been completed and are ready for sale. This account corresponds to the Merchandise Inventory account of a merchandising business. Any changes in the Finished Goods Inventory account are reflected in the Cost of Goods Sold section of the income statement. As you can see in the Kramer Manufacturing Corporation's income statement for 19X9, shown on page 4, the balance of the Finished Goods Inventory account at the beginning of the fiscal period is added to the cost of goods manufactured to determine total cost of goods available for sale. The balance in the Finished Goods Inventory account on December 31 represents completed goods on hand at the end of the fiscal period. It is subtracted from the total goods available for sale to obtain the cost of goods sold. (See page 4.)

THE PURPOSE OF COST ACCOUNTING

Although the income statement and the statement of cost of goods manufactured are valuable in guiding business decisions, they do not supply enough information to achieve the greatest efficiency and profit under competitive conditions. The figures represent *total* costs, which are too broad to permit more than general conclusions. Alert management, interested in showing a larger profit, will ask itself vital questions that these totals cannot answer. Some of these questions might be as follows:

- Is our plant operating efficiently and economically?
- Which of our costs are out of line, and how can they be controlled?
- Are our sales prices set realistically in relation to costs?
- What is the unit cost of each type of product being manufactured?

The answers to such questions require detailed data based on computations that will pinpoint unit costs of products and processes. This is one of the major functions of cost accounting. Through modern systems of cost accounting, it is possible to know how much it costs to construct, manufacture, or sell goods, or to render various services. The ability to make specific and detailed identification and measurement of cost elements permits management to *reach decisions* and to *evaluate results* with greater intelligence.

Estimating and Bidding

In certain trades, a knowledge of the costs of doing business is needed to estimate a job or to bid for other jobs or contracts. The order generally goes to the lowest bidder. Under competitive pressure, the decisive difference in a bid may be as little as a fraction of a cent per unit. Attempting to bid without detailed cost information can mean losing the job, or it can mean winning the job but having to perform the work at a loss. Either result is undesirable.

Planning, Budgets, and Control

The cost accounting system also provides vital information needed to plan *future operations.* Cost data help resolve questions relating to proposed projects or policies, such as the following:

- Should we build a new plant or modernize the old one?
- How far can we go in lowering prices to increase our volume of sales?
- What will be the effect on costs of automating part of our factory operations?

Cost accounting is also used in preparing a company's budget. A **budget** is the overall financial plan for future activities. It is even possible to compute flexible budgets that will tell what the costs for any volume of output should be. Then actual costs can be compared with a realistic budgeted amount.

Standard cost procedures are helpful in evaluating the results of operations. Unit costs are projected on the basis of standard conditions. These standards are often based on the past experience of the firm or on statistics from the industry. Then, as actual costs are incurred, they are compared with these standard costs. The differences between the two sets of cost figures can be noted and investigated while there is still time to take remedial action.

From this brief discussion, it is obvious that cost accounting is one of the most valuable management tools to *control operations.* Knowledge of the costs of making and selling the firm's products or services helps management weigh the various courses of action before any final commitments are made. Once operations begin, cost accounting reveals how efficiently the work is being done, where the strong and weak spots are, and how to improve performance.

The cost of making a product is one of the most critical factors in a firm's ability to meet the competition. With cost information to support the decisions, management can issue directives, perform follow-up activities, and obtain the operating results that ensure prosperity and growth for the enterprise.

TYPES OF COST SYSTEMS

One type of accounting system is needed to accumulate costs of goods manufactured when products are produced in jobs or lots of varying quantities and types. A different type of system is used when there is a continuous flow of goods of identical or similar characteristics throughout the manufacturing process. The job order cost system has been developed for the first type of operation, and the process cost system for the second.

Job Order Cost System

The **job order cost system** accumulates costs applicable to each specified job order or lot of similar goods manufactured on a specific order for stock or for a customer. When production on a job begins, the job is assigned a number, and a form called a *job cost sheet* is set up. As direct materials are used, their costs are entered on the job cost sheet. Similarly, direct labor costs incurred on a job are recorded periodically. When the job is completed (or periodically as the job is worked on), manufacturing overhead costs applicable to the job are estimated and entered on the job cost sheet. The job cost sheet, when complete, shows the total cost of the completed job. The cost per unit may then be obtained by dividing the total cost of the job by the number of units completed.

The job order cost system is often used by manufacturers, such as a furniture manufacturer, who produce a variety of products, because such producers need to keep track of each specific order to ensure correct allocation of costs. Also, the actual costs shown on the job cost sheets may be compared with the estimated costs on which the sales prices were based. Any discrepancies or significant variations between estimated costs and actual costs to manufacture are analyzed, and necessary corrective actions are taken to ensure that adequate profit margins are maintained.

Process Cost System

The **process cost system** accumulates costs without attempting to allocate them during the accounting period to specific units of goods being manufactured. At the end of the fiscal period, the average cost per unit is determined by dividing the total number of units produced into the total cost accumulated. Because of this technique, process costing is often referred to as *average costing.* If the process cost system is used, the goods manufactured must be similar in nature so that an average cost will be meaningful. The process cost system is commonly used in such manufacturing operations as cement plants and flour mills, in which the production process is standardized and continuous and the product remains essentially the same from day to day.

In many types of businesses that use process costing, manufacturing consists of a progressive series of distinct operations or processes. Usually each process is carried out in a different department. A unit cost may be computed for each process or department. This departmental unit cost may be a useful tool in measuring and controlling efficiency. The total cost of production is determined by adding up the departmental costs.

Dual Systems

Some manufacturers use both the job order cost system and the process cost system. A dual system is often used when a company makes standard parts or subassemblies continuously and then incorporates them into finished goods built to customer specifications.

A successful manufacturing operation requires more than just a good cost accounting system. It requires ideas and innovative thinking. Consider the story of how a new form of cat litter came about and saved a Wyoming town in the process.

A secretary to a management consultant in Texas suggested to her boss that he put his efforts into developing a better cat litter than what was currently on the market. His company came up with the idea of manufacturing a litter that clumped when wet, making it easier to remove from the cat litter box.

A chemist in Chicago saw the product and thought it was a good idea but contained the wrong raw ingredient. He felt that bentonite, a porous clay that swells and clumps when wet, would be ideal for cat litter. The chemist worked on the best way to make bentonite work in the litter box. He patented a process which makes a litter that is easy on cats' paws and clumps well.

A small mining town in Wyoming that mined sodium bentonite was having hard times because the market for this clay had dried up. When sodium bentonite was needed to manufacture this new cat litter, the town began mining the clay again. The Wyoming town is now booming and cat owners can buy cat litter of the clumping variety throughout the country.

As the result of a secretary's suggestion, mines and manufacturing plants have reopened, new jobs have been created, and consumers have a new product to make their lives easier.

The cost of the parts is accumulated and determined under a process cost system, and the cost of each customer's order for finished goods is computed under a job order cost system.

THE ROLE OF THE COST ACCOUNTANT

A **cost accountant** is a specialist who analyzes the cost recording and reporting needs of a business and devises a system of records and procedures that will meet these needs. This system will include the necessary forms and other records, recordkeeping procedures, controls, summarizing techniques, and formal reporting methods. In addition, the cost accountant provides up-to-date analyses of the operations of the business to help management make rational and meaningful decisions.

A processor of perishable goods and an automobile manufacturer have different needs. Likewise, a large company with several departments manufacturing many products has concerns that are different from those of a small plant making one product. A cost accountant must be able to adapt systems and procedures in order to meet these varying needs.

SELF-REVIEW

1. Describe how an income statement for a merchandising business differs from an income statement for a manufacturing business.
2. Explain how cost of goods manufactured is calculated.
3. What costs are involved in the manufacture of a product? How are these costs classified?
4. What is the difference in operations between a company that uses a job order cost system and a company that uses a process cost system?

Answers to Self-Review

1. The income statements for a merchandising business and a manufacturing business are different in the Cost of Goods Sold section. A merchandising business shows merchandise inventory (both beginning and ending) in the Cost of Goods Sold section, whereas a manufacturing business shows finished goods inventory (beginning and ending). In addition, a merchandising business shows purchases, whereas the manufacturing business shows cost of goods manufactured.
2. Cost of goods manufactured is computed by first adding together the three major cost categories—direct materials, direct labor, and manufacturing overhead. This amount equals the total manufacturing cost. The beginning work in process inventory is then added to total manufacturing cost, and the ending work in process inventory is subtracted to obtain cost of goods manufactured.
3. The costs involved in manufacturing a product include materials, labor, and other costs, called *manufacturing overhead.* Materials and labor that go directly into the product are classified as direct materials and direct labor. All other costs, including indirect materials and indirect labor, are classified as manufacturing overhead.
4. A job order cost system is used when a company manufactures a product to customers' individual specifications. A process cost system is used when all the products manufactured are the same and the production process is standardized and continuous.

PRINCIPLES AND PROCEDURES SUMMARY

- Management must watch costs closely in order to operate efficiently and achieve maximum profits.
- Cost information permits more effective control of operations through the determination of unit costs. A statement of cost of goods manufactured is prepared to further explain the cost of goods sold and support the income statement. Specific, up-to-date, and pertinent cost figures also help management in estimating, planning, budgeting, and evaluating.
- Manufacturing costs are classified under three major headings: direct materials, direct labor, and manufacturing overhead.

■ Manufacturing overhead includes all costs that cannot be easily and conveniently charged to specific products. Manufacturing overhead is subclassified into indirect materials, indirect labor, and other manufacturing overhead.

■ There are two major systems for accumulating costs. The job order cost system is used when goods are produced for a specific order or lot. The process cost system is used when similar goods are produced in a continuous flow. Some firms may use both systems.

■ The cost accountant is an accounting specialist who studies a firm's needs for cost data and devises a cost system that gives management maximum assistance in planning, controlling, and directing operations.

MANAGERIAL IMPLICATIONS

■ Management depends on information provided in the Statement of Cost of Goods Manufactured and on calculations of the unit cost of products to control costs and measure efficiency of operations.

■ To help measure and control costs, manufacturing costs are classified into three categories: direct materials, direct labor, and manufacturing overhead. Costs are accumulated under these classifications and are carefully studied and analyzed as part of the cost control process.

■ The cost accounting system provides information that can be used not only for controlling costs but for planning and budgeting.

■ The cost accountant must be able to choose a cost accounting system that is best adapted to the production process of the business. There are two major cost accumulation systems: job order cost accounting and process cost accounting.

■ The job order system is used in manufacturing situations in which products are manufactured to fill specific orders—for example, an order to manufacture 50 desks to meet unique specifications. Management uses the job order cost system because it provides information about the cost of these 50 specific desks.

■ Process cost accounting is used when production is on a continuous process basis and the products manufactured during a period are identical or almost identical. In this case, the most useful information to management is the average cost of all the units produced during the period. For example, the manager of a manufacturing process turning out plastic sheeting is interested in the cost per square yard of the sheeting.

REVIEW QUESTIONS

1. What are the three major classifications of manufacturing costs?
2. Define the following:
    a. Direct materials
    b. Direct labor
    c. Manufacturing overhead

3. How do prime costs differ from conversion costs?
4. List four examples of manufacturing overhead costs.
5. What is the difference between direct labor and indirect labor? Give an example of each.
6. What is the difference between direct materials and indirect materials? Give an example of each.
7. A retailing business has one inventory account, Merchandise Inventory, listed on its balance sheet. What inventory account(s) appear on the balance sheet of a manufacturing concern?
8. For each of the inventory items listed below, identify on which of the following statement(s) the item will appear: statement of cost of goods manufactured, income statement, or balance sheet.
    a. Raw Materials, beginning inventory balance
    b. Raw Materials, ending inventory balance
    c. Work in Process, beginning inventory balance
    d. Work in Process, ending inventory balance
    e. Finished Goods, beginning inventory balance
    f. Finished Goods, ending inventory balance
9. How does the income statement for a retailing business differ from the income statement for a manufacturing business?
10. In what type of manufacturing operation would the job cost system be used? Where would the process cost system be used?
11. Describe a budget. What is the purpose of preparing a budget?

MANAGERIAL DISCUSSION QUESTIONS

1. How does a cost accounting system help management? Does the statement of cost of goods manufactured provide enough data for decision making? Explain.
2. How are cost accounting records used by management in making contract bids or in estimating the cost of a job?
3. What type of cost systems would you recommend to the management of each of the following types of manufacturing concerns. Why?
    a. Manufacturer of custom-designed mobile homes
    b. Tailor
    c. Company that processes frozen orange juice
    d. Manufacturer of automobiles
    e. Manufacturer of paint
4. What types of manufacturing overhead costs do you think management would closely watch in attempting to control costs? Why?
5. What is the purpose of determining and using standard costs?
6. Explain why an item that is classified as direct materials by one company may be classified as indirect materials by another. Give an example.
7. Classify the following costs of the Best Chocolate Chip Cookie Company as direct materials, direct labor, overhead, selling expense, or administrative expense.
    a. Repair of ovens
    b. Salary of president's secretary

    c. Chocolate chips
    d. Freight charges to ship cookies to customers
    e. Flour
    f. Salaries of employees who box cookies
    g. Cookie boxes
8. What type of manufacturing overhead would you expect to find in the following businesses?
    a. Automobile factory
    b. Electronics factory
    c. Clothing manufacturer
9. Why might a company decide to have a separate inventory account for factory supplies?

EXERCISES

EXERCISE 1–1 **Calculate manufacturing costs and cost of goods manufactured. (Obj. 1).** The costs for Simpson, Inc. for the year ended June 30, 19X9, are given below.

Direct Materials	$60,380
Direct Labor	88,835
Manufacturing Overhead	36,320
Work in Process Inventory, July 1, 19X8	38,840
Work in Process Inventory, June 30, 19X9	34,510

a. What are the manufacturing costs for the year?
b. What is the cost of goods manufactured for the year?

EXERCISE 1–2 **Calculate prime costs and conversion costs. (Obj. 2).** The following costs were incurred by Prime Radio Manufacturers:

Direct Materials	$250,280
Direct Labor	391,320
Manufacturing Overhead	222,492

a. What were the prime costs for the company?
b. What were the conversion costs?

EXERCISE 1–3 **Calculate costs of goods sold and gross profit. (Obj. 7).** The following amounts relate to the Micro-Disk Corporation:

Finished Goods Inventory, April 1, 19X9	$ 88,840
Finished Goods Inventory, April 30, 19X9	82,129
Cost of Goods Manufactured	113,705
Net Sales	157,943

a. Calculate the cost of goods sold.
b. Calculate the gross profit on sales.

EXERCISE 1–4 **Calculate cost of goods manufactured, cost of goods sold, and gross profit. (Objs. 6, 7).** The New England Plumbing Company manufactures water pumps and filters and uses a job cost order accounting system. Cost data for 19X9 are given below.

Raw Materials, January 1, 19X9	$ 448,543
Raw Materials, December 31, 19X9	461,417
Work in Process, January 1, 19X9	383,463
Work in Process, December 31, 19X9	498,182
Finished Goods, January 1, 19X9	321,932
Finished Goods, December 31, 19X9	301,647
Raw Materials Purchases	731,917
Direct Labor	1,182,680
Manufacturing Overhead	814,530
Net Sales	4,708,917

a. Calculate cost of goods manufactured.
b. Calculate cost of goods sold.
c. Calculate gross profit on sales.

EXERCISE 1–5 **Calculate direct materials cost.   (Obj. 1).**   The Auto Products Company maintains a raw materials inventory account for all materials used in its factory operations. Purchases of both direct and indirect materials are debited to this account. The balance on January 1, 19X9, for the raw materials account was $450,837. Purchases of raw materials for the year were $962,091. The ending inventory on December 31, 19X9, was $438,946. Calculate the following:

a. What was the total of the raw materials available for use?
b. What was the cost of raw materials used in factory operations?
c. Materials requisitions show that of the total raw materials used during the year, indirect materials amounted to $73,170. What was the amount of direct materials used during the year?

PROBLEMS

PROBLEM 1–1A **Prepare a statement of cost of goods manufactured. (Obj. 6).** The data for the year ended June 30, 19X9, that follow relate to the Gomez Manufacturing Corporation.

Raw Materials, July 1, 19X8	$ 70,000
Raw Materials, June 30, 19X9	62,000
Work in Process Inventory, July 1, 19X8	34,600
Work in Process Inventory, June 30, 19X9	36,000
Materials Purchases	213,600
Direct Labor	128,200
Indirect Labor	21,080
Payroll Taxes Expense—Factory	12,800
Utilities	26,400
Repairs and Maintenance	6,200
Indirect Materials and Supplies	25,480
Depreciation—Factory Equipment	7,100
Insurance	4,460
Rent—Factory Building	67,000

INSTRUCTIONS Prepare the statement of cost of goods manufactured for the year ended June 30, 19X9.

PROBLEM 1–2A

Prepare a statement of cost of goods manufactured and an income statement. (Objs. 6, 7). The following data pertain to the operations of the Carlson Company, a manufacturer of porch furniture:

	Oct. 1, 19X8	Sept. 30, 19X9
Inventories:		
Finished Goods	$ 25,000	$ 30,000
Raw Materials	152,000	141,000
Work in Process	123,000	127,000
Raw Material Purchases		287,000
Direct Labor		241,000
Indirect Materials and Supplies		52,000
Indirect Labor		87,000
Other Manufacturing Overhead		162,000
Sales		1,250,000
Selling Expenses		270,000
Administrative Expenses		92,000

INSTRUCTIONS

1. Prepare a statement of cost of goods manufactured for the year ended September 30, 19X9.
2. Prepare an income statement.

PROBLEM 1–3A

Prepare a statement of cost of goods manufactured and an income statement. (Objs. 6, 7). The following data pertain to Sam's Chips, Inc.:

	Jan. 1, 19X9	Dec. 31, 19X9
Inventories:		
Finished Goods	$38,400	$ 43,900
Raw Materials	23,825	24,100
Work in Process	16,460	18,280
Direct Labor		73,240
Freight In		14,800
Administrative Expenses		56,890
Indirect Materials and Supplies		14,640
Insurance Expense—Factory		12,760
Depreciation—Plant and Equipment		19,500
Raw Material Purchases		171,820
Payroll Taxes Expense—Factory		18,700
Utilities—Factory		21,600
Property Taxes—Factory		22,080
Repairs and Maintenance—Factory		14,720
Patent Amortization		14,000
Sales		683,450
Selling Expenses		89,340
Waste Removal		5,800

INSTRUCTIONS

1. Prepare a statement of cost of goods manufactured for the year ended December 31, 19X9. NOTE: Freight In should be added to Raw Materials Purchases to determine the Delivered Cost of Raw Materials Purchases.
2. Prepare an income statement.

ALTERNATE PROBLEMS

PROBLEM 1–1B **Prepare a statement of cost of goods manufactured. (Obj. 6).** The data for the year ended July 31, 19X9, that follow relate to the Atlas Phone Corporation.

Raw Materials, August 1, 19X8	$ 48,000
Raw Materials, July 31, 19X9	46,200
Work in Process Inventory, August 1, 19X8	39,600
Work in Process Inventory, July 31, 19X9	33,600
Materials Purchases	180,600
Direct Labor	577,200
Indirect Labor	27,080
Payroll Taxes Expense—Factory	19,800
Utilities	18,400
Repairs and Maintenance	13,200
Indirect Materials and Supplies	26,480
Depreciation—Factory Equipment	9,100
Insurance	12,460
Rent—Factory Building	37,000

INSTRUCTIONS Prepare the statement of cost of goods manufactured for the year ended July 31, 19X9.

PROBLEM 1–2B **Prepare a statement of cost of goods manufactured and an income statement. (Objs. 6, 7).** The following data pertain to the operations of the Kissel Company, a manufacturer of skateboards:

	July 1, 19X8	June 30, 19X9
Inventories:		
Finished Goods	$210,000	$ 290,000
Raw Materials	345,000	358,000
Work in Process	327,000	318,000
Raw Material Purchases		778,000
Direct Labor		512,000
Indirect Materials and Supplies		88,000
Indirect Labor		144,000
Other Manufacturing Overhead		549,000
Sales		2,500,000
Selling Expenses		350,000
Administrative Expenses		90,000

INSTRUCTIONS 1. Prepare a statement of cost of goods manufactured for the year ended June 30, 19X9.
2. Prepare an income statement.

PROBLEM 1–3B **Prepare a statement of cost of goods manufactured and an income statement. (Objs. 6, 7).** The following data pertain to Levine Manufacturing Company:

	April 1, 19X8	**March 31, 19X9**
Inventories:		
Finished Goods	$38,400	$ 63,900
Raw Materials	23,825	45,100
Work in Process	16,460	27,280
Direct Labor		182,240
Freight In		34,800
Administrative Expenses		54,890
Indirect Materials and Supplies		34,640
Insurance Expense—Factory		32,760
Depreciation—Plant and Equipment		39,500
Raw Materials Purchases		191,820
Payroll Taxes Expense—Factory		38,700
Utilities—Factory		41,600
Property Taxes—Factory		42,080
Repairs and Maintenance—Factory		24,720
Patent Amortization		34,000
Sales		803,450
Selling Expenses		89,340
Waste Removal		9,800

INSTRUCTIONS

1. Prepare a statement of cost of goods manufactured for the year ended March 31, 19X9. NOTE: Freight In should be added to Raw Materials Purchases to determine the Delivered Cost of Raw Materials Purchases.
2. Prepare an income statement.

MANAGERIAL DECISION CASE

DeNardo Hat Company sells baseball caps decorated with a wide variety of sports and activity logos. These caps are sold in kiosks located in shopping malls around the country. The company currently purchases the caps it sells, but Joe DeNardo, the president of the company, is considering expanding the company's operations to include the manufacture of baseball caps. Joe believes that if the company manufactured its own caps, it would have better control of the quality and design of the caps. He also thinks that the company could make a greater profit on its sales if it did the manufacturing.

1. Explain how the financial statements of DeNardo Hat Company would change if the company manufactured the caps.
2. What type of cost accounting system would DeNardo Hat Company most likely use if it manufactured the caps? Why?
3. What are the advantages and disadvantages of Joe DeNardo's plan for the company to manufacture the baseball caps it sells?

CHAPTER
2

Job Order Cost Cycle

In Chapter 1 you learned that total manufacturing cost consists of three elements: direct materials, direct labor, and manufacturing overhead. The flow of these costs through the accounting system parallels the flow of products through the manufacturing operations. In this chapter you will begin to learn how a job order manufacturing firm is organized, how the accounting system is designed, and how accounting records and procedures are established to record, transfer, and summarize these manufacturing costs.

WORK FLOW

A firm's cost accounting system parallels its flow of operations. The steps in a typical cycle of operations of a firm that makes and sells its own products are outlined below.

1. **Procurement:** Raw materials and supplies needed for manufacturing are ordered, received, and stored. Direct and indirect factory labor and services are obtained.
2. **Production:** Raw materials are transferred from the storeroom to the factory. Labor, tools, machines, power, and other costs are applied to complete the product.
3. **Warehousing:** Finished goods are moved from the factory to the warehouse to be held until they are sold.
4. **Selling:** Customers are found. Merchandise is shipped from the warehouse. Sales to customers are recorded.

The cost accountant's job is to design a system in which all cost elements are recorded as incurred and then charged to production as the work flows through the operating cycle.

RECORDING COSTS AS INCURRED

As each cost is incurred, it must be recorded in an appropriate general ledger account. Different accounts are needed at different points in the operating cycle. The following information includes typical account titles and numbers:

1. **Procurement:** Accounts must be provided to record the purchase of materials, labor, and overhead. These costs will later be charged to production. Typical general ledger account titles and numbers used for this purpose are Raw Materials 121, Factory Payroll Clearing 500, and Manufacturing Overhead Control 501.
2. **Production:** An account is required to gather procurement costs as they become chargeable to manufacturing operations. This account is Work in Process 122.
3. **Warehousing:** An account must be set up to record the cost of goods that have completed the manufacturing process. This account is Finished Goods 126.
4. **Selling:** The cost of the completed goods that have been sold must be recorded. An account, Cost of Goods Sold 415, is provided in the general ledger for this purpose. Other general ledger accounts, Accounts Receivable 111 and Sales 401, are used for recording the sale to the customer and the credit to income at the selling price.

The illustration on the top of page 23 shows the relationship of these accounts to the steps in the operating cycle.

MATCHING COST FLOW AND WORK FLOW

The provision for special cost accounts sets the stage for the more intricate job of charging costs in accordance with the flow of work. The process can best be understood if analyzed step by step.

1. **Procurement:** Purchases of materials, labor, and overhead are recorded as debits to Raw Materials, Factory Payroll Clearing, and

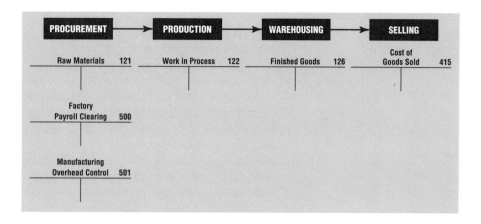

Manufacturing Overhead Control. As these costs are used, or applied, in factory operations, they are credited to these accounts and transferred to production.

2. *Production:* Costs of materials, labor, and overhead transferred into production are debited to Work in Process. As goods are finished and moved from the factory, their total cost is removed from the Work in Process account by a credit entry and charged (debited) to Finished Goods.

3. *Warehousing:* The cost of finished goods transferred from Work in Process is recorded as a debit to Finished Goods. The cost of merchandise shipped from the warehouse to customers is credited to Finished Goods and charged (debited) to Cost of Goods Sold.

4. *Selling:* As indicated above, as finished goods are sold and shipped from the warehouse, their cost is debited to Cost of Goods Sold. At the end of the accounting period, this account is closed by crediting Cost of Goods Sold and debiting Income Summary 399.

The matching of cost and work flow is shown below.

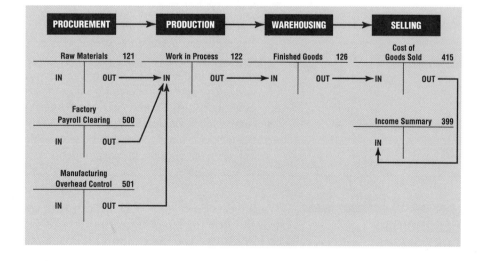

DEPARTMENTAL COST CENTERS

Of the four steps in the operating cycle, production is probably the most complicated to account for and to control. Tons of materials and supplies of every description might be used daily by hundreds of workers who complete a wide variety of processes on countless machines. Total costs are not very useful as indicators of efficiency under such conditions. Therefore, when several operations are performed in the factory, it is customary to group similar activities into departments or cost centers. The cost accounting system is then set up to accumulate and report costs separately by department or cost center. Such reporting matches cost flow with work flow down to the smallest functional unit. The person in charge of the department is then held accountable for its efficient performance. Departmentalization thus helps to provide operating control over manufacturing activities and costs.

Factory operations normally include two types of departments: production and service. A **production department,** or producing department, engages in work directly related to the product. The finishing department in which the products of a furniture factory are painted is an example of a production department. A **service department** serves or assists production departments. For example, the building services department that maintains a plant so that production can be carried on under the best possible working conditions is a service department.

SELF-REVIEW

1. Name the four steps in the operating cycle of a typical manufacturing company.
2. What accounts are needed to record the purchase of materials, labor, and overhead?
3. If a firm had cash sales in addition to credit sales, what additional account would be necessary to record the sale of finished goods?
4. Explain the difference between a production department and a service department.

Answers to Self-Review

1. Procurement, production, warehousing, and selling.
2. The purchase of materials is recorded in the Raw Materials account, labor is recorded in the Factory Payroll Clearing account, and overhead is recorded in the Manufacturing Overhead Control account.
3. Cash. The entry to record the sale of finished goods would consist of a debit to both Cash and Accounts Receivable and a credit to Sales.
4. A production department is engaged in work directly related to the making the product; a service department does not work directly on the product but provides support to the production departments.

RECORDING COST FLOWS

We have seen how a cost accounting system is developed by matching the flow of costs with the flow of factory activities. The next step is to examine the operation of a cost system in a typical manufacturing corporation.

Panorama Windows, Inc., manufactures replacement windows to meet customer specifications. The company offers many styles and colors of maintenance-free windows. Different types of glass such as tempered, privacy, or tinted are available. Most production is carried out to fill specific customer orders, although some standard-size windows are produced and held in inventory for future sales.

When an order is placed with the company, rough measurements of the opening in which the window will be placed are entered into the computer. The computer calculates the necessary window dimensions and generates a multicopy specification sheet that is distributed to each production department. The sheet contains all the information and instructions needed to complete the customer's order.

Organization

The firm is organized into three major divisions: General Administration, Production, and Sales. (See the organization chart below.) The Production Division, which directs factory operations, consists of five departments: three producing departments and two service departments. The three producing departments are Cutting, Framing, and Assembly. The two service departments are Building Services and General Factory.

Cutting Department. In the Cutting Department, large glass sheets are sent through a computerized cutter that cuts the glass with a laser beam. Based on specifications entered into the computer, the exact cuts are plotted by the computer to minimize waste and maximize the use of the material. After the glass is cut, the cut pieces, commonly known as lites, are sent through a specialized glass washer

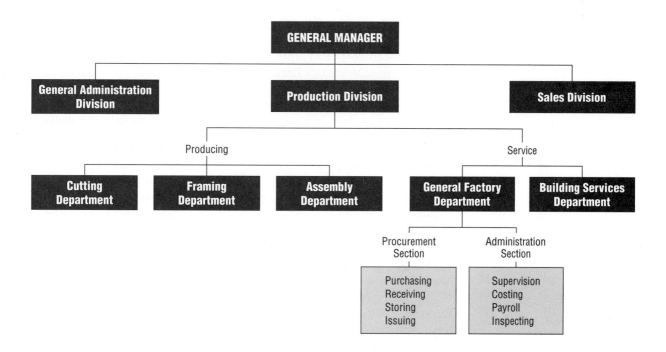

that cleans and dries the lites in one process. After exiting the washer, the lites are stocked in either two-lite or three-lite sections depending on whether the order is for double-pane or triple-pane windows. Special spacers, containing materials to remove moisture, and grids are placed between the lites of glass. The glass units are now ready for sealant.

Before the unit is completely sealed, various gasses are injected into the unit to increase the unit's insulating qualities. When the unit of glass is completely sealed and dried, it is ready for the sash. To make the sash which will encase the unit of glass, extrusions are cut and shaped to specification and then the seams are either welded or mechanically fastened and sealed.

The last step in this department is to unite the glass unit with the sash. The unit is then sent to the Assembly Department.

Framing Department. The Framing Department manufactures the master frame into which the window sashes fit. Here the workers cut various sizes of extrusion to create the header, jambs, and sill that make up the master frame of a window. Since some of the glass and sashes are manufactured to standard dimensions, the Framing Department also creates various head expanders and sill adapters that enable the company's product to be adapted to window openings of various sizes.

In the process of manufacturing the master frame, the department utilizes various types of tools and equipment including miter saws, table saws, and punches that mark the spots for screw and hardware placement. Welders, pneumatic screwdrivers, and sealant guns are also used by the workers in this department. After the master frame has been built, it is sent to the Assembly Department.

Assembly Department. This department performs the final task of uniting the window sashes from the Cutting Department with the master frames from the Framing Department. Workers in the Assembly Department also install hardware on each unit. Window hardware includes nailing fins, locks, keepers, pivot bars and shoes, balance rods, latches, and handles and hinges.

Workers in this department also install screens into the units and combine multiple units, utilizing muntin strips, to fit large openings.

After final inspection, the finished unit is packaged or crated and prepared for shipment.

Building Services Department. This department is responsible for maintaining the building and grounds and performing janitorial services. It also maintains the heating, cooling, electrical, and plumbing systems. Heating and cooling costs, building taxes, building insurance, building depreciation, and similar costs are charged to the Building Services Department.

General Factory Department. This department consists of two sections and performs a variety of activities. The procurement section is responsible for purchasing, receiving, storing, and issuing raw materials and factory supplies. The purchasing agent's staff, the receiving clerk, the storeroom supervisor, and the storeroom clerk make up this section. The administration section includes such personnel as the factory cost clerk, the time clerk, the payroll clerk, inspectors, and the factory superintendent.

Flow of Work

The flow of work at Panorama Windows, as shown below, follows the flow of operations discussed earlier in this part. The various operating divisions, departments, and sections are shown as they relate to the basic steps on the flowchart. Since the General Administration Division is not a direct participant in the flow of costs, it is omitted from this illustration.

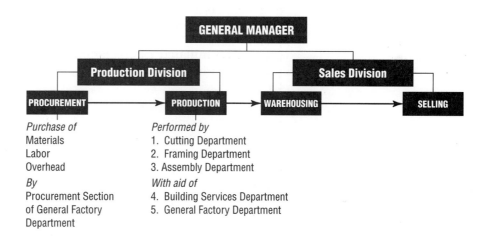

Purchase of
Materials
Labor
Overhead
By
Procurement Section
of General Factory
Department

Performed by
1. Cutting Department
2. Framing Department
3. Assembly Department
With aid of
4. Building Services Department
5. General Factory Department

Chart of Accounts

Panorama Windows, Inc., uses a job order cost system. This system was recommended by Panorama Windows' accountant after a careful study of the organization and manufacturing procedures of the firm. The chart of accounts used is shown on pages 27 and 28.

Most of Panorama Windows' accounts will be familiar to you from your previous courses. Note, however, the new cost accounts below.

121 Raw Materials
122 Work in Process
126 Finished Goods
415 Cost of Goods Sold
500 Factory Payroll Clearing
501 Manufacturing Overhead Control
507 Overapplied or Underapplied Manufacturing Overheads

Flow of Costs

The following examination of the cost flow of Panorama Windows, Inc., for October 19X9 will show how the cost flow matches the work flow.

PANORAMA WINDOWS, INC.
Chart of Accounts

Assets

101 Cash
111 Accounts Receivable
112 Allowance for Doubtful Accounts
121 Raw Materials
122 Work in Process
126 Finished Goods
127 Prepaid Insurance
128 Supplies
131 Land
132 Buildings
133 Accumulated Depreciation—Buildings
134 Machinery and Equipment
135 Accumulated Depreciation—Machinery and Equipment
136 Furniture and Fixtures
137 Accumulated Depreciation—Furniture and Fixtures
141 Patents

Liabilities

201 Vouchers Payable
202 Salaries and Wages Payable
210 Social Security Taxes Payable
211 Medicare Taxes Payable
212 Federal Unemployment Taxes Payable
213 State Unemployment Taxes Payable
214 Employee Income Taxes Payable
215 Group Insurance Deductions Payable
216 Property Taxes Payable
217 Income Taxes Payable

Stockholders' Equity

301 Common Stock
302 Retained Earnings
399 Income Summary

Revenue and Expenses

401 Sales
401 Sales Returns and Allowances
415 Cost of Goods Sold
500 Factory Payroll Clearing

Manufacturing Overhead

501 Manufacturing Overhead Control
502 Manufacturing Overhead—Cutting Department
503 Manufacturing Overhead—Framing Department
504 Manufacturing Overhead—Assembly Department
505 Manufacturing Overhead—Building Services Department
506 Manufacturing Overhead—General Factory Department
507 Overapplied or Underapplied Manufacturing Overhead

PANORAMA WINDOWS, INC.
Chart of Accounts (continued)

Operating Expenses
601 Selling Expenses
611 General Expenses

Other Expenses and Other Income
701 Interest Expense
702 Sales Discount
711 Interest Earned
712 Purchases Discount
713 Miscellaneous Income

Opening Balances. Panorama Windows is an established concern, so the cost accounting system has been in use for some time. Assume that on October 1 these balances appear in the following accounts:

121 Raw Materials $54,254.00
122 Work in Process 43,651.40
126 Finished Goods 36,200.00

These balances are shown in the appropriate general ledger T accounts on the chart below.

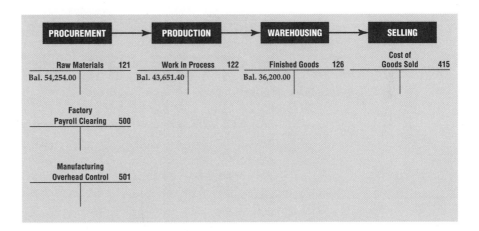

Raw Materials Purchased

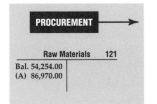

Additional raw materials were purchased during the month of October at a cost of $86,970. The purchase is debited to the asset account, Raw Materials. This entry is shown in general journal form below for illustrative purposes. The transaction would normally be entered in a special journal, such as the voucher register.

19X9	(A)			
Oct. 31	Raw Materials	121	86,970.00	
	Vouchers Payable	201		86,970.00
	Recorded cost of raw materials purchased during the month.			

Letters will be used to identify the general journal entries in this chapter. For example, the effect of this purchase on the Raw Materials account is indicated in the T account beside the general journal entry marked A on page 29.

Raw Materials Used

During the month, raw materials costing $90,419 were used as follows.

Direct Materials, Chargeable to Work in Process	$84,607.35
Indirect Materials, Chargeable to Manufacturing	
Overhead Control	5,811.65
Total	$90,419.00

The required transfer of raw materials costs is shown in general journal form below.

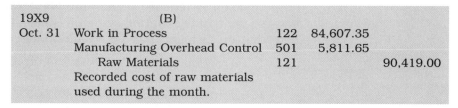

19X9		(B)			
Oct. 31	Work in Process		122	84,607.35	
	Manufacturing Overhead Control		501	5,811.65	
	Raw Materials		121		90,419.00
	Recorded cost of raw materials				
	used during the month.				

The effect on the various cost accounts is indicated on the flow-chart by the entries marked *B*.

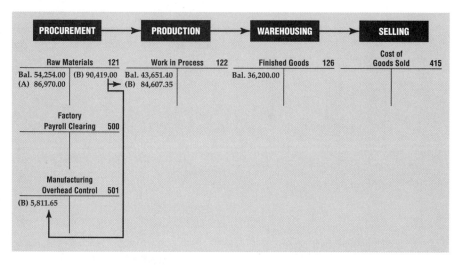

Factory Wages Earned

During the month, wages and salaries totaling $91,884 were earned by the factory employees and charged from the factory payroll register to the Factory Payroll Clearing account, as shown below.

19X9		(C)			
Oct. 31	Factory Payroll Clearing		500	91,884.00	
	Salaries and Wages Payable		202		91,884.00
	Recorded factory payroll for				
	the month.				

The effect on the Factory Payroll Clearing account is indicated by the entry marked *C* in the T accounts below.

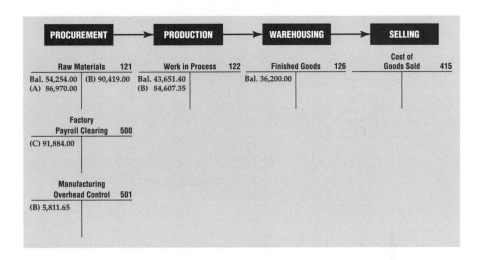

Labor Charged to Operations

An analysis of the records indicates that labor costs of $101,932 should be allocated as follows.

Direct Labor, Chargeable to Work in Process	$ 66,597.00
Indirect Labor, Chargeable to Manufacturing Overhead Control	35,335.00
Total	$101,932.00

The required transfer of labor costs is shown in general journal form shown below.

19X9	(D)			
Oct. 31	Work in Process	122	66,597.00	
	Manufacturing Overhead Control	501	35,335.00	
	Factory Payroll Clearing	500		101,932.00
	Recorded costs of labor used in operations during the month.			

The effect on the various cost accounts is indicated by the entries marked D in the T accounts on page 32. The balance of the Factory Payroll Clearing account represents wages earned but not yet paid.

Manufacturing Overhead Costs

In addition to the indirect materials (B) and indirect labor (D), other overhead costs, such as utilities, insurance, and depreciation, totaling $23,086.81 incurred during the month were charged from various journals. The entry to record these costs in shown on page 32 in general journal form. The effect on the Manufacturing Overhead Control account is shown in the T accounts by the entry marked *E* in the T accounts on page 32.

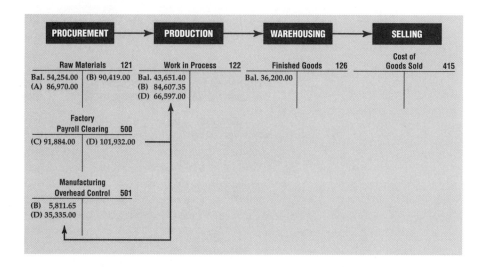

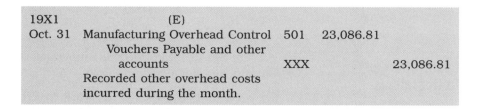

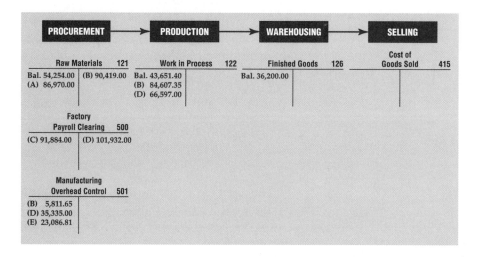

Manufacturing Overhead Applied to Products

It is estimated that overhead costs totaling $61,628.31 are chargeable to jobs worked on during the month of October. An estimate of overhead applicable to each job must be made because it is impossible to determine the exact amount applicable at this point in the process. (The estimation process is explained later.) The required transfer is shown in general journal form on page 33.

19X9		(F)			
Oct. 31	Work in Process		122	61,628.31	
	Manufacturing Overhead Control	501			61,628.31
	Recorded overhead applied to jobs during the month.				

The effect of the transfer is shown in the related T accounts below by the entries marked *F*. Remember that the credit to Manufacturing Overhead Control 501 is an estimate. There will usually be a small balance in the account. A debit balance means that less overhead was charged, or applied, to production than the total costs incurred. This is called **underapplied overhead.** If the estimated overhead transferred is greater than the actual costs incurred, Manufacturing Overhead Control will have a credit balance. This is called **overapplied overhead.** (The proper handling of underapplied or overapplied overhead will be discussed in later chapters.)

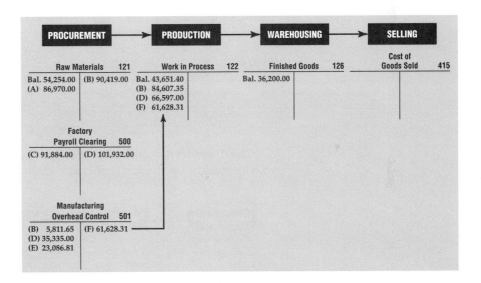

Transfer of Finished Goods

During the month, some jobs were completed and transferred to the finished goods warehouse. These jobs cost $225,155.28. This flow of goods is shown by a debit to Finished Goods 126 and a credit to Work in Process 122. The transfer is shown in the T accounts by the entries marked *G* on the top of page 34.

19X9		(G)			
Oct. 31	Finished Goods		126	225,155.28	
	Work in Process		122		225,155.28
	Transferred cost of jobs completed during the month.				

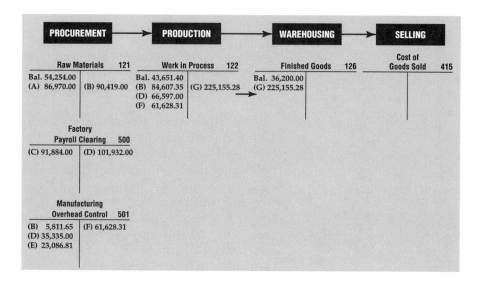

Sale of Finished Goods

During the month, finished goods costing $221,690.78 were sold to various customers. The entry to record this flow is shown in general journal form as follows:

19X9	(H)			
Oct. 31	Cost of Goods Sold	415	221,690.78	
	Finished Goods	126		221,690.78
	Recorded cost of goods sold during the month.			

The transfer is shown in the Finished Goods and Cost of Goods sold accounts by the entries marked *H*.

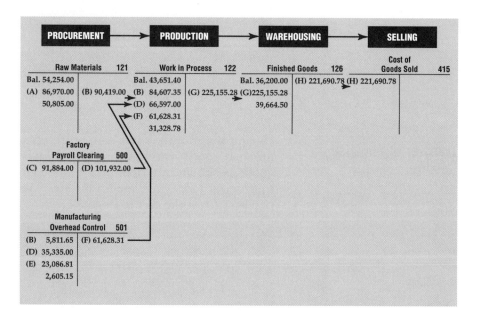

INSPECTION OF ACCOUNTS

Examine the postings in the T accounts and follow the directional arrows at the bottom of page 34 to observe the flow of costs.

Entries B, D, and F appear as credits representing the flow of costs out of Raw Materials 121, Factory Payroll Clearing 500, and Manufacturing Overhead Control 501 and as debits representing the flow of costs into Work in Process 122.

Entry G shows the flow of costs out of Work in Process 122 into Finished Goods 126.

Entry H represents a cost flow out of Finished Goods 126 into Cost of Goods Sold 415. Also note the closing balances in the three inventory accounts.

At this point you should be able to work Exercises 2–1 to 2–4 and Problems 2–1A, 2–2A, 2–4A, 2–1B, 2–2B, and 2–4B.

121 Raw Materials	$50,805.00
122 Work in Process	31,328.28
126 Finished Goods	39,664.50

The handling of the underapplied overhead represented by the balance of Manufacturing Overhead Control 501 ($2,605.15 Dr.) will be explained in later chapters.

END-OF-PERIOD STATEMENTS

The cost accounts in the general ledger contain essential figures needed to complete the statement of cost of goods manufactured and the income statement. The statement of cost of goods manufactured is supported by a schedule of manufacturing overhead, which shows details of individual overhead items. As you will learn later, these detailed figures for manufacturing overhead are obtained from subsidiary accounts.

PANORAMA WINDOWS, INC.
Statement of Manufacturing Overhead
Month Ended October 31, 19X9

Actual Overhead Costs Incurred		
Indirect Materials	$ 5,811.65	
Indirect Labor	35,335.00	
Payroll Taxes Expense	8,539.15	
Depreciation—Buildings	2,250.00	
Depreciation—Equipment	3,460.00	
Repairs and Maintenance	2,543.60	
Utilities	4,283.75	
Insurance	974.05	
Property Taxes	621.00	
Other Taxes	415.26	
Total Actual Overhead Costs Incurred		$64,233.46
Deduct Underapplied Overhead for October		2,605.15
Manufacturing Overhead Applied		$61,628.31

PANORAMA WINDOWS, INC.
Statement of Cost of Goods Manufactured
Month Ended October 31, 19X9

Direct Materials		
Raw Materials Inventory, Oct. 1	$ 54,254.00	
Materials Purchases	86,970.00	
Total Materials Available	$141,224.00	
Deduct Raw Materials Inventory,		
Oct. 31	50,805.00	
Total Materials Used	$ 90,419.00	
Deduct Indirect Materials Used	5,811.65	
Direct Materials Used		$ 84,607.35
Direct Labor		66,597.00
Manufacturing Overhead Applied		61,628.31
Total Manufacturing Cost		$212,832.66
Add Work in Process Inventory,		
Oct. 1		43,651.40
		$256,484.06
Deduct Work in Process Inventory,		
Oct. 31		31,328.78
Cost of Goods Manufactured		$225,155.28

PANORAMA WINDOWS, INC.
Income Statement
Month Ended October 31, 19X9

Revenue		
Sales		$298,761.80
Cost of Goods Sold		
Finished Goods Inventory, Oct. 1	$ 36,200.00	
Add Cost of Goods Manufactured	225,155.28	
Total Goods Available for Sale	$261,355.28	
Deduct Finished Goods Inventory,		
Oct. 31	39,664.50	
Cost of Goods Sold		221,690.78
Gross Profit on Sales		$ 77,071.02
Operating Expenses		
Selling Expenses	$ 18,969.30	
General Expenses	13,847.60	
Total Operating Expenses		32,816.90
Net Income Before Income Taxes		$ 44,254.12
Provision for Income Taxes		6,638.12
Net Income After Income Taxes		$ 37,616.00

BUSINESS HORIZON

Application of Job Order Cost Accounting

The use of job order cost accounting concepts reaches beyond the manufacture of industrial and household products to the world of high fashion jewelry. The House of Cartier, founded in Paris in 1847 by Louis François Cartier, is an international firm known for the elegant and distinctive jewelry it has created for sale to its customers around the world.

A look into the archives of the company demonstrates the principles of job order cost accounting as applied to the design and production of fine jewelry. Cartier has designed jewelry for the rich and famous for the past century. Its archives are filled with job order record books that describe custom-made pieces created for royalty and millionaires including famous people such as Woolworth heiress Barbara Hutton, Aga Khan III, financier J. P. Morgan, Marjorie Merriweather Post, and Harold McCormick, president of International Harvester Company.

As the first step in the process of creating a new piece of jewelry, designers would sketch a design for the customer's order. After the sketch was approved, a detailed color drawing was made. The drawing would include a list of the gemstones and metals to be used, such as rubies, diamonds, emeralds, sapphires, and topaz, and gold, silver, or platinum. Estimated costs of the materials were detailed, and precise instructions for the construction of the item were included. The raw materials—various gems and metals—were then selected and put into production as wax molds were made and the final piece assembled by the firm's artisans. A Cartier registration number and signature were engraved on each completed piece. In order to have a record of the firm's work, the finished item was photographed and plaster casts were made before delivery to the customer. Files were kept of all items sold to a customer so that there would be no duplication of items received by the customer or sold to other customers.

Today there are many artists who work to produce one-of-a-kind jewelry and decorative objects. Whether the items they make are expensive or inexpensive, whether the operation is large or small, job order concepts need to be applied in order to keep track of costs and determine selling price and profit.

SELF-REVIEW

1. Is the total cost of raw materials used charged to Work in Process? If not, explain.
2. Identify several factory costs that would be charged to Manufacturing Overhead Control.
3. Is a credit balance in the Manufacturing Overhead Control account at the end of the accounting period identified as underapplied overhead or as overapplied overhead?
4. What is the entry to record the transfer of finished goods to the warehouse?
5. What does the balance in the Work in Process account at the end of the accounting period represent?

Answers to Self-Review

At this point you should be able to work Exercise 2–5 and Problems 2–3A and 2–3B.

1. No, only the cost of materials directly used in making the product is charged to Work in Process. The remaining cost of materials represents indirect materials which are charged to Manufacturing Overhead Control.
2. Manufacturing overhead costs include indirect materials; indirect labor; cost of repairs to machinery; factory payroll taxes; depreciation of factory buildings, machinery, and equipment; power and light costs; factory insurance; and factory property taxes.
3. Overapplied overhead.
4. The entry is a debit to Finished Goods and a credit to Work in Process.
5. The balance in the Work in Process account represents the cost of products that are not finished and require additional processing in the next accounting period.

PRINCIPLES AND PROCEDURES SUMMARY

- A cost accounting system parallels the flow of operations.
- The four steps in the typical operating cycle of a manufacturer are procurement, production, warehousing, and selling.
  - Procurement is the purchase of materials, labor, and overhead items for use in the factory.
  - Production consists of the actual manufacturing of goods.
  - Warehousing is the movement of finished goods into the warehouse to await sale.
  - Selling includes finding customers and making shipments of merchandise.
- The costs involved in the various steps of the operating cycle are recorded in general ledger accounts, such as Raw Materials, Factory Payroll Clearing, Manufacturing Overhead Control, Work in Process, Finished Goods, and Cost of Goods Sold.
- As work flows from one step to another, costs flow into and out of accounts related to these steps. This is called *matching cost flow and work flow.*
- When manufacturing involves a number of operations, the cost accounting system may accumulate costs by department or by cost center. This arrangement pinpoints responsibility for performance.
- The cost accountant develops a firm's cost accounting system to fit its organization and flow of work. The chart of accounts makes provision for appropriate cost accounts in the general ledger.
- Steps in the cost flow of a manufacturing operation are:
  - Start with the beginning balances in the three inventory accounts, Raw Materials, Work in Process, and Finished Goods.
  - Additional raw materials are purchased; some are used in manufacturing as direct and indirect materials.
  - Factory wages and salaries are earned and allocated as direct and indirect labor charges.

- Other manufacturing overhead costs are recorded as incurred.
- At the end of the month, estimated overhead costs are applied to Work in Process.
- The cost of goods that have been completed is transferred from Work in Process to Finished Goods.
- The cost of goods sold is charged to Cost of Goods Sold.
- The statement of cost of goods manufactured and the income statement utilize figures supplied by the special cost accounts in the general ledger.

MANAGERIAL IMPLICATIONS

- Every successful manufacturing business must have a cost accounting system that will enable the calculation of a meaningful total cost of goods manufactured and also a meaningful cost per unit of product.
- The accounting system must have a chart of accounts that reflects the cycle of operations: procurement, production, warehousing, and selling. The accounts should make it easy to match the flow of costs with the flow of work in the business.
- In order to control costs, the production function is organized into two types of departments: production departments and service departments. Production departments engage in work directly related to products; service departments assist production departments. This organization facilitates the control of costs.
- As materials, labor, and overhead are used, the costs are accumulated in a "Work in Process account." Under the job order cost accounting system, when a job is completed (or at the end of the month) the cost of the completed job is removed from the Work in Process account and transferred to Finished Goods, and when the units are sold their cost is transferred to Cost of Goods Sold.
- At the end of the month a Statement of Cost of Goods Manufactured, summarizing all of the information about products manufactured during the period, is prepared. This statement is of great importance to management in evaluating performance of factory operations.

REVIEW QUESTIONS

1. What are the four basic steps in a typical cycle of operations for a manufacturing firm?
2. What general ledger account(s) are used in recording costs during each of the following steps: (a) procurement, (b) production, (c) warehousing, and (d) selling?
3. The costs of materials, labor, and overhead transferred into production are debited to which account?

4. The total cost of finished goods is removed from Work in Process and transferred to which account?
5. Of the four steps in the production cycle, which step is usually the most complicated to account for and to control? Why?
6. How does a production department differ from a service department? Give an example of each type of department.
7. What does a debit balance in the Manufacturing Overhead Control account at the end of an accounting period represent? What does a credit balance represent?
8. What does the ending balance in the Work in Process account represent?
9. Which inventory account or accounts of a manufacturing company appear on the statement of cost of goods manufactured, and which appear on the income statement?
10. What does the beginning balance in the Finished Goods account represent?

MANAGERIAL DISCUSSION QUESTIONS

1. How does departmentalization aid management in controlling costs?
2. Why is it important that cost accounting systems reflect the flow of costs?
3. Why is good organization important in cost control?
4. Describe how the three inventory accounts assist management in controlling manufacturing operations and production.

EXERCISES

EXERCISE 2–1   **Analyze work in process.   (Obj. 3).**   Work in Process for the Dallas Manufacturing Company is recorded on the T-account below.
a. What are the manufacturing costs for the month?
b. What is the cost of goods manufactured during the month?
c. What is the ending inventory balance?

Work in Process			
Jan. 1 Balance	84,390	Jan. 31 Transferred to	
31 Materials	258,714	Finished Goods	705,226
31 Labor	309,167		
Jan. 31 Mfg. Overhead	140,281		

EXERCISE 2–2   **Analyze manufacturing overhead.   (Obj. 5).**   During May the Manufacturing Overhead Control account for Gray Manufacturers had various debit postings that totaled $66,493 and a credit posting for $69,736. Was the manufacturing overhead for the month overapplied or underapplied? By what amount?

EXERCISE 2–3   **Identify work flow procedures.   (Obj. 1).**   For each procedure identify the steps in the manufacturing cycle in which it occurs: procurement, production, warehousing, or selling.

a. Materials are requisitioned and transferred to the factory.
b. An order is sent to a supplier to obtain more raw materials.
c. A customer's order is received and filled.
d. The weekly payroll is recorded.
e. Finished goods are placed in the appropriate storage areas.
f. New employees are interviewed and hired by the personnel department.
g. Finished goods are shipped to the customer.
h. Manufacturing overhead costs are estimated and charged to the product.
i. A shipment of raw materials arrives and is unpacked.

EXERCISE 2–4   **Analyze manufacturing transactions.   (Obj. 3).**   Eight transactions in the manufacturing process are recorded in the T accounts below. Each transaction is coded by a letter and may be spread over several accounts. Describe what happened in each transaction.

Raw Materials				Work in Process				Vouchers Payable				Factory Payroll Clearing			
(A)	35,000	(B)	28,000	(B)	26,000	(G)	58,500			(A)	35,000	(C)	33,000	(D)	33,000
				(D)	25,000					(E)	3,300				
				(F)	14,200										

Finished Goods				Salaries and Wages Payable		Manufacturing Overhead Control				Cost of Goods Sold	
(G)	58,500	(H)	49,700		(C)	33,000	(B)	2,000	(F)	14,200	(H)	49,700
							(D)	8,000				
							(E)	3,300				

EXERCISE 2–5   **Calculate the missing amounts in the following three independent situations.   (Obj. 6)**

	(A)	(B)	(C)
Direct Materials	$ 50,526	$32,918	_____
Direct Labor	30,816	40,223	$ 64,200
Manufacturing Overhead	_____	36,792	46,268
Total Manufacturing Costs	100,100	_____	192,112
Beginning Work in Process	10,419	6,812	_____
Ending Work in Process	_____	7,262	20,456
Cost of Goods Manufactured	100,697	_____	189,772

PROBLEMS

PROBLEM 2–1A   **Record manufacturing costs.   (Obj. 2).**   Miller Corporation manufactures industrial springs and coils that are sold to other companies for assembling into machinery. The following costs were incurred during the month of August 19X9:

Raw materials purchased: $162,640

Raw materials used: direct materials, $110,290; indirect materials, $22,340

Factory wages earned: $72,720

Factory wages allocated: direct labor, $57,820; indirect labor, $14,900

Voucher recorded for manufacturing overhead costs incurred: $18,200

Depreciation on factory building: $20,430

Depreciation on factory equipment: $5,840

Manufacturing overhead costs applied to jobs worked on: $79,423

Finished goods transferred to warehouse: $242,863

Finished goods sold and shipped to customers: $218,392 (cost)

Finished goods sold and billed to customers: $298,892 (selling price)

INSTRUCTIONS　Prepare the general journal entries dated August 31, 19X9.

PROBLEM 2–2A　**Recording and posting manufacturing costs.　(Obj. 2).**　Consolidated Lamp Company manufactures desk lamps. The total manufacturing costs for July 19X9 are as follows:

Raw materials purchased: $102,340

Raw materials used: direct materials, $83,005; indirect materials, $26,715

Factory wages earned: $138,240

Factory wages allocated: direct labor, $104,620; indirect labor, $33,620

Other overhead costs incurred: $29,568 (credit the total to Vouchers Payable 201)

Estimated manufacturing overhead costs applied to jobs worked on: $87,829

Finished goods transferred to warehouse: $271,783

Finished goods sold and shipped to customers: $275,333

Finished goods sold and billed to customers: $382,257 (selling price)

INSTRUCTIONS
1. Prepare the general journal entries to record each of the costs. Date the entries July 31, 19X9.
2. Post the general journal entries to the general ledger accounts. The general ledger accounts 121, 122, and 126 have the following opening balances at July 1, 19X9: Raw Materials 121, $86,280 Dr.; Work in Process 122, $68,837 Dr.; Finished Goods 126, $42,090 Dr. *Save your working papers for use in Problem 2-3A.*

PROBLEM 2–3A　**Prepare financial statements.　(Objs. 6, 7).**　This problem is a continuation of Problem 2-2A.

INSTRUCTIONS

1. Prepare the statement of cost of goods manufactured.
2. Prepare the income statement. Assume selling expenses of $49,741; administrative expenses of $21,800; and estimated federal income taxes of $14,153.

PROBLEM 2–4A   **Analyze journal entries. (Obj. 2).** Wisconsin Cheese Company, which uses a job order cost accounting system, recorded the following journal entries during March 19X9:

19X9			
Mar. 31	Raw Materials	830,710.00	
	Vouchers Payable		830,710.00
31	Work in Process	682,340.00	
	Manufacturing Overhead Control	64,950.00	
	Raw Materials		747,290.00
31	Factory Payroll Clearing	764,240.00	
	Salaries and Wages Payable		764,240.00
31	Work in Process	691,570.00	
	Manufacturing Overhead Control	72,670.00	
	Factory Payroll Clearing		764,240.00
31	Manufacturing Overhead Control	407,060.00	
	Vouchers Payable		407,060.00
31	Work in Process	558,120.00	
	Manufacturing Overhead Control		558,120.00
31	Finished Goods	1,735,290.00	
	Work in Process		1,735,290.00
31	Cost of Goods Sold	1,529,640.00	
	Finished Goods		1,529,640.00
31	Accounts Receivable	2,247,424.00	
	Sales		2,247,424.00

INSTRUCTIONS   Describe each transaction that took place.

ALTERNATE PROBLEMS

PROBLEM 2–1B   **Record manufacturing costs. (Obj. 2).** The Alamo Manufacturing Corporation uses the job order cost system in the manufacturing of its finished product. The costs for the month of April 19X9 follow:

Raw materials purchased: $182,460
Raw materials used: direct materials, $120,290; indirect materials, $24,630
Factory wages earned: $92,740
Factory wages allocated: direct labor, $77,820; indirect labor, $14,920
Voucher recorded for manufacturing overhead costs incurred: $22,800
Depreciation on factory building: $30,490
Depreciation on factory equipment: $7,480
Manufacturing overhead costs applied to jobs worked on: $108,360
Finished goods transferred to warehouse: $281,460

Finished goods sold and shipped to customers: $198,150
Finished goods sold and billed to customers: $297,225 (selling price)

INSTRUCTIONS Prepare the general journal entries dated April 30, 19X4.

PROBLEM 2–2B **Record and post manufacturing costs. (Obj. 2).** The Western Paint Company manufactures paints for industrial use. The total manufacturing costs for the month of January 19X9 follow:

Raw materials purchased: $202,750
Raw materials used: direct materials, $188,240; indirect materials, $22,650
Factory wages earned: $306,800
Factory wages allocated: direct labor, $241,590; indirect labor, $65,210
Other overhead costs incurred: $88,720 (credit the total to Vouchers Payable 201)
Estimated manufacturing overhead costs applied to jobs worked on: $174,340
Finished goods transferred to warehouse: $581,350
Finished goods sold and shipped to customers: $572,510
Finished goods sold and billed to customers: $908,776 (selling price)

INSTRUCTIONS
1. Prepare the general journal entries to record each of the costs. Date the entries January 31, 19X9.
2. Post the general journal entries to the general ledger accounts. The general ledger accounts 121, 122, and 126 have the following opening balances at January 1, 19X9: Raw Materials 121, $64,820 Dr.; Work in Process 122, $83,920 Dr.; Finished Goods 126, $66,200 Dr. *Save your working papers for use in Problem 2–3B.*

PROBLEM 2–3B **Prepare financial statements. (Objs. 6, 7).** This problem is a continuation of Problem 2–2B.

INSTRUCTIONS
1. Prepare the statement of cost of goods manufactured.
2. Prepare the income statement. Assume selling expenses of $184,922, administrative expenses of $85,200, and estimated federal income taxes of $22,430.

PROBLEM 2–4B **Analyze journal entries. (Obj. 2).** The Mining Equipment Company, which uses a job order cost system, recorded the following journal entries during June 19X9:

June 30	Raw Materials	590,360.00	
	Vouchers Payable		590,360.00
30	Work in Process	475,820.00	
	Manufacturing Overhead Control	58,040.00	
	Raw Materials		533,860.00
30	Factory Payroll Clearing	688,713.00	
	Salaries and Wages Payable		688,713.00

June	30	Work in Process	583,980.00	
		Manufacturing Overhead Control	104,733.00	
		Factory Payroll Clearing		688,713.00
June	30	Manufacturing Overhead Control	86,190.00	
		Vouchers Payable		86,190.00
June	30	Work in Process	257,310.00	
		Manufacturing Overhead Control		257,310.00
June	30	Finished Goods	1,185,200.00	
		Work in Process		1,185,200.00
June	30	Cost of Goods Sold	1,037,540.00	
		Finished Goods		1,037,540.00
June	30	Accounts Receivable	1,944,680.00	
		Sales		1,944,680.00

INSTRUCTIONS Describe each transaction that took place.

MANAGERIAL DECISION CASE

The Novelty Mug Company was formed recently to manufacture plastic mugs that are custom-decorated with logos designed to customer specifications. The first step in the manufacturing process is molding plastic into the shape of a mug. The second step is applying the logo to the mugs. The final step in the manufacturing process is putting the mugs in an attractive box suitable for gift-giving.

The company has purchased a small building in which to conduct its operations. A portion of the building will contain the factory and have a small staff to handle maintenance and cleaning, factory payroll, and purchasing, receiving, and storing materials. The rest of the building will be occupied by the sales staff and the administrative offices. The president of the company will oversee all operations.

1. Describe the flow of costs for the Novelty Mug Company's manufacturing operations.
2. How does having an organization chart help control operations?
3. Prepare an organization chart for the Novelty Mug Company.

C H A P T E R

3

Purchasing Materials

Chapter 2 presented the elements of the job order cost cycle and how they relate to each other. The figures that flowed through Panorama Windows' general ledger cost accounts were provided in summary form. In the remaining chapters in this part, you will find out first where the cost figures originated. You will then study the detailed procedures and records required to account for materials purchased and used. Finally, you will examine the procedures used to account for labor and manufacturing overhead.

NEED FOR CONTROL OF MATERIALS

In most manufacturing businesses, the cost of raw materials is a major part of the total manufacturing cost of each product. Decisions regarding materials and their management are based on product knowledge, good judgment, and accurate, up-to-the-minute data. Here are just a few of the problems involved:

- Quality and cost of materials must meet the specifications on which sales prices are based.
- Correct quantities and types of materials must be on hand at the right time for production to proceed on schedule.
- Materials must be protected from loss or theft.
- Funds must not be tied up in inventory when they could be used more profitably elsewhere.
- Risks of spoilage and obsolescence must be minimized.
- Costs of materials handling and storage must be kept to a minimum.

Specific procedures and methods for controlling materials vary from company to company. Size, organization, and type of goods produced are some of the factors involved. Most modern systems of inventory control include the following features:

- Formal procedures for ordering and paying for materials.
- Physical safeguards for receiving, storing, and issuing materials.
- Perpetual inventory system to provide an ongoing record of the quantity and value of each type of material received and issued and the balance on hand.

You are already familiar with the size, structure, and operations of Panorama Windows, Inc. Panorama Windows' accounting system is designed to achieve maximum internal control. This chapter deals with the procedures for purchasing raw materials. Note that purchases are charged to Raw Materials 121. In order to simplify the discussion on materials, it is assumed that manual records are maintained at Panorama Windows. In reality, many records used in purchasing, storing, issuing, and controlling inventory are maintained on computers. Computerized records and procedures related to materials are discussed later in this chapter and in Chapters 4 and 5. Both manual and automated systems require careful attention to internal control.

MATERIALS PURCHASING PROCEDURES

The responsibility for purchasing materials is given to the **purchasing agent.** This person must buy materials in correct quantities, at the proper time, and at the most economical cost to the company. At Panorama Windows, the purchasing agent's staff is part of the procurement section of the General Factory Department. In a larger organization, a whole department might be required to conduct purchasing activities.

The purchasing staff keeps informed of various sources of supply, negotiates purchase contracts, prepares purchase orders, and follows through on delivery. The routine work of the purchasing staff begins with the receipt of a purchase requisition.

Reorder Routine

Let us trace the typical reorder routine step by step. To determine when an item has reached a level at which it should be reordered, Panorama Windows considers these factors:

- The rate at which the material is used.
- The amount of time it takes for the material to be delivered from the supplier after an order has been placed. This is known as the **lead time.**
- The minimum level of material that should be on hand to ensure that the company does not run out of the material. This is known as **safety stock.**

For example, the **reorder point** for W-206 brass lock assemblies is 200. Panorama Windows wants to have at least 100 brass lock assemblies on hand at all times. Since 20 locks are used in production each day and it takes five days to receive an order, the reorder point is calculated as follows.

20 locks (daily usage) × 5 days (lead time)	100
Plus safety stock	100
Reorder point	200

If an order for brass lock assemblies is processed as expected within five days, then the new lock assemblies should arrive at Panorama Windows as the inventory reaches the safety stock level of 100. Even if the order is delayed, there will still be 100 lock assemblies on hand to meet production requirements.

The standard quantity to be ordered varies from item to item. It should reflect the quantity necessary to get the best price while keeping inventory at an appropriate level to ensure uninterrupted production. To determine this quantity, it is necessary to consider the costs of placing an order as well as the costs of carrying the items in the inventory. The cost of placing an order includes:

- Costs of maintaining the purchasing department
- Cost of operating the receiving department
- Costs of processing an order

The cost of carrying items in the inventory includes:

- Costs of handling and storing material
- Insurance costs
- Losses due to theft, obsolescence, and spoilage
- Costs of maintaining inventory records

To determine the most advantageous number of units to order, a special formula called the **economic order quantity (EOQ)** has been developed. It is computed as follows:

$$\text{EOQ} = \sqrt{\frac{2 \times \text{annual requirements} \times \text{cost of an order}}{\text{cost to carry a single item}}}$$

If Panorama Windows' cost to order is $1.08, the cost to carry an item in inventory if $.75; and if the firm requires 5,000 brass lock assemblies during the year, then the EOQ of 120 is calculated as follows:

$$\text{EOQ} = \sqrt{\frac{2 \times 5{,}000 \times 1.08}{.75}}$$

$$= \sqrt{\frac{10{,}800}{.75}}$$

$$= \sqrt{14{,}400}$$

$$= 120$$

The calculation of the total cost to order and carry materials at various order sizes is shown below. An examination of this table shows that an order size of 120 units produces the lowest *total* cost. Order sizes below 120 and above 120 produce higher total costs. This happens because, as the order size increases, the total cost to order decreases and the total cost to carry increases. The EOQ is the point at which the total of these two costs is at a minimum.

Order Size	Number of Orders	Total Cost to Order	Average Inventory	Total Cost to Carry	Total Cost to Order and Total Cost to Carry
	(5,000/ Order Size) (Rounded)	($1.08 × No. of Orders)	(Order Size ÷ 2)	(Average Inventory × $.75)	
80	62.00	66.96	40.00	30.00	96.96
100	50.00	54.00	50.00	37.50	91.50
120	**42.00**	**45.36**	**60.00**	**45.00**	**90.36**
140	36.00	38.88	70.00	52.50	91.38
160	31.00	33.48	80.00	60.00	93.48

SELF-REVIEW

1. Assume that a company's production requires 400 pounds of steel each day, that it takes four days to receive steel from the supplier, and that the company wants to have 400 pounds of steel on hand at all times. Calculate the reorder point.
2. Assume that a company uses 10,000 pounds of plastic each year, that its cost to carry a pound of plastic in inventory is $.30, and that its cost to place an order is $1.35. Calculate the EOQ.

Answers to Self-Review

1. 400 lb × 4 days = 1,600 lb + 400 lb = 2,000 lb.

2. $$\text{EOQ} = \sqrt{\frac{2 \times 10{,}000 \times 1.35}{.30}}$$

$$= \sqrt{\frac{27{,}000}{.30}}$$

$$= \sqrt{90{,}000}$$

$$= 300$$

At this point you should be able to work Exercises 3–1 and 3–2 and Problems 3–4A and 3–4B.

Purchase Requisition

Once the number of W-206 brass lock assemblies reaches 200, the storeroom supervisor completes a purchase requisition requesting that 120 lock assemblies be ordered. A **purchase requisition** is a properly approved (authorized), written request for materials. An original and one copy of the purchase requisition are made, as shown below. The original is sent to the purchasing unit as a request for the materials. The copy is retained in the storeroom files. Some companies require that three or more copies be completed for various uses.

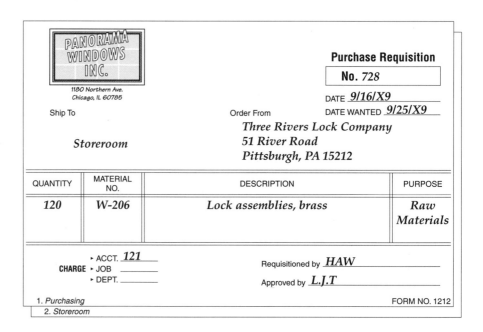

Purchase Order

When the purchasing staff receives the purchase requisition, a source of supply must be selected. Three Rivers Lock Company is the regular supplier of W-206 brass lock assemblies because this firm owns exclusive patent rights. Under other circumstances, several suppliers might be asked to quote prices or make bids. In choosing a supplier, the purchasing agent considers factors such as dependability, quality of material, delivery date, and price.

After the supplier has been chosen, the purchasing agent prepares a purchase order as shown on page 51. The **purchase order** represents written authorization to the supplier to ship the specified material. This form contains all necessary details, such as delivery date, method of shipment, unit price, and account number to be charged. The number of copies prepared varies from company to company. At Panorama Windows, five copies of the purchase order are prepared.

The original is sent to the supplier. Two copies are kept by the purchasing unit in an unfilled order file. One copy is returned to the storeroom as verification. The storeroom clerk compares the purchase order with the requisition and places the purchase order in an on-

PANORAMA WINDOWS INC.

1180 Northern Ave.
Chicago, IL 60785

Purchase Order

No. 1101

THIS NUMBER MUST APPEAR
ON ALL PACKAGES AND PAPERS
RELATING TO THIS ORDER.

DATE __9/20/X9__

To

- *Three Rivers Lock Company*
- *51 River Road*
- *Pittsburgh, PA 15212*

Ship To

- *Panorama Windows, Inc.*
- *1180 Northern Ave.*
- *Chicago, IL 60785*

SHIP TO	DATE WANTED	SHIP VIA	F.O.B.	TERMS
storeroom	*9/25/X9*	*truck*	*Pittsburgh*	*2/30, net 60*

QUANTITY	DESCRIPTION	UNIT PRICE	AMOUNT
120	*Lock assemblies, brass*	*$17.00*	*$2,040.00*

SUBJECT TO TERMS AND CONDITIONS ON THE REVERSE SIDE OF THIS PURCHASE ORDER

▸ ACCT. *121*

CHARGE ▸ JOB _____

▸ DEPT. _____

By *Teresa Keller*
PURCHASING AGENT

1. Supplier
2. Purchasing
3. Purchasing
4. Storeroom
5. Receiving

FORM NO. 1213

order file. The final copy is sent to the receiving department to tell the receiving clerk when the materials should arrive. This procedure allows time for any preparations that would be needed to receive the shipment, such as designating space for the materials in the storeroom. Panorama Windows' internal control system requires that all purchase order forms be prenumbered. The purchasing agent must complete a purchase order for every purchase. At the end of each month, the cost accountant verifies that all numbered forms either have been sent to suppliers, as shown by the copies, or are on hand. This ensures that purchase orders are used only for authorized purposes.

Receiving Report

When the materials are received from the supplier, they go to the receiving clerk. The receiving clerk is responsible for unpacking them, checking quantities and physical condition, and delivering them to the storeroom. Some materials may be of such a technical nature that laboratory tests must be conducted to make sure that they meet all specifications. In this case, the receiving clerk merely counts the items to make sure of the quantities. Laboratory personnel test the materials and send a report on the results to the purchasing unit.

The receiving clerk's copy of the purchase order is a **blind copy.** This means that it does not indicate the quantities ordered. A blind copy ensures an independent check of quantities by the receiving clerk. After counting and inspecting the materials, the clerk prepares a receiving report. The **receiving report** shows all details of the shipment, including comments on the condition of the materials received.

Note that the receiving clerk has indicated on Receiving Report 207, shown below, that 20 lock assemblies were rejected because they were damaged in shipment. All descriptions must agree with the purchase order descriptions to avoid confusion and errors. Some companies merely prepare additional blind copies of the purchase order to serve as the receiving report. This saves the time needed for the receiving clerk to write a description of the material.

Panorama Windows requires four copies of the receiving report. The original and one copy are sent to the purchasing unit, where they

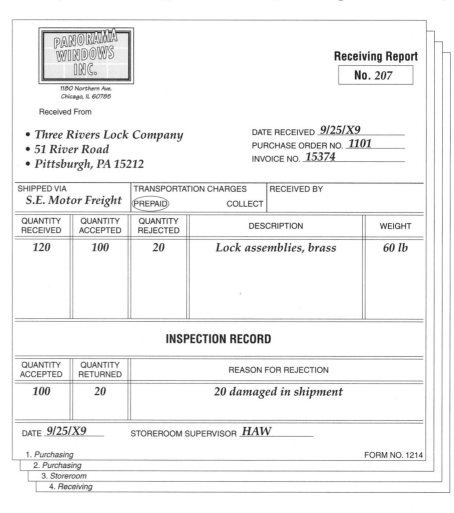

are compared with the purchase order and the supplier's invoice. One copy accompanies the materials to the storeroom for comparison with the purchase order and entry in the storeroom records. The storeroom supervisor signs the final copy to confirm that the materials have reached the storeroom. This copy is then kept in the receiving clerk's permanent file.

The storeroom clerk records the receipt of raw materials in a subsidiary ledger, the **materials ledger,** by making an entry on the appropriate **materials ledger card.** Materials are also called *stores;* therefore, the materials ledger is sometimes referred to as the *stores ledger.* A separate card, like the one shown below, is kept for each type of material. The card shows receipts, issues, and balance on hand, along with identification, control data, and even cost figures in some systems.

MATERIALS LEDGER CARD

MATERIAL *Lock assemblies, brass* REORDER POINT *200*
NUMBER *W-206* REORDER QUANTITY *120*

DATE	REFERENCE	RECEIVED			ISSUED			BALANCE		
		UNITS	PRICE	AMOUNT	UNITS	PRICE	AMOUNT	UNITS	PRICE	AMOUNT
Sept. 16 19X9	*Bal.*							175	17 00	2 975 00
25	*P01101*	100	17 00	1 700 00				275	17 00	4 675 00

Comparing Documents

When the **invoice** is received from the supplier, it is sent to the purchasing unit. The invoice will often arrive before the shipment. Many companies prefer this because it allows for verification of the purchase order before the shipment is accepted. The purchasing unit holds the invoice and the purchase order in the open purchase order file until the receiving report is available for comparison. The purchasing unit compares the supplier's invoice (purchase invoice) with the purchase order and receiving report to make sure of certain points:

- Goods ordered must have been received in good condition and be those listed on the invoice.
- Terms, unit prices, shipping charges, and other details must agree with order specifications.
- Computations must be correct.

If all documents agree, a member of the staff of the purchasing unit staples together one copy each of the invoice, receiving report, and purchase order and places them in a completed purchases file alphabetically by supplier. Next, a disbursement voucher like the one shown on page 54 is completed (adjusted to reflect value of damaged items rejected), and a second set of supporting documents is attached to it. (Panorama Windows normally requests billing in duplicate.) Then the voucher is formally approved and sent to the accounting unit for recording.

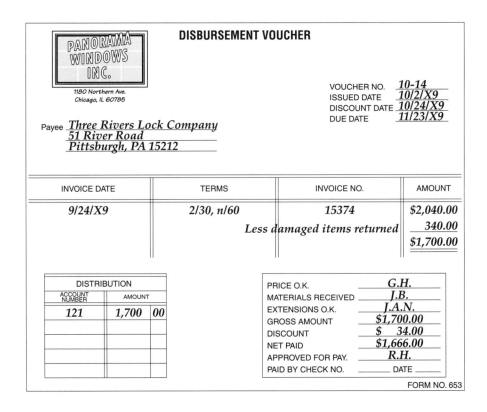

DISBURSEMENT VOUCHER

PANORAMA WINDOWS INC.

1180 Northern Ave.
Chicago, IL 60785

VOUCHER NO.	_10-14_
ISSUED DATE	_10/2/X9_
DISCOUNT DATE	_10/24/X9_
DUE DATE	_11/23/X9_

Payee *Three Rivers Lock Company*
51 River Road
Pittsburgh, PA 15212

INVOICE DATE	TERMS	INVOICE NO.	AMOUNT
9/24/X9	*2/30, n/60*	*15374*	*$2,040.00*
		Less damaged items returned	*340.00*
			$1,700.00

DISTRIBUTION		
ACCOUNT NUMBER	AMOUNT	
121	*1,700*	*00*

PRICE O.K.	*G.H.*
MATERIALS RECEIVED	*J.B.*
EXTENSIONS O.K.	*J.A.N.*
GROSS AMOUNT	*$1,700.00*
DISCOUNT	*$ 34.00*
NET PAID	*$1,666.00*
APPROVED FOR PAY.	*R.H.*
PAID BY CHECK NO.	DATE

FORM NO. 653

Recording the Voucher

When the voucher, invoice, and attached papers reach the accounting unit, the voucher clerk compares quantities, verifies extensions and footings, computes discounts, and checks all other computations. The voucher clerk also checks that all supporting documents are included in the file and that they are properly approved and signed. This double-checking is another part of the internal control system.

After verifying the account distribution against the purchase order, the voucher clerk enters the purchase in the **voucher register,** as shown on page 55. (Vouchers are often prenumbered for control purposes.) A purchase of direct materials, such as W-206 brass lock assemblies, or indirect materials, such as factory supplies, is entered as a debit in the Raw Materials column and as a credit in the Vouchers Payable column, as shown on page 55.

Note that the summary totals from the October voucher register of Panorama Windows were the source of Entry A in Chapter 2, debiting Raw Materials.

At this point you should be able to work Exercises 3–3 to 3–5.

After the entry is made in the voucher register, the voucher is sent to the treasurer's office. Here it is filed in the unpaid vouchers file according to the last date on which the discount may be taken.

Paying the Voucher

Before the due date, the voucher is removed from the unpaid vouchers file. An employee on the treasurer's staff prepares a check for the net amount of the voucher. The check is then entered in the check regis-

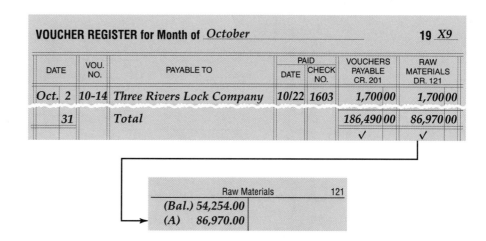

ter. The employee marks the voucher "Paid" by using a rubber stamp and enters the check number and date paid on the voucher. The check is mailed to the supplier (Three Rivers Lock Company), and the voucher is returned to the voucher clerk. The voucher clerk enters the check number and date of payment in the voucher register.

The voucher, with invoice and supporting documents, is then placed in the paid vouchers file.

At this point you should be able to work Problems 3–1A, 3–3A, 3–1B, and 3–3B.

PRINCIPLES OF INTERNAL CONTROL

The purchasing procedures used by Panorama Windows are practical and efficient. They also follow important principles of internal control.

- A request for a purchase must be made by an authorized person.
- A purchase order must be prepared and approved by an authorized person after a purchase requisition has been received.
- All materials received must be carefully checked to see that they correspond to those ordered and are in good condition.
- Payment is made only after proper approval.
- Various steps in the purchasing procedure are delegated to different persons to lessen the risk of fraud or error.
- In order to account for all steps in the purchasing process, all documents are prenumbered.

Flow of Documents in a Materials Purchasing System

The flowchart on page 56 illustrates the flow of documents related to materials purchasing. The arrows indicate which departments receive copies of the documents. The flowchart shows how the documents related to a purchase are collected and used to prepare a disbursement voucher. The disbursement voucher is then the basis for the journal entries to record the purchase and the payment of the invoice.

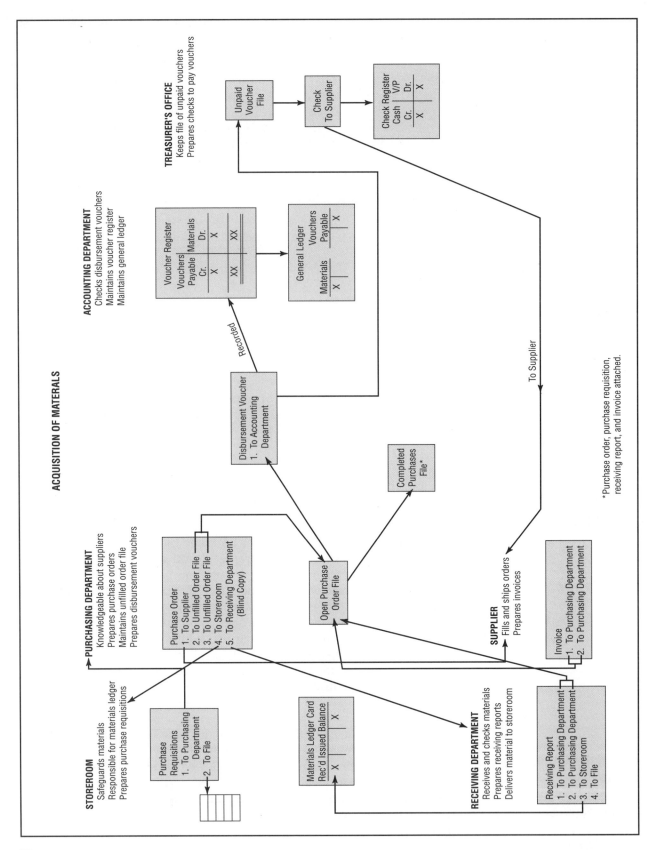

ACQUISITION OF MATERIALS

STOREROOM
Safeguards materials
Responsible for materials ledger
Prepares purchase requisitions

PURCHASING DEPARTMENT
Knowledgeable about suppliers
Prepares purchase orders
Maintains unfilled order file
Prepares disbursement vouchers

ACCOUNTING DEPARTMENT
Checks disbursement vouchers
Maintains voucher register
Maintains general ledger

TREASURER'S OFFICE
Keeps file of unpaid vouchers
Prepares checks to pay vouchers

RECEIVING DEPARTMENT
Receives and checks materials
Prepares receiving reports
Delivers material to storeroom

SUPPLIER
Fills and ships orders
Prepares invoices

Unpaid Voucher File

Check To Supplier

Check Register
Cash | V/P
Dr.
X
Cr.
X

Voucher Register
Vouchers Payable | Materials
Cr. | Dr.
X | X
| XX

General Ledger
Vouchers Payable
| X

Materials
X |

Recorded

Disbursement Voucher
1. To Accounting Department

Completed Purchases File*

To Supplier

Open Purchase Order File

Purchase Order
1. To Supplier
2. To Unfilled Order File
3. To Unfilled Order File
4. To Storeroom
5. To Receiving Department (Blind Copy)

Invoice
1. To Purchasing Department
2. To Purchasing Department

Purchase Requisitions
1. To Purchasing Department
2. To File

Materials Ledger Card
Rec'd Issued Balance
X | | X

Receiving Report
1. To Purchasing Department
2. To Purchasing Department
3. To Storeroom
4. To File

*Purchase order, purchase requisition, receiving report, and invoice attached.

56

SELF-REVIEW

1. What document is used when a department needs to reorder material? What document is sent to the supplier authorizing shipment of the material?
2. What is the function of the receiving report?
3. Why is it important to have a Balance column on the materials ledger card?
4. Why is it necessary to attach the purchase requisition, purchase order, and receiving report to the disbursement voucher?

Answers to Self-Review

1. A purchase requisition is used to reorder material; a purchase order is sent to the supplier.
2. The receiving report shows that the material has been received. It indicates the number of items received and the condition of the items.
3. The Balance column on the materials ledger card acts as a perpetual inventory of the item. An up-to-date balance of each item permits management to plan more efficiently. For example, knowing the balance of an item will facilitate reordering before the stock of the item is depleted.
4. Attaching the purchase requisition, purchase order, and receiving report to the disbursement voucher is part of good internal control. The purchase requisition, purchase order, and receiving report show that the purchase was properly authorized and that the materials received were the ones that were requisitioned and ordered. A record of all the documents related to a purchase lessens the risk of fraud or error.

SPECIAL PURCHASING PROCEDURES

The normal purchasing procedures can easily be adapted to meet special circumstances.

Bill of Materials

Sometimes several jobs requiring the same materials are started at about the same time. The usual quantities on hand of standard stores items may not be sufficient. To avoid this problem, the production manager may prepare a bill of materials when a new sales order is received. The **bill of materials** lists all materials required on the job and the date they will be needed, as shown on page 58. This record enables the storeroom supervisor to check the quantity of material on hand to make sure that enough is available. To avoid costly delays, the purchasing staff may be asked to buy more materials in advance. The bill of materials used by some companies contains columns for unit costs and total costs. Such a bill may later be used as a materials requisition.

Debit and Credit Memorandums

Occasionally, damaged or defective materials are received. These items are usually returned to the supplier immediately. A note of the return is made on the receiving clerk's copy of the purchase order and on the receiving report. The purchasing agent will then prepare a debit

Bill of Materials
Plainview Manufacturing Corp.
Plainview, NY 10699

Job _110_
To Be Started _Nov. 10, 19X9_
WILL REQUIRE THE FOLLOWING MATERIALS:

Date _October 8, 19X9_
For _Goldberg Stores_

UNITS	MATERIAL NO.	DESCRIPTION	MATERIALS ISSUED	
			UNIT COST	TOTAL COST
500	K-25	Leg braces		
500	T-16	Kander frames, 24" × 48"		
500	L-22	Mica tops, 30" × 60"		

Materials Received by _____
Date _____

G. Stanopoulos
Department Head

memorandum. The **debit memorandum** is a notice to the vendor of a deduction from the invoice for the cost of the returned materials, as shown below. (Accounting for materials returned after the voucher has been recorded is discussed in Chapter 4.)

There are some cases, too, when not all the materials ordered and shown on the invoice are actually received. If the supplier indicates that the remainder will be sent later, all documents may be held un-

PANORAMA WINDOWS INC.
1180 Northern Ave.
Chicago, IL 60785

Debit Memorandum

No. _D-3269_

To
• *Three Rivers Lock Company*
• *51 River Road*
• *Pittsburgh, PA 15212*

DATE _9/26/X9_
INVOICE NO. _15374_
INVOICE DATE _9/24/X9_
PURCHASE ORDER NO. _1101_
OUR STOCK NO. _K-193_

We have debited your account as follows:

QUANTITY	DESCRIPTION	UNIT PRICE	AMOUNT
20	Lock assemblies, brass	$17.00	$340.00

EXPLANATION: _Damaged in shipment. Returned 9/25/X9._

RETURNED VIA _S. E. Motor Freight_

T. Keller
PURCHASING AGENT

FORM NO. 1215

til the balance of the materials is received. If the supplier indicates that the balance will not be shipped within a satisfactory period of time, the materials received may be returned. In most cases, however, the buyer will keep the goods. The purchasing agent will issue a debit memorandum to the vendor for the amount of the goods short.

Sometimes a supplier ships more materials than were ordered. If the materials are not needed, the purchasing agent normally authorizes their return. Sometimes, however, they are kept for future use. In this case, if the materials have not been included in the vendor's invoice, the purchasing agent prepares a **credit memorandum** for the additional cost. (Many companies will amend the purchase order to include the extra goods shipped instead of issuing a credit memorandum.)

At this point you should be able to work Problems 3–2A and 3–2B.

Computerized Materials Purchases System

An on-line materials purchases system allows a company to have up-to-date information available and to improve the organization's purchasing process.

A computerized purchases system has an inventory file, a supplier file, and an open purchase order file in its memory. Upon receipt of a purchase requisition, the purchasing agent scans the supplier file and chooses a supplier. The computer prepares a purchase order, and the purchase order information is added to the open purchase order file.

When the order arrives, the receiving room clerk counts the items and enters the number of items into the receiving room terminal (also indicating which, if any, raw materials must be returned). The computer compares the items ordered (stored in the open purchase order file) with the items received, prepares a receiving report, and updates the open purchase order file, the inventory file, and the supplier file.

In addition to improving the processing of requisitions, a computerized system can provide information about purchases to the various users of the system.

CHANGING TECHNOLOGY IN MATERIALS PURCHASING

New technologies can help companies reduce or eliminate the time and paperwork associated with the purchase of materials. Companies can consider the benefits and costs of the following:

Electronic Data Interchange

Electronic data interchange (EDI) is a system that makes possible the intercompany computer-to-computer transmission of business forms. With EDI, standard forms such as purchase orders and invoices can be transmitted electronically between supplier and purchaser, eliminating paper processing and mailing time.

Connecting EDI with electronic funds transfer (EFT), in order to pay an invoice, is increasing in popularity. The purchaser of materials can send an electronic remittance advice to its bank instead of sending a check to the supplier. The purchaser's bank uses EFT to transfer the funds and remittance advice to the supplier's bank, which notifies the supplier of the payment.

Direct Debits

A company can instruct its bank to pay certain invoices by making automatic withdrawals from its accounts and transferring the funds to the supplier's bank account. Direct debits are often used for utility, freight, and insurance payments. Some companies object to this procedure because they do not want funds to be withdrawn from their accounts when they do not know in advance how much will be withdrawn.

Corporate Purchasing Cards

A corporate procurement card (CPC), or corporate purchasing card, program allows employees to use corporate credit cards for inexpensive purchases of items relating to repairs, maintenance, and operating expenses. The company determines which employees will be permitted to use the cards and sets a maximum dollar amount such as $500 or $1,000 for each transaction or sets a maximum monthly amount.

The use of CPCs helps a company save time in preparing and processing purchase requisitions and purchase orders for inexpensive items. Time is also saved in handling the payment for such purchases; the total amount due on all the credit cards for a particular month can be paid with one check. Some advantages of the CPC system are the following: the purchasing department has more time to focus on efficient ordering of large material purchases, the accounting department spends less time on transaction processing, departments get needed goods faster, and employees authorized to use CPCs feel trusted and gain confidence.

Integrated Supply Management

In an integrated supply management system, the supplier takes responsibility for all or part of the inventory for maintenance and repair supplies and tools (indirect materials) for the company. The supplier actually purchases and owns the company's inventory of supplies. In some plans, the supplier also assumes responsibility for delivering supplies to the workstations. The advantage to the company is less investment in inventory, reduced recordkeeping, less time needed to obtain items, and often lower prices and better-quality materials.

PRINCIPLES AND PROCEDURES SUMMARY

- Raw materials must be carefully controlled so that a firm's large investment in materials will be protected and enough raw materials will be on hand to meet production schedules.
- Purchasing involves the buying of materials in correct quantities, at the proper time, and at the most economical cost to the company. Purchasing procedures are performed by a purchasing unit headed by the purchasing agent.

- The purchasing cycle consists of the following steps:
  - A purchase requisition is prepared by the storeroom supervisor or the production manager.
  - A purchase order is issued.
  - When materials are received from the supplier, payment of the bill is authorized.
  - The purchase is recorded in the voucher register.
  - A check in settlement of the invoice is issued and recorded in the check register.
- Many of the steps in the purchasing cycle can be handled by a computer.
- All purchasing procedures should reflect the following key principles of internal control:
  - Requests for purchases must be made only by authorized persons.
  - Purchase orders must be properly approved.
  - All materials received must be carefully counted and inspected.
  - Payment should be made only upon proper approval.
  - Purchasing responsibilities should involve a number of persons, so that the risk of fraud or error is reduced.
- Special recording procedures can be used for handling damaged, lost, or defective materials, and for shortages and overages in shipment.

MANAGERIAL IMPLICATIONS

- Because in most manufacturing businesses the cost of material is a major part of manufacturing costs, management is very concerned with the control of materials and the development of efficient materials purchasing and handling procedures.
- Successful management develops standards for the frequency of ordering raw materials and the most economic order quantities. The goal is to keep materials inventories at the lowest level possible, consistent with economic order quantities, the ready availability of materials and other factors. Correct types and quantities of materials must be kept on hand, but with the least possible amount of funds invested in inventories.
- To achieve the above goals, appropriate procedures must be developed for ordering, paying for, receiving and storing materials. Computer systems have greatly enhanced and simplified the installation and operation of those procedures, providing instantaneous data about inventories and providing inexpensive control systems.
- Computer equipment has permitted even small manufacturers to adopt sophisticated inventory purchasing and control systems that help achieve the goal of having minimum, but adequate, quantities of inventory on hand at all times.

REVIEW QUESTIONS

1. List three factors in determining techniques for controlling materials.
2. How does a purchase requisition differ from a purchase order?
3. What is a receiving report?
4. What is the formula for computing the economic order quantity (EOQ)?
5. What individual costs are considered in determining the total cost to place an order? What individual costs are considered when computing the total cost to carry an item in inventory?
6. Why is a *blind copy* of the purchase order sent to the receiving department?
7. What type of information is shown on a materials ledger card?
8. What procedures should be followed before an entry is made in the voucher register to record the purchase of raw materials?
9. Define *bill of materials*.
10. What document is prepared to inform the supplier of a deduction from an invoice for the cost of goods returned to the supplier?
11. Which departments are responsible for each of the following procedures?
    a. Issuing purchase requisitions
    b. Issuing purchase orders
    c. Recording approved vouchers
    d. Preparing checks to pay vouchers
    e. Counting goods received

MANAGERIAL DISCUSSION QUESTIONS

1. What are some advantages of maintaining a materials ledger?
2. Under what circumstances would a bill of materials be prepared?
3. Before a disbursement voucher is recorded and approved for payment, copies of the purchase requisition, purchase order, receiving report, and purchase invoice should be compared and double-checked for accuracy. Why?
4. List at least three procedures for purchasing materials that should be followed in order to achieve good internal control. Explain how each helps in achieving internal control.
5. Why is it important for management to have complete and current data on the cost of materials?
6. Prepare a table that shows each step in the purchasing process, who is responsible for each step, and any documents or reports that would be produced during each step. Use the following column headings in the preparation of the table.

   Step in Purchasing Materials
   Person/Department
   Documents/Reports

EXERCISES

EXERCISE 3–1 **Calculate the reorder point. (Obj. 3).** The Siegel Company uses 8,000 pounds of Material ST400 every day in production. It it takes 12 days for an order to be delivered and if the company always wants to have a 3-day supply on hand, what is the point at which it should reorder Material ST400?

EXERCISE 3–2 **Calculate the economic reorder quantity. (Obj. 3).** The West Lake Corporation has determined that the cost to place an order for aluminum couplings is $5 and the cost to carry this item in inventory is $8. If 8,000 couplings are required for production each year, calculate the economic order quantity (EOQ).

EXERCISE 3–3 **Calculate the ending balance from a materials ledger card. (Obj. 6).** Calculate the ending balance of Material No. 45867 (6-inch iron brackets) based on the following information from the materials ledger card:

	Units	Amount per Unit
Beginning balance	178	$13.60
Issued	156	13.60
Received	218	13.60

EXERCISE 3–4 **Calculate the amount of a disbursement voucher. (Obj. 8).** Voucher No. 10-16 was prepared from a purchase invoice for $46,840 and a debit memorandum for $2,800 (for damaged goods returned). What is the gross amount of the voucher?

EXERCISE 3–5 **Calculate the net amount of disbursement vouchers. (Obj. 8).** Calculate the *net* amount of the following disbursement vouchers:
a. Gross amount of invoice: $42,730; terms: 3/10, n/30; debit memorandum: $4,380.
b. Gross amount of invoice: $116,708; terms: 4/20, n/60; debit memorandum: $5,460.

PROBLEMS

PROBLEM 3–1A **Record raw materials purchases. (Objs. 4–9).** Western Manufacturers, 231 West Superior Street, Duluth, Minnesota 55802, has an effective system of internal control. During April 19X9, the following transactions took place.

Apr. 4 Purchase Requisition 278 is received in the purchasing department. Purchase Order 644 is issued. The following materials are requisitioned and ordered:

Units	Material No.	Description	Purpose
4,390	603	2′ × 4′ plastic sheeting	Stores
840	622	3′ × 5′ plastic sheeting	Stores
1,890	642	4′ × 6′ plastic sheeting	Stores

14 All materials listed on Purchase Order 644 are received. Receiving Report 703 is completed.

14 All materials listed on Receiving Report 703 go to the storeroom.

19 Debit Memorandum 385 is prepared.

19 Supplier's Invoice 4-539 (shown below) is received. Disbursement Voucher 4-740 is prepared and sent to the accounting department.

QUALITY PRODUCTS, INC.

565 MORGAN AVENUE
PITTSBURGH, PA 15219
(412) 555-8720

SOLD TO   Western Manufacturers
231 West Superior Sreet
Duluth, MN 55802

	INVOICE DATE	INVOICE NUMBER
	4/17/X9	*4-539*

DATE OF ORDER	CUST. ORDER NO.	TERMS	SHIPPED VIA	F.O.B.
April 4, 19X9	*644*	*2/10, n/30*	*Industrial Freight Co.*	*Duluth*

QUANTITY	D E S C R I P T I O N	UNIT PRICE	EXTENSION	TOTAL
4,390	*603 – 2' × 4' plastic sheeting*	*$1.20*	*$5,268.00*	
840	*622 – 3' × 5' plastic sheeting*	*1.90*	*1,596.00*	
1,890	*642 – 4' × 6' plastic sheeting*	*2.60*	*4,914.00*	*$11,778.00*

INSTRUCTIONS

1. Issue Purchase Order 644 to Quality Products, Inc., 565 Morgan Avenue, Pittsburgh, Pennsylvania 15219. This firm supplies the standard stores that are listed on Purchase Requisition 278. Request delivery to the storeroom on April 24 via motor freight. The terms are 2/10, n/30 f.o.b. Duluth. The unit prices are $1.20 for each $2' \times 4'$ plastic sheet, $1.90 for each $3' \times 5'$ plastic sheet, and $2.60 for each $4' \times 6'$ plastic sheet. The purchase is charged to Raw Materials 121. Sign your name as the purchasing agent.

2. As the receiving clerk, issue Receiving Report 703. Note that 140 of the $2' \times 4'$ sheets are being returned to the supplier because of imperfections in the sheets. They need not be replaced. The weights are $\frac{1}{10}$ (.10) of a pound each for the $2' \times 4'$ sheets, $\frac{1}{4}$ (.25) of a pound each for the $3' \times 5'$ sheets, and $\frac{1}{2}$ (.50) of a pound each for the $4' \times 6'$ sheets. Record the weights of the goods accepted. The shipment is delivered by the Industrial Freight Company on April 14, 19X9. Charges are prepaid. Sign your name under *Received by*.

3. Assume that you are the storeroom supervisor. Sign Receiving Report 703 indicating that the materials have been turned over to the storeroom. Post the receipt of the materials to the materials ledger cards. Note the previous balances and the reorder points given on page 65.

Material	Balance		Reorder Point
No.	Units	Amount	
603	2,540	$3,048.00	2,540
622	600	1,140.00	600
642	960	2,496.00	960

4. Assume that you are the purchasing agent. Prepare Debit Memorandum 385 for 140 imperfect sheets returned to the supplier via motor express.

5. As the purchasing agent, compare the supplier's invoice (shown on page 64) with Purchase Order 644 and Receiving Report 703. Prepare Disbursement Voucher 4-740.

6. You represent the accounting department. Complete the first five lines of the verification block. Lines 1 to 3 require your initials to show that the verification has been completed.

7. Discuss the steps Western Manufacturers has taken to ensure that it has an effective system of internal control over purchasing materials.

PROBLEM 3–2A **Journalize raw materials purchases.** **(Obj. 9).** The following are transactions of the Bentley Company for the month of October 19X9.

Oct. 4 Purchase Requisition 1275 for 6,800 units of Material 254 is prepared by the storeroom clerk. The material is to be ordered from the Westmoreland County Corporation for $26.50 per unit. Terms are 1/10, n/30.

  5 Purchase Order 10-48 is completed for materials requisitioned on Requisition 1275.

  21 Materials ordered from the Westmoreland County Corporation on Purchase Order 10-48 are received. Of the 6,800 units received, 620 are rejected for imperfections and returned at once. Receiving Report 10-11 is prepared. The purchase invoice is included in the carton.

  21 A debit memorandum to the Westmoreland County Corporation for materials returned is prepared.

  21 Materials received today from the Westmoreland County Corporation are transferred to the storeroom and entered in the materials ledger.

  24 Disbursement Voucher 10-141 to the Westmoreland County Corporation is prepared for the amount owed on the firm invoice.

  25 A check to the Westmoreland County Corporation for the amount due, less discount, is prepared and mailed.

INSTRUCTIONS Record in general journal form the transactions needing entries.

PROBLEM 3–3A **Record disbursement vouchers.** **(Obj. 9).** The following vouchers were recorded by the Pierce Manufacturing Company during the month of November 19X9. For each voucher, determine the amount of the voucher and record it in a voucher register. Foot the columns.

a. Voucher 11-1 payable to the Transatlantic Supply Company. The invoice was for 1,270 units of Material 4-87 at $11.82 each. The receiving report indicates that 1,270 were received. None were defective.

b. Voucher 11-2 payable the Murray Corporation. The invoice was for 4,938 units of Material 4-113 at $8.93 each and 5,200 units of Material 4-189 at $11.58 each. The receiving report indicates that all materials ordered were received. However, 230 units of Material 4-189 were damaged in transit and were returned to the supplier. A debit memorandum was prepared.

c. Voucher 11-3 payable to Great Plains, Ltd. The invoice was for 2,650 units of Material 6-28 at $6.86 each. The receiving report indicates that only 2,200 units were received. A debit memorandum for the shortage was prepared.

d. Voucher 11-4 payable to the Armstrong Manufacturing Corporation. The invoice was for the following: 6,800 units of Material 3-87 at $7.50 each; 7,423 units of Material 5-83 at $10.30 each; 6,150 units of Material 4-97 at $8.54 each; and 4,600 units of Material 4-30 at $5.20 each. The receiving report indicates that the units ordered were received except for Material 4-97, which was 900 units short. In addition, 200 units of Material 3-87 were defective and were returned to the supplier. A debit memorandum was prepared.

PROBLEM 3–4A   **Calculate the economic order quantity and the recorder point. (Obj. 3).** The following information relates to materials purchases for the Edwards Company:

	Material A	**Material B**
Annual demand for material	4,000 lb	63,375 lb
Cost to place an order	$10	$10
Cost to carry an item	$2	$3
Safety stock	250 lb	750 lb
Lead time	20 days	10 days
Daily usage	15 lb	250 lb

INSTRUCTIONS

1. Calculate the economic order quantity (EOQ) for each material.
2. Calculate the reorder point for each material.
3. How many days late can an order be before the Edwards Company will run out of each material?
4. How many times during the year will the Edwards Company have to place an order?

ALTERNATE PROBLEMS

PROBLEM 3–1B   **Record raw materials purchases. (Objs. 4–9).** Western Manufacturers, 231 West Superior Street, Duluth, Minnesota 55802, has an effective system of internal control. During May 19X9, the following transactions took place.

May 2 Purchase Requisition 589 is received in the purchasing unit. Purchase Order 644 is issued. The materials requisitioned and ordered are as follows:

Unit	Material No.	Description	Purpose
4,390	603	2' × 4' plastic sheeting	Stores
840	622	3' × 5' plastic sheeting	Stores
1,890	642	4' × 6' plastic sheeting	Stores

16 All materials listed on Purchase Order 644 are received. Receiving Report 703 is completed.

16 All materials listed on Receiving Report 703 go to the storeroom.

17 Debit Memorandum 385 is prepared.

17 Supplier's Invoice 5-86 (shown below) is received. Disbursement Voucher 5-740 is prepared and sent to the accounting department.

PORTLAND SUPPLY COMPANY

1605 SW 4TH AVENUE
PORTLAND, OR 97201
(503) 555-1120

SOLD TO   Western Manufacturers
          231 West Superior Sreet
          Duluth, MN 55802

	INVOICE DATE	INVOICE NUMBER
	5/14/X9	*5-85*

DATE OF ORDER	CUST. ORDER NO.	TERMS	SHIPPED VIA	F.O.B.
May 2, 19X9	*644*	*2/15, n/45*	*MRL Delivery Corp.*	*Duluth*

QUANTITY	DESCRIPTION	UNIT PRICE	EXTENSION	TOTAL
4,390	*603 – 2' × 4' plastic sheeting*	*$1.20*	*$5,268.00*	
840	*622 – 3' × 5' plastic sheeting*	*1.90*	*1,596.00*	
1,890	*642 – 4' × 6' plastic sheeting*	*2.60*	*4,914.00*	*$11,778.00*

INSTRUCTIONS

1. Issue Purchase Order 644 to the Portland Supply Company, 1605 SW 4th Avenue, Portland, Oregon 97201. This firm supplies the standard stores that are listed on Purchase Requisition 589. Request delivery to the storeroom on May 16 via motor freight. The terms are 2/15, n/45, f.o.b. Duluth. The unit prices are $1.20 for each 2' × 4' plastic sheet, $1.90 for each 3' × 5' plastic sheet, and $2.60 for each 4' × 6' plastic sheet. The purchase is charged to Raw Materials 121. Sign your name as the purchasing agent.

2. Assume that you are the receiving clerk and issue Receiving Report 703. Note that 210 of the 2' × 4' sheets and 60 of the 4' × 6' sheets are being returned to the supplier because they were cracked. The weights are $\frac{1}{20}$ (.05) of a pound each for the 2' × 4'

sheets, $\frac{1}{10}$ (.10) of a pound each for the 3′ × 5′ sheets, and $\frac{1}{4}$ (.25) of a pound each for the 4′ × 6′ sheets. Record the weights of the goods accepted. The shipment is delivered by the MRL Delivery Corporation on May 16, 19X9. Charges are prepaid. Sign your name in the *Received by* space.

3. Assume that you are the storeroom supervisor. Sign Receiving Report 703 indicating that the materials have been turned over to the storeroom. Post the receipt of the materials to the materials ledger cards. Note the previous balances and the reorder points.

Material No.	Balance Units	Balance Amount	Reorder Point
603	2,540	$3,048.00	2,540
622	600	1,140.00	600
642	960	2,496.00	960

4. Assume that you are the purchasing agent. Prepare Debit Memorandum 385 for the damaged sheets returned to the supplier via motor express.

5. As the purchasing agent, compare the supplier's invoice (shown on page 67) with Purchase Order 644 and Receiving Report 703. Prepare Disbursement Voucher 5-740.

6. You represent the accounting department. Complete the first five lines of the verification block. Lines 1 to 3 require your initials to show that the verification has been completed.

7. Discuss the steps Western Manufacturers has taken to ensure that it has an effective system of internal control over purchasing materials.

PROBLEM 3–2B   **Journalize raw materials purchases.   (Obj. 9).**   The following are transactions of the Industrial Light Manufacturing Company for the month of May 19X9. Record in general journal form those transactions that require entries.

May   3   Purchase Requisition 801 for 1,450 units of Material 46 is prepared by the storeroom clerk. The material is to be ordered from Scalice Associates at a cost of $3.90 per unit. Terms are 2/10, n/30.

   4   Purchase Order 4063 is completed for the materials specified on Purchase Requisition 801.

   23   Materials ordered on Purchase Order 4063 are received. Of the 1,450 units received, 20 are rejected because they have imperfections and are immediately returned. Receiving Report 926 is prepared. The purchase invoice is included in the carton.

   23   A debit memorandum to Scalice Associates for materials returned is prepared.

   23   Materials received today from Scalice Associates (except those returned) are transferred to the storeroom and entered in the materials ledger.

24 Disbursement Voucher 5-62 to Scalice Associates is prepared for the amount owed on the firm's invoice.

25 A check to Scalice Associates for the amount due, after discount, is prepared and mailed.

PROBLEM 3–3B **Record disbursement vouchers.** **(Obj. 9).** The following vouchers were recorded by the St. Mortiz Company during the month of February 19X9. For each voucher, determine the amount of the voucher and record it in the voucher register. Foot the columns.

a. Voucher 2-1 payable to the Pensacola Supply Company. The invoice was for 11,400 units of Material A187 at $1.42 each. The receiving report indicates that 10,900 units were received. None were defective.

b. Voucher 2-2 payable to Sun Systems, Inc. The invoice was for 7,600 units of Material C135 at $3.58 each and 6,350 units of Material G658 at $1.05 each. The receiving report indicates that all materials ordered were received. However, 600 units of Material G658 were damaged in transit and were returned to the supplier. A debit memorandum was prepared.

c. Voucher 2-3 payable to the Eagle Best Corporation. The invoice was for 2,900 units of Material H730 at $5.10 each. The receiving report indicates that only 2,700 units were received. A debit memorandum for the shortage was prepared.

d. Voucher 2-4 payable to the Sioux Falls Metals Company. The invoice was for the following: 5,400 units of Material R870 at $2.86 each; 4,940 units of Material P965 at $4.82 each; 8,125 units of Material J560 at $1.40 each; and 6,450 units of Material L385 at $3.27 each. The receiving report indicates that the units ordered were received except for Material J560, which was 520 units short. In addition, 350 units of Material R870 were defective and were returned to the supplier. A debit memorandum was prepared.

PROBLEM 3–4B **Calculate the economic order quantity and the reorder point.** **(Obj. 3).** The following information relates to materials purchases for the Williams Company:

	Material A	Material B
Annual demand for material	120,000 lb	12,500 lb
Cost to place an order	$30	$20
Cost to carry an item	$20	$8
Safety stock	900 lb	2,800 lb
Lead time	2 days	8 days
Daily usage	300 lb	280 lb

INSTRUCTIONS
1. Calculate the economic order quantity (EOQ) for each material.
2. Calculate the reorder point for each material.
3. How many days late can an order be before the Williams Company will run out of each material?
4. How many times during the year will the company have to place an order?

MANAGERIAL DECISION CASE

The All-Pro Paint Company packages enamel paint for automobile touch-up work. The paint is packaged in 1-ounce glass bottles. A small steel bearing is placed in each paint-filled bottle to aid in mixing the paint when the bottle is shaken. The bottles come in boxes of 12 dozen bottles, and the steel bearings come in boxes of 1,000 bearings.

The purchasing department prepares serially numbered purchase orders. The original is sent to the supplier. Two copies are kept by the purchasing department and are filled numerically in an open purchase order file. An exact copy of the purchase order is sent to the receiving clerk. When a delivery of materials is received, the receiving clerk writes *OK* beside the item on the purchase order and returns the copy to the purchasing department.

When the receiving clerk has time, the boxes containing the small bottles are opened and counted. If a box contains any broken bottles, the receiving clerk calls the supplier and asks for replacements.

Rather than count the steel bearings, the receiving clerk weighs them and converts the weight into number of bearings using a conversion table.

Discuss the strengths and weaknesses of All-Pro's internal control over its purchasing procedures.

C H A P T E R
4

Storing and Issuing Materials

Internal control procedures for purchasing must be matched by similar procedures for storing and issuing materials in order to truly safeguard the company's investment in inventory. These precautionary measures are necessary to avoid damage, waste, theft, spoilage and obsolescence. Physical controls begin the moment that the materials are delivered to the storeroom, and continue to be applied during storage and issuance. Written controls begin with the receiving report and recording in the materials ledger, and continue through entries to record issuance and use.

OBJECTIVES

1. Analyze and record transactions involving the receiving, storing, and issuing of materials.
2. Prepare materials requisitions.
3. Maintain the materials ledger.
4. Maintain a materials requisition journal.
5. Maintain a job cost sheet for each specific job.
6. Maintain a departmental overhead analysis sheet for each department.
7. Maintain a returned materials journal.
8. Prepare returned materials reports.
9. Maintain a voucher register.
10. Explain the principles of internal control that should be present in materials issuance procedures.

NEW TERMS

Bin tag (p. 72)
Departmental overhead analysis sheet (p. 74)
Job cost sheet (p. 74)
Materials requisition (p. 72)
Materials requisition journal (p. 74)
Return shipping order (p. 78)
Returned materials journal (p. 77)
Returned material report (p. 76)

STORAGE

At Panorama Windows, Inc., admission to the storeroom area is carefully restricted to the personnel under the immediate supervision of the storeroom supervisor. The storeroom supervisor is responsible for the materials ledger, for the protection of materials in the storeroom, and for identification of the materials. Each type of material is assigned a number, indicating the type of material and its location. Materials are stored in a systematic manner in bins, on racks, or on shelves.

Attached to each bin or rack is a bin tag. The **bin tag** is an informal but carefully maintained record showing the quantities of the materials received, issued, and on hand at all times. The bin tag for W-206 brass lock assemblies is shown below.

			FORM NO. 14
BIN TAG			
Material No. _W-206_		**Location** _Bin K-7_	
Reorder Point _200_			
Description _Brass lock assemblies_			
DATE	QUANTITY RECEIVED	QUANTITY ISSUED	BALANCE
_9/1_			_285_
_9/4_		_30_	_255_
_9/5_		_50_	_205_
_9/5_		_10_	_195_
_9/16_		_20_	_175_
_9/25_	_100_		_275_
_10/1_		_55_	_220_
_10/6_		_(5)_	_225_

ISSUANCE

The use of all materials must be limited to properly authorized purposes.

Materials Requisition

No material may be issued from Panorama Windows' storeroom without a written form called a **materials requisition.** The materials requisition is prepared in duplicate by the department head or job supervisor. The requisition for the withdrawal of brass lock assemblies from the storeroom indicates the quantity, material number, description, and job number to which the materials are to be charged. (In the case of indirect materials, the requisition shows the department to which the materials are to be charged.)

DELIVER TO _Assembling Dept._	Materials Requisition

CHARGE ► ACCT. _122_
CHARGE ► JOB _101_
CHARGE ► DEPT. _____

No. _802_

DATE _10/1/X9_

QUANTITY	MAT. NO.	DESCRIPTION	UNIT PRICE	AMOUNT
55	W-206	_Brass lock assemblies_	$17 00	$935 00

ENTERED ON MATERIALS LEDGER CARD	ENTERED IN MATERIALS REQUISITION JOURNAL	ENTERED ON JOB COST SHEET	ENTERED ON DEPT. OVERHEAD ANAL. SHEET

Approved By _J.E.T_	Delivered By _T.R._	Received By _J.E.T_

FORM NO. 1217

Upon receipt of the materials requisition, the storeroom supervisor issues the materials and makes the necessary notations on the requisition. One copy is filed as a receipt, and the second copy is given to the storeroom clerk. The storeroom clerk enters the unit price and computes and enters the total amount.

Materials Ledger

After completing the cost computations on the requisition, the storeroom clerk records the entry in the Issued section of the materials ledger card, computes the new quantity on hand, and records it in the Balance section.

A materials ledger card is kept for each type of material on hand. Each card serves as a perpetual inventory record. The materials ledger is a subsidiary ledger verified against the Raw Materials control account in the general ledger. At the end of the accounting period, the sum of the dollar amount balances on the materials ledger cards should equal the balance of the control account.

MATERIALS LEDGER CARD

MATERIAL _Brass lock assemblies_ REORDER POINT _200_
NUMBER _W-206_ REORDER QUANTITY _120_

DATE	REFERENCE	RECEIVED			ISSUED			BALANCE		
		UNITS	PRICE	AMOUNT	UNITS	PRICE	AMOUNT	UNITS	PRICE	AMOUNT
Sept. 16 19X9	Bal.							175	17 00	2 975 00
25	P01101	100	17 00	1 700 00				275	17 00	4 675 00
Oct. 1	R802				55	17 00	935 00	220	17 00	3 740 00

Materials Requisition Journal

Once the information from the requisition has been recorded on the related materials ledger card, the requisition is forwarded to the cost clerk, who journalizes the transaction in the **materials requisition journal** so that the effect of the issuance will be ultimately reflected in the general ledger cost accounts. The journal (see below) shows how two typical entries might appear in the materials requisition journal.

MATERIALS REQUISITION JOURNAL

FOR MONTH OF _October_   19 _X9_   PAGE _10_

DATE	REQ. NO.	✔	JOB OR DEPT.	WORK IN PROCESS DR. 122	MFG. OHD. CONTROL DR. 501	RAW MATERIALS CR.121
Oct. 1	802	✔	101	935 00		935 00
3	808	✔	1		92 50	92 50
31	Total	✔		85,469 95	6,014 65	91,484 60

Special journals, such as a materials requisition journal, are often used in a job order system. Some firms like Panorama Windows, Inc., find that special journals improve the efficiency of the journalizing process when compared to using only a general journal. These special journals are used to avoid writing the many long and repetitious entries involved in issuing and using materials. Internal control also improves because the recording process can be shared by several employees. Additional special journals will be discussed later in this chapter and in other chapters.

Job Cost Sheet

The cost clerk's next step is to post the information from the requisition to the Materials section of the proper **job cost sheet.** The illustration below shows that Requisition 802 is charged to Job 101 on October 1.

Departmental Overhead Analysis Sheet

Since indirect materials cannot be charged to a specific job, information is posted from a requisition for such materials to the Indirect Materials section of the **departmental overhead analysis sheet.** A separate sheet is maintained for each department. The illustration

JOB COST SHEET

CUSTOMER _Nelson Construction Company_   JOB _101_
DESCRIPTION _Customer specs on file_   DATE STARTED _10/1/X9_
QUANTITY _100_   DATE COMPLETED _____

MATERIALS			DIRECT LABOR							MANUFACTURING OVERHEAD APPLIED							
					MILLING		ASSEMBLY		FINISHING				MILLING		ASSEMBLY		FINISHING
DATE	REQ. NO.	AMOUNT	DATE	REF.	HRS.	AMOUNT	HRS.	AMOUNT	HRS.	AMOUNT	DATE	REF.	HRS. RATE	AMOUNT	HRS. RATE	AMOUNT	HRS. RATE AMOUNT
10/1	R802	935 00															

			01	02	03	04	05	06	07	08	09 OTHER	
DATE	**REF.**	**TOTAL**	INDIRECT MATERIALS	INDIRECT LABOR	PAYROLL TAXES	DEPRECIATION	REPAIRS & MAINT.	UTILITIES	INSURANCE	OTHER TAXES	ITEM	AMOUNT
Oct. 3	R808	92 50	92 50									

DEPARTMENTAL OVERHEAD ANALYSIS SHEET
Department *Framing* — Month of *October* 19 *X9*

At this point you should be able to work Exercises 4–1 to 4–3.

above shows Requisition 808 charged to the Framing Department on October 3. The numbered columns classify the type of overhead involved.

PRINCIPLES OF INTERNAL CONTROL

Panorama Windows' procedures for storing and issuing materials reflect important principles of internal control.

- Admittance to the storage area is restricted.
- Materials ledger cards, covering all receipts and issues, are maintained.
- Each type of material is clearly identified, stored in a particular place, and carefully protected while in storage.
- Materials are issued only upon proper written authorization.
- The accounting system permits a periodic check of the materials ledger against the balance of the Raw Materials control account.
- Several different persons are involved in storage and issuance operations.

Flow of Documents Related to Issue of Materials

The flowchart on page 76 illustrates the flow of documents related to the issuance of materials. The arrows indicate where the information from the materials requisition is entered in storeroom records and in accounting department records.

SELF-REVIEW

1. Which general ledger control account is supported by the materials ledger cards?
2. What account(s) is debited when a materials requisition for direct materials is recorded in the materials requisition journal? What account(s) is credited?
3. Why should materials be issued only upon proper written authorization?
4. Name three places where a materials requisition for direct materials is recorded.

Answers to Self-Review

1. The Raw Materials account is supported by the materials ledger cards.
2. Work in Process is debited; Raw Materials is credited.
3. Requiring materials to be issued only with proper written authorization ensures that the materials are used appropriately for company purposes and not for noncompany purposes.
4. A materials requisition for direct materials is recorded in the materials ledger card, job cost sheet, and materials requisition journal.

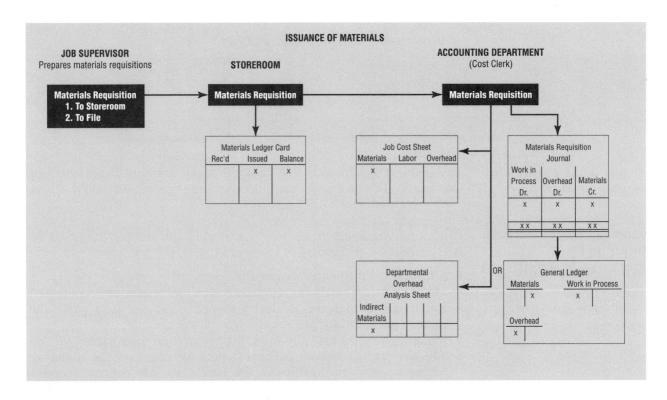

SPECIAL ISSUING PROCEDURES

A complete and well-designed system for the control of materials issuance also includes provision for special situations.

Bill of Materials

In some cases, all the materials for a job will be issued at one time, and the bill of materials (discussed in Chapter 3) serves as a requisition.

Return of Materials to Storeroom

Sometimes materials that have been issued are returned to the storeroom. This may result from requisitioning too much material, withdrawing the wrong materials, or other reasons. All returned materials must be accompanied by a returned materials report, which is very similar to the materials requisitions. At Panorama Windows, the **returned materials report,** shown on page 77, is prepared in duplicate. The report may be filled out either in the department that originally requisitioned the materials or by the storeroom supervisor.

After the storeroom supervisor checks the returns, the bin tag is adjusted by showing the number of units returned in parentheses in the Quantity Issued column. This is illustrated on page 72. The number of units returned is added to the balance. Then, the returned materials report is given to the storeroom clerk, who follows the steps listed below.

1. Enters the unit and total cost figures on the report. The unit cost figure is the same as that used when the materials were charged out.

```
                                              Returned Materials Report
                                              No. 48
           ► ACCT. 122
  CREDIT   ► JOB   101                         DATE 10/6/X9
           ► DEPT. _____                    DEPT. Assembling

  QUANTITY    MAT. NO.        DESCRIPTION            UNIT COST    AMOUNT

     5        W-206       Brass lock assemblies


  REASON FOR RETURN: Excess issue                  Authorized By K.P.

  Entered on          Entered on        Entered on              Received By
  Materials Ledger Card Job Cost Sheet   Dept. Overhead Anal. Sheet
                                                                T.R.
                                                             FORM NO. 1218
```

2. Makes an entry in parentheses in the Issued section of the materials ledger card. The new quantity and cost amounts are then entered in the Balance section of the card, as shown below.
3. Sends the returned materials report to the cost clerk.

These steps are illustrated in the following materials ledger card.

MATERIALS LEDGER CARD

MATERIAL _Brass lock assemblies_ REORDER POINT _200_
NUMBER _W-206_ REORDER QUANTITY _120_

DATE	REFERENCE	RECEIVED			ISSUED			BALANCE		
		UNITS	PRICE	AMOUNT	UNITS	PRICE	AMOUNT	UNITS	PRICE	AMOUNT
19X9 Sept. 16	Bal.							175	17 00	2 975 00
25	P01101	100	17 00	1 700 00				275	17 00	4 675 00
Oct. 1	R802				55	17 00	935 00	220	17 00	3 740 00
6	RM48				(5)	17 00	(85 00)	225	17 00	3 825 00

The cost clerk completes two important entries.

1. An entry in parentheses in the Indirect Materials column of the departmental overhead analysis sheet or in the Materials section of the appropriate job cost sheet, as shown on page 78.
2. An entry covering the return in the **returned materials journal,** as shown on page 78.

The totals of the columns of the materials requisition journal and the returned materials journal are posted in summary form to the appropriate general ledger accounts at the end of the month.

JOB COST SHEET

Customer _Nelson Construction Company_ Job _101_
Description _Customer specs on file_ Date Started _10/1/X9_
Quantity _100_ Date Completed _____

	MATERIALS				DIRECT LABOR								MANUFACTURING OVERHEAD APPLIED								
DATE	REQ. NO.	AMOUNT	DATE	REF.	MILLING		ASSEMBLY		FINISHING		DATE	REF.	MILLING			ASSEMBLY			FINISHING		
					HRS.	AMOUNT	HRS.	AMOUNT	HRS.	AMOUNT			HRS.	RATE	AMOUNT	HRS.	RATE	AMOUNT	HRS.	RATE	AMOUNT
10/1	R802	935 00																			
10/2	R804	2805 00																			
10/6	RM48	(85 00)																			

RETURNED MATERIALS JOURNAL
for Month of _October_ 19 _X9_ Page _10_

DATE	REPT. NO.	✔	JOB OR DEPT.	WORK IN PROCESS CR. 122		MFG. OHD. CONTROL CR. 501		RAW MATERIALS DR. 121	
Oct. 6	48	✔	101	85	00			85	00
12	49	✔	3			7	00	7	00
31	Total	✔		862	60	203	00	1,065	60

For the sake of simplicity, Entry B in Chapter 2 (see page 30) reflected the net effect of the summary postings from these journals, computed as follows:

	Work in Process	Manufacturing Overhead	Raw Materials
Summary Posting From MRJ	$85,469.95	$6,014.65	$91,484.60
Deduct Summary Posting From RMJ	862.60	203.00	1,065.60
Net Amount, Entry B	$84,607.35	$5,811.65	$90,419.00

Return of Materials to Supplier

Occasionally, it may be necessary to return materials to the supplier after they are placed in the storeroom. If materials are to be returned, the purchasing unit sends the storeroom supervisor a **return shipping order** authorizing the return and also prepares a debit memorandum. (Returns were also discussed in Chapter 3.) One copy each of the return shipping order and the debit memorandum is kept by the purchasing unit. The shipping unit receives a copy of the return shipping order as authorization to return the merchandise to the supplier. One copy each of the shipping order and the debit memorandum is sent to the accounting unit for its records. The storeroom clerk receives a copy of the debit memorandum. This copy is used in making an entry in parentheses in the materials ledger (in the Received column) showing the return.

If the return is made before the voucher register is closed for the month, the original entry is corrected by making a notation in paren-

				PAID		VOUCHERS		RAW	
DATE		VOU. NO.	PAYABLE TO	DATE	CHECK NO.	PAYABLE CR. 201		MATERIALS DR. 121	
Nov.	3	11-9	Scranton Steel Co.			(75	00)	(75	00)
						1,000	00	1,000	00

VOUCHER REGISTER for Month of _November_   19 _X9_

theses for the amount of the return on the same line as the original entry. This is shown above.

At the end of the month, the parenthetical entries are totaled separately. Then these totals are posted as a debit to Vouchers Payable and a credit to Raw Materials.

If the voucher register has been closed for the month in which the purchase was entered, a new voucher is issued and recorded. Vouchers Payable 201 is debited for the original amount and is also credited for the revised amount; the difference is credited to Raw Materials 121.

Materials Reserved and on Order

In a large business in which many jobs are started and many purchase orders and materials requisitions covering a variety of materials are processed, the materials ledger cards may be expanded to give more information and better control. Three additional columns are often added. These are the On Order, Reserved Quantity, and Free Quantity columns. An expanded materials ledger card with these columns is shown below.

The On Order column shows the number of units on order and the date of each order. When the order is filled, the storeroom clerk draws a line through the entry. Panorama Windows does not use an On Order column because the number of different materials in stock

MATERIALS LEDGER CARD

Material _Metal brackets_   **Reorder Point** _250_
Number _R-648_   **Reorder Quantity** _200_

DATE	REFERENCE	ON ORDER	RECEIVED			ISSUED			BALANCE			RESERVED QUANTITY	FREE QUANTITY
			UNITS	PRICE	AMOUNT	UNITS	PRICE	AMOUNT	UNITS	PRICE	AMOUNT		
Jan. 1 [19X9]	Bal.								300	1 00	300 00		300
8	PO-608	150	150	1 00	150 00				450	1 00	450 00		450
12	R-243					200	1 00	200 00	250	1 00	250 00		250
13	PO-625	200											
16	BM-116								250	1 00	250 00	100	150
20	PO-625		200	1 00	200 00				450	1 00	450 00		350
25	BM-116					100	1 00	100 00	350	1 00	350 00		350

is small. The filed copy of the purchase order provides the needed information.

The Reserved Quantity column simply indicates that materials will be needed for a forthcoming job. This column tells the storeroom clerk and storeroom supervisor that additional units of the materials must be ordered before the quantity on hand is down to the normal reorder point. When reserved materials are issued, a line is drawn through the entry in the Reserved Quantity column, The Free Quantity column shows the balance on hand less any reserved quantities. Panorama Windows does not use the expanded materials ledger card. At Panorama Windows, a reserved stock tag is clipped to the materials ledger card. This tag shows the amount that will be needed and when the job is to be started if the amount is unusually large.

SELF-REVIEW

1. How are materials returned to the storeroom entered on the materials ledger card?
2. What account(s) is debited when a returned materials report for indirect materials is recorded in the returned materials journal? What account(s) is credited?

Answers to Self-Review

At this point you should be able to work Exercises 4–4 and 4–5 and Problems 4–1A to 4–5B.

1. Materials returned to the storeroom are recorded in the Issued section of the materials ledger card as a negative amount (in parentheses). Revised quantity and cost amounts are entered in the Balance section.
2. Manufacturing Overhead Control is debited; Work in Process is credited.

COMPUTERIZED MATERIALS ISSUANCE

Many companies use a computer system to help track the issue of materials.

In a typical computerized system, the storeroom supervisor enters the material number and the quantity from a materials requisition, a returned materials report, or a return shipping order into a computer terminal in the storeroom. The computer uses this information, together with cost data stored in its memory, to process a completed materials requisition.

The computer system also uses the quantity and material number to update the inventory file for that material and to determine whether more units should be ordered. For example, if the amount of material issued on the material requisition causes the balance to drop below the reorder point, the computer automatically produces a purchase order to reorder the material.

A computerized system helps facilitate up-to-date inventory records, simplifies processing of purchase orders, and provides stronger internal control over materials issuance.

PRINCIPLES AND PROCEDURES SUMMARY

- A firm's procedures for storing and issuing materials must have a variety of internal controls to protect the investment that the firm has in these items.
- Materials on hand must be carefully identified, stored, recorded, and preserved by the storeroom supervisor and the storeroom staff. Materials are issued only upon written receipt of a materials requisition. When materials have been issued, entries are recorded on the materials ledger card, the materials requisition journal, and the job cost sheet or departmental overhead analysis sheet.
- Special issuing procedures are used when all materials required on a job are issued at one time, when materials are returned to the storeroom or to the supplier, and when the materials are to be reserved for a future job.
- A perpetual inventory system operates to record and control both receipts and issues of materials. Entries are made on materials ledger cards as follows:
  - *Materials purchased:* Entry recorded as goods are received. Data taken from receiving report and purchase order.
  - *Materials issued:* Entry recorded as goods are issued. Data taken from materials requisition.
  - *Materials returned to storeroom:* Entry recorded as goods are returned. Data taken from returned materials report.
  - *Materials returned to supplier:* Entry recorded as goods are sent back. Data taken from debit memorandum.
- Related entries are made in the Raw Materials account in the general ledger as follows:
  - *Materials purchased:* Summary posting at end of period from voucher register's Raw Materials column.
  - *Materials issued:* Summary posting at end of period from total of Raw Materials column in materials requisition journal.
  - *Materials returned to storeroom:* Summary posting at end of period from total of Raw Materials column in returned materials journal.
  - *Materials returned to supplier:* Summary entry at end of period from parenthetical entry total of voucher register's Raw Materials column.
- At the end of the period, the balance of the Raw Materials account should equal the total of the dollar amount balances on the materials ledger cards.

MANAGERIAL IMPLICATIONS

- Here are some basic concepts about storing and issuing raw materials that are used by successful, well-run manufacturing companies.
- Access to areas in which raw materials are stored is restricted to authorized personnel.

■ Proper authorization must be given for all materials issued.

■ Appropriate entries are recorded in materials records when materials are received and are issued, so that the records reflect, at all times, accurate information about the materials on hand.

■ All materials issued from the storeroom and all materials returned to it are properly entered in the service department accounts or in the job order cost sheets.

■ Checks should be made monthly to make sure that detailed records, such as the materials ledger, agrees with the general ledger Raw Materials account.

■ Each company should determine the exact journals, ledgers, and detailed records relating to raw materials that the company needs and should develop procedures that are appropriate to the company's organizational structure and operation.

REVIEW QUESTIONS

1. How does a bin tag differ from a materials ledger card?
2. What is a materials requisition?
3. List the three places where a materials requisition for direct materials must be recorded. List three places where a materials requisition for indirect materials must be recorded.
4. What is a returned materials report? How does a returned materials report differ from a return shipping order?
5. Describe the procedures used in recording materials requisitions and returned materials reports on materials ledger cards.
6. What is the purpose of an On Order column on a materials ledger card?
7. Describe the procedure followed in recording information in the Reserved Quantity column of an expanded materials ledger card.
8. Indicate the sequence in which the following documents would be prepared:
   a. Purchase invoice
   b. Bill of materials
   c. Return shipping order
   d. Purchase requisition
   e. Materials requisition
   f. Purchase order
9. What are the sources for the debit entries in the Raw Materials account in the general ledger? What are the sources for the credit entries?

MANAGERIAL DISCUSSION QUESTIONS

1. How are materials requisitions used in controlling the materials inventory?
2. What procedures should be used in storing and issuing materials to achieve good internal control?
3. What would be the advantage of using a materials requisition journal?

4. What information can management obtain from the On Order and Reserved Quantity columns of an expanded materials ledger card? Why is this useful?
5. Why is it necessary to maintain departmental overhead analysis sheets for each production and service department?
6. Which accounting records and forms would provide information to management that would be useful in analyzing high indirect materials costs in the factory?
7. What are job cost sheets, and what types of data do they provide to management?

EXERCISES

EXERCISE 4–1 **Calculate materials costs. (Obj. 5).** Calculate the materials cost for Job 620 from the job cost sheet information given below.

Requisitions		Returned Materials Reports	
476	$898.00	39	$78.00
493	35.97	43	9.50
497	328.00	48	46.80
503	648.35		
514	55.87		

EXERCISE 4–2 **Calculate ending inventory balances. (Obj. 3).** Compute the ending balance and the cost of the ending inventory of Raw Material 4-89, which has a unit price of $6.80. The materials ledger card shows the following data:

	Units		Units
Beginning balance	7,990	Issuances	2,560
Purchases	3,300		675
	6,200		1,250
			360
			1,680

EXERCISE 4–3 **Journalize materials requisitions. (Obj. 4).** During May 19X9, Cummin's Pools had requisitions totaling $74,490 for direct materials and $8,160 for indirect materials. Prepare the entry in general journal form to record the cost of materials requisitioned for the month.

EXERCISE 4–4 **Journalize returned materials reports. (Obj. 7).** During August 19X9, Jones Products Inc. had returned $6,740 in direct materials and $590 in indirect materials. Prepare the entry in general journal form to record the cost of the materials returned to the storeroom for the month.

EXERCISE 4–5 **Journalize a return shipping order. (Obj. 3).** The Schmidt Manufacturing Company returned materials totaling $2,412.20 to its supplier, Martinez Inc. Prepare the entry in general journal form for materials returned.

PROBLEMS

PROBLEM 4–1A

Record in the materials ledger. (Obj. 3). Patio Enclosures Inc. manufactures patio and deck enclosures. Their 4-foot by 6-foot thermal cover, Material T-46, costs $84.50. The following transactions occurred during the month of May 19X9, for receipts, issuances, and returns of Material T-46. The reorder point for Material T-46 is 60 units, and the reorder quantity is 130 units.

May	1	Beginning balance	56
	4	PO308	130
	10	R408	25
	15	R490	115
	16	RM48	22
	19	R518	12
	23	PO315	130
	27	RS204	10
	29	R691	62
	30	RM65	15

INSTRUCTIONS

Record the purchase orders, materials requisitions, returned shipping order, and returned materials reports in the materials ledger card.

PROBLEM 4–2A

Journalize and post raw materials transactions. (Objs. 4, 9). The raw materials transactions of the Vermont Corporation for the month of May 19X9 are listed below. First, record the beginning balance in the Raw Materials account. Then record the transactions in the materials requisition journal and the voucher register. Total the columns in the journals and post the totals to the Raw Materials account.

May	1	Beginning inventory of raw materials	$156,488
	4	Disbursement Voucher 5-1 for raw materials purchased from Prime Supply Company	58,186
	8	Materials Requisition 416 for direct materials used on Job 20	26,122
	14	Materials Requisition 417 for direct materials used on Job 21	49,662
	17	Disbursement Voucher 5-2 for raw materials purchased from Amos Corporation	56,443
	21	Materials Requisition 418 for indirect materials used in Finishing Department	16,640
	24	Materials Requisition 419 for direct materials used on Job 21	32,115
	26	Disbursement Voucher 5-3 for raw materials purchased from Tri-State Company	39,822
	29	Returned Shipping Order 28 for materials to Tri-State Company (voucher register has not been closed)	3,900

PROBLEM 4–3A **Processing source documents. (Objs. 1–9).** The Maxwell Corporation manufactures aluminum ladders. The procedures for receiving and issuing materials include the following:

Receiving. A copy of the receiving report accompanies the materials to the storeroom, where it is signed by the storeroom supervisor to show that the materials were received in that area. The storeroom clerk records the receipt of raw materials by posting to the materials ledger cards. The receiving report and the supplier's invoice are checked against the purchase order. A voucher is completed, approved, and entered in the voucher register. Materials returned to the supplier are covered by a return shipping order and a debit memorandum. The debit memorandum is posted to the materials ledger cards and the voucher register.

Issuing. Materials are issued after an approved materials requisition is received in the storeroom. Unit costs are entered and extended on the requisition. The issue is posted to the materials ledger cards and recorded in the materials requisition journal. The requisition is posted to the proper job cost sheet or the departmental overhead analysis sheet. Materials returned to the storeroom are accompanied by a returned materials report. After the returned materials are checked in, they are posted to the materials ledger cards and recorded in the returned materials journal. The returned materials report is posted to the proper job cost sheet or the departmental overhead analysis sheet.

During December 19X9 the following transactions take place:

Dec. 1 Materials Requisitions 814 is received by the storeroom supervisor, and the materials are issued. The materials requisitioned are for use in the Layout Department on Job 762 for the Singer Supply Company. Job 762 calls for 300 six-foot aluminum ladders. The materials requisitioned are as follows:

> 300 units R-6 side rails, 6'
> 150 units S-12 steps, 4″ × 12″
> 300 units S-15 steps, 4″ × 15″
> 150 units T-612 tops, 6″ × 12″

6 Receiving Report 615 (for Purchase Order 703) is completed by the receiving clerk. Since this report is not shown in this problem, the data to be posted to the materials ledger cards can be found on Disbursement Voucher 12-01, shown on page 86, to which you should refer.

6 Disbursement Voucher 12-01 is received.

10 Materials Requisition 815 is received by the storeroom supervisor, and the materials are issued. The materials requisitioned are for use in the Layout Department on

			Disbursement Voucher	

No. *12-01*

PAYEE ▶ *Tools-for-You Distributors, Inc.*
716 Delaware Avenue
Buffalo, NY 14209

VOUCHER DATE: *12/6/X8*
TERMS: *n/30*
DISCOUNT DATE: _____
DATE DUE: *1/6/X9*

INVOICE DATE	INVOICE NUMBER	DESCRIPTION		AMOUNT	
11/28/X8	*284*	*6,000 Steps, 4″ × 12″, S-12*	*@$.45*	*$2,700*	*00*
		4,600 Steps, 4″ × 15″, S-15	*.60*	*2,760*	*00*
			TOTAL	*$5,460*	*00*

DISTRIBUTION	
ACCT. NO.	AMOUNT
121	*$5,460.00*

PRICE O.K.   *B.A.C*
MATERIAL RECEIVED _____
EXTENSIONS O.K.   *F.C.D.*
GROSS AMOUNT _____
DISCOUNT _____
NET PAID _____
APPROVED FOR PAY _____
PAID BY CHECK NO. ____ DATE ___

Job 763 for the Construction Supplies company. Job 763 calls for 250 eight-foot aluminum ladders. The materials requisitioned are as follows:

    250 units R-8 side rails, 8′
    125 units S-12 steps, 4″ × 12″
    375 units S-15 steps, 4″ × 15″
    125 units T-612 tops, 6″ × 12″

INSTRUCTIONS
1. If you are not using the *Study Guide and Working Papers*, open the materials ledger by recording the opening balances on the materials ledger cards. The December balances are as follows:

Material	Reorder Point	Reorder Quantity	Balance		
			Units	Price	Amount
B-10 elbow braces	6,000	13,000	5,485	$ .35	$1,919.75
R-6 side rails, 6′	3,000	8,000	1,970	1.15	2,265.50
R-8 side rails, 8′	1,900	3,850	2,025	1.40	2,835.00
S-12 steps, 4″ × 12″	2,500	6,000	1,910	.45	859.50
S-15 steps, 4″ × 15″	2,500	4,600	1,700	.60	1,020.00
T-612 tops, 6″ × 12″	2,400	5,000	1,440	.75	1,080.00
W-125 washers, $\frac{1}{4}$″ flat (box of 100)	300 boxes	940 boxes	675	.80	540.00

2. Prepare the materials requisitions.

3. Process the materials requisitions, receiving report data, and the disbursement voucher data through all the procedures adopted by the Maxwell Corporation. The additional records needed are job cost sheets, a departmental overhead analysis sheet, a voucher register, a materials requisition journal, and a returned materials journal. *Keep all your records for use in Problem 4–4A.*

PROBLEM 4–4A   **Process source documents.   (Objs. 1–9).**   This problem is a continuation of Problem 4–3A. The following additional transactions take place:

Dec. 16   Receiving Report 616 (for Purchase Order 704) is completed by the receiving clerk. Since this report is not shown, the data to be posted to the materials ledger cards can be found on Disbursement Voucher 12-02, shown below, to which you should refer.

   16   Disbursement Voucher 12-02 is received.

Disbursement Voucher

No. *12-02*

PAYEE ▶ *Aloha Supplies International*
142 Merchant Street
Honolulu, HI 96813

VOUCHER DATE: *12/16/X8*
TERMS: *3/15, n/45*
DISCOUNT DATE: *12/31/X8*
DATE DUE: *1/30/X9*

INVOICE DATE	INVOICE NUMBER	DESCRIPTION		AMOUNT
12/10/X8	1AX475	5,000 Tops, 6″ × 12″, T-612	@$.75	$3,750 00
			TOTAL	$3,750 00

DISTRIBUTION	
ACCT. NO.	AMOUNT
121	$3,750.00

PRICE O.K.   *B.A.C*
MATERIAL RECEIVED _____
EXTENSIONS O.K.   *F.C.D.*
GROSS AMOUNT _____
DISCOUNT _____
NET PAID _____
APPROVED FOR PAY _____
PAID BY CHECK NO. _____ DATE _____

---

   18   Materials Requisition 816 is received by the storeroom supervisor, and the materials are issued. The materials are for the Assembly Department (Account 502). They consist of 25 boxes of W-125 washers $\frac{1}{4}$″ flat (box of 100).

   20   Receiving Report 617 (for Purchase Order 705) is completed by the receiving clerk. Since this report is not shown, the data to be posted to the materials ledger cards

can be found on Disbursement Voucher 12-03, shown below, to which you should refer.

20 Disbursement voucher 12-03 is received.

Disbursement Voucher

No. *12-03*

PAYEE ▶ *Providence Hardware Corp.*
21 Westminster Street
Providence, RI 02903

VOUCHER DATE: *12/20/X8*
TERMS: *2/10, n/30*
DISCOUNT DATE: *12/30/X8*
DATE DUE: *1/19/X9*

INVOICE DATE	INVOICE NUMBER	DESCRIPTION		AMOUNT	
12/18/X8	*48-818*	*13,000 Elbow braces, B-10*	*@$.35*	*$4,550*	*00*
			TOTAL	*$4,550*	*00*

DISTRIBUTION	
ACCT. NO.	AMOUNT
121	*$4,550.00*

PRICE O.K. *B.A.C*
MATERIAL RECEIVED _____
EXTENSIONS O.K. *F.C.D.*
GROSS AMOUNT _____
DISCOUNT _____
NET PAID _____
APPROVED FOR PAY _____
PAID BY CHECK NO. _____ DATE _____

---

20 Materials Requisition 817 is received by the storeroom supervisor, and the materials are issued. The materials are for the Layout Department on Job 762 and are for the following items:

   300 units R-6 side rails, 6′
   150 units S-12 steps, 4″ × 12″
   300 units S-15 steps, 4″ × 15″
   150 units T-612 tops, 6″ × 12″

21 Returned Materials report 84 is received by the storeroom supervisor. The accompanying materials are 25 S-15 steps, an excess quantity requisitioned in error on Job 763. The materials are returned to the storeroom.

INSTRUCTIONS
1. Prepare the materials requisitions.
2. Prepare the returned materials report.
3. Process all documents through all the procedures followed by the Maxwell Corporation. Use the records provided in Problem 4–3A as needed. *Keep all your records for use in Problem 4–5A.*

PROBLEM 4–5A   **Process source documents.   (Objs. 1–9).** This problem is a continuation of Problems 4–3A and 4–4A. The following additional transactions take place.

Dec. 22   Materials Requisition 818 is received by the storeroom supervisor, and the materials are issued. The materials are for Layout Department for use on Job 763 and include the following:

> 200 units R-8 side rails, 8′
> 100 units S-12 steps, 4″ × 12″
> 300 units S-15 steps, 4″ × 15″
> 100 units T-612 tops, 6″ × 12″

27   Return Shipping Order 108 (not shown) and the debit memorandum (not shown) dated December 20, 19X8, are received from the purchasing unit. The data to be posted to the materials ledger cards can be found on Disbursement Voucher 12-04, shown below, to which you should refer.

27   Disbursement Voucher 12-04 is received.

28   Materials Requisition 819 is received by the storeroom supervisor, and the materials are issued. The materials are for the Layout Department on Job 764 for the O'Dell

---

Disbursement Voucher

No. *12-04*

PAYEE ▶ *AlumLite Developers, Inc.*
2010 Bunker Hill Drive
Baton Rouge, LA 70808

VOUCHER DATE: <u>*12/27/X8*</u>
TERMS: _____
DISCOUNT DATE: _____
DATE DUE: _____

INVOICE DATE	INVOICE NUMBER	DESCRIPTION	AMOUNT	
		To correct Disbursement Voucher 11-24, November 21, 19X8, for excess quantity of materials received, per Return Shipping Order 108, December 20, 19X8, and debit memorandum, December 20, 19X8; copies attached. @$.45	$1,125	00
			360	00
	Returned Material	*800 Steps, 4″ × 12″, S-12* AMOUNT	$ 765	00

DISTRIBUTION	
ACCT. NO.	AMOUNT
201	*$1,125.00* Dr.
201	*765.00* Cr.
121	*360.00* Cr.

PRICE O.K.   *B.A.C*
MATERIAL RECEIVED _____
EXTENSIONS O.K.   *F.C.D.*
GROSS AMOUNT   _____
DISCOUNT   _____
NET PAID   _____
APPROVED FOR PAY _____
PAID BY CHECK NO. _____ DATE _____

Company. Job 764 calls for 300 eight-foot aluminum ladders. The materials requisitioned are as follows:

300 units R-8 side rails, 8′
150 units S-12 steps, 4″ × 12″
450 units S-15 steps, 4″ × 15″
150 units T-612 tops, 6″ × 12″

INSTRUCTIONS

1. Complete the materials requisitions.
2. Process all documents through all the procedures followed by the Maxwell Corporation. Use the records provided in Problems 4–3A and 4–4A.
3. Prove the accuracy of your work by footing and cross-footing all money columns in the voucher register and the materials requisition journal. Double-rule the columns.
4. Post from the voucher register, the materials requisition journal, and the returned materials journal to the Raw Materials account. NOTE: If you are not using the *Study Guide and Working Papers,* open the Raw Materials account by recording the December 1 balance of $10,519.75.
5. Prepare a schedule listing each material in the materials ledger and its ending balance. The total of this schedule should equal the ending balance in the Raw Materials account.

ALTERNATE PROBLEMS

PROBLEM 4–1B

Record in the materials ledger. (Obj. 3). The Chatham Bottling Corporation manufactures six styles of bottles that use a variety of tops. The cork top, Material C-478, costs $3.80 each. The reorder point for Material C-478 is 2,800 units, and the reorder quantity is 2,500 units. The following transactions occurred during the month of September 19X9, for the receipts, issuances, and returns of Material C-478.

Sept.	1	Beginning balance	2,460
	3	PO8-39	2,500
	6	R812	550
	9	R830	840
	12	RM65	30
	16	R861	1,120
	22	PO8-79	2,500
	25	RSO103	50
	30	R920	400
	30	RM83	10

INSTRUCTIONS

Record the purchase orders, materials requisitions, returned shipping order, and returned materials reports in the materials ledger card.

PROBLEM 4–2B

Journalize and post raw materials transactions. (Objs. 4, 9). The raw materials transactions of the Hartman Corporation for the month of March 19X9 are listed below. First, record the beginning balance in the Raw Materials account. Then record the transactions in the materials requisition journal and the voucher register. Total the columns in the journals and post the totals to the Raw Materials account.

Mar.	1	Beginning inventory of raw materials	$5,680
	5	Disbursement Voucher 3-1 for raw materials purchased from the Riverfront Company	4,805
	9	Materials Requisition 509 for direct materials used on Job 405	2,850
	16	Materials Requisition 510 for direct materials used on Job 406	3,925
	19	Disbursement Voucher 3-2 for raw materials purchased from New England Supply Company	3,450
	22	Materials Requisition 511 for indirect materials used in Assembly Department	950
	25	Materials Requisition 512 for direct materials used on Job 405	4,180
	27	Disbursement Voucher 3-3 for raw materials purchased from Green & Company	2,470
	28	Returned Shipping Order 30 for materials returned to Green & Company (voucher register has not been closed)	660

PROBLEM 4–3B   **Process source documents.   (Objs. 1–9).**   The Maxwell Corporation manufactures aluminum ladders. The procedures for receiving and issuing materials include the following:

Receiving. A copy of the receiving report accompanies the materials to the storeroom, where it is signed by the storeroom supervisor to show that the materials were received in that area. The storeroom clerk records the receipt of raw materials by posting to the materials ledger card. The receiving report and the supplier's invoice are checked against the purchase order. A voucher is completed, approved, and entered in the voucher register. Materials returned to the supplier are covered by a return shipping order and a debit memorandum. The debit memorandum is posted to the materials ledger cards and the voucher register.

Issuing. Materials are issued after an approved materials requisition is received in the storeroom. Unit costs are entered and extended on the requisition. The issue is posted to the materials ledger cards and recorded in the materials requisition journal. The requisition is posted to the proper job cost sheet or the departmental overhead analysis sheet. Materials returned to the storeroom are accompanied by a returned materials report. After the returned materials are checked in, they are posted to the materials ledger cards and recorded in the returned materials journal. The returned materials report is posted to the proper job cost sheet or the departmental overhead analysis sheet.

During December 19X9, the following transactions take place:

Dec. 1 Materials Requisition 814 is received by the storeroom supervisor, and the materials are issued. The materials requisitioned are for use in the Layout Department on Job 762 for the HandiHome Hardware Company. Job 762 calls for 250 six-foot aluminum ladders. The materials requisitioned are as follows:

> 250 units R-6 side rails, 6′
> 125 units S-12 steps, 4″ × 12″
> 250 units S-15 steps, 4″ × 15″
> 125 units T-612 tops, 6″ × 12″

6 Receiving Report 615 (for Purchase Order 703) is completed by the receiving clerk. Since this report is not shown in this problem, the data to be posted to the materials ledger cards can be found on Disbursement Voucher 12-01, shown on page 86, to which you should refer.

6 Disbursement Voucher 12-01 is received.

10 Materials Requisition 815 is received by the storeroom supervisor, and the materials are issued. The materials requisitioned are for use in the Layout Department on Job 763 for the Waterbury Supply Company. Job 763 calls for 180 eight-foot aluminum ladders. The materials requisitioned are as follows:

> 180 units R-8 side rails, 8′
> 90 units S-12 steps, 4″ × 12″
> 270 units S-15 steps, 4″ × 15″
> 90 units T-612 tops, 6″ × 12″

INSTRUCTIONS

1. If you are using the *Study Guide and Working Papers,* open the materials ledger by recording the opening balances on the materials ledger cards.
2. Prepare the materials requisitions.

Material	Reorder Point	Reorder Quantity	Balance Units	Balance Price	Balance Amount
B-10 elbow braces	6,000	13,000	5,485	$ .35	$1,919.75
R-6 side rails, 6′	3,000	8,000	1,970	1.15	2,265.50
R-8 side rails, 8′	1,900	3,850	2,025	1.40	2,835.00
S-12 steps, 4″ × 12″	2,500	6,000	1,910	.45	859.50
S-15 steps, 4″ × 15″	2,500	4,600	1,700	.60	1,020.00
T-612 tops, 6″ × 12″	2,400	5,000	1,440	.75	1,080.00
W-125 washers, $\frac{1}{4}$″ flat (box of 100)	300 boxes	940 boxes	675	.80	540.00

3. Process the materials requisitions, receiving report data, and the disbursement voucher data through all the procedures adopted by the Maxwell Corporation. The additional records needed are job cost sheets, a departmental overhead analysis sheet, a voucher reg-

ister, a materials requisition journal, and a returned materials journal. *Keep all your records for use in Problem 4–4B.*

PROBLEM 4–4B **Process source documents. (Objs. 1–9).** This problem is a continuation of Problem 4–3B. The following additional transactions take place:

Dec. 16 Receiving Report 616 (for Purchase Order 704) is completed by the receiving clerk. Since this report is not shown, the data to be posted to the materials ledger cards can be found on Disbursement Voucher 12-02, shown on page 87, to which you should refer.

16 Disbursement Voucher 12-02 is received.

18 Materials Requisition 816 is received by the storeroom supervisor, and the materials are issued. The materials are for the Assembly Department (Account 502). They consist of 40 boxes of W-125 washers, $\frac{1}{4}''$ flat (box of 100).

20 Receiving Report 617 (for Purchase Order 705) is completed by the receiving clerk. Since this report is not shown, the data to be posted to the materials ledger cards can be found on Disbursement Voucher 12-03, shown on page 88, to which you should refer.

20 Disbursement Voucher 12-03 is received.

20 Materials Requisition 817 is received by the storeroom supervisor, and the materials are issued. The materials are for the Layout Department on Job 762 and are for the following items:

250 units R-6 side rails, 6′
125 units S-12 steps, 4″ × 12″
150 units S-15 steps, 4″ × 15″
125 units T-612 tops, 6″ × 12″

21 Returned Materials Report 84 is received by the storeroom supervisor. The accompanying materials are 25 S-15 steps, an excess quantity requisitioned in error on Job 763. The materials are returned to stock.

INSTRUCTIONS
1. Prepare the materials requisitions.
2. Prepare the returned materials report.
3. Process all documents through all the procedures followed by the Maxwell Corporation. Use the records provided in Problem 4–3B as needed. *Keep all your records for use in Problem 4–5B.*

PROBLEM 4–5B **Process source documents. (Objs. 1–9).** This problem is a continuation of Problems 4–3B and 4–4B. The following additional transactions take place:

Dec. 22 Materials Requisition 818 is received by the storeroom supervisor, and the materials are issued. The materials are for the Layout Department for use on Job 763 and include the following:

> 100 units R-8 side rails, 8'
> 50 units S-12 steps, 4″ × 12″
> 150 units S-15 steps, 4″ × 15″
> 50 units T-612 tops, 6″ × 12″

27 Return Shipping Order 108 (not shown) and the debit memorandum (not shown) dated December 20, 19X8, are received from the purchasing unit. The data to be posted to the materials ledger cards can be found on Disbursement Voucher 12-04, shown on page 89, to which you should refer.

27 Disbursement Voucher 12-04 is received.

28 Materials Requisition 819 is received by the storeroom supervisor, and the materials are issued. The materials are for the Layout Department on Job 764 for the O'Dell Company. Job 764 calls for 250 eight-foot aluminum ladders. The materials requisitioned are as follows:

> 250 units R-8 side rails, 8'
> 125 units S-12 steps, 4″ × 12″
> 375 units S-15 steps, 4″ × 15″
> 125 units T-612 tops, 6″ × 12″

INSTRUCTIONS

1. Prepare the materials requisitions.
2. Process all documents through all the procedures adopted by the Maxwell Corporation. Use the records provided in Problems 4–3B and 4–4B as needed.
3. Prove the accuracy of your work by footing and cross-footing all money columns in the voucher register and the materials requisition journal. Double-rule the columns.
4. Post from the voucher register, the materials requisition journal, and the returned materials journal to the Raw Materials account. NOTE: If you are not using the *Study Guide and Working Papers*, open the Raw Materials account by recording the December 1 balance of $10,519.75.
5. Prepare a schedule listing each material in the materials ledger and its ending balance. The total of this schedule should equal the ending balance in the Raw Materials account.

MANAGERIAL DECISION CASE

The management of the Cupelli Manufacturing Corporation has asked you to review its internal control procedures related to raw materials inventory. You have discovered the following problem areas.

Purchase Orders. Most purchase orders were prepared as a result of a written purchase requisition. However, some have a notation such as "As per phone conversation with MJN," and there is no supporting purchase requisition. In addition, the materials ledger cards do not contain reorder points or quantities. It is not uncommon for the factory to run out of raw materials and to be unable to obtain them from the storeroom. Several jobs have not been completed because the company is waiting for the delivery of the necessary raw materials.

Materials Requisitions. Requisitions from last month have yet to be processed on the materials ledger cards and on the job cost sheets. The company does not use returned materials reports; the excess materials are merely returned to the storeroom by the factory personnel. Also, the storeroom does not have limited access. You have observed several factory workers removing raw materials on their own and returning to the factory. They did not prepare requisitions. The factory workers have indicated that often they are "in a hurry and cannot be bothered" with completing requisitions.

Storeroom Procedures. The storeroom is not organized according to types of raw materials. During your inspection, you have found that several raw materials have more than one bin location. In addition, the storeroom workers have reported that they have difficulty in locating the raw materials and waste time searching through the storeroom. No special precautions are taken to safeguard some very valuable metals; these metals are located in the same bin area as other metals of low value.

Prepare a report to management in which you recommend procedures to improve the company's internal control over materials. Where appropriate, explain how these procedures will improve the company's cost accounting records.

C H A P T E R
5

Controlling and Valuing Inventory

In the previous two chapters, prices of materials were purposely kept constant to simplify your initial experience with materials ledger card procedures. However, prices normally vary from one purchase to the next, and it is often impossible to tell the specific purchase from which an issue is made. In this chapter you will learn how the accountant prices issues of materials. You will also learn how physical inventories of materials are taken and valued and how inventory adjustments are recorded.

COSTING: A COMPLEX PROBLEM

The partially completed materials ledger card below shows unit prices ranging from $10 to $17.50.

How would you price the issue of 150 units? How would you value the 25 units on hand? The valuation directly affects the amount of profit or loss reported for the accounting period. If other factors remain the same, the higher the ending inventory valuation (and therefore the lower the cost of goods sold), the larger the reported profit will be, or the smaller the reported loss. The lower the ending inventory valuation (and therefore the higher the costs of goods sold), the smaller the reported profit, or the larger the reported loss.

MATERIALS LEDGER CARD

MATERIAL _Balance Rods_ REORDER POINT _100_

NUMBER _R-268_ REORDER QUANTITY _50_

DATE	REFERENCE	RECEIVED			ISSUED			BALANCE		
		UNITS	PRICE	AMOUNT	UNITS	PRICE	AMOUNT	UNITS	PRICE	AMOUNT
Jan 1 19XX	Bal.							25	10 00	250 00
4	PO-1701	50	15 00	750 00				25 } 50	10 00 15 00	1000 00
8	PO-1709	50	15 00	750 00				25 100	10 00 15 00	1750 00
15	PO-1721	50	17 50	875 00				25 100 50	10 00 15 00 17 50	2625 00
20	R-216				150	?		25	?	

INVENTORY COSTING METHODS

Since most manufacturers keep perpetual inventory records, unit costs and total costs should be computed each time materials are received or issued. The primary basis of inventory valuation is cost. Because unit prices often vary from one purchase to another, the accountant must make an assumption about the flow of costs. For inventory valuation purposes, it is not necessary that the method used to measure cost flows be related to the physical flow of goods. The accountant will choose the inventory valuation method that best meets the needs of the company. The method selected will determine what unit prices are used to price issues of materials and what cost of goods sold and ending inventory values will be reported.

One assumption the accountant can make is that the first materials purchased (the oldest or earliest) are the first materials used. The materials on hand are therefore assumed to be the last ones purchased. This is the **first in, first out (FIFO) method** of costing. Another assumption is that the last materials purchased (the most recent) are the first materials used. Then the materials on hand are assumed to be the first ones purchased. This is the **last in, first out (LIFO) method** of costing. The **moving average method** may also be used. In this method all the costs are commingled and an average cost is computed with each new purchase and assigned to materials issued and on hand.

In order to learn how each of these assumptions would be applied, refer to the following transactions relating to Material K-26, hinges.

Feb. 1 The beginning balance on hand is 150 units, costing $15 each; total cost, $2,250.

6 150 units are purchased on Purchase Order 87 at $15.50 each; total cost, $2,325.

10 180 units are issued for use on Requisition 103.

21 150 units are purchased on Purchase Order 109 for $15.60; total cost, $2,340.

23 160 units are issued for use on Requisition 116.

25 10 units are returned to the storeroom as noted on Returned Materials Report 13. These units had been issued on February 10 for use on Requisition 103.

First In, First Out Method

The materials ledger card below shows the transactions relating to Material K-26 recorded as if the FIFO method were used. The price to be used for each issue must be individually determined.

MATERIALS LEDGER CARD
(FIFO Cost Method)

MATERIAL *Hinges*   REORDER POINT _150_

NUMBER _K-26_   REORDER QUANTITY _150_

DATE	REFERENCE	RECEIVED			ISSUED			BALANCE		
		UNITS	PRICE	AMOUNT	UNITS	PRICE	AMOUNT	UNITS	PRICE	AMOUNT
19XX Feb. 1	Bal.							150	15 00	2 250 00
6	PO-87	150	15 50	2 325 00				150} 150}	15 00 15 50	4 575 00
10	R-103				150} 30}	15 00 15 50	2 715 00	120	15 50	1 860 00
21	PO-109	150	15 60	2 340 00				120} 150}	15 50 15 60	4 200 00
23	R-116				120} 40}	15 50 15 60	2 484 00	110	15 60	1 716 00
25	RM-13				(10)	15 50	(15 500)	10} 110}	15 50 15 60	1 871 00

- The issue of 180 units on February 10 includes all the 150 units from the beginning inventory (150 units at $15 each) plus 30 of the units purchased on February 6 (30 units at $15.50 each).
- The issue of 160 units on February 23 includes the remaining 120 units from the February 6 purchase (120 units at $15.50 each) plus 40 units purchased on February 21 (40 units at $15.60 each).
- The 10 excess units returned to the storeroom on February 25 are priced at $15.50 because they relate to the issue of February 10 and are assumed to be part of the group of 30 units. The job finally will be charged only with the costs that would have been charged if the correct quantity had been issued on February 10 (150 units at $15 each + 20 units at $15.50 each).
- Of the 120 units on hand at February 25, all except the 10 units returned are priced at the *most recent cost*, $15.60 per unit.

Arguments in favor of the first in, first out method are that it is easier and less costly to use because FIFO requires less recordkeeping than the LIFO method; that it reflects the actual physical flow of goods in most cases; and that the inventory shown on the balance sheet is more relevant because it includes the most recent costs and is an approximation of replacement cost.

A strong argument against the first in, first out method is that it does not match current costs against current sales revenue. Under this method, the ending inventory is priced at the most recent costs, leaving the items comprising the cost of goods sold to be priced at the oldest costs. Therefore, when net income is computed, the cost of goods sold that is matched against the current sales does not include the most recent costs. In periods of rising prices, this can lead to distortions in net income because the cost of goods sold is understated. A lower cost of goods sold means less is subtracted from sales, resulting in a higher net income and higher taxes.

Last In, First Out Method

The same transactions for Material K-26 would have different value if the LIFO method were used.

MATERIALS LEDGER CARD
(LIFO Cost Method)

MATERIAL *Hinges* REORDER POINT *150*
NUMBER *K-26* REORDER QUANTITY *150*

DATE	REFERENCE	RECEIVED			ISSUED			BALANCE		
		UNITS	PRICE	AMOUNT	UNITS	PRICE	AMOUNT	UNITS	PRICE	AMOUNT
Feb. 1	Bal.							150	15 00	2250 00
6	PO-87	150	15 50	2325 00				150⎫ 150⎭	15 00 15 50	4575 00
10	R-103				150⎫ 30⎭	15 50 15 00	2775 00	120	15 00	1800 00
21	PO-109	150	15 60	2340 00				120⎫ 150⎭	15 00 15 60	4140 00
23	R-116				150⎫ 10⎭	15 60 15 00	2490 00	110	15 00	1650 00
25	RM-13				(10)	15 00	(150 00)	10⎫ 110⎭	15 00 15 00	1800 00

- The issue of 180 units on February 10 consists of the 150 units purchased on February 6 (150 units at $15.50 each) plus 30 units from the beginning inventory (30 units at $15 each). Note that some accountants prefer to list the issues in reverse order. That is, they would show 30 units at $15 each followed by 150 units at $15.50 each. The sequence used here enables you to compare the FIFO and LIFO methods more easily.
- The issue of 160 units on February 23 consists of the 150 units purchased on February 21 (150 units at $15.60 each) plus 10 units from the beginning inventory (10 units at $15 each).
- The 10 excess units returned to the storeroom on February 25 relate to the issue of February 10 and are assumed to be part of the

group of 30 units (the oldest). Thus the job finally will be charged only with the costs that would have been charged if the correct quantity had been issued (150 units at $15.50 each + 20 units at $15 each).

■ All the 120 units on hand on February 25 (10 + 110) are priced at the *earliest cost,* $15 per unit. Note that these units would normally be recorded together as 120 units at $15 each. They are recorded separately here so that you can quickly compare FIFO and LIFO methods.

The major argument in favor of the last in, first out method is that current costs are matched against current revenue, since the cost of goods sold when LIFO is used contains the most recent costs. Therefore, the net income figure is a better measure of current earnings.

LIFO is popular in times of rising prices since inventories under LIFO are lower than under FIFO, resulting in lower profits and, thus, lower taxes. Also, the use of LIFO in times of rising prices can improve the cash flow of a company because taxes, which must be paid in cash, will be lower. A company that uses the LIFO method for federal income tax purposes is also required to use it on financial accounting statements.

Critics point out that the inventory value under the LIFO method reflects old costs. Therefore, the inventory value of the balance sheet would not be relevant because it would bear little relationship to the costs that would be incurred to replace the inventory. During periods of falling prices, inventory costs would be higher, and the related profits and taxes would be higher. An inventory liquidation (a voluntary or involuntary reduction in the number of units in the inventory during an accounting period) when prices are rising will also produce higher income and higher taxes. Some accountants may oppose the method because it usually represents an unrealistic physical flow of goods. However, as stated earlier, the physical flow of goods does not have to correspond to the inventory costing method used.

Moving Average Method

Neither the FIFO nor the LIFO method is entirely satisfactory for valuing inventory under all circumstances. Therefore, the cost accountant may employ the moving average method as a compromise. Under this method, the units and cost of each new purchase are added to the balances already on hand when the purchase is received, and a new average cost per unit is computed. At the time materials are issued, they are charged out at this new average cost until another purchase is received or a return is recorded, when a new average cost per unit is calculated. The same transactions used to illustrate FIFO and LIFO show different values if the moving average method is used. (See page 101.)

■ The 180 units issued on February 10 are priced at $15.25 per unit (the unit price appearing in the Balance section on the line above).
■ The 160 units issued on February 23 are priced at $15.44 per unit ($4,170 divided by 270).

MATERIALS LEDGER CARD
(Moving Average Cost Method)

MATERIAL _Hinges_ REORDER POINT _150_
NUMBER _K-26_ REORDER QUANTITY _150_

DATE	REFERENCE	RECEIVED			ISSUED			BALANCE		
		UNITS	PRICE	AMOUNT	UNITS	PRICE	AMOUNT	UNITS	PRICE	AMOUNT
Feb. 1	Bal.							150	1500	225000
6	PO-87	150	1550	232500				300	1525	457500
10	R-103				180	1525	274500	120	1525	183000
21	PO-109	150	1560	234000				270	1544	417000
23	R-116				160	1544	247040	110	1544	169960*
25	RM-13				(10)	1525	(15250)	120	1543	185210

*Adjusted for rounding difference, $1.20.

- The 10 excess units returned to the storeroom on February 25 are priced at $15.25 because they are related to the issue of February 10. Again, the job finally will be charged for the same amount as it would have been had the correct quantity been issued in the first place.
- The 120 units remaining in stock on February 25 are valued at $15.43, the current average price.

One major advantage of the moving average method is that it minimizes the influence of wide fluctuations in the purchase price of materials during the period. However, an average cost cannot be related to any individual purchase, and it may be desirable to have a more specific method of cost determination.

At this point you should be able to work Exercises 5–1 to 5–3 and Problems 5–1A to 5–2B.

Valuation at Cost or Market, Whichever Is Lower

The methods of inventory valuation that have been discussed so far have been based on cost. Accountants generally believe that the asset valuation used on the balance sheet should be conservative; that is, when alternative accounting methods are available, the accountant should select the one that is least likely to overstate asset value. If the market value of raw materials has declined, the company will probably have trouble selling its products at the usual prices. If the price decline is especially severe, the manufacturer may even have to sell the products at a loss. Consequently, accountants may prefer to value raw materials inventory according to the **cost or market, whichever is lower, rule.** *Market* should be interpreted as the cost of replacing materials. It is not the selling price. When the market price (replacement cost) of an item has declined below the original cost, the accountant values it at market price instead of at cost. This method reflects the lower current value on the books so that assets are not overstated.

Market price—for the purpose of applying the rule of cost or market, whichever is lower—might be described as the price at which

SELF-REVIEW

1. Given the data below, compute the ending inventory balance using the following inventory valuation methods: (a) first in, first out (FIFO), (b) last in, first out (LIFO), and (c) moving average. Round dollar amounts to nearest dollar.

Beginning Balance	40 units at $150 each
Purchase Order	60 units at $155 each
Materials Requisition	50
Purchase Order	60 units at $170 each
Materials Requisition	65

2. If prices are rising, will the ending inventory be higher under the FIFO method or the LIFO method?

Answers to Self-Review

1. (a) FIFO Method—$7,650

Received	Issued	Balance
		40 × $150 = $6,000
60 × $155 = $9,300		40 × $150 }= $15,300 60 × $155
	40 × $150 }= $7,550 10 × $155	50 × $155 = $7,750
60 × $170 = $10,200		50 × $155 }= $17,950 60 × $170
	50 × $155 }= $10,300 15 × $170	45 × $170 = $7,650

(b) LIFO Method—$6,775

Received	Issued	Balance
		40 × $150 = $6,000
60 × $155 = $9,300		40 × $150 }= $15,300 60 × $155
	50 × $155 = $7,750	40 × $150 }= $7,550 10 × $155
60 × $170 = $10,200		40 × $150 10 × $155 }= $17,750 60 × $170
	60 × $170 }= $10,975 5 × $155	40 × $150 }= $6,775 5 × $155

(c) Moving Average Method—$7,290

Received	Issued	Balance
		40 × $150 = $6,000
60 × $155 = $9,300		100 × $153 = $15,300
	50 × $153 = $7,650	50 × $153 = $7,650
60 × $170 = $10,200		110 × $162 = $17,820
	65 × $162 = $10,530	45 × $162 = $7,290

2. The ending inventory will be higher using the FIFO method.

the material could be bought (at the inventory date) through the usual channels and in the usual quantities. In some cases, current market prices are quoted in trade publications. In other cases, a recent purchase may give a price that is reasonably close to current market. In still other circumstances, quotations for use in valuation may be obtained from the firm's regular suppliers. (There are upper and lower limits imposed on the determination of the market price; implementation of these limits is beyond the scope of the text.)

There are several ways of applying the rule of cost or market, whichever is lower.

Lower of Cost or Market by Item. Under one plan, the cost of each item in inventory is determined according to an acceptable valuation method. Current market price is also determined for each material. Then the basis of valuation (the lower figure) is identified for each and is multiplied by the quantity on hand to obtain the value at the lower of cost or market. The lower valuation figure for each item is used to determine the value of the inventory as a whole, as shown below.

Lower of Cost or Market by Item

Description	Quantity	Cost per Unit	Market Price per Unit	Valuation Basis	Lower of Cost or Market
Material A	100	$1.00	$1.10	Cost	$100
Material B	200	1.50	1.20	Market	240
Inventory Valuation					$340

Lower of Total Cost or Total Market. Another method of valuation is to determine the total cost and the total market value of the entire inventory. The lower of these total figures is then used as the inventory valuation, as shown below.

Lower of Total Cost or Total Market

Description	Quantity	Cost per Unit	Market Price per Unit	Total Cost	Total Market
Material A	100	$1.00	$1.10	$100	$110
Material B	200	1.50	1.20	300	240
				$400	$350
Inventory Valuation					$350

If the prices of some materials have risen and others have declined, this procedure gives a less conservative valuation than the by-item procedure. However, those who prefer this method say that only the total inventory figure need be presented conservatively.

Lower of Total Cost or Total Market by Group. A variation on the preceding plan is to classify inventory materials by group or department and to determine the lower of total cost or total market for each classification. The lower figure (cost or market) for each group is added to the lower figure for each of the other groups to obtain the total inventory valuation. Assuming that Materials A and B in the preceding example constitute Group I and that Materials C and D constitute Group II, the basic computations required for the group total method are as follows:

Lower of Total Cost or Total Market by Group

Description	Quantity	Cost per Unit	Market Price per Unit	Total Cost	Total Market
Group I					
Material A	100	$1.00	$1.10	$100	$110
Material B	200	1.50	1.20	300	240
Total Group I				$400	$350*
Group II					
Material C	30	$0.70	$0.60	$ 21	$ 18
Material D	150	0.60	0.80	90	120
Total Group II				$111*	$138

*Lower figures for inventory valuation.

Obviously, market ($350) is the lower basis for valuation of the materials in Group I, and cost ($111) is the lower basis for valuation of the materials in Group II. The value of inventory Groups I and II combined would be $461 ($350 + $111). This valuation is between those obtained under the other two methods, as shown below.

Lower of Cost or Market by Item

Material	Basis	Valuation
A	Cost	$100
B	Market	240
C	Market	18
D	Cost	90
Inventory Valuation		$448

Lower of Total Cost or Total Market by Group

Material	Basis	Valuation
Group I (A and B)	Market	$350
Group II (C and D)	Cost	111
Inventory Valuation		$461

Lower of Total Cost or Total Market

Material	Cost	Market
A	$100	$110
B	300	240
C	21	18
D	90	120
Inventory Valuation	$511	$488*

*Lower figure for inventory valuation.

Valuation by the lower of total cost or total market by group produces middle-of-the road figures. It does not reflect individual fluctuations the way the lower of cost or market by item method does. But it does not offset market increases against market declines as much as the total cost or total market procedure does. The most commonly used method is the lower of cost or market by item, which produces the most conservative (lowest) inventory valuation.

APPLYING THE RULE OF COST OR MARKET, WHICHEVER IS LOWER

When market value is lower than cost, the inventory would be written down; that is, the inventory would be adjusted to show the lower value. This procedure is common except when selling prices are expected to be unaffected by the decline in replacement costs. In such a situation, a write-down of inventory would amount to a fictitious loss. Therefore, cost rather than market would be used. There is also some controversy over when a loss should be recorded. Some accountants believe that the loss should not be reflected on the books until the transactions actually take place. Others prefer that the loss be recorded to prevent overstatement of assets on the balance sheet.

When a company adjusts inventory to show the lower value, two procedures may be used if perpetual inventory records are kept.

1. Each materials ledger card may be adjusted to show the new unit values.
2. A valuation account may be set up to reduce the total value of the inventory to market. The individual materials ledger cards are not changed and continue to reflect cost.

Under the first procedure each materials ledger card is adjusted according to the lower of cost or market value. The cards are then totaled to determine the new valuation. The loss is recorded by a general journal entry debiting an account called *Loss on Reduction of Inventory to Market* and crediting Raw Materials. After this entry is posted, the total of the materials ledger cards will agree with the balance of the Raw Materials account in the general ledger. This method results in an increase to the cost of goods sold for the difference between the cost and the market value and does not show the inventory loss as a separate item on the income statement.

A second procedure, which overcomes this objection and identifies the inventory loss as a separate item on the income statement, uses a valuation account that serves a purpose similar to that of Allowance for Uncollectible Accounts. This valuation account is usually called *Allowance for Reduction of Inventory to Market*. It is adjusted at the end of each fiscal period to value the inventory at the lower of cost or market.

To illustrate how this valuation technique is applied, assume the following data for 19X8 (the first year of operations) and 19X9:

	Dec. 31, 19X8	Dec. 31, 19X9
Inventory at Cost, per Materials Ledger Cards	$180,000	$210,000
Inventory at Market Value	174,000	208,000

On December 31, 19X8, an adjusting entry is made to set up the valuation account for $6,000, the difference between inventory cost and market value. (See page 106.)

```
19X8
Dec. 31  Loss on Reduction of Inventory
              to Market                          XXX  6,000.00
              Allowance for Reduction of
                  Inventory to Market            XXX           6,000.00
         Recorded loss resulting from decline
         in market value of inventory.
```

In practice, the Loss on Reduction of Inventory to Market account is treated as an adjustment of the cost of goods sold on the income statement, although there is some argument for showing it as an adjustment of either the cost of raw materials used or the manufacturing overhead. Treating the loss as an adjustment of the cost goods sold is very simple and eliminates the necessity for allocating the loss among the raw materials, work in process, and finished goods inventories. A partial income statement showing the loss as an adjustment of the cost of goods sold is shown here.

Dixon Electronic Manufacturers, Inc.
Partial Income Statement
Year Ended December 31, 19X8

Revenue		
Sales (Net)		$3,400,000
Cost of Goods Sold		
Finished Goods Inventory, Jan. 1	-0-	
Add Cost of Goods Manufactured (at Cost)	$2,940,000	
Total Goods Available for Sale	$2,940,000	
Deduct Finished Goods Inventory, Dec. 31 (at Cost)	180,000	
	$2,760,000	
Add Loss on Reduction of Inventory to Market	6,000	
Cost of Goods Sold		2,766,000
Gross Profit on Sales		$ 634,000

The Allowance for Reduction of Inventory to Market account is shown on the balance sheet as a deduction from inventory.

Dixon Electronic Manufacturers, Inc.
Partial Balance Sheet
December 31, 19X8

Inventory, at Cost	$180,000	
Deduct Allowance for Reduction of Inventory to Market Value	6,000	
Inventory, at Lower of Cost or Market		$174,000

At the end of later periods, the allowance account will again be adjusted to reflect inventory value at that time. For example, at the end of 19X9, the allowance account of $6,000 should be reduced to

$2,000, which is the difference then existing between cost, $210,000, and current market value, $208,000. To reduce the balance of the allowance account from $6,000 to $2,000, you must debit the allowance account for $4,000, the difference between these amounts. This adjustment is shown below in general journal form.

19X9		
Dec. 31 Allow. for Reduction of Inv. to Market XXX	4,000.00	
Recovery From Decrease in Allow.		
for Reduction of Inv. to Market XXX		4,000.00
Recorded recovery resulting from		
adjustment of allowance account.		

The recovery account will be shown on the income statement as a reduction in the cost of goods sold, as shown below.

Dixon Electronic Manufacturers, Inc.
Partial Income Statement
Year Ended December 31, 19X9

Revenue		
Sales (Net)		$3,900,000
Cost of Goods Sold		
Finished Goods Inventory, Jan. 1	$ 180,000	
Add Cost of Goods Manufactured (at Cost)	3,650,000	
Total Goods Available for Sale	$3,830,000	
Deduct Finished Goods Inventory, Dec. 31 (at Cost)	210,000	
	$3,620,000	
Deduct Recovery From Decrease in Allowance		
for Reduction of Inventory to Market	4,000	
Cost of Goods Sold		3,616,000
Gross Profit on Sales		$ 284,000

The allowance account balance of $2,000 at the end of 19X9 will again be treated as a deduction from the inventory at cost on the balance sheet.

If the cost of the inventory should exceed the market value, the valuation account is no longer needed. An entry would be made to close Allowance for Reduction of Inventory to Market by debiting that account for its current balance and crediting Recovery From Decrease in Allowance for Reduction of Inventory to Market. The inventory would be shown on the balance sheet at cost; inventory is not written up above cost.

INVENTORY MANAGEMENT

A primary objective of inventory controls is to achieve maximum profits by keeping the investment in materials inventory at the lowest level consistent with efficient manufacturing operations. Procedures such as holding larger quantities of materials in storage than are needed

SELF-REVIEW

1. How can the lower of cost or market method be applied to inventory?
2. What accounting theory justifies the use of the lower of cost or market method?
3. What adjusting entry is needed to value the raw materials inventory at the lower of cost or market if the ending inventory at cost is $87,450 and the market value is $76,120?

Answers to Self-Review

1. The lower of cost or market method can be applied by (1) cost or market of individual items, (2) total cost or total market of entire inventory, or (3) total cost or total market of groups of inventory items.
2. The lower of cost or market method is justified by the accounting concept of conservatism, which says that it is better to understate than overstate the value of an asset.
3. The adjusting entry needed is as follows:

Loss on Reduction of Inventory to Market	11,330	
Allowance for Reduction of Inventory to Market		11,330

At this point you should be able to work Exercises 5–4 to 5–11 and Problems 5–3A to 5–5B.

for normal operations, or purchasing required materials earlier than they are needed for manufacture, tie up working capital unnecessarily. This can cause loss of profits that otherwise could be earned by investment of capital in other ways or for different purposes.

CUTOFF DATE

Accuracy in reporting costs of ending materials, work in process, and finished goods inventories is essential to the preparation of reliable financial statements. For ending inventories to be valued as accurately as possible, it is necessary that all costs associated with the items included be recorded. In order to ensure that these costs have been recorded, businesses establish a **cutoff date** for including transactions in a specified period. The cutoff date is usually the last day of the company's fiscal year or the end of an interim period such as a calendar quarter or month.

The accountant examines transactions just before and just after the cutoff date to determine whether they are properly classified. All transactions associated with items in the ending inventories are included in the current period. Transactions affecting events after the cutoff date either are not included or are entered as deferred items.

Since Panorama Windows operates on the calendar-year basis, December 31 becomes the annual cutoff date for those transactions that are to be included in the current year. For example, all invoices for materials received on or before December 31 must be entered in the materials ledger and posted to the materials ledger cards. The same principle applies to accounting for labor and overhead transactions.

PERIODIC PHYSICAL INVENTORY

The perpetual inventory system provides routine internal control over materials. Still, in spite of carefully planned procedures and controls, some differences often occur between the quantity of a material on hand and the quantity shown on the materials ledger card. In order to detect these errors and to correct the records, it is necessary to count the materials on hand periodically and to compare this actual count with the materials ledger cards. A physical inventory can be scheduled in one of two ways.

1. At the end of an accounting period, such as a year, all production is halted and the employees count and tally materials on hand. The plant does not resume operations until the inventory is completed and verified.

2. A less disruptive procedure is the **continuous or cycle inventory method.** Under this plan, only a few materials are counted each day. A schedule is developed so that all materials will be inventoried at least once each year. Materials that are difficult to measure accurately or that are highly susceptible to theft are inventoried two or more times a year. Some large companies have full-time inventory crews conducting the inventory on a scheduled basis. This avoids overtime work and eliminates errors that occur when untrained people are used.

Inventory-Taking Technique

Panorama Windows uses a regular end-of-year inventory by actual count, weight, or measurement to check its perpetual inventory system. These are the steps in taking inventory:

1. Serially numbered inventory tags are prepared in advance for each material and for each shelf, stack, or bin in which the material is stored. (See page 110.)

2. Tags are attached to the materials to be inventoried.

3. An inventory checker proceeds to count, weigh, or measure each material, recording the count and the date on the inventory tag. This count is often made several days before the official inventory date (the cutoff date). Receipts and issues after the count are recorded on the inventory tag in order to reflect the current balance on hand.

4. Inventory sheets are prepared in advance. The materials to be inventoried are listed on the sheets, usually in the same order as they are physically stored. The material number, description, location, and unit cost are entered. Much of this information is obtained from the materials ledger card.

5. On the inventory date, a checker counts, weighs, or measures each material and records the count on the inventory sheet. This count is completely independent of the first count, which was recorded on the inventory tag.

6. A supervisor or another checker then compares the count (or balance) shown on the inventory tag with the count shown on the

INVENTORY TAG	FORM NO. 15

No. _35_

Material _Pivot Bars_
Material No. _2-307_   Location _Bin 3_
Quantity _400_   Date _12/26/X9_
Counted by _N. Z._   Verified by _G. H._
Unit Price _____
Total Value _____
Priced by _____ Checked by _____

DATE	RECEIVED AFTER COUNT	ISSUED AFTER COUNT	BALANCE
12/27	200		600

inventory sheet. Differences are immediately reconciled so that the inventory sheet contains an actual count, double-checked for accuracy.

7. The inventory sheets are sent to a clerk, who compares the actual counts shown on the sheets with the balances shown on the materials ledger cards. This clerk also verifies the unit costs listed on the inventory sheets. (The inventory tags remain attached to the materials.)

8. Materials are recounted if unusually large differences are noted, and corrections are made.

9. Entries on the inventory sheets are extended, the extensions are totaled, and the complete inventory is summarized, as shown below.

INVENTORY _December 31, 19X9_			**Page** _9_		

Sheet No. _1_   **Department** _Assembling_   **Priced By** _P. O._
Listed by _F. K._   **Location** _Factory Bldg. A_   **Extended by** _T. L._
Checked by _N. Z._

TAG NO.	MATERIAL NO.	DESCRIPTION	QUANTITY	UNIT COST	EXTENDED TOTAL
35	2-307	Pivot Bars	400	40	16000
36	L-27	Latches	50	150	7500
37	I-16	Keepers	250	61	15250
		TOTAL			131219

10. All inventory computations are independently double-checked.
11. Inventory differences are summarized in an inventory shortage and overage report.
12. The materials ledger cards are corrected to show the actual count and value.
13. The general ledger accounts are adjusted to show the actual inventory valuation.
14. Reasons for inventory differences are looked into. Action is taken to prevent large differences from recurring.

Adjustment of Inventory

Adjusting for an inventory shortage or overage is done in two steps:

1. The individual materials ledger cards must be corrected. A shortage is recorded by an entry in the Issued section of the materials ledger card for the material found to be short. The cost is computed on the regular costing basis (FIFO, LIFO, or moving average) as though the missing materials were being charged out on a requisition on the closing date of the period. An overage is entered in the Received section of the materials ledger card. The cost to be used is the cost of the last issue of that material.

2. A general journal entry is made to adjust the firm's ledger accounts for the net shortage or overage. If the net total inventory shortage at Panorama Windows, as revealed by the periodic physical inventory, were $835, this adjustment amount would be journalized as a debit to Manufacturing Overhead Control and a credit to Raw Materials. The amount of the shortage is also entered under Indirect Materials on the departmental overhead analysis sheet of the General Factory Department, which is responsible for the control of raw materials.

   At Panorama Windows, the adjusting entry is made on a general journal voucher, as shown below, rather than in the more familiar general journal. Panorama Windows, like most large businesses, finds that using a separate voucher for each journal entry is more efficient and convenient. Vouchers are numbered for control purposes. The

JOURNAL VOUCHER Date _Dec. 31,_ 19 _X9_ No. _12-37_					
ACCOUNT	ACCT. NO.	✓	DEBIT	CREDIT
Manufacturing Overhead Control	501		835 00	
Raw Materials	121			835 00
EXPLANATION				
Recorded net inventory shortage per schedule.				
PREPARED BY C.J.S.	AUDITED BY JB		APPROVED BY RM	

first portion of the number represents the month, and the second portion, the sequence of the entry within the month. General journal vouchers are kept in numeric order in a binder. There is very little difference between the general journal with which you are familiar and the collection of journal vouchers (one entry to a page) used by Panorama Windows.

Computer-Assisted Physical Inventory

When a business has a computerized perpetual inventory system, the computer can assist with the process of taking the physical inventory. The inventory sheets can be prepared by the computer. The materials to be inventoried are listed on individual sheets along with their material numbers, description, and locations. This information comes from the inventory files in the computer's memory. On the day of the physical inventory, the inventory checkers record the amount of each material on the appropriate inventory sheet. Then the count and material number for each item are entered into the computer.

A company can further streamline the process of taking a physical inventory with the use of bar codes and scanners. To implement this technology, bar-coded labels are attached to all materials when they are delivered to the storeroom. On the day of the physical inventory, inventory checkers are given small, handheld devices that scan the bar codes, thus feeding the type and number of items into the device's memory. The information in the scanner is then downloaded to the company's computer. This method saves time by eliminating the need to manually input inventory counts into the computer from the inventory sheets.

Regardless of how inventory counts are obtained and entered into the computer, the next step is for the computer to compare the count for each item with the balance carried in the computer's inventory files. Differences are recorded in an error and exception file. This file is specifically set up to store the difference between the physical inventory amounts and the inventory balances recorded in the accounting records. A list of exceptions can be printed for evaluation by the accountant.

Many companies have a policy of examining exceptions only if they exceed a certain level. For example, a company may investigate items only if the difference between the physical count and the inventory balance in the computer file is greater than 5 percent. The computer is programmed to produce an exception report listing all items whose differences are greater than 5 percent. Management can use this report to investigate inventory losses.

When the count for all inventory items is complete, the computer can update the inventory records to reflect any changes that have been brought to light by the physical count.

Reasons for Inventory Shortages and Overages

Some differences are almost certain to occur in inventory records under the pressure of large-scale operations. Some reasons for these differences might be the following:

- Failure to complete required paperwork at each step of the flow of materials
- Failure to post receipts
- Failure to post issues
- Incorrect posting of receipts and issues
- Computation errors in day-to-day posting
- Errors in recognizing the correct cutoff dates

Other differences, such as the following, arise from the nature of the material or from storage conditions:

- Spoilage as a result of natural processes or from poor storage conditions.
- Shrinkage due to such natural causes as dehydration.
- Computation errors arising from different units of measurement for receipts and issues. For example, material might be bought by the ton but issued by the pound.

The following differences require special attention:

- Losses due to theft of materials by employees
- Losses arising from theft by outsiders owing to inadequate plant protection
- Losses due to short weight or short measure, often involving collusion between suppliers and receiving and purchasing personnel
- Losses due to unnecessary or deliberate scrapping of materials that are still useful

Since a firm's raw materials represent a large investment, any loss may involve a great deal of money. Accountants must be consistently on guard to see that the business's resources are protected. Knowledge of what conditions to look for is essential if safeguards are to be used effectively.

SELF-REVIEW

1. Why is it important for a company to establish a cutoff date for recording transactions?
2. Name two ways in which a company can schedule the taking of a physical inventory.
3. An inventory shortage is charged to what account and what department?

Answers to Self-Review

1. Establishing a cutoff date ensures that transactions at the end of an accounting period are recorded in the appropriate period.
2. A company can schedule a specific time, usually at the end of the accounting period, to stop production and count all materials at one time, or it can schedule the counting of materials on an ongoing basis throughout the accounting period.
3. An inventory shortage is charged to the Manufacturing Overhead Control account and to the General Factory Department.

Just-in-time inventory techniques were first utilized by Japanese industry and have become popular with manufacturers in the United States.

General Motors was one of the first U.S. manufacturers to implement the method. JIT requires that materials and components needed to assemble a car arrive at the plant when they are needed—not before, not afterward, but *just in time*. In order for this strategy to work, GM is geographically close to its suppliers. At one of its locations, 99 percent of the parts needed to build a car are within 300 miles of the factory, 93 percent are within 200 miles, and 83 percent are within 100 miles. Ideally, GM wants suppliers to deliver parts directly to the assembly line.

Just in time should cut both costs and production time. At GM the JIT concept reduced handling of a fender from 22 times to 6 times; the total distance a fender had to be moved was reduced from 8,000 feet to 140 feet; and a 10-day fender inventory was reduced to 8 hours.

JUST-IN-TIME INVENTORY MANAGEMENT

The **just-in-time (JIT) concept** is a recent innovation in inventory management that focuses on reducing the cost of inventory. JIT manufacturing involves restructuring the production process—from receiving new material to shipping the finished product—so that every material arrives at the right place on the assembly line "just in time" to be used. Instead of large inventories being maintained, the JIT approach depends on suppliers delivering orders regularly and on time; thus, raw materials arrive just in time to be placed into production.

When a JIT system is implemented, inventory is reduced to a minimum. Therefore, JIT requires reliable suppliers who can deliver a quality product on time. A company needs to develop a good relationship with its suppliers. Some companies require suppliers to be located geographically close to their plants in order to keep transportation delays to a minimum.

By decreasing inventory levels, a company has less working capital tied up in inventory and needs less warehouse space in which to store the inventory. Also, the risk of inventory items becoming obsolete or physically deteriorating is lessened.

Because JIT requires efficient coordination of all production processes, it usually results in reduced production time, thereby enabling a company to be more flexible in meeting customer needs. The method should also help a company to improve the quality of goods produced and have better control over spoiled or lost units.

There are risks in establishing a JIT system. If materials are not delivered on time, the entire manufacturing operation may have to shut down. For example, a strike at a supplier's location can cause a company to halt operations because the supplier cannot deliver materials. Defective materials may also cause a slowdown or halt to operations because there is no safety stock to fall back on. The benefits of a JIT system are lost if a company has to suspend operations because of lack of orders. JIT requires that all components of the production process work efficiently; if any one part of the process fails, the benefits are diminished.

PRINCIPLES AND PROCEDURES SUMMARY

- The perpetual inventory system provides a complete record of receipts, issues, and balances of materials on hand, item by item. The quantity computations can be made easily enough, but the pricing or valuation process is difficult. Prices paid for materials fluctuate from purchase to purchase. Furthermore, it is difficult to relate an issue or a balance on hand to a specific purchase.
- The cost accountant resolves the problem of pricing by applying a recognized method of valuation. Methods of costing inventory include:
    - The first in, first out (FIFO) method, which assumes that the oldest materials are used first.
    - The last in, first out (LIFO) method, which assumes that the newest materials are used first.
    - The moving average method, with which a new average cost is calculated after each receipt of materials.
- Each inventory costing method has some advantages and limitations. The accountant will recommend the method that best fits the firm's needs.
- Valuation of the inventory at the end of the fiscal period may be based on actual cost or according to the rule of cost or market, whichever is lower.
- The accuracy of the perpetual inventory must be checked from time to time by an actual physical count. Some firms take inventory periodically; others use the continuous or cycle method.
- After the count has been fully verified, the inventory sheets are extended, totaled, and double-checked for accuracy. Inventory differences are summarized on an inventory shortage or overage report. In turn, the materials ledger cards are corrected and general ledger account balances are adjusted. Reasons for differences are determined, and corrective action is taken to prevent recurrence.
- A computer can speed up and simplify the process of taking inventory.

MANAGERIAL IMPLICATIONS

- Management must give appropriate attention not only to controls over the purchase, storage, and issuance of raw materials and the maintenance of a perpetual inventory system but also to inventory flow assumptions for costing purposes.
- Raw material inventories may be costed on the basis of the first in, first out (FIFO) assumption, the last in, last out (LIFO) assumption, or the moving average assumption. The method chosen will affect both the ending raw materials inventory shown on the balance sheet and the cost of raw materials charged into production.
- Raw materials inventories normally are valued on the basis of the lower of cost or market. The lower of cost or market rule is often

applied to groups of inventory items but may be applied on an item-by-item basis or on the basis of the inventory as a whole.

■ Good control procedures require the taking of a periodic inventory to verify the perpetual records even if a perpetual inventory is maintained.

■ Taking a physical inventory is a time-consuming project, so the accountant and management must develop efficient systems for counting or weighing the materials.

■ Frequently there are discrepancies between the perpetual inventory records and the physical count. If these differences are excessive and recurring, it is important that the reasons be determined and steps taken to correct the problem. Excessive shortages may indicate theft or the discarding of damaged inventory.

REVIEW QUESTIONS

1. What is a major advantage of using a perpetual inventory system?
2. The materials on hand always are considered to be from the last ones purchased under what method of inventory costing?
3. The materials on hand always are considered to be from the first ones purchased under what method of inventory costing?
4. Which inventory costing method charges current costs against current revenue?
5. When must a new unit cost be calculated under the moving average method?
6. What are the three ways that the lower of cost or market method can be applied to inventory items?
7. When the lower of cost or market method is applied to the raw materials inventory, which method results in the lowest possible value for the inventory? Which method results in the highest value?
8. Why are general journal vouchers often used in place of recording transactions in a general journal?
9. How is a loss on the reduction of inventory to market value shown on the income statement? How is a recovery from a decrease in the allowance for the reduction of inventory to market value shown?
10. What is a physical inventory?
11. Inventory shortage may be caused by spoilage, and inventory overages may be caused by duplicate postings prepared by two employees. What are three other causes of shortages and overages?

MANAGERIAL DISCUSSION QUESTIONS

1. In a period of rising prices, what effect would the use of FIFO have on the net income and the taxes of a company? What effect would LIFO have on the net income and the taxes?

2. Discuss the relationship between the physical flow of goods and the inventory costing method used.

3. A company that maintains an effective perpetual inventory system should take a periodic physical inventory. Why?

4. Management is concerned about the rise in inventory shortages. Suggest some security methods and internal control procedures that could be adopted to minimize the inventory shortages.

5. What are the benefits of using continuous or cycle inventory procedures?

6. Why would management want to adopt the lower of cost or market rule?

7. What is the importance to management of adhering to a clearly established inventory cutoff date?

8. How does an inventory exception report aid management in efficient inventory control?

EXERCISES

EXERCISE 5–1   **Calculate the ending inventory balance and cost using FIFO.   (Obj. 1).**   The data given below relate to Material 408, 6-inch cloth zippers used by the Elite Leather Goods Company. Based on this data, determine the ending inventory balance and cost using the FIFO inventory valuation method.

Beginning Balance	480 at $4.80 each
Purchase Order 301	600 at $4.90 each
Requisition 469	175
Requisition 493	225
Requisition 504	280
Purchase Order 960	400 at $4.95 each
Requisition 529	310
Returned Material Report 24 (from Requisition 504)	20

EXERCISE 5–2   **Calculate the ending inventory balance and cost using LIFO.   (Obj. 2).**   Based on the data given in Exercise 5–1, determine the ending inventory balance and cost using the LIFO inventory valuation method.

EXERCISE 5–3   **Calculate the ending inventory balance and cost using the moving average method.   (Obj. 3).**   Based on the data given in Exercise 5–1, determine the ending inventory balance and cost using the moving average inventory valuation method.

EXERCISE 5–4   **Calculate inventory value using the lower of cost or market method.   (Obj. 4).**   The data given on page 118 relates to the raw materials inventory of the Edgewood Lighting Company. Determine the value of the inventory if the lower of cost or market method is applied to the individual inventory items.

	Units	Costs	Market
Group I			
Material A	460	$1.40	$1.30
Material B	830	.85	.90
Group II			
Material C	1,290	1.20	1.45
Material D	580	.65	.55

EXERCISE 5–5 **Calculate inventory value by group using the lower of cost or market method. (Obj. 6).** Based on the data given in Exercise 5–4, determine the value of the inventory if the lower of cost or market method is applied to the inventory by groups.

EXERCISE 5–6 **Calculate inventory value using the lower of cost or market method. (Obj. 5).** Based on the data given in Exercise 5–4, determine the value of the inventory if the lower of cost or market method is applied to the inventory as a whole.

EXERCISE 5–7 **Present inventory on the balance sheet at the lower of cost or market. (Obj. 7).** The following information is obtained from the records of the Century Square Corporation:

Inventory (at Cost): $392,780
Allowance for Reduction of Inventory to Market Value: $11,650

Show the balance sheet presentation for these accounts.

EXERCISE 5–8 **Calculate the cost of goods sold. (Obj. 7).** From the data presented below, determine the cost of goods sold to be shown on the income statement of the Langley Corporation for the month of September 19X9.

Finished Goods, September 1, 19X9	$ 52,720
Finished Goods, September 30, 19X9	59,240
Cost of Goods Manufactured	182,960
Loss on Reduction of Inventory to Market	3,270

EXERCISE 5–9 **Calculate the cost of goods sold. (Obj. 7).** From the data presented below, determine the cost of goods sold to be shown on the income statement of the Omega Manufacturing Company for the month of June 19X9.

Finished Goods, June 1, 19X9	$145,270
Finished Goods, June 30, 19X9	138,380
Cost of Goods Manufactured	402,910
Recovery From Decrease in Allowance for Reduction of Inventory to Market	5,360

EXERCISE 5–10 **Journalize inventory at the lower of cost or market. (Obj. 7).** The Forbes Company has decided to value its raw materials inventory at the lower of cost or market. The Raw Materials account has an ending balance of $90,760. The market value of the raw materials is $86,160. Record the necessary general journal entry to value the inventory at the lower of cost or market.

EXERCISE 5–11   **Journalize inventory at the lower of cost or market. (Obj. 7).** At the end of the current fiscal year, the Raw Materials account for the Martinez Manufacturing Company has a balance of $296,369. The company has been using the lower of cost or market method for several years. The Allowance for Reduction of Inventory to Market Value account has a balance of $8,930. The market value of the raw materials at the end of the year is $291,250. Record the adjusting entry needed to value the raw materials at the lower of cost or market.

PROBLEMS

PROBLEM 5–1A   **Use different inventory costing methods. (Objs. 1–3).** The Allegheny Manufacturing Company uses a perpetual inventory system to control materials. Data relating to Material S-8 during January 19X9 are given below.

Jan.   1   Balance, 150 units at $4.00 each.
      6   Received 200 units at $4.05 each, Purchase Order 74.
    12   Issued 225 units, Requisition 18.
    14   Received 250 units at $4.10 each, Purchase Order 83.
    17   Issued 200 units, Requisition 23.
    31   Issued 40 units, Requisition 29.

INSTRUCTIONS   Enter the beginning balance on a materials ledger card for each of the three inventory valuation methods: FIFO, LIFO, and moving average. Record each of the transactions on each of the materials ledger cards. Round unit costs to the nearest cent under the moving average costing method.

PROBLEM 5–2A   **Use different inventory costing methods. (Objs. 1–3).** Mt. Lebanon Office Furniture Company, a manufacturer of office equipment, uses a perpetual inventory system to control materials. During July 19X9, the following transactions took place in completing an order for chairs and desks:

July   1   Issued 110 units of Material B-42 on Materials Requisition 320.
      3   Received 650 units of Material B-42 at $1.02 and 650 units of Material R-18 at $.65. These goods were ordered on Purchase Order 517.
      6   Issued 175 units of Material R-18 on Materials Requisition 347.
      8   Issued 150 units of Material B-42 on Materials Requisition 362.
    12   Issued 80 units of Material B-18 on Materials Requisition 463.
    26   Received 650 units of Material R-18 at $.59. These goods were ordered on Purchase Order 617.
    31   Issued 210 units of Material B-42 and 382 units of Material R-18 on Materials Requisition 822.

INSTRUCTIONS

1. The number of units on hand, the unit price, and the total amount of July 1, 19X9, are given below. Record each of the transactions on materials ledger cards. Use the FIFO method of inventory costing.

Material	Reorder Point	Reorder Quantity	Balance Units	Balance Price	Balance Amount
B-42 Seats, Plywood	300	650	271	$.95	$257.45
R-18 Tops, Plastic	300	650	83	.70	58.10

2. Record each of the transactions on materials ledger cards. Use the LIFO method of inventory costing.
3. Record each of the transactions on materials ledger cards. Use the moving average method of inventory costing. Compute new unit prices only after each new purchase of materials. Carry your computations to three decimal places.

PROBLEM 5-3A

Calculate inventory value at the lower of cost or market. (Objs. 4–6). The following data pertain to the raw materials inventory for the High Meadow Trail Bike Company on December 31, 19X9:

	Quantity	Cost per Unit	Market Price per Unit
Group I—Wheels			
Type 1	100	$10.00	$11.00
Type 2	200	15.00	13.00
Type 3	120	16.00	15.00
Group II—Spoke Assemblies			
Type A	120	5.00	4.50
Type B	110	7.50	7.25
Type C	25	6.00	6.30

INSTRUCTIONS

Determine the amount to be reported as the inventory valuation at cost or market, whichever is lower, under each of the following methods: (1) lower of cost or market for each item, (2) lower of total cost or total market, and (3) lower of total cost or total market by groups.

PROBLEM 5-4A

Calculate inventory value at the lower of cost or market and make journal entries. (Obj. 7). The Jensen Novelty Company uses a perpetual inventory system. On April 30, 19X8, its balance sheet included the following items related to the raw materials inventory:

Raw Materials Inventory, at Cost	$587,250
Deduct Allowance for Reduction of Inventory to Market	41,320
Raw Materials Inventory, at Lower of Cost or Market	$545,930

INSTRUCTIONS

1. One year later, on April 30, 19X9, the perpetual inventory account showed a balance of $593,480. The market value of the inventory on that date was determined to be $550,220. Give the entry in general journal form to adjust the allowance accounts on April 30, 19X9.
2. Assume the same facts as in Instruction 1, except that the market value on April 30, 19X9, was determined to be $580,110. Give the journal entry to adjust the allowance account.

3. Assume the same facts as in Instruction 1, except that the market value on April 30, 19X9, was determined to be $596,360. Give the journal entry to adjust the allowance account.

PROBLEM 5–5A   **Calculate inventory at the lower of cost or market and make journal entries. (Obj. 7).** The following information relates to the raw materials inventory of the Mancuso Manufacturing Corporation on June 30, 19X7: Raw Materials Inventory (at Cost), $731,800; Raw Materials Inventory (Market Value), $758,200.

INSTRUCTIONS   1. Record the journal entry needed on June 30, 19X7, assuming that the company wants to report the raw materials inventory on its balance sheet using the lower of cost or market valuation method.
2. Record the general journal entry needed the next year on June 30, 19X8, assuming the following: The balance of the Raw Materials inventory account is $696,210; the market value is $683,510; the company uses the lower of cost or market valuation method.
3. At the end of the following year, June 30, 19X9, the balance of the Raw Materials inventory account is $675,480 and the market value is $679,350. Record the necessary journal entry, assuming that the company still uses the lower of cost or market method of valuing its inventory.
4. Show the balance sheet presentation for the raw materials inventory and related accounts for 19X7, 19X8, and 19X9.

PROBLEM 5–6A   **Prepare an income statement. (Obj. 7).** The fiscal year for the Wellesley Corporation ends on January 31, 19X9. Use the data below to prepare an income statement for the current year.

Sales	$1,385,720
Sales Returns and Allowances	34,643
Finished Goods, February 1, 19X8	94,310
Finished Goods, January 31, 19X9	98,570
Cost of Goods Manufactured	833,270
Selling Expenses	185,417
Administrative Expenses	118,823
Loss on Reduction of Inventory to Market	18,365
Provision for Income Taxes	98,490

ALTERNATE PROBLEMS

PROBLEM 5–1B   **Use different inventory costing methods. (Objs. 1–3).** The Mellon Manufacturing Company uses a perpetual inventory system to control materials. Data relating to Material J-2 during January 19X9 are given below.

Jan.   1   Balance, 1,000 units at $12.50 each.
         5   Issued 400 units, Requisition 917
         9   Received 600 units at $14 each, Purchase Order 16.
        13   Issued 850 units, Requisition 944.

22 Received 600 units at $14.50 each, Purchase Order 23.

29 Issued 250 units, Requisition 984.

INSTRUCTIONS Enter the beginning balance on a materials ledger card for each of the three inventory valuation methods: FIFO, LIFO, and moving average. Record each of the transactions on each of the materials ledger cards. Round unit costs to the nearest cent under the moving average costing method.

PROBLEM 5–2B **Use different inventory costing methods. (Objs. 1–3).** Conroy Furniture, a manufacturer of office equipment, uses a perpetual inventory system to control materials. During July 19X9, the following transactions took place in completing an order for chairs and desks:

July 1 Issued 135 units of Material B-42 on Materials Requisition 711.

   3 Received 650 units of Material B-42 at $.88 and 650 units of Material R-18 at $.76. These goods were ordered on Purchase Order 426.

   4 Issued 135 units of Material R-18 on Materials Requisition 735.

   7 Issued 165 units of Material B-42 and 165 units of Material R-18 on Materials Requisition 749.

  12 Issued 80 units of Material B-42 and 80 units of Material R-18 on Materials Requisition 763.

  21 Issued 304 units of Material B-42 on Materials Requisition 796.

  26 Received 650 units of Material B-42 at $.85 and 650 units of Material R-18 at $.79. These goods were ordered on Purchase Order 471.

  31 Issued 210 units of Material B-42 and 383 units of Material R-18 on Materials Requisition 822.

INSTRUCTIONS 1. The number of units on hand, the unit price, and the total amount on July 1, 19X9 are given below. Record each of the transactions on materials ledger cards. Use the FIFO method of inventory costing.

| | | | Balance | | |
Material	Reorder Point	Reorder Quantity	Units	Price	Amount
B-42 Seats, Plywood	300	650	271	$.95	$257.45
R-18 Tops, Plastic	300	650	83	.70	58.10

2. Record each of the transactions on materials ledger cards. Use the LIFO method of inventory costing.

3. Record each of the transactions on materials ledger cards. Use the moving average method of inventory costing. Compute new unit prices only after each new purchase of materials. Carry your computations to three decimal places.

EXERCISE 5–3B **Calculate inventory value at the lower of cost or market. (Objs. 4–6).** The following data pertain to the raw materials inventory for the Universal Auto Company on December 31, 19X9:

	Quantity	Cost per Unit	Market Price per Unit
Group I—Frames			
Type 1	250	$ 3.00	$ 3.20
Type 2	400	4.40	4.20
Type 3	370	2.00	2.10
Group II—Assemblies			
Type A	40	170.00	182.00
Type B	20	410.00	400.00
Type C	50	153.00	144.00

INSTRUCTIONS Determine the amount to be reported as the inventory valuation at cost or market, whichever is lower, under each of the following methods: (1) lower of cost or market for each item, (2) lower of total cost or total market, and (3) lower of total cost or total market by groups.

PROBLEM 5–4B **Calculate inventory value at the lower of cost or market and make journal entries. (Obj. 7).** The Hiland Appliance Company uses a perpetual inventory system. On April 30, 19X8, its balance sheet included the following items related to the raw materials inventory:

Raw Materials Inventory, at Cost	$132,820
Deduct Allowance for Reduction of Inventory to Market	10,570
Raw Materials Inventory, at Lower of Cost or Market	$122,250

INSTRUCTIONS
1. One year later, on April 30, 19X9, the perpetual inventory account showed a balance of $123,970. The market value of the inventory on that date was determined to be $108,930. Give the entry in general journal form to adjust the allowance accounts on April 30, 19X9.
2. Assume the same facts as in Instruction 1, except that the market value on April 30, 19X9, was determined to be $118,160. Give the journal entry to adjust the allowance account.
3. Assume the same facts as in Instruction 1, except that the market value on April 30, 19X9, was determined to be $126,130. Give the journal entry to adjust the allowance account.

PROBLEM 5–5B **Calculate inventory at the lower of cost or market and make journal entries. (Obj. 7).** The following information relates to the raw materials inventory of the Cercone Manufacturing Corporation on June 30, 19X7: Raw Materials Inventory (at Cost), $648,100; Raw Materials Inventory (Market Value), $619,500.

INSTRUCTIONS
1. Record the general journal entry needed on June 30, 19X7, assuming that the company wants to report the raw materials inventory on its balance sheet using the lower of cost or market valuation method.
2. Record the general journal entry needed the next year on June 30, 19X8, assuming the following: The balance of the Raw Materials inventory account is $592,620; the market value is $581,220; the company uses the lower of cost or market valuation method.

3. At the end of the following year, June 30, 19X9, the balance of the Raw Materials inventory account is $602,260 and the market value is $614,050. Record the necessary journal entry, assuming that the company still uses the lower of cost or market method of valuing its inventory.
4. Show the balance sheet presentation for the raw materials inventory and related accounts for 19X7, 19X8, and 19X9.

PROBLEM 5–6B   **Prepare an income statement. (Obj. 7).**   The fiscal year for the Haskell Corporation ends on January 31, 19X9. Use the data below to prepare an income statement for the current year.

Sales	$2,105,600
Sales Returns and Allowances	48,400
Finished Goods, February 1, 19X8	99,310
Finished Goods, January 31, 19X9	108,670
Cost of Goods Manufactured	1,271,107
Selling Expenses	243,682
Administrative Expenses	218,238
Loss on Reduction of Inventory to Market	27,427
Provision for Income Taxes	88,288

MANAGERIAL DECISION CASE

Part A. The Snyder Supply Company uses the FIFO method in valuing its inventories. At the end of the current fiscal year, management is considering adopting a new method in inventory valuation. The following comparative schedule was prepared showing the inventory costs under the FIFO, LIFO, and moving average methods for the ending inventory on December 31, 19X9.

	FIFO	LIFO	Moving Average
Raw Materials Inventory	15,890	$13,750	$14,805
Work in Process Inventory	28,750	25,840	26,030
Finished Goods Inventory	16,960	14,280	15,340

Prepare a recommendation to management on which of the three methods the company should use in valuing inventory. Indicate in your recommendation the effect that the inventory value would have on the cost of goods manufactured and on the income statement and the balance sheet.

Part B. Assume the same facts as above. However, management has indicated to you that the market value of its raw materials has declined by 10 percent. What effect, if any, would this fact have on your recommendation to management?

6

Timekeeping and Payroll

Labor costs are a major cost element in many manufacturing operations. These costs must be carefully controlled if management is to be effective. A typical system of accounting for labor costs includes keeping records of time worked, computing and recording earnings, and charging costs to production. In this chapter, you will learn about timekeeping, computing, and recording procedures as they relate to the payment of wages. The amounts involved are debited to the Factory Payroll Clearing account. Charging labor costs to production will be covered in the next chapter.

OBJECTIVES

1. Explain and demonstrate how to keep records of time worked by factory employees.
2. Differentiate between and compute overtime premium earnings and overtime earnings.
3. Compute gross and net earnings of individual employees.
4. Prepare a payroll register, including computations of gross earnings, taxes and other deductions, and net earnings of several employees.
5. Prepare the journal entry to record employee earnings and deduction liabilities.
6. Prepare journal entries to record payments of period payrolls.

NEW TERMS

Individual earnings records (p. 130)
Medicare tax (p. 128)
Overtime compensation (p. 127)
Overtime premium (p. 127)
Payroll register (p. 126)
Social security tax (p. 127)
Time card (p. 126)
Timekeeping (p. 126)

TIMEKEEPING PROCEDURES

The procedure for keeping records of the time worked by each employee is called **timekeeping.** The time records serve as a basis for calculating gross wages. From these amounts, appropriate deductions are computed to determine employees' net pay. These records also serve as the basis to compute the employer's payroll taxes. Panorama Windows' timekeeping procedures contain the basic payroll elements found in typical manufacturing operations.

Time Cards

A **time card** is prepared for each employee by the payroll unit. Time cards are placed in a rack next to a time clock near the plant entrance. When employees enter the factory, they select their time cards and insert them in the clock to record the time of arrival. Employees then replace their cards in the rack. Each time employees enter or leave the plant, they record their time in or out in this way. At the end of each week, all time cards are collected from the rack and sent to the timekeeping unit so that the payroll clerks can compute the total hours worked by each worker. The time card for the week ending October 5 for Donald Jones, an employee in the Assembly Department, is shown below.

| NAME | *Donald Jones* |
| NO. | *16* |

WEEK ENDING *OCTOBER 5, 19X9*

	REGULAR				EXTRA		
Hrs.	In	Out	In	Out	In	Out	Hrs.
8	≥07₅₅	≥12₀₁	≥12₅₉	≥17₀₀			
8	₽07₅₇	₽12₀₀	₽12₅₈	₽17₀₃			
8	≥07₅₉	≥12₀₅	≥12₅₉	≥17₀₀			
8	₣07₅₅	₣12₀₃	₣12₅₅	₣17₀₅			
8	ᴸ07₅₈	ᴸ12₀₀	ᴸ12₅₇	ᴸ17₀₁	ᴸ17₃₀	ᴸ19₃₀	2

PAYROLL PROCEDURES

The number of hours worked each day by hourly wage rate employees is transferred from the time card to the weekly factory **payroll register.** After all hours worked by each employee during the week have been entered in the payroll register, regular earnings, overtime

Weekly Factory Payroll Register

premium earnings, and total earnings are computed and extended. Appropriate deductions are made and entered in the proper columns, and the net pay for each employee is determined, as shown below. Some companies, like Panorama Windows, may also show a distribution of gross earnings into direct and indirect labor. (Classification of gross earnings into direct and indirect labor is discussed in Chapter 7.)

PAYROLL REGISTER		Week Beginning _Oct. 1,_ 19 _X9_				and ending _Oct. 5,_ 19 _X9_				Paid _Oct. 8,_ 19 _X9_		

EMPLOYEE	EXEMPTIONS	MARITAL STATUS	HOUR BY DAY S M T W T F S	HOURS WORKED TOTAL OVERTIME	RATE PER HOUR	REGULAR EARNINGS	OVERTIME PREMIUM	GROSS AMOUNT	CUMULATIVE EARNINGS	SOCIAL SECURITY	MEDICARE	FUTA	SOCIAL SECURITY	MEDICARE	FEDERAL INCOME TAX WITH.	OTHER	NET AMOUNT	DIRECT LABOR	INDIRECT LABOR
Jones, D.	2	M	8 8 8 10	42 2	1050	44100	1050	45150	1650000	45150	45150		2844	677	6773	800	34056	44100	1050
Nunez, M.	2	M	8 8 8 8 8	40	825	33000		33000	1056000	33000	33000		2079	495	4950	800	24676	33000	
Powell, S.	1	S	8 8 8 8 8 4	44 4	625	27500	1250	28750	960000	28750	28750		1811	431	4313	800	21395	27500	1250
Shu, W.	1	S	8 8 8 8 8	40	1200	48000		48000	668000	48000	48000	32000	3024	720	7200	800	36256	48000	
Taylor, B.	3	M	8 8 8 8 8	40	1500	60000		60000	2160000	60000	60000		3780	900	9000	800	45520	60000	
Totals						2074760	67840	2142600	8792560 0	2142600	2142600	248000	134984	32139	321390	20000	1634087	1649800	492800

Overtime Compensation. Firms engaged in interstate commerce are subject to the Fair Labor Standards Act, which regulates wages and working hours of employees. This law requires that employees be paid at one and a half times the regular hourly rate for all time worked in excess of 40 hours in any one work week; that is, in certain circumstances an employee is entitled to receive **overtime compensation.** For example, suppose that an employee with a pay rate of $8 per hour works 44 hours during a week. Four hours are overtime (subject to payment in excess of the regular rate). During these 4 hours the employee earns his or her regular rate of $8 per hour plus an overtime premium of $4 per hour. Thus the employee's total pay for 4 hours of overtime is $48 ($12 × 4 hours), of which $32 ($8 × 4 hours) is the regular rate and $16 ($4 × 4 hours) is the **overtime premium.**

The problem arises as to whether the overtime premium should be charged to specific jobs as direct labor or should be charged as manufacturing overhead. When charged as overhead, the overtime premium is spread over all jobs worked on during the year. Panorama Windows, like most manufacturers, charges all overtime premium to manufacturing overhead. Some companies, however, compute overtime premium on a daily basis and charge it to specific jobs.

Deductions From Employees' Earnings. Deductions are required from employees' wages under the Federal Insurance Contributions Act (FICA), commonly referred to as the *Social Security Act*. The rate of **social security tax** and the earnings base to which it applies are both changed frequently. In this textbook, a social security rate of 6.3

percent is assumed on a base of $66,000 during the year. The social security tax base means that, after an employee's yearly earnings reach a maximum amount (the base), social security tax is no longer deducted from his or her wages. For example, a employee whose year-to-date earnings reached $66,000 at the end of October would not have social security tax deducted from his or her gross wages in November and December.

Deductions are also required from employees' wages for the medicare tax. The **medicare tax** is closely related to the social security tax; in fact, prior to 1992 it was part of the social security tax (or FICA) tax. The tax rate for medicare has changed frequently. A medicare tax rate of 1.5 percent is assumed in this textbook. The medicare tax, unlike the social security tax, is applied to the *total* earnings of an employee; that is, there is no upper earnings limit for medicare taxes.

Another deduction is for the employee's federal income tax withholding. The income tax deduction is usually found by consulting income tax withholding tables. The amount withheld varies with the individual's earnings and marital status and with the number of allowances, or exemptions, claimed.

Most states, and many local governments, require a deduction from employees' earnings for state and local income taxes. Certain states require additional deductions to provide unemployment compensation insurance or sickness and disability benefits. Because rates and earnings bases vary from state to state and locality to locality, deductions for state and local taxes have been omitted from the payroll register example.

The taxes deducted by the employer from the employee's earnings are remitted at the proper time to the appropriate governmental agencies or depositories as designated by law. A business may also deduct amounts for group life insurance, hospitalization insurance, union dues, uniforms, retirement plan contributions, and various other purposes. All amounts deducted must be remitted by the employer to the insurance companies, the unions, or other appropriate organizations in payment of the obligations for which the money was withheld.

Semimonthly Factory Payroll

A separate semimonthly payroll register is used by Panorama Windows to record payment for some factory supervisors and managers. These people earn fixed monthly salaries payable in two installments on the fifteenth and last day of the month. The semimonthly payroll register is similar to the weekly payroll register.

Posting From the Payroll Register

At the end of the payroll period, the total gross earnings and the totals for each of the various liabilities are posted directly from the payroll registers (see the total line on the payroll register) to the general ledger accounts. The effect of this procedure is shown in general journal form for the week ended October 5. (See next page.)

19X9				
Oct. 5	Factory Payroll Clearing	500	21,426.00	
	Social Security Taxes Payable	210		1,349.84
	Medicare Taxes Payable	211		321.39
	Employee Income Taxes Payable	214		3,213.90
	Group Insurance Payable	215		200.00
	Salaries and Wages Payable	202		16,340.87
	Recorded weekly factory payroll, Oct. 1–5.			

Panorama Windows' Factory Payroll Clearing account 500 is shown below with entries posted from the weekly payrolls of October 5, 12, 19, and 26 and from the semimonthly payrolls of October 15 and 31. The posting reference *WP* refers to the weekly payroll register; *SP* refers to the semimonthly payroll register.

			Factory Payroll Clearing			**NO.** _500_	
DATE	EXPLANATION	POST. REF.	DEBIT	CREDIT		BALANCE	DR. CR.
19 X9							
Oct. 5		WP	21,426 00			21,426 00	DR.
12		WP	19,129 00			40,555 00	DR.
15		SP	5,545 00			46,100 00	DR.
19		WP	20,074 00			66,174 00	DR.
26		WP	20,165 00			86,339 00	DR.
31		SP	5,545 00			91,884 00	DR.

Not shown in the illustration (but explained in detail in the next chapter) are wages of $10,788 earned during the period of October 27 through 31, but not paid in October.

Paying the Payroll

Panorama Windows uses a special bank account for payroll payments. The payroll clerk initiates a voucher for the net amount of the payroll and forwards it to the voucher clerk, who completes the voucher and records it in the voucher register. The entry is a debit to Salaries and Wages Payable 202 and a credit to Vouchers Payable 201. The voucher then goes to the treasurer, who issues a check on the regular bank account for the amount of the voucher and enters it in the check register. This check is deposited to the special payroll bank account.

The payroll liabilities are paid with checks drawn on the regular bank account.

Individual Earnings Records

An employer is required to keep an **individual earnings record** for each employee. This record is the basis for the preparation of various year-end payroll reports, such as Form W-2, the Wage and Tax Statement, which is sent to each employee to aid in the preparation of his or her annual income tax returns.

At this point you should be able to work Exercises 6–1 to 6–5 and Problems 6–1A to 6–3B.

The information for this record is taken from the payroll register at the end of each pay period. The individual earnings record for Donald Jones is shown below. In many companies the payroll register, the individual earnings records, and the paychecks are prepared simultaneously through the use of special forms or by computer.

Name *Jones, Donald*   Soc. Sec. No. *160-14-0730*

Address *902 Fox Lane, Chicago, IL 60699*   Withholding Allow. *2*

Employee No. *16*   Marital Status *M*   Date of Birth *10/12/XX*

PERIOD	WEEK ENDED	HOURS WORKED TOTAL HOURS	HOURS WORKED O.T. HOURS	RATE PER HOUR	EARNINGS REGULAR	EARNINGS OVER. PREM.	EARNINGS TOTAL	CUM. TOTAL	DEDUCTIONS SOCIAL SEC.	DEDUCTIONS MEDICARE	DEDUCTIONS FEDERAL INC. TAX WITH.	DEDUCTIONS OTHER	NET PAID
	Carried Forward							1099275					
27	7/6	40		10 50	42000		42000	1141275	2646	630	6300	800	31624
28	7/13	40		10 50	42000		42000	1183275	2646	630	6300	800	31624
29	7/20	40		10 50	42000		42000	1225275	2646	630	6300	800	31624
30	7/27	40		10 50	42000		42000	1267275	2646	630	6300	800	31624
	July				168000		168000		10584	2520	25200	3200	126496
31	8/3	40		10 50	42000		42000	1309275	2646	630	6300	800	31624
32	8/10	40		10 50	42000		42000	1351275	2646	630	6300	800	31624
33	8/17	40		10 50	42000		42000	1393275	2646	630	6300	800	31624
34	8/24	41	1	10 50	43050	525	43575	1436850	2745	654	6536	800	32840
35	8/31	40		10 50	42000		42000	1478850	2646	630	6300	800	31624
	August				211050	525	211575		13329	3174	31736	4000	159336
36	9/7	40		10 50	42000		42000	1520850	2646	630	6300	800	31624
37	9/14	40		10 50	42000		42000	1562850	2646	630	6300	800	31624
38	9/21	40		10 50	42000		42000	1604850	2646	630	6300	800	31624
39	9/28	42	2	10 50	44100	1050	45150	1650000	2844	677	6773	800	34056
	September				170100	1050	171150		10782	2567	25673	3200	128928
	3rd Quarter				549150	1575	550725		34696	8261	82609	10400	414760
40	10/5	42	2	10 50	44100	1050	45150	1695150	2844	677	6773	800	34056

FLOW OF PAYROLL COSTS

The flowchart on page 131 illustrates the flow of costs associated with timekeeping. The flowchart shows that the first step in the process is to transfer data about employee hours from time cards to the payroll register. The next step is completion of the payroll register. The in-

FLOW OF PAYROLL COSTS

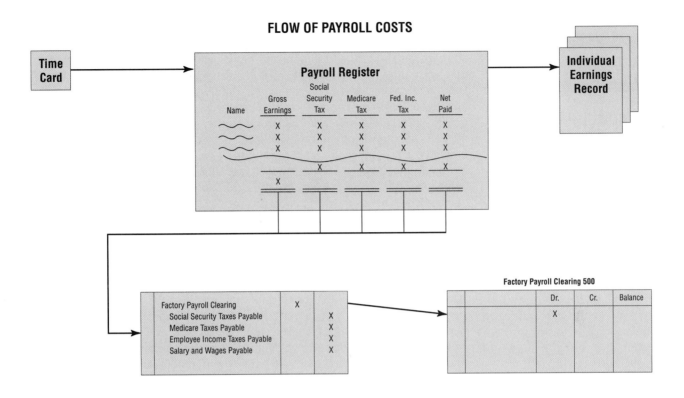

formation from the payroll register flows in two directions: Amounts relating to individual employees are recorded on the individual earnings record, and summary totals are used to prepare a journal entry to record the payroll. Finally, total gross earnings are posted to the Factory Payroll Clearing account.

COMPUTERIZED PAYROLL

Because of the repetitive nature of the calculations involved with payroll, many companies computerize their payroll records. A company can either have its own computerized payroll system or contract with an outside payroll service bureau to handle this function for it.

If a company decides to have a service bureau process its payroll, it must first supply the bureau with basic personnel data about its employees such as name and address, marital status, number of withholding allowances, and hourly pay rate. Then, each pay period, the company tells the service bureau the number of hours each employee worked. The bureau calculates the payroll and delivers to the company a completed payroll register and payroll checks for all employees. The bureau also keeps an individual earnings record for each employee and prepares all necessary quarterly and yearly payroll tax returns.

There are several advantages to this method of processing payroll:

BUSINESS HORIZON

Speeding Up Payroll With Computers

Bathtub Rings, Inc., a manufacturer of shower curtain rings, shower curtains, soap dishes, and other items for the bath, has been having trouble getting its payroll out in a timely manner. Product manufacturing is done at the Detroit, Michigan, and Charlotte, North Carolina, factories. Currently, factory employees are paid two weeks after they have earned their wages. First, payroll data must be gathered at the factories and mailed to the home office in Atlanta, Georgia, for processing. After the payroll has been processed, the paychecks must be sorted and mailed back to the factories for distribution. Many workers have voiced dissatisfaction at having to wait two weeks before being paid. In order to keep employee morale high, management wants to remedy the problem.

The solution, as Bathtub Rings sees it, is to put computer terminals in each of the factories. These terminals would have the capacity to send information to and receive information from the company's central computer in Atlanta.

The terminal at the entrance to each factory will be equipped with an optical scanner that is able to read information, such as an employee identification number, from a bar-coded identification card (similar to a credit card) issued to each employee. Upon arriving at work, an employee will insert (swipe) his or her identification card through the factory's optical scanner. The scanner will read the employee number from the card, and the computer will record the employee's arrival time. The employee's exit time will be recorded in the same way at the end of the day.

On Thursday of each week, the hours worked during the week by each employee will be sorted according to employee number by the central computer. On Friday morning, after Thursday night processing, paycheck data will be sorted according to the factory and then by employee number and sent back to the factory terminals. Checks will be printed out at each factory and distributed on Friday afternoon.

This solution is appealing for several reasons: With the new system, employees will be paid the day after the week in which they have earned wages. This should boost morale considerably. Another benefit is that the labor information available to management for analysis is much more current. In addition, because there is less manual processing of payroll data, payroll data should be more accurate and payroll processing costs should be reduced.

1. For a medium-sized or small company, it may be less expensive and more convenient to pay an outside firm to do the payroll than it is to invest in computer equipment to handle the payroll.
2. Since the employees in the service bureau are in the payroll business, it is easier for them to stay up to date about the frequent changes in tax rates.
3. Confidentiality of payroll is more likely to be maintained when the payroll function is performed outside the company.

SELF-REVIEW

1. What is the name of the record that keeps track of the hours worked by an hourly employee?
2. Calculate the regular earnings, overtime premium, and gross earnings for an employee who works 44 hours during the week and has an hourly wage rate of $12.
3. Calculate the net pay for the employee described in Self-Review Question No. 2 assuming the same social security and medicare tax rates as used in the text and federal income tax withheld of $65.
4. Prepare the journal entry to record the payroll of the employee described in Self-Review Questions 1 and 2.

Answers to Self-Review

1. Time card

2. 44 hours × $12 = $528.00   Regular Earnings
    4 hours × $ 6 = 24.00   Overtime Premium
                   $552.00   Gross Earnings

3. Gross earnings $552.00
   Social security tax ($552.00 × 6.3%) $34.78
   Medicare tax ($552.00 × 1.5%)   8.28
   Federal income tax   65.00   108.06
      Net Pay $443.94

4. Factory Payroll Clearing   552.00
      Social Security Taxes Payable   34.78
      Medicare Taxes Payable   8.28
      Employee Income Taxes Payable   65.00
      Salaries and Wages Payable   443.94

PRINCIPLES AND PROCEDURES SUMMARY

- There are three phases in accounting for labor costs:
  - Keeping track of time worked
  - Computing and recording earnings
  - Charging costs to production
- The timekeeping process uses time clocks and time cards.
  - Once the record of hours worked is available, the data can be transferred to the payroll register.
  - At the end of the pay period, the hours are totaled, and pay and deductions are computed to complete the payroll.
  - The total gross earnings are then debited to the Factory Payroll Clearing account, with offsetting credits to various liability accounts.
- Many businesses pay their employees by special payroll check.
  - Under this system, a voucher is prepared and a check is issued to cover the net payroll. The check is then deposited in a separate payroll bank account, and payroll checks are drawn against the balance.

MANAGERIAL IMPLICATIONS

- Accounting for labor costs is important because these costs make up a very high portion of total manufacturing costs. In addition, federal and state employment laws and federal and state payroll taxes require accurate, detailed records of salaries and wages.
- It is important that the payroll records for all workers reflect proper withholdings for social security taxes, medicare taxes, and employee income tax withheld.
- The payroll register shows the hours worked, the hourly wage rate of each employee, and all payroll deductions for hourly employees during the pay period. Similarly, payroll registers are maintained for workers who are paid on a salary basis. At the end of the month, the total figures from the payroll registers are posted to the general ledger accounts. The cost accountant is intensely interested in the accuracy of the information in the payroll register.

NOTE: *For all questions, exercises, and problems, use a social security tax rate of 6.3 percent on the first $66,000 in wages and a medicare tax rate of 1.5 percent on total wages.*

REVIEW PROBLEM

Calculate net pay and prepare journal entries. Jane Miller worked the following hours for the week ended August 7, 19X9: Monday, 8 hours; Tuesday, 8 hours; Wednesday, 9 hours; Thursday, 8 hours; Friday, 8 hours; and Saturday, 4 hours. Her hourly rate is $10. The federal income tax applicable to Jane is 15 percent. She has $7 per week deducted from her wages for group insurance.

INSTRUCTIONS

1. Compute Jane's gross earnings.
2. Compute Jane's net pay.
3. Prepare general journal entries to record the payroll, the issuance of a voucher to pay the net payroll, and payment of the voucher.

ANSWER

1. 45 × $10.00 = $450 regular earnings
   5 × $ 5.00 = <u> 25</u> overtime premium
   <u>$475</u> gross earnings

2. Gross earnings $475.00

Social Security tax ($475 × 6.3%)	$ 29.93	
Medicare tax ($475 × 1.5%)	7.13	
Federal income tax ($475 × 15%)	71.25	
Group insurance deduction	<u>7.00</u>	115.31
Net pay		359.69

3. | | | |
|---|---:|---:|
| Factory Payroll Clearing | $475.00 | |
| Social Security Taxes Payable | | 29.93 |
| Medicare Taxes Payable | | 7.13 |

Employee Income Taxes Payable		71.25
Group Insurance Deduction Payable		7.00
Salaries and Wages Payable		359.69
Vouchers Payable		359.69
Vouchers Payable	359.69	
Cash		359.69

REVIEW QUESTIONS

1. Define *timekeeping*.
2. What is overtime premium?
3. What are two methods for recording overtime premium?
4. What is the difference between gross pay and net pay?
5. What types of information and payroll calculations are shown on the payroll register?
6. What deductions are employers required by law to make from an employee's gross wages?
7. What accounts are debited and credited in the journal entry to record the payroll? What is the source of the amounts used in this entry?
8. What accounts are debited and credited in the journal entries to record the payment of the payroll?
9. What information is contained in an individual earnings record? Why is it necessary for a company to keep these records?

MANAGERIAL DISCUSSION QUESTIONS

1. Why should management be concerned with the overtime premium paid to employees?
2. What types of deductions are required by law? What deductions are optional?
3. What technology can replace a time clock and time cards and speed up payroll processing?

EXERCISES

EXERCISE 6–1   **Calculate gross earnings.** **(Obj. 3).** Determine the amount of gross pay for Sonia Grammer, who worked 46 hours in one week at a rate of $9 an hour. Show the amount of regular earnings and overtime premium if she is paid one and a half times the regular rate for hours worked in excess of 40.

EXERCISE 6–2   **Determine deductions.** **(Obj. 3).** Calculate the amount of social security and medicare and federal income tax to be withheld from an employee's gross pay of $1,300 if all earnings are taxable for social security and medicare taxes and the federal income tax rate is 15 percent.

EXERCISE 6–3   **Calculate net pay.   (Obj. 3).**   Based on the data that follow, what is the net pay for Mike Chin for the week ended June 16, 19X9?

Hours and rate	42 hours worked at $8 an hour
Earnings to date	$14,000
Federal income tax	15% of earnings

EXERCISE 6–4   **Calculate social security taxes.   (Obj. 3).**   Determine the amounts of social security tax to be deducted under the following assumptions:
a. Alice Hernandez earned gross wages of $1,500 for the week and has wages to date of $42,500.
b. Assume that Alice's wages to date are $65,000.
c. Assume that Alice's wages to date are $66,800.

EXERCISE 6–5   **Prepare journal entries.   (Obj. 5).**   Wilmington Gardening Supplies manufactures pots for plants and small garden tools. The weekly payroll for the factory totaled $25,900. The employees' share of the social security tax was $1,632, the medicare tax was $388, and the federal income taxes were $3,700. Prepare the journal entries to record the weekly payroll for February 1 through February 7, to record the voucher to pay the payroll, and to record the payment of the voucher.

PROBLEMS

PROBLEM 6–1A   **Compute gross earnings.   (Obj. 3).**   From the following data, compute the regular earnings (for regular and overtime hours), overtime premium earnings, and gross earnings of each employee at Pacific Timbers, Inc., for the week ended May 7, 19X9. All employees are paid at the regular hourly rate for the first 40 hours worked during the week. The rate for hours worked in excess of 40 is one and half times the regular rate. The rate for hours worked on Sunday is twice the regular rate.

Employee	Su	M	Tu	W	Th	F	Sa	Hourly Rate
				Hours Worked				
J. Ho	—	8	8	7	9	8	—	$10.80
F. Mitchell	4	8	8	8	8	10	—	8.50
H. O'Neill	—	8	8	10	8	8	4	7.10
W. Timmons	—	8	8	8	8	9	4	6.50

PROBLEM 6–2A   **Prepare a payroll register and the journal entry to record the payroll.   (Objs. 4, 5).**   The Braun Corporation is a manufacturing concern that employs six people on an hourly basis. The following data relate to the week ended October 31, 19X9:

Employee	Hours Worked							Hourly Rate	Cumulative Total Through October 24, 19X9
	Su	M	Tu	W	Th	F	Sa		
K. Cheminski	—	8	8	8	8	8	—	$14.00	$21,900
W. Greco	—	8	9	8	8	9	4	26.00	49,200
A. Kurda	—	8	10	8	8	9	—	17.50	29,600
T. Nasser	—	8	10	8	8	9	—	10.30	15,890
L. Stoner	—	8	8	8	9	8	4	8.50	13,560
R. Westerman	—	8	8	8	8	8	—	23.00	46,180

INSTRUCTIONS

1. Prepare the payroll register for the week ended October 31, 19X9. For this problem, assume that the federal income tax withheld is a flat rate of 15 percent of gross earnings. Group insurance is $10 per employee. Show total earnings as regular earnings plus overtime premium earnings. Employees are paid one and one-half times the regular rate for hours worked over 40.
2. Prepare in general journal form the entry to record the payroll, using the account titles shown in your textbook.

PROBLEM 6–3A **Prepare payroll entries. (Obj. 5).** Data for the payroll for the California Chemical Corporation for the week ended April 20, 19X9, are shown below:

Total gross earnings	$548,140
Social security taxes withheld	34,533
Medicare taxes withheld	8,222
Employee income taxes withheld	84,200
Group insurance deductions	6,400

INSTRUCTIONS Prepare the following entries in general journal form.

1. An entry to record the weekly payroll.
2. An entry to record the issuance of a voucher to pay the net payroll.
3. An entry to record payment of the voucher.

ALTERNATE PROBLEMS

PROBLEM 6–1B **Compute gross earnings. (Obj. 3).** From the following data, compute the regular earnings (for regular and overtime hours), overtime premium earnings, and gross earnings of each employee at Texas Oil, Inc., for the week ended July 14, 19X9. All employees are paid at the regular hourly rate for the first 40 hours worked during the week. The rate for hours worked in excess of 40 is one and a half times the regular rate. The rate for hours worked on Sunday is twice the regular rate.

Employee	Hours Worked							Hourly Rate
	Su	M	Tu	W	Th	F	Sa	
K. Akanian	—	8	9	8	9	10	—	$ 9.80
F. Costanzo	—	8	8	8	—	10	4	8.70
S. Harper	3	8	8	9	8	8	—	6.00
B. Rosen	—	8	8	8	8	9	2	11.00

PROBLEM 6–2B

Prepare a payroll register and the journal entry to record the payroll. (Objs. 4, 5). The Jackson Corporation is a manufacturing concern that employs six people on an hourly basis. The following data relate to the week ended May 31, 19X9:

	Hours Worked							Hourly	Cumulative Total Through
Employee	Su	M	Tu	W	Th	F	Sa	Rate	May 24, 19X9
T. Ehrhardt	—	8	8	9	8	8	—	$13.00	$ 8,300
J. Gaydos	—	8	9	8	8	9	4	25.00	16,000
B. Mariani	—	8	10	8	8	9	—	18.40	11,700
A. Peters	—	8	10	8	8	9	—	10.30	6,180
L. Scheller	—	8	8	8	9	8	4	7.50	4,800
S. Turk	—	8	8	8	8	10	—	19.50	12,480

INSTRUCTIONS

1. Prepare the payroll register for the week ended May 31, 19X9. For this problem, assume that the federal income tax withheld is a flat rate of 15 percent of gross earnings. Group insurance is $10 per employee. Show total earnings as regular earnings plus overtime premium earnings. Employees are paid one and one-half times the regular rate for hours worked over 40.
2. Prepare in general journal form the entry to record the payroll, using the account titles shown in your textbook.

PROBLEM 6–3B

Prepare payroll entries. (Obj. 5). Data for the payroll for the Sloan Book Corporation for the week ended November 20, 19X9, are shown below.

Total gross earnings	$101,200
Social security taxes withheld	6,375
Medicare taxes withheld	1,518
Employee income taxes withheld	15,800
Group insurance deductions	3,600

INSTRUCTIONS

Prepare the following entries in general journal form.

1. An entry to record the weekly payroll.
2. An entry to record the issuance of a voucher to pay the net payroll.
3. An entry to record payment of the voucher.

MANAGERIAL DECISION CASE

Food Movers is a small manufacturer of grocery store shopping carts. The company has 20 employees who normally work a 5-day, 40-hour week.

In April, the company experienced an accelerated rate of demand for its product. As a result, all employees worked 8 hours of overtime each Saturday in April in order to eliminate the backlog orders.

In May, Grand Markets, one of Food Movers' largest customers, placed a rush order for 50 shopping carts. The carts had to be ready for delivery in a week in order to be available for the opening of one of Grand Markets' new stores. All the employees worked overtime every evening during the second week in May to meet this deadline.

In June, there was a severe thunderstorm causing a 2-hour electrical power outage. The employees stayed and worked 2 hours of overtime to make up for the lost time.

How should overtime be charged in April? In May? In June?

Charging Labor Costs Into Production

I n the last chapter, you learned the various recording phases of accounting for labor costs. This chapter will explain the other half of the operation—how labor costs are charged to production.

1. Explain the function of a time ticket and list the information included on a time ticket.
2. Explain how the analysis of time tickets and the analysis of semimonthly payroll are prepared and used.
3. Post direct labor costs from the analysis of time tickets to job cost sheets.
4. Post indirect labor costs from the analysis of time tickets and the analysis of semimonthly payroll to appropriate departmental overhead analysis sheets.
5. Determine wages unpaid at the end of the accounting period.
6. Prepare the monthly summary of factory wages.
7. Prepare the entry to transfer direct and indirect labor costs to production.
8. Determine and record the flow of costs into and out of the Factory Payroll Clearing account.
9. Determine and record the various payroll taxes levied against the employer and the employer's costs for fringe benefits.

Analysis of semimonthly factory payroll (p. 145)
Analysis of time tickets (p. 143)
Federal unemployment insurance tax (FUTA tax) (p. 150)
Fringe benefits (p. 154)
Idle time (p. 142)
State unemployment insurance tax (SUTA tax) (p. 151)
Summary of factory wages (p. 147)
Time ticket (p. 141)

LABOR COST ANALYSIS

In Chapter 2, Entry D on the flowchart showed that direct labor costs are charged to Work in Process 122 and indirect labor costs are charged to Manufacturing Overhead Control 501. In order to charge the correct amount of labor costs to Work in Process and to Manufacturing Overhead Control, total wages must be allocated between direct labor and indirect labor. The steps Panorama Windows uses to allocate wages between direct and indirect labor are described in this chapter.

Time Tickets

The first step in allocating labor costs between direct and indirect labor is the preparation of a **time ticket.** The time card shown in Chapter 6 on page 126 indicates the total hours worked by the employee each day, but it does not show the jobs worked on or what type of work was performed. Since labor costs are charged to specific jobs or departments, some record showing how time was used must be prepared. Time tickets, sometimes called *job time cards,* are used for this purpose (see below).

The time ticket shows the employee's name and number, the department worked in, jobs worked on, time spent on each job, and type of work performed. Panorama Windows computes time on the job to the nearest quarter hour, although some companies keep more exact records. For example, time on the job could be measured to the nearest tenth of an hour.

At Panorama Windows, both direct and indirect workers paid an hourly wage rate (weekly payroll) are required to prepare daily time tickets indicating their activities. Workers who earn a fixed monthly salary (semimonthly payroll) are not required to prepare time tickets.

TIME TICKET

EMPLOYEE NAME   *Donald Jones*

EMPLOYEE NUMBER   *8045*

DEPARTMENT   *Assembly*

DATE   *October 1, 19X9*

JOB/DEPT. NUMBER	TIME STARTED	TIME FINISHED	TOTAL HOURS	WORK PERFORMED	
				CODE	DESCRIPTION
99	8:00	9:30	1.5	822	Install screens
101	9:30	12:00	2.5	690	Attach hardware
002	1:00	2:00	1.0	052	Repair machine
002	4:30	5:00	0.5	099	Safety meeting
TOTAL HOURS			8.0		

Their earnings are classified as indirect labor, and each employee of this type usually works in only one department.

The time ticket used by Panorama Windows is a card with columns in which the employee can record information about each activity performed during the day. This includes the job or department number, the time an activity is started and finished, the total hours spent on an activity, and a description of work performed, in both numeric code and written form. All this data, except for the written description, is in numeric form so that it can easily be processed by computer. At the end of the day, the time tickets are collected and the numeric information from the time tickets is entered into the company's computer. The computer has been programmed to process the data from the time tickets and generate, on a weekly basis, an analysis of time tickets (see page 143).

The time ticket for Donald Jones, shown on page 141, indicates that his employee number is 8045 and that he works in the Assembly Department. For October 1, 19X9, Donald indicated each different job he worked on and the amount of time he spent on each job. For example, from 8:00 to 9:30 he performed direct labor on Job 99, installing screens, and from 1 to 2 he repaired machinery, classified as indirect labor.

Although the filling out of time tickets may seem to be a burdensome task, the procedure is really quite simple and employees can easily complete their time tickets as the work day progresses. To facilitate the process, each employee has a booklet listing the codes to be assigned to each task. Employees complete a time ticket for each day worked.

The exact format and procedures for completing and processing time tickets vary depending on the product and organization of the company and the extent to which the company's operations are computerized (see "Computerized Labor Cost Analysis" later in this chapter). Employees may complete time tickets on a weekly basis; they may, in some cases, enter time ticket data directly into a computer.

Idle Time.   It is not always possible to charge every hour an employee spends in the factory to a specific job or department. Some nonproductive, or **idle time,** is bound to occur, even though a well-managed plant succeeds in keeping it to a minimum. The method of charging idle time varies according to its nature and extent. At Panorama Windows, the short time spent during the morning and afternoon rest periods is not considered idle time. It is absorbed into whatever job the employee is working on at the time of the break. Sometimes a longer period is involved, such as an hour lost waiting for materials, for assignment to a new job, or for a machine to be repaired. These idle time costs are considered manufacturing overhead. Idle time is entered on the time ticket in exactly the same way time spent on a job is entered—but using the code for idle time. At the end of each week an analysis of idle time is prepared for review by the production manager or line supervisor, who takes appropriate action. A partial analysis of idle time is shown on the top of page 143.

ANALYSIS OF IDLE TIME					
JOB/DEPT. NUMBER	TIME STARTED	TIME FINISHED	TOTAL HOURS	WORK PERFORMED	
				CODE	DESCRIPTION
002	4:00	4:30	0.5	999	Power outage

Analysis of Time Tickets

Each week an analysis is made of the time tickets that were filled out by the hourly employees. The **analysis of time tickets** shows the direct labor costs incurred on each job by each department and the total direct labor costs for each department. It also indicates the indirect labor costs for each department. Postings are made from this summary to the job cost sheets and to the departmental overhead analysis sheets. The analysis of time tickets for the week ended October 5 is shown below.

PANORAMA WINDOWS, INC.
Analysis of Time Tickets
Week Ended October 5, 19X9

DIRECT LABOR

JOB	CUTTING HOURS	CUTTING AMOUNT	FRAMING HOURS	FRAMING AMOUNT	ASSEMBLY HOURS	ASSEMBLY AMOUNT	TOTAL
98					175	$1,552.60	$ 1,552.60
99			35	$ 596.40	120	1,363.60	1,960.00
100			80	852.00	130	1,208.00	2,060.00
101	290	$1,902.00	220	1,580.00	55	420.00	3,902.00
102	16	510.00	300	2,788.00	-0-	-0-	3,298.00
103	40	524.00	60	774.00	-0-	-0-	1,298.00
104	150	1,068.00	-0-	-0-	-0-	-0-	1,068.00
105	55	687.00	-0-	-0-	-0-	-0-	687.00
106	-0-	-0-	40	672.40	-0-	-0-	672.40
Total	551	$4,691.00	735	$7,262.80	480	$4,544.20	$16,498.00

INDIRECT LABOR

DEPARTMENT	REGULAR EARNINGS	OVERTIME PREMIUM	TOTAL
Cutting	$ 441.60	$338.40	$ 780.00
Framing	654.00	284.00	938.00
Assembly	564.00	354.00	918.00
Building Services	924.00	-0-	924.00
General Factory	1,368.00	-0-	1,368.00
Total	$3,951.60	$976.40	$4,928.00

SUMMARY

Direct Labor	$16,498.00
Indirect Labor	4,928.00
Total	$21,426.00

The analysis indicates that the direct labor used on Job 101 in the Cutting Department amounted to 290 hours, at a cost of $1,902. In the Framing Department, 220 hours of direct labor were expended at a cost of $1,580. In the Assembly Department, 55 hours of direct labor were used on this job, at a cost of $420. These figures are posted directly from the analysis of time tickets to the job cost sheet for Job 101. The posting reference *TTA* stands for "time ticket analysis" (see the job cost sheet below).

JOB COST SHEET

CUSTOMER *Nelson Construction Company*
DESCRIPTION *Customer specs on file*
QUANTITY *100*

JOB *101*
DATE STARTED *10/1/X9*
DATE COMPLETED

| MATERIALS | | | DIRECT LABOR | | | | | | | MANUFACTURING OVERHEAD APPLIED | | | | | | | | | | |
DATE	REQ. NO.	AMOUNT	DATE	REF.	CUTTING HRS.	AMOUNT	FRAMING HRS.	AMOUNT	ASSEMBLY HRS.	AMOUNT	DATE	REF.	MILLING HRS.	RATE	AMOUNT	ASSEMBLY HRS.	RATE	AMOUNT	FINISHING HRS.	RATE	AMOUNT
10/1	R802	935 00	10/5	TTA	290	1902 00	220	1580 00	55	420 00											
10/2	R804	280 5 00																			
10/6	RM48	(85 00)																			

The analysis of time tickets for the week also shows that total indirect labor costs of $780 were incurred in the Cutting Department. This amount is posted directly from the analysis to the Cutting Department overhead analysis sheet shown below.

DEPARTMENTAL OVERHEAD ANALYSIS SHEET

Department *Cutting*

Month of *October* 19 *X9*

DATE		REF.	TOTAL	01 INDIRECT MATERIALS	02 INDIRECT LABOR	03 PAYROLL TAXES	04 DEPRECIATION	05 REPAIRS & MAINT.	06 UTILITIES	07 INSURANCE	08 OTHER TAXES	09 OTHER ITEM	AMOUNT
Oct.	3	R808	106 25	106 25									
	5	TTA	780 00		780 00								

The overtime premium for each department includes overtime worked by employees classified as direct labor and employees classified as indirect labor. The summary of direct and indirect labor will be the same as the total gross wages shown in the payroll register for that week.

Analysis of Semimonthly Payroll

The semimonthly payroll is also analyzed and data entered into the computer. This payroll represents the wages earned by employees, such as custodial workers and factory office personnel, who are on a fixed monthly salary. Their earnings are classified as indirect labor and are entered in the departmental overhead analysis sheets. The **analysis of semimonthly factory payroll** for Panorama Windows for the period ended October 15 is shown below.

PANORAMA WINDOWS, INC.
Analysis of Semimonthly Factory Payroll
Period Ended October 15, 19X9

DEPARTMENT	INDIRECT LABOR
Cutting	$ -0-
Framing	-0-
Assembly	-0-
Building Services	1,580.00
General Factory	3,965.00
Total	$5,545.00

The indirect wages paid in each department are entered in the Indirect Labor column of the appropriate departmental overhead analysis sheet.

DEPARTMENTAL OVERHEAD ANALYSIS SHEET

Department *Building Services* Month of *October* 19 *X9*

DATE		REF.	TOTAL	01 INDIRECT MATERIALS	02 INDIRECT LABOR	03 PAYROLL TAXES	04 DEPRECIATION	05 REPAIRS & MAINT.	06 UTILITIES	07 INSURANCE	08 OTHER TAXES	09 OTHER ITEM	AMOUNT
Oct.	5	TTA	924 00		924 00								
	15	SP	1580 00		1580 00								

DEPARTMENTAL OVERHEAD ANALYSIS SHEET

Department *General Factory* Month of *October* 19 *X9*

DATE		REF.	TOTAL	01 INDIRECT MATERIALS	02 INDIRECT LABOR	03 PAYROLL TAXES	04 DEPRECIATION	05 REPAIRS & MAINT.	06 UTILITIES	07 INSURANCE	08 OTHER TAXES	09 OTHER ITEM	AMOUNT
Oct.	5	TTA	1368 00		1368 00								
	15	SP	3965 00		3965 00								

Analysis of Unpaid Wages

The last day of the weekly pay period usually differs from the last day of the fiscal period. Therefore it is necessary to prepare an analysis of time tickets at the end of the month for those labor costs that have been incurred since the last weekly payroll date but have not yet been paid. For example, the last day of the month may fall on a Wednesday, but employees are paid every Friday. Thus, labor costs incurred on Monday, Tuesday, and Wednesday, the days worked since the last pay date, must be accounted for. In this way, production is charged with all labor costs in the month in which they are incurred. The analysis of time tickets for the period October 27 through 31 is shown below. The direct labor costs are posted to the job cost sheets. The indirect labor costs are posted to the departmental overhead analysis sheets.

PANORAMA WINDOWS, INC.
Analysis of Time Tickets
October 27–31, 19X9

DIRECT LABOR

JOB	CUTTING HOURS	CUTTING AMOUNT	FRAMING HOURS	FRAMING AMOUNT	ASSEMBLY HOURS	ASSEMBLY AMOUNT	TOTAL
108	45	$ 295.00	140	$1,012.00	150	$1,125.00	$2,432.00
109	70	459.00	100	723.00	75	563.00	1,745.00
110	90	590.00	80	578.00	45	337.00	1,505.00
111	85	557.00	75	542.00	-0-	-0-	1,099.00
112	30	198.00	35	255.00	-0-	-0-	453.00
Total	320	$2,099.00	430	$3,110.00	270	$2,025.00	$7,234.00

INDIRECT LABOR

DEPARTMENT	REGULAR EARNINGS	OVERTIME PREMIUM	TOTAL
Cutting	$ 487.00	-0-	$ 487.00
Framing	495.00	-0-	495.00
Assembly	447.00	-0-	447.00
Building Services	507.00	-0-	507.00
General Factory	878.00	-0-	878.00
Total	$2,814.00	-0-	$2,814.00

SUMMARY

Direct Labor	$ 7,234.00
Indirect Labor	2,814.00
Total	$10,048.00

TRANSFERRING LABOR COSTS TO PRODUCTION

Entries are made during the month to transfer labor costs to job cost sheets and departmental overhead analysis sheets. These transfers are recorded in the general ledger accounts at the end of the month.

Summary of Factory Wages

At the end of the month it is also necessary to prepare a summary of all factory wages earned. The **summary of factory wages** consists of the time ticket analyses and the semimonthly payroll analyses that have been prepared and posted to the job cost sheets and departmental overhead analysis sheets during the month. (See below.)

PANORAMA WINDOWS, INC.
Summary of Factory Wages
October 19X9

PAYROLL PERIOD	CUTTING DIRECT LABOR	CUTTING INDIRECT LABOR	FRAMING DIRECT LABOR	FRAMING INDIRECT LABOR	ASSEMBLY DIRECT LABOR	ASSEMBLY INDIRECT LABOR	BUILDING SERVICES	GENERAL FACTORY	TOTAL
Oct. 1–5	$ 4,691.00	$ 780.00	$ 7,262.80	$ 938.00	$ 4,544.20	$ 918.00	$ 924.00	$ 1,368.00	$ 21,426.00
6–15	4,236.00	648.00	5,427.00	610.00	4,150.00	640.00	1,057.00	2,361.00	19,129.00
1–5	-0-	-0-	-0-	-0-	-0-	-0-	1,580.00	3,965.00	5,545.00
13–19	4,972.00	376.00	5,566.00	762.00	4,197.00	684.00	1,131.00	2,386.00	20,074.00
20–26	4,566.00	477.00	5,376.00	945.00	4,375.00	752.00	1,250.00	2,424.00	20,165.00
16–31	-0-	-0-	-0-	-0-	-0-	-0-	1,580.00	3,965.00	5,545.00
27–31	2,099.00	487.00	3,110.00	495.00	2,025.00	447.00	507.00	878.00	10,048.00
Total	$20,564.00	$2,768.00	$26,741.80	$3,750.00	$19,291.20	$3,441.00	$8,029.00	$17,347.00	$101,932.00

SUMMARY

Direct Labor	$ 66,597.00
Indirect Labor	35,335.00
Total	$101,932.00

The summary of factory wages for October shows total direct labor costs of $66,597 and total indirect labor costs of $35,335. At the end of the month these amounts are transferred to production, as shown on the general journal voucher below.

JOURNAL VOUCHER	Date Oct. 31,	19 X9	No. 10-48			
ACCOUNT		ACCT. NO.	✓	DEBIT	CREDIT	
Work in Process		122		66597 00		
Manufacturing Overhead Control		501		35335 00		
Factory Payroll Clearing		500	✓		101932 00	
Charged labor costs to production for the month.						
PREPARED BY NV		AUDITED BY BJ			APPROVED BY MP	

After the factory labor costs have been charged to production, the Factory Payroll Clearing account appears as shown below.

	Factory Payroll Clearing					NO. 500	
DATE	EXPLANATION	POST. REF.	DEBIT	CREDIT	BALANCE	DR. CR.	
19 X9							
Oct. 5		WP	21,426 00		21,426 00	DR.	
12		WP	19,129 00		40,555 00	DR.	
15		SP	5,545 00		46,100 00	DR.	
19		WP	20,074 00		66,174 00	DR.	
26		WP	20,165 00		86,339 00	DR.	
31		SP	5,545 00		91,884 00	DR.	
31		J10-48		101,932 00	10,048 00	CR.	

Balance of Factory Payroll Clearing

The credit to Factory Payroll Clearing ($101,932) consists of October earnings, both paid and unpaid (October 27–31), as follows:

	Paid	Unpaid	Total
Direct Labor Chargeable to Work in Process	$59,363	$ 7,234	$ 66,597
Indirect Labor Chargeable to Manufacturing Overhead Control	32,521	2,814	35,335
Total Labor Credited to Factory Payroll Clearing	$91,884	$10,048	$101,932

The Factory Payroll Clearing account has been debited for the gross amount of factory wages paid during the month ($91,884). It is credited for the total amount of wages charged to production during the month ($101,932) through the general journal entry. The balance of the Factory Payroll Clearing account after these postings ($10,048 Cr.) represents the amount of factory wages earned and charged to production but unpaid on October 31. This balance, representing unpaid wages at the end of the month, will be shown on the balance sheet as a current liability called Accrued Wages Payable. Some accountants prefer to make a formal journal entry debiting Factory Payroll Clearing and crediting Salaries and Wages Payable 202 at the end of the month for the amount of unpaid wages.

When the next payroll is prepared for the week of October 27 through November 2, the total earnings shown in the payroll register ($19,020) is debited to Factory Payroll Clearing, as shown on page 149. Of this amount, $10,048 represents the unpaid wages on October 31 that were charged to production in October. The remaining $8,972 represents wages earned on November 1 and 2 and will be charged to production at the end of November, as shown on page 149.

At this point you should be able to work Exercises 7–1 and 7–2.

Factory Payroll Clearing						NO.	500	
DATE	EXPLANATION	POST. REF.	DEBIT		CREDIT	BALANCE		DR. CR.
19 X9								
Nov. 1	Balance	✓				10,048	00	CR.
2		WP	19,020	00		8,972	00	DR.

FLOW OF COSTS

Labor costs flow into the Factory Payroll Clearing account as a result of timekeeping and computing procedures. Costs flow out of the account as the direct and indirect labor costs are applied to production. The flowchart below illustrates the flow of labor costs. Each of the steps is identified by number.

1. Record the number of hours worked each day by each employee on a time card.
2. Record the hours and type of work performed each day by each employee on a time ticket.

FLOW OF LABOR COSTS

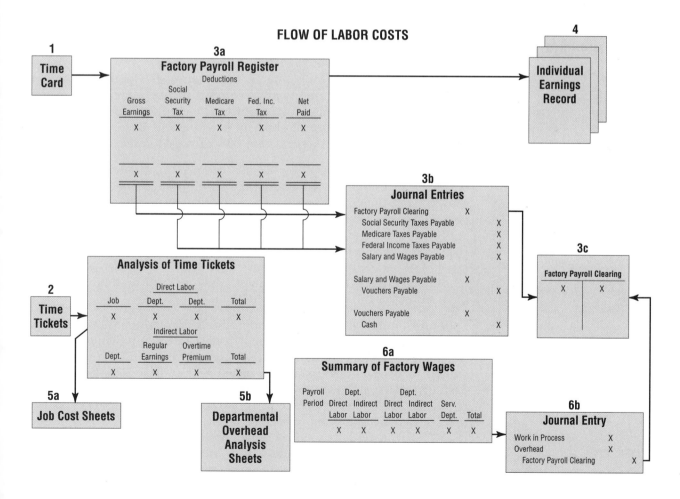

3. Record the total earnings, deductions, and net pay of all employees for a payroll period in the payroll register. Post the totals from the payroll register to the appropriate general ledger accounts.
4. Post the earnings, deductions, and net pay for each employee to an individual earnings record, which provides cumulative figures for the year.
5. Charge the direct labor costs to the individual job sheets. Enter the indirect labor costs on the departmental overhead analysis sheets by means of postings from analyses of weekly and semimonthly payrolls and analysis of end-of-month unpaid earnings.
6. Prepare a general journal voucher based on the monthly labor summary to charge labor costs to production. Post the amounts to the Work in Process account, the Manufacturing Overhead Control account, and the Factory Payroll Clearing account.

SPECIAL LABOR COST PROBLEMS

The labor costs discussed so far were accounted for in the normal routine of preparing time cards, time tickets, periodic analyses, and payroll summaries. Certain other labor costs require special accounting procedures.

Employer's Payroll Taxes

The employer normally must pay four payroll taxes: social security tax, medicare tax, federal unemployment tax, and state unemployment tax.

Social Security Tax. Under the Federal Insurance Contributions Act (FICA), the employer is currently required to pay a tax equal to the amount levied for social security against the employee. Because of frequent changes in the social security tax rate and base, an assumed rate of 6.3 percent on the first $66,000 of wages is used in this text.

Medicare Tax. The employer is also required to "match" (pay a tax equal to the amount levied against the employee) the medicare tax deducted from the employees' wages. A medicare tax rate of 1.5 percent on all wages is assumed in this textbook.

Since a company pays the social security tax and medicare tax at the same rate and on the same taxable wages as its employees do, the amount of tax the firm owes is usually the same as that deducted from employees' wages. Small adjustments may need to be made because of rounding of individual tax deductions.

Federal Unemployment Tax. Under the Federal Unemployment Tax Act (FUTA), the federal government levies an unemployment tax. In this text, the **federal unemployment insurance tax (FUTA tax)** is assumed to be 6.2 percent and is based on the first $7,000 of gross earnings paid each employee during the calendar year. However, a credit, not to exceed 5.4 percent, is allowed against the federal tax for taxes levied by states for unemployment insurance. As a result, the net FUTA rate actually paid by most employers is .8 percent (6.2 percent − 5.4 percent = .8 percent). Both the rate and the base are subject to change. It is important to note that this tax is *not* paid by the employee, only by the employer.

State Unemployment Tax. The typical **state unemployment insurance tax (SUTA tax)** on the employer is 5.4 percent of the first $7,000 of gross earnings paid each employee during the calendar year, although it may be higher or lower. Most states allow credits against the tax due through a merit rating given for a stable employment record. This merit, or experience, rating system may reduce the effective tax rate. State unemployment tax rates and bases are subject to change and will vary from state to state. In this discussion, we will assume that because of a stable employment record the effective SUTA rate for Panorama Windows is 3.8 percent.

Charging Payroll Taxes. It is customary for the accountant to charge all employer's payroll taxes on factory earnings to manufacturing overhead. Panorama Windows, Inc., uses a typical four-step procedure, as outlined below, to enter payroll taxes in the accounting records of the firm.

1. The payroll unit prepares a monthly summary of taxable wages by department, as shown below. Taxable wages may differ from total wages (page 147) since some employees may have earned wages

---

PANORAMA WINDOWS, INC.
Summary of Taxable Factory Wages
October 19X9

WAGES SUBJECT TO SOCIAL SECURITY AND MEDICARE TAXES

PAYROLL PERIOD	CUTTING	FRAMING	ASSEMBLY	BUILDING SERVICES	GENERAL FACTORY	TOTAL
Oct. 1–5	$ 4,171	$ 6,763	$ 4,164	$ 924	$ 1,368	$ 17,390
6–12	5,637	6,819	5,313	1,147	2,400	21,316
1–15	-0-	-0-	-0-	1,565	3,740	5,305
13–19	5,544	6,919	4,922	1,211	2,343	20,939
20–26	5,393	6,309	5,704	1,080	2,662	21,148
16–31	-0-	-0-	-0-	1,556	3,643	5,199
27–31	2,586	3,605	2,472	507	878	10,048
Total	$23,331	$30,415	$22,575	$7,990	$17,034	$101,345

WAGES SUBJECT TO FEDERAL AND STATE UNEMPLOYMENT COMPENSATION TAXES

PAYROLL PERIOD	CUTTING	FRAMING	ASSEMBLY	BUILDING SERVICES	GENERAL FACTORY	TOTAL
Oct. 1–5	$ 734	$1,301	$ 843	$271	$ 261	$ 3,410
6–12	856	1,003	778	152	284	3,073
1–15	-0-	-0-	-0-	98	383	481
13–19	725	821	594	110	178	2,428
20–26	670	926	532	86	221	2,435
16–31	-0-	-0-	-0-	80	297	377
27–31	490	503	408	87	96	1,584
Total	$3,475	$4,554	$3,155	$884	$1,720	$13,788

over the maximum amounts subject to social security and unemployment taxes.

2. This summary becomes the basis for calculating payroll taxes expense for the period, as shown below.

PANORAMA WINDOWS, INC.
Summary of Factory Payroll Taxes
October 19X9

| | SOCIAL SECURITY AT 6.3% | MEDICARE AT 1.5% | UNEMPLOYMENT TAXES | | TOTAL |
| | | | STATE AT 3.8% | FEDERAL AT 0.8% | |
DEPARTMENT					
Cutting	$1,469.86	$ 349.96	$132.05	$ 27.80	$1,979.67
Framing	1,916.15	456.23	173.05	36.43	2,581.86
Assembly	1,422.22	338.62	119.89	25.24	1,905.97
Building Services	503.37	119.85	33.59	7.07	663.88
General Factory	1,073.14	255.51	65.36	13.76	1,407.77
Total	$6,384.74	$1,520.17	$523.94	$110.30	$8,539.15

3. The payroll taxes for each department are posted to the departmental overhead analysis sheets from the summary of factory payroll taxes. (See page 168.)

4. A general journal voucher is prepared so that the taxes payable may be recorded in the general ledger accounts, as shown below.

At this point you should be able to work Exercises 7–3 and 7–4 and Problems 7–1A to 7–3B.

Some companies do not attempt to compute the exact amount of payroll taxes chargeable to each department. Instead, the total monthly payroll taxes expense is simply allocated to the departments on the

JOURNAL VOUCHER	Date *Oct. 31,*		19 *X9*	No. *10-49*	
ACCOUNT	ACCT. NO.	✓	DEBIT	CREDIT	
Manufacturing Overhead Control	*501*		8539 15		
Social Security Taxes Payable	*210*			6384 74	
Medicare Taxes Payable	*211*			1520 17	
Federal Unemployment Taxes Payable	*212*			523 94	
State Unemployment Taxes Payable	*213*			110 30	
EXPLANATION					
Recorded employer's payroll taxes on factory wages for the month.					
PREPARED BY *NV*	AUDITED BY *BJ*		APPROVED BY *MP*		

Computerized Labor Cost Analysis

Uniform Attire, Inc., manufactures uniforms for professional sports teams and large hotel and restaurant chains. The process of making uniforms and shipping them is done in three departments: cutting, sewing, and shipping. Each factory worker is assigned to only one department. Since work is being done for specific clients, the management of Uniform Attire believes that it is very important to keep track of the production costs that relate to each job. The company has developed the computerized system described below to gather and analyze client labor costs.

Each of the factory departments is equipped with a computer terminal that is connected to a central computer. The terminals are equipped with badge readers. When ready to begin a task, an employee inserts his or her badge into the badge reader and keys in a code representing a job for a particular client. For example, if Clara Suarez is going to begin cutting the uniforms ordered by the Regency Inn, she will insert her badge and key in 1264, the code identifying the client. The computer will note the time the job was started, the fact that it was started by Clara Suarez in the Cutting Department, and that the job pertains to the Regency Inn order. When Clara Suarez finishes working on the job, she will again insert her badge into the terminal and key in the client code. Now the *computer* will note the time the job was finished and will compute the time spent on it by Clara Suarez.

At any time, a partial job cost sheet can be printed out on the computer. Such a report is shown below. The data that have been collected will be used to prepare the payroll, update the general ledger, and prepare an analysis of labor cost.

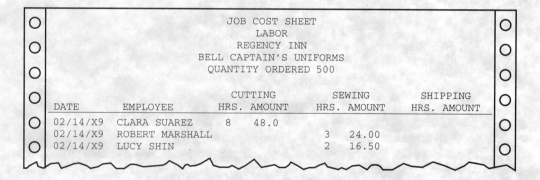

Management believes that this system has several advantages: production information is available on a timely basis, factory workers spend more time producing and less time recording their production, and the accounting staff can analyze costs of production to see where operations can become more efficient.

basis of the total wages earned in each. Although this procedure is not exact, it will usually result in reasonably accurate cost allocations.

Fringe Benefit Costs

In recent years there has been a tremendous growth in the cost of **fringe benefits** related to salaries and wages. Fringe benefits include vacation and holiday pay, pension plan contributions, hospitalization insurance, and group life insurance, to mention only a few. At Panorama Windows, Inc., such costs are charged to Manufacturing Overhead Control 501. They are entered on the appropriate departmental overhead analysis sheets as they are incurred. For example, if a factory employee is paid while on vacation, the earnings are charged to Manufacturing Overhead Control. They are entered on the overhead analysis sheet of the department in which the employee regularly works. This procedure is the most common one. A few companies, however, do classify the fringe benefits associated with direct labor as part of the direct labor cost rather than as manufacturing overhead.

SELF-REVIEW

1. Joe Marshall, a custodian for Safeway, Co., did not complete a time ticket for the week ending Jan. 15. How should his time be recorded?
2. The last day of the fiscal period is Tuesday, March 31, 19X9, but the last pay date for the month was Thursday, March 26. What actions should you take?
3. Calculate the employer's payroll taxes from the following data:

Gross Wages:	683,879
Taxable wages for Social Security:	623,975
Taxable wages for Medicare	683,879
Taxable wages for FUTA and SUTA	75,214

4. Record the general journal entry needed to recognize the payroll tax liability.

Answers to Self-Review

1. Joe is not required to complete a time ticket. As a custodian, his time is recorded as indirect labor.
2. An analysis of time tickets will be prepared. Labor costs for the days worked from Thursday, March 27, and Tuesday, March 31, will be charged in the month in which they were incurred.
3. Social Security (623,975 × .063) 39,310.43
   Medicare (683,879 × .015) 10,258.19
   FUTA (75,214 × .008) 601.71
   SUTA (75,214 × .038) 2858.14
4. Manufacturing Overhead Control 53,028.47
       Social Security Taxes Payable 39,310.43
       Medicare Taxes Payable 10,258.19
       FUTA Taxes Payable 601.71
       SUTA Taxes Payable 2858.14

PRINCIPLES AND PROCEDURES SUMMARY

- After employee earnings are computed through various time-keeping and recording operations, they are analyzed for further cost processing.
- Data obtained by such analyses are the basis for charging labor costs to specific jobs (direct) or to departments (indirect).
- At the end of the month payroll costs must be transferred to production through a general journal entry.
  - Direct labor costs are debited to Work in Process.
  - Indirect labor costs are debited to Manufacturing Overhead Control.
  - The total costs are credited to the Factory Payroll Clearing account.
- Additional labor costs are the various payroll taxes levied upon the employer and the numerous fringe benefits that may be provided for the employees. In most systems of cost accounting, these expenses are debited to Manufacturing Overhead Control.

MANAGERIAL IMPLICATIONS

- The time tickets showing the hours worked by each production worker on each job are the source of labor costs that are entered on job order cost sheets—the records that accumulate the costs of each job. It is therefore very important that employees accurately and completely record time data on the tickets.
- The accountant prepares a summary of all factory wages at the end of each month. This summary shows all wages earned by employees in each department. This is the source of data for a journal entry transferring labor costs from the Factory Payroll Clearing account to the Work in Process account and Manufacturing Overhead Control.
- Employee payroll taxes must be properly deducted from each paycheck and remitted, along with the employer's payroll taxes, at the proper time. The payroll taxes that must be matched by the employer include the social security tax and medicare tax. Federal unemployment tax and state unemployment tax are paid only by the employer. Management must exercise great care in making sure that all taxes are properly computed and paid on time.
- Another cost related to labor (both direct labor and indirect labor) is that of fringe benefits (employee retirement plans, health and life insurance, and vacation pay, for example). Today, fringe benefits make up a large part of total labor-related costs, often running to as much as 35 percent of salaries and wages paid. The magnitude of these costs, plus close governmental scrutiny, makes it necessary for management to devote a great deal of oversight to all such costs.

NOTE: *For all questions, exercises, problems, and case, use a social security tax rate of 6.3 percent on the first $66,000 in wages and a medicare tax rate of 1.5 percent on total wages. Also use FUTA tax of 0.8 percent on the first $7,000 in wages and a SUTA tax of 3.8 percent on the first $7,000 of wages.*

REVIEW QUESTIONS

1. How do time cards differ from time tickets?
2. What types of data are found on the weekly analysis of the time tickets?
3. What are some causes of idle time? How should long periods of idle time be recorded?
4. To what subsidiary records are direct labor costs and indirect labor costs posted?
5. What general ledger account is debited for direct labor costs? What account is debited for indirect labor costs?
6. How does an analysis of time tickets differ from a summary of factory wages?
7. At the end of the month, after all postings are made, the Factory Payroll Clearing account has a $6,190 credit balance. What does this credit balance represent, and where is it shown on the financial statements?
8. List the four payroll taxes incurred by employers.
9. What general ledger account is charged with the total employer's payroll taxes liability incurred on the wages of factory employees?
10. What are fringe benefits? How are they typically accounted for?

MANAGERIAL DISCUSSION QUESTIONS

1. What uses are made of data obtained from time tickets?
2. Why should management analyze idle time?
3. What effect would the omission of recording unpaid wages at the end of the month have on the financial statements for a manufacturer? What problems would this omission cause management?
4. Discuss two ways in which a manufacturing firm can allocate payroll taxes to factory departments.
5. What problems might management face in attempting to assign payroll taxes and fringe benefit costs to specific jobs?
6. What uses can management make of the data concerning hours and the amount of direct labor costs recorded on the job cost sheet?
7. At the end of the month, after all postings have been made, the Factory Payroll Clearing account would typically have a credit balance. What would a zero balance indicate? What would a debit balance indicate?

EXERCISES

EXERCISE 7–1 **Calculate the balance of the Factory Payroll Clearing account. (Obj. 8).** At the Norris Company, the Factory Payroll Clearing account shows debits totaling $254,690 made during the month and a credit of $286,520 made at the end of the month.
a. What is the balance of the Factory Payroll Clearing account?
b. Is it a debit or credit balance?
c. What does this balance represent?

EXERCISE 7–2 **Distribute wages earned. (Obj. 7).** Record the general journal entry for Casco Metals Inc. to distribute the following wages earned during the month of November: direct labor, $178,348; indirect labor, $32,180.

EXERCISE 7–3 **Journalize the employer's payroll taxes. (Obj. 9).** For the month of May, the Winston Materials Company incurred the following four payroll taxes:

Social security taxes	$35,856
Medicare taxes	8,605
FUTA taxes	962
SUTA taxes	3,859

Record the general journal entry needed to recognize the payroll taxes liability.

EXERCISE 7–4 **Calculate the employer's payroll taxes. (Obj. 9).** Calculate the employer's payroll taxes for Peter Wong, Inc. for the month of April 19X9 from the following data:

Gross wages	$650,300
Taxable wages for social security	562,310
Taxable wages for medicare	650,300
Taxable wages for FUTA and SUTA	81,280

PROBLEMS

PROBLEM 7–1A **Journalize payroll and payroll tax entries. (Objs. 8, 9).** The data and instructions given below relate to Memphis Furniture Company for the month of August 19X9. The beginning credit balance of the Factory Payroll Clearing account on August 1 was $9,720, representing unpaid wages earned by employees during the last two days of July.

INSTRUCTIONS 1. Set up a Factory Payroll Clearing account and enter the beginning balance.
2. Journalize the summary of weekly and semimonthly payroll paid during the month. Use the account titles in your textbook with the data shown here.

Total gross wages	$84,380
Income taxes withheld	12,700
Social security taxes withheld	5,316
Medicare taxes withheld	1,266
Group insurance deductions	1,680
Pension plan contributions	4,200

3. Journalize the charging of labor costs to production. The summary of factory wages for the month shows $62,140 for direct labor and $19,460 for indirect labor.
4. Journalize the employer's payroll taxes. The wages subject to unemployment taxes were $43,580.
5. Post the journal entries to the Factory Payroll Clearing account.
6. Explain where the balance of the Factory Payroll Clearing account on July 31 is shown on the financial statements.

PROBLEM 7–2A

Summarize factory payroll taxes. (Obj. 9). A summary of taxable factory wages of the Sunshine Corporation for the month of March 19X9 is shown below.

	Wages Subject To:	
Department	**Social Security and Medicare Taxes**	**Federal and State Unemployment Taxes**
Factory Supply	$52,800	$20,130
Factory Administration	53,260	12,110
Cutting	72,380	28,640
Assembly	79,910	33,750
Finishing	84,620	30,970

INSTRUCTIONS

1. Compute the employer's payroll taxes to be charged to each department. Use the data to prepare the summary of factory payroll taxes for March 19X9.
2. Prepare an entry in general journal form to record the taxes. Use the account titles in your textbook.

PROBLEM 7–3A

Journalize payroll entries. (Objs. 7–9). Prepare the necessary general journal entries for Martinez Machines, Inc., a manufacturer of small engines, for the month of September 19X9. Note that Martinez pays its hourly employees twice a month.

Sept. 15 The payroll for the first half of September for the hourly factory workers totaled $32,500. Deductions: social security taxes, $2,047; medicare taxes, $487; federal income taxes, $4,900.

15 Issued a voucher to pay the net payroll.

15 Recorded payment of the voucher.

30 The payroll for the second half of September for the hourly factory workers totaled $33,200. Deductions: social security taxes, $2,092; medicare taxes, $498; federal income taxes, $5,120.

30 Issued a voucher to pay the net payroll.

30 Recorded payment of the voucher.

30 Recorded distribution of the factory wages earned during the entire month of September. The summary of factory wages showed total direct labor at $46,240 and total indirect labor at $19,460.

30 Recorded employer's payroll tax liability for the month as follows: social security taxes, $4,139; medicare taxes, $985; federal unemployment taxes, $342; state unemployment taxes, $2,837.

PROBLEM 7–4A **Process payroll records: comprehensive problem. (Objs. 3–9).** Dolls, Unlimited, manufactures a variety of dolls. Since the last day of the normal payroll period falls on September 30, there are no accrued wages payable and no analysis of time tickets for a partial pay period. The following reports have been prepared:

DOLLS, UNLIMITED
Analysis of Time Tickets
Week Ended September 30, 19X9

DIRECT LABOR

JOB	MOLDING HOURS	MOLDING AMOUNT	ASSEMBLY HOURS	ASSEMBLY AMOUNT	PAINTING HOURS	PAINTING AMOUNT	TOTAL
479			460	$2,208	272	$1,360	$ 3,568
480			263	1,262	184	920	2,182
481	210	$1,071	216	1,036	133	665	2,772
482	308	1,570	79	379	-0-	-0-	1,949
483	96	490	-0-	-0-	-0-	-0-	490
Total	614	$3,131	1,018	$4,885	589	$2,945	$10,961

INDIRECT LABOR

DEPARTMENT	REGULAR EARNINGS	OVERTIME PREMIUM	TOTAL
Molding	$ 456	$162	$ 618
Assembly	508	98	606
Painting	461	184	645
Building Services	610	-0-	610
General Factory	684	-0-	684
Total	$2,719	$444	$3,163

SUMMARY

Direct Labor	$10,961
Indirect Labor	3,163
Total	$14,124

DOLLS, UNLIMITED
Analysis of Semimonthly Factory Payroll
Period Ended September 30, 19X9

DEPARTMENT	INDIRECT LABOR
Molding	$ -0-
Assembly	-0-
Painting	-0-
Building Services	3,426
General Factory	4,082
Total	$7,508

DOLLS, UNLIMITED
Summary of Factory Payroll Taxes
September 19X9

	SOCIAL		UNEMPLOYMENT TAXES		
DEPARTMENT	SECURITY AT 6.3%	MEDICARE AT 1.5%	STATE AT 3.8%	FEDERAL AT .8%	TOTAL
Molding	$1,243.12	$ 295.98	$ 349.15	$ 94.10	$1,982.35
Assembly	1,271.47	302.73	429.82	115.72	2,119.74
Painting	1,126.82	268.29	286.12	77.03	1,758.26
Building Services	581.74	138.51	134.16	36.11	890.52
General Factory	818.87	194.97	232.10	62.49	1,308.43
Total	$5,042.02	$1,200.48	$1,431.35	$385.45	$8,059.30

INSTRUCTIONS

NOTE: If you are using the *Study Guide and Working Papers,* the beginning data from Instructions 1 to 5 and 8a and 8b have already been recorded for you.

1. Set up the following job cost sheets:

   Job 479, Delta Department Store, 200 units, started Sept. 10
   Job 480, Educational Toys, 300 units, started Sept. 18
   Job 481, Peter Pan Toy Store, 350 units, started Sept. 25
   Job 482, O'Malley's Specialty Store, 200 units, started Sept. 27
   Job 483, Ramirez Toy Shop, 150 units, started Sept. 27

2. Set up the following departmental overhead analysis sheets:

   Molding Department
   Assembly Department
   Painting Department
   Building Services Department
   General Factory Department

3. a. Set up the following general ledger accounts:

   Work in Process 122
   Social Security Taxes Payable 210

Medicare Taxes Payable 211
Federal Unemployment Taxes Payable 212
State Unemployment Taxes Payable 213
Factory Payroll Clearing 500 (enter the Sept. 1 credit
    balance of $8,930)
Manufacturing Overhead Control 501

b. Record the following debits in the Factory Payroll Clearing
account. Compute the balances.

Date	Post. Ref.	Debits
Sept. 2	WP	$13,740
9	WP	16,190
15	SP	7,320
16	WP	14,950
23	WP	15,130

4. Indirect labor charges for the weeks ended September 2, 9, 16,
   and 23 are given below. Post these charges by week to the departmental overhead analysis sheets set up in Instruction 2.

	Molding	Assembly	Painting	Building Services	General Factory
Sept. 2 TTA	$435	$392	$225	$ 386	$ 479
9 TTA	573	415	462	518	833
15 TTA	—	—	—	2,840	4,480
16 TTA	486	512	548	724	1,160
23 TTA	532	583	597	730	1,280

5. The direct labor charges have been taken from the analysis of
   time tickets for the week ended September 23. Post the data to
   the job cost sheets set up in Instruction 1.

	Molding		Assembly		Painting	
Job	Hours	Amount	Hours	Amount	Hours	Amount
479 TTA	125	$ 638	66	$317	16	$ 79
480 TTA	116	592	57	274	12	60
481 TTA	173	882	74	355	—	—
	414	$2,112	197	$946	28	$139

6. a. Post the data from the analysis of time tickets for the week
      ended September 30, 19X9, to the job cost sheets set up in
      Instruction 1 and the departmental overhead analysis sheets
      set up in Instruction 2.
   b. Post the total amount of this weekly payroll directly as a debit
      to Factory Payroll Clearing 500 set up in Instruction 3. Omit
      posting the credit side of the entry.

7. a. Post the amounts from the analysis of semimonthly factory
      payroll for the period ended September 30, 19X9, to the de-
      partmental overhead analysis sheets set up in Instruction 2.
   b. Post the total amount of this semimonthly payroll directly as
      a debit to Factory Payroll Clearing 500. Omit posting the credit
      side of the entry.

8. Prepare the summary of factory wages for the month of September.
   a. Enter in the appropriate columns the following departmental direct labor charges for each payroll period:

Payroll Period	Molding	Assembly	Painting
Sept. 1–2	$1,048	$1,253	$ 592
3–9	4,810	3,873	4,706
1–15	-0-	-0-	-0-
10–16	4,672	3,284	3,564
17–23	3,427	4,379	3,602

   b. Enter in the appropriate columns the departmental indirect labor charges from the data given in Instruction 4.
   c. Enter the departmental direct labor charges from the analysis of time tickets for the week ended September 30.
   d. Enter the departmental indirect labor charges from the analysis of time tickets for the week ended September 30.
   e. Enter the departmental indirect labor charges from the analysis of semimonthly factory payroll for the period ended September 30, 19X9.
   f. Total all columns, crossfoot to prove, and double rule. Prepare the Summary section.
9. a. Prepare a general journal voucher to transfer all direct and indirect labor costs for the month to production. (Voucher 9-33.)
   b. Post this journal voucher to the general ledger accounts.
10. Post the amounts from the summary of factory payroll taxes (use the reference SPT) to the departmental overhead analysis sheets set up in Instruction 2.
11. a. Prepare the general journal voucher to record taxes payable (Voucher 9-34.)
    b. Post this journal voucher to the general ledger accounts.
12. Foot all hour and amount columns of the job cost sheets and summarize the data in a schedule showing the totals for each job by department.
13. Foot the amount columns of the departmental overhead analysis sheets and summarize the data in a schedule showing the total for each department by type of cost.
14. Check the extensions of the general ledger account balances, and prepare a schedule showing the name and number of each account, the balance, and whether the balance is a debit or credit.

ALTERNATE PROBLEMS

PROBLEM 7–1B **Journalize payroll and payroll tax entries. (Objs. 8, 9).** The data and instructions given below relate to the Commodore Company for the month of July 19X9. The beginning credit balance of the Factory Payroll Clearing account on July 1 is $13,550, representing unpaid wages earned by employees during the last three days of June.

INSTRUCTIONS
1. Set up a Factory Payroll Clearing account and enter the beginning balance.
2. Journalize the summary of weekly and semimonthly payroll paid during the month. Use the account titles in your textbook with the data shown here.

Total gross wages	$102,400
Income taxes withheld	18,250
Social security taxes withheld	6,451
Medicare taxes withheld	1,536
Group insurance deductions	2,300
Pension plan contributions	5,630

3. Journalize the charging of labor costs to production. The summary of factory wages for the month shows $71,680 for direct labor and $20,740 for indirect labor.
4. Journalize the employer's payroll taxes. The wages subject to unemployment taxes were $61,310.
5. Post the journal entries to the Factory Payroll Clearing account.
6. Explain where the balance of the Factory Payroll Clearing account on July 31 is shown on the financial statements.

PROBLEM 7–2B **Summarize factory payroll taxes. (Obj. 9).** A summary of taxable factory wages of Swanson & Company for the month of May 19X9 is shown below.

	Wages Subject To:	
Department	Social Security and Medicare Taxes	Federal and State Unemployment Taxes
General Factory	$39,350	$11,460
Building Maintenance	36,470	10,290
Cutting	42,780	15,340
Molding	46,280	16,040
Finishing	44,780	19,260

INSTRUCTIONS
1. Compute the employer's payroll taxes to be charged to each department. Use the data to prepare the summary of factory payroll taxes for May 19X9.
2. Prepare an entry in general journal form to record the taxes. Use the account titles in your textbook.

PROBLEM 7–3B **Journalize payroll entries. (Objs. 7–9).** Prepare the necessary general journal entries for Chicago Manufacturing, Inc., a manufacturer of small appliances, for the month of November 19X9. Note that Chicago Manufacturing pays its hourly employees twice a month.

Nov. 15   The payroll for the first half of November for the hourly factory workers totaled $67,300. Deductions: social security taxes, $4,240; medicare taxes, $1,010; federal income taxes, $10,780.

15   Issued a voucher to pay the net payroll.

15   Recorded payment of the voucher.

30   The payroll for the second half of November for the hourly factory workers totaled $69,600. Deductions: social

security taxes, $4,385; medicare taxes, $1,044; federal income taxes, $10,490.

30 Issued a voucher to pay the net payroll.

30 Recorded payment of the voucher.

30 Recorded distribution of the factory wages earned during the entire month of September. The summary of factory wages showed total direct labor at $105,412 and total indirect labor at $31,488.

30 Recorded the employer's payroll tax liability for the month as follows: social security taxes, $8,625; medicare taxes, $2,054; federal unemployment taxes, $562; state unemployment taxes, $4,745.

MANAGERIAL DECISION CASE

Pounds-a-Way, Inc., is a manufacturer of exercise equipment for home use. Because of an increase in interest in physical fitness, demand for home-exercise equipment is booming, and Pounds-a-Way has received an unprecedented number of orders. The current factory staff, consisting of two supervisors and twelve factory workers, has been unable to meet this increase in demand in its standard 40-hour work week. As a result, Pounds-a-Way has a backlog of unfilled orders.

Paulo Monti, president of the company, is anxious to fill these orders as quickly as possible so that the company will benefit from the boom and not lose customers to competitors. He is trying to decide whether to ask the current employees to work 8 hours of overtime on Saturdays until the backlog is satisfied or to hire three additional workers to work a 40-hour week. He asks you, the company's accountant, for your advice.

A study of the records and operating procedures at Pounds-a-Way reveals the following:

■ The supervisors each earn $15 an hour, and the twelve factory workers each earn $9 an hour.

■ No employee has reached the yearly maximum for social security, FUTA, or SUTA.

■ Employees who have worked for the company at least 18 months are covered by a company-paid pension plan. All current employees have been with the company for more than 2 years. Pounds-a-Way contributes an amount equal to 6 percent of an employee's gross wages to the pension plan.

■ The company pays $35 a week for each employee, regardless of length of service, for a hospitalization insurance plan.

■ New employees will be hired at $7 an hour.

■ To help the supervisors train the new employees, one of the current factory workers would be promoted to assistant supervisor and receive a raise of $2 an hour.

1. To assist Paulo Monti in making his decision, prepare a schedule showing the cost of each alternative.

2. What additional information would be useful in making this decision? What nonmonetary factors should be considered?

8

Departmentalizing Overhead Costs

In a job cost system, the costs of direct materials and direct labor are charged to specific jobs. All other costs, including indirect materials and indirect labor, are charged to manufacturing overhead. In this chapter, you will learn how the many other manufacturing costs are classified, recorded, summarized, and distributed. Chapters 9 and 10 will explain the steps involved in charging overhead costs to production.

OBJECTIVES

1. Classify and record manufacturing overhead costs by department to achieve control of overhead costs.
2. Prepare the journal entry to record monthly fixed overhead charges.
3. Compute the basis for allocation of service department costs.
4. Prepare a worksheet to prorate service department costs to other service departments and to the production departments.
5. Prepare journal entries to record the distribution of overhead costs.

NEW TERMS

Distribution memorandum (p. 169)
Fixed costs (p. 170)
Schedule of departmental overhead costs (p. 171)
Schedule of monthly fixed overhead costs (p. 170)

TYPES OF MANUFACTURING OVERHEAD COSTS

Manufacturing overhead includes all factory costs other than direct materials and direct labor. Here is a partial listing of the most common costs in a typical factory operation.

Indirect Materials

Shop supplies
Lubricants
Cleaning supplies
Factory office supplies
Small tools
Packaging materials
Items used in small amounts in the manufacturing process

Indirect Labor

Factory line supervisors
Factory clerical workers
Factory payroll clerks
Factory superintendents
Janitors
Receiving clerks
Storeroom supervisors
Storeroom clerks
Purchasing employees
Idle-time costs of direct workers
Overtime premium of direct workers (unless the time is identified with a specific job)

Other Manufacturing Overhead

Employee fringe benefits
Payroll taxes
Workers' compensation insurance
Factory utilities
Rent of factory building, warehouse, and equipment
Depreciation of factory building and equipment
Fire and casualty insurance
Property taxes
Group insurance for factory employees
Repairs and maintenance
Spoiled goods

CONTROL OF MANUFACTURING OVERHEAD COSTS

The size of a company, how it is organized, and the types of products manufactured are key factors that have an important bearing upon the method used to account for manufacturing overhead costs. A small company producing only one product or a few products may simply keep a separate general ledger account for each manufacturing overhead cost. If there are many different types of overhead costs, manufacturing overhead analysis sheets would be maintained. These analysis sheets function as a subsidiary ledger that is controlled by the Manufacturing Overhead Control account in the general ledger. This account summarizes that data in the analysis sheets.

DEPARTMENTALIZATION OF OVERHEAD

Separate Control Accounts

In large businesses it is necessary to divide the factory operations into departments. The departments become the centers for effective control of costs. There are two methods of achieving cost departmentalization.

One method is to maintain a control account for each different manufacturing overhead cost. In a subsidiary ledger, analysis sheets are used to show the amount chargeable to each department.

For example, a control account for indirect labor throughout the factory may be set up, such as the one below.

	Indirect Labor								**NO.** *650*	
				DEPARTMENTAL ANALYSIS						
DATE	EXPLANATION	POST. REF.	CUTTING	FRAMING	ASSEMBLY	BUILDING SERVICES	GENERAL FACTORY	TOTAL		
Oct. [19X9] *5*	*Time tkt. anal.*	*TTA*	780 00	938 00	918 00	924 00	1368 00	4928 00		
12	*Time tkt. anal.*	*TTA*	648 00	610 00	640 00	1057 00	2361 00	5316 00		
15	*Semimo. pay.*	*SP*				1580 00	3965 00	5545 00		
19	*Time tkt. anal.*	*TTA*	376 00	762 00	684 00	1131 00	2386 00	5339 00		
26	*Time tkt. anal.*	*TTA*	477 00	945 00	752 00	1250 00	2424 00	5848 00		
31	*Semimo. pay.*	*SP*				1580 00	3965 00	5545 00		
31	*Time tkt. anal.*	*TTA*	487 00	495 00	447 00	507 00	878 00	2814 00		
			2768 00	3750 00	3441 00	8029 00	17347 00	35335 00		

A record of the indirect labor costs charged to each department in the factory is maintained in a subsidiary ledger made up of analysis sheets.

When there are many different types of overhead costs, it is necessary to have a large number of general ledger accounts. This procedure of posting to the control accounts then becomes inefficient.

Single Control Accounts

The second method of achieving cost departmentalization is to set up one control account for all manufacturing overhead costs. (This cuts down on the number of accounts in the general ledger.) The subsidiary ledger may organize costs in two ways: by type of cost or by department.

Subsidiary Ledger by Type of Cost. A subsidiary ledger account may be kept for each manufacturing overhead cost. For example, a separate account would be established for indirect materials. This arrangement eliminates many entries in the general ledger and accumulates data by type of cost. It does not, however, accumulate the total factory overhead by departments. Departmental totals are needed at the end of the accounting period. Additional analysis is required to obtain this information.

DEPARTMENTAL OVERHEAD ANALYSIS SHEET

Department _Cutting_ Month of _October_ 19 _X9_

	DATE	REF.	TOTAL	01 INDIRECT MATERIALS	02 INDIRECT LABOR	03 PAYROLL	04 DEPRECIATION	05 REPAIRS & MAINT.	06 UTILITIES	07 INSURANCE	08 PROPERTY TAXES	09 OTHER ITEM	AMOUNT
	Oct. 3	R812	206 30	206 30									
	5	TTA	780 00		780 00								
	12	TTA	648 00		648 00								
	14	R827	237 55	237 55									
	19	TTA	376 00		376 00								
Ⓐ	21	10-789	661 15					661 15					
	26	TTA	477 00		477 00								
	27	10-804	16 20									Permit	16 20
	27	J10-27	115 03									Spoilage	115 03
	31	TTA	487 00		487 00								
	31	R906	588 15	588 15									
	31	SPT	1 979 66			1 979 66							
Ⓒ	31	J10-38	1 351 00				1 220 00			38 00	93 00		
Ⓑ	31	10-832	984 15						984 15				
	31	J10-44	270 00							270 00			
	Total		9 177 19	1 032 00	2 768 00	1 979 66	1 220 00	661 15	984 15	308 00	93 00		131 23

Subsidiary Ledger by Department. The subsidiary ledger accounts may also take the form of departmental overhead analysis sheets. This is the practice at Panorama Windows because it offers the most efficient control of costs. Each sheet contains special columns for recording common types of overhead costs such as those listed below.

Indirect materials
Indirect labor
Payroll taxes
Depreciation
Repairs and maintenance
Utilities
Insurance
Property taxes

Each sheet also contains another column for entering infrequent costs. The departmental overhead analysis sheet for the Cutting Department for the month of October is shown above.

RECORDING OVERHEAD COSTS

Entries for indirect materials from material requisitions and indirect labor from labor time analyses are recorded on departmental overhead analysis sheets. Other manufacturing overhead costs are posted from disbursement vouchers (purchases from outsiders) and at the end of the month from general journal vouchers (adjusting entries to cover accrued or deferred costs).

Voucher Register Entries

The cost of repairs, utilities, or other overhead items purchased from outsiders is usually obtained from an invoice. A control routine similar to the one relating to the purchase of direct materials (described in Chapter 3) follows:

1. The invoice is compared with the purchase order, and all computations are checked.
2. A voucher is prepared, including a notation of the department to be charged.
3. Upon approval of the voucher, the purchase is entered in the voucher register as a debit to Manufacturing Overhead Control and as a credit to Vouchers Payable (or Accounts Payable).
4. The cost clerk charges the cost to the appropriate departmental overhead analysis sheet.

For example, on October 21 Panorama Windows received an invoice for $661.15 from Beechwood Repair Company for repairs to equipment in the Cutting Department. The voucher register entry would be as follows:

VOUCHER REGISTER for Month of _October_   19 _X9_

DATE	VOU. NO.	PAYABLE TO	PAID DATE	PAID CHECK NO.	VOUCHERS PAYABLE CR. 201	MFG. OHD. CONTROL DR. 501
Oct. 21	10-789	Beechwood Repair Co.			661 15	661 15

Since only one department is involved in this transaction, the name of the department is noted on the invoice. This information guides the cost clerk to charge the amount to the correct departmental overhead analysis sheet (see Item A on the departmental overhead analysis sheet shown on page 168). If the invoice applies to more than one department, the cost distribution is noted on the invoice.

Another procedure is to prepare an analysis of the invoice, known as a **distribution memorandum,** indicating how the cost is to be distributed. This analysis is then sent to the cost clerk, to be entered in the departmental overhead analysis sheets. For example, Panorama Windows' utility bill for October totals $4,283.75. The invoice is entered in the voucher register as shown:

VOUCHER REGISTER for Month of _October_   19 _X9_

DATE	VOU. NO.	PAYABLE TO	PAID DATE	PAID CHECK NO.	VOUCHERS PAYABLE CR. 201	MFG. OHD. CONTROL DR. 501
Oct. 21	10-789	Beechwood Repair Co.			661 15	661 15
27	10-832	Western Utilities			4283 75	4283 75

Then the cost accountant prepares a distribution memorandum for the cost clerk. The distribution memorandum shows how much of the total amount of the voucher is to be allocated to each department. The first three digits of the account number indicate the department to be charged, and the last two digits represent the number of the expense column to be charged. For example, the distribution memorandum shown below shows that $984.15 is to be charged to utilities expense (06) on the departmental overhead analysis sheet for the Cutting Department (see Item B on the departmental overhead analysis sheet shown on page 168).

DISTRIBUTION MEMORANDUM

PANORAMA WINDOWS INC.

1180 Northern Ave.
Chicago, IL 60785

REFERENCE _Voucher 10-832_   DATE _10/27/X9_

ITEM _Utilities (06)_   AMOUNT _$4,283.75_

Comments:

DISTRIBUTION	
ACCOUNT NO.	AMOUNT
502-06	$ 984 15
503-06	550 55
504-06	585 96
505-06	1,483 06
506-06	680 03
TOTAL	$ 4,283 75

By _____ _J. T._
COST ACCOUNTANT

FORM NO. 654

General Journal Vouchers

Most of the manufacturing overhead costs recorded by end-of-period adjusting entries involve **fixed costs** that do not vary from month to month. For example, depreciation, taxes, and insurance usually remain constant each month. These fixed costs are recorded by adjusting entries. To speed up the journalizing of the adjustments and to facilitate posting to the departmental overhead analysis sheets, the cost accountant prepares a **schedule of monthly fixed overhead costs,** as shown on page 171.

A journal voucher can be quickly prepared from this schedule. See page 171.

The schedule is attached to the journal voucher, and the cost clerk then posts the data to the departmental overhead analysis sheets (see Item C on the departmental overhead analysis sheet shown on page 168).

PANORAMA WINDOWS, INC.
Schedule of Monthly Fixed Overhead Charges
Year 19X9

DEPARTMENT	DEPRECIATION OF MACHINERY AND EQUIPMENT	DEPRECIATION OF BUILDINGS	PROPERTY TAXES	PROPERTY INSURANCE	TOTAL
Cutting	$1,220.00		$ 93.00	$ 38.00	$1,351.00
Framing	327.40		52.22	13.30	392.92
Assembly	574.00		63.10	22.00	659.10
Building Services	376.00	$2,250.00	260.50	57.00	2,943.50
General Factory	962.60		152.18	70.70	1,185.48
Total	$3,460.00	$2,250.00	$621.00	$201.00	$6,532.00

JOURNAL VOUCHER	Date Oct. 31,	19 X9	No. 10-38		
ACCOUNT	ACCT. NO.	✓	DEBIT	CREDIT	
Manufacturing Overhead Control	501		6532 00		
Accum. Depr.–Buildings	133			2250 00	
Accum. Depr.–Machinery and Equipment	135			3460 00	
Property Taxes Payable	216			621 00	
Prepaid Insurance	127			201 00	

EXPLANATION

Recorded monthly adjustments for fixed factory costs.

PREPARED BY NV | AUDITED BY BJ | APPROVED BY MP

SUMMARY SCHEDULE OF DEPARTMENTAL COSTS

At this point you should be able to work Exercises 8–1 and 8–2 and Problems 8–1A and 8–1B.

At the end of the month, the cost clerk totals the departmental overhead analysis sheets. The clerk then prepares a schedule showing the total amount of each type of cost incurred in each department. The **schedule of departmental overhead costs** for the month of October is shown on page 172.

When all charges have been entered for the month, the subsidiary ledger should agree with its related control account. The total amount of overhead shown on the departmental overhead analysis sheets will equal the total charges (debits) in the general ledger account Manufacturing Overhead Control 501.

ALLOCATING OVERHEAD TO JOBS

You have seen where all the debit entries in the Manufacturing Overhead Control account come from and how they are entered on departmental overhead analysis sheets. Now the credit side of the control

PANORAMA WINDOWS, INC.
Schedule of Departmental Overhead Costs
October 19X9

COST	CUTTING	FRAMING	ASSEMBLING	BUILDING SERVICES	GENERAL FACTORY	TOTAL
Indirect Materials	$1,032.00	$1,254.65	$1,750.20	$ 722.30	$ 1,052.50	$ 5,811.65
Indirect Labor	2,768.00	3,750.00	3,441.00	8,029.00	17,347.00	35,335.00
Payroll Taxes	1,979.66	2,581.87	1,905.97	663.88	1,407.77	8,539.15
Depreciation	1,220.00	327.40	574.00	2,626.00	962.60	5,710.00
Repairs & Mainten.	661.15	136.54	262.90	1,119.05	363.96	2,543.60
Utilities	984.15	550.55	585.96	1,483.06	680.03	4,283.75
Insurance	308.00	145.55	193.80	134.60	192.10	974.05
Property Taxes	93.00	52.22	63.10	260.50	152.18	621.00
Other Costs	131.23	50.67	119.67	23.76	89.93	415.26
Total	$9,177.19	$8,849.45	$8,896.60	$15,062.15	$22,248.07	$64,233.46

account must be examined. Much more is involved than simply transferring the total manufacturing overhead costs to Work in Process in a quick journal entry. This procedure would produce only a vague total cost of production. The goal of cost accounting is to obtain specific, precise unit cost data. The overhead costs must be associated with products or jobs so that the transfer (the cost flow) will actually parallel the work flow. Distributing overhead costs to departments is the first step in this overall allocation process.

DISTRIBUTING SERVICE DEPARTMENT COSTS

Service departments help producing departments and other service departments to operate efficiently. But service departments do not produce goods themselves. The manufacturing overhead expense charged to service department operations must be redistributed to where goods are produced. (These goods produce the revenue needed to pay for costs.)

Service department costs should be distributed in proportion to the services provided. There are usually as many separate distribution computations as there are service departments.

Order of Allocation

A service department often provides some service to other service departments as well as to producing departments. For example, the Building Services Department of Panorama Windows provides cleaning, maintenance, and repair services for all other departments. The General Factory Department serves all other departments, including the Building Services Department, by purchasing, receiving, and issuing materials and supplies and by providing recordkeeping and general administrative services. This mutual exchange of services might cause difficulty in apportioning service department costs because the apportionment and reapportionment could be repeated endlessly. For example, unless some workable rule is adopted, the accountant may be faced with the problem of apportioning part of the Building Services Department costs to the General Factory Department and part of the General Factory Department costs to the Building Services Department. Panorama Windows solves this problem by adopting some generally accepted rules:

1. Distribute first the costs of the service department that serves the greatest number of other departments.
2. Distribute second the costs of the service department that serves the next greatest number of other departments.
3. Follow this procedure until all service department costs are distributed.
4. If no one department serves a larger number of other service departments, apportion the costs of the service department with the largest expenditures first.
5. Once the costs of a service department have been apportioned, no further costs are prorated to it.

Another method is to apportion the cost of each service department only to producing departments, with no prorating of service department costs to other service departments. This saves time and work but often results in an inaccurate cost apportionment.

Basis for Allocation

The costs of each service department are redistributed by ratios that express the relationship between the service provided and some functional factor or basis. For example, building service costs may be redistributed according to floor area occupied by other departments. This guideline is logical because the larger the area, the more sweeping, cleaning, heating, cooling, and other services required. On the other hand, since general factory expenses include the costs of factory management, it would be equally logical to allocate these costs in proportion to the amount or value of the labor or labor and materials that are being supervised and controlled. Thus direct labor costs, direct labor hours, and even conversion costs may be used as meaningful bases. (Other bases are described in Chapter 9.)

Allocating Building Services Department Costs. At Panorama Windows, the costs of the Building Services Department are apportioned first because it provides service to all other departments. (The General Factory Department primarily serves the producing departments.) This apportionment at the end of the month is made on the basis of the factory floor space occupied by each of the other departments, as indicated below (square feet per department ÷ total square feet = percentage).

Department	Square Feet Occupied	Percent
General Factory	16,200	30
Cutting	10,800	20
Framing	15,120	28
Assembly	11,880	22
Total	54,000	100

On this basis, the manufacturing overhead costs of the Building Services Department for October, totaling $15,062.15 (from the schedule on page 172), will be prorated to the other departments, as follows:

Department	Dollars		Percent		Amount
General Factory	$15,062.15 ×		30	=	$ 4,518.65
Cutting	15,062.15 ×		20	=	3,012.43
Framing	15,062.15 ×		28	=	4,217.40
Assembly	15,062.15 ×		22	=	3,313.67
Total			100		$15,062.15

Allocating General Factory Department Costs.   The General Factory Department costs are distributed among the producing departments on the basis of total direct labor costs in the producing departments. The direct labor costs for October, taken from the monthly summary of factory wages (shown on page 147), are apportioned as shown below (direct labor cost per department ÷ total direct labor costs = percentage).

Department	Direct Labor Cost	Percent
Cutting	$20,564.00	30.8783
Framing	26,741.80	40.1547
Assembling	19,291.20	28.9670
Total	$66,597.00	100.0000

The General Factory Department costs totaling $26,766.72 ($22,248.07 charged directly to the department as shown on page 172, plus $4,518.65 from the apportionment of Building Services Department costs) are then prorated according to these percentages of total direct labor costs.

Department	Dollars		Percent		Amount
Cutting	$26,766.72 ×		30.8783	=	$ 8,265.11
Framing	26,766.72 ×		40.1547	=	10,748.10
Assembly	26,766.72 ×		28.9670	=	7,753.51
Total			100.0000		$26,766.72

The allocations of service department costs are summarized on a worksheet, as shown on page 175.

After the worksheet is completed, the prorations are entered on the various departmental overhead analysis sheets so that the producing department analysis sheets will reflect all manufacturing overhead. The October analysis sheet for the Cutting Department after all service department costs have been apportioned is shown on page 175. Note that the total column must equal the total of all individual columns.

Panorama Windows, Inc.
Worksheet for Prorating Service Department Costs
Month Ended October 31, 19X9

ITEM	BASIS OF PRORATION	BUILDING SERVICES	GENERAL FACTORY	CUTTING	FRAMING	ASSEMBLY	TOTAL
Balance of ov. an. sheets		15 062 15	22 248 07	9 177 19	8 849 45	8 896 60	64 233 46
Prorate Bldg. Ser.	floor space	(15 062 15)	4 518 65	3 012 43	4 217 40	3 313 67	
Prorate Gen. Fact.	dir. labor		(26 766 72)	8 265 11	10 748 10	7 753 51	
Total		0 00	0 00	20 454 73	23 814 95	19 963 78	64 233 46

DEPARTMENTAL OVERHEAD ANALYSIS SHEET

Department **Cutting** Month of **October** 19 **X9**

DATE	REF.	TOTAL	01 INDIRECT MATERIALS	02 INDIRECT LABOR	03 PAYROLL	04 DEPRECIATION	05 REPAIRS & MAINT.	06 UTILITIES	07 INSURANCE	08 PROPERTY TAXES	09 OTHER ITEM	AMOUNT
Oct. 3	R812	206 30	206 30									
5	TTA	780 00		780 00								
12	TTA	648 00		648 00								
14	R827	237 55	237 55									
19	TTA	376 00		376 00								
21	10-789	661 15					661 15					
26	TTA	477 00		477 00								
27	10-804	16 20									Permit	16 20
27	J10-27	115 03									Spoilage	115 03
31	TTA	487 00		487 00								
31	R906	588 15	588 15									
31	SPT	1 979 66			1 979 66							
31	410-38	1 351 00				1 220 00			38 00	93 00		
31	10-832	984 15						984 15				
31	J10-44	270 00							270 00			
Total		9 177 19	1 032 00	2 768 00	1 979 66	1 220 00	661 15	984 15	308 00	93 00		131 23
31	J10-51	3 012 43									Proration	3 012 43
31	J10-52	8 265 11									Proration	8 265 11
Total		20 454 73	1 032 00	2 768 00	1 979 66	1 220 00	661 15	984 15	308 00	93 00		11 408 77

RECORDING OVERHEAD DISTRIBUTION IN THE GENERAL LEDGER

At the end of the month the distribution of overhead costs is entered in the general ledger by a series of general journal entries.

■ Manufacturing Overhead Control 501 is closed into five special departmental overhead accounts so that the ledger will reflect the same departmentalized data as summarized in the departmental overhead analysis sheets.

JOURNAL VOUCHER	Date _Oct. 31,_		19 _X9_	No. _10-50_	
ACCOUNT	**ACCT. NO.**	**✓**	**DEBIT**	**CREDIT**	
Mfg. Overhead–Cutting Dept.	502	✓	917719		
Mfg. Overhead–Framing Dept.	503	✓	884945		
Mfg. Overhead–Assembly Dept.	504	✓	889660		
Mfg. Overhead–Building Serv. Dept.	505	✓	1506215		
Mfg. Overhead–Gen. Factory Dept.	506	✓	2224807		
Mfg. Overhead Control	501	✓		6423346	

EXPLANATION

Closed out control account and recorded
department costs.

PREPARED BY NV	AUDITED BY BJ	APPROVED BY MP

■ Distributions of service department costs are journalized in order of allocation.
1. Building Services Department costs are allocated to the other four departments as shown below.

JOURNAL VOUCHER	Date _Oct. 31,_		19 _X9_	No. _10-51_	
ACCOUNT	**ACCT. NO.**	**✓**	**DEBIT**	**CREDIT**	
Mfg. Overhead–Gen. Factory Dept.	506	✓	451865		
Mfg. Overhead–Cutting Dept.	502	✓	301243		
Mfg. Overhead–Framing Dept.	503	✓	421740		
Mfg. Overhead–Assembly Dept.	504	✓	331367		
Mfg. Overhead–Building Services Dept.	505	✓		1506215	

EXPLANATION

Prorated Building Services Department costs to
other departments.

PREPARED BY NV	AUDITED BY BJ	APPROVED BY MP

JOURNAL VOUCHER	Date *Oct. 31,*		19 *X9*	No. *10-52*	
ACCOUNT	ACCT. NO.	✓	DEBIT	CREDIT	
Mfg. Overhead–Cutting Dept.	502	✓	826511		
Mfg. Overhead–Framing Dept.	503	✓	1074810		
Mfg. Overhead–Assembly Dept.	504	✓	775357		
Mfg. Overhead–General					
Factory Dept.	506	✓		2676672	
EXPLANATION					
Prorated General Factory Department costs to					
other departments.					
PREPARED BY *NV*	AUDITED BY *BJ*		APPROVED BY *MP*		

2. General Factory Department costs are allocated to the three producing departments as shown above.

After the entries are posted, the Manufacturing Overhead Control and the departmental overhead accounts appear on pages 178 and 179.

SELF-REVIEW

1. Identify the sources of the amounts that are posted to departmental overhead analysis sheets.
2. List typical monthly fixed overhead charges that occur in a manufacturing business.
3. Why is it necessary to allocate service department overhead costs to producing departments?
4. After all the entries to record the distribution of overhead costs have been posted to the general ledger, the balances of the producing departments' overhead accounts will be equal to the debits made to what account?

Answers to Self-Review

1. Amounts are posted to the departmental overhead analysis sheets from the materials requisition journal, time ticket analyses, distribution vouchers, and general journal vouchers.
2. Typical fixed overhead charges are insurance, depreciation, and property taxes.
3. Although service departments do not produce any goods themselves, they are a necessary part of the manufacturing process. If the costs in these departments are not allocated to producing departments, a precise unit cost of a goods cannot be determined.
4. The sum of the balances of all the producing departments' overhead accounts should equal the total of the debits in the Manufacturing Overhead Control account.

At this point you should be able to work Exercises 8–3 to 8–5 and Problems 8–2A to 8–3B.

Manufacturing Overhead Control   NO. 501

DATE		EXPLANATION	POST. REF.	DEBIT		CREDIT		BALANCE		DR. CR.
19	X9									
Oct.	31	Balance	✔					64,233	46	DR.
	31	Close out to other dept. accounts	J10-50			64,233	46	-0-		

Manufacturing Overhead–Cutting Department   NO. 502

DATE		EXPLANATION	POST. REF.	DEBIT		CREDIT		BALANCE		DR. CR.
19	X9									
Oct.	31		J10-50	9,177	19			9,177	19	DR.
	31		J10-51	3,012	43			12,189	62	DR.
	31		J10-52	8,265	11			20,454	73	DR.

Manufacturing Overhead–Framing Department   NO. 503

DATE		EXPLANATION	POST. REF.	DEBIT		CREDIT		BALANCE		DR. CR.
19	X9									
Oct.	31		J10-50	8,849	45			8,849	45	DR.
	31		J10-51	4,217	40			13,066	85	DR.
	31		J10-52	10,748	10			23,814	95	DR.

Manufacturing Overhead–Assembly Department   NO. 504

DATE		EXPLANATION	POST. REF.	DEBIT		CREDIT		BALANCE		DR. CR.
19	X9									
Oct.	31		J10-50	8,896	60			8,896	60	DR.
	31		J10-51	3,313	67			12,210	27	DR.
	31		J10-52	7,753	51			19,963	78	DR.

Manufacturing Overhead–Building Services Department   NO. 505

DATE		EXPLANATION	POST. REF.	DEBIT		CREDIT		BALANCE		DR. CR.
19	X9									
Oct.	31		J10-50	15,062	15			15,062	15	DR.
			J10-51			15,062	15	-0-		

Manufacturing Overhead–General Factory Department					NO. _506_		
DATE	EXPLANATION	POST. REF.	DEBIT		CREDIT	BALANCE	DR. CR.
_19_ _X9_							
Oct. _31_		_J10-50_	_22,248_	_07_		_22,248_ _07_	_DR._
_31_		_J10-51_	_4,518_	_65_		_26,766_ _72_	_DR._
_31_		_J10-52_			_26,766_ _72_	_-0-_	

Note that the total of the balances in Accounts 502, 503, and 504 agrees with the total debits in the Manufacturing Overhead Control account shown on page 178 ($20,454.73 + $23,814.95 + $19,963.78 = $64,233.46).

Flow of Entries to Record Distribution of Overhead Costs

The flowchart below illustrates the flow of actual overhead costs from the Manufacturing Overhead Control account to their final allocation

DISTRIBUTION OF MANUFACTURING OVERHEAD COSTS

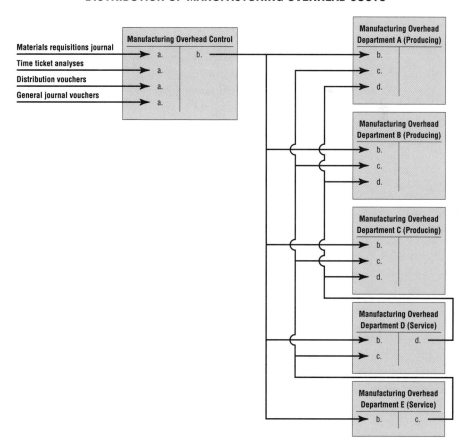

on the Manufacturing Overhead—Producing Department accounts. Letters identify the entries as follows:

a. Entries to record actual overhead costs in the Manufacturing Overhead Control account.
b. Entry to close the Manufacturing Overhead Control account into departmental overhead accounts.
c. Allocation of service department costs to other service departments and to producing departments.
d. Allocation of service department costs to producing departments.

PRINCIPLES AND PROCEDURES SUMMARY

- The most effective way to achieve control of costs is by departmentalization.
- Overhead costs may be departmentalized by one of two methods.
  - A separate control account is used for each cost, and a subsidiary ledger shows the amount chargeable to each department.
  - A single control account is used for all costs, and the subsidiary ledger accounts take the form of an overhead analysis sheet for each department.
- Indirect materials and indirect labor costs are recorded from materials requisitions and labor time analyses. Other manufacturing overhead costs appear in the voucher register or general journal vouchers.
- After total overhead costs are known, they must be associated with specific departments. The steps in this process are to:
  - Prepare a general journal entry to close the Manufacturing Overhead Control account (501) and charge each department with its overhead costs as shown on the schedule of departmental overhead costs.
  - Distribute the service department costs to the producing departments on a special proration worksheet.
  - Record the distribution of service department overhead on the appropriate departmental overhead analysis sheets.
  - Prepare general journal voucher entries that distribute service department overhead to producing departments. These entries are posted to the departmental manufacturing overhead accounts in the general ledger.
- When the steps listed above are completed,
  - The service department manufacturing overhead accounts (505 and 506) will be closed.
  - The balance in the manufacturing overhead account of each producing department (502, 503, and 504) should agree with the total on that department's overhead analysis sheet.

MANAGERIAL IMPLICATIONS

- Overhead costs must be carefully controlled. In addition, they must be accumulated and charged to the cost of goods manufactured during each period in a way that reflects the benefits provided by the overhead costs. The key to proper control and allocation of over-head is accumulating overhead on a departmentalization basis.

■ Departmentalization involves identifying overhead with specific pro-duction departments to the extent possible. If an overhead cost, for example, indirect materials or indirect labor, can be identified specifically with a production department, it should be entered on a departmental overhead analysis sheet for that department. This places responsibility for control of such an overhead cost directly on the production department manager.

   ■ All other overhead costs should be charged to an appropriate nonproducing department (service department).

   ■ The manager of each department is responsible for the overhead charged to that department. Again, the goal is to secure control of overhead costs.

■ The accumulated costs of each service department are allocated to the department to which it provides service. This may mean that some service department costs are allocated between other service departments as well as production departments. At the end of the allocation process, all service department costs will have been allocated to production departments.

■ In evaluating the efficiency of department managers, it must be kept in mind that some costs (for example, property taxes) cannot be controlled by the department manager. Similarly, the head of a production department may not be responsible for some of the service department costs that have been allocated to the producing department.

REVIEW QUESTIONS

1. If a company establishes a single manufacturing overhead con-trol account, what two forms can be used for the subsidiary ledger accounts?
2. What is a distribution memorandum?
3. In preparing a distribution memorandum, Panorama Windows, Inc., used an account distribution code. What two items are in-cluded in this code?
4. Do all manufacturing overhead costs require a cash payment? Explain.
5. What are the sources of postings to the departmental overhead analysis sheets?
6. What are typical fixed costs that occur in a factory?
7. What is a schedule of departmental overhead costs? When is it prepared?
8. What do the debit postings in a Manufacturing Overhead Control account represent?
9. To what departments are service department overhead costs dis-tributed? Why?
10. What is the purpose of a worksheet for prorating service de-partment costs?

11. Why are special departmental overhead accounts established at the end of the month in the general ledger?
12. At the end of the month, the total of the departmental overhead analysis sheets should equal the balance of what account?

MANAGERIAL DISCUSSION QUESTIONS

1. What is the advantage to management in having manufacturing overhead costs departmentalized?
2. If management is reviewing the overhead costs of a department, which of the costs listed under Other Manufacturing Overhead on page 166 would be most likely to merit close attention? Why?
3. Should management rely on allocated overhead costs from service departments in considering the efficiency of producing departments? Explain.
4. To what extent would the head of a production department be accountable to management for the cost of equipment depreciation? Explain.
5. Why should management have the costs of service departments distributed to producing departments?
6. Describe the two methods of establishing overhead control accounts in the general ledger.

EXERCISES

EXERCISE 8–1 **Allocate manufacturing overhead costs. (Obj. 3).** The Raider Manufacturing Company received an invoice for $34,230 for repairs. The allocation is as follows: 60 percent of the repairs were performed in the Cutting Department, 30 percent in the Shaping Department, 4 percent in the Assembly Department, and 6 percent in the Finishing Department.

EXERCISE 8–2 **Record manufacturing overhead costs. (Obj. 5).** For the month of May 19X9, the depreciation expense for the factory building was $21,700, the depreciation expense for factory machinery and equipment was $14,800, and the cost of insurance expired on the factory was $9,500. Prepare the entry on May 31, 19X9, at the Sea Crest Company to record these manufacturing overhead costs for the month of May 19X9.

EXERCISE 8–3 **Select the basis for manufacturing cost allocation. (Obj. 3).** The Gracie Dish Corporation allocates Building Services Department overhead on the basis of the amount of floor space occupied by each producing department in the factory. The Mixing Department occupies 4,000 square feet, the Molding Department occupies 6,000 square feet, and the Finishing Department occupies 10,000 square feet. Calculate the amount that should be allocated to each of these producing departments based on the square footage occupied if the Building Services Department incurs $75,400 in overhead costs.

EXERCISE 8–4   **Select the basis for manufacturing cost allocation. (Obj. 3).** The Fun Toy Corporation allocates the General Factory Department overhead on the basis of direct labor costs incurred by each producing department in the factory. The Cutting Department incurred $7,020 in direct labor costs, the Shaping Department incurred $4,680 in direct labor costs, and the Assembly Department incurred $11,700 in direct labor costs. Determine the amount that should be allocated to each producing department if the General Factory Department incurs overhead costs of $68,400.

EXERCISE 8–5   **Record the allocation of manufacturing overhead. (Obj. 5).** The departmental overhead analysis sheets of Bridgeville Metal, Inc., for the month of August showed the following overhead amounts:

Cutting Department	$16,480
Pressing Department	20,260
Finishing Department	16,290
Building Services Department	9,720
General Factory Department	7,890

A worksheet was prepared to allocate the overhead of the service departments to the producing departments. The allocations were as follows:

Building Services Department:

To General Factory Department	$1,665
To Cutting Department	2,176
To Pressing Department	3,342
To Finishing Department	2,537

General Factory Department:

To Cutting Department	$2,783
To Pressing Department	3,310
To Finishing Department	3,462

a. Record the general journal entry to close the Manufacturing Overhead Control account.
b. Record the general journal entries to allocate the overhead of the service departments to the producing departments.

PROBLEMS

PROBLEM 8–1A   **Complete departmental overhead analysis sheets. (Obj. 1).** Wilmington Supply manufactures concrete blocks. The factory is divided into five departments. The Mixing Department, the Shaping Department, and the Finishing Department are producing departments. The Maintenance Department and the General Factory Department are service departments. During September 19X9, the following transactions affecting the Mixing Department take place:

Sept. 4 The weekly analysis of time tickets shows direct labor costs of $6,900 and indirect labor costs of $2,060.

5 Indirect materials costing $206 are issued on Materials Requisition 764.

6 Voucher 9-033 for repairs to machinery (total cost $215) is prepared.

8 Voucher 9-082 for the water bill (total cost $157) is prepared.

11 The weekly analysis of time tickets shows direct labor costs of $7,300 and indirect labor costs of $2,100.

12 Indirect materials costing $188 and direct materials costing $616 are issued on Materials Requisition 817.

15 Voucher 9-105 for allocation of electricity (total cost $540) is prepared.

15 The semimonthly payroll records show supervisors' salaries totaling $2,370 (use reference PR9-3).

18 The weekly analysis of time tickets shows direct labor costs of $6,800 and indirect labor costs of $2,450.

19 Indirect materials costing $205 are issued on Materials Requisition 862.

25 The weekly analysis of time tickets shows direct labor costs of $7,320 and indirect labor costs of $1,840.

26 Indirect materials costing $198 are issued on Materials Requisition 894.

30 The semimonthly payroll records show supervisors' salaries totaling $2,650 (use reference PR9-6).

30 General journal vouchers are prepared as follows: No. 9-7, insurance, $265; No. 9-8, payroll taxes, $2,840; No. 9-9, property taxes, $750; No. 9-12, depreciation, $1,890.

INSTRUCTIONS

1. Enter the overhead expense items given in the transactions on the departmental overhead analysis sheet.
2. Prove the accuracy of your work by footing and crossfooting all money columns.

PROBLEM 8–2A

Complete a worksheet for prorating service department costs and make journal entries. (Objs. 4, 5). Information for prorating service department costs of the M. Marino Corporation for the month of July 19X9 is given below.

Department	Square Feet Occupied	Direct Labor Hours
General Factory	1,400	
Stores	2,400	
Grinding	5,600	3,680
Mixing	4,800	2,300
Finishing	3,200	3,220

	Service Departments		Producing Departments			
Overhead Item	General Factory	Stores	Grinding	Mixing	Finishing	Total
Indirect Labor	$ 6,300	$2,500	$ 3,400	$2,390	$2,780	$17,370
Payroll Taxes	179	184	287	174	204	1,028
Supplies	87	56	35	49	62	289
Property Taxes	1,245	1,852	1,520	1,324	1,720	7,661
Depreciation	1,325	1,400	2,260	1,104	1,156	7,245
Utilities	2,089	1,850	1,854	2,160	2,017	9,970
Insurance	1,000	500	750	750	750	3,750
Repairs	112	168	86	160	107	633
Totals	$12,337	$8,510	$10,192	$8,111	$8,796	$47,946

INSTRUCTIONS

1. Complete the worksheet for prorating service department costs. The General Factory Department costs are prorated on the basis of floor space occupied. The Stores Department costs are then allocated to the producing departments on the basis of direct labor hours. Round allocated amounts to the nearest whole dollar.
2. Give the general journal entries to close the Manufacturing Overhead Control account into the departmental manufacturing overhead accounts and to prorate the service department costs.

PROBLEM 8–3A **Distribute service department costs, make journal entries, and post to accounts. (Objs. 4, 5).** Data for prorating service department costs for the Lorraine Watch Corporation for November 19X9 are given below.

Account Number	Department	Overhead Expenses	Allocation of Maintenance Department	Allocation of General Factory Department
502	Preparing	$ 6,544	25%	30%
503	Assembly	7,241	35%	40%
504	Finishing	6,428	25%	30%
505	Maintenance	3,129		
506	General Factory	3,418	15%	
	Total	$26,760	100%	100%

INSTRUCTIONS

1. Open a departmental overhead analysis sheet for each department using the balances for overhead expenses given above. Open a general ledger account for Manufacturing Overhead Control 501 with a debit balance of $26,760.
2. Prepare the worksheet for prorating service department costs. Use the proration percentages given above. Allocate Maintenance Department costs first; then allocate General Factory Department costs. Round the amounts to the nearest dollar. Post the allocations to the departmental overhead analysis sheets. Total the departmental overhead analysis sheets.

3. Prepare the general journal vouchers to distribute the service departments' costs to the other departments. Begin with journal Voucher 11-37.
   a. Close the Manufacturing Overhead Control account into the special departmental overhead accounts.
   b. Allocate Maintenance Department costs to the other four departments.
   c. Allocate General Factory Department costs to the three producing departments.
4. Post the general journal entries to the general ledger accounts. (NOTE: The balance in each general ledger account should agree with the total on the corresponding departmental overhead analysis sheet.)

ALTERNATE PROBLEMS

PROBLEM 8–1B **Complete departmental overhead analysis sheets. (Obj. 1).** Bancroft Supply manufactures storage equipment. The factory is divided into five departments. The Preparing Department, the Assembly Department, and the Finishing Department are producing departments. The Maintenance Department and the General Factory Department are service departments. During October 19X9, the following transactions affecting the Preparing Department take place:

Oct. 4 The weekly analysis of time tickets shows direct labor costs of $2,900 and indirect labor costs of $790.

5 Indirect materials costing $205 are issued on Materials Requisition 472.

6 Voucher 10-28 for repairs to machinery (total cost $207) is prepared.

8 Voucher 10-36 for the water bill (total cost $172) is prepared.

11 The weekly analysis of time tickets shows direct labor costs of $3,300 and indirect labor costs of $740.

12 Indirect materials costing $85 and direct materials costing $860 are issued on Materials Requisition 514.

15 Voucher 10-47 for allocation of electricity (total cost $225) is prepared.

15 The semimonthly payroll records show supervisors' salaries totaling $1,025 (use reference PR9-3).

18 The weekly analysis of time tickets shows direct labor costs of $3,050 and indirect labor costs of $721.

19 Indirect materials costing $128 are issued on Materials Requisition 533.

25 The weekly analysis of time tickets shows direct labor costs of $4,401 and indirect labor costs of $835.

26 Indirect materials costing $108 are issued on Materials Requisition 561.

30 The semimonthly payroll records show supervisors' salaries totaling $1,025 (use reference PR9-6).

30 General journal vouchers are prepared as follows: No. 10-9, insurance, $245; No. 10-10, payroll taxes, $970; No. 10-14, property taxes, $300; No. 10-16, depreciation, $970.

INSTRUCTIONS

1. Enter the overhead expense items given the transactions in the departmental overhead analysis sheet.
2. Prove the accuracy of your work by footing and crossfooting all money columns.

PROBLEM 8–2B **Complete a worksheet for prorating service department costs and make journal entries. (Objs. 4, 5).** Information for prorating service department costs of the Pressley Corporation for the month of March 19X9 is given below.

Department	Square Feet Occupied	Direct Labor Hours
General Factory	1,200	
Stores	3,000	
Shaping	12,000	4,500
Assembly	6,000	3,000
Finishing	9,000	2,500

	Service Departments		Producing Departments			
Overhead Item	General Factory	Stores	Shaping	Assembly	Finishing	Total
Indirect Labor	$ 7,100	$3,100	$4,300	$3,250	$3,970	$21,720
Payroll Taxes	277	254	352	263	248	1,394
Indirect Materials	200	250	325	200	260	1,235
Property Taxes	160	185	520	225	270	1,360
Depreciation	1,020	2,100	2,600	2,100	650	8,470
Power and Light	540	365	340	575	140	1,960
Heat	335	260	345	310	135	1,385
Insurance	254	124	118	273	136	905
Repairs	320	128	242	140	262	1,092
Totals	$10,206	$6,766	$9,142	$7,336	$6,071	$39,521

INSTRUCTIONS

1. Complete the worksheet for prorating service department costs. The General Factory Department costs are prorated on the basis of floor space occupied. The Stores Department costs are then allocated to the producing departments on the basis of direct labor hours. Round allocated amounts to the nearest whole dollar.
2. Give the general journal entries to close the Manufacturing Overhead Control account into the departmental manufacturing overhead accounts and to prorate the service department costs.

PROBLEM 8–3B **Distribute service department costs, make journal entries, and post to accounts. (Objs. 4, 5).** Data for prorating service department costs for the Braun Corporation for August 19X9 are given below.

Account Number	Department	Overhead Expenses	Allocation of Maintenance Department	Allocation of General Factory Department
502	Preparing	$ 9,356	26%	32%
503	Assembly	10,417	30%	36%
504	Finishing	8,729	27%	32%
505	Maintenance	3,824		
506	General Factory	5,261	17%	
	Total	$37,587	100%	100%

INSTRUCTIONS

1. Open a departmental overhead analysis sheet for each department using the balances for overhead expenses given above. Open a general ledger account for Manufacturing Overhead Control 501 with a debit balance of $37,587.

2. Prepare the worksheet for prorating service department costs. Use the proration percentages given above. Allocate Maintenance Department costs first; then allocate General Factory Department costs. Round the amounts to the nearest dollar. Post the allocations to the departmental overhead analysis sheets. Total the departmental overhead analysis sheets.

3. Prepare the general journal vouchers to distribute the service departments' costs to the other departments. Begin with journal Voucher 8-37.

   a. Close the Manufacturing Overhead Control account into the special departmental overhead accounts.

   b. Allocate Maintenance Department costs to the other four departments.

   c. Allocate General Factory Department costs to the three producing departments.

4. Post the general journal entries to the general ledger accounts. (NOTE: The balance in each general ledger account should agree with the total on the corresponding departmental overhead analysis sheet.)

MANAGERIAL DECISION CASE

The Prairie Corporation is a furniture manufacturer that is beginning its first month of operations. You have been hired to work in the cost accounting department and to establish procedures for recording factory costs. The factory is organized into three producing departments and two service departments.

Cutting Department.   All wood is cut into the appropriate pieces for assembling.

Assembly Department. All pieces of wood are received from the Cutting Department and are assembled into the various pieces of furniture. The wood is either glued or screwed into place.

Finishing Department. The unfinished furniture is transferred to this department, where it is sanded, stained, and polished. From this department it is transferred to Finished Goods.

Building Maintenance Department. The employees in this department are responsible for cleaning each of the producing departments at the end of the day. In addition, they clean the tools used and perform any required repairs and sharpening.

General Factory Department. This department is responsible for the payroll of all employees. This responsibility includes recording time cards and time tickets. The cost accounting records are also maintained by this department. These include materials ledger cards, job cost sheets, and finished goods and stock ledger cards. Daily materials requisitions are recorded and posted to the appropriate records.

1. Which service department costs would you allocate first? Why?
2. What basis would you suggest be used to allocate the Building Maintenance Department costs and the General Factory Department costs to be producing departments? Why?
3. Using the information below, prepare a report for the corporate controller explaining how you would prorate the costs of the service departments to the producing departments. Include a table indicating the basis of allocation. Show any percentages that would be used. (Carry percents to 5 places and round to 4 places.) Also, determine the sequence in which the costs of the service departments will be allocated. Give reasons for all your recommendations.

Department	Square Feet Occupied	Number of Employees
Cutting	3,750	20
Assembly	5,000	40
Finishing	3,250	40
Building Maintenance	1,200	10
General Factory	1,000	10

9

Setting Overhead Rates

After manufacturing overhead costs have been accumulated by departments, they must be allocated to jobs or products. In this chapter, you will learn how the cost accountant selects bases for allocating the departmentalized overhead costs to specific units of production.

OBJECTIVES

1. Explain the purpose and theory of overhead application rates.
2. Explain the considerations involved in selecting the period and basis and in determining whether single or departmental rates should be used in allocating overhead costs.
3. Compute overhead application rates using a number of different bases.
4. Prepare the worksheet for prorating estimated service department overhead to producing departments.
5. Calculate the amounts of manufacturing overhead to be applied to specific jobs.

NEW TERMS

Basis (p. 191)
Overhead application rate (p. 191)

PURPOSE OF OVERHEAD RATES

Management cannot wait until the end of the year, or even until the end of the month, to find out how much a particular job costs. Cost data are most useful when they are immediately available. They can then be used to evaluate efficiency, to suggest changes in procedures, and to help in setting profitable selling prices. The cost accountant is usually expected to report the total cost of a job as soon as it is finished. At this time the actual total overhead costs are not available. For example, various bills, such as telephone or utility bills, may not arrive before a job is completed. The accountant must devise a method for rapidly and reliably estimating the overhead costs applicable to the completed job. Since these costs are not yet fully known, predetermined overhead rates are used for estimating overhead costs.

DETERMINING THE OVERHEAD RATE

The basic procedure for determining an overhead rate is quite simple. First, a relationship is found between the company's total overhead costs and some second factor or **basis** that relates to the overhead costs of the job in a realistic way. The basis must also be accurately measurable. The basis for allocating overhead might be an amount or quantity, such as direct labor costs, materials costs, or direct labor hours. The ratio between the total overhead costs and the basis* is called the **overhead application rate.** For example, assume that total overhead costs for the coming year are estimated at $100,000 and direct labor costs are expected to total $200,000. Direct labor costs are used as the basis for allocating overhead. The ratio of the overhead to the basis is 1:2 ($100,000:$200,000). The corresponding overhead application rate would be 50 percent of the direct labor costs ($100,000 ÷ $200,000).

Once the overhead application rate has been determined, the overhead on each job is estimated by determining the basis amount on the job and applying the rate. For example, with a 50 percent rate, the overhead amount charged to a job with direct labor costs of $3,000 would be $1,500 ($3,000 × .50).

FACTORS THAT AFFECT RATE SETTING

Even though the basic process of application is simple, the actual allocation of overhead costs will be strongly affected by several factors. One consideration is the length of the period over which the rate is to be computed. Another is whether a single rate is used for all factory overhead or whether separate rates are used for each producing department. The basis chosen for formulating the rate also affects the allocation.

Length of the Period

Most manufacturers use an annual period as a basis for determining rates. A shorter period for averaging costs is not satisfactory because wide variations can occur from period to period. These variations are due to changes in season, volume, and so forth. For example, heating costs are incurred only in the cold months. However, these costs should be averaged over the entire year.

*It depends on whether the basis is expressed in dollars or a measure of activity.

Similar distortions in unit costs arise because some fixed costs remain constant each month regardless of volume. For example, assume an overhead rate based on direct labor hours. If depreciation for a month is $10,000 and expected direct labor hours that month are 40,000, the overhead rate includes an amount equal to 25 cents per hour of labor for depreciation cost. However, if the expected labor hours are only 20,000 in the following month, the rate for the month will include 50 cents per direct labor hour for depreciation. Since volume does normally vary from month to month, an overhead rate computed each month would be changing constantly. With such a system, identical products manufactured in different months would be assigned varying overhead costs.

Fluctuating costs also complicate any attempt to use monthly costs in arriving at overhead rates. For example, repair costs may be extremely high in certain months of the year and low in others. The fact that the repair costs were actually incurred in certain months does not mean that products manufactured during that time should bear all repair costs. These costs are applicable to all goods produced during the year. In fact, some companies close down operations at certain times while repairs are made.

Many accountants argue that neither a monthly period nor a yearly period is long enough to establish overhead rates. They advise the use of a normal cost and normal volume for computing overhead rates based on a period of time sufficiently long to level out both seasonal and yearly fluctuations in volume and costs. Although the use of a normal overhead rate has much theoretical justification, it is very hard to determine "normal" volume and "normal" costs.

Departmental and Factory Rates

A small plant with only one or a few similar departments manufacturing very few types of goods may successfully use a single common rate for the entire factory. However, if several different types of products are manufactured, or if all products do not go through all departments, a single rate is not appropriate. Nor is a single rate suitable if some departments perform largely machine operations and other departments use primarily hand labor. In such a case, separate rates must be used for each of the producing departments.

TYPES OF OVERHEAD RATE BASES

The primary purpose of using a predetermined overhead rate is to charge a fair share of overhead costs to each job. A number of bases for determining overhead rates may be used in computing factorywide rates and in setting departmental rates. The most common bases are as follows:

Units of production
Materials costs
Machine hours

Direct labor hours
Direct labor costs

The cost and production figures used in the calculations are usually derived from budget estimates. To demonstrate the computation procedure for each basis, the following budgeted data are given for a hypothetical producing department:

Manufacturing overhead costs for the year	$ 48,000
Number of units of production in the year	12,000 units
Direct material costs for the year	$240,000
Machine hours for the year	6,000 hours
Direct labor hours for the year	20,000 hours
Direct labor costs for the year	$100,000

Units of Production Basis

Overhead may be applied on the basis of the number of units manufactured during the period. The estimated manufacturing overhead costs are divided by the estimated total number of units of production to get the overhead cost to be applied to each unit of production.

$$\frac{\text{Estimated Manufacturing Overhead Costs}}{\text{Estimated Units of Production}} = \text{Overhead Cost per Unit of Production}$$

Using the figures given above,

$$\frac{\$48,000}{12,000} = \$4 \text{ per unit}$$

Therefore, if a job of 600 units were produced, the overhead applied to the job would be $2,400 (600 × $4).

Unfortunately, the units of production basis has limited application. The rate is meaningful only if the manufacturing process is a simple one and only if one type, or a few very similar types, of goods are produced. For instance, if Product A requires 20 hours to be produced and Product B requires 2 hours, it would be inappropriate to base overhead on units of production. Product A is obviously going to require more overhead.

Materials Costs Basis

Overhead may be applied on the basis of the cost of direct materials used to produce the product. The estimated manufacturing overhead costs are divided by the estimated direct materials costs. This calculation gives the percentage of materials costs to be applied as overhead.

$$\frac{\text{Estimated Manufacturing Overhead Costs}}{\text{Estimated Direct Materials Costs}} = \text{Percentage of Materials Costs}$$

Again, using the figures given above.

$$\frac{\$48,000}{\$240,000} = 20\% \text{ of materials costs}$$

Therefore, if direct materials consumed on a specific job cost $11,000, the overhead applied to that job would be $2,200 ($11,000 × .20).

For materials costs to make a good rate basis, each article manufactured must require approximately the same amount of materials, or materials usage must be distributed uniformly through the manufacturing process. In practice, most overhead costs bear little relationship to materials used, so this basis is seldom appropriate.

Machine Hours Basis

Overhead may be applied as a rate for each machine hour. When work is performed primarily by machines, a large part of the manufacturing overhead costs consists of depreciation, power, repairs, and other costs associated with machinery. Thus, a logical relationship exists between the use of the machinery and the amount of cost incurred. To determine this basis, divide the estimated manufacturing overhead costs by the estimated number of machine hours to get the rate for each machine hour.

$$\frac{\text{Estimated Manufacturing Overhead Costs}}{\text{Estimated Machine Hours}} = \text{Rate per Machine Hour}$$

Using the figures given on page 193.

$$\frac{\$48,000}{6,000} = \$8 \text{ per machine hour}$$

Therefore, if a job required 200 machine hours, the overhead costs applied would be $1,600 (200 × $8).

In a highly automated factory where machines perform most of the work and each item goes through a similar sequence of machines, this basis makes sense. However, a machine hours basis is not accurate if different kinds of machines are used for various products. In such a case, variations in original costs, operating costs, machine speed, and labor costs would make this rate inappropriate as an overall formula. A further objection to this method is the additional clerical work required to keep a record of the number of machine hours used on each job.

Direct Labor Hours Basis

Overhead may be applied as a rate for each direct labor hour. This widely used method assumes that overhead costs tend to vary with the number of hours of direct labor used. The estimated manufacturing overhead costs are divided by the estimated number of direct labor hours to obtain an application rate for each hour.

$$\frac{\text{Estimated Manufacturing Overhead Costs}}{\text{Estimated Direct Labor Hours}} = \text{Rate per Direct Labor Hour}$$

Using the figures given on page 193.

$$\frac{\$48,000}{20,000} = \$2.40 \text{ per direct labor hour}$$

Therefore, if a job required 1,125 direct labor hours to be completed, the overhead applied would be $2,700 (1,125 × $2.40).

The direct labor hours basis is usually appropriate if labor operations are a major part of the production process and the wage rates paid different workers vary considerably. As a general rule, there is a correlation between total manufacturing overhead costs and the number of direct labor hours worked. However, the direct labor hours method requires a record of the number of direct labor hours spent on each job, which may necessitate additional recordkeeping. Total labor costs are part of normal factory records; however, a separate computation of total hours is not always made.

Direct Labor Costs Basis

Overhead may be applied as a percentage of the cost of direct labor. This method is the most widely used overhead application basis because it is simple and easy to use. Information concerning direct labor costs of each department and each job is available from the payroll records and the time tickets. Labor costs are normally accumulated by jobs as a routine cost accounting procedure, so no extra clerical work is involved. The estimated manufacturing overhead costs are divided by the estimated direct labor costs. This calculation results in the percentage of direct labor costs.

$$\frac{\text{Estimated Manufacturing Overhead Costs}}{\text{Estimated Direct Labor Costs}} = \text{Percentage of Direct Labor Costs}$$

Using the figures given on page 193.

$$\frac{\$48,000}{\$100,000} = 48\% \text{ of direct labor costs}$$

Therefore, if direct labor costs incurred on a particular job totaled $3,000, the applied overhead would be $1,440 ($3,000 × .48).

The direct labor costs basis is not generally used in cases where a large proportion of overhead costs relates to the use of machinery. Also, if hourly wage rates vary widely between different workers on the same job or in the same department, the method will result in a larger amount of overhead being charged to those jobs on which higher-paid workers are used. Just because an employee is paid more does not necessarily mean that the employee will use more heat, light, power, and so on in producing the product.

SELECTING THE OVERHEAD BASIS

The overhead rate basis selected by a company will depend on many considerations. Factors that affect the choice include the type of goods produced, amount of machinery employed, organization of the firm, type of labor used, wage rates paid, and cost and time involved in collecting the necessary data. Certain guiding principles should be observed in selecting a basis.

■ The rate should be easily computed.

■ The factor chosen as the basis must be one that can easily be measured for each job.

■ There must be some direct relationship between the amount of overhead costs incurred and the factor chosen as the basis.

■ The basis should be representative of the overhead costs applicable to each unit.

■ Departmental rates should be used if possible. As a result, a number of different bases may be selected to meet the needs of different departments.

SELF-REVIEW

1. Name common bases used to determine overhead application rates. What bases are most widely used?
2. What period of time is used to determine an overhead application rate?
3. Buffet Corporation has annual manufacturing overhead costs of $70,000. Using the following data, calculate overhead application rates based on machine hours, direct labor costs, and direct labor hours.

Machine hours for the year	10,000 hours
Direct labor costs for the year	$175,000
Direct labor hours for the year	25,000 hours

Answers to Self-Review

1. Common bases used to determine overhead application rates are units of production, materials costs, machine hours, direct labor costs, and direct labor hours. Direct labor costs and direct labor hours are the most widely used bases.
2. The time period used is a year.
3. The overhead application rates are:

Machine hours	$70,000/10,000 = $7.00 per machine hour
Direct labor costs	$70,000/$175,000 = 40% of direct labor costs
Direct labor hours	$70,000/25,000 = $2.80 per direct labor hour

SETTING RATES

After a careful study of all pertinent considerations, the cost accountant at Panorama Windows has developed bases for the application of overhead costs.

Length of Rate Period

Panorama Windows bases its predetermined overhead rates on the estimated overhead costs and volume for a one-year period. In December, a budget is prepared for the coming year. This becomes the basis for computing the departmental overhead rates. The budgeted costs of the three producing departments and the two service departments for 19X9 are shown on page 197.

PANORAMA WINDOWS, INC.
Overhead Budgets
Year 19X9

COST	CUTTING	FRAMING	ASSEMBLY	BUILDING SERVICES	GENERAL FACTORY	TOTAL
Indirect Materials	$ 20,653	$ 16,600	$ 37,675	$ 8,195	$ 13,490	$ 96,613
Indirect Labor	52,790	47,170	66,780	70,265	134,860	371,865
Payroll Taxes	24,235	25,885	26,965	10,615	14,815	102,515
Depreciation	18,150	7,425	14,646	27,820	15,100	83,141
Repairs & Maintenance	5,830	3,200	6,360	4,715	9,370	29,475
Utilities	10,780	4,935	5,940	16,240	7,930	45,825
Insurance	4,235	4,680	5,080	3,120	2,715	19,830
Property Taxes	1,685	695	1,535	3,400	1,925	9,240
Other	1,825	1,290	1,480	960	2,700	8,255
Total	$140,183	$111,880	$166,461	$145,330	$202,905	$766,759
Estimated Direct Labor Hours	32,000	40,000	28,000			
Estimated Direct Labor Costs	$220,500	$301,350	$213,150			

The accountant completes the worksheet shown below to prorate estimated service department costs to the producing departments. After the budgeted overhead costs of the service departments are prorated to the producing departments, the overhead rates for the three producing departments are computed.

Panorama Windows, Inc.

Worksheet for Prorating Service Department Overhead

Year Ended December 31, 19X9

ITEM	BASIS OF PRORATION	BUILDING SERVICES	GENERAL FACTORY	CUTTING	FRAMING	ASSEMBLY	TOTAL
Est. dir. dept.							
Overhead costs		145330 00	202905 00	140183 00	111880 00	166461 00	766759 00
Prorate Bldg. Ser.	floor space*	(145330 00)	43599 00	29066 00	40692 00	31973 00	
Prorate Gen. Fact.	direct labor†		(246504 00)	73951 00	101067 00	71486 00	
Total		0 00	0 00	243200 00	253639 00	269920 00	766759 00

*General Factory, 30%; Cutting, 20%; Framing, 28%; Finishing, 22% (percentage calculated in Chapter 8).
†Cutting, $220,500 (30%); Framing, $301,350 (41%); Assembly, $213,150 (29%); Total, $735,000.
 All amounts are rounded to nearest whole dollar.

Extent of Rate Application

Panorama Windows uses a separate overhead rate for each producing department because the operations in each are so different.

Selection of Rate Basis

In each of the producing departments, the predetermined overhead rate is based on direct labor hours. This method has been selected because of the number of different types of direct workers employed in each of the three departments and because their hourly wage rates vary considerably. Operations performed on each job also vary widely.

COMPUTING DEPARTMENTAL RATES

Separate computations are required for each of Panorama Windows' producing departments. Using the direct labor hours basis, each department's budgeted manufacturing overhead for the year is divided by that department's estimated direct labor hours for the year to determine the application rate.

Cutting Department Overhead Rate

Total budgeted overhead of the Cutting Department for the year 19X9 is $243,200, including allocated service department costs (see the proration worksheet on page 197). The total direct labor hours for the year are estimated to be 32,000. The departmental rate is computed as follows:

$$\frac{\text{Manufacturing Overhead, \$243,200}}{\text{Direct Labor Hours, 32,000}} = \$7.60 \text{ per Direct Labor Hour}$$

Framing Department Overhead Rate

The budgeted overhead for the Framing Department is $253,639, based on an expected 40,000 direct labor hours. The departmental rate is computed as follows:

$$\frac{\text{Manufacturing Overhead, \$253,639}}{\text{Direct Labor Hours, 40,000}} = \$6.34 \text{ per Direct Labor Hour}$$

Assembly Department Overhead Rate

At this point you should be able to work Exercises 9–1 to 9–5 and Problems 9–1A to 9–4B.

The budgeted overhead for the Assembly Department is $269,920, based on an expected 28,000 direct labor hours. The departmental rate is computed as follows:

$$\frac{\text{Manufacturing Overhead, \$269,920}}{\text{Direct Labor Hours, 28,000}} = \$9.64 \text{ per Direct Labor Hour}$$

PRINCIPLES AND PROCEDURES SUMMARY

■ Management needs cost information as soon as a job is finished. Instead of waiting for the end of a fiscal period, when the actual cost totals are available, the cost accountant estimates overhead costs for each job.

- Five major types of bases are used for computing overhead rates:
  - Units of production
  - Materials costs
  - Machine hours
  - Direct labor hours
  - Direct labor costs
- The direct labor costs basis is used by about half the manufacturers in the United States. Whatever basis is used, the application rate is determined by dividing the estimated overhead costs by the basis chosen.
- An accountant should be guided by the following criteria in choosing a rate basis:
  - The rate should be easily computed.
  - The factor chosen as the basis must be easily measurable.
  - There must be a direct relationship between the amount of overhead costs incurred and the factor chosen as the basis.
  - The basis should be representative of overhead costs applicable to each unit.
  - The rate should meet specific departmental needs.
  - The cost to collect the necessary data should be reasonable.
- The figures for the application rate are obtained from budget estimates. For example, if direct labor hours are selected as the rate basis, the estimated number of direct labor hours is divided into the estimated departmental overhead costs (after service department costs have been allocated to producing departments) to determine an overhead application rate for each labor hour.

MANAGERIAL IMPLICATIONS

- Management cannot wait until the end of the year or other accounting period to get a measure or an estimate of the manufacturing overhead applicable to goods worked on during the period. For this reason, overhead application rates are developed to charge each job with the estimated overhead applicable to the job.
- Overhead application rates are based on the relationship between overhead costs and some other factor that can be accurately measured for each job. For example, it may be determined that there is a relationship between the overhead costs in a department and the number of direct labor hours worked in that department. The overhead applicable to a job might then be estimated on the basis of the number of hours worked on the job and the estimated overhead rate per hour. This permits the determination of a job's total cost at the time the job is completed.
- It is important that overhead application bases be chosen that reflect, as closely as possible, the overhead costs incurred. It may be necessary to use a different application base for each department in order to get the best match between costs and the application base.

■ Historically, direct labor hours or direct labor costs have been most frequently used as application bases. However, the cost accountant should always be alert for more representative application bases. For example, in today's manufacturing economy, a large part of overhead relates to the use of machinery and equipment. As a result, machine hours used may be a suitable base for allocating costs.

REVIEW QUESTIONS

1. What is the purpose of using predetermined manufacturing overhead rates?
2. List two factors that affect the setting of manufacturing overhead rates.
3. What are the five most common bases used in establishing manufacturing overhead rates?
4. Which of these five bases is used most often? Why?
5. Why is the materials costs basis rarely used?
6. What is the major limitation in using the units of production basis or manufacturing overhead rates?
7. How is the overhead application rate calculated under the machine hours basis?
8. What calculation is used when determining the overhead application rate under the direct labor hours method? The direct labor costs method?
9. In selecting a basis for manufacturing overhead rates, what are four guidelines that should be followed?

MANAGERIAL DISCUSSION QUESTIONS

1. Why are individual departmental overhead rates often used rather than one single factorywide rate? What are the advantages to management in using departmental rates?
2. What basis should be used in calculating overhead rates in a business in which production volume varies greatly from year to year? Why?
3. Under what circumstances would you recommend to management that it use the machine hours basis for setting manufacturing overhead rates?
4. Discuss the difference between the direct labor hours basis and the direct labor costs basis. Under what circumstances should each method be used by management in determining overhead rates?

EXERCISES

EXERCISE 9–1   **Calculate overhead rates.   (Obj. 3).**   For the current year, 19X9, the estimated manufacturing overhead for the Preparing Department is $196,000. The estimated number of units of production is 280,000.

The company uses the units of production basis for overhead rates. How much overhead should be applied to (a) Job 320 for 1,480 units and (b) Job 352 for 3,160 units?

EXERCISE 9–2 **Calculate overhead rates. (Obj. 3).** Job 670 calls for 1,200 units to be produced. The estimate of manufacturing overhead for the year for the Cutting Department is $42,000. The company expects that direct materials will be $600,000 and total machine hours will be 250,000. Job 670 incurred $5,300 in direct materials and used 3,284 machine hours. How much manufacturing overhead should be applied to Job 670 if the company uses (a) the materials costs basis and (b) the machine hours basis?

EXERCISE 9–3 **Calculate overhead rates. (Obj. 3).** Using the data below, calculate the amount of manufacturing overhead to be applied to Job 792 for 460 units, if (a) the direct labor hours basis is used and (b) the direct labor costs basis is used.

Estimated manufacturing overhead for the year	$296,772
Estimated direct labor hours	353,300 hours
Estimated direct labor costs	$370,965
Job 792: direct labor hours used	1,580 hours
Job 792: direct labor costs incurred	$ 1,770

EXERCISE 9–4 **Calculate overhead rates. (Obj. 3).** The United Tailors Company used the direct labor costs basis in establishing overhead rates for its producing departments. For the year 19X9, the company estimated the following manufacturing overhead budgets:

Building Services	$48,860
Department 101	75,300
Department 102	83,800
Department 103	78,518

Building Services is a service department that assists the producing departments. Its overhead is allocated to the producing departments on the basis of floor space occupied. The floor space occupied by each department is given below.

	Square Feet Occupied	Direct Labor Costs
Department 101	2,660	$154,000
Department 102	1,900	148,860
Department 103	3,040	125,239

Determine the manufacturing overhead rates for each department for the year. Carry your answers to six decimal places, round to five, and then change to percents.

EXERCISE 9–5 **Calculate overhead rates. (Obj. 3).** Assume the same facts as in Exercise 9–4, except that the United Tailors Company uses the direct labor hours basis for overhead rates. Determine the rates for the year if the estimated direct labor hours are as shown below. Round the rates to three decimal places.

	Hours
Department 101	120,000
Department 102	150,000
Department 103	87,000

PROBLEMS

PROBLEM 9–1A

Calculate departmental overhead rates. (Obj. 3). A summary of the budget data for the Assembly Department of the Vera Cruz Company for the year 19X9 is given here.

Manufacturing overhead costs	$372,600
Units of production	155,000 units
Direct materials costs	$436,170
Direct labor costs	$525,760
Direct labor hours	119,000 hours
Machine hours	77,260 hours

INSTRUCTIONS

Determine the manufacturing overhead application rates under each of the following bases. Round percents to three decimal places and rates to the nearest whole cent.
a. Units of production
b. Direct materials costs
c. Machine hours
d. Direct labor hours
e. Direct labor costs

PROBLEM 9–2A

Calculate and apply manufacturing overhead. (Obj. 3). A summary of budget data for the Jones Manufacturing Group for the year 19X9 is given below.

Manufacturing overhead costs	$792,450
Direct materials costs	$463,970
Direct labor costs	$584,200
Direct labor hours	109,300 hours
Machine hours	83,890 hours

INSTRUCTIONS

1. Use each of the following bases to determine the overhead application rate. Round to three decimal places except for percents, which should be carried to six places and rounded to five.
   a. Materials costs
   b. Direct labor costs
   c. Direct labor hours
   d. Machine hours
2. Prepare a schedule showing the amount of overhead that would be applied to Job 53 using each application rate. Assume the following data for the job:

Direct materials costs	$5,617
Direct labor costs	$6,790
Direct labor hours	1,780 hours
Machine hours	562 hours

PROBLEM 9–3A **Complete a worksheet for prorating service department costs. (Obj. 4).** DLM Dress Manufacturers, Inc. is divided into service departments and producing departments. The Warehousing Department, which carries out receiving, storing, and shipping functions, and the Maintenance Department are service departments. The Cutting, Sewing, and Finishing Departments are producing departments. The Maintenance Department serves the other departments in proportion to the area occupied by each department.

Department	Square Feet Occupied
Warehousing	10,500
Cutting	17,500
Sewing	14,000
Finishing	28,000

The costs of the Warehousing Department are allocated to the producing departments on the basis of the number of materials requisitions processed.

Department	Number of Materials Requisitions
Cutting	3,920
Sewing	5,880
Finishing	4,200

INSTRUCTIONS 1. Prepare a worksheet for prorating estimated service department costs for the year 19X9. The budgeted departmental overhead is as follows:

Department	Estimated Direct Departmental Overhead Costs
Maintenance	$29,210
Warehousing	21,390
Cutting	35,870
Sewing	41,552
Finishing	26,760

2. Summarize your computations for the bases and the prorations on three-column analysis paper. (Keep your papers for use in Problem 9–4A.)

PROBLEM 9–4A **Compute overhead applications rates. (Obj. 4).** This problem is a continuation of Problem 9–3A. The following data are provided:

Basis	Cutting	Sewing	Finishing
Direct Labor Costs	$85,000	$90,000	$110,000
Direct Labor Hours	24,000 hours	30,000 hours	27,000 hours
Machine Hours	6,600 hours	9,000 hours	8,300 hours

INSTRUCTIONS

1. Compute three overhead application rates for each of the three producing departments, using the data above. Show your computations in equation form. Carry your answers to three decimal places except for percents. Carry percents to six decimal places, and then round to five.
2. Which overhead application rate would you choose for each department? Why?

ALTERNATE PROBLEMS

PROBLEM 9–1B **Calculate departmental overhead rates.** **(Obj. 3).** A summary of the budget data for the Finishing Department of the Best Hardware Company for the year 19X9 is given here.

Manufacturing overhead costs	$936,840
Units of production	450,000 hours
Direct materials costs	$738,540
Direct labor costs	$845,920
Direct labor hours	220,000 hours
Machine hours	84,500 hours

INSTRUCTIONS Determine the manufacturing overhead application rates under each of the following bases. Round percents to three decimal places and rates to the nearest whole cent.
a. Units of production
b. Direct materials costs
c. Machine hours
d. Direct labor hours
e. Direct labor costs

PROBLEM 9–2B **Calculate and apply manufacturing overhead.** **(Obj. 3).** A summary of budget data for the Smith Manufacturing Group for the year 19X9 is given below.

Manufacturing overhead costs	$196,560
Direct materials costs	$ 86,400
Direct labor costs	$159,310
Direct labor hours	79,300 hours
Machine hours	16,050 hours

INSTRUCTIONS 1. Use each of the following bases to determine the overhead application rate. Round to three decimal places except for percents, which should be carried to six places and rounded to five.
a. Materials costs
b. Direct labor costs

c. Direct labor hours

d. Machine hours

2. Prepare a schedule showing the amount of overhead that would be applied to Job 61 using each application rate. Assume the following data for the job.

Direct materials costs	$11,375
Direct labor costs	$12,650
Direct labor hours	840 hours
Machine hours	230 hours

PROBLEM 9–3B

Complete a worksheet for prorating service department costs. (Obj. 4). The Utah Western Shirt Company, Inc. is divided into service departments and producing departments. The Warehousing Department, which carries out receiving, storing, and shipping functions, and the Maintenance Department are service departments. The Cutting, Sewing, and Finishing Departments are producing departments. The Maintenance Department serves the other departments in proportion to the area occupied by each department.

Department	Square Feet Occupied
Warehousing	9,300
Cutting	15,500
Sewing	19,840
Finishing	17,360

The costs of the Warehousing Department are allocated to the producing departments on the basis of the number of materials requisitions processed.

Department	Number of Materials Requisitions
Cutting	968
Sewing	1,364
Finishing	2,068

INSTRUCTIONS

1. Prepare a worksheet for prorating estimated service department costs for the year 19X9. The budgeted departmental overhead is as follows:

Department	Estimated Direct Departmental Overhead Costs
Maintenance	$40,540
Warehousing	29,480
Cutting	43,410
Sewing	59,620
Finishing	35,372

2. Summarize your computations for the bases and the prorations on three-column analysis paper. (Keep your papers for use in Problem 9–4B.)

PROBLEM 9–4B **Compute overhead application rates. (Obj. 4).** This problem is a continuation of Problem 9–3B. The following data are provided:

Basis	Cutting	Sewing	Finishing
Direct Labor Costs	$77,400	$82,000	$32,800
Direct Labor Hours	30,000 hours	60,000 hours	70,000 hours
Machine Hours	20,400 hours	7,100 hours	5,900 hours

INSTRUCTION 1. Compute three overhead application rates for each of the three producing departments, using the data above. Show your computations in equation form. Carry your answers to three decimal places except for percents. Carry percents to six decimal places, and then round to five.
2. Which overhead application rate would you choose for each department? Why?

MANAGERIAL DECISION CASE

Outdoor Manufacturers makes hatchets, knives, and other tools for use by campers and hikers. Its employees work in three departments: Machining, Polishing, and Assembly. In the Machining Department, robots are used to handle the metals, and one employee monitors the operations. The employees of the Polishing Department clean and polish the blades. In the Assembly Department, employees inspect each blade for defects and attach wooden handles and the firm's decals.

As the cost accountant, you have been asked to determine the overhead application basis most appropriate for each department. In a short written report, present your suggestions on the methods to use and your reasons for choosing each basis.

Applying Manufacturing Overhead

The overhead application rates that were computed in the last chapter can now be used to allocate manufacturing overhead costs to specific units of production. Allocation is done in two steps. First, estimated manufacturing overhead costs for individual jobs are computed by departments and recorded on the job cost sheets. Then the total overhead accumulated during the month is charged to production by posting from the manufacturing overhead applied journal to the Work in Process account in the general ledger.

OBJECTIVES

1. Record manufacturing overhead applied to specific jobs by making entries on job cost sheets and in the manufacturing overhead applied journal.
2. Charge manufacturing overhead to production by posting from the manufacturing overhead applied journal to the general ledger accounts.
3. Prepare and record the entries to close the departmental Manufacturing Overhead account balances to the general ledger Overapplied or Underapplied Manufacturing Overhead account.
4. Calculate the amount of overapplied or underapplied overhead.
5. Explain the income statement treatment and balance sheet presentation of overapplied and underapplied manufacturing overhead on interim statements.
6. Prepare the general journal entry to close the Overapplied or Underapplied Manufacturing Overhead account to the Cost of Goods Sold account.
7. Analyze overapplied and underapplied overhead and determine volume and spending variances.

NEW TERMS

Fixed costs (p. 217)
Manufacturing overhead applied journal (p. 208)
Overapplied overhead (p. 210)
Spending variance (p. 217)
Underapplied overhead (p. 210)
Variable costs (p. 217)
Volume variance (p. 217)

ENTRIES ON JOB COST SHEETS

Panorama Windows uses the direct labor hours basis for overhead application. The amount of overhead to be charged to each job is calculated by multiplying the number of direct labor hours worked on the job in each department by the predetermined departmental overhead rate. The amount of overhead thus computed is then entered in the Manufacturing Overhead Applied section of the individual job cost sheet. This entry may be made when a job is completed or at the end of the month if the job is still in process. (Some companies apply overhead to jobs each week.)

Applying Overhead to Completed Jobs

At the end of the week in which the job is finished, the labor hours data are taken from the weekly analysis of the time tickets and forwarded to the cost accounting unit. Suppose that the job cost sheet for Job 101, completed October 18, shows the following total direct labor hours after all time tickets have been recorded:

Cutting Department	290 hours
Framing Department	220 hours
Assembly Department	320 hours

If the predetermined departmental overhead rates computed in the last chapter (page 198) are used, the overhead applied to this job for these departments in October is as follows:

Cutting Department, 290 hours at $7.60 per hour = $2,204.00
Framing Department, 220 hours at $6.34 per hour = $1,394.80
Assembly Department, 320 hours at $9.64 per hour = $3,084.80

These amounts are entered in the appropriate columns of the Manufacturing Overhead Applied section of the job cost sheet, as shown on page 209.

Applying Overhead to Jobs in Process

Job cost sheets for jobs still in process are brought up to date at the end of the month by applying overhead based on the direct labor hours recorded during the month. The total number of hours is multiplied by the predetermined overhead application rate for each department. The resulting applied overhead cost is entered in the Manufacturing Overhead Applied section on the job cost sheets.

ENTRIES IN THE GENERAL LEDGER

At the end of the month, entries are made in the general ledger accounts to reflect the estimated manufacturing overhead charged to production. In some companies, the information for this entry is obtained by totaling the overhead entries that have been made on the job cost sheets during the month. However, Panorama Windows simplifies this process by keeping a **manufacturing overhead applied journal.** Each time an entry for overhead is made on a job cost sheet, the entry is also recorded in the manufacturing overhead applied journal, as shown on page 209.

JOB COST SHEET

CUSTOMER _Nelson Construction Co._

DESCRIPTION _Customer specs on file_

QUANTITY _100_

JOB _101_

DATE STARTED _10/1/X9_

DATE COMPLETED _10/18/X9_

| MATERIALS | | | DIRECT LABOR | | | | | | | | | MANUFACTURING OVERHEAD APPLIED | | | | | | | | | | |
| DATE | REQ. NO. | AMOUNT | DATE | REF. | CUTTING | | FRAMING | | ASSEMBLY | | DATE | REF. | CUTTING | | | FRAMING | | | ASSEMBLY | | |
					HRS.	AMOUNT	HRS.	AMOUNT	HRS.	AMOUNT			HRS.	RATE	AMOUNT	HRS.	RATE	AMOUNT	HRS.	RATE	AMOUNT
10/1	R802	935 00	10/5	TTA	290	1902 00	220	1580 00	55	420 00	10/18	MOA 10	290	7.60	2204 00	220	6.34	1394 80	320	9.64	3084 80
10/2	R804	2805 00	10/12	TTA					95	685 00											
10/6	RM48	(85 00)	10/17	TTA					170	1215 00											
10/8	R809	1598 00																			
10/8	R817	119 00																			
10/16	R843	41 00																			
10/17	R848	27 00																			
10/18	R852	34 00																			
Total					220		320														

TOTAL COST $ _____

UNITS PRODUCED _____

SUMMARY

MATERIALS $ _____

LABOR—MILLING _____

MANUFACTURING OVERHEAD APPLIED JOURNAL

FOR MONTH OF _October_ 19 _X9_ PAGE _10_

| DATE | | JOB. NO. | WORK IN PROCESS DR. 122 | | CUTTING CR. 502 | | FRAMING CR. 503 | | ASSEMBLY CR. 504 | |
					HOURS	AMOUNT	HOURS	AMOUNT	HOURS	AMOUNT
Oct.	18	101	6,683	60	290	2,204 00	220	1,394 80	320	3,084 80
	31	Total	61,628	31	2,775.4	21,093 03	3,688.0	23,381 91	1,779.4	17,153 37
						(✓)		(✓)		(✓)

This journal is totaled, and the totals are posted to the appropriate general ledger accounts at the end of the month.

To illustrate the effect of these postings, they are shown in general journal form here.

19X9			
Oct. 31 Work in Process		122	61,628.31
Manufacturing Overhead—Cutting Department		502	21,093.03
Manufacturing Overhead—Framing Department		503	23,381.91
Manufacturing Overhead—Assembly Department		504	17,153.37
Applied departmental manufacturing overhead for the month.			

Posting to Departmental Manufacturing Overhead Accounts

After the totals have been posted to the general ledger from the manufacturing overhead applied journal, the departmental manufacturing overhead accounts involved appear as follows:

Manufacturing Overhead–Cutting Department   NO. 502

DATE		EXPLANATION	POST. REF.	DEBIT		CREDIT		BALANCE		DR. CR.
19	X9									
Oct.	31		J10-50	9,177	19			9,177	19	DR.
	31		J10-51	3,012	43			12,189	62	DR.
	31		J10-52	8,265	11			20,454	73	DR.
	31		MOA10			21,093	03	638	30	CR.

Manufacturing Overhead–Framing Department   NO. 503

DATE		EXPLANATION	POST. REF.	DEBIT		CREDIT		BALANCE		DR. CR.
19	X9									
Oct.	31		J10-50	8,849	45			8,849	45	DR.
	31		J10-51	4,217	40			13,066	85	DR.
	31		J10-52	10,748	10			23,814	95	DR.
	31		MOA10			23,381	91	433	04	DR.

Manufacturing Overhead–Assembly Department   NO. 504

DATE		EXPLANATION	POST. REF.	DEBIT		CREDIT		BALANCE		DR. CR.
19	X9									
Oct.	31		J10-50	8,896	60			8,896	60	DR.
	31		J10-51	3,313	67			12,210	27	DR.
	31		J10-52	7,753	51			19,963	78	DR.
	31		MOA10			17,153	37	2,810	41	DR.

The credit balance in Account 502 represents **overapplied overhead.** This occurs because the overhead applied (the amount credited) is more than the actual overhead costs incurred (the amounts debited) for this department. The situation is reversed in the other two departments, and the overhead applied (the amount credited) is less than the actual overhead costs incurred (the amounts debited). The resulting debit balance represents **underapplied overhead.** The net debit underapplied balance in these three accounts is $2,605.15 (a debit balance of $433.04 plus a debit balance of $2,810.41 minus a credit balance of $638.30), which is the same as the debit balance of Manufacturing Overhead Control 501, shown in Chapter 2 (page 34).

Use of Overhead Applied Accounts

Instead of crediting the applied overhead costs directly to the departmental manufacturing overhead accounts, some cost accountants prefer to credit special departmental overhead applied accounts. In this way, the applied overhead costs are kept separate from the actual costs, which appear as debits in the manufacturing overhead accounts. If Panorama Windows used this method, the postings from the manufacturing overhead applied journal would be recorded in the departmental overhead applied accounts as shown below.

	Manufacturing Overhead Applied–Cutting Department					NO. _XXX_	
DATE	EXPLANATION	POST. REF.	DEBIT	CREDIT	BALANCE	DR. CR.
19 X9						
Oct. 31		MOA10		21,093 03	21,093 03	CR.

	Manufacturing Overhead Applied–Framing Department					NO. _XXX_	
DATE	EXPLANATION	POST. REF.	DEBIT	CREDIT	BALANCE	DR. CR.
19 X9						
Oct. 31		MOA10		23,381 91	23,381 91	CR.

	Manufacturing Overhead Applied–Assembly Department					NO. _XXX_	
DATE	EXPLANATION	POST. REF.	DEBIT	CREDIT	BALANCE	DR. CR.
19 X9						
Oct. 31		MOA10		17,153 37	17,153 37	CR.

The overhead applied accounts are then closed into the departmental manufacturing overhead accounts. The final result of this procedure is exactly the same as though applied overhead costs had been credited directly to the manufacturing overhead accounts.

OVERAPPLIED OR UNDERAPPLIED OVERHEAD

The typical cost accounting system includes several provisions for the appropriate treatment of overapplied and underapplied manufacturing overhead.

Monthly Procedure

At Panorama Windows, the balances of the departmental manufacturing overhead accounts are closed at the end of each month into Overapplied or Underapplied Manufacturing Overhead 507 in the

1. To what general ledger accounts are the totals of each column in the manufacturing overhead applied journal posted at the end of the month?
2. What does a debit balance in a departmental manufacturing overhead account represent? A credit balance?

Answers to Self-Review

1. The totals are posted as a debit to Work in Process and credits to the Manufacturing Overhead accounts for each producing department.
2. A debit balance in a departmental manufacturing overhead account represents underapplied overhead. In other words, the amount of overhead applied was less than the actual overhead costs incurred. A credit balance represents the opposite: The amount of overhead applied was more than the actual overhead costs incurred.

At this point you should be able to work Exercises 10–1 and 10–2 and Problems 10–1A and 10–1B.

general ledger. The general journal voucher prepared to close the three departmental overhead accounts at the end of October is shown below.

The Overapplied or Underapplied Manufacturing Overhead account is not closed monthly. Instead, it reflects the cumulative overapplied or underapplied overhead to date, as shown on page 213.

The debit balance of $1,588.40 represents the excess of cumulative actual overhead costs over cumulative applied overhead costs for the months of January through September. The debit of $2,605.15 posted to Account 507 on October 31 (to close the departmental manufacturing overhead accounts for October) increases the cumulative underapplied manufacturing overhead to $4,193.55 for the first ten months of the year, as shown on page 213.

JOURNAL VOUCHER	Date _Oct. 31,_	19 _X9_	No. _10-54_		
ACCOUNT	**ACCT. NO.**	✓	**DEBIT**	**CREDIT**
Overapplied or Underapplied				
Mfg. Overhead	507		2605 15	
Mfg. Overhead–Cutting Dept.	502		638 30	
Mfg. Overhead–Framing				
Dept.	503			433 04
Mfg. Overhead–Assembly				
Dept.	504			2810 41
EXPLANATION				
Closed out departmental manufacturing overhead				
accounts at end of the month.				
PREPARED BY _GAR_	AUDITED BY _KC_		APPROVED BY _SH_	

Overapplied or Underapplied Manufacturing Overhead				NO.	507	
DATE	EXPLANATION	POST. REF.	DEBIT	CREDIT	BALANCE	DR. CR.
19 X9						
Oct. 1	*Balance*	✓			1,588 40	DR.
31		J10-54	2,605 15		4,193 55	DR.

Flow of Entries to Record Applied Overhead Costs

The flowchart below is a continuation of the flowchart presented in Chapter 8. The entry to illustrate the flow of applied overhead from the Manufacturing Overhead—Producing Department accounts to the Work in Process account is shown. Also shown is the entry to close the Manufacturing Overhead—Producing Department accounts to the Overapplied or Underapplied Manufacturing Overhead account. Letters to identify the entries are listed on the next page.

APPLICATION OF OVERHEAD TO WORK IN PROCESS

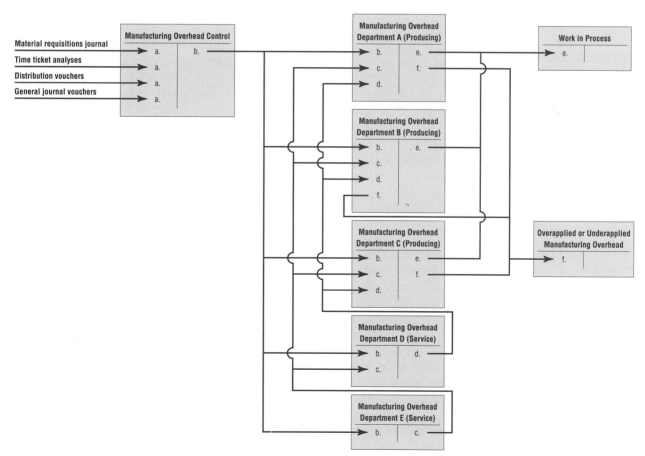

e. Entry to charge applied overhead to Work in Process.

f. Entry to close Manufacturing Overhead—Producing Department to the Overapplied or Underapplied Manufacturing Overhead account.

Balance Sheet Presentation

The actual overhead incurred will seldom equal the overhead applied during any one month, but the two overhead amounts should be close at the end of the year (assuming that accurate estimates were made). Amounts of overapplied overhead during some months of the year are expected to be offset by underapplied overhead during other months. Thus during the year, the cumulative amounts of overapplied or underapplied manufacturing overhead are considered to be amounts related to future months of the year. Any debit balance in Account 507 represents underapplied manufacturing overhead. This amount is considered a deferred charge and is shown under Prepaid Expenses on the interim balance sheet. Any credit balance during the year, representing overapplied manufacturing overhead, is shown on the interim balance sheet as a deferred credit. At the end of the year, any balance of underapplied or overapplied manufacturing overhead is closed into Cost of Goods Sold. Thus the balance will not appear on the end-of-year balance sheet.

Income Statement Presentation

As previously pointed out, the cumulative underapplied manufacturing overhead does not appear on income statements prepared during the year. The amount is carried forward as a deferred charge or deferred credit on the interim balance sheets. The Cost of Goods Sold section of the monthly income statement (see page 215) includes the Cost of Goods Manufactured during the current period. In turn, the Statement of Cost of Goods Manufactured (see page 237) shows direct materials used, direct labor, and manufacturing overhead applied.

End-of-Year Procedures

At the end of the year, Overapplied or Underapplied Manufacturing Overhead 507 must be closed. Any balance at the end of the year represents a discrepancy between overhead costs applied to goods worked on during the year and the actual overhead costs that were incurred in producing these goods.

From the viewpoint of accounting theory, the overapplied or underapplied overhead should be allocated proportionately to all goods that have been worked on during the year. Some of the goods are still in process, some are in finished goods, and some have already been sold. Thus the overapplied or underapplied balance should logically be allocated or subdivided among Work in Process, Finished Goods, and Cost of Goods Sold. However, this procedure is so difficult and time-consuming that the theoretical benefits obtained usually do not warrant the amount of work involved. In addition, most of the goods worked on during the year have probably been transferred to finished goods and sold to customers, so that most of the overapplied or underapplied overhead would be closed into Cost of Goods Sold. For these reasons, it is customary to close any balance of Overapplied or Underapplied Manufacturing Overhead at the end of the year into Cost of Goods Sold.

The following entry is required to close any balance of overapplied manufacturing overhead at the end of the year:

19X9			
Dec. 31	Overapplied or Underapplied		
	Manufacturing Overhead	507	XXX.XX
	Cost of Goods Sold	415	XXX.XX
	Closed overapplied manufacturing		
	overhead at end of year.		

When there is a balance of underapplied manufacturing overhead at the end of the year, the entry shown below is required to close the account.

19X9			
Dec. 31	Cost of Goods Sold	415	XXX.XX
	Overapplied or Underapplied		
	Manufacturing Overhead	507	XXX.XX
	Closed underapplied manufacturing		
	overhead at end of year.		

The overapplied or underapplied overhead is included in the Cost of Goods Sold section of the yearly income statement. It is shown below as an adjustment of Cost of Goods Sold. (Some accountants prefer to show it as an adjustment of Cost of Goods Manufactured.) If overhead has been underapplied, less overhead was charged to production than was actually incurred. Therefore, Cost of Goods Sold is understated, and the amount of the understated overhead is added to Cost of Goods Sold on the income statement. If overhead has been

---

PANORAMA WINDOWS, INC.
Income Statement
Year Ended December 31, 19X9

Revenue		
Sales		$3,648,000
Cost of Goods Sold		
Finished Goods Inventory, Jan. 1	$ 37,300	
Add Cost of Goods Manufactured	2,602,680	
Total Goods Available for Sale	$2,639,980	
Deduct Finished Goods Inventory, Dec. 31	34,800	
Cost of Goods Sold	$2,605,180	
Add Underapplied Overhead for Year	1,060	
Cost of Goods Sold (Adjusted)		2,606,240
Gross Profit on Sales		$1,041,760

overapplied, the opposite is true and more overhead was charged to production than was incurred. Therefore, Cost of Goods Sold is overstated, and the amount of overstated overhead is subtracted from Cost of Goods Sold.

SELF-REVIEW

1. To what account are the departmental manufacturing overhead accounts closed at the end of the month?
2. How is underapplied manufacturing overhead shown on an interim balance sheet? How is overapplied manufacturing overhead shown?
3. To what account is the Overapplied or Underapplied Manufacturing Overhead account closed at the end of the year?
4. At the end of the year, what effect would underapplied manufacturing overhead have on cost of goods sold? What effect would overapplied manufacturing overhead have?

Answers to Self-Review

1. Departmental manufacturing overhead accounts are closed at the end of the month to the Overapplied or Underapplied Manufacturing Overhead account.
2. Underapplied manufacturing overhead is shown as a deferred charge under Prepaid Expenses, and overapplied overhead is shown as a deferred credit.
3. Overapplied or Underapplied Manufacturing Overhead is closed to Cost of Goods Sold at the end of the year.
4. Underapplied manufacturing overhead would mean that less overhead was charged to production than was actually incurred. Therefore, cost of goods sold would be understated. Overapplied overhead would give the opposite effect: More overhead would be charged to production than was actually incurred, resulting in cost of goods sold being overstated.

At this point you should be able to work Exercises 10–3 to 10–5 and Problems 10–2A, 10–5A, 10–2B, and 10–5B.

Analysis of Overapplied or Underapplied Overhead

Management wants to know why overhead costs applied differ from the actual overhead costs incurred during the fiscal period. An analysis of the underapplied or overapplied overhead is more meaningful when used in the context of a flexible budgeting and standard cost system, such as the one discussed in Part 3. A brief summary of the basic ideas involved, however, will help show how the difference between actual costs and applied costs might be examined and explained.

The actual and applied overhead for the Cutting Department and the Assembly Department of Panorama Windows, Inc., for the month of October 19X9 are repeated below.

	Actual Costs	Applied Costs	Underapplied or (Overapplied)
Cutting Department	$20,454.73	$21,093.03	$ (638.30)
Assembly Department	19,963.78	17,153.39	2,810.39

In Chapter 9 you learned that the Cutting Department and Assembly Department overhead rates were determined as follows:

$$\text{Overhead Rate, Cutting Dept.} = \frac{\text{Budgeted Overhead for Year, \$243,200}}{\text{Budgeted Direct Labor Hours, 32,000 hours}}$$

$$= \$7.60 \text{ per hour}$$

$$\text{Overhead Rate, Assembly Dept.} = \frac{\text{Budgeted Overhead for Year, \$269,920}}{\text{Budgeted Direct Labor Hours, 28,000 hours}}$$

$$= \$9.64 \text{ per hour}$$

Cutting Department Overapplied Overhead. An examination of the budgeted overhead of the Cutting Department for the year shows that $147,817 of the budgeted costs are **fixed costs.** That is, they do not vary substantially (in total) regardless of fluctuations in the number of labor hours worked during the year. The remaining budgeted costs of $95,383 are **variable costs.** These costs tend to vary in proportion to the number of direct labor hours worked during the year. (Procedures for separating fixed and variable costs are discussed in Chapter 20.) Thus, out of the total overhead application rate of $7.60 per hour, $4.6193 per hour is for estimated fixed costs, as shown below. The balance, $2.9807 per hour, is for estimated variable costs.

$$\frac{\$147,817}{32,000 \text{ hours}} = \$4.6193 \text{ per hour}$$

If the actual direct labor hours worked in the department in a given month are equal to the number of direct labor hours budgeted (2,666.7 hours, or 32,000 hours per year divided by 12 months), the amount of fixed overhead charged to work in process for the month should be exactly equal to the actual fixed costs of $12,318 incurred in the month ($147,817 divided by 12 months). However, if fewer than 2,666.7 hours are worked during the month, the fixed costs applied will be less than the actual fixed overhead costs, which will remain unchanged at $12,318. Thus, the fixed overhead costs will be *underapplied*. On the other hand, if there are more than 2,666.7 hours of direct labor during the month, the fixed overhead costs applied will exceed $12,318. In this case, the fixed overhead will be *overapplied*. There will be underapplied fixed overhead of $4.6193 for each hour less than 2,666.7 hours of direct labor used during the month. For each hour of direct labor over 2,666.7 employed during the month, fixed overhead will be overapplied by $4.6193.

This overapplication or underapplication of fixed overhead results from the fact that the number of labor hours actually worked during the month deviates from the estimated number of labor hours used in determining the overhead rate. This deviation is known as a **volume variance.** The remainder of the underapplied or overapplied overhead represents the amount by which actual expenditures exceed the amount that should have been spent for overhead based on the number of hours worked. This amount is often called a **spending variance.**

The $638.30 of overapplied overhead in the Cutting Department for October can be analyzed as follows:

Volume Variance:
Fixed overhead applied ($4.6193 × 2,775.4) $12,820.41*
Fixed overhead budgeted   12,318.00
    Volume Variance (favorable) $502.41
Spending Variance:
Actual overhead for month $20,454.73
Budgeted overhead for hours worked:
Fixed $12,318.00
Variable (2,775.4 × $2.9807)   8,272.62*
    Total budgeted   20,590.62
      Spending Variance (favorable)   135.89
Total Variance (favorable) $638.30

*Adjusted for rounding, $.01.

These variances are called *favorable* because the actual overhead costs were less than the costs applied to production.

Assembly Department Underapplied Overhead. The $2,810.41 of underapplied overhead is the Assembly Department for October can be analyzed in the same way as done for the Cutting Department.

A $269,920 yearly overhead budget was used in setting the Assembly Department overhead rate for the year. Fixed costs accounted for $164,651 of the total yearly overhead budget ($13,721 per month). The balance of $105,269 budgeted for the year represented variable costs. Thus, the $9.64 per labor hour overhead rate includes $5.8804 per hour of fixed costs ($164,651 divided by 28,000 hours) and $3.7596 per hour of variable costs ($105,269 divided by 28,000 hours). An unfavorable volume variance of $3257.42 and a favorable spending variance of $447.03 can be computed.

Volume Variance:
Fixed overhead applied ($5.8804 × 1779.4) $10,463.58*
Fixed overhead budgeted   13,721.00
    Volume Variance (unfavorable) $3,257.42
Spending Variance:
Actual overhead for month $19,963.78
Budgeted overhead for hours worked:
Fixed $13,721.00
Variable (1779.4 × $3.7596)   6,689.81*
    Total budgeted   20,410.81
      Spending Variance (favorable)   (447.03)
    Total Variance (unfavorable) $2,810.39

*Adjusted for rounding, $.02.

At this point you should be able to work Problems 10–3A to 10–4B.

These variances are called *unfavorable* because the actual costs were more than the costs applied to production. The concept of variance analysis will be examined more closely in Chapters 22 and 23.

PRINCIPLES AND PROCEDURES SUMMARY

- The major steps in the process of charging manufacturing overhead costs to production are outlined here for review.
  - Service department costs are distributed to producing departments on the basis of the service provided (Chapter 8).
  - An appropriate rate basis is selected for use in cost allocation (Chapter 9). A difference basis may be used to allocate the costs of each department.
  - Departmental application rates are computed (Chapter 9).
  - Application rates are used to charge manufacturing overhead costs to jobs completed or in process (Chapter 10).
  - The amount of overhead applied to each job is entered in the manufacturing overhead applied journal. The totals of this journal are posted to the appropriate departmental overhead accounts and to the Work in Process account at the end of month.
  - The balances of the departmental overhead accounts are closed monthly into an Overapplied or Underapplied Manufacturing Overhead account. This account remains open during the year and is shown on the interim balance sheets as a deferred charge or deferred credit.
  - At the end of the year, any balance of Overapplied or Underapplied Manufacturing Overhead is closed into Cost of Goods Sold and is included in the Cost of Goods Sold section of the income statement.
- Overapplied or underapplied manufacturing overhead is analyzed to determine what part, if any, is due to variations between the volume of activity planned and the volume of activity actually achieved and what part, if any, resulted from a lack of control over the manufacturing costs incurred.

MANAGERIAL IMPLICATIONS

- Manufacturing overhead may be applied at the time a job is completed so that management immediately will have available cost data that may be used in measuring profit or loss on a job, evaluating cost control, and making other managerial decisions.
- At the end of the month, overhead is applied to each job still in process (and to jobs that were completed during the month if overhead was not applied when the job was completed).
- Most manufacturing companies using job order cost accounting maintain a manufacturing overhead applied journal, which accumulates overhead applied during the month and facilitates the posting to the Work in Process account and the Manufacturing Overhead Applied account.
- Usually the difference between actual overhead costs and the overhead costs applied to jobs during the year is carried forward on a

monthly basis and the underapplied overhead or overapplied overhead is shown in the balance sheet as a deferred charge or deferred credit. At the end of the year the underapplied or overapplied overhead is closed. As a matter of practicality, the balance is usually closed into Cost of Goods Sold.

■ Management is very interested in why there is a difference between actual overhead and applied overhead. One useful analytic tool is a technique for dividing the total variance between a volume variance and a spending variance. For cost control purposes, the spending variance is more important because it compares the actual overhead with the budgeted overhead for the number of hours worked. This provides management with a measure of how well the department manager has controlled spending.

REVIEW QUESTIONS

1. When are manufacturing overhead costs recorded on the job cost sheet?
2. The job cost sheets are subsidiary records for what control account in the general ledger?
3. Explain the procedure for using a manufacturing overhead applied journal. What is an advantage of using this journal?
4. What does a debit posting to a departmental manufacturing overhead account represent? What does the credit posting at the end of the month represent?
5. After all the postings are recorded at the end of the month, the Manufacturing Overhead—Framing Department account has a debit balance. What does this balance represent?
6. What does a credit balance in a departmental manufacturing overhead account represent?
7. Is the Overapplied or Underapplied Manufacturing Overhead account closed at the end of the month? Explain.
8. How is the account Overapplied or Underapplied Manufacturing Overhead presented on interim monthly financial statements?
9. To what account is the Overapplied or Underapplied Manufacturing Overhead account closed? When?
10. What does a favorable variance represent? What does an unfavorable variance represent?

MANAGERIAL DISCUSSION QUESTIONS

1. How does management benefit from having manufacturing overhead applied to jobs as the work is being done?
2. Assume that at the end of the month the manufacturing overhead was not applied to the job cost sheets for the jobs being worked on but not completed. What effect would this omission have on the financial statements prepared at the end of the month?

3. What suggestions would you make to management to correct a volume variance and a spending variance?
4. Describe the presentation of overapplied or underapplied overhead on the income statement at the end of the year.

EXERCISES

EXERCISE 10–1   **Apply manufacturing overhead costs. (Obj. 1).** Job 219 was completed on July 12, 19X9. The job cost sheet indicates that 128 direct labor hours were spent on Job 219 in the Cutting Department and 162 hours were spent on it in the Finishing Department. If the manufacturing overhead rates are $1.52 per direct labor hour for the Cutting Department and $1.87 per direct labor hour for the Finishing Department, how much manufacturing overhead should be added to the job cost sheet for Job 219?

EXERCISE 10–2   **Journalize applied manufacturing overhead costs. (Obj. 2).** For the month of September 19X9, the following manufacturing overhead costs were applied on the job cost sheets for the Calgary Supply Corporation:

Shearing Department	$43,670.25
Molding Department	29,372.45
Finishing Department	34,258.44

Prepare the general journal entry to record the manufacturing overhead costs applied for the month.

EXERCISE 10–3   **Journalize overapplied or underapplied overhead. (Obj. 6).** At the end of May, after posting has been done, the following account balances appear in the general ledger of the Baldwin Plastic Company:

Manufacturing Overhead—Department 102	$1,324.63 Dr.
Manufacturing Overhead—Department 103	1,746.81 Cr.
Manufacturing Overhead—Department 104	897.11 Cr.
Manufacturing Overhead—Department 105	749.35 Dr.

Prepare the general journal entry to close the overhead accounts and to record the overapplied or underapplied overhead for the month.

EXERCISE 10–4   **Close Overapplied or Underapplied Manufacturing Overhead. (Obj. 6).** Prepare the necessary general journal entry to close the Overapplied or Underapplied Manufacturing Overhead account under each of the following assumptions:
a. The Overapplied or Underapplied Manufacturing Overhead account has a debit balance of $1,830.46.
b. The Overapplied or Underapplied Manufacturing Overhead account has a credit balance of $1,057.28.

EXERCISE 10–5   **Calculate the Cost of Goods Sold. (Obj. 5).** Determine the amount of Cost of Goods Sold (Adjusted) to be shown on the income statement of the Gregory Company from the following data:

Finished Goods, July 1, 19X8	$152,820
Finished Goods, June 30, 19X9	168,290
Cost of Goods Manufactured	379,340
Overapplied or Underapplied	
Manufacturing Overhead	1,630 Dr. Balance

PROBLEMS

PROBLEM 10–1A   **Complete a job cost sheet. (Obj. 1).**   The partially completed job cost sheet prepared at the Swansen Manufacturing Company for Job 4-09 is given below. (This sheet is reproduced in the *Study Guide and Working Papers*. If you are using the workbook, do all the following activities there.)

JOB COST SHEET

CUSTOMER *Watson Stores, Inc.*   **JOB** *4-09*
DESCRIPTION *Style 2357, mixed colors*   **DATE STARTED** *4/12/X9*
QUANTITY *300 dozen*   **DATE COMPLETED** *4/24/X9*

MATERIALS			DIRECT LABOR									MANUFACTURING OVERHEAD APPLIED									
					CUTTING		SEWING		FINISHING					CUTTING			SEWING			FINISHING	
DATE	REQ. NO.	AMOUNT	DATE	REF.	HRS.	AMOUNT	HRS.	AMOUNT	HRS.	AMOUNT	DATE	REF.	HRS.	RATE	AMOUNT	HRS.	RATE	AMOUNT	HRS.	RATE	AMOUNT
4/12	R385	150 00	4/14	TTA	120																
4/12	R391	125 00	4/21	TTA	55		95														
4/16	R404	175 00	4/28	TTA			64		113												
4/17	R408	42 05																			
4/17	R415	36 10																			
4/19	R422	14 87																			
4/21	R425	22 18																			
4/21	R428	19 87																			
4/23	R432	54 37																			
4/24	R435	9 98																			

INSTRUCTIONS
1. Compute and enter the departmental direct labor costs on the job cost sheet for Job 4-09. The labor rates are as follows: Cutting Department, $7.10 per hour; Sewing Department, $9.98 per hour; and Finishing Department, $10.70 per hour.
2. The Swansen Manufacturing Company applies overhead to work in process on the basis of direct labor hours. Use the overhead application rates given below to determine the manufacturing overhead to be applied to each department. Record the applied overhead on the job cost sheet for Job 4-09.

Cutting Department	$8.25 per direct labor hour
Sewing Department	6.42 per direct labor hour
Finishing Department	9.20 per direct labor hour

3. Total all columns and draw a double rule. Complete the Summary and Total Cost sections of the job cost sheet for Job 4-09.

PROBLEM 10–2A **Record applied manufacturing overhead. (Objs. 2, 3).** The Clancy Manufacturing Company completed five jobs during April 19X9. The company applies overhead to work in process on the basis of direct labor hours and has calculated the following overhead application rates:

Cutting Department	$2.17 per direct labor hour
Sewing Department	1.62 per direct labor hour
Finishing Department	1.63 per direct labor hour

The manufacturing overhead account balances in the ledger are as follows:

Manufacturing Overhead—Cutting Department	$1,580.11 Dr.
Manufacturing Overhead—Sewing Department	1,430.66 Dr.
Manufacturing Overhead—Finishing Department	872.11 Dr.
Overapplied or Underapplied Manufacturing Overhead	306.82 Cr.

INSTRUCTIONS 1. a. Compute the manufacturing overhead to be applied to each department for each of the jobs completed in April. Use the following data:

Date	Job No.	Cutting	Sewing	Finishing
Apr. 9	4-01	450 hours	136 hours	102 hours
14	4-02	75 hours	130 hours	80 hours
18	4-03	100 hours	155 hours	55 hours
23	4-04	125 hours	110 hours	95 hours
29	4-05	135 hours	125 hours	115 hours

   b. Record the jobs in the manufacturing overhead applied journal.
   c. Prove the accuracy of your work by footing and crossfooting all columns of the manufacturing overhead applied journal. Enter the totals and draw a double rule.
2. Post the totals of the manufacturing overhead applied journal to the departmental manufacturing overhead accounts in the general ledger and extend the balance of each account.
3. a. Prepare the general journal voucher to close the departmental manufacturing overhead accounts into the Overapplied or Underapplied Manufacturing Overhead account. Number the voucher 4-17.
   b. Post General Journal Voucher 4-17 to the general ledger accounts and extend the balance of each account.

PROBLEM 10–3A

Compute overhead and analyze volume and spending variances. (Objs. 4, 5, 7). Selected data for the Beverly Hills Manufacturing Company for the year 19X9 follow:

	Budgeted for Year	Actual for Year
Direct Labor Hours	260,000	248,300
Manufacturing Overhead		
Fixed	$ 585,000	$ 578,400
Variable	1,092,000	1,039,940
Total Overhead	$1,677,000	$1,618,340

Overhead is applied on the basis of direct labor hours.

INSTRUCTIONS

1. Compute the overhead application rate.
2. Compute the applied overhead for the year.
3. Compute the total overapplied or underapplied overhead for the year.
4. Analyze the total overapplied or underapplied overhead into a volume variance and a spending variance.

PROBLEM 10–4A

Analyze underapplied or overapplied overhead. (Objs. 4, 5, 7). Vineland Manufacturers uses the direct labor hours method for applying manufacturing overhead. The overhead application rate for 19X9 is $5.49 per hour, based on anticipated fixed costs of $272,250 and anticipated variable costs of $633,600, with an expected volume of 165,000 labor hours.

During the year, the company actually operated for 168,630 hours, incurring fixed overhead of $283,400 and variable overhead of $647,426.67.

INSTRUCTIONS

1. Compute the total underapplied or overapplied overhead for the year.
2. Analyze the total overapplied or underapplied overhead into a volume variance and a spending variance.

PROBLEM 10–5A

Prepare an income statement. (Obj. 5). For the fiscal year 19X9, the Santa Monica Machinery Corporation accumulated the following data:

Sales	$824,384
Sales Returns and Allowances	32,714
Finished Goods, July 1, 19X8	82,844
Finished Goods, June 30, 19X9	85,834
Cost of Goods Manufactured	448,721
Overapplied or Underapplied Overhead	4,190 Dr. Balance
Selling Expenses	94,348
Administrative Expenses	72,200
Provision for Income Taxes	80,650

INSTRUCTIONS

Prepare an income statement for the Santa Monica Machinery Corporation for the year ended June 30, 19X9.

ALTERNATE PROBLEMS

PROBLEM 10–1B **Complete a job cost sheet. (Obj. 1).** The partially completed job cost sheet prepared at the Brooklyn Manufacturing Company for Job 4-09 is given below. (This sheet is reproduced in the *Study Guide and Working Papers*. If you are using the workbook, do all the following activities there.)

JOB COST SHEET

CUSTOMER *Watson Stores, Inc.*   JOB *4-09*
DESCRIPTION *Style 2357, mixed colors*   DATE STARTED *4/12/X9*
QUANTITY *300 dozen*   DATE COMPLETED *4/24/X9*

\multicolumn{3}{MATERIALS}			\multicolumn{DIRECT LABOR}										\multicolumn{MANUFACTURING OVERHEAD APPLIED}											

DATE	REQ. NO.	AMOUNT	DATE	REF.	CUTTING HRS.	AMOUNT	SEWING HRS.	AMOUNT	FINISHING HRS.	AMOUNT	DATE	REF.	CUTTING HRS.	RATE	AMOUNT	SEWING HRS.	RATE	AMOUNT	FINISHING HRS.	RATE	AMOUNT
4/12	R385	150 00	4/14	TTA	120																
4/12	R391	125 00	4/21	TTA	55		95														
4/16	R404	175 00	4/28	TTA			64		113												
4/17	R408	42 05																			
4/17	R415	36 10																			
4/19	R422	14 87																			
4/21	R425	22 18																			
4/21	R428	19 87																			
4/23	R432	54 37																			
4/24	R435	9 98																			

INSTRUCTIONS

1. Compute and enter the departmental direct labor costs on the job cost sheet for Job 4-09. The labor rates are as follows: Cutting Department, $7.50 per hour; Sewing Department, $8.25 per hour; and Finishing Department, $9.30 per hour.
2. The Brooklyn Manufacturing Company applies overhead to work in process on the basis of direct labor hours. Use the overhead application rates given below to determine the manufacturing overhead to be applied to each department. Record the applied overhead on the job cost sheet for Job 4-09.

   Cutting Department $5.15 per direct labor hour
   Sewing Department   3.48 per direct labor hour
   Finishing Department   7.75 per direct labor hour

3. Total all columns and draw a double rule. Complete the Summary and Total Cost sections of the job cost sheet for Job 4-09.

PROBLEM 10–2B **Record applied manufacturing overhead. (Objs. 2, 3).** The Webster Manufacturing Company completed five jobs during April 19X9. The company applies overhead to work in process on the basis of direct labor hours and has calculated the following overhead application rates:

Cutting Department	$2.17 per direct labor hour
Sewing Department	1.62 per direct labor hour
Finishing Department	1.63 per direct labor hour

The manufacturing overhead account balances in the ledger are as follows:

Manufacturing Overhead—Cutting Department	$1,580.11 Dr.
Manufacturing Overhead—Sewing Department	1,430.66 Dr.
Manufacturing Overhead—Finishing Department	872.11 Dr.
Overapplied or Underapplied Manufacturing Overhead	306.82 Cr.

INSTRUCTIONS

1. a. Compute the manufacturing overhead to be applied to each department for each of the jobs completed in April. Use the following data:

Date	Job No.	Cutting	Sewing	Finishing
Apr. 9	4-01	201 hours	248 hours	192 hours
14	4-02	175 hours	159 hours	113 hours
18	4-03	86 hours	150 hours	86 hours
23	4-04	96 hours	160 hours	54 hours
29	4-05	135 hours	125 hours	115 hours

   b. Record the jobs in the manufacturing overhead applied journal.
   c. Prove the accuracy of your work by footing and crossfooting all columns of the manufacturing overhead applied journal. Enter the totals and draw a double rule.
2. Post the totals of the manufacturing overhead applied journal to the departmental manufacturing overhead accounts in the general ledger and extend the balance of each account.
3. a. Prepare the general journal voucher to close the departmental manufacturing overhead accounts into the Overapplied or Underapplied Manufacturing Overhead account. Number the voucher 4-22.
   b. Post General Journal Voucher 4-22 to the general ledger accounts and extend the balance of each account.

PROBLEM 10–3B

Compute overhead and analyze volume and spending variances. (Objs. 4, 5, 7). Selected data for the Portland Manufacturing Company for the year 19X9 follow:

	Budgeted for Year	Actual for Year
Direct Labor Hours	60,000	62,400
Manufacturing Overhead		
Fixed	$ 42,000	$ 42,000
Variable	168,000	171,100
Total Overhead	$210,000	$213.100

Overhead was applied on the basis of direct labor hours.

INSTRUCTIONS

1. Compute the overhead application rate.
2. Compute the applied overhead for the year.
3. Compute the total overapplied or underapplied overhead for the year.
4. Analyze the total overapplied or underapplied overhead into a volume variance and a spending variance.

PROBLEM 10–4B **Analyze underapplied or overapplied overhead. (Objs. 4, 5, 7).** Garfield Manufacturers uses the direct labor hours method for applying manufacturing overhead. The overhead application rate for 19X9 is $8.60 per hour, based on anticipated fixed costs of $348,000 and anticipated variable costs of $684,000, with an expected volume of 120,000 labor hours.

During the year, the company actually operated for 115,800 hours, incurring fixed overhead of $348,000 and variable overhead of $637,880.

INSTRUCTIONS

1. Compute the total underapplied or overapplied overhead for the year.
2. Analyze the total overapplied or underapplied overhead into a volume variance and a spending variance.

PROBLEM 10–5B **Prepare an income statement. (Obj. 5).** For the fiscal year 19X9, the Lorenzo Machinery Corporation accumulated the following data:

Sales	$960,540
Sales Returns and Allowances	43,780
Finished Goods, July 1, 19X8	98,730
Finished Goods, June 30, 19X9	94,520
Cost of Goods Manufactured	641,191
Overapplied or Underapplied Overhead	3,531 Cr. Balance
Selling Expenses	65,496
Administrative Expenses	82,526
Provision for Income Taxes	58,652

INSTRUCTIONS Prepare an income statement for the Lorenzo Machinery Corporation for the year ended June 30, 19X9.

MANAGERIAL DECISION CASE

Wrap-It-Up, Inc., manufactures gift wrap for all occasions from Christmas to birthdays to weddings. However, most of its output (70 percent) has a Christmas motif. Because of the lead time needed to get the gift wrap into stores for the Christmas season, production of Christmas-related wrapping paper occurs in March, April, and May. During these months, company employees often work many hours of overtime to get the product ready for shipment. During the rest of the year, production drops back to normal as the company focuses on the production of other types of gift wrap.

In an attempt to capture a larger share of the gift wrap market, Wrap-It-Up has recently added designers to its staff, increased the number of designs it offers, and modernized its production line with new automated machinery.

Margaret Dreiser, president of the company, is concerned about the wide fluctuations in the amount of overhead applied each month. She is aware that applied overhead is twice as high in some months as it is in other months (see below). "How can that be?" she asks. In addition, she points out that total applied overhead is also much higher than the actual overhead costs for the year, resulting in a large adjustment at the end of the year to Cost of Goods Sold for overapplied overhead.

Wrap-It-Up uses a single overhead application rate based on direct labor hours. Budgeted overhead costs are based on the previous year's actual overhead costs.

Month	Applied Overhead
January	$ 89,500
February	92,400
March	190,800
April	206,100
May	197,500
June	110,700
July	104,300
August	98,700
September	145,800
October	123,400
November	113,900
December	86,300
Total	$1,559,400

Total actual overhead costs for the year were $1,294,520.

What reasons can you suggest for the monthly fluctuations in applied overhead? What changes would you suggest that Wrap-It-Up make in determining its overhead application rate?

11

Completing the Cost Cycle

When jobs have been completed, the finished goods are moved from the factory to the warehouse. Since the flow of costs must follow the flow of the goods, the cost of completed jobs is transferred from the Work in Process account to the Finished Goods account in the general ledger. Later, when finished goods are sold, their cost is transferred to the Cost of Goods Sold account. In this chapter, you will learn how warehousing and selling operations are controlled through cost records and reports.

OBJECTIVES

1. Prepare and record the accounting entries required in the job order cost cycle.
2. Complete a job cost sheet including the entries and cost calculations required on completion of a job.
3. Explain and illustrate the flow of work and accompanying flow of costs through job order manufacturing operations.
4. Explain and illustrate the roles and relationships of the three typical inventory accounts and their subsidiary records.
5. Prepare a statement of cost of goods manufactured and a related schedule of manufacturing overhead costs.
6. Prepare an income statement for a manufacturing concern.

NEW TERMS

Completed jobs journal (p. 230)
Finished goods ledger (p. 232)
Sales journal (p. 233)

RECORDING COMPLETION OF JOBS

After completion of a job, the final entries covering materials, labor, and overhead are recorded on the job cost sheet (see below).

Then the following steps are performed:

1. All columns on the job cost sheet are totaled, and the amounts are entered in the Summary section.
2. The total cost is computed and entered.
3. The unit cost is determined and recorded.

JOB COST SHEET

CUSTOMER *Nelson Construction Company*
DESCRIPTION *Customer specs on file*
QUANTITY *100*

JOB *101*
DATE STARTED *10/1/X9*
DATE COMPLETED *10/18/X9*

| MATERIALS | | | DIRECT LABOR | | | | | | | | MANUFACTURING OVERHEAD APPLIED | | | | | | | | | | |
DATE	REQ. NO.	AMOUNT	DATE	REF.	CUTTING HRS.	AMOUNT	FRAMING HRS.	AMOUNT	ASSEMBLY HRS.	AMOUNT	DATE	REF.	CUTTING HRS.	RATE	AMOUNT	FRAMING HRS.	RATE	AMOUNT	ASSEMBLY HRS.	RATE	AMOUNT
10/1	R802	935 00	10/5	TTA	290	1902 00	220	1580 00	55	420 00	10/20	MOA 10	290	7.60	2204 00	220	6.34	1394 80	320	9.64	3084 80
10/2	R804	2805 00	10/12	TTA					95	685 00											
10/6	RM48	(85 00)	10/19	TTA					170	1215 00											
10/8	R809	1598 00																			
10/8	R817	119 00																			
10/16	R843	41 00																			
10/17	R848	27 00																			
10/18	R852	34 00																			
Total		5474 00			290	1902 00	220	1580 00	320	2320 00			290		2204 00	220		1394 80	320		3084 80

TOTAL COST $ *17,959.60*
UNITS PRODUCED *100*
COST PER UNIT $ *179.60*
COMMENTS:

Contract Price $18,200.00

SUMMARY	
MATERIALS	$ *5,474.00*
LABOR—MILLING	*1,902.00*
LABOR—ASSEMBLY	*1,580.00*
LABOR—FINISHING	*2,320.00*
OVERHEAD—MILLING	*2,204.00*
OVERHEAD—ASSEMBLY	*1,394.80*
OVERHEAD—FINISHING	*3,084.60*
TOTAL	$ *17,959.60*

Completed Jobs Journal

The job cost sheet is removed from the job cost ledger after the final calculations have been made. An entry to record the completion of the job is made in a special journal called a **completed jobs journal** (page 231).

At the end of the month, the total of the completed jobs journal is debited to Finished Goods and credited to Work in Process. The effect is shown on page 231.

COMPLETED JOBS JOURNAL
for Month of _October_   19 _X9_   Page ___10___

DATE		JOB NO.	MANUFACTURED FOR	FINISHED GOODS DR. 126 WORK IN PROCESS CR. 122 ✔	AMOUNT
Oct.	3	98	_Richard Wholesale Supply Co._	✓	26,573 82
	9	99	_Yorktown School District_	✓	48,628 05
	15	100	_Stock (Double-Hung 327)_	✓	11,743 20
	18	101	_Nelson Construction Co._	✓	17,959 60
	31		_Total_		225,158 28

19X9				
Oct. 31	Finished Goods	126	225,155.28	
	Work in Process	122		225,155.28
	Transferred cost of jobs completed during the month.			

When the transfer is posted, the balance of the Work in Process account, $31,328.78 (below), is the same as shown in the T account in Chapter 2.

Work in Process   NO. ___122___

DATE		EXPLANATION	POST. REF.	DEBIT	CREDIT	BALANCE	DR. CR.
19 X9							
Oct.	1	_Balance_	✓			43,651 40	DR.
	31	_Direct Materials Issued_	MR10	85,469 95		129,121 35	DR.
	31	_Direct Labor_	J10-48	66,597 00		195,718 35	DR.
	31	_Dir. Mat. Ret. to Storeroom_	RM10		862 60	194,855 75	DR.
	31	_Manufacturing Overhead Applied_	MOA10	61,628 31		256,484 06	DR.
	31	_Cost of Goods Completed_	CJ10		225,155 28	31,328 78	DR.

Proving the Job Cost Ledger

The balance of Work in Process 122 must equal the total of all costs charged to goods still in process at the end of the month. The cost accountant prepares a proof, in the form of a schedule of work in process, listing the uncompleted jobs and the costs that have been charged to them.

PANORAMA WINDOWS, INC.				
Schedule of Work in Process				
October 31, 19X9				
JOB	MATERIALS	LABOR	OVERHEAD	TOTAL
109	$4,492.08	$3,349.00	$3,019.06	$10,860.14
110	4,119.15	2,851.25	2,619.10	9,589.50
111	2,458.74	1,973.60	1,846.70	6,279.04
112	2,040.64	1,313.67	1,245.79	4,600.10
Total	$13,110.61	$9,487.52	$8,730.65	$31,328.78

Finished Goods Ledger

In the journal entry illustrated on page 231, finished goods costing $225,155.28 were transferred from Work in Process 122 to Finished Goods 126. Some of these goods were manufactured to customers' specifications (custom orders), and other goods were manufactured to be held for future sale (goods for stock). The treatment of custom orders will be discussed later in this chapter.

The completion of goods for stock is recorded in a **finished goods ledger** as well as in the completed jobs journal. This subsidiary ledger (Finished Goods 126 is the control account in the general ledger) consists of a stock ledger card for each type of product that the firm manufactures for stock. The design of the stock ledger card is very similar to the design of the materials ledger card discussed in Chapter 3. In fact, many companies use the same form for both ledgers.

The completion of 40 double-hung sash windows (Stock 327) at Panorama Windows is recorded as shown below.

STOCK LEDGER CARD

MATERIAL *Double-hung sash windows*   NUMBER *327*

DATE	REFERENCE	RECEIVED			SOLD			BALANCE		
		UNITS	PRICE	AMOUNT	UNITS	PRICE	AMOUNT	UNITS	PRICE	AMOUNT
19X9 Oct. 1	Bal.							20	28 00	5620 00
6	S-611				14	28 00	3934 00	6	28 00	1686 00
15	J-100	40	29 358	11743 20				6 } 40 }	28 00 29 358	13429 20

RECORDING SALES OF FINISHED GOODS

Operations flow from warehousing to selling. As goods are sold, they are shipped from the warehouse to the customers. The costs being recorded must be transferred from Finished Goods to Cost of Goods Sold to parallel this flow.

Sales From Stock

When finished goods that have been manufactured for stock are sold to a customer, the warehouse clerk receives a copy of the sales invoice. This invoice tells the clerk that goods have been sold and that an

At this point you should
be able to work Exer-
cises 11–1 to 11–3.

SELF-REVIEW

1. What accounts are debited and credited to record the transfer of completed goods to the warehouse?
2. The total of all the costs assigned to uncompleted jobs is equal to the balance of which general ledger account?
3. What is the name of the subsidiary ledger in which finished goods manufactured for stock are recorded?

Answers to Self-Review

1. Finished Goods is debited and Work in Process is credited to record the transfer of completed goods to the warehouse.
2. This total is equal to the balance of the Work in Process account.
3. Finished goods manufactured for stock are recorded in the finished goods ledger.

entry should be made in the finished goods ledger to show the sale of the goods and to record the new balance of goods on hand. Assume that on October 20, Panorama Windows sells 10 double-hung sash windows (Stock 327) at $380 each. The sale would be recorded on the stock ledger card as follows. (Note that the FIFO method of inventory valuation is used.)

STOCK LEDGER CARD

MATERIAL *Double-hung sash windows*   **NUMBER** *327*

DATE	REFERENCE	RECEIVED UNITS	RECEIVED PRICE	RECEIVED AMOUNT	SOLD UNITS	SOLD PRICE	SOLD AMOUNT	BALANCE UNITS	BALANCE PRICE	BALANCE AMOUNT
Oct. 1	Bal.							20	28100	562000
6	S-611				14	28100	393400	6	28100	168600
15	J-100	40	29358	1174320				6} 40}	28100 29358	1342920
20	S-621				6} 4}	28100 29358	286032	36	29358	1056888

As the entry on the stock ledger card is made, the cost of goods sold ($1,686.00 + $1,174.32 = $2,860.32) is entered on the Accounting Department's copy of the invoice. The information on the invoice copy then serves as the basis for an entry in a specially designed **sales journal** (page 234), in which both sales price (10 × $380 = $3,800) and cost of goods sold are recorded. (In some companies, cost data are entered on the shipping documents rather than on the invoice copy.)

Sales of Custom Orders

When a firm completes a job that has been manufactured to fill a customer's specifications, it ships the goods at once and records an entry in the sales journal. The sales journal on the middle of page

SALES JOURNAL		for Month of _October_			19 _X9_	Page _10_	
DATE	INVOICE NUMBER	CUSTOMER'S NAME	TERMS	✓	ACCOUNTS REC. DR. 111 SALES CR. 401	COST OF GOODS SOLD DR. 415 FINISHED GOODS CR. 126	
Oct. 3	610	Richard Wholesale Supply Company	n/30	✓	32,340 00	26,573 82	
6	611	Kible Supply	n/30	✓	5,670 60	4,362 00	
9	612	Yorktown School District	n/30	✓	61,785 10	48,628 05	
20	621	The Window Mart	n/30	✓	3,800 00	2,860 32	

234 shows a sale that Panorama Windows made to the Nelson Construction Company on October 18 for goods produced on Job 101.

Since the special-order goods never actually enter the warehouse stock, they are not picked up in the finished goods subsidiary ledger.

SALES JOURNAL		for Month of _October_			19 _X9_	Page _10_	
DATE	INVOICE NUMBER	CUSTOMER'S NAME	TERMS	✓	ACCOUNTS REC. DR. 111 SALES CR. 401	COST OF GOODS SOLD DR. 415 FINISHED GOODS CR. 126	
Oct. 3	610	Richard Wholesale Supply Company	n/30	✓	32,340 00	26,573 82	
6	611	Kible Supply	n/30	✓	5,670 60	4,362 00	
9	612	Yorktown School District	n/30	✓	61,785 10	48,628 05	
20	621	The Window Mart	n/30	✓	3,800 00	2,860 32	
18	622	Nelson Construction Co.	n/30	✓	18,200 00	17,959 60	
31		Total			298,761 80	221,690 78	

At the end of the month, the column totals of the sales journal are posted to the general ledger accounts. The effects of these postings are shown below in general journal form.

```
19X9
Oct. 31   Accounts Receivable        111   298,761.80
             Sales                   401              298,761.80
          Recorded sales for month.
      31  Cost of Goods Sold         415   221,690.78
             Finished Goods          126              221,690.78
          Recorded cost of goods sold
          during October.
```

Proving the Finished Goods Account

The firm's inventory of finished goods is a valuable asset that requires close watching. Therefore, at the end of each month, the cost accountant will prove the finished goods ledger to the control account, Finished Goods, in the general ledger.

		Finished Goods				NO.	126	
DATE		EXPLANATION	POST. REF.	DEBIT	CREDIT	BALANCE		DR. CR.
19 X9								
Oct. 1		Balance	✓			36,200	00	DR.
31		Cost of Goods						
		Completed	CJ10	225,155 28		261,355	28	DR.
31		Cost of Goods Sold	S10		221,690 78	39,664	52	DR.

The finished goods ledger is subsidiary to the Finished Goods account in the general ledger. Thus, at the end of the period, the total of the individual balances of the stock ledger cards should always agree with the balance of the control account. A schedule of finished goods is prepared from the subsidiary ledger at that time to prove it to the control account.

PANORAMA WINDOWS, INC.
Schedule of Finished Goods
October 31, 19X9

STOCK	STOCK NO.	UNITS	AMOUNT
Bay Windows	312	20	$ 8,806.00
Bow Windows	325	35	8,140.00
Eyebrow Windows	326	70	12,149.62
Double-Hung Sash Windows	327	36	10,568.88
Total			$39,664.50

Periodic inventories of finished goods must be taken. The procedures are much like those for taking inventory of raw materials, discussed on pages 109 to 112. Shortages of finished goods are usually charged to Cost of Goods Sold 415.

SELF-REVIEW

1. What two amounts are recorded in the sales journal for all products sold by the company?
2. The total of the balances on the stock ledger cards is equal to the balance of which general ledger account?

At this point you should be able to work Exercises 11–4 and 11–5 and Problems 11–3A to 11–4B.

Answers to Self-Review

1. Both the sales price and the cost of manufacturing the product are recorded in the sales journal.
2. This total is equal to the balance of the Finished Goods account.

BUSINESS HORIZON

Computerized Cost Accumulation

Using the computer to accumulate costs associated with the manufacturing process gives management immediate access to cost data and permits quick reaction to costing and pricing problems.

Consider the cost accounting system in place at the Bake House, Inc., a wholesale bakery supplying baked goods on a daily basis to local restaurants, clubs, hotels, and caterers. Bake House currently has five lines of bakery products: bread, dinner rolls, hamburger and hot dog buns, hoagie rolls, and doughnuts. Each line passes through three production stages: mixing, baking, and packaging.

Bake House has computerized its product costing and inventory systems. As materials, labor, and manufacturing overhead are added to the production process of a particular product, job costs are accumulated in a work-in-process file. Material quantities are input into the computer at the mixing station by passing the bar code on each bag or package of ingredients under an optical scanner as the materials are added to the product. Labor time is accumulated as workers in each of the production stages insert their badges into badge-reading terminals. The computer calculates materials and labor costs by multiplying the cost of materials or labor rates (stored in the computer's memory) by the quantity of materials used or hours worked. The computer also calculates overhead costs by multiplying standard overhead rates by labor hours.

When work on a product, such as hoagie rolls, is completed for the day, the costs related to hoagie rolls are transferred by the computer from the hoagie rolls work in process cost file to the finished goods inventory master file. As the rolls physically move from the bakery into the warehouse, another scanner reads the bar code on each finished box of hoagie rolls that is complete and ready to be moved. This signals the computer to reduce the work in process file and increase the finished goods file for the hoagie rolls.

Thus, the cost of any of the five products manufactured by Bake House is available to management at any time; the cost data can be called up on computer terminals, or computer printouts can be read. If costs appear to be too high at any stage of production, management can make changes in the production process. Management can also analyze costs for each product line. These costs may suggest that the prices of certain product lines should be raised or lowered. Timely information such as this may give the firm a pricing edge over its competition.

MANUFACTURING COSTS ON FINANCIAL STATEMENTS

The manufacturing costs for a fiscal period are reported in the form of a summary total in the Cost of Goods Sold section of the income statement as shown on page 237.

The details supporting the Cost of Goods Manufactured ($225,155.28) are shown in the statement of cost of goods manufactured.

PANORAMA WINDOWS, INC.
Income Statement
Month Ended October 31, 19X9

Revenue		
Sales		$298,761.80
Cost of Goods Sold		
Finished Goods Inventory, Oct. 1	$ 36,200.00	
Add Cost of Goods Manufactured	**225,155.28**	
Total Goods Available for Sale	$261,355.28	
Deduct Finished Goods Inventory,		
Oct. 31	39,664.50	
Cost of Goods Sold		221,690.78
Gross Profit on Sales		$ 77,071.02
Operating Expenses		
Selling Expenses	$ 18,969.30	
General Expenses	13,847.60	
Total Operating Expenses		32,816.90
Net Income Before Income Taxes		$ 44,254.12
Provision for Income Taxes		6,638.12
Net Income After Income Taxes		$ 37,616.00

PANORAMA WINDOWS, INC.
Statement of Cost of Goods Manufactured
Month Ended October 31, 19X9

Direct Materials		
Raw Materials Inventory, Oct. 1	$ 54,254.00	
Materials Purchases	86,970.00	
Total Materials Available	$141,224.00	
Deduct Raw Materials Inventory,		
Oct. 31	50,805.00	
Total Materials Used	$ 90,419.00	
Deduct Indirect Materials Used	5,811.65	
Direct Materials Used		$ 84,607.35
Direct Labor		66,597.00
Manufacturing Overhead Applied		61,628.31
Total Manufacturing Cost		$ 212,832.66
Add Work in Process Inventory,		
Oct. 1		43,651.40
		$ 256,484.06
Deduct Work in Process Inventory,		
Oct. 31		31,328.78
Cost of Goods Manufactured		**$225,155.28**

Only manufacturing overhead applied is shown on the statement of cost of goods manufactured. A supplementary schedule, the schedule of manufacturing overhead, is prepared, giving the details of the actual overhead costs incurred and the underapplied or overapplied overhead for the period. Another option is to show all the details of manufacturing overhead directly on the statement of cost of goods manufactured.

PANORAMA WINDOWS, INC. Schedule of Manufacturing Overhead Month Ended October 31, 19X9	
Actual Overhead Costs Incurred	
Indirect Materials	$ 5,811.65
Indirect Labor	35,335.00
Payroll Taxes	8,539.15
Depreciation—Buildings	2,250.00
Depreciation—Equipment	3,460.00
Repairs and Maintenance	2,543.60
Utilities	4,283.75
Insurance	974.05
Property Taxes	621.00
Other Overhead Costs	415.26
Total Actual Overhead Costs Incurred	$64,233.46
Deduct Underapplied Overhead for October	2,605.15
Manufacturing Overhead Applied	$61,628.31

At this point you should be able to work Problems 11–1A, 11–2A, 11–5A, 11–1B, and 11–2B.

The statements shown above and on page 237 are the same as the statements illustrated in Chapter 2. You have now learned how every figure on the statement of cost of goods manufactured is developed.

PRINCIPLES AND PROCEDURES SUMMARY

■ When a factory completes a job, all costs are totaled, and the total cost of the job is transferred from Work in Process to Finished Goods. If the goods are manufactured for stock, the cost of the completed goods is also recorded in the finished goods ledger.
■ The sale of merchandise from stock is recorded as follows:
  ■ A deduction is made on the appropriate stock ledger card.
  ■ The sales price and the cost of the goods sold are recorded in the sales journal.
■ At the end of the month, summary postings are made from the sales journal to transfer the total cost of the goods sold during month as a debit to Cost of Goods Sold and a credit to Finished Goods and to transfer the total sales for the month as a debit to Accounts Receivable and a credit to Sales.

- Also at the end of the month, the finished goods ledger is proved to its control account, Finished Goods. The accountant prepares a schedule of finished goods, the total of which should agree with the balance of the control account in the general ledger.
- The cost of goods manufactured appears on the financial statements of the firm in two ways:
  - In the Cost of Goods Sold section of the income statement, these costs are represented by a summary total.
  - In the statement of cost of goods manufactured, all facts are supplied in detail.
- Accounting for the completion of goods and for the sale of goods are the last two phases of the typical job order cost accounting cycle.

MANAGERIAL IMPLICATIONS

- Accounting records are designed to save time and effort. For this reason, with job order cost accounting a completed jobs journal accumulates information to be used to remove the costs of completed jobs from the Work in Process account and transfer the costs to Finished Goods.
- If the goods manufactured are not sold immediately on completion, they are entered on a stock ledger card. The stock ledger cards make up the finished goods subsidiary ledger in the Finished Goods account.
- If a job has been completed to fill a customer's order, the products normally are not entered on stock ledger cards.
- At the end of each month, the Finished Goods account is proved by comparing its balance with the total of the stock ledger cards. If the account does not balance with the stock ledger cards, the accountant must determine the reason and correct the difference.
- As part of the control cycle, inventories of finished goods must be taken periodically and compared with the stock ledger cards. Again, any difference must be explained and corrected as part of the accountant's control procedures.

REVIEW QUESTIONS

1. What general ledger account is charged for the cost of jobs completed? Is the entry a debit or a credit to this account?
2. What information does a completed jobs journal provide? What is the source for entries in this journal? Describe a typical entry.
3. Work in Process is a control account in the general ledger. The balances in what subsidiary records must equal the balance of this account?
4. Why is a schedule of work in process prepared?
5. What is the control account for the finished goods ledger?
6. Why should a physical inventory of finished goods be taken?
7. How are shortages of finished goods accounted for?

8. When finished goods are sold, what two amounts must be recorded in the sales journal? Describe a typical entry.
9. Are special-order goods entered in the finished goods ledger? Explain.
10. Which inventory accounts appear on the statement of cost of goods manufactured? On the income statement? On the balance sheet?

MANAGERIAL DISCUSSION QUESTIONS

1. What are the benefits of using special journals such as the completed jobs journal?
2. When a job is completed, management should review the job cost sheet. Which cost items would management look at most closely? Why?
3. What are the limitations on the usefulness to management of the statement of cost of goods manufactured? Why?
4. What are the advantages of maintaining a perpetual inventory record for finished goods?
5. If the monthly schedule of manufacturing overhead shows that overhead was overapplied or underapplied, what additional information about this item would management want to have?

EXERCISES

EXERCISE 11-1   **Total job costs.   (Obj. 2).**   The O'Brien Manufacturing Company finished Job 357 for 350 engines on July 30, 19X9. The following costs were recorded on the job cost sheet:

Materials	$46,560
Labor—Milling	38,890
Labor—Assembly	42,350
Labor—Finishing	34,238
Overhead—Milling	11,560
Overhead—Assembly	14,167
Overhead—Finishing	10,007

Complete the following calculations. (You may want to review Chapter 1 on prime and conversion costs.)
a. What are the prime costs for this job?
b. What are the conversion costs?
c. Determine the total cost for this job and the unit cost for each engine.

EXERCISE 11-2   **Journalize the cost of completed jobs.   (Obj. 2).**   At the end of June, the total of the completed jobs journal was $673,930. Prepare the entry in general journal form to record the cost of the completed jobs.

EXERCISE 11-3   **Analyze Work in Process account postings.   (Obj. 4).**   The Work in Process account for the Welsh Supply Corporation is shown on page 241. All journal entries for the month of November have been posted. Describe each of the six postings.

Work in Process					NO.	122	
DATE	EXPLANATION	POST. REF.	DEBIT	CREDIT	BALANCE		DR. CR.
19 X9							
Nov. 1	(a)	✓			35,790	65	DR.
30	(b)	MR11	65,830 20		101,620	85	DR.
30	(c)	J11-38	82,438 56		184,059	41	DR.
30	(d)	RM11		1,463 90	182,595	51	DR.
30	(e)	MOA11	58,741 82		241,337	33	DR.
30	(f)	CJ11		202,812 38	38,524	95	DR.

EXERCISE 11–4   **Record cost of goods sold and sales. (Obj. 5).**   For the month of May 19X9, the Carnegie Steel Corporation sold goods that cost $1,256,240 to produce. The corporation billed its customers $1,984,820 for these goods. Prepare the entries in general journal form record the cost of goods sold and the sales for the month.

EXERCISE 11–5   **Calculate gross profit. (Obj. 6).**   The sales journal for the Nevada Machine Company is shown below.

SALES JOURNAL		for Month of May		19 X9	Page 5		
DATE	INVOICE NUMBER	CUSTOMER'S NAME	TERMS	✓	ACCOUNTS REC. DR. 111 SALES CR. 401	COST OF GOODS SOLD DR. 415 FINISHED GOODS CR. 126	
May 4	501	Washington Supply Co.	n/30	✓	23,400 00	15,212 80	
8	502	Page & Orlez Co.	n/30	✓	36,250 00	23,562 68	
10	503	Riverton Wholesale Co.	n/30	✓	25,850 00	16,921 53	
15	504	Flatlands Machine Corp.	n/30	✓	43,150 00	48,390 15	
22	505	Rosenberg Supply Co.	n/30	✓	34,200 00	22,237 83	
29	506	Davis Industrial Supply	n/30	✓	18,400 00	7,692 71	
		Total			181,250 00	134,017 70	
					(111) (401)	(415) (216)	

a. Calculate the amount of gross profit (or loss) for each job and the total gross profit for the month.

b. What was the gross profit percentage for the total sales for the month?

PROBLEMS

PROBLEM 11–1A   **Journalize manufacturing cost transactions. (Obj. 1).**   The Wilson Company is a manufacturer of fire alarm equipment. During the month of July 19X9, the firm had the following transactions and incurred the following costs:

a. Raw materials were purchased on credit for $24,570.

b. Direct materials costing $19,530 and indirect materials costing $11,780 were used during the month.

c. Factory wages paid during the month totaled $23,650. The deductions were: social security taxes, $1,490; medicare taxes, $355; federal income taxes, $3,548; and group insurance premiums, $496.

d. Direct labor costs were $22,430 and indirect labor costs were $2,530, as shown on the summary of factory wages for the month.

e. Vouchers for various types of manufacturing overhead costs totaled $8,220 and were recorded in the voucher register.

f. Depreciation for the month was $9,700 on the factory building and $4,500 on factory equipment and tools.

g. Expired factory insurance for the month totaled $810.

h. Accrued property taxes on the factory for the month were $1,595.

i. Employer's payroll taxes were: social security taxes, $1,490; medicare taxes, $355; federal unemployment taxes, $180; and state unemployment taxes, $370.

j. Manufacturing overhead applied to the job cost sheets during the month totaled $24,650.

k. Jobs completed and transferred to finished goods cost $47,340.

l. Cost of goods sold during the month was $39,245. The sales were made on credit for $53,970. (Prepare two separate entries.)

INSTRUCTIONS Prepare the general journal entries to record the above transactions. Date the entries July 31.

PROBLEM 11–2A **Journalize and post transactions. (Obj. 1).** The Chan Company manufactures a single product. On June 1, 19X9, the company's inventory accounts showed the following balances:

Raw Materials	$52,300
Work in Process	50,500
Finished Goods	73,000

Transactions that occurred during the month of June are summarized below.

a. Raw materials were purchased on credit for $100,380.

b. Direct materials costing $88,120 and indirect materials costing $9,380 were used during the month.

c. Factory wages earned during June totaled $67,200. (Credit Salaries and Wages Payable 202; payroll taxes should be ignored.)

d. Direct labor costs for the month amounted to $49,000, and indirect labor costs amounted to $18,200.

Additional factory costs incurred are as follows:

e. Employer's payroll taxes, $4,610 (credit Taxes Payable 212).

f. Machinery repairs, $1,720 (credit Vouchers Payable 201).

g. Depreciation for the month on the factory building, $3,080; on factory equipment, $5,600.

h. Factory insurance expired, $590.

i. Property taxes accrued, $2,378.

j. Manufacturing overhead chargeable to Work in Process is estimated at $47,115.

k. Jobs completed and transferred to finished goods cost $186,755.

l. Cost of goods sold during the month, $197,015. Price of goods sold (on credit) during the month, $262,555. (Prepare two entries.)

INSTRUCTIONS

1. Open accounts for Raw Materials 121, Work in Process 122, Finished Goods 126, Sales 401, Cost of Goods Sold 415, Factory Payroll Clearing 500, and Manufacturing Overhead Control 501.
2. Enter the beginning balances in the three inventory accounts.
3. Record the above transactions in general journal form. Date the entries June 30.
4. Post to the accounts provided. (No accounts have been opened for some asset and liability items.)
5. Prepare a schedule of manufacturing overhead costs showing the underapplied or overapplied overhead and the overhead applied to production, and prepare a statement of cost of goods manufactured.
6. Prepare an income statement for the month, assuming that selling expenses totaled $30,880 and the general and administrative expenses totaled $13,600.

PROBLEM 11–3A

Complete a job cost sheet. **(Obj. 2).** Built-Rite Manufacturers uses a job order cost system. The data below applies to Job 6-6B, which is for 150 Model MT-4 tables ordered by the Belmont Furniture Store. The job was started on June 10, 19X9.

Materials

June 10, Requisition 314, $1,500
June 15, Requisition 331, $520
June 20, Requisition 360, $160
June 22, Returned Materials Report 18, $32 (materials returned to storeroom)

Labor

Week ended June 14:
  Milling department, 120 hours, $630
  Assembly Department, 55 hours, $325
Week ended June 21:
  Milling Department, 30 hours, $157.50
  Assembly Department, 110 hours, $561
Week ended June 28:
  Assembly Department, 12 hours, $63
  Finishing department, 45 hours, $229.50

The job was completed on June 26, and overhead was applied as follows:

Milling Department	$4.05 per direct labor hour
Assembly Department	4.30 per direct labor hour
Finishing Department	6.80 per direct labor hour

INSTRUCTIONS

Complete a job cost sheet for this job.

PROBLEM 11–4A

Record finished jobs and sales. **(Obj. 1).** The Durand Company is a manufacturer of warm-up suits. It manufactures standard gray men's, women's, and children's models for stock. In addition, the Durand Company accepts custom orders from colleges and universities to produce warm-up suits in the schools' colors.

On March 1, 19X9, the company's inventory accounts showed the following balances:

Work in Process $6,215
Finished Goods 4,375

On March 1, 19X9, the finished goods ledger included three stock ledger cards, with the following information:

Number	Stock Item	Balance
100	Men's Warm-Up Suits	100 at $20 each
101	Women's Warm-Up Suits	125 at $15 each
102	Children's Warm-Up Suits	50 at $10 each

Transactions relating to completion and sales of warm-up suits for the month of March were as follows:

Mar. 4 Completed Job 20 for 60 men's warm-up suits at a cost of $20 each and transferred the goods to the warehouse.

7 Completed Job 21 for 50 women's warm-up suits at a cost of $15 each and transferred the goods to the warehouse.

11 Completed Job 22 for 24 blue and white warm-up suits for Granville College and shipped the goods to the customer. Issued Invoice 109. The cost to manufacture was $18 each, and the price was $27 each.

14 Sold 30 women's warm-up suits to the Lindberg Department Store at a price of $23 each. Issued Invoice 110.

17 Sold 75 men's warm-up suits to the Western Sporting Goods Store for $30 each. Issued Invoice 111.

19 Completed Job 23 for 45 children's warm-up suits at a cost of $10 each and transferred the goods to the warehouse.

25 Completed Job 24 for 15 red and gold women's warm-up suits for Northern Utah University and shipped the goods to the customer. Issued Invoice 112. The cost to manufacture was $16 each, and the price was $24 each.

27 Completed Job 25 for 120 men's warm-up suits at a cost of $20 each and transferred the goods to the warehouse.

29 Sold 100 men's warm-up suits at a price of $30 each to the Timberline Pro Shop. Issued Invoice 113.

INSTRUCTIONS

1. Open general ledger accounts for the following: Accounts Receivable 111, Work in Process 122, Finished Goods 126, Sales 401, and Cost of Goods Sold 415. Enter the March 1, 19X9, balances in the inventory accounts.

2. Open stock ledger cards in the finished goods ledger as follows: Men's Warm-up Suits, Number 100; Women's Warm-up Suits, Number 101; and Children's Warm-up Suits, Number 102. Enter the March 1, 19X9, balances.

3. Record the March transactions in the completed jobs journal and the sales journal. Use page number 12.

4. Post the jobs manufactured for stock to the finished goods ledger.
5. Post the summary totals of the completed jobs journal and the sales journals to the general ledger accounts.
6. Prepare a schedule of finished goods. This schedule should agree with which account in the general ledger?

PROBLEM 11–5A   **Analyze manufacturing cost transactions. (Obj. 3).** NOTE: The transaction listing for this problem is provided only in the *Study Guide and Working Papers*.

This problem illustrates the flow of work in job order cost accounting and the flow of costs through the accompanying general ledger accounts. Selected transactions for Panorama Windows are given in the first column of the forms in the *Study Guide and Working Papers*.

INSTRUCTIONS   Analyze each transaction given in the *Study Guide and Working Papers*. Insert a check mark in the appropriate debit or credit column of the general ledger accounts affected. Transaction 1 has been completed as an example.

ALTERNATE PROBLEMS

PROBLEM 11–1B   **Journalize manufacturing cost transactions. (Obj. 1).** Bentley's Custom Wood Shop is a manufacturer of custom-designed furniture. During the month of July 19X9, the firm had the following transactions and incurred the following costs:

a. Raw materials were purchased on credit for $33,720.
b. Direct materials costing $24,050 and indirect materials costing $8,470 were used during the month.
c. Factory wages paid during the month totaled $52,140. The deductions were: social security taxes, $3,285; medicare taxes, $782; federal income taxes, $7,821; and group insurance premiums, $620.
d. Direct labor costs were $44,060 and indirect labor costs were $10,865, as shown on the summary of factory wages for the month.
e. Vouchers for various types of manufacturing overhead costs totaled $30,290 and were recorded in the voucher register.
f. Depreciation for the month was $1,820 on the factory building and $395 on the factory equipment and tools.
g. Expired factory insurance for the month totaled $2,090.
h. Accrued property taxes on the factory for the month were $4,270.
i. Employer's payroll taxes were: social security taxes, $3,285; medicare taxes, $782; federal unemployment taxes, $317; and state unemployment taxes, $1,564.
j. Manufacturing overhead applied to the job cost sheets during the month totaled $63,155.
k. Jobs completed and transferred to finished goods cost $123,265.
l. Cost of goods sold during the month was $110,500. The sales were made on credit for $135,915. (Prepare two separate entries.)

INSTRUCTIONS   Prepare the general journal entries to record the above transactions. Date the entries July 31.

PROBLEM 11–2B

Journalize and post transactions. (Obj. 1). The Nadal Company manufactures a single product. On June 1, 19X9, the company's inventory accounts showed the following balances:

Raw Materials $34,570
Work in Process 24,800
Finished Goods 41,600

Transactions that occurred during the month of June are summarized below.

a. Raw materials were purchased on credit for $40,400.
b. Direct materials costing $37,071 and indirect materials costing $8,250 were used during the month.
c. Factory wages earned during June totaled $56,265. (Credit Salaries and Wages Payable 202; payroll taxes should be ignored.)
d. Direct labor costs for the month amounted to $45,800, and indirect labor costs amounted to $12,592.
Additional factory costs incurred are as follows:
e. Employer's payroll taxes, $7,720 (credit Taxes Payable 212).
f. Machinery repairs, $3,540 (credit Vouchers Payable 201).
g. Depreciation for the month on the factory building, $690; on factory equipment, $4,140.
h. Factory insurance expired, $420.
i. Property taxes accrued, $910.
j. Manufacturing overhead chargeable to Work in Process is estimated at $29,017.
k. Jobs completed and transferred to finished goods cost $114,157.
l. Cost of goods sold during the month, $127,422. Price of goods sold (on credit) during the month, $150,290. (Prepare two entries.)

INSTRUCTIONS

1. Open accounts for Raw Materials 121, Work in Process 122, Finished Goods 126, Sales 401, Cost of Goods Sold 415, Factory Payroll Clearing 500, and Manufacturing Overhead Control 501.
2. Enter the beginning balances in the three inventory accounts.
3. Record the above transactions in general journal form. Date the entries June 30.
4. Post to the accounts provided. (No accounts have been opened for some asset and liability items.)
5. Prepare a schedule of manufacturing overhead costs showing the underapplied or overapplied overhead and the overhead applied to production, and prepare a statement of cost of goods manufactured.
6. Prepare an income statement for the month, assuming that selling expenses totaled $15,800 and the general and administrative expenses totaled $7,720.

PROBLEM 11–3B

Complete a job cost sheet. (Obj. 2). The Crane Desk Company uses a job order cost system. The data below applies to Job 11-24, which is for 600 Model F-108 desks ordered by the Mott Office Equipment Store. The job was started on November 14, 19X9.

Materials

November 14, Requisition 811, $4,016
November 19, Requisition 825, $1,055
November 24, Requisition 840, $179
November 27, Returned Materials Report 64, $60 (materials returned to storeroom)

Labor

Week ended November 14:
  Milling Department, 130 hours, $728
Week ended November 21:
  Milling Department, 95 hours, $532
  Assembly Department, 40 hours, $232
Week ended November 28:
  Assembly Department, 55 hours, $319
  Finishing Department, 90 hours, $540

The job was completed on November 27, and overhead was applied as follows:

Milling Department	$4.85 per direct labor hour
Assembly Department	3.60 per direct labor hour
Finishing Department	6.40 per direct labor hour

INSTRUCTIONS   Complete a job cost sheet for this job.

PROBLEM 11–4B   **Record finished jobs and sales. (Obj. 1).** The Walko Company is a manufacturer of desk sets. It manufactures standard desk sets for stock. In addition, the Walko Company accepts custom orders from colleges and universities to produce desk sets imprinted with the schools' logos.

On April 1, 19X9, the company's inventory accounts showed the following balances:

Work in Process	$7,512
Finished Goods	4,375

On April 1, 19X9, the finished goods ledger included three stock ledger cards, with the following information:

Number	Stock Item	Balance
134	Leather Desk Sets, Gold Trim	100 at $20
135	Leather Desk Sets, Plain	125 at $15
136	Plastic Desk Sets, Plain	50 at $10

Transactions relating to completion and sales of desk sets for the month of April were as follows:

Apr. 6   Completed Job 51 for 70 leather desk sets, gold trim, at a cost of $20 each and transferred the goods to the warehouse.

8 Completed Job 52 for 40 leather desk sets, plain, at a cost of $15 each and transferred the goods to the warehouse.

13 Completed Job 53 for 24 desk sets with school logo for Mississippi College and shipped the goods to the customer. Issued Invoice 403. The cost to manufacture was $17 each, and the price was $29 a dozen.

17 Sold 35 leather desk sets, plain, to Indorato Office Supply Company at a price of $24 a dozen. Issued Invoice 404.

19 Sold 80 leather desk sets, gold trim, to the Omega Gift Store for $30 each. Issued Invoice 405.

23 Completed Job 54 for 45 plastic desk sets, plain, at a cost of $10 each and transferred the goods to the warehouse.

26 Completed Job 55 for 20 desk sets with school logo for Northern Utah University and shipped the goods to the customer. Issued Invoice 406. The cost to manufacture was $16 each and the price was $24 each.

28 Completed Job 56 for 130 leather desk sets, gold trim, at a cost of $20 each and transferred the goods to the warehouse.

30 Sold 110 leather desk sets, gold trim, at a price of $30 each to the Braun Department Store. Issued Invoice 407.

INSTRUCTIONS

1. Open general ledger accounts for the following: Accounts Receivable 111, Work in Process 122, Finished Goods 126, Sales 401, and Cost of Goods Sold 415. Enter the April 1, 19X9, balances in the inventory accounts.
2. Open stock ledger cards in the finished goods ledger as follows: Leather Desk Sets, Gold Trim, Number 100; Leather Desk Sets, Plain, Number 101; and Plastic Desk Sets, Plain, Number 102. Enter the April 1, 19X9, balances.
3. Record the April transactions in the completed jobs journal and the sales journal. Use page number 12.
4. Post the jobs manufactured for stock to the finished goods ledger.
5. Post the summary totals of the completed jobs journal and the sales journals to the general ledger accounts.
6. Prepare a schedule of finished goods. This schedule should agree with which account in the general ledger?

MANAGERIAL DECISION CASE

Glass Works is a small manufacturer of one-of-a-kind contemporary glass art. Several artists are employed by Glass Works to produce the glass artwork the company sells.

The only records the company kept of the objects made during January were job cost sheets showing the material cost and labor cost of each job. A summary of these costs is given on page 249.

Job Number	Material Cost	Labor Cost	Status of Job
1*	$160	$600	Sold, January 16
2	140	500	Completed, January 18
3	90	670	Sold, January 20
4	250	420	Completed, January 25
5	205	260	Still in process, January 31
6	115	150	Still in process, January 31

*Job 1 was started in December. Costs charged to Job 1 in December were: materials, $40; labor, $80; overhead, $40. There were no finished goods on January 1.

Glass Works applies overhead to each job at 50 percent of labor cost. The glass art objects produced are priced to generate a 60 percent gross profit. Using the above data, compute the following:

a. Cost of each job worked on during January
b. Balance of Work in Process on January 31
c. Balance of Finished Goods on January 31
d. Cost of Goods Manufactured for January
e. Cost of Goods Sold for January

Prepare an income statement for Glass Works for January. Selling expenses were $1,735, and administrative expenses were $825. The company's tax rate is 30 percent.

Job Order Cost Accounting

You have learned how to account for the basic elements of manufacturing costs. This practice set combines these various techniques and principles in a practical application for Porch and Garden Company, Inc. You will be required to perform the duties not only of the cost accountant but also of the storeroom clerk, voucher clerk, and other factory personnel.

PORCH AND GARDEN COMPANY, INC.

Porch and Garden Company, Inc., is a manufacturer of outdoor furniture for the porch, deck, and garden. The company fabricates metal and plastic chairs and tables in a variety of styles and sizes. These tables and chairs are popular because they are sturdy, easy to handle, and able to withstand the weather. Production is divided between custom orders and standard models manufactured for stock.

The Production Division consists of three producing departments and two service departments. The producing departments are Shaping, Assembly, and Finishing. The service departments are Building Services and General Factory. The production process begins in the Shaping Department, where metal and plastic are shaped into the component parts that make up the finished product. These parts are transferred to the Assembly Department, where they are assembled. In the Finishing Department, a variety of finishes are applied to the assembled chairs and tables. The Building Services and General Factory departments perform activities similar to those described for Panorama Windows in this text. Finished products are sold to department stores, specialty shops, and discount outlets across the country.

COST ACCOUNTING SYSTEM

Porch and Garden's cost accounting system includes a number of journals, ledgers, and cost accounting forms. All forms required are found in the *Study Guide and Working Papers*. Entries have been made on these forms where indicated. If you are not using the *Study Guide and Working Papers*, you will have to record on appropriate forms all the data shown on pages 259 to 265 of this text.

JOURNALS

The seven journals used for making original entries are listed here, as are the initials to be used for posting references.

Voucher Register	VR
Materials Requisition Journal	MR
Returned Materials Journal	RM

Manufacturing Overhead Applied Journal   MOA
Completed Jobs Journal   CJ
Sales Journal   S
General Journal (vouchers)   J

GENERAL LEDGER

The firm's chart of accounts includes the following accounts, relating to the flow of manufacturing costs. The balances as of June 1, 19X9, are given.

121   Raw Materials, $50,784.00
122   Work in Process, $13,728.73
126   Finished Goods, $28,648.70
401   Sales, $-0-
415   Cost of Goods Sold, $-0-
500   Factory Payroll Clearing, $20,480
501   Manufacturing Overhead Control, $-0-
502   Manufacturing Overhead—Shaping Department, $-0-
503   Manufacturing Overhead—Assembly Department, $-0-
504   Manufacturing Overhead—Finishing Department, $-0-
505   Manufacturing Overhead—Building Services Department, $-0-
506   Manufacturing Overhead—General Factory Department, $-0-
507   Overapplied or Underapplied Manufacturing Overhead, $5,194.00 Dr.

The June 1 balances and the postings occurring between June 1 and June 25 have been recorded in the general ledger accounts.

SUBSIDIARY LEDGERS

Four subsidiary cost ledgers are used, and the necessary forms are provided in the *Study Guide and Working Papers*. Porch and Garden uses the FIFO method of costing all inventories.

Materials Ledger. In order to simplify the work in this practice set, the materials ledger, which actually contains several dozen materials ledger cards, has been condensed to four cards showing the activities up to the close of business on June 25. (See pages 261 and 262.) You will make detailed entries for Materials T-23 (glass tops, circular), L-16 (legs, plastic), and P-42 (polishing cloths). All other materials are summarized in total on the fourth materials ledger card, and no entries are required on it.

Job Cost Ledger. The job cost ledger currently consists of four job cost sheets. Job 211 was begun in May; Jobs 218, 219, and 220 were started in June. Various entries have been posted through June 25.

Departmental Overhead Analysis Sheets. Overhead analysis sheets are provided for each of the five departments in the organization: Shaping, Assembly, Finishing, Building Services, and General Factory.

The first entry on each sheet summarizes the postings of June 1 through June 25.

Finished Goods Ledger. The finished goods ledger consists of three stock ledger cards showing all postings through June 25. (See pages 264 and 265.) You will make entries involving two types of finished goods—chairs (Stock 129) and tables (Stock 458)—as required during the remainder of the month. All other types of finished goods are summarized on the third card, and no entries are required on it.

TRANSACTIONS

Record the following daily transactions in the proper journals. Post to the subsidiary ledgers daily.

JUNE 26

Materials Issued. Requisition 613 for 30 units of Material T-23 for Job 211. Requisition 614 for 100 units of Material L-16 for Job 218.

When you record a requisition for direct materials, you will perform the duties of both the storeroom clerk and the cost clerk. (See Chapter 4.) The following recording steps are required:

1. Compute the cost and enter the requisition on the materials ledger card.
2. Record the appropriate entries in the materials requisition journal.
3. Post to the job cost sheet.

JUNE 27

Materials Received. 400 units at $15.95 each of Material L-16, obtained on Purchase Order 2194, from the Century Plastic Company, Voucher 6-72.

When you record receipts of materials, you will perform the work normally assigned to the storeroom clerk and the voucher clerk. (See Chapter 3.) The following recording steps are required:

1. Record the receipt on the materials ledger card.
2. Enter the voucher in the voucher register.

Materials Issued. Requisition 615 for 18 units of Material T-23 for Job 220.

JUNE 28

Materials Issued. Requisition 616 for 150 units of Material L-16 for Job 219. Requisition 617 for 100 units of Material P-42 for the Finishing Department.

Remember that issues of indirect materials require a different recording procedure. (See Chapter 4.)

1. Enter the issue on the materials ledger card.
2. Record the issue in the materials requisition journal.
3. Post to the departmental overhead analysis sheet.

Sale of Finished Goods. Sold 55 chairs (Stock 129) to the Hornes Department Store for $160.50 each on Invoice 716; terms 2/10, n/30.

For sales, the following recording steps are required. (See Chapter 11.)

1. Enter the issue on the finished goods stock ledger card.
2. Record the sale in the sales journal.

JUNE 29

Materials Issued. Requisition 618 for 450 units of Material T-23 for Job 219. Requisition 619 for 100 units of Material P-42 for the Finishing Department.

Materials Received. 1,000 units at $2.25 each of Material T-23, obtained on Purchase Order 2195, from the Ambridge Glass Company, Voucher 6-73.

Services Received. Repairs to equipment in the Shaping Department performed by South Hills Repair for $290, Voucher 6-74.

For transactions of this type, the following recording steps are required (see Chapter 8):

1. Enter the voucher in the voucher register.
2. Post to the departmental overhead analysis sheet.

Sale of Finished Goods. Sold 100 tables (Stock 458) to Ryan Discount Centers for $32 each on Invoice 717; terms 2/10, n/30.

JUNE 30

Materials Issued. Requisition 620 for 300 units of Material T-23 for Job 218. Requisition 621 for 200 units of Material P-42 for the Finishing Department.

Materials Returned to Storeroom. 20 units of Material T-23, originally issued on June 26, Requisition 613, for Job 211. Returned Materials report 70 has been prepared.

Complete the entries normally made by the storeroom clerk and the cost clerk. (See Chapter 4.) The following recording steps are required:

1. Determine the cost and make the entry (in parentheses) in the Issued section of the materials ledger card.
2. Post to the job cost sheet.
3. Record the return in the returned materials journal.

Sale of Finished Goods. Sold 50 tables (Stock 458) to the Garden Design Company for $32 each on Invoice 718; terms 2/10, n/30.

Services Received. Utilities for factory operations in June, payable to Edison Utilities, Voucher 6-75. The cost of $2,062 should be allocated as follows to the departments:

Shaping	$502
Assembly	90
Finishing	190
Building Services	903
General Factory	377

INTERIM PROCEDURES

Complete the necessary recording and posting relating to the weekly and semimonthly payrolls.

WEEKLY PAYROLL REGISTER

The weekly payroll register for June 24 through 30 shows the following:

Gross earnings	$26,490.00
Social security taxes withheld	1,668.89
Medicare taxes withheld	397.36
Income taxes withheld	4,503.35
Group insurance withheld	364.66

Record the payroll using a general journal voucher (6-1), since the factory payroll register is not provided. Then post the gross earnings to the Factory Payroll Clearing account. Other items are not posted because no accounts are provided for them.

ANALYSIS OF TIME TICKETS

All analysis of the time tickets for the week ended June 30 is shown on page 251. The following recording steps are required:

1. Post direct labor to the job cost sheets.
2. Post indirect labor to the departmental overhead analysis sheets.

SEMIMONTHLY PAYROLL REGISTER

The semimonthly payroll register for June 16 through June 30 shows the following:

Gross earnings	$6,056.00
Social security taxes withheld	381.53
Medicare taxes withheld	151.40
Income taxes withheld	1,211.20
Group insurance withheld	160.56

Enter as you did the weekly payroll, using a general journal voucher (6-2).

ANALYSIS OF SEMIMONTHLY PAYROLL

An analysis of the semimonthly payroll for June 16 through June 30 shows the following charges to be posted to the respective departmental overhead analysis sheets:

Building Services	$1,756
General Factory	4,300
	$6,056

PORCH AND GARDEN COMPANY, INC.
Analysis of Time Tickets
Week Ended June 30, 19X9

DIRECT LABOR

JOB	SHAPING HOURS	SHAPING AMOUNT	ASSEMBLY HOURS	ASSEMBLY AMOUNT	FINISHING HOURS	FINISHING AMOUNT	TOTAL
211			185	$1,526.80	110	$1,248.00	$ 2,774.80
218	113	$ 958.00	133	1,103.90	148	1,702.00	3,763.90
219	235	2,021.00	356	2,954.80	240	2,760.00	7,735.80
220	285	2,451.00	165	1,369.50	-0-	-0-	3,820.50
	633	$5,430.00	839	$6,955.00	498	$5,710.00	$18,095.00

INDIRECT LABOR

DEPARTMENT	REGULAR EARNINGS	OVERTIME PREMIUM	TOTAL
Shaping	$ 900.00	$529.00	$1,429.00
Assembly	1,530.00	-0-	1,530.00
Finishing	833.00	426.00	1,259.00
Building Services	1,842.00	-0-	1,842.00
General Factory	2,335.00	-0-	2,335.00
	$7,440.00	$955.00	$8,395.00

END-OF-MONTH PROCEDURES

The end-of-month procedures for Porch and Garden will be completed in the order in which you studied the cost accounting elements: materials, labor, and manufacturing overhead.

MATERIALS

Total the following journals and post to the appropriate general ledger accounts:

1. Voucher register
2. Materials requisition journal
3. Returned materials journal

LABOR

A summary of factory wages for the month must be completed before labor costs can be charged to production.

1. Enter the weekly payroll figures for the week ended June 30 and the semimonthly payroll for the period ended June 30 in the partially completed monthly summary provided. (See page 265.)
2. Total the summary and compute the total direct labor and indirect labor.
3. Prepare a general journal voucher (6-3) to transfer the cost of labor used during the month from Factory Payroll Clearing 500

to Work in Process 122 (direct labor) and to Manufacturing Overhead Control 501 (indirect labor).

4. Post to the general ledger accounts supplied.

Next, the employer's payroll taxes for the month must be entered in the accounting records. The summary of taxable factory wages for June follows. (NOTE: SUTA is used for state unemployment insurance tax.)

PORCH AND GARDEN COMPANY, INC.
Summary of Taxable Factory Wages
June 19X9

| | WAGES SUBJECT TO | | |
DEPARTMENT	SOCIAL SECURITY TAX	MEDICARE TAX	FUTA AND SUTA TAXES
Shaping	$ 30,085.00	$ 30,085.00	$ 3,785.00
Assembly	35,774.00	35,774.00	4,105.00
Finishing	30,397.00	30,397.00	2,384.00
Building Services	11,231.00	11,231.00	750.00
General Factory	18,003.00	18,003.00	1,045.00
	$125,490.00	$125,490.00	$12,069.00

1. Prepare a summary of payroll taxes for June similar to the one shown on page 152 of the textbook. Use the following rates: social security, 6.3 percent; medicare, 1.5 percent; FUTA, .8 percent; and SUTA, 3.8 percent.
2. Post from the schedule to the departmental overhead analysis sheets.
3. Prepare a general journal voucher (6-4) to record the payroll taxes.
4. Post to the general ledger account Manufacturing Overhead Control 501.

MANUFACTURING OVERHEAD

Overhead costs include both fixed and variable elements. Use the schedule of monthly fixed overhead charges for Porch and Garden shown on page 257 as a basis for the following steps:

1. Prepare a general journal voucher (6-5) to record the fixed overhead costs.
2. Post to the Manufacturing Overhead Control account.
3. Post to the departmental overhead analysis sheets.

Workers' compensation insurance is estimated as follows for the departments:

Shaping	$224
Assembly	260

PORCH AND GARDEN COMPANY, INC.
Schedule of Monthly Fixed Overhead Charges
Year 19X9

DEPARTMENT	DEPRECIATION OF MACHINERY AND EQUIPMENT	DEPRECIATION OF BUILDINGS	PROPERTY TAXES	PROPERTY INSURANCE	TOTAL
Shaping	$1,156.00	-$0-	$ 83.00	$ 48.00	$1,287.00
Assembly	237.00	-$0-	55.00	15.00	307.00
Finishing	621.00	-$0-	75.00	25.00	721.00
Building Services	284.00	$1,520.00	275.00	44.00	2,123.00
General Factory	884.00	-$0-	143.00	62.00	1,089.00
Total	$3,182.00	$1,520.00	$631.00	$194.00	$5,527.00

Finishing	184
Building Services	58
General Factory	96

To enter these costs, perform the following steps:

1. Prepare a general journal voucher (6-6) to record workers' compensation insurance. Credit Workers' Compensation Insurance Payable 218.
2. Post to the Manufacturing Overhead Control account.
3. Post to the departmental overhead analysis sheets.

APPLYING OVERHEAD TO COMPLETED GOODS

Overhead costs are ordinarily applied to finished goods as soon as possible after the factory operations are completed. Jobs 218 and 219 were completed on June 30. Perform the following procedures for each job:

1. Compute and enter the applied overhead on the job cost sheets. The following overhead rates are to be used:

Shaping	$8.50 per direct labor hour
Assembly	7.80 per direct labor hour
Finishing	8.40 per direct labor hour

2. Record the amount of overhead applied in the manufacturing overhead applied journal.
3. Total all columns of the job cost sheets and complete the summary block on the job cost sheets.

APPLYING OVERHEAD TO WORK IN PROCESS

Jobs 211 and 220 are incomplete at the end of June. Use the following procedures to apply overhead to these jobs:

1. Compute and enter the overhead to be applied for the month on the job cost sheets. Use the overhead rates given above for Jobs 218 and 219.

2. Record the amount of overhead applied in the Manufacturing overhead applied journal.
3. Foot the columns of the job cost sheets.

SUMMARY OF MANUFACTURING OVERHEAD COSTS

Manufacturing overhead costs are drawn together by completing a monthly summary, as follows:

1. Total the departmental overhead analysis sheets.
2. Prepare a schedule of departmental overhead costs similar to the one shown on page 172 of this textbook.
3. Prepare a general journal voucher (6-7) to close Manufacturing Overhead Control 501 into the departmental manufacturing overhead accounts.
4. Post to the general ledger accounts involved.

ALLOCATING SERVICE DEPARTMENT COSTS

The allocation of the cost of service departments to the producing departments is made easier by the preparation of a worksheet similar to the one shown on page 175 of the textbook. Building Services Department costs are to be allocated on the basis of floor space occupied, as indicated below.

Department	Square Feet	Percent
General Factory	15,600	20
Shaping	23,400	30
Assembly	14,040	18
Finishing	24,960	32
Total	78,000	100

General Factory Department costs are to be allocated on the basis of the direct labor costs shown by the factory wage summary for June that you have already prepared.

1. Complete the allocation worksheet.
2. Prepare general journal vouchers (6-8 and 6-9) to apportion the service department costs to the producing departments.
3. Post to the general ledger accounts.

OVERAPPLIED AND UNDERAPPLIED OVERHEAD

Since the month's activities are complete, total the manufacturing overhead applied journal to prepare the way for the following steps:

1. Post the totals to the Work in Process account and to the appropriate departmental overhead accounts in the general ledger.
2. Close the balances of the departmental overhead accounts into Overapplied or Underapplied Manufacturing Overhead 507 by doing the following:
   a. Prepare a general journal voucher (6-10).
   b. Post the entry to the general ledger accounts involved. (The balance of Account 507 is continued from month to month.)

COMPLETION OF JOBS

Jobs 218 and 219 were completed during the period, and all costs have been totaled and summarized on the job cost sheets. Therefore, the following steps are to be performed:

1. Record completion of the two jobs in the completed jobs journal.
2. Total the completed jobs journal and post.
3. Since Job 218 was for stock, record the receipt of 100 chairs (Stock 129) on the finished goods stock ledger card.

SALE OF FINISHED GOODS

Job 219 was manufactured for the Quality Outdoor Furniture Company and is shipped immediately upon completion, on June 30. The sale, amounting to $40,300, is covered by Invoice 719; terms 2/10, n/30.

1. Enter the sale in the sales journal.
2. Since this is the final sale of the month, total the sales journal.
3. Post to the accounts supplied.

SCHEDULES

Schedules are prepared to prove the balances of the subsidiary ledgers to their control accounts in the general ledger before any financial statements are prepared.

1. Prepare a schedule of raw materials. Compare the total with the balance of Raw Materials 121.
2. Prepare a schedule of work in process. Compare the total with the balance of Work in Process 122.
3. Prepare a schedule of finished goods. Compare the total with the balance of Finished Goods 126.

STATEMENTS

The final cost data are now ready for inclusion in the monthly financial statements. Assume selling expenses of $12,658.00 and general expenses of $9,894.00, estimate federal income tax at 15 percent of net income for the period, and complete the following statements:

1. Schedule of manufacturing overhead for June.
2. Statement of cost of goods manufactured for June.
3. Income statement covering June operations.

VOUCHER REGISTER for Month of _June_   **19** _X9_   **Page** _11_

DATE	VOU. NO.	PAYABLE TO	PAID DATE	CHECK NO.	VOUCHERS PAYABLE CR. 201	RAW MATERIALS DR. 121	MFG. OHD. CONTROL DR. 501	✓	OTHER DEBITS AMOUNT
June 1-25	6-1 to 6-71	_Various_			79 247 34	49 349 02	1 798 32		28 100 00

MATERIALS REQUISITION JOURNAL
for Month of June   19 X9   PAGE 11

DATE	REQ. NO.	✔	JOB OR DEPT.	WORK IN PROCESS DR. 122	MFG. OHD. CONTROL DR. 501	RAW MATERIALS CR.121
June 1-25	540-612		Var.	44 3 9 9 00	3 1 0 5 18	47 5 0 4 18

RETURNED MATERIALS JOURNAL
for Month of June   19 X9   Page 11

DATE	REPT. NO.	✔	JOB OR DEPT.	WORK IN PROCESS CR.122	MFG. OHD. CONTROL CR. 501	RAW MATERIALS DR. 121
June 1-25	61-69		Var.	2 9 8 70	3 1 90	3 3 0 60

MANUFACTURING OVERHEAD APPLIED JOURNAL
for Month of June   19 X9   PAGE 11

DATE	JOB. NO.	WORK IN PROCESS DR. 122	SHAPING DEPT. CR. 502 HOURS	SHAPING DEPT. CR. 502 AMOUNT	ASSEMBLY DEPT. CR. 503 HOURS	ASSEMBLY DEPT. CR. 503 AMOUNT	FINISHING DEPT. CR. 504 HOURS	FINISHING DEPT. CR. 504 AMOUNT
June 9	210	3 4 2 9 60			122	9 5 1 60	295	2 4 7 8 00
9	209	4 6 1 6 50	139	1 1 8 1 50	225	1 7 5 5 00	200	1 6 8 0 00
16	210	10 6 4 5 00	310	2 6 3 5 00	510	3 9 7 8 00	480	4 0 3 2 00
16	216	4 1 9 5 50	123	1 0 4 5 50	70	5 4 6 00	310	2 6 0 4 00
16	214	7 7 0 0 00	290	2 4 6 5 00	375	2 9 2 5 00	275	2 3 1 0 00
23	217	9 3 6 7 00	370	3 1 4 5 00	550	4 2 9 0 00	230	1 9 3 2 00
23	213	4 7 3 7 50	245	2 0 8 2 50	195	1 5 2 1 00	135	1 1 3 4 00
23	215	3 6 8 8 00	220	1 8 7 0 00	120	9 3 6 00	105	8 8 2 00

COMPLETED JOBS JOURNAL
for Month of June   19 X9   Page 11

DATE	JOB NO.	MANUFACTURED FOR	FINISHED GOODS DR. 126 WORK IN PROCESS CR. 122 ✔	AMOUNT
June 9	210	Stock 122 (Other Finished Goods)	✓	6 9 1 6 40
9	209	Patio Place		1 8 4 9 4 20
16	210	Rainbow Decks		1 9 9 4 1 85
16	216	Stock 129	✓	3 2 9 4 5 30
16	214	Apple Furniture Company		3 1 6 3 3 37
23	217	Butler Outdoor Furniture Co.		1 5 3 7 4 34
23	213	Stock 157 (Other Finished Goods)	✓	1 1 2 4 9 55
23	215	Stock 337 (Other Finished Goods)	✓	1 2 5 9 8 31

SALES JOURNAL for Month of *June* 19 *X9* Page *11*

DATE		INVOICE NUMBER	CUSTOMER'S NAME	TERMS	✓	ACCOUNTS REC. DR. 111 SALES CR. 401	COST OF GOODS SOLD DR. 415 FINISHED GOODS CR. 126
June	1-25	695-715	*Various*	✓	✓	15 334 86 63	11 744 43 82

Factory Payroll Clearing   NO. *500*

DATE	EXPLANATION	POST. REF.	DEBIT	CREDIT	BALANCE	DR. CR.
June *19X9* 1	*Balance*	✓			20480 00	CR.
2		WP	26590 00		6110 00	DR.
9		WP	25937 00		32047 00	DR.
15		SP	6056 00		38103 00	DR.
16		WP	27384 00		65487 00	DR.
23		WP	27457 00		92944 00	DR.

MATERIALS LEDGER CARD

MATERIAL *Legs, plastic*   REORDER POINT *225*
NUMBER *L-16*   REORDER QUANTITY *400*

DATE	REFERENCE	RECEIVED			ISSUED			BALANCE		
		UNITS	PRICE	AMOUNT	UNITS	PRICE	AMOUNT	UNITS	PRICE	AMOUNT
June *19X9* 25	*Bal.*							225	14 50	3 262 50

MATERIAL *Glass tops, circular*   REORDER POINT *550*
NUMBER *T-23*   REORDER QUANTITY *1,000*

DATE	REFERENCE	RECEIVED			ISSUED			BALANCE		
		UNITS	PRICE	AMOUNT	UNITS	PRICE	AMOUNT	UNITS	PRICE	AMOUNT
June *19X9* 25	*Bal.*							580	2 18	1 264 40

MATERIAL *Polishing cloths*   REORDER POINT *500*
NUMBER *P-42*   REORDER QUANTITY *500*

DATE	REFERENCE	RECEIVED			ISSUED			BALANCE		
		UNITS	PRICE	AMOUNT	UNITS	PRICE	AMOUNT	UNITS	PRICE	AMOUNT
June *19X9* 25	*Bal.*							1,000	88	880 00

MATERIAL _All other materials_
NUMBER _____

REORDER POINT _____
REORDER QUANTITY _____

DATE	REFERENCE	RECEIVED UNITS	PRICE	AMOUNT	ISSUED UNITS	PRICE	AMOUNT	BALANCE UNITS	PRICE	AMOUNT
June 25 19X9	Bal.									47551 54

JOB COST SHEET

CUSTOMER _Zanesville Furniture Company_
DESCRIPTION _Customer's specs on file_
QUANTITY _300_

JOB _211_
DATE STARTED _5/16/X9_
DATE COMPLETED _____

DATE	REQ. NO.	MATERIALS AMOUNT	DATE	REF.	SHAPING HRS.	AMOUNT	ASSEMBLY HRS.	AMOUNT	FINISHING HRS.	AMOUNT	DATE	REF.	SHAPING HRS. RATE	AMOUNT	ASSEMBLY HRS. RATE	AMOUNT	FINISHING HRS. RATE	AMOUNT
6/1	Bal.	1254 74	6/1	TTA		521 72					6/1	Bal		446 30				
6/2	R540	768 50	6/2	TTA	35	218 75												
6/8	R551	696 00	6/9	TTA	110	687 50	33	198 00										
6/21	R589	29 00	6/16	TTA	35	218 75	65	390 00										
			6/23	TTA			100	600 00	65	422 50								

JOB COST SHEET

CUSTOMER _Stock_
DESCRIPTION _Chairs, 129_
QUANTITY _100_

JOB _218_
DATE STARTED _6/12/X9_
DATE COMPLETED _____

DATE	REQ. NO.	MATERIALS AMOUNT	DATE	REF.	SHAPING HRS.	AMOUNT	ASSEMBLY HRS.	AMOUNT	FINISHING HRS.	AMOUNT	DATE	REF.	SHAPING HRS. RATE	AMOUNT	ASSEMBLY HRS. RATE	AMOUNT	FINISHING HRS. RATE	AMOUNT
6/12	R566	2610 00	6/16	TTA	71	443 75												
6/13	R568	203 00	6/23	TTA	71	443 75	67	402 00										
6/18	R574	232 00																
6/23	R606	58 00																

JOB COST SHEET

CUSTOMER _Quality Outdoor Furniture Company_ **JOB** _219_
DESCRIPTION _Customer's specs on file_ **DATE STARTED** _6/19/X9_
QUANTITY _150_ **DATE COMPLETED** _____

MATERIALS			DIRECT LABOR								MANUFACTURING OVERHEAD APPLIED										
					SHAPING		ASSEMBLY		FINISHING				SHAPING			ASSEMBLY			FINISHING		
DATE	REQ. NO.	AMOUNT	DATE	REF.	HRS.	AMOUNT	HRS.	AMOUNT	HRS.	AMOUNT	DATE	REF.	HRS.	RATE	AMOUNT	HRS.	RATE	AMOUNT	HRS.	RATE	AMOUNT
6/19	R581	2750 00	6/23	TTA	60	3750 00	18	108 00													
6/20	R588	284 50																			
6/22	R601	27 40																			
6/23	R609	175 80																			

JOB COST SHEET

CUSTOMER _Cornell Department Store_ **JOB** _220_
DESCRIPTION _Customer's specs on file_ **DATE STARTED** _6/21/X9_
QUANTITY _120_ **DATE COMPLETED** _____

MATERIALS			DIRECT LABOR								MANUFACTURING OVERHEAD APPLIED										
					SHAPING		ASSEMBLY		FINISHING				SHAPING			ASSEMBLY			FINISHING		
DATE	REQ. NO.	AMOUNT	DATE	REF.	HRS.	AMOUNT	HRS.	AMOUNT	HRS.	AMOUNT	DATE	REF.	HRS.	RATE	AMOUNT	HRS.	RATE	AMOUNT	HRS.	RATE	AMOUNT
6/21	R591	2870 40	6/23	TTA	25	156 25															
6/22	R598	55 20																			

DEPARTMENTAL OVERHEAD ANALYSIS SHEET

Department _Shaping (1)_ **Month of** _June_ **19** _X9_

DATE		REF.	TOTAL	01 INDIRECT MATERIALS	02 INDIRECT LABOR	03 PAYROLL TAXES	04 DEPRECIATION	05 REPAIRS & MAINT.	06 UTILITIES	07 INSURANCE	08 OTHER TAXES	09 OTHER ITEM	AMOUNT
June	1-25	Var.	5151 56	602 69	4254 00			225 72				Various	74 15

DEPARTMENTAL OVERHEAD ANALYSIS SHEET

Department _Assembly (2)_ **Month of** _June_ **19** _X9_

DATE		REF.	TOTAL	01 INDIRECT MATERIALS	02 INDIRECT LABOR	03 PAYROLL TAXES	04 DEPRECIATION	05 REPAIRS & MAINT.	06 UTILITIES	07 INSURANCE	08 OTHER TAXES	09 OTHER ITEM	AMOUNT
June	1-25	Var.	5308 16	702 66 (11 20)	4473 00			29 30				Various	114 40

DEPARTMENTAL OVERHEAD ANALYSIS SHEET

Department _Finishing (3)_   Month of _June_   19 _X9_

DATE	REF.	TOTAL	01 INDIRECT MATERIALS	02 INDIRECT LABOR	03 PAYROLL TAXES	04 DEPRECIATION	05 REPAIRS & MAINT.	06 UTILITIES	07 INSURANCE	08 OTHER TAXES	09 OTHER ITEM	AMOUNT
June 1-25	Var.	5 926 15	944 80 (13 85)	4 624 00			226 15				Various	95 05

DEPARTMENTAL OVERHEAD ANALYSIS SHEET

Department _Building Services (4)_   Month of _June_   19 _X9_

DATE	REF.	TOTAL	01 INDIRECT MATERIALS	02 INDIRECT LABOR	03 PAYROLL TAXES	04 DEPRECIATION	05 REPAIRS & MAINT.	06 UTILITIES	07 INSURANCE	08 OTHER TAXES	09 OTHER ITEM	AMOUNT
June 1-25	Var.	8 396 23	320 18 (6 85)	7 633 00			383 50				Various	66 40

DEPARTMENTAL OVERHEAD ANALYSIS SHEET

Department _General Factory (5)_   Month of _June_   19 _X9_

DATE	REF.	TOTAL	01 INDIRECT MATERIALS	02 INDIRECT LABOR	03 PAYROLL TAXES	04 DEPRECIATION	05 REPAIRS & MAINT.	06 UTILITIES	07 INSURANCE	08 OTHER TAXES	09 OTHER ITEM	AMOUNT
June 1-25	Var.	12 436 50	484 85	11 368 00			435 25				Various	148 40

FINISHED GOODS LEDGER

MATERIAL _Chairs_
NUMBER _129_

DATE	REFERENCE	RECEIVED UNITS	PRICE	AMOUNT	SOLD UNITS	PRICE	AMOUNT	BALANCE UNITS	PRICE	AMOUNT
June 1 19X9	Bal.							30	107 30	3 219 00
9	S702				20	107 30	2 146 00	10	107 30	1 073 00
16	J113	50	106 43	5 321 50				10 } 50 }	107 30 106 43	6 394 50

MATERIAL _Tables_
NUMBER _458_

DATE	REFERENCE	RECEIVED UNITS	PRICE	AMOUNT	SOLD UNITS	PRICE	AMOUNT	BALANCE UNITS	PRICE	AMOUNT
June 1 19X9	Bal.							360	23 64	8 510 40

MATERIAL _All other finished goods_
NUMBER _Various_

DATE	REFERENCE	RECEIVED			SOLD			BALANCE		
		UNITS	PRICE	AMOUNT	UNITS	PRICE	AMOUNT	UNITS	PRICE	AMOUNT
June 1 19X9	Bal.									2782880

Porch and Garden Company, Inc.
Summary of Factory Wages
June 19X9

PAYROLL PERIOD	SHAPING		ASSEMBLY		FINISHING		BUILDING SERVICES	GENERAL FACTORY	TOTAL
	DIRECT LABOR	INDIRECT LABOR	DIRECT LABOR	INDIRECT LABOR	DIRECT LABOR	INDIRECT LABOR			
June 1-2	112700	31500	176100	37300	104900	55000	42000	51500	611000
3-9	579500	108500	624000	125000	595000	144500	186700	230500	2593700
1-15	000	000	000	000	000	000	175600	430000	605600
10-16	652000	142500	746000	122500	596500	117000	174500	187400	2738400
17-23	553000	142900	735500	162500	584000	145900	184500	237400	2745700

C H A P T E R

12

Scrap, Spoiled Goods, and Defective Goods

In the manufacturing activities discussed so far, it has been assumed that the materials issued were completely used up in the production of finished goods. However, in almost every factory certain losses of materials occur as an inevitable part of normal operations. Materials lost may take the form of scrap, spoiled goods, or defective goods.

A cost accounting system must provide for recording these losses, so that the unit cost figures will be as accurate as possible. The accounting technique varies according to the type of loss involved.

ACCOUNTING FOR SCRAP

Scrap is the residue of manufacturing processes. In a radio assembly plant, it might include bits and pieces of wire and solder. In a metal toy factory, it would include blanks and countless fragments produced by punch-press operations. In a sawmill, it would be sawdust, bark, and discarded end pieces. Other scrap materials are paper, wood, or metal shavings; cloth remnants and clippings; and chemical sediments.

Scrap material has value. It is normally stored in a shed, hopper car, or pile until a marketable quantity is collected. Then it is sold to scrap dealers, other industries, or individuals. The cost accountant considers how much the scrap is worth, how fast it accumulates, and other factors in selecting a procedure for recording it.

Low-Value Scrap

If the value of the scrap is low and if it is sold at irregular intervals, customarily no entry is made in the accounts until the scrap is sold.

Credit to Miscellaneous Income. At the time of sale, the simplest recording procedure is to debit Cash or Accounts Receivable and to credit Miscellaneous Income. A sale for cash is recorded in the cash receipts journal. A sale on credit is entered on a general journal voucher, as shown below.

JOURNAL VOUCHER	Date Oct. 9,	19 X9	No. 10-10		
ACCOUNT	ACCT. NO.	✓	DEBIT	CREDIT	
Accounts Receivable	111		260 00		
Miscellaneous Income	713			260 00	
EXPLANATION					
Sold scrap materials.					
PREPARED BY ANG	AUDITED BY KLM		APPROVED BY PON		

Because of the difficulty of identifying scrap with a specific job or department, this is the procedure used by most manufacturers. Some firms, however, prefer to apply the proceeds from the sale of scrap to the cost of producing the product. There are two methods that may be used to accomplish this.

Credit to a Specific Job. Sometimes it is possible to determine the specific job from which the scrap accumulated. If so, and if the job requires a long time to complete, the proceeds from the sale are subtracted from the cost of the materials that have been charged to that job. The debit is to Cash or Accounts Receivable as before, but the credit is to Work in Process, as shown in the general journal form on page 268.

19X9			
Oct. 9	Accounts Receivable	111	260.00	
	Work in Process	122		260.00
	Sold scrap materials arising from Job 141.			

The credit amount is also recorded in the Materials column of the job cost sheet as an entry in parentheses to indicate that the cost reduction is an offset against previous charges, as shown below.

JOB COST SHEET

CUSTOMER *Stock*
DESCRIPTION *Conference Table #479*
QUANTITY _____

JOB *141*
DATE STARTED *9/6/X9*
DATE COMPLETED _____

MATERIALS			DIRECT LABOR								MANUFACTURING OVERHEAD APPLIED										
					MILLING		ASSEMBLY		FINISHING				MILLING			ASSEMBLY			FINISHING		
DATE	REQ. NO.	AMOUNT	DATE	REF.	HRS.	AMOUNT	HRS.	AMOUNT	HRS.	AMOUNT	DATE	REF.	HRS.	RATE	AMOUNT	HRS.	RATE	AMOUNT	HRS.	RATE	AMOUNT
9/6	R906	2700.00	9/12	TTA	200	1300.00															
9/8	R911	1350.00	9/18	TTA	100	675.00	65	462.00													
9/15	R920	162.00	9/24	TTA					75	518.00											
9/20	R924	108.00	10/6	TTA					75	542.00											
10/1	R935	270.00	10/13	TTA					30	205.00											
10/9	J10-10	(260.00)																			

Credit to Manufacturing Overhead. If the scrap cannot be identified with a specific job, the proceeds from the sale may be used to reduce product costs by crediting Manufacturing Overhead Control, as shown in the general journal form below.

19X9			
Oct. 9	Accounts Receivable	111	260.00	
	Manufacturing Overhead Control	501		260.00
	Sold scrap materials arising from the			
	Milling Department.			

The credit to Manufacturing Overhead Control is also recorded on the departmental overhead analysis sheet as an entry in parentheses, as shown on page 269.

This procedure assumes that the scrap can be associated with a specific producing department. If this cannot be done, a common practice is to credit the proceeds from the sale as a reduction of the costs of a service department.

High-Value Scrap

The valuable scrap material (such as precious metal shavings) that results from certain industrial processes requires special care in control and storage. For this reason, a **scrap report** is prepared when scrap is moved from the factory floor to storage, as shown on page 269.

DEPARTMENTAL OVERHEAD ANALYSIS SHEET

Department _Milling_   ...h of _October_   19 _X9_

DATE		REF.	TOTAL		01 INDIRECT MATERIALS		02 INDIRECT LABOR		07 INSURANCE		08 OTHER TAXES		09 OTHER ITEM	09 OTHER AMOUNT	
Oct.	4	R943	121	00	121	00									
	6	TTA	265	00			265	00							
	7	R948	27	00	27	00									
	9	J10-10	(260	00)									Scrap	(260	00)

Scrap Report

OLD DUTCH IRONWORKS
Plainview, Texas 79016   **No.** _80248_

DATE _11/5/X9_   Department _Cutting_

ITEM NO.	DESCRIPTION	QUANTITY	UNIT VALUE	TOTAL VALUE
	Metal cuttings	_500 lbs._		

Delivered by _____ K. N. _____   Storeroom Clerk _____

FORM NO. 517

SCRAP INVENTORY LEDGER CARD

MATERIAL _Metal Cuttings_

DATE	REFERENCE	RECEIVED UNITS	RECEIVED PRICE	RECEIVED AMOUNT	ISSUED UNITS	ISSUED PRICE	ISSUED AMOUNT	BALANCE UNITS	BALANCE PRICE	BALANCE AMOUNT
19X9 Nov. 5	SR 80248	500 lbs.								

The storeroom supervisor, who controls the scrap in storage, prepares a scrap inventory ledger card for each type of scrap. This card resembles a materials ledger card, as shown above.

Fluctuating Value. When the market price for a scrap material changes frequently, the value of the scrap inventory is uncertain. In this instance, the scrap inventory ledger card will show only the quantity on hand. When the scrap is sold, the proceeds are debited to Cash or Accounts Receivable and credited to Miscellaneous Income, Work in Process, or Manufacturing Overhead Control. If the dollar amount is large, it should be identified with the product costs whenever possible. Most accountants would therefore not use the Miscellaneous Income account. If Work in Process is credited, the amount must also be recorded on the job cost sheet. If Manufacturing Overhead Control is used, an entry must be made on the departmental overhead analysis sheet.

Stable Value.   When the market price for scrap material remains at a fairly constant level, the scrap report and the scrap inventory ledger card may show the market value as well as the quantity. Also, a new general ledger account, called *Scrap Inventory,* is opened. As soon as the scrap materials are moved from the factory floor, this account is debited for the estimated market value. The credit is to Work in Process, Manufacturing Overhead Control, or rarely, Miscellaneous Income.

19X9				
Nov. 25	Scrap Inventory	118	250.00	
	Work in Process	122		250.00
	Transferred 500 pounds of metal cuttings			
	from factory to storeroom.			

Entries must be made on the job cost sheet if Work in Process is used or on the departmental overhead analysis sheet if Manufacturing Overhead Control is used.

When the scrap is sold, an entry is made debiting Accounts Receivable or Cash and crediting Scrap Inventory.

19X9				
Nov. 28	Accounts Receivable	111	250.00	
	Scrap Inventory	118		250.00
	Sold scrap at recorded value.			

Sale at Different Value.   Sometimes scrap is sold for more or for less than the value at which it is recorded. Any difference between the sales price and the recorded value is treated as an adjustment to the account that was originally credited (Work in Process, Manufacturing Overhead Control, or Miscellaneous Income). For example, if the scrap in the illustration above were sold for only $225, the entry to record the sale would be as follows:

At this point you should be able to work Exercises 12–1 to 12–3 and Problems 12–1A, 12–2A, 12–4A, 12–1B, 12–2B, and 12–4B.

19X9				
Nov. 28	Accounts Receivable	111	225.00	
	Work in Process	122	25.00	
	Scrap Inventory	118		250.00
	Sold scrap at less than recorded value.			

ACCOUNTING FOR SPOILED GOODS

Goods that have been damaged through imperfect machining or processing, so that they do not measure up to quality standards or specifications, are called **spoiled goods.** Spoiling occurs in batches or in isolated instances, whereas scrap is inevitable and recurs constantly in specific manufacturing processes. In some cases, spoiled goods may be sold as **seconds.** For example, textile and shoe manufacturers often produce goods with slight defects that are sold as seconds at substantial discounts. In other instances, spoiled goods must be discarded as waste.

The basic problem in accounting for spoiled goods is how the loss due to spoilage should be charged. The loss may be charged to manufacturing overhead and thus spread over all jobs worked on during the period. Or the loss may be charged to the particular job from which the spoiled goods were recovered.

If spoilage occurs often and is a regular part of the manufacturing process, it is not logical to charge the loss to a specific job merely because that job happened to be the one on which the spoilage occurred. On the other hand, if the spoilage is caused by unusual standards, specifications, or processes required for a particular job, that one job should bear the spoilage loss.

Loss Charged to Manufacturing Overhead

Most manufacturers charge routine, recurring spoilage to Manufacturing Overhead Control. To see how this procedure works, the system used by Bentley's Works of Wood, a manufacturer of living room furniture, is examined below.

Assume that Job 161 calls for the production of 259 unpainted end tables (Model T). These tables were put into production in the Milling Department, and the costs accumulated to date are as follows:

	Total	Per Unit
Materials	$4,191.20	$16.7648
Labor		
Milling Department	499.20	1.9968
Assembly Department	361.00	1.6640
Finishing Department	55.00	
Manufacturing Overhead		
Milling Department	493.00	1.9720
Assembly Department	345.20	1.6024
Finishing Department	55.40	
Total	$6,000.00	$24.0000

Suppose that an inspector discovers that the lumber used in ten of the tables was improperly cured. These tables are spoiled goods that may be sold as seconds. If a dealer in unpainted furniture buys the tables for $10 each (a loss of $14 per table), the following steps are required:

1. A **spoiled goods report** is completed listing the quantity and the dollar value, as shown on page 272.
2. A general journal entry is prepared, as shown on page 272, to do the following:
   a. Record the estimated sales value of the spoiled goods as a debit to a Spoiled Goods Inventory account (10 × $10 = $100).
   b. Record the loss as a debit to Manufacturing Overhead Control (10 × $14 = $140).

```
BENTLEY'S                                         SPOILED
WORKS OF WOOD                                     GOODS
     76 Western Avenue                            REPORT
   Pittsburgh, PA 15212


JOB  161                              REPORT NO.   16
DEPARTMENT  Milling                  DATE  11/27/X9
```

QUANTITY	DESCRIPTION	EST. UNIT VALUE	TOTAL EST. VALUE
10	Model T end tables	10 00	100 00

EXPLANATION: lumber warped, improperly cured.

Department Foreman   K. T.   Received by

FORM NO. 516

c. Transfer the total cost of the spoiled goods from Work in Process by a credit entry (10 × $24 = $240).

```
19X9
Nov. 27   Spoiled Goods Inventory            119   100.00
          Manufacturing Overhead Control     501   140.00
              Work in Process                122            240.00
          Recorded estimated market value of
          spoiled goods (Job 161) and charged
          loss to Manufacturing Overhead—Milling
          Department.
```

3. The loss of $140 is recorded on the overhead analysis sheet for the Milling Department, as shown below.

DEPARTMENTAL OVERHEAD ANALYSIS SHEET

Department Milling

DATE		REF.	TOTAL	01 INDIRECT MATERIALS	02 INDIRECT LABOR	05 REPAIRS & MAINT.	09 OTHER ITEM	AMOUNT
Nov.	3	R1014	185 75	185 75				
	5	TTA	876 00		876 00			
	12	TTA	910 00		910 00			
	14	R1019	90 00	90 00				
	19	TTA	575 00		575 00			
	21	VR12	244 50			244 50		
	26	TTA	414 60		414 60			
	27	J11-27	140 00				Sp. Goods	140 00

JOB COST SHEET

CUSTOMER *Stock*   JOB *161*

DESCRIPTION *Model T End Tables*   DATE STARTED *11/5/X9*

QUANTITY *250*   DATE COMPLETED *11/27/X9*

MATERIALS			DIRECT LABOR							MANUFACTURING OVERHEAD APPLIED											
					MILLING		ASSEMBLY		FINISHING				MILLING			ASSEMBLY			FINISHING		
DATE	REQ. NO.	AMOUNT	DATE	REF.	HRS.	AMOUNT	HRS.	AMOUNT	HRS.	AMOUNT	DATE	REF.	HRS.	RATE	AMOUNT	HRS.	RATE	AMOUNT	HRS.	RATE	AMOUNT
11/5	R691	3950 00	11/5	TTA	75	499 20	56	361 00	8	55 00	11/27	MOA 11	75	6.573	493 00	56	6.163	345 20	8	6.925	55 40
11/7	R712	191 20	11/27	SGR 16		(19 97)		(14 44)		(22 20)					(19 72)			(13 81)			(22 21)
11/12	R778	50 00																			
11/27	SGR 16	(167 65)																			
Total		4023 55				479 23		346 56		52 80					473 28			331 39			53 19

TOTAL COST $ *5,760.00*

UNITS PRODUCED *240*

COST PER UNIT $ *24.00*

COMMENTS:

    10 tables spoiled (4% of original order)

SUMMARY

MATERIALS	$ *4,023.55*
LABOR—MILLING	*479.23*
LABOR—ASSEMBLY	*346.56*
LABOR—FINISHING	*52.80*
OVERHEAD—MILLING	*473.28*
OVERHEAD—ASSEMBLY	*331.39*
OVERHEAD—FINISHING	*53.19*
TOTAL	$ *5,760.00*

4. The credit to Work in Process is recorded on the job cost sheet for Job 161 by entries in parentheses. The credits in the individual cost element columns are computed at 4 percent of previous charges because the quantity of spoiled goods represents 4 percent of the order ($10 \div 250 = .04$). For example, a credit entry of $14.44 (4 percent of the $361 accumulated total) is entered in the Assembly Amount column in the Direct Labor section, as shown above.

    After the above credit is posted, the summary block of the job cost sheet for Job 161 (shown above) is completed. The cost of the remaining 240 tables amounts to $5,760, which is $24 per table ($5,760 \div 240 = 24). Note that $24 per table is the same as the cost would have been if there had been no spoiled goods and 250 good tables had been produced.

Loss Absorbed in the Cost of a Specific Job

If the loss on spoiled goods is to be left as part of the total cost of a specific job, a simple entry is made removing the estimated value of the spoiled goods from Work in Process. If Bentley's Works of Wood had used this procedure, the spoilage on Job 161 would have been recorded as shown on page 274.

19X9				
Nov. 27	Spoiled Goods Inventory	119	100.00	
	Work in Process	122		100.00
	Removed estimated market value of spoiled goods (Job 161) from Work in Process.			

The exact form of the entry on the job cost sheet depends upon whether the value of the spoiled goods is considered a reduction of material costs, labor costs, overhead costs, or all three.

Reduction of Cost Elements. If the cost accountant prefers to record the $100 as a reduction involving each of the cost elements, the estimated value of the spoiled goods must be apportioned. The apportionment is usually done on the basis of the relative amount of cost incurred on the job to date. In the example, the division of the value of the spoiled goods would be made as shown below.

Allocation of Estimated Market Value of Spoiled Goods to Individual Cost Elements

MATERIALS

$$\frac{\text{Materials Cost, \$4,191.20}}{\text{Total Cost, \$6,000.00}} \times \text{Spoiled Goods Value, \$100.00} \quad = \$ \ 69.85$$

LABOR—MILLING DEPARTMENT

$$\frac{\text{Dept. Labor Cost, \$499.20}}{\text{Total Cost, \$6,000.00}} \times \text{Spoiled Goods Value, \$100.00} \quad = \quad 8.32$$

LABOR—ASSEMBLY DEPARTMENT

$$\frac{\text{Dept. Labor Cost, \$361.00}}{\text{Total Cost, \$6,000.00}} \times \text{Spoiled Goods Value, \$100.00} \quad = \quad 6.02$$

LABOR—FINISHING DEPARTMENT

$$\frac{\text{Dept. Labor Cost, \$55.00}}{\text{Total Cost, \$6,000.00}} \times \text{Spoiled Goods Value, \$100.00} \quad = \quad .92$$

OVERHEAD—MILLING DEPARTMENT

$$\frac{\text{Dept. Overhead Cost, \$493.00}}{\text{Total Cost, \$6,000.00}} \times \text{Spoiled Goods Value, \$100.00} = \quad 8.22$$

OVERHEAD—ASSEMBLY DEPARTMENT

$$\frac{\text{Dept. Overhead Cost, \$345.20}}{\text{Total Cost, \$6,000.00}} \times \text{Spoiled Goods Value, \$100.00} = \quad 5.75$$

OVERHEAD—FINISHING DEPARTMENT

$$\frac{\text{Dept. Overhead Cost, \$55.40}}{\text{Total Cost, \$6,000.00}} \times \text{Spoiled Goods Value, \$100.00} = \quad \underline{.92}$$

Total Estimated Market Value $100.00

JOB COST SHEET

CUSTOMER *Stock*
DESCRIPTION *Model T End Tables*
QUANTITY *250*

JOB *161*
DATE STARTED *11/5/X9*
DATE COMPLETED *11/27/X9*

MATERIALS			DIRECT LABOR		MILLING		ASSEMBLY		FINISHING		MANUFACTURING OVERHEAD APPLIED		MILLING			ASSEMBLY			FINISHING		
DATE	REQ. NO.	AMOUNT	DATE	REF.	HRS.	AMOUNT	HRS.	AMOUNT	HRS.	AMOUNT	DATE	REF.	HRS.	RATE	AMOUNT	HRS.	RATE	AMOUNT	HRS.	RATE	AMOUNT
11/5	R691	3950 00	11/5	TTA	75	499 20	56	361 00	8	55 00	11/27	MOA 11	75	6.573	493 00	56	6.163	345 20	8	6.925	55 40
11/7	R712	191 20	11/27	SGR 16		(8 32)		(6 02)		(92)	11/27	SGR 16			(8 22)			(5 75)			(92)
11/12	R778	50 00																			
11/27	SGR 16	(69 85)																			
Total		**4121 35**				**490 88**		**354 98**		**54 08**					**484 78**			**339 45**			**54 48**

TOTAL COST $ *5,900.00*

UNITS PRODUCED *240*

COST PER UNIT $ *24.5833*

COMMENTS:

10 tables spoiled (4% of original order)

SUMMARY

MATERIALS	$ *4,121.35*
LABOR—MILLING	*490.88*
LABOR—ASSEMBLY	*354.98*
LABOR—FINISHING	*54.08*
OVERHEAD—MILLING	*484.78*
OVERHEAD—ASSEMBLY	*339.45*
OVERHEAD—FINISHING	*54.48*
TOTAL	$ *5,900.00*

Based on these computations, entries in parentheses would be made on the job cost sheet, as shown on page 276.

Reduction of Total Cost. A simpler solution is to show one entry in parentheses for the total value of the spoiled goods ($100) on the job cost sheet and to deduct this amount from the total cost of the job. If this is done, it is not necessary to analyze the value of the spoiled goods by department. No special entries are needed in the individual columns of the job cost sheet for each of the various cost elements.

When the $100 is entered as a reduction on the job cost sheet for Job 161, the cost of the remaining tables is $5,900 ($6,000 − $100), or $24.5833 each. Thus, under this method, each of the 240 tables has absorbed $.5833 of the loss on the spoiled goods ($24.5833 − $24 = $.5833, and $.5833 × 240 = $140 loss).

It is obvious that if the product has been processed through several departments, complex computations are required to record the value of the spoiled goods as a reduction involving each of the cost elements. Therefore, most companies use the simpler procedure of reducing the total costs.

```
              SUMMARY
  MATERIALS          $  4,191.20
  LABOR—MILLING         499.20
  LABOR—ASSEMBLY        361.00
  LABOR—FINISHING        55.00
  OVERHEAD—MILLING      493.00
  OVERHEAD—ASSEMBLY    345.20
  OVERHEAD—FINISHING     55.40
  TOTAL              $  6,000.00
  Less Spoiled Goods    (100.00)
       Net Cost      $ 5,900.00
```

At this point you should be able to work Exercises 12–4 and 12–5 and Problems 12–5A and 12–5B.

ACCOUNTING FOR DEFECTIVE GOODS

Units of production that fail to meet production standards but that can be brought up to standard by putting in more materials, labor, and overhead are generally referred to as **defective goods.** The additional costs required to bring these goods up to standard are known as **rework costs.**

Accounting for rework costs may be handled in two ways:

1. The additional manufacturing costs are charged to Manufacturing Overhead Control, and are thus spread over all jobs.
2. The additional costs are charged to the particular job of which they are a part.

Rework Costs Charged to Manufacturing Overhead

If defective goods appear often in a firm's normal operations, the rework costs are usually treated as an addition to manufacturing overhead. The defects may result from mass-production techniques and have no special connection with a specific job or production order. The rework costs applied to goods that became defective through an accident or negligence are also charged to manufacturing overhead. Bentley's Works of Wood uses this method of charging the rework costs of defective goods as manufacturing overhead.

To illustrate the procedure, assume that a specific job of 200 tables is being completed for stock. A quick-dry varnish is applied incorrectly to the tables by a new employee in the Finishing Department. As a result, the varnish on four tables is blotched and must be removed and reapplied. The additional costs of reworking the tables consist of materials, $5; labor, $16; and manufacturing overhead applied, $18.78. These costs are charged to the manufacturing overhead of the Finishing Department.

Accounting for the rework costs is simplified at Bentley's Works of Wood by treating the rework operation as a separate job. Materials, labor, and overhead are charged in the regular manner to the rework job. Cost details are recorded on a new job cost sheet.

When the units have been reprocessed, an entry is made to transfer the rework costs to manufacturing overhead as follows:

19X9				
Nov. 29	Manufacturing Overhead Control		501	39.78	
	Work in Process		122		39.78
	Transferred cost of reworked defective				
	units (Job 153) to Manufacturing Overhead.				

An appropriate entry to record the $39.78 is made in the Other column of the departmental overhead analysis sheet of the Finishing Department.

Treating the rework operation as a separate job permits entries for materials, labor, and overhead to be made in the regular way. It also allows the total costs of a rework operation to be accumulated and reported. Management can then see the cost and take corrective action.

Rework Costs Charged to a Specific Job

If the rework costs are charged to the job of which the defective units are a part, no special accounting procedures are necessary. The additional materials, labor, and overhead are recorded in the normal manner and are entered on the job cost sheet for that job. The final unit costs will reflect both regular and reprocessing costs. Unit costs may vary a great deal from job to job when this method is used.

SELF-REVIEW

1. Texas Supply Company sold scrap material on credit for $580. What general journal entry would the company make if the scrap is to be charged to Job 367?
2. A scrap report should be prepared for what type of scrap materials?
3. What is the term used for spoiled goods that can be sold "as is" at a discount?
4. When are rework costs on defective goods charged to manufacturing overhead?

Answers to Self-Review

1. The general journal entry would be as follows:

Accounts Receivable   580
    Work in Process   580
Sold scrap materials from Job 367.

2. A scrap report would be prepared when the scrap materials have a high value and require extra attention.
3. Spoiled goods that can be sold "as is" are called *seconds*.
4. Rework costs are charged to manufacturing overhead when the defective goods are part of a company's normal operations.

At this point you should be able to work Exercise 12–6 and Problems 12–3A and 12–3B.

PRINCIPLES AND PROCEDURES SUMMARY

- Modern mass-production methods of factory operation often result in some losses of materials as scrap, spoiled goods, and defective goods. The procedure for accounting for these losses varies with the type of loss, value, frequency, and other factors.
- Scrap is material residue from manufacturing operations.
  - If the scrap is of low value and does not occur often, no record is made until it is sold. The simplest recording procedure is to credit the proceeds to Miscellaneous Income.
  - Scrap losses may also be credited to Work in Process or Manufacturing Overhead (with entries in related subsidiary ledgers). The difficulty of identifying the loss with a job or department makes this procedure impractical when a small dollar value is involved.
- High-value scrap is recorded on a scrap report and moved to a storage area. The storeroom supervisor enters the amount of scrap on a scrap inventory ledger card.
  - If the scrap has a stable and easily measurable value, the scrap inventory records will show dollar value as well as quantity.
  - If the scrap does not have a stable and easily measurable value, the records will list quantity only until the scrap is sold. The proceeds from high-value scrap are normally used to reduce Work in Process or Manufacturing Overhead Control.
- Spoiled goods appear less often than scrap. They may be sold as seconds or treated as scrap. There are two methods of charging the losses involved:
  - With the first method, the loss is charged to manufacturing overhead; this spreads the cost over all jobs completed during the period.
  - With the second method, the loss is charged to a particular job when the spoilage is directly related to special processes or when exacting specifications are required for a particular job.
- Defective goods also represent a loss to a firm. However, these items can be reprocessed into salable merchandise. The costs of the reprocessing, known as rework costs, may be charged to manufacturing overhead or added to existing charges against a specific job. The deciding factor is the nature of the defect.
  - If the rework costs are a recurring result of typical production processes, the loss is charged to manufacturing overhead.
  - If the rework costs are unusual and identifiable with a specific job, they should be added to the cost of that job.

MANAGERIAL IMPLICATIONS

- An important task of production management is to minimize spoiled goods, defective goods, and scrap. Scrap is an inherent part of many manufacturing processes. Also, in normal operations it is expected that some defective and spoiled goods will result. However, departmental management is responsible for holding these losses to levels that are deemed to be acceptable.

■ Scrap must be properly controlled. This involves accumulating, storing, and selling the scrap. Several different accounting procedures may be used in accounting for scrap. The accountant should choose a method after considering the value of scrap, the quantity, the handling procedures, and the channel of sale.

■ Spoiled goods are goods that have been damaged in the production process and cannot be completed as normal units. The production process should be carefully studied to get an estimate of the spoilage that is a part of the normal manufacturing process. Actual spoilage should be watched carefully, and if the spoilage exceeds the "normal" amount, the cause should be determined and, if appropriate, the departmental manager should be held responsible. Various procedures can be developed to account for spoiled goods, depending on the magnitude of the spoilage, the frequency of spoilage, the usual sales price of the spoiled goods, and how the goods are sold.

■ Defective goods are units of product that are damaged but can be reworked into normal salable merchandise. Defective goods, like spoiled goods, may in some cases be a normal part of the production process, and that process should be studied to determine the level of defective goods that can be expected under normal conditions. The departmental manager should be held accountable for excessive spoilage.

REVIEW QUESTIONS

1. What are the three categories of lost materials?
2. What is scrap? Give three examples.
3. What are two factors that should be considered by the cost accountant in selecting a procedure for recording scrap?
4. When scrap has a low value, what account is credited for the proceeds of its sale?
5. If scrap can be identified with a special job, what account is credited with the proceeds of its sale?
6. If scrap can be identified with a specific department, what account is credited with the proceeds of its sale?
7. What is a scrap report and when is it used?
8. Scrap may have a high value that changes often. If this is the case, when is the transfer from the factory to the storeroom recorded? What information is given?
9. Scrap may have a high value that is relatively stable. If this is the case, when is the transfer of the scrap from the factory to the storeroom recorded? What information is given?
10. Are gains and losses recorded on the sale of scrap? Explain.
11. What are spoiled goods?
12. What are seconds?

13. What are two ways of accounting for the loss due to spoiled goods?
14. When spoilage is routine and recurring, what account should be charged for the loss?
15. Define *defective goods*. What are rework costs?
16. List two ways of accounting for rework costs.

MANAGERIAL DISCUSSION QUESTIONS

1. When would management want the cost of spoiled goods to be considered as a part of the cost of the specific job on which the spoilage occurred?
2. At the Sampson Company, the cost of spoiled goods averages about 4 percent of the total manufacturing costs. Management learns that the cost of spoiled goods at the Armstrong Supply Company, a competitor that produces a similar product, averages less than 1 percent of the total manufacturing costs. Comment on the managerial implications of this. What factors could cause such a difference?
3. The management of the Phoenix Manufacturing Corporation learns that the cost allocated to spoiled goods on Job 833 totals $3,860. It is also determined that the goods could be sold for $3,450 if additional costs of $950 are incurred. What would be your recommendation to management regarding these goods?
4. When would management want to maintain a perpetual inventory for scrap?

EXERCISES

EXERCISE 12–1 **Record a sale of scrap. (Obj. 1).** On June 15, 19X9, the Cox Manufacturing Company sold scrap with a low value. The scrap was sold on credit for $925, and the company records such proceeds as Miscellaneous Income. Prepare the general journal entry to record this sale.

EXERCISE 12–2 **Record a sale of scrap. (Obj. 1).** The partially completed job cost sheet for Job 351 is shown on page 281. On April 19, 19X9, scrap material was recovered from this job and sold on credit for $475.
a. Prepare the general journal entry to record the sale of this scrap.
b. How should the sale of scrap be recorded on the job cost sheet?
c. What is the total materials cost of Job 351?

EXERCISE 12–3 **Record a sale of scrap. (Obj. 1).** The Wilson Manufacturing Company sold scrap for $1,789 on credit. The scrap was sold on May 31, 19X9, and had accumulated during the month in the Assembly Department, which is to receive credit for the proceeds.
a. Prepare the general journal entry to record the sale of this scrap.
b. How should the sale of the scrap be recorded on the departmental overhead analysis sheet?

JOB COST SHEET

CUSTOMER *Kelley Furniture Store*
DESCRIPTION *Table, Model #384-Walnut*
QUANTITY *100*

JOB *351*
DATE STARTED *4/1/X9*
DATE COMPLETED _____

MATERIALS			DIRECT LABOR		MILLING		ASSEMBLY		FINISHING		MANUFACTURING OVERHEAD APPLIED		MILLING			ASSEMBLY			FINISHING		
DATE	REQ. NO.	AMOUNT	DATE	REF.	HRS.	AMOUNT	HRS.	AMOUNT	HRS.	AMOUNT	DATE	REF.	HRS.	RATE	AMOUNT	HRS.	RATE	AMOUNT	HRS.	RATE	AMOUNT
4/1	R840	800 00	4/4	TTA	85	446 25															
4/2	R871	2145 00	4/11	TTA	110	575 50	38	247 00													
4/6	RM-58	(53 00)	4/17	TTA			125	812 50													
4/12	R892	1827 00																			
4/17	R910	2815 00																			
4/18	RM-61	(82 50)																			
4/19	R953	1135 00																			

EXERCISE 12–4 **Account for spoiled goods. (Obj. 2).** Job 451 was completed on June 25, 19X9. The job was for 300 chairs ordered by the Baker Communications Company. The job cost sheet shows the following costs incurred:

Materials	$6,390
Labor—Milling	2,460
Labor—Assembly	1,875
Labor—Finishing	1,950
Overhead—Milling	2,091
Overhead—Assembly	1,594
Overhead—Finishing	1,658

Upon inspection, 24 chairs were found to be spoiled and could be sold as seconds for $45 each.

a. Prepare the general journal entry to establish the spoiled goods inventory, assuming that the loss is charged to Manufacturing Overhead.

b. Determine the amount of the credits to be recorded in the individual cost element columns of the job cost sheet for Job 451.

EXERCISE 12–5 **Account for spoiled goods. (Obj. 2).** Assume the same facts as in Exercise 12–4 except that the loss is to be absorbed in the cost of Job 451.

a. Prepare the general journal entry to establish the spoiled goods inventory.

b. Determine the amount of the credits to be recorded in the individual cost element columns of the job cost sheet for Job 451.

EXERCISE 12–6 **Account for defective goods. (Obj. 3).** In completing Job 650, 15 units were found to be defective and required rework costs of

$1,578.45. The rework costs were recorded on a new job cost sheet. What general journal entry is needed to transfer the rework costs to manufacturing overhead?

PROBLEMS

PROBLEM 12–1A **Record a sale of scrap. (Obj. 1).** The Cornell Manufacturing Company applies the proceeds from the sale of scrap against the cost of production. On September 4, 19X9, scrap was sold on credit of $782.

INSTRUCTIONS Prepare a general journal entry to record the sale of the scrap in each of the following cases. Use the account names found in your textbook.

1. The firm credits the income from the sale of scrap to Job 848, from which it was derived.
2. The firm credits the income from the sale of scrap to the Manufacturing Overhead Control account for the Forming Department, where the scrap originated.

PROBLEM 12–2A **Record scrap inventory. (Obj. 1).** Webster Metal Manufacturers maintains a Scrap Inventory account for metal scrap recovered from operations in the Cutting Department. On March 15, 19X9, 5,300 pounds of scrap with an estimated market value of $2,385 are transferred from the factory to the storeroom.

INSTRUCTIONS Use the account names found in your textbook to do the following:

1. Prepare the general journal entry to record the storage of the metal scrap. Credit Work in Process.
2. Prepare the general journal entry to record the sale of 1,900 pounds of scrap at $.52 a pound on credit.
3. Prepare the general journal entry to record the sale of 2,100 pounds of scrap at $.39 a pound on credit.

PROBLEM 12–3A **Record spoiled and defective goods. (Objs. 2, 3).** The New Jersey Clothing Company produced 500 units on Job 45 at a unit cost of $15 each. On January 4, 19X9, it is found that 17 units have defects and have an estimated sales value of only $6 each.

INSTRUCTIONS Use the account names found in your textbook to do the following:

1. a. Assume that the units are spoiled. Prepare the general journal entry to record the estimated market value of the rejected units. Assume that the spoilage costs are to be charged to Manufacturing Overhead Control.
   b. Compute the unit cost of the remaining finished units.
2. a. Prepare the general journal entry to record the estimated market value of the rejected units. Assume that the spoilage costs are to be absorbed in the cost of the specific job.
   b. Compute the unit cost of the remaining finished units.

3. Assume that the units are defective instead of spoiled. Prepare the general journal entry to record the total rework costs of $35. Also assume that Job 470 is assigned to the necessary rework. The rework is completed on January 4, and the rework costs are to be charged to Manufacturing Overhead Control.

PROBLEM 12–4A **Record a sale of scrap. (Obj. 1).** Crafton Motor Corporation manufactures various types of custom-designed electric motors. Scrap metal is accumulated and periodically sold. The value of this scrap is quite small. Therefore, the company merely collects the material from the factory floor and stores it until it is sold, at which time an entry is made.

Job 748 was in production during the month of July 19X9. Scrap materials from this job were collected and sold on August 10 for $714 on credit.

INSTRUCTIONS Give the general journal entry to record the sale in each of the following cases. Also indicate which subsidiary records would be affected.

1. Sales proceeds to be treated as income.
2. Sales proceeds to be treated as a recovery from the specific job.
3. Sales proceeds to be treated as a reduction of manufacturing overhead.

PROBLEM 12–5A **Record spoiled goods. (Obj. 2).** During the month of March 19X9, the following events involving losses from spoilage took place at the Woodridge Company.

On March 14 a heating mechanism on a cooking machine became defective while Job 743 for 70 units was in production. As a result, four units for which materials had cost $24 were spoiled. Estimated sales value as seconds is $24 each. Total costs accumulated to date on the order are materials, $420; direct labor, $735; and manufacturing overhead, $315.

INSTRUCTIONS 1. Give the general journal entry to have the loss on the four spoiled units absorbed by Job 743.
2. Compute the allocation of the estimated market value of the four spoiled items to the individual cost elements on Job 743.
3. The spoiled items were later sold on March 28 for $75 each on credit. Give the general journal entry to record this sale.

ALTERNATE PROBLEMS

PROBLEM 12–1B **Record a sale of scrap. (Obj. 1).** The Carolina Supply Company applies the proceeds from the sale of scrap against the cost of production. On April 10, 19X9, scrap was sold on credit for $3,120.

INSTRUCTIONS Prepare a general journal entry to record the sale of the scrap in each of the following cases. Use the account names found in your textbook.

1. The firm credits the income from the sale of scrap to Job 829, from which it was derived.

2. The firm credits the income from the sale of scrap to the Manufacturing Overhead Control account for the Fabricating Department, where the scrap originated.

PROBLEM 12–2B **Record scrap inventory. (Obj. 1).** Polinsky Manufacturers maintains a Scrap Inventory account for metal scrap recovered from operations in the Molding Department. On February 15, 19X9, 1,500 pounds of scrap with an estimated market value of $975 are transferred from the factory to the storeroom.

INSTRUCTIONS Use the account names found in your textbook to do the following:

1. Prepare the general journal entry to record the storage of the metal scrap. Credit Work in Process.
2. Prepare the general journal entry to record the sale of 300 pounds of scrap at $.58 a pound on credit.
3. Prepare the general journal entry to record the sale of 500 pounds of scrap at $.72 a pound on credit.

PROBLEM 12–3B **Record spoiled and defective goods. (Objs. 2, 3).** The Fairbanks Machine Company produced 4,000 units on Job 18 at a unit cost of $55 each. On September 8, 19X9, it is found that 60 units have defects and have an estimated sales value of only $34 each.

INSTRUCTIONS Use the account names found in your textbook to do the following:

1. a. Assume that the units are spoiled. Prepare the general journal entry to record the estimated market value of the rejected units. Assume that the spoilage costs are to be charged to Manufacturing Overhead Control.
   b. Compute the unit cost of the remaining finished units.
2. a. Prepare the general journal entry to record the estimated market value of the rejected units. Assume that the spoilage costs are to be absorbed in the cost of the specific job.
   b. Compute the unit cost of the remaining finished units.
3. Assume that the units are defective instead of spoiled. Prepare the general journal entry to record the total rework costs of $585. Also assume that Job 229 is assigned to the necessary rework. The rework is completed on September 8, and the rework costs are to be charged to Manufacturing Overhead Control.

PROBLEM 12–4B **Record a sale of scrap. (Obj. 1).** Ingram Paper Supply manufactures various types of business forms. Scrap paper is accumulated and periodically sold. The value of this scrap is quite small. Therefore, the company merely collects the material from the factory floor and stores it until it is sold, at which time an entry is made.

Job 439, for a large quantity of carbonless invoice forms, was in production during the month of May 19X9. Scrap materials from this job were collected and sold on June 6 for $267 in cash.

INSTRUCTIONS Give the general journal entry to record the sale in each of the following cases. Also indicate which subsidiary records would be affected.

1. Sales proceeds to be treated as income.
2. Sales proceeds to be treated as a recovery from the specific job.
3. Sales proceeds to be treated as a reduction of manufacturing overhead.

PROBLEM 12–5B

Record spoiled goods. (Obj. 2). During the month of November 19X9, the following events involving losses from spoilage took place at the Bennett Tool Company.

On November 8 the control mechanism on an automatic machine become defective while Job 384 for 200 units was in production. As a result, nine units for which materials had cost $198 were spoiled. Estimated sales value as seconds is $55 each. Total costs accumulated to date on the order are materials, $6,600; direct labor, $10,800; and manufacturing overhead, $5,400.

INSTRUCTIONS

1. Give the general journal entry to have the loss on the nine spoiled units absorbed by Job 384.
2. Compute the allocation of the estimated market value of the nine spoiled items to the individual cost elements on Job 384.
3. The spoiled items were later sold on November 29 for $400 each on credit. Give the general journal entry to record this sale.

P A R T
T W O

Process Cost Accounting

13

Process Cost System

In Chapter 2 you learned that a firm's cost accounting system is designed to parallel its flow of operations—procurement, production, warehousing, and selling. In later chapters you learned how a job order cost system is designed and implemented for a company that manufactures products to customer specifications or manufactures dissimilar products in batches or job lots. In this chapter you will be introduced to **process cost accounting,** a cost accounting system that is commonly used by companies that manufacture on a continuous basis only one product or a few almost identical products. When a process cost system is used, a separate Work in Process account is maintained for costs incurred in each producing department or in each process. At the end of the period the costs charged to each department during the period, including costs transferred in from prior departments, are assigned to products worked on in that department during the period. Costs related to products transferred out of the department are charged to the next department, or to Finished Goods Inventory if appropriate.

CHOOSING A COST SYSTEM

A job order cost system is expensive to operate even in a small business because of the work involved in analyzing each cost and recording it on a job cost sheet. For example, all direct materials used and all direct labor costs must be recorded by job number. As a result a job order cost system should be used only when costs incurred must be identified with specific jobs.

The process cost system is used in accounting for costs in mass-production operations such as flour milling, gasoline refining, cement production, and the manufacture of insulating materials for houses. Typically, in such operations all goods are produced for stock rather than for specific customer orders, one unit of production is identical with every other, goods move down the production line in a continuous stream, and all factory procedures are standardized. The identification of specific unit costs is not feasible. Specific identification is not necessary because all units manufactured are identical and are not "made to order." Under these conditions, an average cost per unit is adequate for most control purposes. The **average cost per unit** is obtained by dividing total costs applicable to a producing department by the total number of units produced during the period.

An example of a manufacturing process in which process cost accounting is appropriate is the cement manufacturing industry. Some cement manufacturing plants use a production process consisting of several stages. First, seashells (or some other lime base) are mixed with water and ground in a grinding or preparation department. The resulting lime material is transferred to a mixing department, where it is mixed with a small quantity of a special mud. The resulting slurry is then run through a gas-fired kiln, sometimes called the *cooking department,* and cooked at a high temperature. The cooked materials exit the kiln as small, rocklike pieces, called *clinkers.* The clinkers, along with measured quantities of gypsum and other miscellaneous materials, are then run through another grinding department. The resulting finished product, cement, is run through a bagging department, where bags of some standard size are filled. The bags are then moved to a shipping dock for shipping or are placed in storage in the warehouse. Every bag of cement manufactured is essentially like every other bag, so computation of the average cost per bag manufactured each month is adequate for all costing purposes.

THE FLOW OF PROCESS COSTS

Many procedures and records used in the process cost system are similar to those in job order cost accounting. Here is an overview of the process cost system.

Procurement

Three familiar general ledger accounts are used to record costs as they are incurred: Raw Materials 121, Factory Payroll Clearing 500, and Manufacturing Overhead Control 501.

Materials. Purchases of materials are first recorded in the voucher register and are charged to the Raw Materials account. The raw materials inventory is controlled through the materials ledger. Some firms using process costing do not keep perpetual inventory records for raw materials if there is only one producing department and a single product is manufactured. Instead, a monthly inventory is taken, and the cost of materials used is computed and recorded at that time.

Labor. The same time card and payroll summary procedures are used as in the job order cost system. Gross earnings are charged to the Factory Payroll Clearing account. Since there are no individual jobs, a daily time ticket for each worker is used to accumulate the data required for charging labor costs to the various producing department Work in Process accounts and to the Manufacturing Overhead Control account.

Overhead. Other manufacturing costs are recorded as usual through the payroll register, the voucher register, and general journal vouchers. Details are posted to departmental overhead analysis sheets in the same way as under job order costing. At the end of the month, overhead costs are allocated to producing departments or processes, as explained later.

Production

Costs are charged to Work in Process by one of several arrangements, according to the complexity of the firm's operations.

- A single Work in Process account may be used by a company that has only one producing department.
- Departmental Work in Process accounts are generally used if production flows through several departments. Separate cost figures for each process might also be desirable, if more than one process is carried out in a department. We will assume in this text that a department is established for each major manufacturing process. This is the most commonly used procedure and is the one used here.
- A separate Work in Process account for each of the three cost elements (materials, labor, and overhead) incurred in each department may allow more accurate costing if the business produces multiple products. Costs can later be analyzed for identification with each production run.
- A Work in Process account for each product may be used if a number of products are processed in the same department. This is rarely done, however, because materials, labor, and overhead apply to all products being manufactured in the department.

Let us examine the procedures involved in the second plan—using departmental Work in Process accounts—which is the most common procedure for accumulating costs and assigning them to products. A firm with three producing departments might have the following Work in Process accounts:

123 Work in Process—Department 1
124 Work in Process—Department 2
125 Work in Process—Department 3

Producing departments are often given the names of the processes performed in them. For example, a department might be called the *Mixing Department* because raw materials are mixed in that department.

Costs are charged against (applied to) production as follows:

Materials. Issues of materials are made by an authorized requisition, and each requisition is recorded in a materials requisition journal. As materials are issued, their cost is recorded in the appropriate column in the materials requisition journal. The journal contains a column for each producing department and a column for manufacturing overhead. The totals of the columns in the materials requisition journal are posted to the producing department Work in Process accounts or to Manufacturing Overhead Control. Direct materials are charged to the Work in Process account of the department requisitioning the materials. Indirect materials issued to a producing department may be charged, along with direct materials, to the department's Work in Process account. Alternatively, depending on the manufacturing process and the company's desire for more precise detailed accounting, indirect materials requisitioned by producing departments may be charged to Manufacturing Overhead Control. Materials issued to nonproducing departments, such as the Building Services Department, are always charged to Manufacturing Overhead Control. The manufacturing overhead analysis sheets show the amount of indirect materials charged to Manufacturing Overhead Control that is applicable to each department.

The charging of costs of materials used in the manufacturing process is depicted in this flowchart.

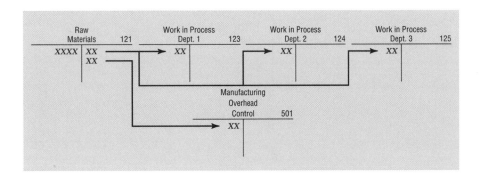

Labor. Labor costs are transferred from the Factory Payroll Clearing account to the departmental Work in Process accounts and the Manufacturing Overhead Control account monthly or weekly on the basis of an analysis of labor costs by departments. The labor charges are obtained from monthly summaries of earnings by departments. As with materials costs, many accountants do not distinguish between direct and indirect labor costs incurred in producing departments. They prefer to charge all labor costs, both direct and indirect, that can be identified with a producing department directly to the Work in Process account for that department. Factory labor costs that relate to service departments are charged to the Manufacturing Overhead Control account.

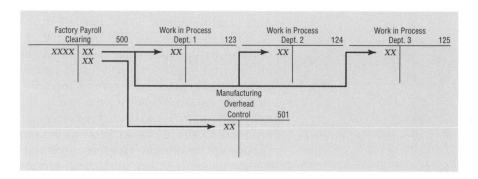

Overhead. Manufacturing overhead costs that have been accumulated and classified in departmental overhead analysis sheets during the period (usually a month) are allocated to producing departments or processes. Some overhead costs may be identified directly with producing departments. Other overhead costs must be allocated to producing departments on some predetermined basis. For example, the overhead analysis sheets may show the amounts of indirect labor and indirect materials attributable directly to each producing department. However, costs related to building occupancy (depreciation, taxes, insurance, repairs, custodial services, and so on) must be allocated to the producing departments on some logical and reasonable basis. The charging of overhead costs to the Work in Process accounts is shown in the flowchart below.

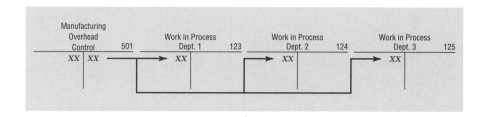

Flow of Costs From One Department to the Next

Costs are transferred from one process to the next process as the product moves toward completion. This cost flow is achieved by crediting a producing department's Work in Process account for the related costs of products completed in that department and transferred out to the next department and debiting the costs to the Work in Process account of the department to which the products are transferred. The costs to be transferred from one department to another or to finished goods are taken from the cost of production report, discussed on page 296.

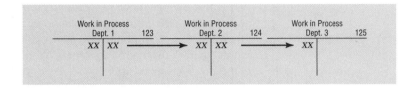

Warehousing

When the goods are finished and transferred to the warehouse to await sale, their cost is debited to Finished Goods 126. The corresponding credit is posted to the Work in Process account of the last department in the producing sequence.

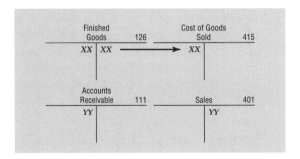

Selling

The cost of products sold is debited to Cost of Goods Sold 415 and credited to Finished Goods 126. In turn, Sales 401 is credited for the selling price, and Cash or Accounts Receivable is debited.

ILLUSTRATION: CHARGING COSTS INTO PRODUCTION IN A PROCESS COST ACCOUNTING SYSTEM

In the preceding paragraphs we have described the flow of manufacturing costs through the accounts of a business using the process cost accounting system. Let us now look at an example of how the procedures and records you have studied are used in practice by examining the records of Apex Computer Designs. This company was recently incorporated by three former employees of a manufacturing company that went out of business. The goal of the owners of the new business is to become a large manufacturer of desks, credenzas, hutches, PC workstations, and other computer furniture. One of the owners was a sales representative for the former employer and has consulted with

SELF-REVIEW

1. Would a process cost accounting system be satisfactory for a building contractor who constructs commercial buildings? Explain.
2. Would a process cost accounting system be satisfactory for a petrochemical plant that produces plastic sheeting 24 hours per day? Explain.
3. Ace Company uses four separate manufacturing processes in producing its sole product. Each process is located in a separate producing department. There are also three nonproducing departments whose costs are treated as manufacturing overhead. How many Work in Process accounts would the company be likely to use?
4. Why is it possible under the process cost system to charge indirect labor and indirect materials in a production department to Work in Process instead of to Manufacturing Overhead?
5. In a process cost accounting system, which accounts are debited and which account is credited when materials are issued from the storeroom?

Answers to Self-Review

1. A process cost system would not be satisfactory for a building contractor who constructs commercial buildings. Each commercial building is different and requires special consideration. A process cost system is best used when there is continuous production of identical products or items that are very similar.
2. Yes. Continuous production of the same product is a production system for which a process cost accounting system is ideal.
3. A Work in Process account is used for each producing department. Thus the company would be likely to have four Work in Process accounts.
4. All costs relating directly to a department are charged to that department, to be assigned to units produced in that department. Since indirect materials and indirect labor are applicable only to the one department, the costs should be assigned to units produced in that department.
5. The Work in Process account of the department in which the materials are used is debited for the cost of materials issued from the storeroom. Indirect materials may be charged to Manufacturing Overhead Control.

purchasing agents of several discount stores who were former customers. As a result of these discussions and the assurance that some of the discount stores will buy their product, the owners of the new business have decided that initially they will manufacture a single style of high-quality credenzas, made of natural materials. After it has established its reputation and increased the size of its marketing network, Apex will expand its line of products. The company has acquired a building, purchased equipment and inventory, hired personnel, and so on, and as of January 1, 19X9, it began production. For the foreseeable future, only one product will be manufactured; therefore, the company's owners and its accountant have decided to use the process cost system. The next paragraphs trace the costs incurred and the costs charged into production during the month of January 19X9.

(The transfer of costs between producing departments and to Finished Goods will be examined in Chapter 14.)

Procurement

The cost records relating to the procurement functions are the same as those used in a job order cost accounting system. The same three general ledger accounts used to record costs incurred are:

121 Raw Materials
500 Factory Payroll Clearing
501 Manufacturing Overhead Control

Purchases of materials are recorded in the purchases journal, a materials ledger is maintained, weekly and semimonthly payroll registers are prepared in the same way as in a job order system, and a voucher register is maintained.

Production

Production flows through three producing departments:

- **The Fabrication Department:** In this department, construction materials are cut into standard sizes and then shaped and prepared for assembly.
- **The Assembly Department:** The fabricated materials are assembled into credenzas in this department; screws, nuts and bolts, and other fastening devices are used in this part of the process.
- **The Completion Department:** In this department the credenzas are sanded, painted, lacquered, and polished.

Departmental work in process accounts are maintained. This means that a separate Work in Process account is opened for each department. The accounts are:

123 Work in Process—Fabrication Department
124 Work in Process—Assembly Department
125 Work in Process—Completion Department

The use of three Work in Process accounts permits the pinpointing of responsibility for production costs to the individual department managers.

Costs are charged into production as materials and services are used in factory operations. The materials requisition journal, monthly payroll summary, voucher register, and general journal vouchers are used to do this. All materials issued are recorded in the materials requisition journal. The **materials requisition journal** contains a column for accumulating the costs of the direct materials requisitioned by each producing department, which are charged to the Work in Process account for each department, and for accumulating the costs of the indirect materials, which are charged to Manufacturing Overhead Control. A payroll summary provides the basis for charging salaries and wages to the departments.

During the month, overhead costs are accumulated in Manufacturing Overhead Control 501 and on the departmental overhead analysis sheets in exactly the same manner as under the job order cost system. These postings come from the materials requisition journal, the payroll summary, the voucher register, and general journal vouchers. At the end of the month, service department overhead costs are allocated to producing departments on a worksheet, as shown on page 300. Then Manufacturing Overhead Control 501 is closed directly into the three departmental Work in Process accounts by an entry on a general journal voucher. (Some companies do not close the overhead account into Work in Process but instead use an overhead application to "apply" overhead, in the same way that you have studied for job order cost accounting.)

PRODUCTION REPORT

At the end of each month a **production report** is prepared for each department by the manager of the department. A production report shows the number of units that were in process in the department at the start of the month, the number of units begun during the month, the number of units transferred out of the department during the month, the number of units still in work in process at the end of the month, and the state of completion of the units still in process at the end of the month.

Cost of Production Report

Based on the production report and the information about costs incurred during the month, a **cost of production report** is prepared for each department at the end of the month. The cost of production report summarizes the costs incurred in the department, the average cost per unit of product, the total costs of products completed and transferred out of the department, and the costs related to the ending inventory of work in process in each department. The cost of production report is not considered further in this chapter, but will be examined in detail in the next three chapters.

Warehousing

Cost procedures related to warehousing are almost the same as those in job order costing. One difference is that the cost of goods completed is transferred from Work in Process—Completion Department (the last department in the manufacturing process) to Finished Goods Inventory by an entry on a general journal voucher rather than by an entry in a completed jobs journal. One summary entry is made at the end of the month to record the cost of all goods completed during the month.

Selling

All recording steps for sales are similar to those used when goods are sold from stock under the job order cost system. The Finished Goods Inventory account is credited, and the Cost of Goods Sold account is debited for the cost of products sold. Accounts Receivable is debited,

Developing an Appropriate Accounting System Is Not Always an Easy Matter

In an accounting textbook it is convenient to assume that a manufacturing process is simple and straightforward, so that it is easy to understand why a company would use either job order cost accounting or process cost accounting. In the "real world," the manufacturing process is not so simple. Most manufacturing companies simply don't make a single product of the same size, shape, color, and so on. For example, a manufacturer of jeans makes pants of different sizes, different colors, and different styles—all on the same processing line and perhaps during the same day. The problem facing the accountant is typical: How should unit costs be calculated? Is it necessary to determine the cost of jeans of different sizes and different colors? (The major factor in answering this question is how much additional cost of materials is involved. If the difference in cost of materials between jeans of different sizes is small, it may be decided that all sizes will be treated as a single product.) Should costs be accumulated for each individual pattern of jeans? (In this case, the major factor may be one of both additional materials and additional labor.) In any event, process cost accounting seems to be the logical answer, but if it is decided to attempt to determine the cost for each style of jeans, for example, it will be necessary to study the manufacturing process carefully. It might be necessary to treat each run of jeans of a particular style as a "job" and to apply job order cost accounting to that run.

This mixture of styles, sizes, colors, and so on, encountered in the jeans manufacturing process is typical of most manufacturing situations. A manufacturer of television sets makes sets of different sizes, different technical characteristics, different features, and so on. Again, the accountant is faced with the problem of developing a system that provides the most accurate measure of unit cost but, at the same time, is practical to implement.

One lesson is clear from these examples. A cost accountant must understand the manufacturing process thoroughly before attempting to develop and implement an accounting system to determine unit costs.

and the Sales account is credited for the selling price of the products sold.

JANUARY TRANSACTIONS

Before making a detailed study of Apex Computer Designs' procedures, let us review the data on the use of materials, labor, and overhead during January 19X9.

Materials

Requisitions for direct and indirect materials have been recorded in the materials requisition journal. The requisitions for indirect materials are also posted to the related departmental overhead analysis sheets. At the end of the month, the journal totals are posted in summary form in order to charge the costs of those materials to factory operations. The materials requisition journal on page 298 shows that the total cost of materials issued in January was $88,660.

MATERIALS REQUISITION JOURNAL

FOR MONTH OF *January*   19 _X9_   PAGE _1_

| DATE | | REQ. NO. | ✔ | WORK IN PROCESS | | | MFG. OVERHEAD CONTROL DR. 501 | | RAW MATERIALS CR.121 | |
				FABRICATION DEPT. DR. 123	ASSEMBLY DEPT. DR. 124	COMPLETION DEPT. DR. 125				
Jan.	2	1	✓	1,854 40					1,854	00
	2	2	✓				90 00		90	00
	3	3	✓		926 36				926	36
	31	Total	✓	54,000 00	21,120 00	6,320 00	7,220 00		88,660	00
				✓	✓	✓	✓		✓	

At this point you should be able to work Exercise 13–1.

Labor

Total charges posted from the payroll registers to the Factory Payroll Clearing account for gross salaries, and wages paid are $133,464. A summary of daily time tickets for the month shows that, of the total labor costs for the month ($150,264), direct labor earnings are $112,824 and indirect labor earnings are $37,440. The amounts chargeable to the various departments are obtained from the regular monthly summary of wages prepared by the payroll unit. The direct labor costs are debited to the related departmental Work in Process accounts. The total of indirect labor costs is debited to Manufacturing Overhead Control 501. Factory Payroll Clearing is credited for the total actual earnings of $150,264. A journal voucher is used to make the necessary entry, as shown below.

JOURNAL VOUCHER   Date _Jan. 31,_   19 _X9_   No. _1-40_

ACCOUNT	ACCT. NO.	✓	DEBIT	CREDIT
Work in Process–Fabrication Dept.	123	✓	3848000	
Work in Process–Assembly Dept.	124	✓	4148000	
Work in Process–Completion Dept.	125	✓	3286400	
Manufacturing Overhead Control	501	✓	3744000	
Factory Payroll Clearing	500	✓		15026400

EXPLANATION
Charged labor cost to production for the month.

PREPARED BY MXH	AUDITED BY AC	APPROVED BY LM

At this point you should be able to work Exercises 13–2 and 13–3.

The balance of $16,800 in the Factory Payroll Clearing account represents unpaid wages at the end of the month.

	Factory Payroll Clearing				NO. 500	
DATE	EXPLANATION	POST. REF.	DEBIT	CREDIT	BALANCE	DR. CR.
19 X9						
Jan. 5		WP	32,960 00		32,960 00	DR.
12		WP	32,664 00		65,624 00	DR.
15		SP	5,120 00		70,744 00	DR.
19		WP	28,800 00		99,544 00	DR.
26		WP	28,800 00		128,344 00	DR.
31		SP	5,120 00		133,464 00	DR.
31		J1-40		150,264 00	16,800 00	CR.

Overhead

Total manufacturing overhead costs incurred during January are $75,756.

	Manufacturing Overhead Control				NO. 501	
DATE	EXPLANATION	POST. REF.	DEBIT	CREDIT	BALANCE	DR. CR.
19 X9						
Jan. 31	Indirect Materials	MR1	7,220 00		7,220 00	DR.
31	Indirect Labor	J1-40	37,448 00		44,660 00	DR.
31	Other overhead	J1-51	11,792 00		56,452 00	DR.
31	Other costs	VR-1	19,304 00		75,756 00	DR.

The department analysis sheets show the following overhead costs for each department:

Facilities	$18,400
General Factory	22,686
Fabrication	18,940
Assembly	5,558
Completion	10,172

Charging these costs to production is a two-step process. First, a worksheet (shown on page 300), almost identical to the one you studied in Chapter 8 (page 175), is prepared to allocate service department costs to the three producing departments.

Second, the figures from the worksheet allocation are entered in a general journal voucher to close Manufacturing Overhead Control 501 into the three departmental Work in Process accounts. (No overhead application rate is used in this procedure because overhead costs are expected to be incurred evenly throughout the year, production is expected to occur evenly throughout the year, and all costs are to be absorbed by the units produced.)

At this point all three elements of manufacturing costs—materials, labor, and overhead—have been charged to work in process. These

Apex Computer Designs

Worksheet for Prorating Service Dept. Costs

Month Ended January 31, 19X9

ITEM	BASIS OF PRORATION	FACILITIES	GENERAL FACTORY	FABRICATION	ASSEMBLY	COMPLETION	TOTAL
Bal. of dept.							
Ov. an. sheets		18 400 00	22 686 00	18 940 00	5 558 00	10 172 00	75 756 00
Prorate Fact.	*floor space**	(18 400 00)	5 520 00	3 680 00	5 152 00	4 048 00	
Prorate Gen. Fact.	*direct labor†*		(28 206 00)	9 620 00	10 370 00	8 216 00	
Total		- 0 -	- 0 -	32 240 00	21 080 00	22 436 00	75 756 00

*General Factory, 30%; Fabrication, 20%; Assembly, 28%; Completion, 22%.
†Fabrication, $38,480 (34.1063%); Assembly, $41,480 (36.7652%); Completion, $32,864 (29.1286%).
 Total, $112,824.

JOURNAL VOUCHER Date __*Jan. 31,*__ 19 _X9_ No. _1-52_

ACCOUNT	ACCT. NO.	✓	DEBIT	CREDIT
Work in Process–Fabrication Dept.	123	✓	32 240 00	
Work in Process–Assembly Dept.	124	✓	21 080 00	
Work in Process–Completion Dept.	125	✓	22 436 00	
Manufacturing Overhead Control	501	✓		75 756 00

EXPLANATION

Closed out control account and recorded

department costs.

PREPARED BY *MXH*	AUDITED BY *AC*	APPROVED BY *LM*

At this point you should be able to work Exercises 13–4 to 13–6 and Problems 13–1A and 13–1B.

charges are shown in the departmental Work in Process accounts below. The charges are made more easily and directly under the process cost system because many time-consuming details, such as those relating to job cost sheets and time tickets, are no longer required.

FLOW OF COSTS THROUGH WORK IN PROCESS ACCOUNTS TO COST OF GOODS SOLD

Earlier in this chapter you learned that in a process cost system the flow of costs through the accounts parallels the flow of products through the manufacturing processes, and then to the Finished Goods Inventory and ultimately into Cost of Goods Sold. In the following four chapters we shall examine in detail how the accountant determines the costs to be transferred from one producing department to the next

		Work in Process–Fabrication Department				NO.	123	
DATE		EXPLANATION	POST. REF.	DEBIT	CREDIT	BALANCE		DR. CR.
19 X9								
Jan. 31		Materials	MR1	54,000 00		54,000	00	DR.
31		Labor	J1-40	38,480 00		92,480	00	DR.
31		Overhead	J1-52	32,240 00		124,720	00	DR.

		Work in Process–Assembly Department				NO.	124	
DATE		EXPLANATION	POST. REF.	DEBIT	CREDIT	BALANCE		DR. CR.
19 X9								
Jan. 31		Materials	MR1	21,120 00		21,120	00	DR.
31		Labor	J1-40	41,480 00		62,600	00	DR.
31		Overhead	J1-52	21,080 00		83,680	00	DR.

		Work in Process–Completion Department				NO.	125	
DATE		EXPLANATION	POST. REF.	DEBIT	CREDIT	BALANCE		DR. CR.
19 X9								
Jan. 31		Materials	MR1	6,320 00		6,320	00	DR.
31		Labor	J1-40	32,864 00		39,184	00	DR.
31		Overhead	J1-52	22,436 00		61,620	00	DR.

producing department or to finished goods, because that calculation is the essential element of process cost accounting. However, in order to illustrate the flow of costs, the following journal entries for Apex Computer Designs at the end of January 19X9 are given:

- Transfer of units of product from the Fabrication Department to the Assembly Department
- Transfer of units of product from the Assembly Department to the Completion Department
- Transfer of units of product from the Completion Department to Finished Goods Inventory
- The sale of units and the related cost of goods sold

Transfer of Product From Fabrication Department to Assembly Department

During January, 880 units of product were transferred from the Fabrication Department to the Assembly Department. The cost accountant determined (as will be explained in Chapter 14) that the costs of the 880 units totaled $103,840. In general journal form, the entry to record the transfer would be:

```
19X9
Jan. 31   Work in Process—Assembly
              Department                    124   103,840
                  Work in Process—Fabrication
                      Department            123            103,840
              Recorded transfer of units of product.
```

Transfer of Product From Assembly Department to Completion Department

Similarly, at the end of January the cost accountant determined that 820 units of product had been transferred from the Assembly Department to the Completion Department and that the cost of those 820 units totaled $176,792. The entry, in summarized general journal form, to record this transfer would be:

```
19X9
Jan. 31   Work in Process—Completion
              Department                    125   176,792
                  Work in Process—Assembly
                      Department            124            176,792
              Recorded transfer of units of product.
```

Transfer of Product From Completion Department to Finished Goods Inventory

During January, 780 units of product were completed and transferred from the Completion Department to Finished Goods Inventory. Based on the assumptions and procedures used by the cost accountant, the cost of these 780 units was $229,008. The entry, in general journal form, to record the completion and transfer of the units is:

```
19X9
Jan. 31   Finished Goods Inventory         126   229,008
                  Work in Process—Completion
                      Department            125            229,008
              Recorded completion and transfer
              of 780 units to Finished Goods.
```

Recording Sales and Cost of Goods Sold

Entries to record sales of products and the related cost of the units sold are exactly the same as those you learned in studying job order cost accounting. Assume that 400 credenzas were sold and shipped during the month of January at a price of $375 each, for a total selling price of $150,000. Since this is the first month of production for Apex, all the credenzas sold came from the January production. As you have just seen, each unit produced in January had an average cost of $293.60. Thus, the 400 units sold had total cost of $117,440 (400 × $293.60 = $117,440). Entries to record the sales and cost of sales during January would be:

19X9				
Jan. 31	Accounts Receivable	112	150,000	
	Sales	301		150,000
	Recorded sales of credenzas during January.			

19X9				
Jan. 31	Cost of Goods Sold	302	117,440	
	Finished Goods Inventory	126		117,440
	Recorded cost of credenzas sold during January.			

SELF-REVIEW

1. In what journal are requisitions for direct materials recorded? Indirect materials?
2. Explain how the materials requisition journal is organized to facilitate posting to the work in process accounts.
3. What is a cost of production report?
4. Is it always necessary to use an overhead application rate under the process cost system? Explain.
5. Postings from the payroll register of the Alberta Company to its Factory Payroll Clearing account totaled $184,000 for the month of September. However, a summary of the time tickets for September showed that actual labor earnings for the month totaled $192,000, which was credited to Factory Payroll Clearing at the end of September. What does the $8,000 difference in these two figures represent?

Answers to Self-Review

1. Requisitions for both direct and indirect materials are entered in the materials requisition journal.
2. The materials requisition journal contains a column for each producing department and a column for manufacturing overhead control. At the end of the month, the total in each column is posted to the appropriate general ledger account.
3. The cost of production report for a producing department summarizes the costs incurred in the department, the average cost per unit of product, the total costs of products completed and transferred out of the department, and the costs related to the ending inventory of work in process in each department.
4. It is not necessary to use an overhead application rate under the process cost accounting system unless overhead costs occur irregularly or production occurs irregularly during the year.
5. The $8,000 difference between actual labor earnings and the earnings recorded in the payroll register represents wages that have been incurred but not yet paid.

At this point you should be able to work Exercises 13–7 to 13–9 and Problems 13–2A and 13–2B.

In this chapter you received an overall view of how the process cost accounting system works. In the next four chapters we will examine some of the more technical aspects of the system and how the most important calculations are made.

PRINCIPLES AND PROCEDURES SUMMARY

- The process cost system is used by companies that manufacture on a continuous basis only one or a few products that are homogeneous.
  - The system is ideal for accounting for costs in mass-production or repetitive operations.
  - Industries such as soft drink processing and bottling, cement factories, petroleum refining, and flour milling use process cost accounting.
  - Typically in manufacturing operations using process cost accounting, all goods are produced for stock, one unit of production is identical with others, factory procedures are standardized, and goods move through production processes in a constant stream.
  - Procurement of materials, labor, and overhead is accounted for in the same way under process cost accounting as in job order cost accounting.
  - The procedures for charging costs into production in a process cost system are very similar to those in a job order cost system. However, there is no job order cost sheet in a process cost system.
    - Direct materials placed in production are charged to departmental Work in Process accounts.
    - Indirect materials issued to producing departments may be charged directly to the department's Work in Process account or to the Manufacturing Overhead account.
    - Direct labor costs are charged to departmental Work in Process accounts.
    - Indirect labor costs in a producing department may be charged to the department's Work in Process account or to the Manufacturing Overhead account.
    - At the end of the period Manufacturing Overhead is analyzed and closed into the departmental Work in Process accounts.
- At the end of the period a cost of production report is prepared for each department. The report summarizes the costs charged to the department and the costs that are transferred out of the department.
- The procedures for accounting for completed goods and for goods sold are identical to those in a job order cost accounting system. The Work in Process account for the final manufacturing department is credited, and the Finished Goods Inventory is debited, for the cost of goods completed. Cost of Goods Sold is debited, and Finished Goods Inventory is credited, for the cost of products sold. Accounts Receivable is debited, and Finished Goods Inventory is credited, for the sales price of products sold.

MANAGERIAL IMPLICATIONS

- It is very important for management to receive the most reasonable and reliable information about product costs, especially about costs per unit.
- Unit costs are used for many purposes, including the measurement of efficiency and cost control, setting prices, and determining inventory valuation.
- The cost accountant must understand which type of cost accounting system should be used in different types of manufacturing situations.
- Process cost accounting generally provides the most useful product cost information when only one product is being manufactured, procedures are standardized, and production occurs in a continuous stream through different processes.
- Process cost accounting also provides the best information about operations in such circumstances, so that costs can be monitored and controlled.
- Process cost accounting is easier and less expensive to use than a job order cost system, because process cost accounting requires fewer time-consuming detailed records, such as the job order cost sheet.

REVIEW QUESTIONS

1. Under what circumstances is the process cost accounting system appropriate?
2. Why is the job order cost ledger eliminated under the process cost accounting system?
3. In what journal are requisitions for indirect materials recorded if the process cost system is used?
4. Why is it sometimes possible under the process cost system to charge indirect materials issued to producing departments to the Work in Process accounts, rather than to Manufacturing Overhead?
5. Under the job order cost accounting system, the daily time ticket for each worker whose wages are classified as direct labor shows the number of the job worked on. What does the time ticket for such workers show if the process cost system is used?
6. A Work in Process account may be used for each producing department. What other arrangements for Work in Process accounts might be used?
7. Under what circumstances would it be reasonable under a process cost system *not* to use an overhead application rate?
8. A company has three Work in Process accounts reflecting the flow of products. To what account are costs transferred from the final Work in Process account?
9. Under what circumstances would a company having four producing departments and using a process cost system debit the

cost of raw materials requisitioned to all four of its Work in Process accounts?

10. How does the procedure for allocating the costs of service departments to the producing departments differ under process costing and job order costing?

MANAGERIAL DISCUSSION QUESTIONS

1. Under what conditions might management decide that a process cost system is appropriate?

2. The Brooks Company must decide whether to manufacture a variety of products to customer specifications or to manufacture a single, uniform product. What are the advantages of each alternative?

3. Assume that you are a cost accountant. The management of the firm where you work has asked how the accounts differ under process and job order cost accounting. How would you answer this question?

4. Your employer manufactures iron products. Most of the products are made on special order to meet customer specifications. Management has asked you whether a process cost accounting system could be used. How would you answer this question?

5. Flores Steel Products manufactures decorative wall paneling used in commercial buildings. Three basic processes are used in manufacturing the panels. Almost all the paneling sold is finished to meet the purchasers' specifications, although one standard plain panel is manufactured for sale to a large number of "home stores." All products go through the first two processes; however, in the final process the panels are finished and decorated to meet customers' specifications. On the basis of this brief description, what cost accounting system(s) should the company consider adopting? Explain.

6. Process cost accounting is sometimes described as a procedure for computing the average cost of products manufactured. Suppose that the management of the firm by which you are employed asks you whether this system is satisfactory as a tool for controlling costs. What is your reply to management?

7. A company using the process cost system has a highly automated factory. Three times each year the factory is closed for one week to perform preventive maintenance on the factory equipment. The company charges overhead, including repair and maintenance costs, directly to the Work in Process accounts. Do you think that the company is using the appropriate method to account for overhead? Explain.

8. Some companies using a process cost accounting system maintain a perpetual inventory for raw materials. Less frequently, some companies do not keep a perpetual inventory but instead rely on a physical count. What can you see as the advantages and disadvantages of each of these methods for determining ending inventory and cost of goods sold?

EXERCISES

EXERCISE 13–1 **Make a journal entry to record materials requisitions. (Obj. 6).** Atomizer Associates uses the process cost system. The details of three materials requisitions issued during January 19X9 follow. Give the entry in general journal form to record the issue of these materials. Ignore account numbers. (Indirect materials are not charged directly to Work in Process.)

- Requisition 105 for direct materials for use in the Lathing Department (122), a producing department, $1,560.
- Requisition 110 for indirect materials used in the Lathing Department, $76. (Ignore account numbers.)
- Requisition 162 for cleaning materials used in the Building Services Department, a service department, $48.

EXERCISE 13–2 **Make a journal entry to charge labor costs to departments. (Obj. 6).** A summary of the factory wages at Long Beach Chemical Products for the month of August shows the following costs. Give the entry in general journal form to charge the labor costs to the departments. (Ignore account numbers.)

Mixing Department	$40,000
Cooking Department	20,000
Compounding Department	60,000
Manufacturing Overhead	70,000

EXERCISE 13–3 **Make a journal entry to charge labor costs to departments. (Obj. 6).** The Mustafa Corporation uses a process cost system. During its first month of manufacturing operations, it had total labor costs of $30,000 applicable to the producing departments. These costs were charged to the Factory Payroll Clearing account. An analysis shows that $17,000 was applicable to the Press Department, $4,500 to the Tooling Department, and $8,500 to the Finishing Department. Give the journal entry to charge labor costs to production. (Ignore account numbers.)

EXERCISE 13–4 **Allocate service department costs (Obj. 5).** The Imir Company allocates the cost of its Building Services Department to the producing departments on the basis of square feet of floor space occupied. The Mixing Department occupies 9,000 square feet, the Cooking Department occupies 2,250 square feet, and the Blending Department occupies 3,000 square feet. The costs of the Facilities and Maintenance Department for March 19X9 totaled $11,400. How much should be allocated to each producing department?

EXERCISE 13–5 **Prepare a worksheet to prorate service department costs; prepare a journal entry to charge service department costs to producing departments. (Objs. 5, 6).** The balances of the departmental overhead analysis sheets of Alomar Products for August 19X9 show the following costs. The direct labor cost and the percentage of floor space occupied by each producing department are also shown.

Department	Cost	Percentage of Floor Space	Direct Labor Costs
Building Facilities	$15,000		
General Factory	12,000	30	
Mixing	14,000	25	$40,000
Cooking	3,000	28	20,000
Compounding	5,000	17	60,000

a. Prepare a worksheet for prorating service department costs, similar to the one on page 300. The overhead cost of the Building Facilities Department is allocated on the basis of the percentage of space occupied. The overhead cost of the General Factory Department is allocated on the basis of direct labor costs.

b. Based on the worksheet prepared in Instruction a, give the general journal entry to close Manufacturing Overhead Control into the three departmental Work in Process accounts. (Ignore account numbers.)

EXERCISE 13–6   **Allocate and journalize service department costs.   (Objs. 5, 6).** For the month of July 19X9, the Isaacs Manufacturing Company had the direct labor costs shown below. The overhead costs of $3,600 incurred by the Facilities Department are allocated to the three other departments on the basis of floor space occupied. The overhead costs of $9,300 incurred by the General Services Department plus the allocated costs of the Facilities Department are allocated on the basis of direct labor costs.

Department	Floor Space	Direct Labor Costs
General Services	2,000 square feet	
Cutting	7,000 square feet	$12,000
Finishing	5,000 square feet	$30,000

a. What amount of the costs of the Facilities Department should be allocated to each of the other departments?

b. What amount of the total General Services Department Costs, including all allocated Facilities Department Costs, should be allocated to each production department?

EXERCISE 13–7   **Record completion of goods.   (Obj. 7).**   The last department in the production process of Samuelson Coated Cable Company is the Coating Department. At the end of June the cost of goods completed during the month was determined to be $114,000. Give the general journal entry to record the cost of goods completed during the month. (Ignore account numbers.)

EXERCISE 13–8   **Make journal entries for sales and cost of goods sold.   (Obj. 7).** During the month of June the total sales of the Midway Company were $233,000. The cost of those goods was $151,000. Give the general journal entries to record the sales and the cost of goods sold. (Ignore account numbers.)

EXERCISE 13-9   **Make journal entries for sales and cost of goods sold. (Obj. 7).** During March 19X9 the Berne Manufacturing Company had total sales of $1,200,000. The goods were sold at a gross profit rate of 15 percent on sales. Give the journal entries to record the sales and the cost of goods sold.

PROBLEMS

PROBLEM 13-1A   **Record procurement of materials, labor, and overhead; allocate service department costs; charge manufacturing costs into production. (Objs. 4, 5, 6).** The management of McIntosh Furniture, Inc., a producer of school desks, uses a process cost accounting system. During May 19X9 the following data appear in the firm's records: Page 5 of the voucher register shows a debit of $18,604 to Raw Materials 121 and a debit of $2,476 to Manufacturing Overhead Control 501. Page 5 of the materials requisition journal shows issues of raw materials as follows:

Distribution	Amount
Cutting Department	$ 7,250
Assembly Department	5,628
Finishing Department	1,618
Manufacturing Overhead Control	1,468
Total Raw Materials Issued	$15,964

The weekly payroll register shows labor costs as follows:

Date	Amount
May 5	$3,840
12	3,756
19	3,904
26	3,874

The monthly payroll register shows salaries of $5,058. Accrued wages and salaries on May 31 were $2,194. The monthly summary of labor costs shows the distribution of the charges as follows:

Distribution	Amount
Cutting Department	$5,528
Assembly Department	6,414
Finishing Department	7,628
Manufacturing Overhead Control	3,056

The schedule of monthly fixed overhead charges contains the following figures:

Overhead	Amount
Insurance	$ 170
Taxes	1,564
Depreciation	866

INSTRUCTIONS

1. Set up the following general ledger accounts:

121	Raw Materials
132	Work in Process—Cutting Department
133	Work in Process—Assembly Department
134	Work in Process—Finishing Department
137	Finished Goods Inventory
500	Factory Payroll Clearing
501	Manufacturing Overhead Control

2. Post the debit entries from the voucher register to the appropriate general ledger accounts.
3. Post the distribution of raw materials from the materials requisition journal to the appropriate general ledger accounts.
4. Post the debit entries for each week from the weekly payroll register to the appropriate general ledger account.
5. Post the debit entry from the monthly payroll register to the appropriate general ledger account.
6. Prepare a general journal voucher to record accrued salaries and wages on May 31. (Credit Salaries and Wages Payable. Number the voucher 5-10. Post to the debit account.
7. Prepare a general journal voucher to charge labor costs to production. Number the voucher 5-11. Post to the general ledger accounts.
8. Post the debit entries from the schedule of monthly fixed overhead charges to the appropriate general ledger account.
9. Complete the worksheet for prorating the costs of the Factory Services Department to the producing departments. Prorate on the basis of 45 percent to Cutting, 35 percent to Assembly and 20 percent to Finishing. Round calculations to the nearest whole dollar. The overhead analysis sheet shows the following totals for overhead in each department:

Factory Services Department	$1,386
Cutting Department	1,962
Assembly Department	3,212
Finishing Department	3,040

10. Prepare the general journal voucher to apportion manufacturing overhead to the producing departments. Number the voucher 5-12. Post to the general ledger accounts.

PROBLEM 13–2A

Record procurement of materials, labor, and overhead; allocate service department costs; charge manufacturing costs into production; record completion and sale of product. (Objs. 4, 5, 6, 7).
The Great Midwest Manufacturing Company uses the process cost system. Selected general ledger accounts and balances as of January 1, 19X9, are listed below.

111	Accounts Receivable	$120,000
121	Raw Materials	200,000
123	Work in Process—Cleaning Department	-0-

124	Work in Process—Mixing Department	-0-
126	Finished Goods	280,000
201	Vouchers Payable	260,000
202	Salaries and Wages Payable	-0-
204	Other Accounts	-0-
401	Sales	-0-
415	Cost of Goods Sold	-0-
500	Factory Payroll Clearing	-0-
501	Manufacturing Overhead Control	-0-

INSTRUCTIONS

1. Enter the January 1, 19X9, balances in the general ledger accounts.
2. The transactions for January 19X9 are listed below. Record the January transactions in general journal form. Date all entries January 31. Start with journal page 1.
   a. Purchased raw materials for $214,000 on credit.
   b. Issued materials from the storeroom as follows:

      To Cleaning Department, $182,000
      To Mixing Department, $26,000
      To Service Departments, $9,000

   c. Recorded labor costs of $183,000 at the payroll dates.
   d. Recorded accrued wages on January 31, $9,000. (Credit Salaries and Wages Payable.)
   e. Charged labor costs to production as follows:

      To Cleaning Department, $61,000
      To Mixing Department, $106,000
      To Service Departments, $25,000

   f. Incurred $4,000 in miscellaneous manufacturing overhead costs, such as power, lighting, taxes, and repairs. (Credit Other Accounts.)
   g. Allocated manufacturing overhead costs equally between the two producing departments.
   h. Transferred goods costing $202,000 from the Cleaning Department to the Mixing Department.
   i. Transferred goods costing $351,000 from the Mixing Department to Finished Goods Inventory.
   j. Sold goods for $520,000 on credit in January.
   k. Goods sold in January cost $400,000.
3. Post the January transactions to the accounts listed.

ALTERNATE PROBLEMS

PROBLEM 13–1B **Record procurement of materials, labor, and overhead; allocate service department costs; charge manufacturing costs into production. (Objs. 4, 5, 6).** The Unicorn Company, which produces a medicinal compound, uses the process cost accounting system.

During April 19X9 the following data appear in the firm's records: Page 4 of the voucher register shows a debit of $16,471 to Raw Materials 121 and a debit of $1,770 to Manufacturing Overhead Control 501. Page 4 of the materials requisition journal shows issues of raw materials as follows:

Distribution	Amount
Grinding Department	$ 6,200
Compounding Department	4,750
Packaging Department	906
Manufacturing Overhead Control	1,620
Total Raw Materials Issued	$13,476

The weekly payroll register shows labor costs as follows:

Date	Amount
Apr. 5	$2,375
12	2,638
21	2,874
26	2,518

The monthly payroll register shows salaries of $3,895. Accrued salaries and wages at the end of the month were $1,712. The monthly summary of labor costs shows the distribution of the charges as follows:

Distribution	Amount
Grinding Department	$4,805
Compounding Department	3,251
Packaging Department	4,620
Manufacturing Overhead Control	3,336

The schedule of monthly fixed overhead charges contains the following figures:

Overhead	Amount
Insurance	$218
Taxes	847
Depreciation	486

INSTRUCTIONS

1. Set up the following general ledger accounts:

121	Raw Materials
132	Work in Process—Grinding Department
133	Work in Process—Compounding Department
134	Work in Process—Packaging Department
137	Finished Goods Inventory
500	Factory Payroll Clearing
501	Manufacturing Overhead Control

2. Post the debit entries from the voucher register to the appropriate general ledger accounts.
3. Post the distribution of raw materials from the materials requisition journal to the appropriate general ledger accounts.

4. Post the debit entries for each week from the weekly payroll register to the appropriate general ledger account.
5. Post the debit entry from the monthly payroll register to the appropriate general ledger account.
6. Prepare a general journal voucher to record accrued wages. (Credit Salaries and Wages Payable.) Number the voucher 4-10. Post to the debit account.
7. Prepare a general journal voucher to charge labor costs to production. Number the voucher 4-11. Post to the general ledger accounts.
8. Post the debit entries from the schedule of monthly fixed overhead charges to the appropriate general ledger account.
9. Complete the worksheet for prorating the costs of the Factory Services Department to the producing departments. Prorate on the basis of 34 percent to Grinding, 25 percent to Compounding, and 41 percent to Packaging. Round calculations to the nearest whole dollar. The overhead analysis sheet shows the following totals for overhead in each department.

Factory Services Department	$2,885
Grinding Department	1,897
Compounding Department	1,561
Packaging Department	1,934

10. Prepare the general journal voucher to apportion manufacturing overhead to the producing departments. Number the voucher 4-12. Post to the general ledger accounts.

PROBLEM 13–2B

Record procurement of materials, labor, and overhead; allocate service department costs; charge manufacturing costs into production; record completion and sale of product. (Objs. 4, 5, 6, 7).
The Antonelli Plastics Company uses the process cost system. General ledger accounts and balances as of January 1, 19X9, are listed below.

111	Accounts Receivable	$160,000
121	Raw Materials	240,000
123	Work in Process—Blending Department	-0-
124	Work in Process—Cooking Department	-0-
126	Finished Goods	360,000
201	Vouchers Payable	760,000
202	Salaries and Wages Payable	-0-
204	Other Accounts	-0-
401	Sales	-0-
415	Cost of Goods Sold	-0-
500	Factory Payroll Clearing	-0-
501	Manufacturing Overhead Control	-0-

INSTRUCTIONS

1. Enter the January 1, 19X9, balances in the general ledger accounts.
2. The transactions for January 19X9 are listed below. Record the January transactions in general journal form. Date all entries January 31. Start with journal page 1.

a. Purchased raw materials for $218,000 on credit.
b. Issued raw materials from the storeroom as follows:

   To Blending Department, $204,000
   To Cooking Department, $14,000
   To Service Departments, $18,000

c. Recorded labor costs of $262,000 at the payroll dates.
d. Recorded accrued wages on January 31, $26,000. (Credit Salaries and Wages Payable.)
e. Charged labor costs to production as follows:

   To Blending Department, $52,000
   To Cooking Department, $174,000
   To Service Departments, $36,000

f. Incurred $32,000 in miscellaneous manufacturing overhead costs, such as repairs, power, lighting, and taxes. (Credit Other Accounts.)
g. Allocated manufacturing overhead costs to the producing departments as follows:

   To Blending Department, $36,000
   To Cooking Department, $50,000

h. Transferred goods costing $292,000 from the Blending Department to the Cooking Department.
i. Transferred goods costing $474,000 from the Cooking Department to Finished Goods Inventory.
j. Sold goods for $655,000 on credit in January.
k. Cost of goods sold in January, $504,000.

3. Post the January transactions to the accounts listed.

CHAPTER
14

Production Data and Cost Flow

The systematic accumulation of costs for each process or department, discussed in Chapter 13, is the first phase in determining unit costs. The second phase is to find the total production for each process during the period. Once the production data are available, an average unit cost for the process may be established by dividing the total cost by the total units of output. The **cost of production report** summarizes all information about production and costs in the department during the period. In this chapter you will learn how to prepare a cost of production report for a department when there is no beginning work in process.

OBJECTIVES

1. Understand periodic production reports and explain how they are used in computing the cost of goods completed in a process cost accounting system.
2. Use the percentage of completion of the ending inventory, as shown in the periodic production report, to compute equivalent units of production.
3. Use equivalent units of production to calculate the costs of materials, labor, and overhead in ending inventory and in goods transferred out of the department when there was no beginning work in process.
4. Prepare a departmental cost of production report.
5. Prepare journal entries to charge costs into production and to record the costs of products transferred out of a department.

NEW TERMS

Cost of production report (p. 315)
Equivalent units of production (p. 316)

DEPARTMENTAL PRODUCTION REPORTS

Departmental managers are responsible for achieving the production goals assigned to their departments. They direct and control the performance of the workers so that the desired output is achieved on schedule and according to specifications. Production records are an inevitable and necessary part of this managerial activity. The departmental manager uses these production records to prepare periodic production reports in order to make managerial decisions.

The manager of each producing department at Apex Computer Designs is required to submit a monthly production report. This report includes the following data, as illustrated below for the Fabrication Department of Apex for the month of January 19X9, the first month of manufacturing operations for the company:

1. Number of units started in production
2. Number of units completed and transferred to the next department
3. Number of units remaining in process
4. Stage of completion of the ending work in process

FABRICATION DEPARTMENT
Monthly Production Report
January 19X9

Quantity

Started in Production—Current Month	1,080
Transferred Out to Next Department	880
Work in Process—Ending	200

Stage of Completion of Ending Work in Process

Materials	complete
Labor	80%
Overhead	80%

The last section of the report, which contains an estimate of the stage of completion of the work still in process at the end of the month, warrants special attention. Production efforts and the related costs are expended during the month on incomplete as well as on fully processed goods. This fact must be recognized in the reports and statements because the average cost must consider all units worked on during the month. The manager draws on past experience to estimate the stage of completion of the ending work in process inventory.

EQUIVALENT UNITS OF PRODUCTION

The cost accountant uses the manager's stage-of-completion estimate to equate the incomplete and completed goods in terms of a common denominator, or common units of measure. This common denominator is **equivalent units of production** for each cost element. Units of incomplete products are converted to equivalent production units by multiplying the number of units in process by the percentage of completion. Thus 200 units that are estimated to be 80 percent completed as to labor and overhead are equivalent to 160 completed units (200 × .80 = 160).

From the monthly production report of the Fabrication Department, shown on page 316, the equivalent production for each cost element (materials, labor, and overhead) is computed as shown below.

FABRICATION DEPARTMENT
Equivalent Units of Production Computations
Month of January 19X9

Materials

Transferred Out to Next Department	880
Work in Process—Ending (200 credenzas × 100%)	200
Equivalent Production for Materials	1,080

Labor and Manufacturing Overhead

Transferred Out to Next Department	880
Work in Process—Ending (200 × 80%)	160
Equivalent Production for Labor and Overhead	1,040

Materials

The equivalent production for materials (1,080) is the sum of the number of units completed and transferred to the next department (880) and the number of units remaining in process (200). This is because the manager's estimate of completion shows that all materials needed to process these units in the Fabrication Department have been issued and charged to the Work in Process account.

Labor and Overhead

The equivalent production for labor and manufacturing overhead involves two factors. The first factor is the 880 units transferred to the next department, which are *100 percent complete* in terms of labor and manufacturing overhead. The second factor is the 200 credenzas still in process, which are estimated to be *80 percent complete* as to both labor and manufacturing overhead. Completing 80 percent of the work on 200 units is equivalent to performing 100 percent of the work on 160 units (200 × .80 = 160). The resulting equivalent production is 1,040 credenzas (880 + 160). This figure means that enough labor and overhead have been expended on a total of 1,080 credenzas (some only partly finished) to have fully completed 1,040 credenzas if the costs had been expended entirely on the smaller number of units.

Although this example assumes that labor and overhead in the ending work in process are at the same stage of completion, this is not always true. If the two elements are at different stages of completion, it will be necessary to make separate calculations of equivalent units of production for the two elements.

In the next section of this chapter you will learn how equivalent units are used to compute the cost of goods transferred out of a department and the cost of the ending inventory in the department.

SELF-REVIEW

1. Who should prepare the monthly production report for a department? Why?
2. Why is it often necessary to compute equivalent units of production when a process cost system is used?
3. Explain why labor and overhead would not be fully completed in the ending work in process inventory even though materials might be 100 percent complete.
4. Are labor and overhead always at the same stage of completion in the ending work in process inventory?
5. At the end of the month 2,200 units of product are in process. The departmental manager estimates that 90 percent of materials costs and 60 percent of labor and overhead costs have been added. Compute the equivalent units of materials, labor, and overhead in ending work in process.

Answers to Self-Review

1. The manager of the production department should prepare the production report because the manager has first-hand knowledge of the status of the work in process and other experience and training that should be invaluable in determining the stage of completion.
2. It is usually necessary to compute equivalent units of production because, in order to determine a meaningful cost per unit, the work in process must be considered. Since not all the work has been completed on the work in process, it is necessary to convert these units to a unit of measure that is comparable to the units that were completed in the department.
3. Frequently, all materials are added at the start of the producing process in a department. However, labor and overhead costs are incurred throughout the entire month in working on the raw materials. Even in departments in which materials are not added at the start of production, they may be added at times that have no relationship to the stage of completion of labor and overhead.
4. Labor and overhead may not be at the same stage of completion. Although overhead costs are generally assumed to have a relationship to labor, some other factor (such as machine hours) may be more important in determining the stage of completion of overhead.

At this point you should be able to work Exercises 14–1 and 14–2.

5. Materials: 2,200 units × 90 percent = 1,980 equivalent units. Labor and overhead: 2,200 units × 60 percent = 1,320 equivalent units.

COST OF PRODUCTION REPORT

The cost data accumulated in the Work in Process accounts (see page 320) and the equivalent production data now available make it possible to compute an average unit cost for each equivalent unit of production for materials, labor, and overhead. If the average cost per equivalent unit of each of the three elements is applied to the number of units completed and transferred out of the department during the month, the total cost of product transferred out is determined. Similarly, if the cost per equivalent unit of each element is multiplied by the number of equivalent units of that element in the ending work in process inventory, the total cost of the ending inventory can be determined.

The cost of production report for Apex Computer Designs' Fabrication Department is shown below. The report contains two sections: the Quantity Schedule and the Cost Schedule.

FABRICATION DEPARTMENT
Cost of Production Report
Month of January 19X9

QUANTITY SCHEDULE	UNITS
(a) Quantity to Be Accounted For:	
Started in Production—Current Month	1,080
Total to Be Accounted For	1,080
(b) Quantity Accounted For:	
Transferred Out to Next Department	880
Work in Process—Ending	200
Total Accounted For	1,080

COST SCHEDULE	TOTAL COST	E.P. UNITS	UNIT COST
(c) Costs to Be Accounted For:			
Costs in Current Department			
Materials	$ 54,000.00 ÷	1,080 =	$ 50.00
Labor	38,480.00 ÷	1,040 =	37.00
Overhead	32,240.00 ÷	1,040 =	31.00
Total Costs to Be Accounted For	$124,720.00		$118.00
(d) Costs Accounted For:			
(*1*) Transferred Out to Next Department	$103,840.00 =	880 ×	$118.00
(*2*) Work in Process—Ending			
Materials	$ 10,000.00 =	200 ×	$ 50.00
Labor	5,920.00 =	160 ×	37.00
Overhead	4,960.00 =	160 ×	31.00
Total Work in Process	$ 20,880.00		
Total Costs Accounted For	$124,720.00		

Quantity Schedule

The Quantity Schedule section is divided into two parts. The first half, (a) Quantity to Be Accounted For, shows the number and source of the units handled during the month. Since January 19X9 is the first month of Apex Computer Designs' operation, production of all units was started during the current month. The second half, (b) Quantity Accounted For, shows what happened to the units reported in the first half of the Quantity Schedule. In this instance, 880 units were completely processed and transferred out to the next department, and 200 units remained on hand at the end of the month. The two parts of the Quantity Schedule complete a reconciliation of physical units *to be* accounted for with physical units that *are* accounted for.

Cost Schedule

The first part of the Cost Schedule, (c) Costs to Be Accounted For, shows the total cost to be accounted for. It also shows the cost of each element per equivalent unit of production and the total cost of each equivalent unit.

■ The total costs come from the general ledger account Work in Process—Fabrication Department 123, shown on page 301 and reproduced below.

Work in Process–Fabrication Department					NO.	123	
DATE	EXPLANATION	POST. REF.	DEBIT	CREDIT	BALANCE		DR. CR.
19 X9							
Jan. 31	_Materials_	_MR1_	_54,000 00_		_54,000_	_00_	_DR._
31	_Labor_	_J1-40_	_38,480 00_		_92,480_	_00_	_DR._
31	_Overhead_	_J1-52_	_32,240 00_		_124,720_	_00_	_DR._

■ The unit cost of each element is computed by dividing the total cost of the element by the related equivalent production units shown on the departmental equivalent production report (page 317). In the case of materials, all units are considered to be 100 percent complete. The total materials cost of $54,000 is divided by 1,080 units to give a unit cost of $50 for materials in the fabricating process.

■ In the case of labor and overhead, the total cost for each element (from the general ledger) is divided by the 1,040 equivalent production units (from the equivalent production report) to give the unit costs, $37.00 and $31.00, for these elements in process.

■ After the unit cost for each of the three elements has been computed, the unit costs are added to determine the cumulative total cost per equivalent unit, $118 ($50 + $37 + $31). The cumulative total cost for all units, $124,720, shown on the cost of production report, agrees with the balance of the general ledger account Work in Process—Fabrication Department 123.

■ The unit cost for each element and the total unit cost are then used in the second part of the Cost Schedule.

The second part of the Cost Schedule, (d) Costs Accounted For, relates costs to the production operations of the period.

■ The total cost of the units completely processed and transferred out to the next department is calculated in Part 1 of Section (d), Transferred Out to Next Department. The cumulative unit cost determined in the previous half of the Cost Schedule ($118) is multiplied by the number of units transferred out (880) from the Quantity Schedule. The result is a total cost of $103,840 for units transferred to the Assembly Department Schedule during the month.

■ Part 2 of Section (d), Work in Process—Ending, shows the cost of the work remaining in process at the end of the month. The unit cost for each element, computed in Section (c), is multiplied by the equivalent units of that element in the ending work in process. The total cost of the materials in the work in process is computed by multiplying the materials element unit cost of $50 by 200 equivalent units (200 units of product to which all materials have been added, shown as the second item on the equivalent production report on page 317) for a total of $10,000. The labor cost in ending work in process, $5,920, is computed by multiplying the labor element unit cost of $37 by the 160 equivalent units of production in process (shown on the cost of production report on page 317). Similarly, overhead in the ending work in process is determined to be $4,960 (160 equivalent units multiplied by $31 per equivalent unit). When all three elements have been costed in this manner, the total cost of the work in process is found to be $20,880.

At this point you should be able to work Exercises 14–3 and 14–4.

The Cost Schedule is designed to reconcile total cost figures. The total costs incurred in the production process must agree with the total costs related to both the units that were fully completed and those that were partially completed during the month. If small errors occur as a result of rounding off numbers, the cost of goods transferred out of the department, as shown in Part 1 of Section (d) of the Cost Schedule, is adjusted to absorb the rounding error. Technically, a portion of the rounding error should be allocated to work in process. However, this would require a great deal of effort and would not have a meaningful result, because typically most of the costs apply to work transferred out of the department during the month. As a result, adjust the cost of units transferred out for the amount of the rounding error.

FLOW OF UNITS AND COSTS—SUBSEQUENT DEPARTMENTS

From the Fabrication Department, the product moves into the Assembly Department and then to the Completion Department. Equivalent units are computed, and a cost of production report is prepared for each department.

Assembly Department

Monthly Production Report. The second department in Apex Computer Designs' production sequence is the Assembly Department. The 880 units transferred out of the Fabrication Department become the input for the Assembly Department's operations during the month. These units appear in the Assembly Department's monthly production report, as shown below.

ASSEMBLY DEPARTMENT Monthly Production Report January 19X9	
Quantity	
Transferred In From Prior Department	880
Transferred Out to Next Department	820
Work in Process—Ending	60
Stage of Completion of Ending Work in Process	
Materials	complete
Labor	50%
Overhead	50%

SELF-REVIEW

1. What are the two sections of the Quantity Schedule in a cost of production report?
2. What is the source of the data for the Quantity Schedule?
3. What is the source of the data for the Cost Schedule in a cost of production report?
4. How is the unit cost for each cost element computed?
5. How is the ending work in process amount for each cost element determined?
6. What two cost figures make up the Total Costs Accounted For in the cost of production report?

Answers to Self-Review

1. The two sections of the Quantity Schedule in a cost of production report are Quantity to Be Accounted For (which shows all the units that were available to be worked on in the department) and the Quantity Accounted For, which shows what happened to the quantity that had to be accounted for.
2. The source of data for the Quantity Schedule is the departmental production report.
3. The source of data for the Cost Schedule is the departmental Work in Process account.
4. The unit cost for each element is determined by dividing the total cost of that element by the number of equivalent units for the element.
5. The ending work in process for each element is determined by multiplying the equivalent units of production for the element in the ending work in process by the number of equivalent units of that element in process.
6. The Total Costs Accounted For section is made up of the cost of the goods transferred out of the department during the period and the ending work in process.

Equivalent Units of Production.   Not all units in the Assembly Department are completely processed before January 31. Equivalent units of production must, therefore, be computed from the production data supplied by the departmental manager. The equivalent production computations are shown below.

ASSEMBLY DEPARTMENT
Equivalent Production Computations
Month of January 19X9

Materials
Transferred Out to Next Department	820
Work in Process—Ending (60 credenzas × 100%)	60
Equivalent Production for Materials	880

Labor and Manufacturing Overhead
Transferred Out to Next Department	820
Work in Process—Ending (60 credenzas × 50%)	30
Equivalent Production for Labor and Overhead	850

At this point you should be able to work Problems 14–1A and 14–1B.

Cost of Production Report. The equivalent production unit data, shown on page 322, and the costs accumulated in the account Work in Process—Assembly Department 124 (shown on page 301 and reproduced below) provide the information needed to complete the cost of production report for the second department.

Work in Process–Assembly Department					NO. 124	
DATE	EXPLANATION	POST. REF.	DEBIT	CREDIT	BALANCE	DR. CR.
19 X9						
Jan. 31 Materials		MR1	21,120 00		21,120 00	DR.
31 Labor		J1-40	41,480 00		62,600 00	DR.
31 Overhead		J1-52	21,080 00		83,680 00	DR.

The first part of the Quantity Schedule, (a) Quantity to Be Accounted For, reflects the receipt of 880 units from the Fabrication Department. The second part, (b) Quantity Accounted for, shows what was done with them. Of the 880 units, 820 were fully processed and transferred out to the Completion Department. The remaining 60 units are still in process at the end of the month.

This time the first part of the Cost Schedule, Costs to Be Accounted For, includes the total cost transferred in from the prior department as well as costs, by elements, incurred in the current department. The figures on the Costs in Prior Department line are the same as those in Part 1 of Section (d) in the cost of production report of the Fabrication Department, shown on page 319. The total costs incurred in the current department are taken from Work in Process—Assembly Department 124, shown above.

Other current department cost data are determined as follows:

■ The unit cost of each element in the current department is computed by dividing the equivalent units of production into the total cost of that element. In the case of materials, all units are again considered to be 100 percent complete. Thus $21,120 divided by 880 gives a unit cost of $24 for materials in the Assembly Department. In the case of labor and overhead, the total cost of each element is divided by the 850 equivalent units of production (from the equivalent production schedule) to give unit costs of $48.80 and $24.80 for labor and overhead in the assembly process. Thus the total cost added per equivalent unit of completed product in the Assembly Department is $97.60.
■ The costs in the current department (both unit and total costs) are added to the prior department costs to obtain new cumulative total costs to be accounted for. The cost of production report shows that total costs incurred to date amount to $187,520 and that the average unit cost incurred to date is $215.60.
■ The unit cost for each element and the total unit cost are used to complete the second part of the Cost Schedule, costs accounted for.

ASSEMBLY DEPARTMENT
Cost of Production Report
Month of January 19X9

QUANTITY SCHEDULE	UNITS
(a) Quantity to Be Accounted For:	
Transferred In From Prior Department	880
Total to Be Accounted For	880
(b) Quantity Accounted For:	
Transferred Out to Next Department	820
Work in Process—Ending	60
Total Accounted For	880

COST SCHEDULE	TOTAL COST		E.P. UNITS		UNIT COST
(c) Costs to Be Accounted For:					
Costs in Prior Department	$103,840.00	=	880	×	$118.00
Costs in Current Department					
Materials	$21,120.00	÷	880	=	$24.00
Labor	41,480.00	÷	850	=	48.80
Overhead	21,080.00	÷	850	=	24.80
Total Costs in Current Dept.	83,680.00				$ 97.60
Total Costs to Be Accounted For	$187,520.00				$215.60
(d) Costs Accounted For:					
(1) Transferred Out to Next Department:	$176,792.00	=	820	×	$215.60
(2) Work in Process—Ending Costs in					
Prior Department	$ 7,080.00	=	60	×	$118.00
Costs in Current Department					
Materials	1,440.00	=	60	×	24.00
Labor	1,464.00	=	30	×	48.80
Overhead	744.00	=	30	×	24.80
Total Work in Process	$ 10,728.00				
Total Costs Accounted For	$187,520.00				

Costs are accounted for in the second section of the Cost Schedule—Section (d)—as follows:

- The cost of the goods transferred out to the Completion Department (Part 1) is determined by multiplying the unit cost of $215.60 by the 820 units transferred ($215.60 × 820 = $176,792). This total cost figure will ultimately flow into Work in Process—Completion Department 125 in the general ledger.
- The cost of the work in process is again determined (in Part 2) by multiplying the unit costs of the various elements by the number of equivalent units of each element.
- Note that work in process costs in the Assembly Department must now include the $118 unit cost that originated in the Fabrication Department. Later we will examine the journal entry to record this transfer of costs.

At this point you should be able to work Exercises 14–4 to 14–8 and Problems 14–2A and 14–2B.

When all costs have been computed and added, the cost of the work remaining in process amounts to $10,728. Also note that the total costs to be accounted for have been reconciled with the total costs accounted for ($187,520).

Completion Department

Monthly Production Report. The third department in Apex Computer Designs' production sequence is the Completion Department. The 820 units transferred out of the Assembly Department become the basis of the Completion Department's operations during the month as shown below.

COMPLETION DEPARTMENT
Monthly Production Report
January 19X9

Quantity

Transferred In From Prior Department	820
Transferred Out to Finished Goods	780
Work in Process—Ending	40

Stage of Completion of Ending Work in Process

Materials	25%
Labor	25%
Overhead	25%

Equivalent Units of Production. At the end of the month, the equivalent units of production must be calculated because not all units are fully completed during the month. The schedule of equivalent units of production is shown below.

COMPLETION DEPARTMENT
Equivalent Production Computations
Month of January 19X9

Materials, Labor, and Manufacturing Overhead

Transferred Out to Finished Goods	780
Work in Process—Ending (40 credenzas × 25%)	10
Equivalent Production for Materials, Labor, and Overhead	790

Cost of Production Report. The costs accumulated in the Work in Process—Completion Department 125 account (page 326) are used with the equivalent production unit data to prepare the cost of production report. The cost of production report is shown on page 326.

In the Quantity Schedule, the entire quantity to be accounted for (820 units) was received from the Assembly Department. A total of 780 units were then fully processed and transferred to Finished Goods, leaving 40 units in process.

In the Cost Schedule, the costs to be accounted for are determined in the same way they were accounted for in the Fabrication and Assembly Departments.

Work in Process–Completion Department					**NO.** _125_		
DATE	EXPLANATION	POST. REF.	DEBIT	CREDIT	BALANCE	DR. CR.	
19 X9							
Jan. *31*	*Materials*	*MR1*	*6,320* *00*		*6,320* *00*	*DR.*	
31	*Labor*	*J1-40*	*32,864* *00*		*39,184* *00*	*DR.*	
31	*Overhead*	*J1-52*	*22,436* *00*		*61,620* *00*	*DR.*	

■ The figures on the line Costs in Prior Department are the same as those shown on the line Transferred Out to Next Department in Part 1 of Section (d) in the cost of production report of the Assembly Department shown on page 324.

COMPLETION DEPARTMENT
Cost of Production Report
Month of January 19X9

QUANTITY SCHEDULE	UNITS
(a) Quantity to Be Accounted For:	
Transferred In From Prior Department	820
Total to Be Accounted For	820
(b) Quantity Accounted For:	
Transferred Out to Finished Goods	780
Work in Process—Ending	40
Total Accounted For	820

COST SCHEDULE	TOTAL COST		E.P. UNITS		UNIT COST
(c) Costs to Be Accounted For:					
Costs in Prior Department	$176,792.00	÷	820	=	$215.60
Costs in Current Department					
Materials	$ 6,320.00	÷	790	=	$8.00
Labor	32,864.00	÷	790	=	41.60
Overhead	22,436.00	÷	790	=	28.40
Total Costs in Current Department	$ 61,620.00				$ 78.00
Total Costs to Be Accounted For	$238,412.00				$293.60
(d) Costs Accounted For:					
(1) Transferred Out to Finished Goods	$229,008.00	=	780	×	$293.60
(2) Work in Process—Ending Costs in					
Prior Department	$ 8,624.00	=	40	×	215.60
Costs in Current Department					
Materials	80.00	=	10	×	8.00
Labor	416.00	=	10	×	41.60
Overhead	284.00	=	10	×	28.40
Total Work in Process	$ 9,404.00				
Total Costs Accounted For	$238,412.00				

- Costs in Current Department are taken from the Work in Process—Completion Department account.
- The unit cost of each element is computed by dividing the equivalent production units into the total cost.
- Prior departmental costs are added to current departmental costs (both total and unit) to obtain total and unit cumulative costs ($238,412 and $293.60) per equivalent unit of production in the department.
- The unit cost of each element and the cumulative total unit cost figures are used, along with the equivalent unit quantities, to complete Section (d) of the report, as follows:

  Costs are accounted for in Section (d) as follows:

- The first costs accounted for are those relating to the 780 completed units transferred to Finished Goods. The value of these completed credenzas is computed by multiplying the unit cost of $293.60 by the 780 units involved.
- The cost of the work remaining in process is again computed by using previously determined prior department unit costs and the unit cost for each element in the current department. When all amounts are totaled, the total cost of the work in process is found to be $9,404.

RECORDING DEPARTMENTAL TRANSFERS

The departmental cost of production reports supply the figures that the cost accountant needs to record the flow of costs in the accounting records. Part 1 of Section (d) in the Cost Schedule portion of each cost of production report shows the cost of credenzas transferred to the next department.

Each transfer is formally recorded in the accounting records by a general journal voucher entry. The entry to transfer the $103,840 cost of the 880 units from the Fabrication Department to the Assembly Department is shown below. The information for this entry comes from the cost of production report for the Fabrication Department found on page 319.

JOURNAL VOUCHER	Date _Jan. 31,_		19 _X9_	No. _1-53_	
ACCOUNT		ACCT. NO.	✓	DEBIT	CREDIT
Work in Process–Assembly Dept.		124		10384000	
Work in Process–					
Fabrication Dept.		123			10384000
EXPLANATION					
Recorded transfer of 880 units from Fabrication Department					
to Assembly Department.					
PREPARED BY *MXH*	AUDITED BY *AC*			APPROVED BY *LM*	

The entry to record the transfer of 820 units costing $176,792 from the Assembly Department to the Completion Department is as follows:

JOURNAL VOUCHER	Date _Jan. 31,_		19 _X9_	No. _1-54_	
ACCOUNT	**ACCT. NO.**	✓	**DEBIT**	**CREDIT**	
Work in Process–Completion Dept.	125		176792 00		
Work in Process–Assembly Dept.	124			176792 00	

EXPLANATION
Recorded transfer of 820 units from Assembly Department
to Completion Department.

PREPARED BY _MXH_	AUDITED BY _AC_	APPROVED BY _LM_

The entry for the third transfer, of 780 units with a cost of $229,004, from the Completion Department to Finished Goods is handled in the same way. The information for this entry comes from the cost of production report for the Completion Department.

JOURNAL VOUCHER	Date _Jan. 31,_		19 _X9_	No. _1-55_	
ACCOUNT	**ACCT. NO.**	✓	**DEBIT**	**CREDIT**	
Finished Goods Inventory	126		229008 00		
Work in Process–Completion					
Department	125			229008 00	

EXPLANATION
Recorded completion and transfer of 780 units to
Finished Goods Inventory

PREPARED BY _MXH_	AUDITED BY _AC_	APPROVED BY _LM_

Process Controls—An Example

As you have learned, process cost accounting is used in industries in which one product or a few almost identical products are manufactured on a continuous basis. In such situations, the quality of products and the efficiency of operations depend on continuous monitoring of the production process and the monitoring of costs. The following example of process controls indicates why such monitoring is important. This illustration will help you understand the types of controls that might be used in other, similar manufacturing situations.

Manitou Pharmaceutical Laboratories (MPL) is a manufacturer of over-the-counter and prescription drugs. The production of chemicals for the drugs is a continuous activity. A mistake in the production process or a slight deviation from the formula for a particular chemical could damage the drugs, causing batches of drugs to be wasted. Because the production process allows only slight room for error, and because errors can be so expensive, MPL uses a computerized process control system in its production.

A process control system monitors production, checking key variables such as air temperature, humidity, chemical temperature, and chemical flow to detect deviations from allowable levels. If a deviation is detected, corrective action is taken immediately either by the system or by an operator. This helps prevent the production of a substandard product.

The monitor in a process control system is a computer. Two other components of process control are sensors and an actuator. Sensors gather information about the key variables of the production process. The computer compares this information with the predetermined limits for each of these variables and determines whether any corrective action is necessary. If corrective action is needed, the computer instructs the actuator to make the adjustments. The corrections are then monitored, and the process reevaluated by the computer.

Frequent process measurement and control ensure a quality product and minimize variances between actual and expected production costs that are caused by inefficiency and errors. However, frequent process control also means high computing costs. Therefore, the number of times the process is sampled must be balanced against the cost of sampling and the time required. Thus, production costs become an important factor in the quality control process. In addition to analyzing production costs, the cost accountant must monitor the costs of the system itself. However, this extra bit of work is more than offset by the benefits of the system to MPL.

MPL uses a software program with its process control system that provides the cost accountant with comparative data for cost control purposes. The information will be timely enough for management to act in a manner that will allow the company to remain competitive in the marketplace.

S E L F - R E V I E W

1. A company has three departments. In order, they are the Mixing Department, the Bottling Department, and the Sterilization Department. When the cost of production report for the Bottling Department is prepared, what source will the cost accountant use for Costs Transferred in From Prior Department?
2. If, because of rounding, the total of Costs Accounted For does not equal the Costs to Be Accounted For, what disposition should the accountant generally make of the difference?
3. What account is debited for the cost of products transferred out of the final department in the production process?
4. How is the figure *equivalent units of production for labor* used in preparing the cost of production report?
5. Why does the process cost accounting system lend itself to controlling costs and measuring efficiency?
6. The cost of production report for the Cracking Department in a refinery shows Work in Process—Ending of $220,000. In what general ledger account should this balance be found after all closing entries are made and posted?

Answers to Self-Review

1. The data for costs transferred into a department from a prior department are found on the cost of production report of the preceding department under Costs Transferred Out to . . .
2. Rounding errors are accounted for by adjusting the cost of units transferred out of the department to the next department or to finished goods.
3. The costs transferred out of the final production department are debited to Finished Goods Inventory.
4. The equivalent units of production for labor is divided into the total labor cost to arrive at the labor cost per equivalent unit. The cost per equivalent unit for labor is multiplied (as a part of the total cost per unit) by the number of units transferred out, to arrive at the cost of goods transferred out. The unit cost is also multiplied by the equivalent units of labor in the ending inventory of work in process to arrive at the cost of the ending inventory.
5. The process cost accounting system provides a means for determining unit costs for each element of production during the period and also for the total cost of producing a unit. The costs for one period may be compared with those for other period as a measure of efficiency and cost control.
6. This balance should be found in the Work in Process—Cracking Department account.

PROOF OF WORK IN PROCESS

After the transfer entries are posted, the balance remaining in the Work in Process accounts (shown on page 331) is the same as the value of the total work in process computed in Part 2 of Section (d) of each departmental cost of production report.

Work in Process–Fabrication Department						NO. 123
DATE	EXPLANATION	POST. REF.	DEBIT	CREDIT	BALANCE	DR. CR.
19 X9						
Jan. 31	Materials	MR1	54,000 00		54,000 00	DR.
31	Labor	J1-40	38,480 00		92,480 00	DR.
31	Overhead	J1-52	32,240 00		124,720 00	DR.
31	Transferred to Assembly Dept.	J1-53		103,840 00	20,880 00	DR.

Work in Process–Assembly Department						NO. 124
DATE	EXPLANATION	POST. REF.	DEBIT	CREDIT	BALANCE	DR. CR.
19 X9						
Jan. 31	Materials	MR1	21,120 00		21,120 00	DR.
31	Labor	J1-40	41,480 00		62,600 00	DR.
31	Overhead	J1-52	21,080 00		83,680 00	DR.
31	Transferred from Fabrication Dept.	J1-53	103,840 00		187,520 00	DR.
31	Transferred to Completion Dept.	J1-54		176,792 00	10,728 00	DR.

Work in Process–Completion Department						NO. 125
DATE	EXPLANATION	POST. REF.	DEBIT	CREDIT	BALANCE	DR. CR.
19 X9						
Jan. 31	Materials	MR1	6,320 00		6,320 00	DR.
31	Labor	J1-40	32,864 00		39,184 00	DR.
31	Overhead	J1-52	22,436 00		61,620 00	DR.
31	Transferred from Assembly Dept.	J1-54	176,792 00		238,412 00	DR.
31	Transferred to Finished Goods	J1-55		229,008 00	9,404 00	DR.

At this point you should be able to work Exercise 14–9 and Problems 14–3A and 14–3B.

PRINCIPLES AND PROCEDURES SUMMARY

- After costs are accumulated in Work in Process accounts, production data must be assembled for use in computing unit costs.
- The department manager's monthly production report provides information about the quantity started, quantity transferred in and out, and the quantity and stage of completion of products in process at the end of the month.
- The cost accountant then computes the equivalent units of production to show the amount of equivalent production done on both

completed and partially processed units in each department. Equivalent units of production reflect the number of units that could have been started and completed if all units started had been completed and none had been in the ending inventory of work in process.

■ Using the cost figures from the general ledger accounts and the equivalent production unit figures, the cost accountant completes a cost of production report for each process.

■ The cost of production report has two main schedules. The first presents quantity data, and the second gives cost data.

■ The first part of the Quantity Schedule assembles unit data showing units to be accounted for. The second part explains what happened to the units that were handled in the department. Generally, the products were either transferred out of the department or are in the ending work in process inventory in various stages of completion.

■ In the first part of the Cost Schedule, total costs are assembled, and the cost per equivalent unit of production for each element (materials, labor, and overhead) is computed. In addition, the cumulative cost per unit of equivalent production is calculated.

■ The second part of the Cost Schedule accounts for the costs. Some costs relate to units of product that were transferred to the next department or to finished goods during the month. The total of costs transferred out is found by multiplying the cumulative cost per equivalent unit by the number of units of product transferred out.

■ Other costs remain as part of the cost of work in process. The cost of ending work in process is the unit cost of each element's equivalent units of production multiplied by the number of equivalent units of that element still in process.

■ The total cost of goods transferred from one department to the next or to finished goods as shown in the cost of production report is recorded by means of a general journal voucher entry and posted to the general ledger.

■ When all transfers have been recorded, the balance in each Work in Process account should equal the cost of work in process shown in the cost of production report.

MANAGERIAL IMPLICATIONS

■ A process cost system provides information, in the cost of production report, about the average cost of manufacturing products during the period.

■ Unit cost information is of great importance to management. Three of its most important uses are:

■ It is an element or consideration in setting a fair price for products.

■ It is often used to measure managerial efficiency in controlling costs. It is especially useful to compare the unit costs of a period with those of prior periods in order to pinpoint cost changes.

■ A study of the manufacturing process and of costs of materials, labor, and overhead may make it possible to establish a "standard" for what the cost per unit for each element should be under efficient conditions. Comparing actual costs shown in the cost of production report for the period with the standard cost of each element and with the actual unit costs of prior periods may make it possible to detect costs that have gotten "out of line."

■ The process cost system requires less effort than the job order cost system.

REVIEW QUESTIONS

1. What information is contained in the monthly production report? What is the purpose of this report? Who prepares it? Who receives it?
2. What is meant by the term *equivalent units of production?*
3. What are the two major schedules in a cost of production report? Describe each briefly.
4. What information is included in the Quantity Schedule of a cost of production report? What is the source of this information?
5. What is the relationship between a departmental Work in Process account and the department's cost of production report?
6. On a journal voucher, which account is debited and which is credited to record the cost of work transferred from the Fabrication Department to the Assembly Department?
7. Explain what is meant by *Costs in Prior Departments*. What happens to these costs as the products move through production?
8. What is the source of information for recording the flow of costs from one Work in Process account to another? What entry is made to record the flow of costs?
9. With what figures should the balances in the Work in Process accounts agree after the transfer entries are posted?
10. What do you think would be the effect on the cost of production report if a departmental manager overestimated the stage of completion of the ending work in process?

MANAGERIAL DISCUSSION QUESTIONS

1. How does process cost accounting assist in measuring the efficiency of departmental managers?
2. What data are provided to management by the monthly production report for each department?
3. Why is it necessary to estimate the stage of completion of work in process?
4. What is the cost of production report? What information does it contain for management?
5. Is it likely that work in process will be at the same stage of completion for each of the cost elements? Explain.

6. Why should management compare the costs per equivalent unit for one month with those for prior months?
7. What would be the effects of underestimating the stage of completion of the ending work in process in a department?
8. Explain how the results shown in the cost of production report might be used to measure efficiency and cost control in the department.

EXERCISES

EXERCISE 14–1

Compute units started in production. (Obj. 1). Selwyn Rubber Company manufactures foam rubber pads that it markets to carpet retailers and installers. During the month, the Rolling Department completed 10,000 units of the product. The ending work in process inventory was 1,400 units, and there was no beginning inventory. How many units were started in production during the month?

EXERCISE 14–2

Compute equivalent units of production. (Objs. 1, 2). A department had no beginning work in process inventory. During the month, 6,500 units were transferred in from the prior department. Of this amount, 6,000 were completed by the end of the month and transferred to finished goods. The ending work in process inventory was complete as to materials and 40 percent incomplete as to labor and overhead.
a. What is the equivalent production for materials?
b. What is the equivalent production for labor and overhead?

EXERCISE 14–3

Compute equivalent production and cost per unit for materials. (Objs. 1, 2, 3). The cost of materials put into production in a department during the month totaled $249,600. By the end of the month, these materials had been used for 31,200 units, of which 29,000 were completed and transferred out and 2,200 were in process. All materials were added to the units in process.
a. What is the equivalent production for materials?
b. What is the cost per equivalent unit for materials?

EXERCISE 14–4

Compute equivalent production, cost per unit, and ending work in process. (Objs. 1, 2, 3). During the month, 123,000 units were started into production, of which 118,500 units were completed and transferred out during the month. It is estimated that the units in process have had one-third of the labor added. Total labor costs for the month were $60,000.
a. What is the cost per equivalent unit for labor?
b. What is the labor cost applicable to the ending work in process?

EXERCISE 14–5

Compute equivalent production, cost per equivalent unit, and ending work in process. (Objs. 1, 2, 3). The following data are given for the Finishing Department of the Commons Company in January 19X9:

Beginning inventory, 0
Units transferred in during month, 8,000
Units transferred to Finished Goods during month, 7,500
Ending work in process, 500 units (25 percent completed as to labor)
Labor costs incurred for month, $20,968.75

a. What is the equivalent production for labor during the month?
b. What is the labor cost per equivalent unit?
c. What is the labor cost in the ending inventory of work in process?

EXERCISE 14–6   **Compute equivalent production, cost per equivalent unit, and ending work in process.   (Objs. 1, 2, 3).**   The following data are given for the Grinding Department of the Midwest Commercial Tray Company in November 19X9:

Beginning inventory, -0-
Units placed in production during month, 42,000
Units transferred to next department during month, 40,000
Ending work in process, 2,000 units (25 percent complete as to overhead)
Overhead costs incurred for month, $81,405

a. What is the equivalent production for overhead during the month?
b. What is the overhead cost per equivalent unit?
c. What is the overhead cost in the ending inventory of work in process?

EXERCISE 14–7   **Compute equivalent production, cost per equivalent unit, and ending work in process.   (Objs. 1, 2, 3).**   The following data are given for the Assembly Department of the Emory Motor Company in April 19X9:

Beginning inventory, -0-
Units transferred in during month, 30,000
Units transferred out to next department during month, 24,000
Ending work in process, 6,000 units (75 percent complete as to materials)
Material costs incurred for the month, $3,028,124

a. What is the equivalent production for materials during the month?
b. What is the materials cost applicable to the 24,000 units transferred out of the department?
c. What is the materials cost in the ending inventory of work in process?

EXERCISE 14–8   **Compute equivalent production, cost per equivalent unit, costs transferred out, and ending work in process inventory.   (Objs. 1, 2, 3).**   During the month, 3,400 units of product were started into production in a department, of which 3,250 were completed. Of the 3,250 completed units, 125 are still on hand in the department and have not been physically transferred to the next department. There are also 150 units still in process; they are estimated to be one-third complete as to labor and overhead. Overhead for the month was $46,000.

a. What is total overhead cost applicable to the 3,125 units transferred to the next department?

b. What is the overhead cost applicable to the 125 units completed and still on hand?

c. What is the overhead cost applicable to the 150 uncompleted units on hand?

EXERCISE 14–9

Make journal entries to record the transfer of costs. (Obj. 5). The following data are given for the two production departments, the Blending and Finishing Departments, of the Mason Solvent Company for the month of June 19X9. Materials, labor, and overhead charged to production are as follows:

	Materials	**Labor**	**Overhead**
Blending Department	$79,000	$4,000	$21,000
Finishing Department	1,000	3,000	12,500

The costs of work transferred were as follows:

From Blending Department to Finishing Department	$ 90,000
From Finishing Department to Finished Goods	102,000

Give the journal entries to charge the costs to production and to record the transfer of work from the Blending Department to the Finishing Department and from the Finishing Department to Finished Goods.

PROBLEMS

PROBLEM 14–1A

Compute equivalent production. (Obj. 2). The Merriwell Manufacturing Company, which has four producing departments, uses the process cost accounting system. Production data for August 19X9, the first month's operations, are given below.

	Dept. A	Dept. B	Dept. C	Dept. D
Quantity				
Started in Production	9,000			
Transferred In From Prior Department		7,500	7,000	6,300
Transferred Out to Next Department	7,500	7,000	6,300	
Transferred Out to Finished Goods				4,500
Work in Process—Ending	1,500	500	700	1,800
Stage of Completion of Ending Work in Process				
Materials	100%	100%	80%	80%
Labor	20%	40%	30%	80%
Overhead	20%	40%	40%	80%

INSTRUCTIONS

Compute the equivalent units of production for materials, labor, and overhead for each department for the first month.

PROBLEM 14–2A **Compute equivalent production; prepare a cost of production report for department. (Objs. 2, 3, 4).**   The Schmidt Manufacturing Company began operations on June 1, 19X9. During the first month, 4,860 units of product were placed in production in the first department, the Blending Department. Of these, all but 1,000 were completed during the month and transferred out to the second department, the Baking Department. All materials had been added to the 1,000 units in process, but only 75 percent of the labor and overhead had been added. The costs incurred during the month were materials, $121,500; labor, $88,560; and manufacturing overhead, $72,540.

INSTRUCTIONS 1. Prepare a schedule of equivalent production for the Blending Department for the month of June.
2. Prepare a cost of production report for the Blending Department for the month of June.

PROBLEM 14–3A **Compute equivalent production; prepare a cost of production report for three departments; prepare journal entries to charge costs into production; record costs of products transferred out of a department. (Objs. 1, 2, 3, 4).**   The departmental managers of Turner Manufacturing Company have submitted the monthly production reports for August 19X9. These reports have been summarized, and the results are shown below.

	Framing Department	Assembly Department	Completion Department
Quantity			
Started in Production—Current Month	1,580	-0-	-0-
Transferred In From Prior Department	-0-	1,500	1,385
Transferred Out to Next Department	1,500	1,385	-0-
Transferred Out to Finished Goods	-0-	-0-	1,360
Work in Process—Ending	80	115	25
Stage of Completion of Ending Work in Process			
Materials	complete	complete	25%
Labor	60%	85%	25%
Overhead	60%	85%	25%

The materials requisition journal shows issues of raw materials as follows:

Distribution	Amount
Framing Department	$15,800
Assembly Department	30,000
Completion Department	68,300

The monthly payroll register shows the following totals:

Distribution	Amount
Framing Department	$30,960
Assembly Department	29,660
Completion Department	13,660

The schedule of monthly overhead charges from the worksheet for prorating the costs of the Factory Services Department to the producing departments shows the following figures:

Distribution	Amount
Framing Department	$61,920
Assembly Department	14,830
Completion Department	6,830

INSTRUCTIONS

1. Prepare a schedule showing the equivalent units of production for each element in each department.
2. Prepare a cost of production report for each department.
3. a. Prepare general journal vouchers to charge materials, labor, and overhead costs into production. Number the vouchers 8-18, 8-19, and 8-20.
   b. Prepare the general journal voucher to record the transfer of goods from the Framing Department to the Assembly Department. Number the voucher 8-21.
   c. Prepare the general journal voucher to record the transfer of goods from the Assembly Department to the Completion Department. Number the voucher 8-22.
   d. Prepare the general journal voucher to record the completion of goods and the transfer to Finished Goods. Number the voucher 8-23.

ALTERNATE PROBLEMS

PROBLEM 14–1B

Compute equivalent production. (Obj. 1). Oregon Heights Corporation, which has four producing departments, uses the process cost accounting system. Production data for September 19X9, the first month's operations, are given below.

	Dept. A	Dept. B	Dept. C	Dept. D
Quantity				
Started in Production	72,000			
Transferred In From Prior Department		64,000	57,500	50,400
Transferred Out to Next Department	64,000	57,500	50,400	
Transferred Out to Finished Goods				47,600
Work in Process—Ending	8,000	6,500	7,100	2,800
Stage of Completion of Ending Work In Process				
Materials	100%	100%	90%	80%
Labor	20%	40%	60%	80%
Overhead	20%	40%	80%	80%

INSTRUCTIONS Compute the equivalent units of production for materials, labor, and overhead in each department for the month.

PROBLEM 14–2B **Compute equivalent production; prepare a cost of production report for one department. (Objs. 2, 3, 4).** The Daytona Company manufactures one product, involving three processing departments. During the month of May 19X9, the company's first month of production, 72,000 units were placed in production in the first department (the Blending Department), with the following costs added: materials, $146,880; labor, $82,350; and overhead, $48,300. On May 31, 7,500 units were in process in this department, with all materials added and 60 percent of the labor and overhead added.

INSTRUCTIONS 1. Prepare a schedule of equivalent production for the Blending Department for May.
2. Prepare a cost of production report for the Blending Department for May.

PROBLEM 14–3B **Compute equivalent production; prepare a cost of production report for three departments; prepare journal entries to charge costs into production; record costs of products transferred out of a department. (Objs. 1, 2, 3, 4, 5).** The departmental managers of Delta Factories, Inc., have submitted the monthly production reports for September 19X9. These reports have been summarized as follows:

	Trimming Department	Assembly Department	Finishing Department
Quantity			
Started in Production—Current Month	1,800	-0-	-0-
Transferred In From Prior Department	-0-	1,600	1,400
Transferred Out to Next Department	1,600	1,400	-0-
Transferred Out to Finished Goods			1,275
Work in Process—Ending	200	200	125
Stage of Completion of ending Work in Process			
Materials	complete	complete	$66\frac{2}{3}$%
Labor	50%	75%	$66\frac{2}{3}$%
Overhead	50%	75%	$66\frac{2}{3}$%

The materials requisition journal shows issues of raw materials as follows:

Distribution	Amount
Trimming Department	$16,800
Assembly Department	8,400
Finishing Department	3,200

The monthly payroll register shows the following totals:

Distribution	Amount
Trimming Department	$9,250
Assembly Department	7,300
Finishing Department	5,160

The schedule of monthly overhead charges from the worksheet for prorating the costs of the Factory Services Department to the producing departments shows the following figures:

Distribution	Amount
Trimming Department	$4,600
Assembly Department	3,560
Finishing Department	2,500

INSTRUCTIONS

1. Prepare the equivalent production computations for each producing department.
2. Prepare the cost of production report for each department. Round off to three decimal places when calculating unit costs.
3. a. Prepare general journal vouchers to charge materials, labor, and overhead into production. Number the vouchers 9-21, 9-22, and 9-23.
   b. Prepare the general journal voucher to record the transfer of goods from the Trimming Department to the Assembly Department. Number the voucher 9-24.
   c. Prepare the general journal voucher to record the transfer of goods from the Assembly Department to the Finishing Department. Number the voucher 9-25.
   d. Prepare the general journal voucher to record the completion of goods and their transfer to Finished Goods. Number the voucher 9-26.

MANAGERIAL DECISION CASE

The Dehydration Department of the Solomon Chemical Products Corporation typically has little work in process at the end of the month. The controller of the company has studied the cost and production records of the department for the past several years and has expressed concern over the overhead and labor cost behavior in the department. The costs per unit of these elements have increased substantially during the summer months, although materials costs per unit have remained fairly constant in each month. For example, the data below show the costs per equivalent unit during the last 12 months. A similar pattern was found in prior years.

	Cost per Unit		
Month	Materials	Labor	Overhead
January	$15.01	$ 9.00	$3.00
February	14.98	8.87	3.20
March	15.03	9.06	3.15

April	15.05	9.03	3.18
May	15.04	9.07	3.26
June	15.06	11.11	3.43
July	15.05	13.52	4.01
August	15.07	15.04	6.92
September	15.09	9.37	3.37
October	15.08	9.28	3.33
November	15.09	9.37	3.37
December	15.07	9.45	3.34

1. List some other factors that might logically explain this cost behavior.
2. Assume that the controller has investigated the situation and has found the following:
   a. Production workers take their vacations in the summer, especially in July or August. Their vacation pay is treated as direct labor.
   b. During vacation periods, the dehydrators are cleaned and repaired and all costs of these activities are charged to the Dehydration Department's overhead.

The controller expresses the belief that these huge variations in unit cost are misleading and asks you, as cost accountant, to suggest accounting procedures that will yield "more logical" results. Write a brief report responding to the controller's request.

C H A P T E R
15

Average Costing of Work in Process

In the course of normal operations, the producing departments in continuous process industries carry forward inventories of work in process from one month to the next. For example, Apex Computer Designs' general ledger shows Work in Process balances on February 1, 19X9. The accountant must be sure to include these balances when determining the total costs and the unit costs to be accounted for in February.

OBJECTIVES

1. Explain and illustrate the average cost method of handling costs of beginning work in process.
2. Compute equivalent production using the average cost method for beginning work in process.
3. Compute costs per equivalent unit for each element of cost.
4. Compute costs of units transferred out and costs of ending inventory of work in process.
5. Complete a cost of production report using the average cost method for beginning work in process.
6. Prepare a combined cost of production report, assuming the average cost method for beginning work in process.
7. Prepare entries to transfer costs from department to department and from the final department to finished goods.

NEW TERMS

Average cost method (p. 343)
Combined cost of production report (p. 354)
First in, first out (FIFO) method (p. 343)

ACCOUNTING FOR BEGINNING WORK IN PROCESS

Apex Computer Designs' cost accountant considered two generally recognized methods of handling the cost of the beginning work in process inventory: the first in, first out method and the average cost method.

First In, First Out Costing

Under the **first in, first out (FIFO) method,** the partially processed units carried over from the previous month are costed separately from the units started in the current month.

- The costs of the beginning inventory and the additional costs incurred to complete these units are added to obtain the total and unit costs for the carried-over units of production.
- The costs of the units started during the month are assembled separately to obtain a second set of total and unit costs for the new production.
- Transfers are costed on the assumption that the oldest units (first in) will move out first (first out).

This method is explained in detail in Chapter 17.

Average Costing

The **average cost method** combines rather than separates the costs of carried-over and new production.

- The cost of each element (materials, labor, and overhead) applicable to the beginning work in process inventory is added to the cost incurred for that element in the current month.
- A single cumulative total and unit cost for each element is obtained. The costs per equivalent unit for the three elements are added to determine the total unit cost for each unit completed.
- One unit cost figure is used for costing units transferred out of the department.

APPLYING THE AVERAGE COST METHOD—APEX COMPUTER DESIGNS

Apex Computer Designs' ending work in process inventory will usually be small in relation to total monthly production and will vary only slightly from month to month. As a result, there will be little difference between the unit costs computed under the FIFO method and the average cost method. Therefore, the cost accountant decides to adopt the simpler average cost method of accounting for beginning inventories and costs added during the month.

You will learn how this method works step by step as the February costs are calculated. Departments will be studied in the sequence in which materials are processed.

Fabrication Department

The cost data and production data for the Fabrication Department are assembled from the sources described in Chapters 13 and 14. These sources include the materials requisition journal, the summary of time tickets, the department overhead analyses, and the monthly production reports.

	*Work in Process–Fabrication Department* **NO.** _123_

DATE	EXPLANATION	POST. REF.	DEBIT	CREDIT	BALANCE	DR. CR.
19 X9						
Feb. 1	*Balance*	✓			*20,880 00*	*DR.*
28	*Materials*	*MR2*	*39,840 00*		*60,720 00*	*DR.*
28	*Labor*	*J2-50*	*26,487 92*		*87,207 92*	*DR.*
28	*Overhead*	*J2-52*	*22,693 36*		*109,901 28*	*DR.*

Cost Data. The Work in Process—Fabrication Department 123 account shows a balance of $109,901.28 on February 28.

The balance of this account is broken down into cost elements in two simple steps.

1. Analyze the beginning work in process, as given below, by referring to the work in process data in Part 2 of Section (d) of the cost of production report for January (shown on page 346).

Beginning Work in Process	
Materials	$10,000
Labor	5,920
Overhead	4,960
Balance of Account, Jan. 31	$20,880

2. Determine the cost incurred for each element in the current month by referring to the general ledger postings in the Work in Process account.

Current Month	
Materials	$39,840.00
Labor	26,487.92
Overhead	22,693.36
Total Current Month's Costs	$89,021.28

Production Data. The supervisor's production report for the month of February is shown below.

FABRICATION DEPARTMENT
Monthly Production Report
February 19X9

Quantity	
Work in Process—Beginning	200
Started in Production—Current Month	800
Transferred Out to Next Department	820
Work in Process—Ending	180

Stage of Completion of Ending Work in Process	
Materials	complete
Labor	30%
Overhead	30%

Equivalent Production Data. The cost accountant computes the equivalent production for the Fabrication Department in February in the same manner as in January. The 820 credenzas transferred to the Assembly Department are 100 percent complete as to materials, labor, and overhead. The remaining 180 units are also 100 percent complete as to materials, according to the manager's report. However, these credenzas are regarded by the manager as only 30 percent complete in terms of labor and overhead. Thus, the equivalent production for February is computed as 1,000 units for materials and 874 units for labor and overhead (180 × .30 = 54; 54 + 820 = 874), as shown below.

FABRICATION DEPARTMENT
Equivalent Production Computations
Month of February 19X9

Materials

Transferred Out to Next Department	820
Work in Process—Ending (180 credenzas × 100%)	180
Equivalent Production for Materials	1,000

Labor and Manufacturing Overhead

Transferred Out to Next Department	820
Work in Process—Ending (180 credenzas × 30%)	54
Equivalent Production for Labor and Overhead	874

At this point you should be able to work Exercise 15–1.

Cost of Production Report. The cost of production report for February is now completed, as shown on page 346. Several new details should receive special attention:

The first part of the Quantity Schedule—(a) Quantity to Be Accounted For—now starts with Work in Process—Beginning. The total of 200 units is taken from the manager's monthly production report for February. The number of units started into production also comes from the manager's report. No figure is shown as Transferred In From Prior Department because fabrication is the first manufacturing operation.

The second part of the Quantity Schedule—(b) Quantity Accounted For—is completed in the same way as it was for January.

In the first part of the Cost Schedule—(c) Costs to Be Accounted For—there are no figures under Costs in Prior Department because fabrication is the first operation. Under Costs in Current Department, the cost of each element in the beginning work in process is added to the additional cost of that element incurred during the month.

■ The materials cost of the beginning work in process, $10,000, is added to the cost of materials issued during February, $39,840. The total cost of materials, $49,840, is then divided by the equivalent production for materials, 1,000 units. The resulting average unit cost is $49.84.

FABRICATION DEPARTMENT
Cost of Production Report
Month of February 19X9

QUANTITY SCHEDULE	UNITS
(a) Quantity to Be Accounted For:	
Work in Process—Beginning	200
Started in Production—Current Month	800
Transferred In From Prior Department	-0-
Total to Be Accounted For	1,000
(b) Quantity Accounted For:	
Transferred Out to Next Department	820
Transferred Out to Finished Goods	-0-
Work in Process—Ending	180
Total Accounted For	1,000

COST SCHEDULE	TOTAL COST	E.P. UNITS	UNIT COST
(c) Costs to Be Accounted For:			
Costs in Prior Department			
Work in Process—Beginning	-0-		
Transferred In—Current Month	-0-		
Total Prior Department Costs	-0-		
Costs in Current Department			
Materials—Beginning Work in Process	$ 10,000.00		
Added in Current Month	39,840.00		
Total Materials	$ 49,840.00 ÷	1,000 =	49.840
Labor—Beginning Work in Process	$ 5,920.00		
Added in Current Month	26,487.92		
Total Labor	$ 32,407.92 ÷	874 =	37.080
Overhead—Beginning Work in Process	$ 4,960.00		
Added in Current Month	$ 22,693.36		
Total Overhead	$ 27,653.36 ÷	874 =	31.640
Total Costs in Current Department	$109,901.28		$118.560
Total Costs to Be Accounted For	$109,901.28		$118.560
(d) Costs Accounted For:			
Transferred Out to Next Department	$ 97,219.20 =	820 × $118.560	
Transferred Out to Finished Good	-0-		
Total Transferred Out	$ 97,219.20		
Work in Process—Ending			
Costs in Prior Department	-0-		
Costs in Current Department			
Materials	$ 8,971.20 =	180 × $ 49.840	
Labor	2,002.32 =	54 × $ 37.080	
Overhead	1,708.56 =	54 × $ 31.640	
Total Work In Process	$ 12,682.08		
Total Costs Accounted For	$109,901.28		

- The labor cost of the beginning work in process, $5,920, is added to the labor costs incurred in February, $26,487.92, for a total of $32,407.92. Dividing this figure by the equivalent production for labor of 874 units (as computed above) yields an average equivalent unit cost for labor of $37.08.
- The overhead cost of the beginning work in process, $4,960, is added to the overhead cost incurred in February, $22,693.36, for a total of $27,653.36 and an average equivalent unit cost for overhead of $31.64.

The remainder of the Cost Schedule for February is prepared as before.

SELF-REVIEW

1. Under the FIFO method of handling the beginning work in process inventory, what assumption is made about which units are completed first?
2. Under the average cost method of handling the beginning work in process inventory, how is the amount of materials costs in the beginning work in process accounted for?
3. Under the average cost method, will all products completed during the period be assumed to have the same cost, or will a separate cost be computed for units transferred out that came from the beginning inventory and those that were started and finished during the period?
4. Would the difference between the unit costs computed under the FIFO method and the average cost method be greater if the ending inventory of work in process in a business is typically large or typically small?
5. Under the average cost method of accounting for beginning work in process inventory, are separate costs per equivalent unit computed for labor costs in the beginning work in process inventory and for the labor costs added during the period?

Answers to Self-Review

1. Under the FIFO method, it is assumed that the first units completed come from the beginning work in process inventory in the department.
2. Under the average cost method, the materials costs in the beginning work in process are combined with the materials costs incurred during the current period.
3. Under the average cost method, all products completed during the current period are assumed to have the same cost.
4. The difference in unit costs computed under the FIFO method and the average cost method would be large if the ending inventory of work in process is typically large, because of the possibility that large changes in manufacturing costs would be reflected in the ending inventory under the FIFO method.
5. Under the average cost method, the beginning inventory of labor costs and the costs added during the period are combined to determine a total cost for labor, and only cost per equivalent unit for materials is computed.

At this point you should be able to work Exercise 15–2 and Problems 15–1A and 15–1B.

Assembly Department

The February costs for the Assembly Department are found by using procedures very similar to those described for the Fabrication Department. However, certain details are different because assembly is the second process in the manufacturing sequence, and costs from the prior department must be considered.

Cost Data. On February 28 the Work in Process account for the Assembly Department shows a balance of $92,720.80. The balance of this account is made up of cost elements obtained from the following sources:

1. The work in process data in Part (2) of Section (d) of the Cost Schedule portion of the cost of production report for January (shown on page 346). This data shows the costs of the prior department (the Fabrication Department) as well as the costs of the Assembly Department for the January 31 ending work in process inventory. These costs, shown below, become the beginning work in process costs.

Beginning Work in Process	
Costs in Prior Department	$ 7,080
Costs in Current Department	
Materials	1,440
Labor	1,464
Overhead	744
Balance of Account, Jan. 31	$10,728

2. The general ledger postings in the Work in Process account during the current month. These postings total $81,992.80 for February, as shown below.

Current Month	
Materials	$19,820.80
Labor	40,644.00
Overhead	21,528.00
Total Current Month's Costs	$81,992.80

Production Data. The manager of the Assembly Department completes the report shown below.

ASSEMBLY DEPARTMENT
Monthly Production Report
February 19X9

Quantity	
Work in Process—Beginning	60
Started in Production—Current Month	820
Transferred Out to Next Department	840
Work in Process—Ending	40

Stage of Completion of Ending Work in Process	
Materials	complete
Labor	75%
Overhead	75%

Equivalent Production Data. The equivalent production report prepared by the accountant is shown below.

ASSEMBLY DEPARTMENT	
Equivalent Production Computations	
Month of February 19X9	
Materials	
Transferred Out to Next Department	840
Work in Process—Ending (40 credenzas × 100%)	40
Equivalent Production for Materials	880
Labor and Manufacturing Overhead	
Transferred Out to Next Department	840
Work in Process—Ending (40 credenzas × 75%)	30
Equivalent Production for Labor and Overhead	870

At this point you should be able to work Exercise 15–3.

Cost of Production Report. The February cost of production report, shown on page 350, is patterned after the one used in January for the Assembly Department. Note that unit cost computations have been carried to four decimal places (rounded to three) because the number of equivalent production units is not evenly divisible into the total cost. The extra decimal places permit a greater degree of accuracy, which is important when large quantities and values are involved. Some companies carry unit costs to four or more decimal places when large numbers of units are involved. This is because large dollar amounts result when small unit costs are applied to a large number of units.

The first part of the Quantity Schedule—(a) Quantity to Be Accounted For—now shows that 60 units are involved in the beginning work in process. This figure comes from the prior months' production report and can be verified by referring to the January cost of production report on page 324.

In the first part of the Cost Schedule—(c) Costs to Be Accounted For—note the following:

- The Costs in Prior Department section includes the cost of the beginning work in process of $7,080. This figure is picked up from the ending work in process on the January cost of production report (60 × $118). This cost is added to the $97,219.20 transferred in from the Fabrication Department in the current month, resulting in total prior department costs of $104,299.20. This total is divided by the 880 equivalent units involved to obtain a prior department average unit cost of $118.522.

  This average unit cost is different from the $118.56 transferred into the Assembly Department from the Fabrication Department during the month of February. The reason is that the $118.52 figure is an average of the cost of 60 units at $118 in the beginning work in process from January and the 820 units at $118.56 transferred in from the Fabrication Department in February.

At this point you should be able to work Exercises 15–4 and 15–5.

- The Costs in Current Department section shows that each cost element relating to the beginning work in process (obtained from the January cost of production report) is added to the cost incurred for

ASSEMBLY DEPARTMENT
Cost of Production Report
Month of February 19X9

QUANTITY SCHEDULE	UNITS
(a) Quantity to Be Accounted For:	
Work in Process—Beginning	60
Started in Production—Current Month	-0-
Transferred In From Prior Department	820
Total to Be Accounted For	880
(b) Quantity Accounted For:	
Transferred Out to Next Department	840
Transferred Out to Finished Goods	-0-
Work in Process—Ending	40
Total Accounted For	880

COST SCHEDULE	TOTAL COST	E.P. UNITS	UNIT COSTS
(c) Costs to Be Accounted For:			
Costs in Prior Department			
Work in Process—Beginning	$ 7,080.00		
Transferred in—Current Month	97,219.20		
Total Prior Department Costs	$104,299.20 ÷	880	= $118.522
Costs in Current Department			
Materials—Beginning Work in Process	$ 1,440.00		
Added in Current Month	19,820.80		
Total Materials	$ 21,260.80 ÷	880	= $ 24.160
Labor—Beginning Work in Process	$ 1,464.00		
Added in Current Month	40,644.00		
Total Labor	$ 42,108.00 ÷	870	= 48.400
Overhead—Beginning Work in Process	$ 744.00		
Added in Current Month	21,528.00		
Total Overhead	$ 22,272.00 ÷	870	= 25.600
Total Costs in Current Department	$ 85,640.80		$ 98.160
Total Costs to Be Accounted For	$189,940.00		$216.682
(d) Costs Accounted For:			
Transferred Out to Next Department	$182,012.72* =	840	× $216.682
Transferred Out to Finished Goods	-0-		
Total Transferred Out	$182,012.72		
Work in Process—Ending			
Costs in Prior Department	$ 4,740.88 =	40	× $118.522
Costs in Current Department			
Materials	966.40 =	40	× $ 24.160
Labor	1,452.00 =	30	× $ 48.400
Overhead	768.00 =	30	× $ 25.600
Total Work in Process	$ 7,927.28		
Total Costs Accounted For	$189,940.00		

*Adjusted $.16 for rounding.

BUSINESS HORIZON

Cutting Costs by Installing Efficient Purchasing and Inventory Control Practices

Many managers, especially financial managers, view inventories—raw materials, work in process, and finished goods—as an idle investment of capital because they represent funds tied up that could be invested profitably elsewhere. Management is therefore keenly interested in keeping inventory balances at a minimum and, with the assistance of accountants, financial managers, and others in the company, develops many techniques for controlling inventory investment. Some of these techniques are visible not only to people involved in business operations but also to customers. You have already learned some of these techniques in this book.

Economic order quantities (EOQs) may be established for each raw material. Sophisticated EOQ calculations consider the number of inventory units required, the inventory order quantity, the cost of each inventory unit, the fixed cost per order, the holding cost per unit of inventory, and the daily opportunity cost to arrive at an order quantity that will result in the greatest cost savings. Computers make these calculations simple because programs have been developed into which relevant information is fed, with the output being the EOQ.

Inventory control systems are essential to all types of businesses, especially in retail establishments, where there may be thousands of inventory items. You see a modern practical application of the computer in maintaining an up-to-the minute control over inventories. Nowadays, most retail checkout cashiers scan the bar code on each product. This tells the computer the number of the inventory item and the quantity sold. The computer enters this information in a perpetual inventory, so that the decrease in inventory resulting from the sale is recorded immediately. Modern plants similarly maintain on-line inventory control systems.

In Chapter 5 of this book you read about just-in-time (JIT) inventory management, which involves the use of sophisticated information systems by manufacturers and their suppliers. Just-in-time systems work hand in hand with EOQ systems to achieve minimum investment in inventories.

that element during February (from the general ledger). This addition produces a total for each cost element. The total is divided by the equivalent production units for the cost element to determine the cost.

Completion Department

The costs for the Completion Department are found by using the same procedures as described for the Assembly Department.

Cost Data. The Work in Process—Completion Department 125 account shows a balance of $75,094 on February 28.

Reference to prior reports and analysis of ledger entries show that this balance is made up of the following:

Beginning Work in Process	
Costs in Prior Department	$ 8,624.00
Costs in Current Department	
Materials	80.00
Labor	416.00
Overhead	284.00
Balance of Account, Jan. 31	$ 9,404.00

Work in Process–Completion Department					NO. 125	
DATE	EXPLANATION	POST. REF.	DEBIT	CREDIT	BALANCE	DR. CR.
19 X9						
Feb. 1	Balance	✓			9,404 00	DR.
28	Materials	MR2	6,720 00		16,124 00	DR.
28	Labor	J2-50	34,604 00		50,728 00	DR.
28	Overhead	J2-52	24,366 00		75,094 00	DR.

Current Month

Materials	$ 6,720.00
Labor	34,604.00
Overhead	24,366.00
Total Current Month's Costs	$65,690.00

Production Data. The manager of the Completion Department completes the monthly production report.

COMPLETION DEPARTMENT
Monthly Production Report
February 19X9

Quantity

Work in Process—Beginning	40
Started in Production—Current Month	840
Transferred Out to Finished Goods	820
Work in Process—Ending	60

Stage of Completion of Ending Work in Process

Materials	50%
Labor	50%
Overhead	50%

Equivalent Production Data. The equivalent production report for February prepared by the accountant is shown below.

COMPLETION DEPARTMENT
Equivalent Production Computations
Month of February 19X9

Materials, Labor, and Manufacturing Overhead

Transferred Out to Finished Goods	820
Work in Process—Ending (60 credenzas × 50%)	30
Equivalent Production for Materials, Labor, and Overhead	850

At this point you should be able to work Exercise 15–6 and Problems 15–2A and 15–2B.

Cost of Production Report. The Completion Department's cost of production report can now be completed in the usual manner. This report is shown on page 353.

COMPLETION DEPARTMENT
Cost of Production Report
Month of February 19X9

QUANTITY SCHEDULE	UNITS
(a) Quantity to Be Accounted For:	
Work in Process—Beginning	40
Started in Production—Current Month	-0-
Transferred In From Prior Department	840
Total to Be Accounted For	880
(b) Quantity Accounted For:	
Transferred Out to Next Department	-0-
Transferred Out to Finished Goods	820
Work in Process—Ending	60
Total Accounted For	880

COST SCHEDULE	TOTAL COST	E.P. UNITS	UNIT COST
(c) Costs to Be Accounted For:			
Costs in Prior Department			
Work in Process—Beginning	$ 8,624.00		
Transferred In—Current Month	182,012.72		
Total Prior Department Costs	$190,636.72	÷ 880	= $216.632
Costs in Current Department			
Materials—Beginning Work in Process	$ 80.00		
Added in Current Month	6,720.00		
Total Materials	$ 6,800.00	÷ 850	= $ 8.000
Labor—Beginning Work in Process	$ 416.00		
Added in Current Month	34,604.00		
Total Labor	$ 35,020.00	÷ 850	= 41.200
Overhead—Beginning Work in Process	$ 284.00		
Added in Current Month	$ 24,366.00		
Total Overhead	$ 24,650.00	÷ 850	= 29.000
Total Costs in Current Department	$ 66,470.00		$ 78.200
Total Costs to Be Accounted For	$257,106.72		$294.832
(d) Costs Accounted For:			
Transferred Out to Next Department	-0-		
Transferred Out to Finished Goods	$241,762.80* =	820	× $294.832
Total Transferred Out	$241,762.80		
Work in Process—Ending			
Costs in Prior Department	$ 12,997.92 =	60	× $216.632
Costs in Current Department			
Materials	240.00 =	30	× $ 8.000
Labor	1,236.00 =	30	× $ 41.200
Overhead	870.00 =	30	× $ 29.000
Total Work in Process	$ 15,343.92		
Total Costs Accounted For	$257,106.72		

*Adjusted $0.56 for rounding.

COMBINED COST OF PRODUCTION REPORT

Many accountants prefer to use one **combined cost of production report,** as shown on the following page, rather than a separate report for each department. The single report is simpler to prepare, permits quicker cross-checking, and makes it possible to trace transfers from department to department more easily. The combined report makes it easy for the reader to get a quick understanding of the costs of the entire manufacturing process. The equivalent production unit figures are normally omitted from the combined report to save space.

Recording Departmental Transfers

Section (d) in the Cost Schedule of the combined report shows that the following transfers must be recorded at the end of February: Fabrication Department to Assembly Department, $97,219.20; Assembly Department to Completion Department, $182,012.72; Completion Department to Finished Goods, $241,762.80.

The general journal voucher entries needed to complete the transfers are shown below.

JOURNAL VOUCHER Date _Feb. 28,_ 19 _X9_ No. _2-53_				
ACCOUNT	**ACCT. NO.**	**✓**	**DEBIT**	**CREDIT**
Work in Process–Assembly Dept.	124		9721920	
Work in Process–Fabrication Dept.	123			9721920
EXPLANATION				
Recorded cost of 820 units transferred from Fabrication				
Department to Assembly Department for the month.				
PREPARED BY *MXH* AUDITED BY *AC* APPROVED BY *LM*				

JOURNAL VOUCHER Date _Feb. 28,_ 19 _X9_ No. _2-54_				
ACCOUNT	**ACCT. NO.**	**✓**	**DEBIT**	**CREDIT**
Work in Process–Completion Dept.	125		18201272	
Work in Process–Assembly Dept.	124			18201272
EXPLANATION				
Recorded cost of 840 units transferred from Assembly Department				
to Completion Department for the month.				
PREPARED BY *MXH* AUDITED BY *AC* APPROVED BY *LM*				

Combined Cost of Production Report
Month of February 19X9

	Fabrication Department		Assembly Department		Completion Department	
QUANTITY SCHEDULE	UNITS		UNITS		UNITS	
(a) Quantity to Be Accounted for:						
Work in Process—Beginning	200		60		40	
Started in Production—Current Month	800		-0-		-0-	
Transferred In From Prior Department	-0-		820		840	
Total to Be Accounted For	1,000		880		880	
(b) Quantity Accounted For:						
Transferred Out to Next Department	820		840		-0-	
Transferred Out to Finished Goods	-0-		-0-		820	
Work in Process—Ending	180		40		60	
Total Accounted For	1,000		880		880	

	TOTAL COST	UNIT COST	TOTAL COST	UNIT COST	TOTAL COST	UNIT COST
COST SCHEDULE						
(c) Costs to Be Accounted For:						
Costs in Prior Department						
Work in Process—Beginning	-0-		$ 7,080.00		$ 8,624.00	
Transferred In—Current Month	-0-		97,219.20		182,012.72	
Total Prior Department Costs	-0-		$104,299.20	$118.522	$190,636.72	$216.632
Costs in Current Department						
Materials—Beginning Work in Process	$ 10,000.00		$ 1,440.00		$ 80.00	
Added in Current Month	39,840.00		19,820.80		6,720.00	
Total Materials	$ 49,840.00	$ 49.840	$ 21,260.80	$ 24.160	$ 6,800.00	$ 8.000
Labor—Beginning Work in Process	$ 5,920.00		$ 1,464.00		$ 416.00	
Added in Current Month	26,487.92		40,644.00		34,604.00	
Total Labor	$ 32,407.92	$ 37.380	$ 42,108.00	$ 48.400	$ 35,020.00	$ 41.200
Overhead—Beginning Work in Process	$ 4,960.00		$ 744.00		$284.00	
Added in Current Month	22,693.36		21,528.00		$ 24,366.00	
Total Overhead	$ 27,653.36	$ 31.640	$ 22,272.00	$ 25.600	$ 24,650.00	$ 29.000
Total Cost in Current Department	$109,901.28	$118.560	$ 85,640.80	$ 98.160	66,470.00	78.200
Total Costs to Be Accounted For	$109,901.28	$118.560	$189,940.00	$216.682	$257,106.72	$294.832
(d) Costs Accounted For:						
Transferred Out to Next Department	$ 97,219.20	$118.560	$182,012.72*	$216.682	-0-	
Transferred Out to Finished Goods	-0-		-0-		$241,762.80†	$294.832
Total Transferred Out	$ 97,219.20		$182,012.72		$241,762.80	
Work in Process—Ending						
Costs in Prior Department			$ 4,740.88	$118.522	$ 12,997.92	$216.632
Costs in Current Department						
Materials	$ 8,971.20	$ 49.840	966.40	$ 24.160	240.00	$ 8.000
Labor	2,002.32	$ 37.080	1,452.00	$ 48.400	1,236.00	$ 41.200
Overhead	1,708.56	$ 31.640	768.00	$ 25.600	870.00	$ 29.000
Total Work in Process	$ 12,682.08		$ 7,927.28		$ 15,343.92	
Total Costs Accounted For	$109,901.28		$189,940.00		$257,106.72	

*Adjusted $.16 for rounding
†Adjusted $.56 for rounding

JOURNAL VOUCHER	Date _Feb. 28,_		19 _X9_	No. _2-55_	
ACCOUNT	ACCT. NO.	✓	DEBIT	CREDIT
Finished Goods	126		24176280	
Work in Process–Completion				
Department	125			24176280

EXPLANATION
Recorded cost of 820 units transferred from Completion Department
to Finished Goods for the month.

PREPARED BY _MXH_	AUDITED BY _AC_	APPROVED BY _LM_

After the transfer entries are posted, the departmental Work in Process accounts for February appear below.

Proof of Work in Process

Each Departmental Work in Process account balance must agree with the ending work in process cost shown on the corresponding departmental cost of production report for the period. The accountant com-

		Work in Process–Fabrication Department				NO. _123_	
DATE		EXPLANATION	POST. REF.	DEBIT	CREDIT	BALANCE	DR. CR.
19 X9							
Feb.	1	_Balance_	✓			20,880 00	DR.
	28	_Materials_	MR2	39,840 00		60,720 00	DR.
	28	_Labor_	J2-50	26,487 92		87,207 92	DR.
	28	_Overhead_	J2-52	22,693 36		109,901 28	DR.
	28	_Transferred to_					
		Assembly Dept.	J2-53		97,219 20	12,682 08	DR.

		Work in Process–Assembly Department				NO. _124_	
DATE		EXPLANATION	POST. REF.	DEBIT	CREDIT	BALANCE	DR. CR.
19 X9							
Feb.	1	_Balance_	✓			10,728 00	DR.
	28	_Materials_	MR2	19,820 80		30,548 80	DR.
	28	_Labor_	J2-50	40,644 00		71,192 80	DR.
	28	_Overhead_	J2-52	21,528 00		92,720 80	DR.
	28	_Transferred from_					
		Fabrication Dept.	J2-53	97,219 20		189,940 00	DR.
	28	_Transferred to_					
		Completion Dept.	J2-54		182,012 72	7,927 28	DR.

| | | | | Work in Process–Completion Department | | | NO. | 125 | |

DATE		EXPLANATION	POST. REF.	DEBIT		CREDIT		BALANCE		DR. CR.
19	X9									
Feb.	1	Balance	✓					9,404	00	DR.
	28	Materials	MR2	6,720	00			16,124	00	DR.
	28	Labor	J2-50	34,604	00			50,728	00	DR.
	28	Overhead	J2-52	24,366	00			75,094	00	DR.
	28	Transferred from Assembly Dept.	J2-54	182,012	72			257,106	72	DR.
	28	Transferred to Finished Goods Dept.	J2-55			241,762	80	15,343	92	DR.

pares the Work in Process accounts with the cost of production report to make certain that journal entries have been properly posted to the accounts.

Accounting For Sales and Cost of Goods Sold

Under the process cost system, goods manufactured are usually produced for stock. These goods are stored in the warehouse. The receipt of new stock is recorded on finished goods stock ledger cards. At the end of the period, after unit costs have been computed and transfer entries posted, the finished goods stock ledger should be in balance with the amount of its control account in the general ledger, Finished Goods 126.

At this point you should be able to work Exercises 15–6 to 15–8 and Problems 15–3A and 15–3B.

As you studied in Chapters 13 and 14, sales are recorded exactly as in the job order cost system. The sales journal provides space for recording both cost and selling price. At the end of the period, the usual summary postings are completed. Cost of Goods Sold 415 is debited, and Finished Goods 126 is credited. Accounts Receivable 111 (or Cash 101) is debited, and Sales 401 is credited.

PRINCIPLES AND PROCEDURES SUMMARY

- The cost of the ending work in process inventory carried over from one period to the next must be included when unit costs in the new month are determined.
- Two commonly used methods to handle the costs in the beginning inventory of work in process are discussed in this chapter.
  - Under the FIFO method, the partially processed products carried over are costed.
  - Under the average cost method, all costs of each element are combined and an average unit cost is found.
  - The materials costs in beginning inventory are combined with the costs of materials added in the current period. The total is divided by equivalent production of materials to compute an average cost for materials.

SELF-REVIEW

1. How is equivalent production for prior department costs computed when the average costing method is used?
2. How are the costs transferred in from a prior department treated in the cost of production report when the average cost method is used?
3. What advantage is there in having a single cost of production report combining the reports for all producing departments?
4. If the average cost method is used, would it be feasible and desirable to combine the costs in prior departments with the costs of materials incurred in the current department?
5. How does the accountant prove the Work in Process accounts at the end of the month?

Answers to Self-Review

1. The equivalent production for prior department costs—and for each other element of cost—is determined by adding the number of units transferred out of the department and the equivalent units of that element remaining in ending work in process.
2. The beginning inventory of prior department costs and the costs transferred into the department during this period from the prior department are added. To arrive at the unit cost for a prior department, the total prior department cost is divided by the number of equivalent units of prior department costs.
3. The advantage of having a combined cost of production report is that it provides the accountant and management an overview of all manufacturing costs and permits the easy tracing of the flow of costs through the producing departments.
4. It would be possible to combine costs in prior departments only if all materials in the current department were added at the start of the production process. Combining costs would be less informative than showing them separately.
5. The accountant proves the ending Work in Process accounts by comparing the ending inventories shown on the departmental cost of production reports with the work in process general ledger accounts.

- The labor cost in beginning inventory is combined with labor added. The total is divided by equivalent production of labor to compute an average cost for labor.
- The overhead cost in beginning inventory is combined with overhead added. The total is divided by the equivalent production of overhead to compute an average cost for overhead.
- In departments subsequent to the first department, the prior department cost in the beginning inventory is combined with costs transferred in during the current period. The total is divided by equivalent production to compute an average cost for prior department cost.

■ Cost procedures with the average cost method follow a familiar pattern.
  - Cost data is assembled and the production report is prepared.

- The equivalent units are computed.
- The cost of production report is completed.
- The transfers are journalized and posted.
- The accountant may prepare a combined cost report instead of a separate report for each department.
- Under the process cost system, sales and the cost of goods sold are accounted for in the same way as when stock items are sold under the job order cost system.
- The entries to record sales and cost of goods sold are the same, no matter which inventory costing method is used.

MANAGERIAL IMPLICATIONS

- Manufacturers using the process cost system often adopt the average cost method because of its simplicity.
- If the work in process inventories are large in comparison with goods transferred out of the department, there may be significant differences between the costs assigned to ending inventory under the FIFO assumption and under the average cost assumption.
- The average cost method is not as precise as the FIFO method for valuing inventories.
- It is important that the stage of completion of work in process inventories be estimated as accurately as possible. An improper estimate results in a misstatement of cost of products in both the current month and the following month.
- In making cost per equivalent calculations, the accountant must exercise judgment in deciding the number of decimal places to which calculations must be made. The goal is to balance accuracy, the extent of error, and the number of calculations required.
- The combined cost of production report is a tool that expedites the accountant's analysis of departmental costs. Using a combined cost of production report makes it possible for the accountant to easily visualize the flow of costs through the accounts.
- If inventories remain fairly stable in comparison with production, making a comparison of the average costs of the current month with the average costs of prior months may help in analyzing and controlling costs.
- To check the accuracy of the work in process inventories at the end of the month, the accountant should compare the account balances with the cost of production reports.

REVIEW QUESTIONS

1. Explain what is meant by the *average method* of accounting for beginning work in process inventories.
2. What are the main characteristics of the average cost method of handling beginning work in process inventories?

3. How are equivalent units of labor computed if there is a beginning work in process inventory and the average cost method is used?
4. How are equivalent units of prior department costs computed if there is a beginning inventory of work in process?
5. Describe the journal entry used to record the transfer of a product from one producing department to another.
6. Describe the journal entry used to record the transfer of finished goods from the last producing department to the warehouse.
7. A department's beginning inventory of work in process was 1,000 units that were 25 percent complete. During the month, 9,000 units were transferred into the department, 8,600 were completed and transferred out, and the 1,400 on hand were 60 percent complete. What is the equivalent production for the month if the average cost method is used?
8. What is meant by a *transfer entry*?
9. What does the opening balance in the first producing department's Work in Process account represent?
10. Under average costing, why is the amount of each cost element in the beginning work in process inventory combined with the amount of that cost element added during the current period?
11. What is a combined report of departmental production costs? Why is it used?
12. With which general ledger account should the finished goods ledger be in balance?
13. Why does the magnitude of the number of units involved in production affect the number of decimal places to which unit costs are carried?
14. How does the cost of production report for the second department in the production process differ from that of the first department?

MANAGERIAL DISCUSSION QUESTIONS

1. Do you think that the manager of the current department should be responsible for costs incurred in prior departments?
2. Look at the cost of production report of the Fabrication Department on page 346. What figure would mean most to management in measuring the efficiency of labor during the month of February? What figure would probably be the best measure of the performance of the manager of the Fabrication Department?
3. What benefits are there to management from using a combined cost of production report instead of a separate statement for each department?
4. The president of your company has observed that you spend a great deal of time computing equivalent production units and costs per equivalent unit. She suggests that it would be much more efficient for you to ignore the beginning and ending work in process inventories. What is your response? Under what conditions might the president's suggestion be a logical one?

5. Assume that the average cost method is being used. An error was made in the current period's work in process inventory in a department: The ending inventory stage of completion was substantially overstated.
   a. What would be the effect of this error on the number of equivalent units of production?
   b. What would be the effect on the cost of goods transferred out during the period?
   c. That would be the effect on cost of goods completed and transferred out of the department in the following period?

EXERCISES

NOTE: Assume in all the exercises that the company uses the average cost method for costing work in process.

EXERCISE 15–1 **Compute equivalent units of production. (Obj. 2).** The monthly production report made by the manager of the Planing and Sanding Department of Big Foot Furniture Company for September 19X9 contains the following information:

- Beginning inventory, 10,000 units; materials, 25 percent complete; labor and overhead, 50 percent complete.
- Units started this month, 25,000.
- Units transferred to next department during September, 30,000.
- Units in process at the end of September, 5,000; materials, 40 percent complete; labor and overhead, 60 percent complete.

Compute the equivalent units of production for materials, labor, and overhead, assuming that the average cost method is to be used for handling beginning work in process inventory.

EXERCISE 15–2 **Compute equivalent units of production for materials, cost per equivalent unit, cost of units transferred out, and costs of ending work in process. (Objs. 2, 3, 4).** The beginning inventory in the Mixing Department, the first department, consisted of 1,000 units, with materials costs of $2,000. During the period, 15,000 units were started into production in the department. Materials costing $47,290 were added during the period. During the period, 13,500 units were transferred out to the next department, and 2,500 units were ending work in process. It was estimated that 80 percent of the materials had been added in the preceding month to the beginning work in process. The ending work in process was 60 percent complete as to materials.
a. Determine the equivalent units of production for materials.
b. Compute the cost per equivalent unit for materials.
c. Compute the materials cost in the units transferred out during the month.
d. Compute the materials cost in the ending work in process inventory for the Mixing Department.

EXERCISE 15–3   **Compute equivalent units of production. (Obj. 2).** Medical Chemicals, Inc., produces a cough syrup. The beginning work in process inventory in the Blending Department was 1,000 units; the total cost included $1,500 of prior department costs. During the month, 15,000 units were transferred into the department, 13,500 units were transferred out to the next department, and 2,500 units were in the ending work in process inventory.

Compute the equivalent units of production for prior department costs in the Blending Department.

EXERCISE 15–4   **Compute equivalent units of production for labor, cost per equivalent unit, cost of units transferred out, and cost of ending work in process.   (Objs. 2, 3, 4).**   The beginning work in process inventory in the Configuration Department of the Coe Company on August 1, 19X9, was 600 units, to which 60 percent of labor had been applied at a cost of $720. During August, 8,000 units were transferred into the department and 6,800 units were transferred out to the next department. Labor costs of $15,360 were incurred during the month. The 1,800 units in the ending work in process in the Configuration Department were estimated to be 50 percent complete as to labor.
a. Determine the equivalent units of production for labor.
b. Compute the cost per equivalent unit for labor.
c. Compute the labor cost in the units transferred out during the month.
d. Compute the labor cost in the ending work in process inventory for the Assembly Department.

EXERCISE 15–5   **Compute equivalent units of production for overhead, cost per equivalent unit, cost of units transferred out, and cost of ending work in process.   (Objs. 2, 3, 4).**   The beginning work in process inventory in the Grinding Department of Algers Company on March 1, 19X9, was 6,000 units, to which 50 percent of overhead had been applied at a cost of $6,000. During March, 24,000 units were transferred into the department and 25,000 units were transferred out to the next department. Overhead costs of $49,550 were incurred during the month. The 5,000 units in process were estimated to be 80 percent complete as to overhead.
a. Determine the equivalent units of production for overhead.
b. Compute the cost per equivalent unit for overhead.
c. Compute the overhead cost in the units transferred out during the month.
d. Compute the overhead cost in the ending work in process inventory in the Grinding Department.

EXERCISE 15–6   **Compute equivalent units of production for materials, cost per equivalent unit, cost of units transferred out, and cost of ending work in process.   (Objs. 2, 3, 4).**   The beginning work in process inventory in the Cooking Department of Mayfair Syrup Company on April 1, 19X9, was 1,000 units, to which 100 percent of materials had been added at a cost of $2,500. During April, 6,000 units were transferred into the department and 6,700 units were transferred out to finished goods. Materials costs of $15,860 were incurred during the month. The 300 units in the ending work in process were 60 percent complete as to materials.

a. Determine the equivalent units of production for materials.

b. Compute the cost per equivalent unit for materials.

c. Compute the materials cost in the units transferred out to finished goods during the month.

d. Compute the materials cost in the ending work in process inventory for the Cooking Department.

EXERCISE 15–7   **Make a journal entry to transfer costs.   (Obj. 7).**   Total costs incurred in the Blending Department 125 of the Velaquez Corporation during October 19X9 were $74,510. Of this amount, $2,600 is determined to be applicable to the ending work in process and the balance is applicable to work transferred to the Bottling Department 126. Give the journal entry to record the transfer of units between the departments.

EXERCISE 15–8   **Prepare a journal entry to transfer costs.   (Obj. 7).**   The beginning inventory of work in process in the Packaging Department 127 of the McFee Company in March 19X9 was $34,000. Costs incurred in the department during the month totaled $68,000. The cost of products transferred to Finished Goods 130 during the month was $76,000. Give the journal entry to record the transfer of finished products from the Packaging Department to the finished goods storeroom.

PROBLEMS

NOTE: Assume in all the problems that each company uses the average cost method for costing work in process.

PROBLEM 15–1A

Compute equivalent units; compute costs per equivalent unit; compute cost of units transferred out of the department and of ending work in process inventory; prepare a cost of production report.   (Objs. 2, 3, 4, 5).   The Boston Solvent Corporation produces a single product. All materials are added at the beginning of production. On January 1, 19X9, 8,000 pounds of the product were in process in the Refining Department, the first department. During the month of January, 75,000 pounds were placed into production and 71,000 pounds were transferred out to the Toning Department, the second department. On January 31, 12,000 pounds were still in process in the Refining Department. The ending inventory is estimated to be complete as to materials and two-thirds complete as to labor and overhead. Cost data for the month of January are shown below.

	Materials	Labor	Overhead
Beginning Work in Process Inventory	$ 32,000	$ 14,400	$ 7,200
Added During January	228,000	133,040	68,800

INSTRUCTIONS
1. Compute the equivalent units of production for the month of January.
2. Prepare a cost of production report for the Refining Department for the month of January.

PROBLEM 15–2A

Compute equivalent production; compute costs per equivalent unit; compute cost of goods transferred out of the department and cost of ending inventory of work in process; prepare a cost of production report. (Objs. 2, 3, 4, 5). On April 1, 19X9, the beginning inventory of work in process in the Processing Department, the second department in the manufacturing process of the Atlanta Detergent Company, was 1,000 units. Costs in the beginning inventory were as follows: prior department costs, $60,000; materials, $12,000; labor, $12,530; and overhead, $3,160. During April, 3,960 units were transferred in from the Mixing Department at a total cost of $233,640 ($59 each). Additional costs incurred in the Processing Department during April were as follows: materials, $47,520; labor, $93,330; and overhead, $43,474. Of the 4,960 units, 4,690 were completed and transferred out to finished goods. The remaining 270 were still in process on April 30. All materials had been added, but only 25 percent of the labor and 25 percent of the overhead had been added.

INSTRUCTIONS
1. Compute the equivalent units of production for the month of April.
2. Prepare a cost of production report for the Processing Department for the month of April.

PROBLEM 15–3A

Compute equivalent production; compute costs per equivalent unit; compute cost of units transferred out of the department; compute costs of ending inventory of work in process; prepare a combined cost of production report. (Objs. 2, 3, 4, 6). The Andover Company uses a process cost accounting system. All materials in the first department (Blending) are added at the start of production. Raw materials placed into production in the second department (Finishing) are added in proportion to labor and manufacturing overhead. Data for the month of February 19X9 are given below.

	Blending Department	Finishing Department
Costs		
Beginning Work in Process		
Costs in Prior Department	-0-	$3,046
Costs in Current Department		
Materials	$ 1,500	312
Labor	430	263
Manufacturing Overhead	730	291
Current Department Costs—February		
Materials	19,020	7,848
Labor	17,860	5,884
Manufacturing Overhead	16,270	4,908

Quantities		
Beginning Work in Process	150	125
Started in Production	1,250	-0-
Transferred In From Prior Department	-0-	1,225
Transferred Out to Next Department	1,225	-0-
Transferred Out to Finished Goods	-0-	1,200
Ending Work in Process	175	150

Stage of Completion of Work in Process		
Beginning		
Material	complete	$66\frac{2}{3}\%$
Labor and Manufacturing Overhead	25%	$66\frac{2}{3}\%$
Ending		
Material	complete	50%
Labor and Manufacturing Overhead	60%	50%

INSTRUCTIONS
1. Complete the equivalent production computations for each department.
2. Prepare a combined cost of production report for the two departments.
3. Prepare journal vouchers to transfer costs out of the department.

ALTERNATE PROBLEMS

PROBLEM 15–1B   **Compute equivalent units of production; compute costs per equivalent unit of production; compute cost of goods transferred out of the department and of ending work in process; prepare a cost of production report.   (Objs. 2, 3, 4, 5).**   The Gruener Company produces a single product, involving three processing departments. All materials are added at the beginning of production. On June 1, 19X9, 20,000 quarts of the product were in process in the first department. During the month of June, 195,000 quarts were placed into production and 170,000 quarts were transferred out to the next department. The ending work in process inventory is one-half completed. The beginning inventory costs were as follows: materials, $40,000; labor, $18,000; and overhead, $9,000. During June additional costs were as follows: materials, $362,500; labor, $116,300; and overhead, $82,200.

INSTRUCTIONS   Prepare a cost of production report for the first department for the month of June 19X9.

PROBLEM 15–2B   **Compute equivalent production; compute cost per unit of equivalent production; compute cost of goods transferred out of the department during month and of ending work in process inventory; prepare a cost of production report.   (Objs. 2, 3, 4, 5).**   The Memphis Products Company produces a single product. All materials are added in the Formation Department, the first department, at the beginning of production. On September 1, 19X9, 2,000 pounds of the product were in process in the Formation Department. During the month of September, 24,000 pounds were put into production. On September 30, 4,000 pounds were still in process. The ending inventory is estimated to be complete as to materials and 75 percent complete as to labor and overhead. The remainder of the units to be accounted for were transferred to the Cooking Department. Cost data for the month of September are shown below.

	Materials	Labor	Overhead
Beginning Work in Process Inventory	$ 16,200	$ 1,850	$ 3,700
Added During September	201,000	23,916	47,800

INSTRUCTIONS Prepare a cost of production report for the Formation Department for the month of September.

PROBLEM 15–3B **Compute equivalent production; compute costs per equivalent unit; compute cost of goods transferred and of ending inventory; prepare a combined cost of production report; make journal entries to transfer costs out of department. (Objs. 2, 3, 4, 6, 7).** Big Sky Industries uses a process cost accounting system. All materials in the first department (Mixing) are added at the start of production. Raw materials put into production in the second department (Finishing) are added in proportion to labor and manufacturing overhead. Data for the month of July 19X9 are given below.

	Mixing Department	Finishing Department
Costs		
Beginning Work in Process		
Costs in Prior Department	-0-	$26,178
Costs in Current Department		
Materials	$ 6,480	980
Labor	2,610	730
Manufacturing Overhead	1,710	580
Current Department Costs—July		
Materials	$92,520	$10,135
Labor	76,650	8,090
Manufacturing Overhead	62,190	6,770
Quantities		
Beginning Work in Process	1,500	2,400
Started in Production	21,000	-0-
Transferred In From Prior Department	-0-	21,500
Transferred Out to Next Department	21,500	-0-
Transferred Out to Finished Goods	-0-	21,000
Ending Work in Process	1,000	2,900
Stage of Completion of Work in Process		
Beginning Inventory		
Materials	complete	75%
Labor and Manufacturing Overhead	40%	75%
Ending Inventory		
Materials	complete	70%
Labor and Manufacturing Overhead	50%	70%

INSTRUCTIONS 1. Complete the equivalent production computations for each department.
2. Prepare a combined cost of production report for the two departments.

3. Prepare entries in general journal form to record the costs charged to each department, the costs transferred between departments, and the costs transferred out to finished goods. Date the entries July 31. Use the accounts Work in Process—Mixing 123 and Work in Process—Finishing 124. Combine the amounts and accounts in entries whenever possible.

MASTER PROBLEM

Compute equivalent production; compute costs per equivalent unit; compute cost of goods transferred out of the department and of ending inventory; prepare a combined cost of production report; make journal entries to transfer costs. (Objs. 2, 3, 4, 6, 7. The Flatlands Company has three producing departments: the Forming Department, the Assembly Department, and the Finishing Department. The departmental Work in Process accounts are completed for June 19X9 as shown below.

Work in Process–Forming Department   NO. 134

DATE	EXPLANATION	POST. REF.	DEBIT	CREDIT	BALANCE	DR. CR.
19X9						
June 1	Balance	✓			2,824 47	DR.
30	Materials	MR4	10,206 27		13,030 74	DR.
30	Labor	J4-9	4,161 62		17,192 36	DR.
30	Overhead	J4-10	9,345 64		26,538 00	DR.

Work in Process–Assembly Department   NO. 135

DATE	EXPLANATION	POST. REF.	DEBIT	CREDIT	BALANCE	DR. CR.
19X9						
June 1	Balance	✓			5,981 95	DR.
30	Materials	MR4	720 10		6,702 05	DR.
30	Labor	J4-9	6,331 17		13,033 22	DR.
30	Overhead	J4-10	1,152 34		14,185 56	DR.

Work in Process–Finishing Department   NO. 136

DATE	EXPLANATION	POST. REF.	DEBIT	CREDIT	BALANCE	DR. CR.
19X9						
June 1	Balance	✓			1,142 47	DR.
30	Materials	MR4	1,526 20		2,668 67	DR.
30	Labor	J4-9	3,159 82		5,828 49	DR.
30	Overhead	J4-10	3,653 47		9,481 96	DR.

The departmental summaries of the costs of work in process on May 31 are shown below.

	Forming Department	Assembly Department	Finishing Department
Prior Department Costs	-0-	$4,334.56	$1,016.41
Materials	$1,632.48	838.40	22.10
Labor	385.63	331.33	48.18
Overhead	806.36	477.66	55.78
Totals of Work in Process on May 31	$2,824.47	$5,981.95	$1,142.47

The monthly departmental production reports for June 19X9 have been submitted and summarized. The results are shown below.

	Forming Department	Assembly Department	Finishing Department
Quantity			
Work in Process—Beginning	430	630	56
Started in Production—Current Month	1,915	-0-	-0-
Transferred In From Prior Department	-0-	1,975	1,955
Transferred Out to Next Department	1,975	1,955	-0-
Transferred Out to Finished Goods	-0-	-0-	1,970
Work in Process—Ending	370	650	41
Stage of Completion of Ending Work in Process			
Materials	100%	25%	30%
Labor	50%	25%	60%
Overhead	50%	25%	60%

INSTRUCTIONS

1. Prepare the equivalent production computations for the three departments for June 19X9.
2. Prepare the combined cost of production report for June 19X9. Carry the unit costs to nearest one-one hundredth of a cent.
3. a. Prepare the general journal voucher (Number 6-11) to record the transfer of goods from the Forming Department to the Assembly Department.
   b. Prepare the general journal voucher (Number 6-12) to record the transfer of goods from the Assembly Department to the Finishing Department.
   c. Prepare the general journal voucher (Number 6-13) to record the completion of goods and their transfer to Finished Goods 126.

16

Units Lost or Increased in Production

The mass-production techniques and high-speed machinery used in continuous process operations occasionally fail to function properly. Similarly, production workers sometimes make mistakes. Both situations can result in products that are damaged and cannot be completed, and thus a decrease in units of product in process occurs. Losses in the number of units in process may also be due to shrinkage, evaporation, condensation, or other factors that are a normal part of the process.

Manufacturing processes may also produce an increase in the number of units in production through expansion, blending, and other processes. Further, the measurement being used may change during a manufacturing process. For example, the input to the cooking department of a chemical company may be expressed in gallons or barrels, and the output expressed in pounds. These increases or changes in units must be considered so that the final unit cost will relate to the actual output for the period.

CLASSIFYING LOSSES OR SPOILAGE

In almost every month, the manufacturing process at Apex Computer Designs' factory results in a small number of spoiled units.

Spoiled units are units of product that have been damaged or improperly manufactured and cannot be completed as salable products. The spoilage may be due to defective raw materials, problems with the machinery used to work on the product, problems in the operating environment, poor judgment on the part of production personnel, or various other causes. For example, in Apex Computer Designs, in spite of close quality checks, raw materials used in a credenza may be severely defective, with the result that the cost of disassembling the unit and replacing the defective material is so high that it makes sense to discard the credenza rather than rework it.

Processing activities in almost every manufacturing company result in some quantity of spoiled goods. For example, Byproducts Company manufactures an agent used to combat certain nerve disorders. The humidity and temperature in the processing area must be extremely tightly controlled. In spite of sophisticated automatic equipment and vigilance by employees, the humidity or temperature occasionally varies by a small margin. As a result, batches of the compound are made unusable and must be destroyed.

Most of the spoilage in Apex Computer Designs and in Byproducts Company can be classified as **normal spoilage** because it is a common occurrence that is inherent in the manufacturing process. On the other hand, **abnormal spoilage** results from unusual and non-recurring factors, such as a power outage, a fire, or water damage.

Lost units are units of product that are started in production but are not completed. In many cases, the quantity of materials being worked on simply decreases because of the manufacturing process. This may be due to normal spoiled units, as discussed above. As mentioned, evaporation, condensation, shrinkage, leakage, and other factors cause lost units. Losses that result from normal recurring events or factors are frequently referred to as **normal lost units,** and those resulting from nonrecurring and unusual events are called **abnormal lost units.** Both normal lost units and abnormal lost units must be identified and properly accounted for so that the cost per unit of completed product will be computed accurately.

In many manufacturing operations, some units of the product that have been damaged in the production process can be reworked and made into salable units. Damaged products that can be reworked and completed as finished units are referred to as **defective units.** The reworking of course requires additional costs that must be properly accounted for.

ACCOUNTING FOR LOST UNITS

In most companies that use process cost accounting, costs for units lost through normal spoilage are absorbed by the remaining good units produced during the month because lost units are considered a routine part of production. Apex Computer Designs uses this method to account for normal lost units.

Costs related to abnormal spoilage are usually removed from the work in process account and charged to a loss account so that the completed units do not absorb the costs related to lost units. The manner in which lost units are reflected in the accounting records depends on whether the loss occurs in the first department in the production sequence or in a subsequent department.

NORMAL LOSS OF UNITS IN FIRST DEPARTMENT

When normal loss of units occurs in the first department, no special calculations are required. The costs incurred for materials, labor, and overhead are merely spread over the equivalent units of production for each element. Let us assume that in March 19X9 the supervisor of the Fabrication Department at Apex Computer Designs reports that 20 credenzas are badly damaged and are a complete loss. This type of loss is considered by Apex to be normal spoilage. The March cost and production data for the department are assembled in the usual order.

Cost Data

The Work in Process—Fabrication Department 123 account in the general ledger shows a balance of $127,128.80 on March 31. The balance of this account is analyzed as follows:

Beginning Work in Process		
Materials	$ 8,971.20	
Labor	2,002.32	
Overhead	1,708.56	
Balance of Account, Jan. 31		$ 12,682.08
Costs Incurred in Current Month		
Materials	$47,128.80	
Labor	36,313.68	
Overhead	31,004.24	
Total Current Month's Costs		$114,446.72
Balance of Account, Mar. 31		$127,128.80

Production Data

The manager's production report for the month of March is shown on page 372. The 20 units lost in production are reported on the last line of the Quantity section of the monthly production report.

Equivalent Production Data

In computing equivalent production, the cost accountant ignores the normal lost units because all costs must be absorbed by the good units. Only the good units (those transferred out to the next department and those in the ending work in process) are considered.

Cost of Production Report

The March cost of production report, shown on page 373, is very similar to the department's February report. However, note the details given in connection with lost units.

```
┌─────────────────────────────────────────────────────────────────┐
│                    FABRICATION DEPARTMENT                          │
│                   Monthly Production Report                        │
│                     Month of March 19X9                           │
│                                                                   │
│ Quantity                                                          │
│     Work in Process—Beginning              180 credenzas          │
│     Started in Production—Current Month     940                   │
│     Transferred Out to Next Department      960                   │
│     Work in Process—Ending                  140                   │
│     Lost in Production (normal loss)         20                   │
│ Stage of Completion of Work in Process                            │
│     Materials                               complete              │
│     Labor                                      50%                │
│     Overhead                                   50%                │
└─────────────────────────────────────────────────────────────────┘
```

```
┌─────────────────────────────────────────────────────────────────┐
│                    FABRICATION DEPARTMENT                          │
│               Equivalent Production Computations                  │
│                     Month of March 19X9                           │
│                      (Average Costing)                            │
│                                                                   │
│ Materials                                                         │
│     Transferred Out to Next Department                    960     │
│     Work in Process—Ending (140 credenzas × 100%)         140     │
│       Equivalent Production for Materials (average costing) 1,100 │
│ Labor and Manufacturing Overhead                                  │
│     Transferred Out to Next Department                    960     │
│     Work in Process—Ending (140 credenzas × 50%)           70     │
│       Equivalent Production for Labor and Overhead       1,030    │
└─────────────────────────────────────────────────────────────────┘
```

- In the Quantity Schedule, all units are included under Quantity to Be Accounted For. The lost units are reported separately under Quantity Accounted For.
- In the Cost Schedule, the cost of each element in the beginning work in process inventory is combined as usual with the cost incurred during the month. However, note that all costs are absorbed by the good units in determining average unit costs. This is done by dividing the total cost of each element by the equivalent production units. Remember that the lost units were ignored when the equivalent units were computed. The term *equivalent units* actually means **equivalent good units.**

At this point you should be able to work Exercises 16–1 to 16–3 and Problems 16–1A and 16–1B.

NORMAL LOSS OF UNITS IN SUBSEQUENT DEPARTMENTS

When units of a product are lost in departments that work on the product after the first department, the accounting procedures are slightly more complex. The good units must absorb not only all the costs incurred in the department in which the loss occurs, but also the costs incurred in prior departments. Since prior departmental

FABRICATION DEPARTMENT
Cost of Production Report
Month of March 19X9

QUANTITY SCHEDULE	UNITS
(a) Quantity to Be Accounted For:	
Work in Process—Beginning	180
Started in Production—Current Month	940
Transferred In From Prior Department	-0-
Total to Be Accounted For	1,120
(b) Quantity Accounted For:	
Transferred Out to Next Department	960
Transferred Out to Finished Goods	-0-
Work in Process—Ending	140
Lost in Production (Normal Loss)	20
Total Accounted For	1,120

COST SCHEDULE	TOTAL COST	E.P. UNITS	UNIT COST
(c) Costs to Be Accounted For:			
Costs in Prior Department			
Work in Process—Beginning	-0-		
Transferred In—Current Month	-0-		
Total Prior Department Costs	-0-		
Costs in Current Department			
Materials—Beginning Work in Process	$ 8,971.20		
Added in Current Month	47,128.80		
Total Materials	$ 56,100.00	÷ 1,100 =	$ 51.000
Labor—Beginning Work in Process	$ 2,002.32		
Added in Current Month	36,313.68		
Total Labor	$ 38,316.00	÷ 1,030 =	$ 37.200
Overhead—Beginning Work in Process	$ 1,708.56		
Added in Current Month	$ 31,004.24		
Total Overhead	$ 32,712.80	÷ 1,030 =	$ 31.760
Total Costs in Current Department	$127,128.80		$119.960
Total Costs to Be Accounted For	$127,128.80		$119.960
(d) Costs Accounted For:			
Transferred Out to Next Department	$115,161.60	= 960 ×	$119.960
Transferred Out to Finished Goods	-0-		
Total Transferred Out	$115,161.60		
Work in Process—Ending			
Costs in Prior Department	-0-		
Costs in Current Department			
Materials	$ 7,140.00	= 140 ×	$ 51.000
Labor	2,604.00	= 70 ×	$ 37.200
Overhead	2,223.20	= 70 ×	$ 31.760
Total Work in Process	$ 11,967.20		
Total Costs Accounted For	$127,128.80		

SELF-REVIEW

1. What are some common causes of normal lost units?
2. How are manufacturing costs related to normal spoilage or normal lost units accounted for?
3. How does normal spoilage or lost units affect the calculation of equivalent production in a department?
4. What is the difference between spoiled units and defective units?
5. Why can it be said that *equivalent units* actually means *equivalent good units*?

Answers to Self-Review

1. Normal lost units result from such factors as shrinkage, evaporation, and condensation. In addition, the term encompasses normal spoilage caused by routine malfunction or problems with equipment settings and normal human error.
2. Manufacturing costs related to normal spoilage or lost units are absorbed by the good units.
3. Normal spoilage or lost units are ignored in computing equivalent production. Only good units of production are used in the calculation.
4. Spoiled units are units that cannot be finished as products. Defective units are units that can be reworked and completed as units of product.
5. In computing equivalent units of production, normal spoilage is generally ignored. As a result, equivalent production is based on good units only.

costs have already been identified with the total number of units transferred out of the preceding department and into the current department, there must be a recalculation of the unit cost from prior departments. This recalculation of prior department unit costs may be made by merely dividing the total prior departmental costs by the good units. In this case, no separate disclosure is made of the amount of change in the cost per unit resulting from the loss. This procedure is illustrated for Apex Computer Designs' Assembly Department for March. In that month the Assembly Department lost 25 units through breakage. These units cannot be repaired and have no salvage value. Here is how the firm's records are adjusted to reflect the impact of the loss on prior department unit costs.

Cost Data

The Work in Process—Assembly Department 124 account shows a balance of $98,818.88 on March 31. The balance consists of the following costs:

Beginning Work in Process		
Costs in Prior Department	$ 4,740.88	
Costs in Current Department		
Materials	966.40	
Labor	1,452.00	
Overhead	768.00	
Balance of Account, March 1		$ 7,927.28

Current Month
   Materials $22,823.60

Current Month		
Materials	$22,823.60	
Labor	45,152.00	
Overhead	22,916.00	
Total Current Month's Costs		$90,891.60
Balance of Account, Mar. 31		$98,818.88

Production Data

The departmental production report shows the 25 units lost during the period.

ASSEMBLY DEPARTMENT
Monthly Production Report
March 19X9

Quantity	
Work in Process—Beginning	40
Units Started in Production—Current Month	960
Transferred Out to Next Department	925
Work in Process—Ending	50
Lost in Production	25

Stage of Completion of Ending Work in Process	
Materials	100%
Labor	60%
Overhead	60%

Equivalent Production Data

In determining equivalent production, the lost units are again ignored. As before, the result reflects good units only, as shown below in the equivalent production computations for the Assembly Department.

ASSEMBLY DEPARTMENT
Equivalent Production Computations
Month of March 19X9
(Average Costing)

Materials	
Transferred Out to Next Department	925
Work in Process—Ending (50 credenzas × 100%)	50
Equivalent Production for Materials	975

Labor and Manufacturing Overhead	
Transferred Out to Next Department	925
Work in Process—Ending (50 credenzas × 60%)	30
Equivalent Production for Labor and Overhead	955

The Cost of Production Report

The Quantity Schedule of the cost of production report is prepared in the same way as the corresponding section of the Fabrication Department's report. However, several details in the Cost Schedule for

ASSEMBLY DEPARTMENT
Cost of Production Report
Month of March 19X9

QUANTITY SCHEDULE	UNITS
(a) Quantity to Be Accounted For:	
Work in Process—Beginning	40
Started in Production—Current Month	-0-
Transferred In From Prior Department	960
Total to Be Accounted For	1,000
(b) Quantity Accounted For:	
Transferred Out to Next Department	925
Transferred Out to Finished Goods	-0-
Work in Process—Ending	50
Lost in Production	25
Total Accounted For	1,000

COST SCHEDULE	TOTAL COST	E.P. UNITS	UNIT COST
(c) Costs to Be Accounted For:			
Costs in Prior Department			
Work in Process—Beginning	$ 4,740.88		
Transferred In—Current Month	115,161.60		
Total Prior Department Costs	$119,902.48	÷ 975	= $122.977
Costs in Current Department			
Materials—Beginning Work in Process	$ 966.40		
Added in Current Month	22,823.60		
Total Materials	$ 23,790.00	÷ 975	= $ 24.400
Labor—Beginning Work in Process	$ 1,452.00		
Added in Current Month	45,152.00		
Total Labor	$ 46,604.00	÷ 955	= 48.800
Overhead—Beginning Work in Process	768.00		
Added in Current Month	22,916.00		
Total Overhead	$ 23,684.00	÷ 955	= 24.800
Total Costs in Current Department	$ 94,078.00		$ 98.000
Total Costs to Be Accounted For	$213,980.48		$220.977
(d) Costs Accounted For:			
Transferred Out to Next Department	$204,403.63* =	925	× $220.977
Transferred Out to Finished Goods	-0-		
Total Transferred Out	$204,403.63		
Work in Process—Ending			
Costs in Prior Department	$ 6,148.85 =	50	× $122.977
Costs in Current Department			
Materials	1,220.00 =	50	× $ 24.400
Labor	1,464.00 =	30	× $ 48.800
Overhead	744.00 =	30	× $ 24.800
Total Work in Process	$ 9,576.85		
Total Costs Accounted For	$213,980.48		

*Adjusted $.10 for rounding.

the Assembly Department require careful attention because now all costs must be absorbed by only the remaining good units.

■ The total of prior department costs, $119,902.48, is divided by the 975 total equivalent (good) units for an average prior department unit cost of $122.977, as shown on the cost of production report below.
■ The total of each cost element under Costs in Current Department is divided by its equivalent production of good units to obtain the average unit costs shown on the cost of production report.

Some accountants believe that the Costs in Prior Department section should be made more informative. That is, in dealing with lost units, they prefer to show the following:

1. What the unit cost would have been if there had been no lost units.
2. The adjusted unit cost, which is the same as the unit cost obtained by using equivalent *good* units. This is the cost figure shown in the illustration on page 376.
3. The lost-unit cost, which is the difference between what the cost would have been and the adjusted unit cost.

COST SCHEDULE

	TOTAL COST	E.P. UNITS	UNIT COST
(c) Costs to Be Accounted For:			
Costs in Prior Department			
Work in Process—Beginning	$ 4,740.88		
Transferred In—Current Month	115,161.60		
Total Prior Department Costs	$119,902.48 ÷	1,000 =	$119.902
Adjustment for Lost Units (abnormal loss)		25	3.075
Adjusted Prior Department Costs	$119,902.48 ÷	975 =	$122.977

The partial cost of production report illustrated above shows how this expanded presentation of prior department costs would appear in the cost of production report. Note the following items:

■ The Total Prior Department Costs figure is first divided by 1,000 units to compute what the unit cost would have been had there been no lost units. This is the gross number of units worked on during the month, consisting of 40 units from Work in Process—Beginning on March 1 and 960 units transferred in from the Fabrication Department during the month. This calculation yields a unit cost of $119.902 ($119,902.48 ÷ 1,000 units = $119.902 per unit).
■ The Adjusted Prior Department Costs line shows the same total cost ($119,902.48) divided by the 975 equivalent good units only, yielding unit cost of $122.977.
■ The difference between the unit costs ($122.977 − $119.902 = $3.075), called the **lost-unit cost,** is then entered on the Adjustment for Lost Units line in the Unit Cost column to show the increase in unit cost of the good units resulting from the 25 lost units.

At this point you should be able to work Exercises 16–4 to 16–6 and Problems 16–2A to 16–3B.

SELF-REVIEW

1. Explain two ways that the impact of normal lost units on prior department costs can be handled in the cost of production report.
2. In determining equivalent production in a department subsequent to the first department, what consideration is given to lost units?
3. What is meant by the term *lost-unit cost*?
4. Why must there be a recalculation of prior department unit costs when units are lost in the current department?
5. In preparing a cost of production report, it is often necessary to round unit costs. As a result, the Total Costs Accounted For, computed by adding the ending work in process inventory and the cost of units transferred out of the department, may not exactly equal the Total Costs to Be Accounted For. What adjustment is made to make the two numbers agree?

Answers to Self-Review

1. In the cost of production report, the impact of lost units may simply be absorbed by good units, with no disclosure of the effects of the loss on cost per unit of good units. An alternative is to show in Costs to Be Accounted For three items for Prior Department Costs: (1) the average unit costs if there had been no lost units, (2) the average unit costs based on the equivalent units of good production, and (3) the difference between items (1) and (2)—which is the Adjustment for Lost Units.
2. In departments subsequent to the first, lost units are treated in the same way as in the first department, except that the unit costs for work done in the prior department must be adjusted to reflect the lost units.
3. Lost-unit cost is the difference in the cost per equivalent unit for (1) prior department costs based on actual good units in the current department and (2) what the prior department cost per equivalent unit would have been had there been no loss in the current department.
4. There must be a recalculation of prior department costs when units are lost in the prior department because the total prior department costs apply to fewer units than were transferred into the department.
5. Errors resulting from rounding are always absorbed by the units transferred out of the department during the current month.

ABNORMAL LOSS OF UNITS

If units of product are spoiled or ruined because of unusual or abnormal conditions that are not a typical, recurring part of the manufacturing process, it is customary to assign to such goods their usual share of costs as though the spoiled units were good units. Then the cost assigned to the abnormal spoilage is removed from work in process and charged to a special loss account by an entry similar to the following:

Loss From Abnormally Spoiled Units	10,000.00	
Work in Process—Department 2		10,000.00
Charged the cost of abnormal spoilage to		
the loss account.		

Controlling Production While Increasing Distribution of Products

Companies manufacturing standardized products (who are thus good candidates to use process cost accounting) frequently seek to improve their product distribution by using outside distributors to get the product into the hand of retailers. This is especially true in international distribution activities. Manufacturers of soft drink products are typical users of this concept. For example, the Coca-Cola Company manufactures drink concentrate and sells the syrup to bottlers, who appropriately dilute the syrup, bottle the final product, and sell it to retailers. The 1996 annual report of the Coca-Cola Company contains the following references to sales to its bottlers:

2. **BOTTLING INVESTMENTS**
   Coca-Cola Enterprises Inc.
   Coca-Cola Enterprises is the largest soft drink bottler in the world. Our Company owns approximately 45 percent of the outstanding stock of Cola-Cola Enterprises. . . . We also provide certain administrative and other services to Coca-Cola Enterprises under negotiated fee arrangements.

   Coca-Cola Amatil Limited
   We own approximately 36 percent of Coca-Cola Amatil, an Australian-based bottler of our products that operates in 17 countries.

Why do Coca-Cola and other companies use this system of distribution? The answer is contained in the 1996 Coca-Cola Annual Report:

Not even a brand like Coca-Cola sells itself. To make Coca-Cola and our other brands more successful requires a business system capable of selling more soft drinks in more places to more people, overcoming logistical hurdles, creating more value for customers, stimulating consumer demand, and ensuring the finest in quality products.

We have just such a system; it's a true competitive advantage for us, and we take steps to improve it every day.

Increasingly, we are able to bring our Company's resources to bear in partnership with our various bottlers. When the opportunity arises, we are able to invest directly in a bottler and contribute to improving its performance. Often, we later sell our stake, handing off a stronger bottler, with greater capacity for profitable growth, and in turn reap rewards for our share owners.

This entry may be combined with the entry transferring goods out of the current department into the next department or into finished goods inventory.

In the above example it was assumed that abnormal spoilage occurred at the end of the production process. If the spoilage occurs before all the work is completed on the units in the department, to arrive at the appropriate cost for the units spoiled it will be necessary to estimate the amount of work that has been performed on the spoiled units. The prior department costs will, of course, have all been added. Typically, all raw materials to be added in the current department will also have been added. However, the labor and overhead may have been only partially added. It will therefore be necessary to estimate the percentage of completion of the labor and overhead. Fortunately, abnormal spoilage is, by definition, not common. As a result, although you should be aware of the problem arising when abnormal spoilage occurs before the units are completed in the current department, there are more critical cost accounting topics that require attention.

At this point you should be able to work Exercise 16–7 and Problems 16–4A and 16–4B.

DEFECTIVE UNITS AND REWORK COSTS

Defective units are those units of product that are damaged or are somehow imperfect and will require additional work before they can be sold. Defective units are either normal defective units or abnormal defective units. If the defects resulted from normal operations, the costs to rework the units are usually treated simply as additional manufacturing costs and are allocated to all the units in the period during which the rework costs are incurred. This does not require any additional accounting entries. At Apex Computer Designs, for example, in the process of manufacturing computer credenzas, frequently units are scratched and must be refinished (reworked). This is a normal part of the manufacturing process, and the rework costs are simply treated as a part of the costs of the period in which they are incurred. In this case, costs incurred to rework the units are considered part of normal charges to work in process.

If defective units result from some abnormal condition which is not part of the usual manufacturing process, the rework costs should be treated as a loss of the period or as part of the cost of goods sold during the period. For example, suppose that an automatic sprinkling system in the ceiling of the factory broke, causing water damage to a number of credenzas. This event is not part of the normal manufacturing process. The costs to rework these damaged credenzas would be charged to a loss account or to cost of goods sold, rather than treated simply as a normal manufacturing cost.

Defective units are sometimes spoiled (or lost) and cannot be processed, but the salvaged material may be sold as scrap. In this event, it is customary to treat the salvaged material in the same way as a by-product. A **by-product** is a product that has little value compared to other products being manufactured in the process. Accounting for by-products is discussed in Chapter 18.

At this point you should be able to work Exercise 16–8.

ACCOUNTING FOR INCREASES IN UNITS

Because of the nature of Apex Computer Designs' operations, it is not possible for the firm to have unit increases in production during the production process. A credenza may be completely destroyed or only slightly damaged, but a credenza can never be increased to more than the single unit that it started out to be. However, in certain industries, the addition of materials in later departments and the further processing of the product result in an increase in the number of physical units.

Typically, increases in units result from one of two situations. First, additional materials might be added in the department. For example, suppose that in the first manufacturing process a manufacturer of shampoo combined a number of basic ingredients and transferred 20,000 gallons of the mixture to the second department during the current month. In the second department, water and certain inert ingredients were added to the shampoo concentrate, increasing the total mixture to 30,000 gallons. As a result, the output from the second department would be substantially larger than the input to the department.

A second situation in which the number of units increases is one in which the unit of measure changes. Suppose, for example, that the input to the Cooking Department of the Mayfair Chemical Company is 5,000 gallons of dense liquid material. In the department, the material is cooked to a powder and the output is 15,000 pounds of finished product. It is obvious that each gallon of material input resulted in about 3 pounds of finished product.

The accounting problem involved when there is an increase of units during production is the reverse of that caused by lost units. The solution is to spread the total costs among the larger number of units to produce a lower average unit cost. The following example illustrates how most companies account for increases in units of product.

In the first department of Townsend Pesticide Company, the Formulation Department, chemicals are mixed to form an active pesticide ingredient. The resulting mixture is transferred to the Blending Department, where a special oil is blended into the pesticide mixture and further processing takes place. The blended product is transferred to the Packaging Department for bottling, labeling, and packaging.

On April 1, 19X9, there were 1,000 pounds of material in process in the Blending Department. All the oil had been added to make up the 1,000 pounds. During the month, 20,000 pounds of pesticide were transferred into the Blending Department from the Formulation Department and 10,000 pounds of oil base were added. In the month of April, 29,800 pounds of the mixture were transferred to the Packaging Department from the Blending Department, and at the end of the month 1,200 pounds were still on hand in the Blending Department, to which all oil had been added and $66\frac{2}{3}$ percent of labor and overhead had been added.

It is obvious that if the number of Units to Be Accounted For in the Blending Department is to agree with the number of Units Accounted For in the Blending Department, consideration must be given to the increase in units. The cost data, the monthly production report, the equivalent production computations, and the cost of production report for the month of April are given below.

Cost Data

The Work in Process—Blending Department 124 account shows a balance of $252,768 on April 30, 19X9, including costs transferred in from the Formulation Department during April. The costs making up the balance are shown on the next page.

Beginning Work in Process (1,000 units)

Costs in Prior Department	$ 6,310.00	
Cost in Current Department		
Materials	734.00	
Labor	300.00	
Overhead	400.00	
Balance of Account, Mar. 31		$ 7,744.00
Costs Incurred in Current Month		
Materials	$22,578.00	
Labor	18,151.80	
Overhead	24,294.20	
Total Current Month's Costs		65,024.00
Transferred In From Formulation Department		180,000.00
Balance of Account, Apr. 30		$252,768.00

Production Data

The manager's production report for the month shows an increase of 10,000 units of product.

BLENDING DEPARTMENT
Monthly Production Report
April 19X9

Quantity

Work in Process—Beginning	1,000
Transferred In From Prior Department	20,000
Transferred Out to Next Department	29,800
Work in Process—Ending	1,200
Increase in Production	10,000

Stage of Completion of Ending Work in Process

Materials	complete
Labor	$66\frac{2}{3}\%$
Overhead	$66\frac{2}{3}\%$

Equivalent Production Data

The equivalent production report prepared by the accountant is shown on page 383. Note that the number of units indicated as transferred to the next department, 29,800, includes the increase of 10,000 units in this process. Thus, equivalent units means **equivalent expanded units** in this system. (It is assumed that all materials have been added to the beginning inventory of work in process.)

Cost of Production Report

There are several fine points to be noted in the treatment of increased units on the cost of production report shown on page 384.

▪ **Quantity Schedule.** The increase in units is reported under Quantity to Be Accounted For because the units to be accounted for must equal the units accounted for.

BLENDING DEPARTMENT
Equivalent Production Computations
Month of April 19X9
(Average Costing)

Prior Department Costs	
Transferred Out to Next Department	29,800
Work in Process—Ending	1,200
Equivalent Production for Prior Department	31,000
Materials	
Transferred Out to Next Department	29,800
Work in Process—Ending (1,200 × 100%)	1,200
Equivalent Production for Materials	31,000
Labor and Manufacturing Overhead	
Transferred Out to Next Department	29,800
Work in Process—Ending (1,200 × $66\frac{2}{3}$%)	800
Equivalent Production for Labor and Overhead	30,600

■ **Cost Schedule.** The Costs to Be Accounted For section shows the spreading of the costs among the total expanded units so that all costs will be absorbed by all the units produced.

- ■ The Total Prior Department Costs figure, $188,310, is divided by the 31,000 expanded equivalent units to obtain an average unit cost of $6.01.
- ■ The total for each cost element in the Costs in Current Department section is divided by its expanded equivalent units to determine an average unit cost.

Accountants who prefer more detail in the Costs in Prior Department section may show separate physical units and separate unit costs for beginning work in process and work transferred in. (The latter figures are the same as those shown as Transferred Out to Next Department in the cost of production report of the Blending Department.) The partial cost of production report shown below shows the cost per equivalent unit of $9, *based on the 10,000 units transferred into the*

COST SCHEDULE	TOTAL COST		E.P. UNITS		UNIT COST
(c) Costs to Be Accounted For:					
Costs in Prior Department					
Work in Process—Beginning	$ 6,310.00	÷	1,000	=	$6.310
Transferred In—Current Month	180,000.00	÷	20,000	=	$9.000
Adjustment for Increase in Units			10,000	=	$3.000
Adjusted Cost Transferred In—Current Month	$180,000.00	÷	30,000	=	$6.000
Total Prior Department Costs	$186,310.00	÷	31,000	=	$6.010

BLENDING DEPARTMENT
Cost of Production Report
Month of April 19X9

QUANTITY SCHEDULE	UNITS

(a) Quantity to Be Accounted For:

Work in Process—Beginning	1,000
Transferred In From Prior Department	20,000
Increase in Units	10,000
Total to Be Accounted For	31,000

(b) Quantity Accounted For:

Ending Work in Process	29,800
Transferred Out to Finished Goods	1,200
Total Accounted For	31,000

COST SCHEDULE	TOTAL COST	E.P. UNITS	UNIT COST

(c) Costs to Be Accounted For:

Costs in Prior Department

Work in Process—Beginning	$ 6,310.00		
Transferred In—Current Month	180,000.00		
Total Prior Department Costs	$186,310.00	÷ 31,000 =	$6.010

Costs in Current Department

Materials—Beginning Work in Process	$ 734.00		
Added in Current Month	22,578.00		
Total Materials	$ 23,312.00	÷ 31,000 =	$0.752
Labor—Beginning Work in Process	$ 300.00		
Added in Current Month	18,151.80		
Total Labor	$ 18,451.80	÷ 30,600 =	0.603
Overhead—Beginning Work in Process	$ 400.00		
Added in Current Month	$ 24,294.20		
Total Overhead	$ 24,694.20	÷ 30,600 =	0.807
Total Costs in Current Department	$ 66,458.00		$2.162
Total Costs to Be Accounted For	$252,768.00		$8.172

(d) Costs Accounted For:

Transferred Out to Next Department	$243,525.60	= 29,800 × $8.172	

Work in Process—Ending

Costs in Prior Department	$ 7,212.00	= 1,200 × $6.010	

Costs in Current Department

Materials	902,40	= 1,200 × $0.752	
Labor	482.40	= 800 × $0.603	
Overhead	645.60	= 800 × $0.807	
Total Work in Process	$ 9,242.40		
Total Costs Accounted For	$252,768.00		

department during the month. It also shows the cost of $6 per equivalent unit for prior department costs transferred in during the current month based on the *total increased number* of units resulting from the work transferred in ($180,000 ÷ 30,000 units = $6 per unit). The difference of $3 per unit represents the decrease in unit cost resulting from the increase in the number of units. The total prior department cost to be accounted for, $136,310, is unchanged. This amount is divided by the 31,000 equivalent expanded units in order to calculate an average cost of $6.01, as shown previously.

At this point you should be able to work Exercise 16–9 and Problems 16–5A and 16–5B.

Completion of the balance of the report is the same as in other similar illustrations. Adjustments for increases and lost units may be shown on a single combined report as well as presented in the separate departmental reports illustrated.

SELF-REVIEW

1. How does abnormal spoilage differ from normal spoilage?
2. Name two typical causes of abnormal spoilage.
3. How is abnormal spoilage shown in the cost of production report?
4. What special journal entry is required to account for abnormal spoilage?
5. What are some common reasons for an increase in the number of units of products?
6. When units are made defective as a part of the normal manufacturing costs, how are costs to rework the units accounted for?

Answers to Self-Review

1. Abnormal spoilage results from unusual or abnormal conditions that are not a typical, recurring part of the manufacturing process, and normal spoilage is an inherent, recurring part of the process.
2. Abnormal spoilage may result from defective raw materials, a human error, the malfunctioning of equipment, temporary loss of power, and other unusual and unexpected events.
3. Abnormal spoilage is assigned a share of costs, computed as though the spoiled units were good units, but those costs are shown as a separate item in the Costs Accounted For section.
4. The costs related to abnormal spoilage are charged to a Loss From Spoiled Goods account (or to Cost of Goods Sold) and are credited to the Work in Process account of the department in which the spoilage occurred. The cost is computed in the same way as though the units had been completed. The entry may be combined with the entry to transfer products to the next department or to finished goods inventory.
5. Increases in units may occur because of expansion from the manufacturing process, the addition of materials, or a change in the unit of measure of the product in the department.
6. Costs to rework defective units receive no special accounting treatment. They are merely added to other manufacturing costs to arrive at total costs to be accounted for in the department.

PRINCIPLES AND PROCEDURES SUMMARY

- Units of product are often lost in the production process. For accounting purposes, there are two types of losses:
  - Normal losses, resulting from such factors as shrinkage, spoilage, evaporation, and condensation, are an inherent, recurring part of the manufacturing process.
  - Abnormal losses result from factors that do not recur with predictable frequency—for example, from a power outage, the malfunctioning of equipment, and unusual human error.
- Normal losses (or normal spoilage) are generally ignored in computing equivalent units, and all costs are absorbed by the good units.
- Some accountants prefer to show (1) what prior department costs would have been if there had been no normal lost units, (2) the adjusted unit cost considering lost units, and (3) the difference between the two unit costs, which is referred to as *lost-unit cost.*
- Units lost as a result of abnormal conditions are usually assigned the share of costs they would have been assigned if they had not been lost. This amount is then removed from work in process and charged to a loss account.
- In some cases, defective units that occur may be reworked and completed as good units. The additional rework costs are treated in the usual manner as costs to be accounted for in the current department and are charged to the Work in Process account.
- In some industries, the number of units is increased during the production process. In this event, the equivalent units are based on the expanded equivalent units in the department.
- Increases in units of production result in lower average unit cost because total charges are spread among a greater number of units.
- Some accountants prefer to show two unit costs for costs transferred in from the prior department. The first is based on the number of units transferred in before considering increased units. The second is based on the expanded units. The difference between the two is treated as an adjustment for increase in units.

MANAGERIAL IMPLICATIONS

- Management is keenly interested in lost units, because lost units increase the cost of manufacturing good units.
- Management may be unable to eliminate normal spoilage or even to reduce normal losses below an inherent level.
- Management may wish to have a cost of production report that shows an adjustment for lost units separately, so that managers can understand and attempt to control manufacturing costs.
- The accountant and management should carefully investigate abnormally high losses during a month.

■ The amount of detail regarding the unit increase that is shown on the report depends upon the accountant's preference. Detailed presentations supply more information and permit easier cross-checking.

REVIEW QUESTIONS

1. How are units lost in production?
2. What is meant by *shrinkage?*
3. What are *spoiled units?*
4. Are lost units considered in computing equivalent units? Explain.
5. What are *defective units?*
6. *Equivalent units of production* actually refers to *equivalent good units.* Explain.
7. What is the effect of spoiled goods on prior department costs per unit? How does this differ from their effect on the cost per unit in the current department?
8. How does *abnormal* loss of units differ from *normal* loss of units?
9. When units are made defective by abnormal conditions or events, how are costs to rework the units usually accounted for?
10. How should abnormal lost units be treated in computing equivalent production?
11. How can units increase in production?
12. How can the effects of lost units on prior department unit costs be reflected in the cost of production report?

MANAGERIAL DISCUSSION QUESTIONS

1. You are the cost accountant of Ashurst Manufacturing Company. All spoiled units are treated as normal lost units. You have noticed that the percentage of units that are lost has varied considerably, ranging from less than 1 percent of units started in the department to more than 5 percent of units started in the department. What steps, if any, do you think you should take?
2. Why should management be acutely interested in units lost in production?
3. How would you explain to management why some spoilage can be considered normal whereas other spoilage is abnormal?
4. As the cost accountant of Duluth Production Company, you have been asked by your employer to explain why the unit cost of materials increases dramatically in the winter. You have discovered that some of the materials are affected by extremely cold weather and as a result become unusable during the manufacturing process. Your employer asks you whether you should treat this loss as a normal loss or an abnormal loss and how the problem affects costs per unit manufactured. Provide a brief answer.

5. You have discussed with the management of your company the impact of defective units on the cost of each item of product manufactured. One of the company's officers expresses the opinion that the company loses money on reworking defective units. His argument is that the units should bear the normal costs of materials, labor, and overhead and should also bear the additional rework costs. He argues that the defective units should not be reworked but should be discarded to eliminate this loss. What is your response to this proposal?

6. In your company, normal spoiled units are ignored in computing equivalent production and costs per unit. In other words, good units bear all the costs. The company president thinks that this may lead to a lack of control over spoilage. Do you agree? Why or why not?

7. Are normal spoilage and abnormal spoilage accounted for in the same way? If they are handled differently, explain how their treatments differ and why they are treated differently.

8. Assume that during one month your company had abnormally high spoilage. You have recommended that the applicable costs be removed from the current month and allocated over several months. Why?

EXERCISES

NOTE: Assume in all exercises that the average cost method is used.

EXERCISE 16–1 **Compute equivalent units of material and cost per equivalent unit when there are normal losses. (Obj. 2).** Kay Company adds materials at the start of production in the Forming Department. Data related to production in September 19X9 are as follows:

	Units
Work in process on September 1	24,000
Started in September	80,000
Completed and transferred out in September	82,000
Normal spoilage	4,000
Work in process on September 30	18,000

Materials in beginning work in process inventory, $48,500
Cost of materials added during month, $160,500

Assuming the average cost method is used, compute the equivalent units of materials for September.

EXERCISE 16–2 **Compute equivalent units of production and cost per equivalent unit for labor when there are normal losses. (Obj. 2).** The following data pertain to labor used in the Boxing Department of the Emerson Company during July 19X9.

Beginning work in process, 400 units, 50% complete
Started in production, 8,000 units

Transferred out to next department, 7,600 units
Ending work in process, 200 units, 40% complete
Lost in production, 600 units
Labor costs in beginning work in process, $4,000
Cost of labor incurred during the month, $164,000

a. Calculate the equivalent units of production for labor for the month.
b. Calculate the labor cost per equivalent unit of production.

EXERCISE 16–3   **Compute equivalent production and cost per equivalent unit for overhead when there are normal losses. (Obj. 2).** The following data pertains to overhead for the Assembly Department of Austin Electronics Company for September 19X9.

Beginning work in process, 1,000 units 75% complete
Started in production, 12,800 units
Transferred out to next department, 11,600 units
Ending work in process, 2,080 units, 60% complete
Lost in production, 120 units
Overhead in beginning work in process, $1,950
Overhead costs incurred during September, $40,340

a. Compute the equivalent units of production for overhead for the month.
b. Compute the cost per equivalent unit of production for overhead for the month.

EXERCISE 16–4   **Compute equivalent production and cost per equivalent unit for prior department costs when there are normal lost units. (Obj. 2).** On January 1, 19X9, beginning work in process inventory for the Machining Department of the Allen Company was 6,000 units with prior department costs of $18,000. During the month, 30,000 units were transferred into the Machining Department with prior department costs of $90,000. A total of 34,600 units were transferred to the next department, and 1,200 units were in the ending work in process inventory. Some units were lost in production as a normal part of the manufacturing process. Compute the following:
a. Equivalent production for prior department costs for the month.
b. Cost per equivalent unit for prior department costs.
c. The lost-unit cost per unit.

EXERCISE 16–5   **Compute equivalent production and cost per equivalent production for prior department costs when there are normal losses. (Obj. 2).** On March 1, 19X9, the beginning work in process inventory for the Laminating Department of the Istanbul Company was 100 units. The prior department costs for these units were $1,000. During the month, 2,400 units with prior department costs of $26,375 were transferred into the Laminating Department, and 2,300 units were completed and transferred to the next department. The ending work in process inventory was 150 units, and 50 units were lost in production.

a. Compute the equivalent production for prior department costs.

b. Compute the cost per equivalent unit for prior department costs.

c. Show how the Costs in Prior Department section of Costs to Be Accounted For would appear in the cost of production report for March, assuming that there is a separate adjustment for lost units.

d. Compute the Costs in Prior Department to be included in the ending inventory of work in process in the Laminating Department.

EXERCISE 16-6   **Compute equivalent production and cost per equivalent unit for prior department costs when there are normal losses.   (Obj. 2).** On October 1, 19X9, the beginning work in process inventory for the Drying Department of the Apache Company was 14,000 units with prior department costs of $22,800. During October, 65,000 units with prior department costs of $99,000 were transferred into the Drying Department, and 70,000 units were transferred out to the next department. The ending work in process inventory was 8,400 units.

a. Compute the equivalent units for costs in prior departments.

b. Compute the cost per equivalent unit for costs in prior departments for the month of October.

c. What is the amount of prior department costs in the ending work in process inventory?

d. Show how the Costs in Prior Department section of Costs to Be Accounted For would appear in the cost of production report for October, assuming that a separate adjustment for lost units is shown.

EXERCISE 16-7   **Compute equivalent units of production, compute cost per equivalent unit, and record abnormal spoilage.   (Obj. 3).**   Denver Decorative Tray Company adds materials at the start of production in the Forming Department. Data related to materials used in October 19X9 are as follows:

	Units
Work in process on October 1	12,000
Started in October	40,000
Completed and transferred out in October	41,000
Abnormal spoilage	100
Work in process on October 31	11,900

Materials in beginning work in process inventory, $48,000
Cost of materials added during month, $160,000

a. Compute the equivalent units of production for materials for the month.

b. Compute the cost per equivalent unit of production for materials for the month.

c. Give the general journal entry at the end of the month to remove from work in process the materials costs related to the units of abnormal loss. (Ignore labor, overhead, and prior department costs.)

EXERCISE 16-8   **Accounting for reworking of defective units.   (Obj. 6).**   In the Finishing Department of Alamo Reclining Chair Corporation, some reclining chairs are routinely improperly finished and are classified as "defective." These units are refinished and transferred to Finished Goods Inventory. In April 19X9, 14 chairs were judged to be defective and were refinished. It is estimated that the refinishing costs applicable to these chairs are: materials, $280; labor, $640; overhead, $640. How would these costs be accounted for?

EXERCISE 16–9   **Compute equivalent production and cost per equivalent unit when there are increased units.   (Obj. 7).**   On October 1, 19X9, the beginning work in process inventory for the Absorption Department of Beauty Plus Personal Care Products, a cosmetics producer, was 1,000 units with prior department costs of $1,400. During the month, 22,000 units of concentrate with prior department costs of $33,200 were transferred into the Absorption Department. Because of the addition of water to the solution, the number of units was increased. A total of 32,000 units were transferred to the next department, and 2,000 units were in the ending work in process inventory.
a. Compute the equivalent production for prior department costs.
b. Compute the cost per equivalent unit for prior department costs.
c. What is the amount of prior department costs in the ending work in process inventory?

PROBLEMS

PROBLEM 16–1A

Compute equivalent units of production and costs per equivalent unit when there is a normal loss of units; prepare a cost of production report when normal loss has occurred.   (Objs. 2, 4).   The Erie Appliance Company manufactures small appliances. The first producing department is the Assembly Department. The average cost method is used to price the beginning work in process inventory. The cost of normal loss of units is absorbed by the remaining good units. Data relating to costs in the Assembly Department during March 19X9 are shown below.

The balance in the Work in Process account on March 1 consists of the following costs:

Materials	$17,185.28
Labor	3,179.44
Overhead	11,372.16
Total	$31,736.88

Costs in the Assembly Department in March were:

Materials	$395,614.72
Labor	84,369.28
Overhead	235,107.84

The monthly production report for March follows.

ASSEMBLY DEPARTMENT
Monthly Production Report
March 19X9

Quantity

Work in Process—Beginning	400
Units Started in Production—Current Month	9,800
Transferred Out to Next Department	8,880
Work in Process—Ending	920
Lost in Production	400

Stage of Completion of Ending Work in Process

Materials	100%
Labor	50%
Overhead	50%

INSTRUCTIONS

1. Prepare the equivalent production computations for the Assembly Department for March 19X9.
2. Prepare the cost of production report for the Assembly Department for March 19X9. Carry the unit costs to three decimal places. (Do not show a separate entry for lost units.)

PROBLEM 16–2A **Compute equivalent units of production and cost per equivalent unit when there is a normal loss of units; prepare a cost of production report when normal loss has occurred.** **(Objs. 2, 4).** The Jaurez Company uses a process cost system. On May 1, 19X9, the company had 500 units in production in the Mixing Department (the second department). All materials had been added to these units, but processing was only one-half complete. Costs applicable to the beginning work in process inventory follow:

Costs in Prior Department	$20,800
Materials	14,000
Labor	6,000
Overhead	12,000

During the month of May, an additional 10,250 units were transferred into the Mixing Department with prior department costs of $392,800. Additional costs were incurred in the Mixing Department in May as follows:

Materials	$305,600
Labor	234,096
Overhead	447,642

A total of 9,600 units were transferred out to finished goods. The ending work in process inventory consisted of 400 units to which all materials had been added, but on which only 75 percent of the processing had been completed. The other units were lost as normal spoilage in the manufacturing process.

INSTRUCTIONS

1. Prepare the equivalent production computations for the Mixing Department for May 19X9.
2. Prepare the cost of production report for the Mixing Department for May 19X9. Assume that the average cost method of accounting for inventories is used. Do not show a separate adjustment for lost units.

PROBLEM 16–3A

Compute equivalent units of production and cost per equivalent unit when there is a normal loss of units; prepare a cost of production report when there is a normal loss of units. (Objs. 2, 4). The second producing department of the Columbia Basin Manufacturing Company is the Completion Department. The average cost method is used to price its beginning work in process inventory. The cost of lost units is absorbed by the remaining good units. Cost and production information for the month of May 19X9 for the department are shown below.

Costs
    Beginning Work in Process

Costs in Prior Department	$20,040.00
Costs in Current Department	
Material	3,257.00
Labor	2,500.00
Overhead	1,200.00
Total Beginning Work in Process	$26,997.00
Current Department Costs	
Materials	20,425.50
Labor	56,000.00
Overhead	28,000.00
Transferred In From Prior Department	177,184.04

The quantity data for the month of May is summarized in the monthly production report shown below.

COMPLETION DEPARTMENT
Monthly Production Report
May 19X9

Quantity

Work in Process—Beginning	500
Transferred In From Prior Department	4,400
Transferred Out to Next Department	4,600
Work in Process—Ending	150
Lost in Production (normal loss)	150
Stage of Completion of Ending Work in Process	
Materials	80%
Labor	$33\frac{1}{3}$%
Overhead	$33\frac{1}{3}$%

INSTRUCTIONS

1. Prepare the equivalent production computations for the Completion Department for May 19X9.
2. Prepare the cost of production report for the Completion Department for May 19X9. Carry the unit costs to three decimal places. (Do not show a separate entry for lost units.)

PROBLEM 16–4A **Compute equivalent units of production and cost per equivalent unit when there is abnormal spoilage; prepare a cost of production report when there is abnormal spoilage.** (Objs. 2, 3, 4, 5).

The third department in the production process of Cool Air Fan Company is the Finishing Department. Data for the department for the month of April 19X9 are given below.

Costs
Beginning Work in Process	
Costs in Prior Department	$ 4,160
Materials	2,800
Labor	1,200
Overhead	2,400
Costs in Current Department	
Materials	58,400
Labor	46,400
Overhead	92,800
Costs Transferred In From Prior Department	85,300

Quantities
Beginning Work in Process	1,000
Transferred In From Prior Department	20,500
Transferred Out to Finished Goods	19,340
Lost in Production—Normal Spoilage	100
Lost in Production—Abnormal Spoilage	60
Ending Work in Process	2,000

Stage of Completion of Work in Process
Beginning	
Materials	100%
Labor	50%
Overhead	50%
Ending	
Materials	100%
Labor	60%
Overhead	60%

The abnormal spoilage is discovered at the time of final inspection of the units as they leave the department and are transferred to finished goods. It is therefore assumed that the units have been fully processed in the Finishing Department.

INSTRUCTIONS

1. Compute equivalent production units for all elements of production.
2. Prepare a cost of production report for the Finishing Department for the month of April. In the Costs Accounted For section, add a new line just beneath Transferred Out to Finished Goods. Call this

line *Loss From Abnormal Spoilage.* This line will be used to show the cost of the 60 units lost from abnormal spoilage.
3. Make a compound entry in general journal form to record the transfer of units to finished goods and the loss from abnormal spoilage.

PROBLEM 16–5A **Compute equivalent units of production and cost per equivalent unit when there is an increase in units; prepare a cost of production report when there is an increase in units.   (Objs. 7, 8).** Lincoln Company uses a process cost accounting system and the average cost method. The data given below are for the Mixing Department, the second department in the production process, for November 19X9. Because material is added in this department, the number of units is increased during production.

Costs
   Beginning Work in Process

Costs in Prior Department	$24,368
Costs in Current Department	
Materials	2,496
Labor	1,888
Overhead	1,536
Total Work in Process	$30,288

Costs Incurred in Mixing Department	
Materials	62,784
Labor	47,072
Overhead	39,264
Transferred In From Prior Department	633,320

Quantities

Beginning Work in Process in Mixing Department	150
Transferred In From Prior Department	1,225
Transferred Out to Next Department	1,475
Ending Work in Process	100

Stage of Completion of Work in Process

Beginning Inventory of Work in Process	
Materials	$66\frac{2}{3}$%
Labor and Overhead	70%
Ending Inventory of Work in Process	
Materials	80%
Labor and Overhead	75%

INSTRUCTIONS
1. Compute the equivalent units of production for each element.
2. Prepare a cost of production report for the department. (It is not necessary to show an adjustment for increased units separately.)

ALTERNATE PROBLEMS

PROBLEM 16–1B **Compute equivalent units of production and costs per equivalent unit; prepare a cost of production report when there is a normal loss of units.   (Objs. 2, 4).** The Haifa Company makes parts for forging equipment. The first producing department is the Lathing Department. The average cost method is used to process the beginning work in process inventory. The cost of lost units is absorbed by the remaining good units. Cost and quantity data for January 19X9 are given below.

Costs
Beginning Work in Process

Materials	$ 2,148.16
Labor	473.84
Overhead	1,421.52
Total Beginning Work in Process	$ 4,043.52

Current Department Costs

Materials	49,451.84
Labor	10,546.16
Overhead	31,638.48

Quantity data for the month of January are summarized in the following monthly production report.

LATHING DEPARTMENT
Monthly Production Report
January 19X9

Quantity

Work in Process—Beginning	150
Units Started in Production—Current Month	1,200
Transferred Out to Next Department	1,100
Work in Process—Ending	200
Lost in Production	50

Stage of Completion of Ending Work in Process

Materials	100%
Labor	50%
Overhead	50%

INSTRUCTIONS

1. Prepare the equivalent production computations for the Lathing Department for January 19X9.
2. Prepare the cost of production report for the Lathing Department for January 19X9. (Do not show a separate entry for lost units.)

PROBLEM 16–2B

Compute the equivalent units of production and cost per equivalent unit when there is a normal loss of units; prepare a cost of production report when normal loss has occurred. (Objs. 2, 4).
The Cinqo Company uses a process cost system. On May 1, 19X9, the company had 800 units in production in the Boiling Department, the second of three producing departments. All materials had been added to this beginning inventory, but labor and overhead were only 75 percent complete. Costs applicable to the beginning work in process inventory follow:

Costs in Prior Departments	$15,182.00
Materials	2,416.00
Labor	3,360.00
Overhead	1,920.00
Total Beginning Work in Process	$22,878.00

During the month of May, an additional 19,200 units were transferred into the Boiling Department with prior department costs of $143,952. Additional costs were incurred in the Boiling Department as follows:

Materials	$57,059.00
Labor	11,268.00
Overhead	57,920.00

A total of 18,500 units were transferred out to the third department during the month, 1,000 units were still in production at the end of the month, and 500 units were lost in production. This is considered to be a normal loss. All materials had been added to the ending work in process inventory, but labor and overhead were only 70 percent complete.

INSTRUCTIONS
1. Prepare the equivalent production computations for the Boiling Department for May 19X9.
2. Prepare the cost of production report for the Boiling Department for May 19X9, assuming that the average cost method of handling work in process inventory is used. (Do not show an adjustment for lost units.)

PROBLEM 16–3B
Compute equivalent units of production and cost per equivalent unit when there is a normal loss of units; prepare a cost of production report when there is a normal loss of units.   (Objs. 2, 4).
The second producing department of the Little Atlantic Company is the Streaming Department. The average cost method is used to process its beginning work in process inventory. The cost of lost units is absorbed by the remaining good units. The cost data and production data for the Streaming Department for May 19X9 are shown below.

Costs	
Beginning Work in Process	
Costs in Prior Department	$10,020.00
Costs in Current Department	
Materials	1,785.00
Labor	1,250.00
Overhead	600.00
Total Beginning Work in Process	$13,655.00
Current Department Costs	
Materials	10,212.50
Labor	28,000.00
Overhead	13,440.00
Transferred In From Prior Department	83,406.00

The quantity data for the month of May are summarized in the monthly production report shown below.

STREAMING DEPARTMENT
Monthly Production Report
May 19X9

Quantity

Work in Process—Beginning	250
Transferred In From Prior Department	2,200
Transferred Out to Next Department	2,300
Work in Process—Ending	100
Lost in Production (normal loss)	50

Stage of Completion of Ending Work in Process

Materials	100%
Labor	60%
Overhead	60%

INSTRUCTIONS

1. Prepare the equivalent production computations for the Streaming Department for May 19X9.
2. Prepare the cost of production report for the Streaming Department for May 19X9. (Do not show a separate entry for lost units.)

PROBLEM 16–4B **Compute equivalent units of production and cost per equivalent unit when there is abnormal spoilage; prepare a cost of production report when there is abnormal spoilage. (Objs. 2, 3, 4, 5).**
The second department in the production process of New York Plastic Case Company is the Assembly Department. Data for the department for the month of November 19X9 are shown below.

Costs

Beginning Work in Process	
Costs in Prior Department	$ 20,800
Materials	14,000
Labor	6,000
Overhead	12,000
Costs in Current Department	
Materials	264,600
Labor	234,096
Overhead	447,642
Costs Transferred In From Prior Department	392,800

Quantities

Beginning Work in Process	500
Transferred In From Prior Department	9,200
Transferred Out to Next Department	9,200
Lost in Production—Normal Spoilage	60
Lost in Production—Abnormal Spoilage	40

Stage of Completion of Work in Process

Beginning	
Materials	100%
Labor and Overhead	50%
Ending	
Materials	100%
Labor and Overhead	75%

The abnormal spoilage is discovered at the time of final inspection of the units as they leave the department and are transferred to the next department. It is therefore assumed that the units have been fully processed in the Assembly Department.

INSTRUCTIONS

1. Compute equivalent production units for all elements of production.
2. Prepare a cost of production report for the Assembly Department for the month of November. In the Costs Accounted For section, add a new line just beneath Transferred Out to Next Department. Call this line *Loss From Abnormal Spoilage.* This line will be used to show the cost of the 40 units lost from abnormal spoilage.
3. Make a compound entry in general journal form to record the transfer of units to the next department and the loss from abnormal spoilage.

PROBLEM 16–5B

Compute equivalent units of production and cost per equivalent unit when there is an increase in units; prepare a cost of production report when there is an increase in units. (Objs. 7, 8).
The D. Argo Company uses a process cost accounting system and the average cost method. The data given below relate to the Conditioning Department for March 19X9. Because material is added in this department, the number of units is increased during production.

Costs

Beginning Work in Process	
Costs in Prior Department	$12,000
Costs in Current Department	
Materials	2,600
Labor	1,700
Overhead	800
Current Department Costs—March	
Materials	82,775
Labor	49,500
Overhead	22,300
Transferred In From Prior Department—Current Month	64,150

Quantities

Beginning Work in Process	100
Transferred In From Prior Department	1,900
Transferred Out to Next Department	1,800
Ending Work in Process	350

Stage of Completion of Work in Process

Beginning Materials, Labor, and Overhead	60%
Ending Materials, Labor, and Overhead	50%

INSTRUCTIONS

1. Compute the equivalent units of production for each element for the month of March.
2. Prepare the cost of production report for the department for the month of March. (It is not necessary to show an adjustment for increased units separately.)

MANAGERIAL DECISION CASE

On the average, 9,000 hand-decorated picture frames are transferred into the Finishing Department of the Darin Decorative Manufacturing Company each month with prior department costs of $168,750. Of these 9,000 frames, on the average, 8,250 units are transferred out of the department to Finished Goods and 750 are lost in production with no salvage value. The work in process inventory remains constant. Monthly departmental costs include labor, $49,500; overhead, $24,750. The department is currently operating at full capacity. A study has shown that all the spoilage is due to defects in materials added in the prior department. The defects cannot be detected until the work is completed in the Finishing Department. A better quality of materials can be purchased for an additional $3 per unit, decreasing the number of lost units in the Finishing Department from an average of 750 to an average of 300 each month.

INSTRUCTIONS

1. Compute the unit cost of each frame based on the materials presently used.
2. Compute the unit cost of each frame if the more expensive materials are used.
3. Should the more expensive materials be purchased? Explain.

First In, First Out (FIFO) Costing of Work in Process

In Chapter 15 we examined the average cost method of accounting for work in process inventories, and in Chapter 16 we discussed how units lost in production are accounted for under the average cost method. In this chapter we will examine the first in, first out (FIFO) cost method, with the same data used in Chapter 16.

OBJECTIVES

1. Explain and illustrate the FIFO method of accounting for costs of work in process inventories.
2. Compute equivalent production under the FIFO method of accounting for costs of work in process inventories.
3. Compute cost per equivalent unit under the FIFO method of accounting for work in process.
4. Prepare a cost of production report when the FIFO method of accounting for costs of work in process inventories is used.
5. Account for goods lost in production under the FIFO method of accounting for work in process inventories.
6. Compare results obtained by using the average cost method and the FIFO method, explain the differences between the methods, and identify the advantages and disadvantages of each method.

NEW TERMS

First in, first out (FIFO) method (p. 402)

DIFFERENCES BETWEEN AVERAGE COST METHOD AND FIFO COST METHOD

Under the average cost method, no distinction is made between the cost per unit of products that were both started and completed during the current period and those that were completed during this period but on which work was begun in a prior period. Each element of cost in the beginning work in process inventory is combined with the amount of cost of that element added in the current period. The total cost of each element is assigned to all equivalent units of production for that element. This is accomplished by dividing the total costs of the element by the equivalent units of production of that element. As a result, the unit cost for each element is an average of that element's cost in the beginning inventory and the cost added in the current period.

Under the **first in, first out (FIFO) method,** however, the costs of the beginning work in process inventory are kept separate and assigned only to the units that were included in that inventory. Costs incurred during the current period to complete the beginning inventory of work in process are added to the beginning balance of cost. Costs of units that are started and finished in the current period are accumulated and computed separately from the beginning inventory. Units transferred out are identified as having come first from the beginning work in process inventory and then from units that were started or transferred into the department during the current period.

CHOOSING A COSTING METHOD

In Chapter 15 you learned that Apex Computer Designs' cost accountant chose the average cost method of accounting for work in process inventories for the following reasons:

■ The ending work in process inventory was small in relation to the total monthly production.
■ The rate of production was stable, so the work in process inventory was fairly constant.
■ The average cost method is simple to use.

Some accountants, however, prefer to use the FIFO method of accounting for work in process inventories. They cite the following advantages:

■ The unit costs are more accurate because they relate more directly to specific units of product—the units in the beginning inventory and the units started and completed during the period.
■ The unit costs reflect current conditions more clearly because the cost of completed units that were in process at the beginning of the period and the cost of units started during the period are computed separately.
■ Major changes in costs can be monitored easily for control purposes.

Choosing the method that will best fit the firm's accounting system is not difficult as long as the accountant knows how both methods work and understands fully the advantages and disadvantages of each. With the same data used in Chapter 16, including the same cost data for the beginning inventory of work in process, we can examine the procedure and results of the FIFO method. Then we can compare the results with those of the average cost method. Remember that under the FIFO method the costs incurred to complete the beginning work in process inventory are computed separately from the cost of the units started into production during the month.

FABRICATION DEPARTMENT

The cost and production data of the Fabrication Department, the first department of Apex Computer Designs, for March 19X9, the third month of operations of the company, were first discussed in Chapter 16, pages 371 and 372.

Cost Data

The Work in Process—Fabrication Department 123 account on March 31, 19X9, has a balance of $127,128.80, made up of the following costs:

Beginning Work in Process		
Materials	$ 8,971.20	
Labor	2,002.32	
Overhead	1,708.56	
Balance of Account, Mar. 1		$ 12,682.08
Costs Incurred in Current Month		
Materials	$47,128.80	
Labor	36,313.68	
Overhead	31,004.24	
Total Current Month's Costs		$114,446.72
Balance of Account, Mar. 31		$127,128.80

Production Data

The production data of the Fabrication Department for the month of March appears on the monthly production report illustrated below. The Transferred Out to Next Department section shows units from

---

FABRICATION DEPARTMENT
Monthly Production Report
Month of March 19X9

Quantity

Work in Process—Beginning		180
Started in Production—Current Month		940
Transferred Out to Next Department		
From Work in Process—Beginning	180	
Started and Completed in Current Month	780	
Total Transferred Out to Next Department		960
Work in Process—Ending		140
Lost in Production		20

Stage of Completion of Work in Process

	Beginning	Ending
Materials	complete	complete
Labor	30%	50%
Overhead	30%	50%

the beginning work in process inventory and units started and completed in the current month. The latter is determined by subtracting the number of units in the beginning inventory from the total units transferred out of the department (960 − 180 = 780). In this example, it is assumed that all losses are incurred at the start of production; therefore, all losses involve units started in production during the current month.

Equivalent Production Data

The FIFO method of costing separates the costs of new units from the costs of units in the beginning inventory. Equivalent units of production that will be used to determine unit costs must be separated in the same way that the costs will be separated. The equivalent production is therefore computed so that the final figure relates only to work performed in the current month.

Observe the following points about the items in the equivalent production computations for March 19X9, shown below.

- The goal of the calculation is to determine the equivalent units of production for each cost element, reflecting only the work done in the current period.
- The number of equivalent units that can be accounted for is always the sum of (1) the units transferred out, which are 100 percent complete as to all elements, and (2) the equivalent units in the ending work in process, which in this example are 100 percent complete as to materials and 50% percent complete as to labor and overhead.
- Under the FIFO method, the Total Units Accounted For related to each element (1,100 units for materials and 1,030 for labor and

---

FABRICATION DEPARTMENT
Equivalent Production Computations
Month of March 19X9

Materials

Transferred Out to Next Department	960
Work in Process—Ending (140 credenzas × 100%)	140
Total Units Accounted For	1,100
Deduct Units of Work in Prior Month	
(180 credenzas × 100%)	180
Equivalent Production for Materials (FIFO)	920

Labor and Manufacturing Overhead

Transferred Out to Next Department	960
Work in Process—Ending (140 credenzas × 50%)	70
Total Units Accounted For	1,030
Deduct Units of Work in Prior Month	
(180 credenzas × 30%)	54
Equivalent Units of Production for Labor and Overhead (FIFO)	976

overhead) will be the same as the Equivalent Production for each element under the average cost method.

■ To determine the equivalent units of production in the current period under the FIFO method, the number of units of equivalent production of each element in the beginning inventory is subtracted from the total equivalent units of that element. For materials, the 180 units of equivalent production in the beginning inventory are subtracted from the 1,100 equivalent units accounted for (1,100 − 180 = 920). Similarly, the 54 units of equivalent production of labor and overhead in the beginning work in process are subtracted from the 1,030 units accounted for (1,030 − 54 = 976).

Cost of Production Report

Under the FIFO method, the cost of production report retains the two-schedule organization that you have already learned. The differences in the reports under the two methods are examined below. The Quantity Schedule is very similar to the one used with the average cost method. The Cost Schedule, however, is quite different. Refer to page 406.

Quantity Schedule. The second part—(b) Quantity Accounted For—of the Quantity Schedule has been modified to show the source of the units transferred out. Specifically, on the Transferred Out to Next Department subsection, units transferred out are now identified as coming (1) from beginning inventory or (2) from new production. The rest of the Quantity Schedule is the same as when the average cost method is used.

Cost Schedule. The changes in the Cost Schedule are extensive. They are outlined below.

Section (c)—Costs to Be Accounted For:

■ The beginning inventory appears under Costs to Be Accounted For in one total amount, $12,682.08. The cost elements of this work in process are not shown in detail because the entire amount will apply to the completed units that came out of the beginning inventory. The costs in the beginning inventory do not enter into the cost per equivalent unit of production for work done in the current month.

■ The title of the subsection Costs Charged in Current Month reflects continued emphasis on current production and related costs. There is no figure for Transferred In From Prior Department because Fabrication is the first department.

■ The total cost figures for each element under Costs Added in Current Department come from the general ledger account and represent the current month's costs only. Each cost element is divided by the equivalent production units for that element, as computed on page 404, to obtain a unit cost for the month. The total unit cost, $120.201, is the sum of the costs of the elements added in March and does not contain any costs relating to the beginning work in process inventory on March 1.

FABRICATION DEPARTMENT
Cost of Production Report (FIFO)
Month of March 19X9

QUANTITY SCHEDULE	UNITS

(a) Quantity to Be Accounted For:

Work in Process—Beginning	180	
Started in Production—Current Month	940	
Total to Be Accounted For	1,120	

(b) Quantity Accounted For:

Transferred Out to Next Department

From Beginning Work in Process	180	
Started and Completed in Current Month	780	960
Work in Process—Ending		140
Lost in Production		20
Total Accounted For		1,120

COST SCHEDULE	TOTAL COST	E.P. UNITS	UNIT COST

(c) Costs to Be Accounted For:

Beginning Inventory of Work in Process	$ 12,682.08			
Costs in Current Department				
Materials	$ 47,128.80	÷	920	= $ 51.227
Labor	36,313.68	÷	976	= 37.207
Overhead	31,004.24	÷	976	= 31.767
Total Added in Current Department	$114,446.72			$120.201
Total Costs Charged in Current Month	$114,446.72			$120.201
Total Costs to Be Accounted For	$127,128.80			

(d) Costs Accounted For:

Transferred Out to Next Department

From Beginning Work in Process

Beginning Inventory	$ 12,682.08			
Materials Added in Current Month	-0-			
Labor Added in Current Month	4,688.08	=	126	× $ 37.207
Overhead Added in Current Month	4,002.64	=	126	× $ 31.767
Total Cost of Goods From Beginning Work In Process	$ 21,372.80	÷	180	= $118.738
Goods Started and Completed in Current Month	93,756.04*	=	780	× $120.201
Total Cost of Goods Transferred Out	$115,128.84	÷	960	= $119.926

Work in Process—Ending

Costs in Current Department

Materials	$ 7,171.78	=	140	× $ 51.227
Labor	2,604.49	=	70	× $ 37.207
Overhead	2,223.69	=	70	× $ 31.767
Total Work in Process	$ 11,999.96			
Total Costs Accounted For	$127,128.80			

*Adjusted $0.74 for rounding error.

- The amount labeled Total Costs Charged in Current Month includes costs from the prior department (none in this case) and costs added in the current department.
- The amount labeled Total Costs to Be Accounted For is the sum of Beginning Inventory of Work in Process and Total Costs Charged in Current Month.

Section (d)—Costs Accounted For:

- In (d) Costs Accounted For, the Transferred Out to Next Department subsection is presented in detail to facilitate separation of costs relating to the beginning inventory from those connected with goods started and finished in the current month.
- Costs Accounted For starts with the total cost in the beginning inventory.
- No materials were added in the current month because all units were 100 percent complete as to materials at the start of the month.
- The cost of the labor added during the month is computed by multiplying the equivalent units of production for labor required to complete the goods by the related unit cost of current production (as calculated in the previous section). The percentage of completion required is 70 percent (100 percent minus the 30 percent stage of completion at the beginning of the month).

  Units × Percent of Completion Required × Unit Cost = Labor Added
  180 × 70% × $37.207 = $4,688.08

- A similar computation is made to determine the amount of overhead added to the beginning work in process inventory during March.

  Units × Percent of Completion Required × Unit Cost = Overhead Added
  180 × 70% × $31.767 = $4,002.64

- The Total Cost of Goods From Beginning Work in Process (prior period costs plus current period costs added to the Beginning Work in Process) amounts to $21,372.80. This total divided by the 180 equivalent units added gives a unit cost of $118.738. Thus the FIFO method yields a separate unit cost figure for the units in the beginning inventory.
- The FIFO method is applied to determine the number of equivalent units of new production that were transferred out. In March, a total of 960 units were transferred out. The beginning inventory contained 180 units. Since the units in the beginning inventory were the *first in*, they are *first* to be transferred *out*. The difference between the total units transferred out and the beginning inventory represents the number of units of production started and finished in March that were transferred out (960 − 180 = 780). The 780 units are then multiplied by the total unit cost figure applicable to new production, $120.201. This yields the total cost of goods started and finished in the current period, $93,756.78. (However, a rounding adjustment of $.74 decreases this amount to $93,756.04 in the report.)

■ The Total Cost of Goods Transferred Out, $115,128.84, is divided by the total number of units transferred out, 960, to obtain an average unit cost of $119.926. The total cost of $115,128.84 is used in the end-of-month transfer entry. The same total and the related unit cost of $119.926 are recorded on the cost of production report of the next department as Transferred In From Prior Department in the Costs to Be Accounted For section of the Cost Schedule, page 412.

■ One might expect to find each segment of the month's production (beginning inventory and units started and completed in the current month) costed out separately and recorded as two separate transfers in the costs transferred into the next department. However, any attempt to trace these individual segments through the production process would result in confusion and extra record-keeping not justified by the small additional degree of accuracy achieved.

At this point you should be able to work Exercises 17–1 to 17–6 and Problems 17–1A to 17–2B.

■ The presentation of data regarding the ending work in process inventory under the FIFO method is essentially the same as that used with the average cost method. The total of each cost element is determined by multiplying the equivalent production units by the current unit costs for each element. Thus the total of $7,171.78 for materials was computed by multiplying 140 equivalent units by $51.227, the current unit cost for materials. The unit cost of labor ($37.207) and the unit cost of overhead ($31.767) are multiplied by the 70 equivalent units of production for these two elements.

■ The amount labeled Total Costs Accounted For, $127,128.80, is the sum of the total costs transferred out to the next department and the total cost of the ending work in process inventory.

Comparison of Results

An accountant who has completed a detailed comparison of the average cost method (see page 373) and the FIFO method for the Fabrication Department at Apex Computer Designs would note the following:

1. The FIFO method achieves the desired separation of costs. The unit cost of the completed units coming from the beginning inventory, $118.738, is different from the unit cost of new production started and finished in the current period, $120.201.

2. The distinction between unit costs under the FIFO method requires about 50 percent more calculations to pinpoint a difference of about $1.46 (1.2 percent) between Total Cost of Goods From Beginning Work in Process and Goods Started and Completed in Current Month ($120.201 − $118.738 = $1.463).

3. The difference of $.034 between the $119.926 unit cost of goods transferred out computed under the average cost method (page 373) and the average unit cost of $119.960 computed under the FIFO method (page 406) is insignificant.

4. Once the Total Cost of Goods Transferred Out is computed, the FIFO method reverts to an average cost to make accounting easier in the next department.

SELF-REVIEW

1. Which method, the average cost method or the FIFO method, produces unit costs that more directly relate to specific units of product?
2. How does the monthly production report prepared when the FIFO method is used differ from that prepared when the average cost method is used?
3. How does the computation of equivalent production when the FIFO method is used differ from the computation when the average cost method is used?
4. Is the figure shown as Total Units to Be Accounted For when the FIFO method is used different from that when the average cost method is used? Explain.
5. Why is the cost of each segment of the month's production (units from beginning inventory and units started and completed in the current month) not costed out separately in the cost of production report and transferred as a separate amount to the next department?

Answers to Self-Review

1. The FIFO method more nearly relates costs to specific items because the costs applicable to the goods in the beginning work in process inventory are accumulated separately from those started and completed during the current period. Since the beginning inventory costs apply only to those items in that inventory, costs are more nearly matched with units of product under the FIFO method.
2. The major difference in the cost of production report under the two methods is that, with FIFO, the beginning inventory cost for each element is not added to the costs incurred for that element in the current period. Instead, costs applicable to beginning inventory are shown separately from those applicable to units started and completed during this period.
3. When the FIFO method is used, total equivalent units for an element consist of the total of the equivalent units required to complete the beginning work in process, the equivalent units in goods started and completed during the period, and the equivalent units in the ending work in process. Under the average cost method, equivalent units consist of the number of units completed during the period, plus the equivalent units in the ending work in process inventory.
4. The Total Units to Be Accounted For will be the same no matter which costing method is used.
5. To maintain specific records of separate batches of products transferred from one department to another would result in very detailed and complicated recordkeeping that would not be justified by the differences in results obtained.

ASSEMBLY DEPARTMENT

It is now time to find how the FIFO method is applied as goods move from department to department. Let us examine the cost data and production data for the Assembly Department, the second department of Apex Computer Designs, for the month of March 19X9.

Cost Data

The Work in Process—Assembly Department account has a balance of $98,818.88 on March 31. This balance includes the following costs:

Work in Process
    Costs in Prior Department $ 4,740.88
    Costs in Current Department
        Materials   966.40
        Labor   1,452.00
        Overhead   768.00
        Balance of Account, Mar. 1 $ 7,927.28
Current Month
    Materials $22,823.60
    Labor   45,152.00
    Overhead   22,916.00
    Total Current Month's Costs $90,891.60
      Balance of Account, Mar. 31 $98,818.88

Production Data

Again, the monthly production report is the same as the one prepared under the average cost method, except that the units transferred out to the next department are analyzed to show units from the beginning work in process inventory and units started and completed in the current month.

ASSEMBLY DEPARTMENT
Monthly Production Report
Month of March 19X9

Quantity
    Work in Process—Beginning   40
    Started in Production—Current Month   960
    Transferred Out to Next Department
        From Work in Process—Beginning   40
        Started and Completed in Current Month   885   925
    Work in Process—Ending   50
    Lost in Production   25

Stage of Completion of Ending Work in Process

	Beginning	**Ending**
Materials	complete	complete
Labor	75%	60%
Overhead	75%	60%

Equivalent Production Data

The FIFO method of computing equivalent production described in connection with the Fabrication Department is also applied to the Assembly Department. The final figure for each element, shown in the equivalent production computations below, represents work performed in the current month.

Cost of Production Report

Some important aspects of the cost of production report for the Assembly Department are shown and explained on page 411.

> **ASSEMBLY DEPARTMENT**
> **Equivalent Production Computations**
> **Month of March 19X9**
>
> Materials
> | | |
> |---|---:|
> | Transferred Out to Next Department | 925 |
> | Work in Process—Ending (50 credenzas × 100%) | 50 |
> | Total Units Accounted For | 975 |
> | Deduct Units of Work in Prior Month | |
> | (40 credenzas × 100%) | 40 |
> | Equivalent Production for Materials (FIFO) | 935 |
>
> Labor and Manufacturing Overhead
> | | |
> |---|---:|
> | Transferred Out to Next Department | 925 |
> | Work in Process—Ending (50 credenzas × 60%) | 30 |
> | Total Units Accounted For | 955 |
> | Deduct Units of Work in Prior Months | |
> | (40 credenzas × 75%) | 30 |
> | Equivalent Production for Labor and Overhead (FIFO) | 925 |

Quantity Schedule. The Quantity Schedule of the cost of production report follows the pattern previously used for the Fabrication Department, with the exception that the item called Transferred In From Prior Department is used for Started in Production. Additional items are needed in the Cost Schedule since the costs in a prior department must be accounted for in all later departments. Note the following on the report shown on page 412.

Cost Schedule. Certain items in both the Costs to Be Accounted For and the Costs Accounted For sections bear examination.

Section (c)—Costs to Be Accounted For:

- Beginning Inventory of Work in Process is shown separately, in the same way as in the report for the Fabrication Department.
- Under Costs Charged in Current Month, the cost figures labeled Cost of Goods Transferred In are new items on the report. Note that these figures are the same as the ones that appear on the Total Cost of Goods Transferred Out line of the Fabrication Department's report. Remember that the unit cost of $119.926 is an average of the units transferred into the department during the period, even though that figure was based on the calculation of separate costs of producing the units from the beginning inventory of work in process in the Fabrication Department and the cost of goods started and finished during the month in that department.
- The 25 lost units (from the monthly production report) are entered on the line labeled Adjustment for Lost Units. The lost units are deducted from the 960 units transferred in. (It is assumed that the loss occurred at the beginning of production in the department, so that the lost units are from those transferred in during the current month.)

ASSEMBLY DEPARTMENT
Cost of Production Report (FIFO)
Month of March 19X9

QUANTITY SCHEDULE		UNITS
(a) Quantity to Be Accounted For:		
Work in Process—Beginning		40
Started in Production—Current Month		-0-
Transferred In From Prior Department		960
Total to Be Accounted For		1,000
(b) Quantity Accounted For:		
Transferred Out to Next Department		
From Beginning Work in Process	40	
Started and Completed—Current Month	885	925
Work in Process—Ending		50
Lost in Production		25
Total Accounted For		1,000

COST SCHEDULE	TOTAL COST	E.P. UNITS	UNIT COST
(c) Costs to Be Accounted For:			
Beginning Inventory of Work in Process	$ 7,927.28		
Costs Charged in Current Month			
Cost of Goods Transferred In	$115,128.84 ÷	960	= $119.926
Adjustment for Lost Units		25	3.206
Adjusted Prior Department Costs	$115,128.84 ÷	935	= $123.132
Costs Added in Current Department			
Materials	$ 22,823.60 ÷	935	= $ 24.410
Labor	$ 45,152.00 ÷	925	= $ 48.813
Overhead	$ 22,916.00 ÷	925	= $ 24.774
Total Costs Added in Current Department	$ 90,891.60		$ 97.997
Total Costs in Current Department	$206,020.44		$221.129
Total Costs to Be Accounted For	$213,947.72		
(d) Costs Accounted For:			
Transferred Out to Next Department			
From Beginning Work in Process			
Beginning Inventory	$ 7,927.28		
Materials Added in Current Month	-0-		
Labor Added in Current Month	488.13 =	10	× $ 48.813
Overhead Added in Current Month	247.74 =	10	× $ 24.774
Total Cost of Goods From Beginning			
Work in Process	$ 8,663.15 ÷	40	= $216.579
Goods Started and Completed in Current Month	$195,699.86* =	885	× $221.129
Total Cost of Goods Transferred Out	$204,363.01 ÷	925	= $220.933
Work in Process—Ending			
Costs in Prior Department	$ 6,156.60 =	50	× $123.132
Costs in Current Department			
Materials	$ 1,220.50 =	50	× $ 24.410
Labor	1,464.39 =	30	× $ 48.813
Overhead	743.22 =	30	× $ 24.774
Total Work in Process	$ 9,584.71		
Total Costs Accounted For	$213,947.72		

*Adjusted $.69 for rounding error.

- The Adjusted Prior Department Unit Cost is obtained by dividing the 935 units remaining into the total cost ($115,128.84 ÷ 935 = $123.132).
- The difference of $3.206 between the adjusted unit cost of $123.132 and the unit cost transferred in of $119.926 is the change in unit cost resulting from the lost units. This amount is shown on the Adjustment for Lost Units line.
- The same procedure as that described for the Fabrication Department is used in completing the Costs in Current Department section. The cost for each element, as shown in the general ledger, is divided by the related equivalent production units to obtain the unit cost.
- The amount labeled Total Costs to Be Accounted For is the sum of the Beginning Inventory of Work in Process and the Total Costs Charged in Current Month.

Section (d)—Costs Accounted For:

- The computation techniques for the costs that appear in the Transferred Out to Next Department subsection are the same as those for the Fabrication Department. Note that the total cost and unit cost figures for the beginning inventory are again separate from the costs for the new production. The total cost and the unit costs shown on the Total Cost of Goods Transferred Out line will be used in the transfer of costs to the Finishing Department. Remember that the unit cost of $220.933 is an average cost ($204,363.01 ÷ 925).

At this point you should be able to work Exercises 17–7 to 17–9 and Problems 17–3A to 17–4B.

- The only new item under Work in Process—Ending is Costs in Prior Department. The unit cost of $123.132 is taken from Adjusted Prior Department Costs in the first part of the Cost Schedule. It is multiplied by the 50 units of work in process to obtain the total of $6,156.60. All other computations follow the familiar pattern.

DETERMINING APEX COMPUTER DESIGNS' COSTING METHOD

An accountant who completed a detailed comparison of the FIFO method and the average cost method (see page 376) for the Assembly Department at Apex would note the following:

- Use of the FIFO method for the second department has again made extra data and computations necessary on the report.
- The separate unit costs of completed units coming from the beginning work in process inventory and those started during the current period reflect a difference of $4.55 ($221.129 − $216.579 = $4.455), or about 2 percent of the value involved.
- The average cost used for transfer to the next department under the FIFO method is $220.933, compared with $220.977 computed under the average cost method, a difference of slightly less than one-half of 1 cent.
- The value of Apex's inventory is low relative to production.
- Apex's production is stable, and its inventory is fairly constant.

These points convinced Apex's accountant to choose the average cost method of accounting for beginning inventories. These factors make the slightly greater accuracy provided by the FIFO method of minimal importance. Because the average cost method is simple and convenient and its results not greatly different from those arrived at by using the FIFO cost method, it is more satisfactory for Apex.

Using Unit Costs for Control Purposes

At this point you should be able to work the Master Problem.

The unit cost figures shown on the monthly cost of production reports provide useful information to management on how well costs are being controlled. By comparing monthly unit costs, management can detect and promptly investigate meaningful changes. For example, the unit cost of materials in the Assembly Department for March 19X9 is shown in the cost of production report on page 412 as $24.410. If the corresponding cost in April were $25.80, this significant increase would be promptly looked into.

SELF-REVIEW

1. In the cost of production report under the FIFO method, how are lost units treated in computing cost per equivalent unit for costs Transferred In From Prior Department?
2. Under the FIFO costing method, are costs included for Costs in Prior Department in the beginning work in process inventory added to Costs in Prior Department transferred into the current department during the current period?
3. Does the FIFO method require *less* or *more* computational effort than the average cost method?
4. Under the average cost method, how do lost units affect the cost per equivalent unit for materials, labor, and overhead added in the department during the current month?
5. In a cost of production report prepared when the FIFO method is being used, are rounding errors treated as being applicable only to units that were started and completed during the current period?

Answers to Self-Review

1. In computing cost per equivalent unit for costs Transferred In From Prior Department, the costs applicable to the lost units are absorbed by the good units. The total of costs transferred in during the period is absorbed by the good units.
2. No. Under the FIFO method, the costs of the beginning inventory are kept intact as being applicable to those units.
3. The FIFO method requires more computational effort than the average cost method because separate calculations must be made for units that were in process at the start of the period and for those that were started and completed in each department during the period.
4. Because lost units affect the computation of equivalent production, they increase the cost per equivalent unit of production for materials, labor, and overhead added in the current period.
5. Under the FIFO method any adjustment for rounding errors is shown in the cost of production report as applicable to the units started and completed during the current period. However, the adjustment affects the total cost of all units transferred out of the department during the period.

PRINCIPLES AND PROCEDURES SUMMARY

- Under the FIFO method of computing costs of goods completed and of work in process, separate figures are computed for the cost of completed units coming from the beginning work in process and the costs of units started and finished during the period.

- Because of these two separate calculations, some accountants conclude that the FIFO method gives more accurate costs than does average costing.

- The monthly production report prepared under the FIFO method contains the information found on the report under the average cost method. In addition, a production report under the FIFO method shows the number of units from beginning work in process that were transferred out of the department and the number of units transferred out that were started and completed in the department during the period.

- The monthly production report under the FIFO method also shows the stage of completion of not only the ending inventory but also the beginning inventory.

- Under the average cost method, all work done on units transferred out of the department during the period, including the work in the beginning work in process, is used in computing equivalent units. However, under the FIFO method, only work done in the current period is used in computing equivalent production.

- When the FIFO method is used, all cost elements in the beginning inventory of work in process in the Costs to Be Accounted For section of the cost of production report are combined into a single figure.

- In the Costs Accounted For section, the Transferred Out to Next Department subsection separates costs relating to beginning work in process inventory from those relating to units started and finished in the current month.

- The costs applicable to the units completed from beginning inventory and those applicable to units started and finished during the current month are added to get total costs of goods transferred out of the department. That total is divided by the number of units transferred out to get an average cost of goods transferred out of the department. In the next department this total amount and the average unit cost of goods transferred will be shown as Transferred In From Prior Department in the Costs Charged in Current Month subsection.

- Normal losses of units in production are ignored in computing equivalent production and in determining unit costs. As a result, the costs of lost units are absorbed by good units.

- In many situations, there will be little difference between the costs of goods transferred out of the department under the average cost method and the first in, first out method.

MANAGERIAL IMPLICATIONS

■ If manufacturing costs vary significantly during a month, the average cost method might not provide management with adequate information for controlling costs in a process manufacturing system. In that event, the FIFO method might produce more useful information.

■ If ending inventories are small in comparison with the units transferred out of the department during the month, there will be little difference between the average cost method and the FIFO method.

■ The FIFO cost system is more complex and requires more work than the average cost method because it requires separate calculations to be made for the beginning work in process and the units started and completed during the period. It would be especially time-consuming if an effort were made to trace beginning inventories in each department as those units flow through the manufacturing process.

■ A comparison of the costs of units of products transferred out of a department during a month with the costs of units transferred out in prior months will help management detect unfavorable cost trends that might suggest inefficiencies in the operations of a department.

■ The accountant should carefully consider which costing method is more satisfactory—balancing the costs of each method with the benefits of each. Periodically, the accountant should review the decision to use one method or the other.

REVIEW QUESTIONS

1. Briefly describe the FIFO method of determining unit costs.
2. What are some of the advantages of the FIFO method over the average cost method for handling the cost of the work in process inventories?
3. What are some of the disadvantages of the FIFO method?
4. How does the computation of equivalent units of production under the FIFO method differ from the computation under the average cost method?
5. Why is the cost of the beginning work in process inventory separated from costs of current production under the FIFO method?
6. Is the average cost method or the FIFO method of accounting for work in process more difficult? Explain.
7. When the FIFO method is used, how would a firm compute the unit cost of goods transferred out to the next department?
8. Are the differences between the average cost method and the FIFO method likely to be greater when the work in process inventory is large or when it is small compared to the total costs to be accounted for? Explain.

9. When the FIFO method is used, how does the monthly production report differ from the monthly production report prepared under the average cost method?

10. Will the number of equivalent units of production be larger or smaller if the FIFO method is used rather than the average cost method?

MANAGERIAL DISCUSSION QUESTIONS

1. Suppose that management of a company uses cost data in setting the price of the firm's products. In a period of rapid inflation, would the unit cost figures resulting from FIFO be preferable to those resulting from average costing? Explain.

2. Management is interested in detecting and measuring changes in unit labor and overhead costs as quickly as possible. Would the average cost method or the FIFO method be more suitable for this purpose? Explain.

3. The vice president of production of the company where you are employed as cost accountant has suggested that you switch from the average cost method to the FIFO method. The work in process inventory is small and relatively stable. What arguments can you advance against the suggested change?

4. The president of the company at which you are the chief accountant asks you why it is necessary to compute costs on a departmental basis. She suggests that the entire factory be treated as one process and that a single calculation of cost of goods completed and ending work in process inventory be made. Respond to her suggestion.

5. You are employed as cost accountant in a company in which the process cost accounting method is used. The financial vice president is concerned because about 5 percent of the units brought into the Finishing Department are lost in the production process and you have been ignoring these units in your computation of equivalent units; as a result, the costs of these units are absorbed by the good units. She would prefer to remove the costs of the lost units from Work in Process—Finishing Department and charge them to Cost of Goods Sold. What arguments can you make against her suggestion?

6. Explain why equivalent unit computations for work in process are so important under the FIFO method.

EXERCISES

NOTE: Assume in all the exercises that the FIFO method of costing the work in process inventory is used.

EXERCISE 17–1 **Compute equivalent production. (Obj. 2).** The following information is given for the final producing department of the Northwestern Company. Compute the equivalent production for labor.

Beginning work in process inventory, 180 units, 40 percent
   complete as to labor
Transferred in during month, 1,020 units
Transferred out during month, 1,000 units
Work in process, Jan. 31, 200 units, 80 percent complete as to labor

NOTE: The following information applies to Exercises 17–2, 17–3, and
17–4: Toledo Enterprises manufactures a diet soft drink. All materials
are added at the beginning of production in the Mixing Department.
Production data for that department for the month of September 19X9
is as follows:

Beginning work in process, September 1	2,000 gallons
Stage of completion of beginning work in process	
Labor	60%
Overhead	40%
Units started during September	40,000 gallons
Units completed and transferred to next department	38,000 gallons
Stage of ending work in process	
Labor	80%
Overhead	60%

EXERCISE 17–2   **Compute equivalent production. (Obj. 2).** Compute equivalent
production for materials for the month of September 19X9.

EXERCISE 17–3   **Compute equivalent production. (Obj. 2).** Compute equivalent
production for labor for the month of September 19X9.

EXERCISE 17–4   **Compute equivalent production. (Obj. 2).** Compute equivalent
production for overhead for the month of September 19X8.

EXERCISE 17–5   **Compute equivalent production; compute cost per equivalent
unit. (Objs. 2, 3).** The following information is given for the final
producing department of the Northwestern Company.

Beginning work in process inventory, January 1, 19X9, 180 units,
   40 percent complete as to labor
Transferred in during month, 1,020 units
Transferred out during month, 1,000 units
Ending work in process 200 units, 80 percent complete as to labor
Labor cost in the beginning work in process inventory, $7,200
Labor costs incurred during month, $192,664

a. Compute the equivalent units of production for labor.
b. Compute the cost per equivalent unit for labor.
c. Compute the labor costs in the units transferred out of the department during the month.

EXERCISE 17–6   **Compute equivalent production; compute cost per equivalent
unit. (Objs. 2, 3).** The following information is given for the Finishing Department of the Laredo Company, a sheet metal producer,
for the month of May 19X9. Compute the equivalent production for
overhead.

Beginning work in process inventory, 2,400 units, $66\frac{2}{3}$ percent complete as to overhead

Transferred in during month, 9,600 units

Transferred out during month, 8,000 units

Ending work in process inventory, 4,000 units, 75 percent complete as to overhead

a. Compute the equivalent production for overhead for the month of May.

b. Compute the cost per equivalent unit of overhead for the month of May.

EXERCISE 17-7 **Compute equivalent production; compute cost per equivalent unit when there are lost units. (Objs. 2, 3, 5).** The following information is given for the Toning Department of the Burlington Company for the current month.

Beginning work in process inventory, 1,000 units, 100 percent complete as to materials

Transferred in during month, 4,000 units

Transferred out to next department during month, 4,400 units

Ending work in process inventory, 500 units, complete as to materials

Units lost in production, 100 units

Cost of materials in beginning work in process, $4,000

Materials added during period, $16,000

a. Compute the equivalent units of materials for the month.

b. Compute the cost per equivalent of materials for the month.

c. Compute the materials cost in the ending work in process inventory.

EXERCISE 17-8 **Make an adjustment for lost units. (Obj. 5).** The Settling Department had prior department costs of $18,000 in its beginning work in process inventory (100 units) for the current month. During the current month, 1,000 units were transferred into the Settling Department with total prior department costs of $18,740, and 25 units were lost in production. It is assumed that the lost units came from units transferred into the Settling Department this month. There was no ending inventory of work in process. Show how the adjustment for lost units would appear in the cost of production report for the month.

EXERCISE 17-9 **Compute equivalent units of material; compute cost per equivalent unit when there are normal losses; compare results under average costing and FIFO costing. (Objs. 2, 3, 5, 6).** Kay Company adds materials at the start of production in the Forming Department. Data related to production in September 19X9 are as follows:

	Units
Beginning work in process on September 1	24,000
Started in September	80,000
Completed and transferred out in September	82,000
Normal spoilage	4,000
Work in process on September 30	18,000

Materials in beginning work in process inventory, $48,500
Cost of materials added during month, $160,500

a. Assuming that the average cost method is used, compute:
  (1) The equivalent units of materials for September.
  (2) The cost per equivalent unit of materials for September.
b. Assuming that the FIFO cost method is used, compute:
  (1) The equivalent units of production of materials for September.
  (2) The cost per equivalent unit of materials for September.
c. What is the difference in materials cost per equivalent unit for materials under the two methods? Do you consider this to be a significant difference? Explain.

PROBLEMS

NOTE: Assume in each problem that the FIFO method of inventory costing is used.

PROBLEM 17–1A

Compute equivalent units; compute costs per equivalent unit; prepare a cost of production report. (Objs. 2, 3, 4). The Eastern Chemical Corporation produces a single product. On January 1, 19X9, 8,000 pounds of the product were in process in the Cooking Department, the first department. All materials had been added to the beginning inventory, and labor and overhead were estimated to be 60 percent complete. During the month of January, 75,000 pounds were put into production, and 71,000 pounds were transferred to the Mixing Department, the second department. On January 31, 12,000 pounds were still in process in the Cooking Department. The ending inventory is estimated to be complete as to materials and two-thirds complete as to labor and overhead. Cost data for the month of January are shown below.

	Materials	Labor	Overhead
Beginning Work in Process Inventory	$ 32,000	$ 14,400	$ 7,200
Added During January	288,000	230,020	110,558

INSTRUCTIONS

1. Compute equivalent production units in the Cooking Department for the month of January.
2. Prepare a cost of production report for the Cooking Department for the month of January.

PROBLEM 17–2A

Compute equivalent production; compute costs per equivalent unit; prepare a cost of production report. (Objs. 2, 3, 4). Potomac Star Company uses a process cost accounting system. All materials in the first department (Crushing) are placed in production at the start of the manufacturing process. Data for the month of March 19X9 follow:

<u>Costs</u>

Beginning Work in Process		
Costs in Prior Department		-0-
Costs in Current Department		
Materials		$ 6,840
Labor		2,106
Overhead		1,170
Current Department Costs—March		
Materials		95,220
Labor		75,660
Overhead		61,290

<u>Quantities</u>

Beginning Work in Process	1,500
Started in Production	21,000
Transferred Out to Next Department	20,700
Ending Work in Process	1,800

<u>Stage of Completion of Work in Process</u>

Beginning	
Materials	complete
Labor and Overhead	30%
Ending	
Materials	complete
Labor and Overhead	40%

INSTRUCTIONS

1. Complete the equivalent production computation for the Crushing Department.
2. Prepare a cost of production report for the Crushing Department. Carry the unit cost to three decimal places.

PROBLEM 17–3A

Compute equivalent production; compute cost per equivalent unit; prepare a cost of production report; account for lost units. (Objs. 2, 3, 4, 5). The Westerville Company uses a process cost accounting system. On April 1, 19X9, the firm had 1,800 units in process in the Fractionating Department, the second of three producing departments. All materials had been added to this beginning inventory, but labor and overhead were only 60 percent complete. Costs applicable to the beginning work in process inventory follow:

Costs in prior department	$36,304
Materials	8,522
Labor	12,660
Overhead	5,820

During the month of April, an additional 25,000 units were transferred into the department with total prior department costs of $388,704. Also during April, additional costs were incurred in the department as follows:

Materials	$119,140
Labor	36,252
Overhead	105,580

A total of 25,800 units were transferred out to the third department during the month, 800 units were still in production at the end of the month, and 200 units were lost in production. All materials had been added to the ending work in process inventory, but labor and overhead were only 80 percent complete. Assume that the company uses the FIFO method of costing.

INSTRUCTIONS

1. Compute the equivalent production units.
2. Prepare a cost of production report for the Fractionating Department. Show an adjustment of prior department costs for lost units. Assume that the lost units occur at the beginning of production in the department and that all lost units came from the work transferred into the department during the month of April 19X9.

PROBLEM 17–4A **Compute equivalent units of production; compute cost per equivalent unit; compare FIFO and average cost methods.   (Objs. 2, 3, 6).**   The Cracking Department of Samedan Manufacturing Company is the last production department. On June 1, 19X9, 3,000 units of product were in process and were 50 percent complete as to labor. The labor cost in the beginning inventory was $2,000. During the month of June, 7,000 units were transferred in from the prior department. Labor costs incurred in June in the Cracking Department were $4,500. On June 30, 2,500 units of product were in process. The units were 60 percent complete as to labor.

INSTRUCTIONS

1. Compute equivalent units of production for labor for the month of June, assuming that the company uses the FIFO method.
2. Compute the cost per equivalent unit for labor, assuming that the FIFO method is used.
3. Compute equivalent units of production for labor, assuming that the company uses the average cost method.
4. Compute the cost per equivalent unit for labor, assuming that the company uses the average cost method.
5. Explain the difference between the unit cost computed under the FIFO method and the unit cost computed under the average cost method.

ALTERNATE PROBLEMS

PROBLEM 17–1B **Compute equivalent units; compute costs per equivalent unit; prepare a cost of production report.   (Objs. 2, 3, 4).**   The Great Hope Company produces a single product. All materials are added at the beginning of production. On May 1, 19X9, 6,000 pounds of the product were in process in the Cracking Department, the first department. All materials had been added to these units, and it was estimated that two-thirds of the labor and overhead had been added. During the month of May, 57,000 pounds were put into production, and 54,000 pounds were transferred to the Cooking Department, the second department. On May 31, 9,000 pounds were still in process in the

Cracking Department. The ending inventory is estimated to be complete as to materials and two-thirds complete as to labor and overhead. Cost data for the month of May are shown below.

	Materials	Labor	Overhead
Beginning Work in Process Inventory	$ 24,000	$ 10,800	$ 5,400
Added During May	216,000	151,200	78,400

INSTRUCTIONS

1. Compute equivalent units of production for the month.
2. Prepare a cost of production report for the Cracking Department for the month of May.

PROBLEM 17–2B

Compute equivalent production; compute costs per equivalent unit; prepare a cost of production report. (Objs. 2, 3, 4). The Beetles Company uses a process cost accounting system. All materials in the first department (Preparation) are placed in production at the start of the manufacturing process. Data for the month of July 19X9 follow:

Costs
   Beginning Work in Process
     Costs in Current Department

Materials	$ 34,200
Labor	10,530
Overhead	5,850

     Current Department Costs—March

Materials	476,100
Labor	378,000
Overhead	306,450

Quantities

Beginning Work in Process	3,000
Started in Production	42,000
Transferred Out to Next Department	41,400
Ending Work in Process	3,600

Stage of Completion of Work in Process
   Beginning

Materials	complete
Labor and Overhead	30%

   Ending

Materials	complete
Labor and Overhead	40%

INSTRUCTIONS

1. Complete the equivalent production computation for the Preparation Department.
2. Prepare a cost of production report for the Preparation Department. Carry the unit cost to three decimal places.

PROBLEM 17–3B

Compute equivalent production; compute cost per equivalent unit; prepare a cost of production report; account for lost units. (Objs. 2, 3, 4, 5). The Saginaw Corporation uses the FIFO method in its process cost accounting system. On February 1, 19X9, the firm had 3,600 units in process in the Blending Department, the second of two producing departments. All materials had been added to this beginning inventory, but labor and overhead were only 60 percent complete. Costs applicable to the beginning work in process inventory follow:

Costs in prior department	$72,608
Materials	17,044
Labor	25,320
Overhead	11,640

During the month of February, an additional 50,000 units were transferred into the department with total prior department costs of $777,408. Also during February, additional costs were incurred in the department as follows:

Materials	$238,280
Labor	72,504
Overhead	211,160

A total of 51,600 units were transferred out to finished goods during the month, 1,600 units were still in production at the end of the month, and 400 units were lost in production. All materials had been added to the ending work in process inventory, but labor and overhead were only 80 percent complete.

INSTRUCTIONS

1. Compute the equivalent production units.
2. Prepare a cost of production report for the Blending Department. Show an adjustment of prior department costs for lost units. Assume that the lost units occur at the beginning of production in the department and that all lost units came from the work transferred into the department during the month of February 19X9.

PROBLEM 17–4B **Compute equivalent units of production; compute cost per equivalent unit; compare FIFO and average cost methods.   (Objs. 2, 3, 6).**   The Edging Department of Haltom Products, Inc. is the last production department. On December 1, 19X9, 6,000 units of product were in process and were 50 percent complete as to labor. The labor cost in the beginning inventory was $6,000. During the month of December, 14,000 units were transferred in from the prior department. Labor costs incurred in December in the Edging Department were $33,000. During the month, 15,000 units were transferred to finished goods. On December 31, 5,000 units of product were in process. The units were 60 percent complete as to labor.

INSTRUCTIONS

1. Compute equivalent units of production for labor for the month of December, assuming that the company uses the FIFO method.
2. Compute the cost per equivalent unit for labor, assuming that the FIFO method is used.
3. Compute equivalent units of production for labor, assuming that the company uses the average cost method.

4. Compute the cost per equivalent unit for labor, assuming that the company uses the average cost method.
5. Explain the difference between the unit cost computed under the FIFO method and the unit cost computed under the average cost method.

MASTER PROBLEM

The Phoenix Manufacturing Company has two producing departments, the Foundry Department and the Detailing Department. The FIFO method of handling work in process inventories is used. The beginning work in process inventories on July 1, 19X9, were as follows:

	Foundry Department	Detailing Department
Beginning work in process	$ 2,977.20	$ 3,880.15
Costs added in current period		
Materials	10,206.27	720.10
Labor	4,161.62	6,331.17
Overhead	9,345.64	1,152.34

The monthly production reports for July are summarized below.

Summary of Monthly Production Reports

	Foundry Department	Detailing Department
Quantities		
Work in Process—Beginning	340	360
Started in Production—Current Month	1,915	
Transferred In From Prior Department		1,975
Transferred Out To Next Department		
From Beginning Work in Process	340	
Started and Completed in Current Month	1,635	
Transferred to Finished Goods		
From Beginning Work in Process		360
Started and Completed in Current Period		1,595
Work in Process—Ending	280	380
Stage of Completion of Beginning Work in Process		
Materials	100%	50%
Labor	60%	20%
Overhead	60%	20%
Stage of Completion of Ending Work in Process		
Materials	100%	25%
Labor	60%	25%
Overhead	60%	25%

The beginning inventories on July 1 included the following costs.

	Foundry Department	Detailing Department
Prior Department Costs	-0-	$3,443.65
Materials	$1,632.48	38.40
Labor	538.36	331.33
Overhead	806.36	66.67
Total Work in Process, July 1	$2,977.20	$3,880.15

INSTRUCTIONS

1. Prepare the equivalent production computations for the Foundry Department.
2. Prepare a cost of production report for the Foundry Department.
3. Prepare the equivalent production computations for the Detailing Department.
4. Prepare a cost of production report for the Detailing Department.
5. Prepare journal entries to record transfer of units from the Foundry Department (124) to the Detailing Department (125) and from the Detailing Department to Finished Goods (121).

18

Accounting for By-Products

Although Apex Computer Designs makes only one product, many factories produce several different products simultaneously from a single process. In fact, there has been a constant growth in multiple-product processing as a result of tremendous technological advances in recent years. Chapters 18 and 19 will examine accounting procedures for multiple products.

1. Account for the removal and sale of by-products that do not require further processing.
2. Account for the removal, additional processing costs, and sale of by-products that require further processing when by-products are assigned additional processing costs only.
3. Account for the removal, additional processing costs, and sale of by-products that require further processing when the by-products are assigned both common costs and additional processing costs.
4. Prepare cost of production reports where by-products are involved.
5. Record the value of a by-product at the point of separation using the normal net profit or the reversal cost method.
6. Explain and illustrate the computation of net profits on the sale of by-products under different methods of cost assignment.
7. Decide whether a by-product should be sold without further processing or should be further processed before sale.

NEW TERMS

By-products (p. 428)
Co-products (p. 428)
Common costs (p. 428)
Joint costs (p. 428)
Joint products (p. 428)
Main product (p. 428)
Market value at point of separation (p. 438)
Normal net profit method (p. 434)
Reversal cost method (p. 434)

MULTIPLE-PRODUCT PROCESSING

In some cases of multiple-product processing, only one product is of major importance. The other product or products are incidental to production. For example, bone meal and tallow are produced incidentally in meat-packing operations, and sawdust results from the milling of lumber. In other cases, several products of comparable value or importance emerge from a single process. For example, gasoline, jet fuel, kerosene, naphtha, and lubricants all result from petroleum refining.

The accountant classifies multiple products according to their relative importance. If there is one product of high value, it is called the **main product.** Incidental products of little value are usually called **by-products.** Two or more products of significant value are called **joint products,** or **co-products.**

At some point in the sequence of manufacturing operations, multiple products are separated from one another. In accounting for these products, the basic question is how much of the production costs incurred before separation should be allocated to each product. Costs incurred up to the point of separation are called **common costs** or **joint costs.** In this chapter, which discusses accounting for by-products, we will refer to the costs incurred prior to the separation of the main product and by-products as *common costs.* In Chapter 19, which explains how joint products are accounted for, we will refer to the pre-separation costs as *joint costs.*

METHODS OF ACCOUNTING FOR BY-PRODUCTS

A by-product may be sold as a commodity at the time of its separation from the main product, or it may require further processing after separation to prepare it for sale.

By-Products Not Requiring Further Processing

There are two popular methods of accounting for by-products that require no further processing. In the first, the proceeds from the sale of the by-product are considered as other income, and all manufacturing costs are applied to the main product. In the second method, the estimated value of the by-product at the time it is separated from the main product is recorded as the cost of by-product inventory and is credited to the Work in Process account as a reduction in the cost of the main product. (Another method of accounting for a by-product when there is no further processing is to make no entry at the time the by-product is removed; then, when the by-product is sold, the proceeds are credited to the Work in Process account. This method is not frequently used.)

By-Products Requiring Further Processing

There are also two basic methods for accounting for by-products that require further processing after separation from the main product. The difference between these two methods pertains to the costs to be assigned to the by-product. In one method, the by-product is charged only with the additional manufacturing costs incurred after separation. This method assumes that no part of the common costs applies to the by-product. In the other method, part of the common costs is assigned to the by-product, and the by-product is also charged with any additional costs incurred after separation.

Data for a seed processing company, the Harpool Seed Company, will be used to illustrate each of these methods of by-product costing.

HARPOOL SEED COMPANY

The Harpool Seed Company purchases seed grains from growers. The seeds are cleaned, treated, bagged, and stored for resale to wholesalers and retailers. There are three departments in the operation: Separation, Treating, and Packaging.

The operations and costs of the Separation Department during October 19X9 will be used to illustrate and compare the various methods of accounting for by-products. In this department, the grain is weighed and then passed through a series of blowers and screens that separate the seeds into standard sizes. Small seeds, husks, and foreign matter that are sifted out are called *screenings*. These screenings are removed in the separation process and are stored in bins. They are used in preparing mixed feed for livestock.

Cost Data

The general ledger accounts show the following costs incurred in the Separation Department during October:

Materials (Grain)	$40,872
Labor	8,496
Overhead	7,434

Production Data

The manager of the Separation Department supplies the monthly production report shown below. For the sake of simplicity, it is assumed that there is no beginning or ending inventory involved. (The abbreviation *cwt.* shown on this report stands for *hundredweight,* a unit of measure equivalent to 100 pounds.)

SEPARATION DEPARTMENT
Monthly Production Report
Month of October 19X9

Materials Placed in Production	2,950 cwt.
Seed Transferred to Treating Department	2,655 cwt.
Screenings Removed	295 cwt.
Beginning and Ending Inventories of Work in Process	-0-

Equivalent Production Computation

The computation of equivalent production is simplified by the absence of an ending work in process inventory.

SEPARATION DEPARTMENT
Equivalent Production Computations
Month of October 19X9

Transferred to Treatment Department	2,655 cwt.
Work in Process—Ending	-0-
Equivalent Production	2,655 cwt.

BY-PRODUCTS NOT PROCESSED FURTHER

The screenings described earlier are sold by the Harpool Seed Company without any additional processing. The method of accounting for this by-product was chosen by the accountant after consideration of the values and other circumstances involved. As previously discussed, there are two methods that can be used. The proceeds may be treated as other income, or the estimated selling price may be treated as a reduction in the cost of the main product and assigned to the by-product inventory.

Proceeds Treated as Other Income

If the proceeds from the sale of a by-product are small, they are almost always considered as other or miscellaneous income. The accounting treatment is identical to that for scrap sales under the job order cost system. No entry is made until the by-product is sold. At that time Accounts Receivable or Cash is debited and Miscellaneous Income is credited for the amount of the sale. For example, if the 295 cwt. of screenings are sold for $3.40 per cwt. (295 × $3.40 = $1,003) on November 6, the entry, in general journal form, would be as shown below.

19X9				
Nov. 6	Accounts Receivable (or cash)	111	1,003.00	
	Miscellaneous Income	713		1,003.00
	Recorded sale of by-product.			

Analysis of the Method. If this procedure is followed, no cost is assigned or allocated to the by-product. In addition, the sale of the by-product has no effect on the cost of the main product. This sale is not included on the departmental cost of production report that is shown at the top of page 431.

This procedure is simple and practical and requires no computations of the cost of the by-product. However, it does not give a true measure of the net cost of manufacturing the main product because, although the proceeds from the sale of the by-product actually serve to reduce the total manufacturing cost, that reduction is not reflected in the accounts.

Estimated Sales Value Treated as Cost Reduction

If the estimated sales value of the by-product is treated as a reduction in the cost of the main product, the following entry would be made to record the removal of the by-product at the point of separation:

19X9				
Oct. 31	Inventory of By-Product	119	1,003.00	
	Work in Process—Separation Dept.	126		1,003.00
	Recorded by-product at estimated sales			
	value and removed this assigned cost			
	from the main product.			

Analysis of the Method. If this procedure is followed, the cost assigned to the by-product is equal to its estimated sales value. The

SEPARATION DEPARTMENT
Cost of Production Report
Month of October 19X9

QUANTITY SCHEDULE	UNITS
(a) Quantity to Be Accounted For:	
Started in Production—Current Month	2,950
(b) Quantity Accounted For:	
Transferred Out to Next Department	2,655
Screenings Transferred to By-Product Inventory	295
Total Accounted For	2,950

COST SCHEDULE	TOTAL COST	E.P. UNITS	UNIT COST
(c) Costs to Be Accounted For:			
Costs in Current Month			
Materials	$40,887.00 ÷	2,655 =	$15.40
Labor	8,496.00 ÷	2,655 =	3.20
Overhead	7,434.00 ÷	2,655 =	2.80
Total Costs to Be Accounted For	$56,817.00		$21.40
(d) Costs Accounted For:			
Transferred Out to Next Department	$56,817.00 =	2,655 ×	$21.40
Total Costs Accounted For	$56,817.00		

value of the by-product reduces the cost of the main product. This value appears on the cost of production report under Costs Accounted For. It is treated as a reduction in the cost of goods transferred out of the department during the current month. For example, as shown in the cost of production report shown on page 432, the $1,003 reduction in the total cost of goods transferred to the Treating Department results in a reduction of unit cost from $21.40 ($56,817 ÷ 2,655) to $21.022 ($55,814 ÷ 2,655). The adjustment of $.378 appears on the Deduct Value of By-Product Removed line, shown on page 432.

When the by-product is later sold, the Inventory of By-Product 119 account is credited for the recorded estimated value. Any difference between the sales price and the recorded value is recorded as Gain or Loss on Sale of By-Product and is treated as Other Income or Other Expense on the income statement.

For example, if the screenings recorded previously at $1,003 were sold for $980, the entry in general journal form would be as follows:

19X9				
Oct. 31	Cash	101	980.00	
	Gain or Loss on Sale of By-Product	408	23.00	
	Inventory of By-Product	119		1,003.00
	Recorded sale of By-Product at a loss.			

SEPARATION DEPARTMENT
Cost of Production Report
Month of October 19X9

QUANTITY SCHEDULE	UNITS
(a) Quantity to Be Accounted For:	
Started in Production—Current Month	2,950
(b) Quantity Accounted For:	
Transferred Out to Next Department	2,655
Screenings Transferred to By-Product Inventory	295
Total Accounted For	2,950

COST SCHEDULE	TOTAL COST	E.P. UNITS	UNIT COST
(c) Costs to Be Accounted For:			
Costs in Current Month			
Materials	$40,887.00 ÷	2,655 =	$15.400
Labor	8,496.00 ÷	2,655 =	3.200
Overhead	7,434.00 ÷	2,655 =	2.800
Total Costs to Be Accounted For	$56,817.00		$21.400
(d) Costs Accounted For:			
Transferred Out to Next Department	$56,817.00 =	2,655 ×	$21.400
Deduct Value of By-Product Removed	1,003.00		.378
Adjusted Cost of Grain Transferred Out to			
Next Department	$55,814.00 ÷	2,655 =	$21.022
Costs Assigned to By-Product	1,003.00		
Total Costs Accounted For	$56,817.00		

At this point you should be able to work Exercises 18–1 to 18–4 and Problems 18–1A to 18–3B.

This method is simple and does show the net cost of manufacturing the main product. However, the value of the by-product may be difficult to estimate if market prices tend to vary widely. In addition, if market prices vary, the gain or loss resulting from the sale of the by-product may be large.

BY-PRODUCTS PROCESSED FURTHER

In many cases, the manufacturer may find it more profitable to process the by-product further rather than to sell it in the form in which it exists when it is separated from the main product. In some cases, additional processing may be necessary to make the by-product marketable.

Assume that the Harpool Seed Company further processes the screenings instead of selling them at the point of separation. The 295 cwt. of screening is mixed with an equal weight of feed material and milled into a finished feed product. The additional processing costs for the 590 cwt. of finished feed product in the month of October are as follows:

SELF-REVIEW

1. Explain the difference between by-products and joint products.
2. Explain briefly two methods of costing by-products that do not require further processing after separation from the main product.
3. How are by-products reflected in the computation of equivalent production for the main product?
4. Under what conditions would it be appropriate for no value to be assigned to by-products but, instead, for the sales proceeds to be treated as other income?
5. When the estimated sales value of the by-product is treated as a reduction in the cost of the main product, what entry is made if the by-product is sold for more than the estimated sales value?

Answers to Self-Review

1. By-products are products with little value compared to one or more other products being produced as part of the same manufacturing process. Joint products are products that have nearly the same value as one or more other products being produced as part of the same manufacturing process.
2. If a by-product requires no further processing, no value may be assigned to it and the proceeds from its sale may be considered as other income. Under this method, the by-product does not affect the cost of the main product. Alternatively, the estimated sales price of the by-product removed may be credited to the cost of the main product and recorded as a by-product inventory.
3. By-products do not affect the computation of equivalent units of the main product. By-products are ignored in that computation.
4. If the proceeds from the sale of a by-product are small, they may be considered as other income.
5. Any sales proceeds in excess of the amount recorded as by-product inventory is treated as a gain; any amount by which the amount received is less than the inventory cost will be shown as a loss.

Materials	$1,239
Labor	120
Overhead	130
	$1,489

Assignment of Additional Costs Only

If only the additional processing costs after separation are assigned to the by-product, they are debited to a special Work in Process account for the by-product, as shown below.

19X9				
Oct. 31	Work in Process—By-Product	128	1,489.00	
	Raw Materials	121		1,239.00
	Factory Payroll Clearing	500		120.00
	Manufacturing Overhead Control	501		130.00
	Recorded additional costs of processing by-product.			

The Growing Importance of By-Products

In past decades, by-products from manufacturing were often burned or otherwise disposed of because there was no market for them or their sales value was less than the cost to get them ready to market. Many factors have converged to drastically reduce the quantity and variety of by-product destroyed. The most important factors are (1) the development of facilities and processes to convert by-products into usable goods with high market value and (2) the impact of environmental regulations prohibiting or restricting disposition of the products. The lumber industry is a dramatic example of the conversion of by-products into profitable salable products.

Lumber mills cut logs into boards of different sizes. In the process, the bark is first removed from the logs. Until a few years ago, the bark was burned because it had no profitable use and the cost to transport the bark exceeded its value. Now, however, bark is commonly used as a mulch and for other purposes. The bark is cut into smaller pieces, bagged, and sold to nurseries, farm and garden stores, and other retail outlets. In addition to the development of these new product uses, there are now environmental restrictions on burning the bark in many areas. These two factors have been the impetus to turn a wasted scrap item into a profitable by-product.

In the process of cutting logs into lumber, shavings and sawdust are also created. Like bark, these by-products were generally burned as scrap in the past. Burning is no longer allowed in many areas. Sometimes the sawdust is sold as a mulch item in bags, the way bark is. More important, technology has been developed to convert the sawdust and ground shavings into a durable, strong synthetic lumberlike building material, which has proved profitable to many lumber companies.

The list of industries in which formerly destroyed scrap materials have been turned into useful and valuable by-products is constantly growing. You can probably see evidence of such conversions in industries in the area in which you live.

Analysis of the Method. One feature of this procedure is that only the additional costs after separation are charged to the by-product. Another feature is that the value of the by-product has no effect on the costs incurred in the Separation Department before separation of the by-product. This value does not appear on the Separation Department's cost of production report shown on page 435.

This method is widely used because it is simple and practical. However, it is subject to criticism because it understates the total cost of the by-product and overstates the total cost of the main product.

At this point you should be able to work Exercise 18–5.

Common Costs and Additional Costs Assigned

Many accountants prefer to charge to the by-product not only the costs incurred after separation but also part of the common costs so that the by-product will reflect all costs involved in its manufacture. One popular method used to allocate common costs to the by-product is the **normal net profit method** (sometimes called the **reversal cost method**). Another method, but one less frequently used, is to assign to the by-product its estimated fair market value at the point of separation.

SEPARATION DEPARTMENT
Cost of Production Report
Month of October 19X9

QUANTITY SCHEDULE	UNITS
(a) Quantity to Be Accounted For:	
Started in Production—Current Month	2,950
(b) Quantity Accounted For:	
Transferred Out to Next Department	2,655
Screenings Transferred to By-Product Inventory	295
Total Accounted For	2,950

COST SCHEDULE	TOTAL COST	E.P. UNITS	UNIT COST
(c) Costs to Be Accounted For:			
Costs in Current Month			
Materials	$40,887.00 ÷	2,655 =	$15.400
Labor	8,496.00 ÷	2,655 =	3.200
Overhead	7,434.00 ÷	2,655 =	2,800
Total Costs to Be Accounted For	$56,817.00		$21.400
(d) Costs Accounted For:			
Transferred Out to Next Department	$56,817.00 =	2,655 ×	$21.400
Total Costs Accounted For	$56,817.00		

The Normal Net Profit Method or Reversal Cost Method. Under this method, the amount to be allocated to the by-product is computed so that the by-product will yield the normal percentage of profit on sales that the company makes, on the average. To see how this method works, assume the following data:

- The feed by-product can be sold for $5.60 per cwt.
- The selling and administrative expenses will total 10 percent of the sales value.
- The normal net profit of the business is 5 percent of sales.

The estimated cost of the by-product is obtained by working back from the estimated sales value, as shown in the computation below. In the computation, estimated selling and administrative expenses and estimated normal profit are deducted from the total estimated sales price to obtain the total estimated manufacturing cost of $2,808.40. From this figure, the costs after separation are subtracted to arrive at the estimated costs before separation.

Estimated Sales Price of Finished By-Product		
(590 cwt. at $5.60 per cwt.)		$3,304.00
Estimated Selling and Administrative Expenses (10%)	$330.40	
Estimated Normal Net Profit (5%)	115.20	445.60
Total Estimated Manufacturing Cost		$2,808.40
Estimated Manufacturing Cost After Separation		1,489.00
Estimated Manufacturing Cost Before Separation		$1,319.40

Once the cost figures are determined, two general journal voucher entries are required to make the appropriate charges to the Work in Process account of the by-product. The first entry transfers estimated costs incurred before separation. The second entry charges the additional costs after separation to the by-product in the usual manner.

19X9			
Oct. 31	Work in Process—By-Product	128	1,319.40
	Work in Process—Separation Department	126	1,319.40
	Charged cost before separation applicable to by-product		

19X9			
Oct. 31	Work in Process—By-Product	128	1,489.00
	Raw Materials	121	1,239.00
	Factory Payroll Clearing	500	120.00
	Manufacturing Overhead Control	501	130.00
	Recorded additional costs of processing by-product.		

After the transfer entries are posted, the Work in Process accounts appear as shown below. (Detailed costs are shown for purposes of illustration.)

Work in Process–Separation Department   NO. 126

DATE		EXPLANATION	POST. REF.	DEBIT		CREDIT		BALANCE		DR. CR.
19	X9									
Oct.	31	Materials		40,887	00			40,887	00	DR.
	31	Labor		8,496	00			49,383	00	
	31	Overhead		7,434	00			56,817	00	DR.
	31	Transferred to By-Product Inventory				1,319	40	55,497	60	DR.

Work in Process–By-Product   NO. 128

DATE		EXPLANATION	POST. REF.	DEBIT		CREDIT		BALANCE		DR. CR.
19	X9									
Oct.	31	Transfer From Separation Dept.		1,319	40			1,319	40	DR.
	31	Materials		1,239	00			2,558	40	DR.
	31	Labor		120	00			2,678	40	DR.
	31	Overhead		130	00			2,808	40	DR.

Analysis of the Method. If this procedure is followed, both common costs and costs incurred after separation are assigned to the by-product. The transfer of the common costs affects the cost of the main product processed in the Separation Department. Thus, the cost assigned to the by-product before separation appears on the departmental cost of production report. It is shown on the report as a reduction in the cost of the main product.

This method is complicated and often difficult to apply. Theoretically, all costs to sell the by-products should be used in the computation. However, it is almost impossible to determine the normal selling costs that are applicable. Thus, most companies merely consider the incremental selling costs related specifically to the by-product. Other firms consider both the incremental costs and the normal selling expenses, which are assumed to be the same percentage of the by-product's selling price as the normal overall percentage of total selling expenses to total sales. The computations are made from so many estimates that the results may not be sufficiently reliable. Therefore, if the amount of a by-product is small, it may not be worthwhile to use this method because of the time and effort required compared to the benefits received.

At this point you should be able to work Exercises 18–6 and 18–7.

Market Value at Point of Separation Assigned as Cost of By-Product

Some accountants prefer to remove the present market value of the by-product at the point of separation even though the by-product is to be processed further, because the potential sales proceeds given up reflect a cost of the decision to process the by-product further. If this procedure had been followed in the Separation Department of the Harpool Seed Company, the marked value of the by-product at the point of separation (295 cwt. at $3.40 each = $1,003) would be credited to Work in Process—Separation Department and debited to Work in Process—By-Product. The additional processing costs of the by-product, $1,489 (materials, labor, and overhead), would also be charged to the Work in Process—By-Product account.

In other cases, by-products are treated in the same manner as joint products. That is, they are accounted for by one of the methods discussed in the next chapter.

COMPUTING NET PROFIT

Many firms enjoy sizable profits from the sale of their by-products. However, profits are not assured, particularly when further processing is involved, without alert supervision and control. The cost accountant can prepare reports of estimated net profit on by-products to assist management in the appraisal of its by-product policies and operations. However, such estimates must be used with care because the net profit shown on the report will vary according to the method of costing used. For decision-making purposes, the most important measure is a comparison of the net increase in value (excess of increase in sales value over the additional processing costs) if the product is further processed.

At this point you should be able to work Exercises 18–8 and 18–9 and Problems 18–4A to 18–5B.

If only the *additional costs* are assigned to the by-product, the cost of the by-product is understated. Therefore, since the cost is understated, the resulting profit of $1,484.60 on the by-product, as shown in the computation below, is overstated.

Sales (590 cwt. at $5.60 each)		$3,304.00
Manufacturing Costs After Separation		
Materials	$1,239.00	
Labor	120.00	
Overhead	130.00	1,489.00
Gross Profit on Sale of By-Product		1,815.00
Estimated Selling and Administrative		
Expenses		330.40
Estimated Net Profit on By-Product		$1,484.60

Under the normal net profit method, costs assigned to the by-product include common costs as well as costs after separation. The profit computed ($115.20) is much lower than that shown under the previous method.

Sales (590 cwt. at $5.60 each)			$3,304.00
Cost of Sales			
Common Costs		$1,319.40	
Costs Added After Separation			
Materials	$1,239.00		
Labor	120.00		
Overhead	130.00	1,489.00	
Total Cost of Sales			2,808.40
Gross Profit on Sale of By-Product			$ 495.60
Estimated Selling and			
Administrative Expenses			330.40
Estimated Net Profit on By-Product			$ 115.20

If the common costs assigned to the by-product are equal to its present **market value at point of separation** (the estimated selling source of the by-product without further processing), the profit will be $481.60. The computation of the profit on the by-product with this method is as shown below.

Sales (590 cwt. at $5.60 each)			$3,304.00
Cost of Sales			
Common Costs		$1,003.00	
Costs Added After Separation			
Materials	$1,239.00		
Labor	120.00		
Overhead	130.00	1,489.00	
Total Cost of Sales			2,492.00
Gross Profit on Sale of By-Product			$ 812.00
Estimated Selling and			
Administrative Expenses			330.40
Estimated Net Profit on By-Product			$ 481.60

The profit obtained by this method may be interpreted as an increase in the firm's profit resulting from the decision to process the by-product further rather than to sell it in the form it was in at the point of separation. This "profit" figure is an important measure in determining whether a by-product should be further processed.

SELF-REVIEW

1. If a by-product must be further processed after separation from the main product and only additional processing costs are assigned to the by-product, what will be the effect on the cost of the main product?
2. What is meant by the *normal net profit method?*
3. How is the amount of common costs to be assigned to a by-product computed when common costs are to be assigned to by-products on the basis of the normal profit method?
4. If the market value at the point of separation is assigned as cost of a by-product, how are costs of further processing of the by-product accounted for?
5. What are the major disadvantages of the normal net profit method for assigning common costs to a by-product?

Answers to Self-Review

1. If no common costs are charged to the by-product, all of them will be assigned to the main product. As a result, the true cost applicable to the by-product will not be shown.
2. Under the normal net profit method, the common cost to be assigned to the by-product is estimated in such a way that, on the average, the ratio of net profit to selling price of the by-product will reflect the percentage of net profit on net sales that the company makes.
3. From the estimated ultimate sales proceeds of the by-product, the estimated selling and adminstrative expenses related to the by-product, the normal net profit on the sales price, and the estimated manufacturing cost after separation are deducted to arrive at the common costs assigned to the by-product.
4. Further costs of processing a by-product should always become a part of the cost of the by-product.
5. The major disadvantages of the normal net profit method for assigning common costs to a by-product are that it is complex, that assumptions must be made that the rate of selling and administrative expenses and net profit apply equally to all products, and that many estimates must be made.

PRINCIPLES AND PROCEDURES SUMMARY

- Many manufacturing processes yield multiple products. When a product is of substantially greater value than other products it is called a *main product*. If two or more products are of major value, they are called *joint products*. An incidental product that has little value compared to main products is called a *by-product*.
- The major question in accounting for by-products is whether any part of the costs incurred prior to separation (called *common costs*) should be allocated to the by-product.
- By-products that require no further processing are usually accounted for by one of two methods:

- No cost is assigned to the inventory of by-products. When the by-products are sold, the sales proceeds are recorded as other income.
  - The estimated sales value of the by-product is recorded as inventory of by-product, and that amount reduces the cost of the main product.
- Three methods may be used to account for by-products that require further processing:
  - Only additional costs incurred after separation from the main product are charged to the by-product inventory.
  - The estimated cost of the by-product at the point of separation is assigned to the by-product work in process inventory and removed from the cost of the main product. Additional costs incurred after separation from the main product are also charged to the by-product inventory. The cost at the point of separation is often computed by the normal net profit method or reversal cost method.
  - The estimated market value of the product at the point of separation is recorded as by-product inventory value and removed from the cost of the main product. Costs incurred after separation are also charged to the by-product work in process inventory.
- No matter what method is used to assign a value to the by-product inventory, if it is sold for more than that recorded value, a gain is recognized on the sale, and if it is sold for less than that recorded value, a loss will be recorded.
- Each method of handling by-products has advantages and limitations. Statements of estimated profits from by-products are directly affected by the costing method used.

MANAGERIAL IMPLICATIONS

- Although the value of by-products is relatively low, it is important that good records and good controls be maintained for by-product inventories. In addition to the fact that by-products do have value, they sometimes present environmental hazards, especially if they have not been further processed.
- Procedures should be developed for maintaining records, for establishing policies for safeguarding the by-products, and for their disposition through sale or through further processing.
- In general, costs or other values assigned to by-products are estimated. In addition, the assigned costs are somewhat arbitrary, because they depend on the method chosen for assigning the cost.
- One of the most important decisions in dealing with by-products, and one in which the cost accountant can be of special help, is whether to further process by-products or to sell them at the point of separation from the main product. As a general rule, if the increase in selling price resulting from more processing is greater than the additional costs to further process and sell the product, it will be desirable to undertake the additional processing.

REVIEW QUESTIONS

1. What is a by-product?
2. Explain the difference between a by-product and a joint product.
3. What is meant by common costs?
4. Must a part of common costs be allocated to by-products? Explain.
5. If no part of common costs is assigned to by-products when they are moved from the main product's manufacturing process, what will be the value assigned to the Work in Process—By-Product account if the by-product is not further processed after separation?
6. If a company treats the entire sales proceeds from by-products as other income, how does a sale of a by-product affect the cost of goods manufactured for the main product?
7. A company's manufacturing process produces a by-product in its Trimming Department. The by-product is sold without further processing. The estimated market value of the by-product is treated as a reduction in cost of the main product. During the month, a quantity of the by-product with an estimated market value (inventory value) of $4,000 was sold for $3,600. How is the sale recorded?
8. Village Company does not record the value of its by-product until it is sold. Typically, the by-product accumulates for several months before sale. When it is sold, the sales proceeds are credited to the Work in Process—Sedimentation Department, in which the by-product is created and extracted. Give reasons why this method for accounting for a by-product might be undesirable.
9. If a by-product is to be processed further after separation, in what ways might the value of the by-product at the point of separation be determined?
10. Explain in detail the reversal cost method of allocating common costs to by-products.
11. Assume that a by-product from the manufacturing process is accumulated for several months before it is sold. Explain the conditions under which an accountant might make an entry crediting Work in Process for the by-product's estimated value at the time of its removal from factory operations.
12. Assume that a by-product from the manufacturing process is accumulated for several months before it is sold. Explain the conditions under which the accountant might make an entry only when the by-product is sold.

MANAGERIAL DISCUSSION QUESTIONS

1. The company for which you are cost accountant has traditionally sold, without further processing, the by-product resulting from manufacturing the main product. Management has asked you whether the company would be better off financially to process the

by-product further and sell it as a miscellaneous completed product. What information would you need to properly answer this question?

2. Assume that your company's manufacturing process produces a rather large physical volume of by-product. The company has not maintained a perpetual inventory of by-product, but a question has been raised as to whether a perpetual inventory should be kept. What factors should be considered in making this decision?

3. A company's accounts show a net profit of $3,400 on the sale of by-products. Comment on the usefulness of this information to the company's management.

4. Management has asked you whether the existence of a by-product affects the cost of the main product. Give an appropriate answer.

5. What factors should management consider in deciding how to dispose of a by-product?

6. Your manager has looked at your cost accounting book and has observed that the use of some methods of recording by-product results in a higher profit from the sale of by-products than do other methods. He suggests that in order to increase the company's profits, you should choose the method that results in the highest profit from the sale of by-products. Prepare a brief response to his suggestion.

EXERCISES

EXERCISE 18–1 **Record the sale of a by-product not requiring further processing—sales proceeds treated as income. (Obj. 1).**   The Bridgeport Company uses marble and other types of stone in the manufacture of its products. Shavings are gathered and sold to a landscape company as decorative material. During the month of November 19X9, shavings were sold for $183. Give the general journal entry to record the sale if the company treats the proceeds from the sale of the by-product as other income.

EXERCISE 18–2 **Record the value of a by-product not requiring further processing—value credited to work in process. (Obj. 1).**   Each week the George Company accumulates the by-product arising from its manufacturing process and transfers it to a storage area to be sold to a local buyer. The by-product is recorded at its estimated value at the time of removal, and the value is credited to Work in Process. On May 7, 19X9, a quantity of the by-product with an estimated value of $150 was removed from factory operations. Give the entry in general journal form to record the transfer from factory operations to inventory.

EXERCISE 18–3 **Record the value of a by-product not requiring further processing—value credited to work in process. (Obj. 1).**   The manufacturing process in the Trimming Department of the Paige Company results in a by-product. The company accumulates the by-product and periodically sells it. During the month of June 19X9, a quantity of the by-product with an estimated sales value of $900 was recovered. The company treats the estimated value of the by-product as a reduction in the cost of production completed during the current month. The total cost of the 20,000 units completed during the month was $48,000 before considering the by-product.

a. Give the general journal entry to record the removal of the by-product from factory operations and its storage in inventory.

b. Calculate the revised cost per unit of the goods transferred out of the department during the month.

EXERCISE 18–4 **Record the removal and sale of a by-product not requiring further processing. (Obj. 1).** The Carlton Company produces field seed. Screenings, a by-product, are sold to a garden outlet to be used in mulch products. During the month of May 19X9, screenings with an estimated value of $1,250 were removed from factory operations and stored in a warehouse. On June 9, the materials were sold for $1,180. Give the general journal entries to record these facts if the following procedures are used:

a. The company treats the proceeds from the sale as miscellaneous income at the time of sale.

b. The company treats the estimated value of its by-products as a reduction in the cost of the main product at the time of removal.

EXERCISE 18–5 **Account for removal, further processing, and a sale of a by-product—only additional costs assigned. (Obj. 2).** The Kankakee Company assigns to its by-products only the additional cost needed to process them. Give all journal entries related to the by-product that are called for by the following data:

a. During July 19X9, a by-product with an estimated value of $350 was removed from factory operations.

b. The by-product was further processed at a cost of $100 for materials, $200 for labor, and $100 for overhead.

c. The finished by-product was completed and sold for $600.

EXERCISE 18–6 **Compute the value of a by-product using the normal net profit method. (Obj. 5).** In the Decomposing Department of Krum Company, a by-product is removed. The material is further processed and then sold. The company uses the normal net profit method to account for the by-product. Data for December 19X9 follow.

Amount of by-product removed, 10,000 pounds
Estimated sales price of by-product, $2 per pound
Estimated manufacturing cost after separation, $.60 per pound
Estimated selling and administrative expenses, 20 percent of sales price
Estimated normal net profit, 10 percent of sales price

Compute the value to be assigned to the by-product and removed from Work in Process at the point of separation.

EXERCISE 18–7 **Compute the value assigned to a by-product by the reversal cost method. (Obj. 5).** In the Mixing Department of the Toronto Company, scrap materials (a by-product) are removed, further processed, and sold. The company uses the reversal cost method (or normal net profit method) to account for the by-product. Data for April 19X9 follow.

Amount of by-product removed, 4,300 kilograms
Estimated sales price of by-product after further processing, $.70 per kilogram
Estimated processing cost after separation, $.12 per kilogram
Estimated selling expenses, 10 percent of sales price
Estimated normal profit margin, 10 percent of sales price

Compute the value to be assigned to the by-product and removed from Work in Process at the point of separation.

EXERCISE 18–8 **Account for the removal, additional processing, and sale of a by-product; use the normal net profit method to record the value at separation.** **(Objs. 3, 5).** In the Refining Department of Viva Chemicals Corporation, a by-product is recovered. It is further processed after separation and is sold to a medicinal manufacturer as a raw material. During January 19X9, 500 pounds of the by-product were recovered. The by-product is removed from the Work in Process— Refining Department account on the basis of a formula determined in advance for the quarter. Based on an expected sales price of $10 per pound, estimated manufacturing cost after separation of $3 per pound, estimated selling and administrative expenses of 10 percent of the sales price, and a normal profit of 8 percent of selling price, the by-product is transferred from the Refining Department to Work in Process—By-Product, using the normal net profit method. Additional manufacturing costs of $1,600 were incurred on the 500 pounds after separation. The 500 pounds were sold for $9.80 per pound.

a. Give the journal entry to record removal of the 500 pounds from the Refining Department. Use the normal net profit method to determine the cost to be removed.

b. Give the journal entry to record the manufacturing costs incurred after separation, $1,600. Credit Raw Materials, Factory Payroll Clearing, and Manufacturing Overhead Control for $1,600.

c. Give the entry to record completion of the by-product and its transfer to Inventory of By-Product.

d. Give the entry to record the sale of the 500 pounds of by-product for $10 per pound.

EXERCISE 18–9 **Measure the profit from a by-product; decide whether to further process a by-product before sale.** **(Objs. 6, 7).** A company is attempting to decide whether to sell a by-product without additional processing or to process it further. In an effort to answer this question, you have assembled the following data:

Estimated units of by-product per month, 1,500 units
Estimated selling price without further processing, $3.50 per unit
Estimated selling price with further processing, $4.25 per unit
Estimated labor costs to process further, $1,000 per month

Estimated additional material costs to process further, $.30 per unit
Estimated additional overhead costs to process further, $.20 per unit

a. Compute the profit or loss from further processing and selling the by-product, using the approach that you think is appropriate to measure profit.
b. Calculate the difference in income between additional processing and no further processing.
c. Make a recommendation to management to further process or not further process the by-product.

PROBLEMS

PROBLEM 18–1A

INSTRUCTIONS

Account for the removal and sale of a by-product not requiring further processing. (Obj. 1). The Wright Company manufactures a single main product in powdered form. In the Settling Department, certain impurities are removed and become a by-product.

1. On September 1, 19X9, 13,800 kilograms of the by-product recovered in the month of August were in storage awaiting sale. These 13,800 kilograms were sold on September 3 for $.28 per kilogram. Assume that no entry is made for the by-product until it is sold. Give the entry in general journal form, dated September 3, to record the sale for cash of 13,800 kilograms under the following procedures:
   a. The proceeds of the sale are treated as miscellaneous income.
   b. The proceeds of the sale are treated as a reduction in the cost of the main product. (Credit Work in Process—Settling Department 122.)

2. During the month of September, an additional 21,700 kilograms of the by-product were recovered. These were sold on October 6. Instead of following the procedures in Instruction 1, assume that the estimated sales value of the by-product is treated as a reduction in the cost of the main product when it is removed. Give the entries in general journal form to record the following:
   a. Recovery of the 21,700 kilograms during September, assuming an estimated value of $.28 per kilogram. (Date the entry September 30, 19X9.)
   b. Sale on credit of the 21,700 kilograms on October 6 at $.30 per kilogram.

PROBLEM 18–2A

Account for a by-product not requiring further processing. (Obj. 1). The Argyle Corporation manufactures a single product from a plastic material. In the Cutting Department, plastic shavings are created by the manufacturing process and become a by-product. On October 1, 19X9, 7,450 pounds of the plastic by-product recovered in September were in storage. These 7,450 pounds were sold on October 4 for $.30 per pound.

INSTRUCTIONS

1. Assuming that no entry is made for the by-product until it is sold, give the entry in general journal form to record the sale for cash of the 7,450 pounds under the following procedures:
   a. The amount received from the sale is recorded as miscellaneous income.
   b. The amount received from the sale is treated as a reduction in the cost of the main product. (NOTE: Credit Work in Process—Cutting Department 123.)

2. During the month of October 19X9, an additional 10,520 pounds of the plastic by-product were recovered. This amount was sold on November 2, 19X9. Instead of following the procedures given in Instruction 1, assume that the estimated sales value of the by-product is treated as a reduction in the cost of the main product when it is removed. Give the entries in general journal form to record the following:
   a. Recovery of the 10,520 pounds during October assuming an estimated value of $.30 per pound. (Date the entry October 31, 19X9.)
   b. Sale for cash of the 10,520 pounds on November 2 at $.28 per pound.

PROBLEM 18–3A

Record the cost and sale of a by-product not requiring further processing. (Obj. 1). The Harmon Company has three producing departments: The Clinker Department, the Mixing Department, and the Packaging Department. Five percent of the raw materials put into production in the Clinker Department becomes a by-product that has an estimated sales value of $.06 per kilogram. The estimated sales value of the by-product is treated as a reduction in the cost of the main product. During November 19X9, 500,000 kilograms are put into production. There are no beginning and ending inventories. During November 19X9, the following costs are incurred in the Clinker Department:

Cost	Amount	Post Reference
Materials	$80,560.40	MR11
Labor	11,232.32	J11-10
Overhead	7,847.40	J11-11

INSTRUCTIONS

1. Enter the materials, labor, and overhead costs in the Work in Process—Clinker Department account. Open the Inventory of By-Product 128 account.
2. Prepare the general journal voucher to record the removal of the by-product from the Clinker Department. Number the voucher 11-12. Post the voucher to the general ledger accounts opened.
3. Prepare the general journal voucher to record the sale of half the by-product inventory for $776.54 cash. Post the voucher to the Inventory of By-Product account.

PROBLEM 18–4A **Use the normal net profit method; account for the removal, additional processing costs, and sale of by-products that require further processing; compute the profit from the sale of a by-product; decide whether to sell at the point of separation or process further. (Objs. 2, 3, 5, 6, 7).** Freeport Corporation manufactures a material used in transistors. A by-product is recovered in the Completion Department. The by-product is further processed and is sold under the brand name Free Crystals. During the month of July 19X9, total costs incurred in the Completion Department were as follows:

Materials $200,000
Labor   50,000
Overhead   20,000

During the month a total of 5,000 pounds of materials were processed. Of this total, 4,800 pounds were transferred to finished goods and 200 pounds of by-product were recovered. The by-product could be sold for $6 per pound without further processing. In order to make Free Crystals, additional processing costs of $2 per pound for labor and $1 per pound for overhead must be incurred. These costs include packaging and handling costs. Free Crystals is sold for $14 per pound. Selling costs are $1.50 per pound. The 200 pounds recovered in July were processed and sold in August.

INSTRUCTIONS 1. Assume that the company assigns only the additional processing costs to the by-product.
   a. Compute the profit or loss resulting from the sale of the 200 pounds of by-product recovered in July and sold in August.
   b. Compute the cost per pound of the main product produced in July.
2. Assume that the company assigns to the by-product a part of the common costs, using the reversal cost method to determine the common costs to be assigned to the by-product.
   a. Compute the common costs to be assigned to the by-product removed in July. The company's normal net profit margin is 10 percent of sales.
   b. Compute the profit or loss resulting from the sale of the 200 pounds of Free Crystals recovered in July and sold in August.
   c. Compute the cost per unit of main product produced in July.
   d. Was the company wise to choose to further process the by-product rather than sell it at the point of separation? Support your answer to this question with figures.

PROBLEM 18–5A **Compute the cost of a by-product by the normal net profit method; prepare a cost of production report. (Objs. 4, 5).** Production data for the Sorting Department of the Webb Manufacturing Company for the month of June 19X9 are as follows:

	Cost
Work in Process—Beginning	-0-
Costs in Current Month	

Transferred In From Prior Department	$136,000
Costs Added in Current Department	
Materials	-0-
Labor	11,900
Manufacturing Overhead	17,500

	Units
Work in Process—Beginning	-0-
Transferred In From Prior Department	2,000 barrels
Transferred Out to Finished Goods	1,750 barrels
Amount of By-Product Recovered	250 barrels
Work in Process—Ending	-0-

In the Sorting Department, a by-product is recovered and is further processed to form a chemical called *Webbline*. For each barrel of by-product recovered, it is necessary to add an additional barrel of filler to form Webbline. The filler costs $5 per barrel. Each barrel of Webbline requires additional labor costs of $1 and manufacturing overhead of $1.50. (Note that for each barrel of by-product recovered, 2 barrels of Webbline will be produced.) Webbline has an established selling price of $12 per barrel. The normal net profit margin of the company is 8 percent of sales. The estimated selling and administrative expenses are $1 per barrel of Webbline.

INSTRUCTIONS

1. Compute the common cost to be assigned 250 barrels of by-product before separation, using the reversal cost method.
2. Prepare a cost of production report for the Sorting Department for the month of June 19X9, based on the above data.

ALTERNATE PROBLEMS

PROBLEM 18–1B

Account for the removal and sale of a by-product not requiring further processing. (Obj. 1). The Saginaw Chemical Company manufactures a commercial chemical. In the Settling Department, the product is allowed to stand for several hours so that certain impurities will settle to the bottom. The purified chemical is then transferred out to the next department, and the impurities are removed to be sold as a by-product.

INSTRUCTIONS

1. On January 1, 19X9, 3,000 barrels of the by-product recovered in the month of December 19X8 were in storage awaiting sale. These 3,000 barrels were sold on January 8, 19X9, for $6 per barrel. Assume that no entry is made for the by-product until it is sold. Give the entries in general journal form to record the sale for cash of the 3,000 barrels under these procedures.
   a. The proceeds of the sale are treated as miscellaneous income. (Date the entry January 31, 19X9.)

  b. The proceeds of the sale are treated as a reduction in the cost of the main product. (NOTE: Credit Work in Process—Settling Department 122 instead of Miscellaneous Income.)

2. During the month of January 19X9, 2,680 additional barrels of the by-product were recovered. These were sold on February 4. Instead of using the procedures in Instruction 1, assume that the estimated sales value of the by-product is treated as a reduction in the cost of the main product when it is removed. Give the entries in general journal form to record the following:

  a. Removal of the 2,680 barrels during January, assuming an estimated value of $6 per barrel. (Date the entry January 31, 19X9.)

  b. Sale on credit of the 2,680 barrels on February 4 at $5.94 per barrel.

PROBLEM 18–2B   **Record the sale of a by-product not requiring product further processing. (Obj. 1).** The Kemp Milling Company manufactures a single product—flour. In the Cleaning Department, husks and other impurities are removed and become a by-product.

INSTRUCTIONS   1. On May 1, 19X9, 21,000 pounds of the by-product recovered in the month of February were in storage waiting to be sold. These 21,000 pounds were sold on June 3 for $.07 per pound. Assuming that no entry is made for the by-product until it is sold, give the entry in general journal form to record the sale of 21,000 pounds for cash, using the following procedures:

  a. The proceeds of the sale are treated as miscellaneous income.

  b. The proceeds of the sale are treated as a reduction in the cost of the main product. (NOTE: Credit Work in Process—Cleaning Department 122.)

2. During the month of May, an additional 19,500 pounds of the by-product were recovered. These were sold on July 1. Instead of following the procedures in Instruction 1, assume that the estimated sales value of the by-product is treated as a reduction in the cost of the main product when it is removed. Give the entries in general journal form to record the following:

  a. Recovery of the 19,500 pounds in May, assuming an estimated value of $.07 per pound. (Date the entry May 31, 19X9.)

  b. Sale on credit of the 19,500 pounds on July 1 at $.075 per pound.

PROBLEM 18–3B   **Record the cost and the sale of a by-product not requiring further processing; prepare a cost of production report. (Obj. 1).** The Valley Milling Company has three producing departments: the Grinding Department, the Mixing Department, and the Packaging Department. Five percent of the wheat put into production in the Grinding Department becomes a by-product that has an estimated sales value of $2.30 per cwt. The estimated sales value of the by-product is treated as a reduction in the cost of the main product. During July 19X9, 500,000 pounds of wheat were put into production. There were no beginning and ending inventories. During July 19X9, the following costs were incurred in the Grinding Department:

Cost	Amount
Materials	$47,330.00
Labor	7,795.00
Overhead	7,125.00

INSTRUCTIONS

1. Enter the materials, labor, and overhead costs in the Work in Process—Grinding Department account. Open the Inventory of By-Product account.
2. Prepare the general journal voucher to record removal of the by-product from the Grinding Department. Number the voucher 7-12. Post the voucher to the general ledger accounts opened.
3. Prepare the general journal voucher to record the sale of half the by-product inventory for $247.50 cash. Number the voucher 7-13. Use the same account names and numbers that are used in the text. Post the voucher to the Inventory of By-Product account.

PROBLEM 18–4B

Use the reversal cost method to assign costs to a by-product; account for the removal, additional processing costs, and sale of by-products that require further processing; compute the profit from the sale of a by-product; decide whether to sell at the point of separation or process further. (Objs. 2, 3, 5, 6, 7). Okie Corporation manufactures a roofing product. A by-product is recovered in the Texturing Department. The by-product is further processed and is sold as a sealer under the brand name Quick Seal. During the month of May 19X9, total costs incurred in the Texturing Department were as follows:

Materials	$80,000
Labor	10,000
Overhead	8,000

During the month a total of 200,000 pounds of materials were processed. Of this total, 190,000 pounds were transferred to the next department for further processing as a roofing material and 10,000 pounds of by-product were recovered. The by-product could be sold for $.02 per pound without further processing. In order to make Quick Seal, additional processing costs of $.08 per pound for labor and $.04 per pound for overhead must be incurred. These costs include packaging and handling costs. Quick Seal is sold for $.20 per pound. Selling costs are only $.01 per pound. The 10,000 pounds recovered in May were processed and sold in July.

INSTRUCTIONS

1. Assume that the company assigns only the additional processing costs to the by-product.
   a. Compute the profit or loss resulting from the sale of the 10,000 pounds of Quick Seal recovered in May and sold in July.
   b. Compute the cost per pound of the main product produced in May.

2. Assume that the company assigns to the by-product a part of the common costs, using the reversal cost method to determine the common costs to be assigned to the by-product.

   a. Compute the common costs to be assigned to the by-product removed in May. The company's normal net profit margin is 8 percent of sales.

   b. Compute the profit or loss resulting from the sale of the 10,000 pounds of Quick Seal recovered in May and sold in July.

   c. Compute the cost per unit of main product produced in May.

   d. Was the company wise to choose to further process the by-product rather than sell it at the point of separation? Support your answer to this question with figures.

PROBLEM 18–5B

Compute the cost of a by-product by the reversal cost method; prepare a cost of production report. (Objs. 4, 5). Departmental production data for the Preparation Department of the Miami Products Company for the month of April 19X9 are as follows:

	Cost
Work in Process—Beginning	-0-
Costs in Current Month	
Transferred In From Prior Department	$360,000
Costs Added in Current Department	
Materials	-0-
Labor	30,000
Manufacturing Overhead	42,000

	Units
Work in Process—Beginning	-0-
Transferred In From Prior Department	12,000 cwt.
Transferred Out to Next Department	10,000 cwt.
Amount of By-Product	2,000 cwt.
Work in Process—Ending	-0-

In the Preparation Department, a by-product is recovered that reduces the quantity of the main product transferred out. This by-product is transferred to another department, where it is further processed into a product called *Malzena*. For each hundred-pound unit (cwt.) of the by-product recovered from the main product, .5 cwt. of additional material, costing $6 per cwt., must be added. Each cwt. of Malzena requires additional labor costs of $.36 and manufacturing overhead of $.54. (Note that for each cwt. of the by-product recovered, 1.5 cwt. of Malzena will be produced.) Malzena has a sales value of $8.1 per cwt. The normal net profit margin of the company is 6 percent of sales. Estimated selling and administrative expenses are $.42 per cwt. of Malzena.

INSTRUCTIONS

1. Compute the cost to be assigned to the 2,000 cwt. of by-product before separation, using the reversal cost method.

2. Prepare a cost of production report for the Preparation Department for the month of April 19X9, based on the above data.

MANAGERIAL DECISION CASE

The Mayper Company has two producing departments: the Shaving Department and the Polishing Department. In the Shaving Department, shavings are collected and sold as a by-product. Management follows the policy of assigning the market value at the point of separation as the cost of the by-product. Without further processing, the by-product could be sold for $7.50 per kilogram, but selling and administrative expenses of $.17 per kilogram would be incurred. After further processing, the by-product could be sold for $11.70 per kilogram, but selling and administrative expenses of $.23 per kilogram would be incurred. The necessary processing costs for 3,010 kilograms are estimated as follows:

Materials	$2,244
Labor	4,860
Overhead	2,520

1. Prepare a schedule showing the estimated net profit or loss from the sale of 3,010 kilograms of the by-product without further processing.
2. Prepare a schedule showing the estimated net profit or loss from the sale of 3,010 kilograms of the by-product after further processing. Remember to take the common costs of the by-product into consideration as well as the expenses of further processing.
3. Should the by-product be processed further? Explain.

CHAPTER
19

Accounting for Joint Products

When two or more products, both of significant value, result from a single manufacturing process, they are called **joint products.** A joint product is different from a by-product because a by-product has insignificant value compared to the main product or products. Since all joint products from a process are significant, the costing procedures they require are different from those used to account for by-products.

OBJECTIVES

1. Allocate joint costs between products on the basis of physical units.
2. Allocate joint costs between products on the basis of relative sales value.
3. Allocate joint costs between products on the basis of adjusted sales value.
4. Allocate joint costs between products on the basis of assigned weights.
5. Prepare a cost of production report when joint costs are produced.
6. Explain what factors the cost accountant should consider in choosing an allocation basis.

NEW TERMS

Adjusted sales value basis (p. 454)
Assigned weights basis or survey method (p. 454)
Common physical unit basis (p. 454)
Joint costs (p. 454)
Joint products (p. 453)
Relative sales value basis (p. 454)
Split-off point (p. 454)

PROCESSING JOINT PRODUCTS

Sometimes joint products emerging from the manufacturing process can be sold without further processing. For example, in an oil refinery, the refining process will yield gasoline, jet fuel, residual fuel oil, and other products. In other cases, one or more of the products emerging from the joint process may require additional processing to make them salable. An oil well, for instance, may produce crude oil, which must be refined into products such as gasoline and jet fuel (although the producer may sell the oil to a purchaser at the point of its production). The well may also produce natural gas, which can be marketed without additional processing.

BASES FOR ALLOCATING JOINT COSTS

When a firm produces joint products, there is no main product to bear the joint, or common, costs. Each joint product must carry its share of the costs of production. The cost accountant must therefore devise a system for allocating joint costs to the various joint products. **Joint costs** are those costs incurred up to the split-off point of the joint products. The **split-off point** is the point at which two separate physical products emerge.

One of four bases is usually used to assign joint costs to individual products.

■ The **common physical unit basis,** such as gallons, pounds, or feet.
■ The **relative sales value basis,** set to yield a uniform rate of gross profit.
■ The **adjusted relative sales value basis,** reflecting additional processing costs.
■ The **assigned weights basis,** based on technical studies. For example, production managers may conclude, based on their experience or on technical studies, that a unit of one product emerging from a process is more difficult to handle, has greater spoilage, or requires higher selling costs than a unit of the second product from the same process. Based on these studies or on experience, each equivalent unit of the first product may be assigned twice as much cost as the second product.

Each of these methods is discussed and illustrated with data relating to the operations of a chemical manufacturing firm, the Alto Industrial Products Company.

ALTO INDUSTRIAL PRODUCTS COMPANY

The Alto Industrial Products Company manufactures two joint products for use in maintenance and cleaning of machinery—No Rust, a rust retardant, and No Grease, a solvent. These two products are joint products because the manufacturing process automatically results in both being produced, and both have a relatively high value.

The raw chemicals are processed through a single department and are then removed to tanks to await sale. The average cost method is used to account for the work in process inventories.

Cost Data

The Work in Process account in Alto's general ledger shows the following cost information on April 1, 19X9:

Beginning Work in Process
Materials	$4,800
Labor	508
Overhead	752
Balance of Account, Apr. 1	$6,060

Current Month's Costs
Materials	$49,200
Labor	12,232
Overhead	17,868
Total Current Month's Costs	$79,300

Production Data

The production report for April, shown below, contains the usual information. However, note that the quantity of each product manufactured is shown under Transferred Out to Finished Goods.

ALTO INDUSTRIAL PRODUCTS COMPANY
Monthly Production Report
April 19X9

Quantity
Work in Process—Beginning	8,000 liters
Started in Production—Current Month	92,000 liters
Transferred Out to Finished Goods	
No Rust	64,000 liters
No Grease	31,000 liters
Work in Process—Ending	5,000 liters

State of Completion of Ending Work in Process
Materials	complete
Labor	60%
Overhead	60%

Equivalent Production Data

Since all costs have been incurred to process all the products, the total cost must now be allocated to the individual products. Equivalent units of production for joint products are computed in the same way as for a single product. Using the average cost method, the cost accountant at Alto prepares the equivalent production computations in order to assign the total cost to individual products for April. These computations are shown on page 455.

Cost of Production Report

Alto's cost of production report for April is shown on page 456. This report is similar to the ones discussed in Chapter 15 for the average cost system. Let us examine the report to see how it differs from those in Chapter 15.

ALTO INDUSTRIAL PRODUCTS COMPANY
Equivalent Production Computations
Month of April 19X9

Materials

Transferred Out to Finished Goods	95,000 liters
Work in Process—Ending (5,000 liters × 100%)	5,000 liters
Equivalent Production for Materials	100,000 liters

Labor and Manufacturing Overhead

Transferred Out to Finished Goods	95,000 liters
Work in Process—Ending (5,000 liters × 60%)	3,000 liters
Equivalent Production for Labor and Overhead	98,000 liters

Quantity Schedule.   The quantity of each product transferred out to finished goods is shown in Section (b), Quantity Accounted For.

Cost Schedule.   In Section (c), Costs to Be Accounted For, the costs are computed as though a single product were being produced. All the costs incurred must be borne by the two products. Since the liter is the common measure of production, average costs per equivalent liter of production for materials, labor, and overhead are calculated. Both total and unit costs are then added to arrive at the total costs to be accounted for of $85,360 and an average unit cost of $.860 per liter.

Next, in Section (d), Costs Accounted For, a total of 95,000 liters of product is transferred out at a total cost of $81,700. It is at this point that the basic accounting problem arises. How much of the $81,700 total cost of goods produced applies to the 64,000 liters of No Rust produced, and how much applies to the 62,000 liters of No Grease solvent produced? An allocation may be made on several bases: by physical units, by relative sales value, by relative adjusted sales value, or by assigned weights. In the cost of production report shown below for the month of April, joint costs are allocated on the basis of physical units (liters). This allocation method is explained immediately following the cost of production report.

ALLOCATION ON BASIS OF PHYSICAL UNITS

Production in the Alto Industrial Products Company is measured in liters. The cost of production report shows joint costs allocated on the basis of a physical unit (the liter) under Transferred to Finished Goods. The necessary computations appear below.

Total Cost of Product Transferred Out as Computed in the Cost of Production Report	$81,700
Total Number of Liters Transferred Out	95,000

$$\text{Cost per Liter} = \frac{\$81,700}{95,000} = \$.86 \text{ per liter}$$

Cost Applicable to No Rust, 64,000 liters at $.86 each	$55,040
Cost Applicable to No Grease, 31,000 liters at $.86 each	26,660
Total Cost Allocated	$81,700

ALTO INDUSTRIAL PRODUCTS COMPANY
Cost of Production Report
Month of April 19X9

QUANTITY SCHEDULE	LITERS
(a) Quantity to Be Accounted For:	
Work in Process—Beginning	8,000
Started in Production—Current Month	92,000
Total to Be Accounted For	100,000
(b) Quantity Accounted For:	
Transferred Out to Finished Goods	
No Rust	64,000
No Grease	31,000
Total to Finished Goods	95,000
Work in Process—Ending	5,000
Total Accounted For	100,000

COST SCHEDULE	TOTAL COST	E.P. UNITS	UNIT COST
(c) Costs to Be Accounted For:			
Materials—Beginning Work in Process	$ 4,800		
Added in Current Month	49,200		
Total Materials	$54,000 ÷ 100,000 =		$.540
Labor—Beginning Work in Process	$ 508		
Added in Current Month	12,232		
Total Labor	$12,740 ÷ 98,000 =		.130
Overhead—Beginning Work in Process	$ 752		
Added in Current Month	17,868		
Total Overhead	$18,620 ÷ 98,000 =		.190
Total Costs to Be Accounted For	$85,360		$.860
(d) Costs Accounted For:			
No Rust	$55,040 = 64,000 × $.860		
No Grease	26,660 = 31,000 × $.860		
Total Transferred Out	$81,700		
Work in Process—Ending			
Materials	$ 2,700 = 5,000 × $.540		
Labor	390 = 3,000 × $.130		
Overhead	570 = 3,000 × $.190		
Total Work in Process	$ 3,660		
Total Costs Accounted For	$85,360		

Analysis of the Method

Note the following features of this method:

- The physical unit (the liter) is easy to use because the products are measured in liters.
- The cost is easily distributed between the two products.
- The cost of each product is shown in the monthly cost of production report.

- Unit costs for both products are identical because they were computed by dividing the total cost by the total units.
- No consideration is given to relative sales values, special processing or handling required, the content of the product, or other special characteristics.
- Not all costs are directly related to physical quantities.

At this point you should be able to work Exercises 19–1 and 19–2.

SELF-REVIEW

1. How are joint products similar to by-products? How do the two differ?
2. What factor determines whether a product is classified as a joint product or as a by-product?
3. When there are joint products, how are equivalent units of production computed?
4. Under what conditions can the common physical unit method for allocating joint costs be used? What are the major advantages of the common physical unit method?
5. What are the major disadvantages of the common physical unit method for allocating costs?

Answers to Self-Review

1. Joint products are similar to by-products in that both are produced together with other products from a common process. The two differ in that a by-product has very little value in comparison to the main product(s) being produced, whereas each of the two or more joint products has significant value in comparison with other significant products.
2. The factor that determines whether a product is classified as joint product or as a by-product is its value in comparison with other products. To have joint products, there must be two or more products and each must have significant value.
3. Equivalent units of production are based on some factor that can be measured for both products (such as a physical unit, the relative sales value, or the adjusted sales value), or they are computed on the basis of assigned weights.
4. The common physical unit method can be used for the allocation basis when there is some common physical measure of production. The physical measure may be observed directly (such as gallons, pounds, or tons), or it may be based on some indirect measure (such as relative heat content, expressed in British thermal units).
5. The major disadvantages of using common physical measures to allocate joint costs arise from the fact that there may be little relationship between costs and physical units and that the two products may have much different sales prices per unit.

ALLOCATION ON BASIS OF RELATIVE SALES VALUE

The relative sales value method of allocating joint costs is used very often. It is based on the theory that the product with the higher selling price should bear a proportionately higher share of the common costs. Under this procedure, costs are set for each product, so that they will yield a uniform rate of gross profit.

Procedure to Allocate the Costs

The cost accountant for Alto would use a four-step procedure to allocate the costs by this method.

Step 1. Compute the total sales value of the joint products by multiplying the number of units by the unit sales price. For illustrative purposes, assume a sales price per liter of $1.20 for No Rust and $1.60 for No Grease.

Product	No. of Units	Sales Value per Unit	Total Sales Value
No Rust	64,000	$1.20	$ 76,800
No Grease	31,000	1.60	49,600
Total Sales Value			$126,400

Step. 2. Calculate the percentage of total sales value that each product represents by dividing each product's total sales value by the total sales value of all products.

$$\frac{\text{Sales Value of No Rust}}{\text{Sales Value of All Products}} = \frac{\$76,800}{\$126,400} = 60.76\%$$

$$\frac{\text{Sales Value of No Grease}}{\text{Sales Value of All Products}} = \frac{\$49,600}{\$126,400} = \underline{39.24\%}$$

$$100.00\%$$

Step 3. Allocate a portion of the cost to each product by multiplying the total cost assigned to finished products ($81,700) by the percentage computed in Step 2.

Allocated to No Rust	60.76% × $81,700 = $49,640.92
Allocated to No Grease	39.24% × $81,700 = 32,059.08
Total Cost Associated	$81,700.00

Step 4. Determine the unit cost for each product by dividing the total cost of the product by the number of units produced. (Because of the large number of units and the low unit cost, calculations have been carried to five decimal places and rounded to four places.)

$$\frac{\text{Total Cost of No Rust}}{\text{Liters Produced}} = \frac{\$49,640.92}{64,000} = \$.7756 \text{ per liter}$$

$$\frac{\text{Total Cost of No Grease}}{\text{Liters Produced}} = \frac{\$32,059.08}{31,000} = \$1.0342 \text{ per liter}$$

Eventually, the amounts to be allocated are listed in Costs Accounted For, Section (d) of the firm's cost of production report (shown on page 460). Note that the total transferred out ($81,700) is the same as under the physical unit basis, but the total and average unit costs for each product are different. The average unit cost for a liter of No Rust is $.7756, and the average unit cost for a liter of No Grease is $1.0342.

(d) Costs Accounted For:

Transferred Out to Finished Goods

No Rust	$49,640.92 ÷ 64,000 = $ .7756	
No Grease	2,059.08 ÷ 31,000 = $1.0342	
Total Transferred Out	$81,700.00	

Work in Process—Ending

Materials	$ 2,700.00 = 5,000 × $.540	
Labor	390.00 = 3,000 × $.130	
Overhead	570.00 = 3,000 × $.190	
Total Work in Process	$ 3,660.00	
Total Costs Accounted For	$85,360.00	

Analysis of the Method

At this point you should be able to work Exercises 19–3 and 19–4 and Problems 19–1A and 19–1B.

Note the following features of this method:

- The computations are slightly more involved than those required by the physical unit basis.
- Costs are allocated in proportion to what products are worth.
- Both the total and the unit costs are easily allocated to products.

SELF-REVIEW

1. Explain briefly the relative sales value method for allocating joint costs.
2. What is the basic theory underlying the relative sales value of allocation?
3. Is the relative sales value method for allocating joint costs useful in setting the selling prices of products? Explain.
4. What is the main shortcoming of the relative sales method for allocating joint costs?
5. If sales prices change frequently, would the relative sales method be a logical basis for allocating joint costs? Explain.

Answers to Self-Review

1. With the relative sales value method for allocating joint costs, the total sales value of each joint product is computed. The total sales values of all products are added. The part of joint costs to be allocated to a product is the ratio of that product's sales value to the total sales values of all products.
2. The basic theory underlying the relative sales value basis for allocating joint costs is that the product with the higher selling price should bear a proportionately higher share of the common costs.
3. The cost allocated to a product on the basis of relative sales value cannot be used to set prices. Under this method, prices determine the costs to be allocated; costs do not determine prices.
4. The main shortcoming of the relative sales value method for allocating joint costs is that it is based on the assumption that prices determine cost. Also, it ignores the fact that some joint costs may be the result of the special requirements of one of the products in the joint production process.
5. If sales prices changes frequently, the relative sales value method would not be appropriate because it might result in wide differences in costs from month to month.

■ The costs are shown on the monthly cost of production report.
■ There is an implication that selling price determines cost, whereas cost may not be directly related to sales value. Alternatively, costs may determine selling price.
■ It is assumed that all products should yield the same rate of gross profit.
■ Changing prices may produce wide differences in costs from month to month.
■ The method is frequently used when the products do not have the same physical characteristics.

ALLOCATION ON BASIS OF ADJUSTED SALES VALUE

If the joint products must be processed further before sale, the relative sales value method of allocation does not measure the true value of the products at the point of their separation. The additional processing costs must be deducted from the sales value before the cost allocation is made. Similarly, if the costs of selling the products vary widely because of advertising, transportation costs, or different methods of distribution, it may be desirable to deduct the estimated selling costs from the sales prices in order to arrive at adjusted relative sales values to use as the basis for allocation.

To see how this procedure works, assume that the sales price of No Rust remains at $1.20 per liter but that No Grease must be processed further after its separation to make it marketable. The additional costs of processing the 31,000 liters of No Grease during June are labor, $2,015, and overhead, $2,635.

The allocation of the $81,700 of joint costs between the two products would be computed in the same four steps used to allocate costs by relative sales value. In Step 1, however, the cost of any additional processing needed for completion is deducted from the sales value to find the adjusted sales value. The adjusted sales value is then used in later computation steps.

Step 1: Adjusted Sales Value

Product	No. of Units	Sales Value per Unit	Sales Value	Additional Completion Cost	Adjusted Sales Value
No Rust	64,000	$1.20	$76,800	-0-	$ 76,800
No Grease	31,000	1.60	49,600	$4,650	44,950
Total Sales Value					$121,750

Step 2: Percent of Total Value

$$\frac{\text{Sales Value of No Rust}}{\text{Sales Value of All Products}} = \frac{\$76,800}{\$121,750} = 63.08\%$$

$$\frac{\text{Sales Value of No Grease}}{\text{Sales Value of All Products}} = \frac{\$44,950}{\$121,750} = \frac{36.92\%}{100.00\%}$$

Step 3: Allocation of Cost

Allocated to No Rust	63.08% × $81,700 =	$51,536.36
Allocated to No Grease	36.92% × $81,700 =	30,163.64
		$81,700.00

Step 4: Cost per Unit

$$\frac{\text{Total Cost of No Rust}}{\text{Liters Produced}} = \frac{\$51,536.36}{64,000} = \$.8053 \text{ per liter}$$

$$\frac{\text{Total Cost of No Grease}}{\text{Liters Produced}} = \frac{\$30,163.64}{31,000} = \$.9730 \text{ per liter}$$

BUSINESS HORIZON

Who Knows What the Cost of a Joint Product Is?

For decades, cost accountants have argued over how to determine the costs of products resulting from a joint production process—that is, how to determine how much of the joint costs applies to each product emerging from the process. Unfortunately, it is a debate that no one will win because there is simply no scientific answer to the question. Nevertheless, the argument goes on, and over the years certain examples have been used to drive home one argument or the other.

One of the most common examples concerns how the costs of raising and slaughtering a steer for consumption should be allocated between the various "cuts" of beef. The costs of acquiring the young animal, feed, medication, other care, and the slaughtering and butchering are all joint costs. And after the steer is dressed, different kinds of marketable products result: Hamburger, T-bone steaks, rump roasts, round steaks, soup bones, liver and other internal organs, brisket, and other cuts of beef are some of the usual products. The basic problem is that the selling prices per pound of the individual products vary greatly from the choice steaks to the soup bones. When the cost accountant is asked: "What is the cost per pound of this product?" (in reference to hamburger, for example), the wrong question has been asked. The question should be: "What cost are you going to allocate to this product?"

If the total cost of raising and butchering a steer is $750 and the total weight of all products is 600 pounds, the simple answer is that hamburger costs $1.25 per pound, T-bone steak costs $1.25 per pound, and soup bones cost $1.25 per pound. But, if soup bone sells for $.85 per pound, hamburger for $1.25 per pound, and T-bone steak for $3.75 per pound, the profit per pound of T-bone steaks is $2.50, there is neither profit nor loss on hamburger, and the soup bone is being sold at a loss of $.40 per pound. These results seem illogical to most accountants (and to others). Why would the butcher sell products that result in no profit (soup bones and hamburger)? (with each product having the same cost).

At this point the accountant concludes that the literal cost computed for each pound serves no basis for decision making and may not be a reasonable approach to measuring profit. A common conclusion reached is that the steer is raised and butchered to yield all the products that emerge. The total profit on the steer is found by subtracting the total cost from the total selling price. Thus each pound contributes to profit in proportion to its selling price, and the cost should be allocated between each product on the basis of its sales value compared to each other product. Is this the relative sales value method that you have learned in this chapter? Does this truly result in a cost per pound of each product? The answer is no—it results in an *allocated* cost per pound.

The new allocation of costs is shown in Costs Accounted For, Section (d) of the following cost of production report. (The remainder of the cost of production report is identical with the illustration on page 457.) Again, the total and average unit costs for each product are different.

(d) Costs Accounted For:	
No Rust—to Finished Goods	$51,536.36 ÷ 64,000 = $.8052
No Grease—to Next Department	$30,163.64 ÷ 31,000 = $.9730
Total Transferred Out	$81,700.00
Work in Process—Ending	
Materials	$ 2,700.00 = 5,000 × $.540
Labor	390.00 = 3,000 × $.130
Overhead	570.00 = 3,000 × $.190
Total Work in Process	$ 3,660.00
Total Costs Accounted For	$85,360.00

Analysis of the Method

At this point you should be able to work Exercises 19–5 and 19–6 and Problems 19–3A to 19–4B.

Note the following features of the method:

■ The computations are very similar to those made when the relative sales value method is used.
■ The costs may present a truer picture of the values at the point of separation of the products.
■ The procedures involved are simple and relatively easy to apply.
■ The cost allocations are still derived from the market price, which may have little or no relationship to the actual cost.

ALLOCATION ON BASIS OF ASSIGNED WEIGHTS

Each time a method of costing has been analyzed, it has become increasingly evident that there is no single completely accurate and satisfactory basis for allocating joint costs. For this reason, many cost accountants develop their own formulas for apportionment. They consider many factors involved in the manufacturing and marketing processes, such as volume and weight, technical processing, selling costs, and selling prices. They use this survey data to prepare an allocation formula expressed in terms of assigned weights (a percentage, or points) to show how to divide joint costs. This allocation technique is sometimes called the *survey method.*

For example, it may be decided that based on difficulty of handling, volume, and the production manager's understanding of the production process that each liter of No Rust should be assigned a weight of 3 points, and each liter of No Grease a weight of 4 points. Thus the joint costs for April would be allocated between the two products in the ratio of 192,000 to 124,000, as shown on page 464.

Product	Liters Produced	Weight Assigned	Weighted Production	Percent of Total
No Rust	64,000	3	192,000	60.759
No Grease	31,000	4	124,000	39.241
Total Weighted Production			316,000	100.000

Analysis of the Method

At this point you should be able to work Exercises 19–7 and 19–8 and Problems 19–4A and 19–4B.

LIMITATIONS OF JOINT COSTING

Note the following features of this method:

- It may often yield more logical costs than any single allocation basis.
- The determination of weights is complicated, especially when many products are involved.
- Weight assignment is, in the long run, a rather arbitrary process.

It is obviously impossible to allocate joint costs precisely to each product. At best, the cost accountant may determine what appears to be a reasonable cost for each product. In view of the various ways in which costs may be allocated, the resulting figures should be used with extreme caution. For example, it would be completely unrealistic

SELF-REVIEW

1. What is the adjusted sales value method of allocating joint costs?
2. When is it appropriate to use the adjusted sales value method?
3. What is the major shortcoming of the adjusted sales value method?
4. Explain briefly the allocation by assigned weights method for allocating joint costs.
5. If joint costs are assigned on the basis of weights assigned to the products, how are those weights determined?

Answers to Self-Review

1. The adjusted sales value allocation method is designed for use when one or more of the joint products must be processed further after separation. Under this method, the sales price of each product is reduced by the costs incurred after separation.
2. It is appropriate to use the adjusted sales value method when one or more of the products requires additional processing costs after the point of separation.
3. The major shortcoming of the adjusted sales value method is that the costs are derived from the market price, which may bear little relation to actual costs.
4. With the allocation by assigned weights method, each unit of each product is assigned a weight that usually reflects many factors involved in the manufacturing process. These weights are based on engineering information, relative volumes and weights of products, and other factors.
5. Assigned weights are based on the observations of production personnel, the cost accountant, engineers, and others who are in a position to observe and evaluate factors that affect production costs.

in most cases to use these allocated costs as a basis for setting selling prices of individual products or for making other managerial decisions. Joint costing, in the role it usually plays in manufacturing, can probably best be described as a means of estimating a cost figure for valuation of finished goods inventories. Since most manufacturing businesses using process accounting have small inventories of work in process and the inventories do not vary greatly from year to year, the method chosen is not likely to have a great impact on either the income statement or the balance sheet. For management purposes, a cost allocation method is usually chosen because it most nearly provides a cost that is logical and reasonable in the circumstances. Frequently, accountants must rely heavily on the assistance of engineers, production managers, and others in developing a reasonable allocation basis.

PRINCIPLES AND PROCEDURES SUMMARY

- Joint products are produced when two or more products, all of significant value, result from a single manufacturing process.
- A system must be devised to allocate joint costs to the joint products on some equitable and logical basis.
- One of four methods is usually used to allocate joint costs to joint products: physical units, relative sales value, adjusted sales value, or assigned weights.
- Physical units may be used as the basis of allocating costs when the units of production of each product are expressed in the same unit or can be converted to a common unit. This method may not always reflect actual manufacturing costs, and thus the revenue produced from each product may not be accounted for.
- Relative sales value is often used to allocate joint costs on the basis that each product should absorb a part of the costs reflecting the product's sales value. This method is based on the premise that selling prices determine cost and ignores the fact that costs may not be affected by selling price. It also ignores costs that must be incurred on a product after its separation from other products.
- The adjusted sales price basis recognizes that sales value does not reflect value at the point of separation. Postseparation costs are deducted from sales value to arrive at the basis for allocation under this method.
- Sometimes responsible personnel may assign weights to the units of each product that reflect their judgment about the relative importance of each factor in determining joint costs.
- Joint costing is not an exact procedure. Each method produces different costs, and none is completely accurate. The limitations of these methods should be kept in mind when using the figures obtained.
- It is appropriate for the accountant and management to select an allocation basis that is logical and reasonable for the purpose at hand. This means that different allocation bases may be used for different purposes.

MANAGERIAL IMPLICATIONS

- When a basis for allocating joint costs is chosen, the purpose of the allocation must be kept in mind.
- The main reason for allocating joint costs to joint products is to arrive at inventory values for financial reporting purposes and for income tax purposes. For this purpose, it is customary to use either a physical units basis or a relative sales value basis.
- Some common uses of joint cost allocations other than financial reporting and income tax reporting are to determine costs required under contractual arrangements, to provide a cost for intercompany pricing for products transferred between divisions, to compute profits for the purpose of determining managerial bonuses, and (very infrequently) for setting the prices of products.
- In making decisions such as whether to process a joint product further or to sell it at the point of separation, the key question is how additional costs incurred to complete the product compare with the increased value.
- In meeting contractual terms, for example, when a company sells a product under terms that call for a price equal to the product's cost plus some fixed amount or percentage of cost, the cost accountant must make every effort to be sure that the cost allocation method reflects cause and effect.
- In selecting a basis for allocating joint costs, the accountants should consult with engineers, production managers, and other knowledgeable individuals to make sure that the basis chosen is logical and reasonable in the circumstances and for the purpose at hand.

REVIEW QUESTIONS

1. Explain how joint products and by-products are different.
2. At what point in the production process do joint costs occur?
3. Under what circumstances will physical units of measure provide an appropriate basis for allocating joint costs?
4. What are the basic assumptions underlying the sales value method of allocating joint costs?
5. What are the major criticisms of the relative sales value method of allocating joint costs?
6. How does the adjusted sales value method of allocation differ from the relative sales value method?
7. Explain briefly how to apply the adjusted sales value method of allocation.
8. What factors are considered in assigning the weights if joint costs are to be allocated on the basis of assigned weights?
9. If one of the joint products requires further processing and the other one does not, would the relative sales value method be an appropriate allocation method? Explain.

10. Do you think that it would be appropriate for a company to use different allocation methods in allocating joint costs if the results are to be used for different purposes? Explain.

11. How does the monthly production report differ when a manufacturing process produces joint products rather than a single product?

12. Is the method used to compute the equivalent units of production for joint products the same as the method used for a single product? Explain.

MANAGERIAL DISCUSSION QUESTIONS

1. You are chief accountant for your company, which manufactures three joint products. The company president has told you that it is very important for the costs of the three products to be determined accurately because the company is negotiating a contract to sell a substantial part of its product on a cost-plus basis to a major defense contractor. The contract will call for a sales price equal to manufacturing cost, plus 25 percent. What do you think of this proposal? Do you have any suggestions for items to be included in the contract?

2. Your company produces two joint products, both of which are sold at the point of separation. Management is trying to decide whether one of the products should be further processed before being sold. What factors should be considered in making this decision?

3. Your company manufactures three joint products. After separation, the three products are transferred to three different sales organizations in the company. The products are charged to the three organizations on the basis of cost, using an allocation based on physical units. Under what circumstances might this be an appropriate cost-determination method for this purpose? Under what circumstances would it not be an appropriate method?

4. Assume that the only use made of joint product costing in the company for which you work is to arrive at an inventory carrying value and, consequently, the income reported in each period. To what extent does this affect the decision about which cost allocation method to use? Explain.

5. Your company has been using the relative sales value method for allocating joint costs. The products are similar in physical quantity but have substantial differences in price per unit. Management does not understand why the cost of one unit of product A is much greater than that for product B. The president has expressed the idea that relative sales value allocation results in too much profit for the higher-priced product. She has asked you for a one-paragraph written opinion on the proper accounting methodology. Prepare your response.

EXERCISE 19–1   **Allocate joint costs on the basis of physical units.   (Obj. 1).**   As a result of the manufacturing process, the Extraction Department of the Big Sky Company produces two joint products. During March 19X9, the total manufacturing costs of the goods transferred out of the department were $59,920. A total of 12,000 pounds of Ethno, with a sales value of $6 per pound, and 7,000 pounds of Methno, with a sales value of $9 per pound, were produced. Determine the cost per pound of each product if physical units are used as the basis for allocating joint costs.

EXERCISE 19–2   **Allocate joint costs on the basis of physical units.   (Obj. 1).**   The Raif Company produces oil and gas from the same wells. During October 19X9, the total operating costs of a lease were $68,000. Production was 6,000 barrels of oil and 20,000 cubic feet of gas. Each barrel of oil has about 6 times the energy content of a thousand cubic feet (an mcf.) of gas. What total cost should be allocated to the oil produced and to the gas produced if energy content (a physical unit) is to be used as the basis of the allocation?

EXERCISE 19–3   **Allocate joint costs on the basis of relative sales value.   (Obj. 2).**   Assume the same data as in Exercise 1. Determine the cost per pound of each product if relative sales value is used as the basis for allocating joint costs.

EXERCISE 19–4   **Allocate joint costs on the basis of relative sales value.   (Obj. 2).**   Assume the same facts as in Exercise 2. In addition, assume that the oil sold for $20 per barrel and the gas sold for $2 per mcf. What total cost should be allocated to the oil produced and to the gas produced if relative sales value is to be used as the basis of allocation?

EXERCISE 19–5   **Allocate joint costs on the basis of adjusted sales value.   (Obj. 3).**   The total manufacturing costs applicable to two joint products transferred out of a department in July 19X9 were $30,000. As a result of the manufacturing process, 5,000 units of Strano (a finished product) were produced. The sales value of Strano was $6 per unit. In addition, 6,000 units of Therono were produced. Therono must be further processed at an estimated cost of $2 per unit before it can be sold for $7 per unit. Using the adjusted sales value method, compute the total joint costs to be assigned to each product in July 19X9.

EXERCISE 19–6   **Allocate joint costs to products on the basis of physical units, relative sales price, and adjusted relative sales price.   (Objs. 1, 2, 3).**   The following information relates to the costs and production for the Condensing Department of Lawn Products Inc. for the month of July 19X9.

Product	Units Produced
No Bug	10,000 pounds, sales price of $1.50 per pound with no additional manufacturing costs after separation
Ant Rid	10,000 pounds, sales price of $2 per pound with additional manufacturing costs of $.35 per pound after separation

The total manufacturing costs applicable to No Bug and Ant Rid in this department were $21,000. Compute the amount of joint costs to be allocated to each pound of each product using the following bases:
a. Physical units (pounds)
b. Relative sales price
c. Adjusted relative sales price

EXERCISE 19–7

Allocate joint costs on the basis of assigned weights. (Obj. 4). The total costs of two joint products transferred out of the final producing department of the Samuelson Company during June 19X9 were $160,000. As a result of the manufacturing process, 20,000 units of Arotate and 6,000 units of Belmar were produced. Based on the difficulty of handling the products, additional sales efforts necessary, and other factors, the cost accountant has decided to use the survey method to allocate costs. Each unit of Belmar has been assigned a weight of 2, and each unit of Arotate has been assigned a weight of 3. Determine the total cost and the cost per unit to be assigned to each product for the month.

EXERCISE 19–8

Allocate joint costs on the basis of assigned weights. (Obj. 4). At the output of the Steaming Department of Cambridge Corporation, the two joint products must be physically separated. Because of the physical characteristics of one of the products, the separation is quite difficult and requires a great deal of labor. As a result, management and the cost accountant have decided to allocate joint costs on the basis of physical units (pounds) but to assign to each pound of Rawhide a factor of 1.5, and to each pound of the second product, Toppro, a factor of 1. During the month of November 19X9, 5,200 pounds of Rawhide and 4,800 pounds of Toppro were produced. Total joint costs were $16,800. Compute the total cost and the cost per pound to be allocated to each of the products.

PROBLEMS

PROBLEM 19–1A

Allocate joint costs on the basis of relative sales value and physical units. (Objs. 1, 2). The Wyoming Petroleum Company owns a well that produces both crude oil and natural gas. During the year 19X9, the well produced 2,800 barrels of oil, which were sold at $16 per barrel and 80,000 thousand cubic feet (mcf.) of natural gas, which were sold at $2.50 per mcf. Total costs of producing the oil and the gas were $36,000. Two proposals have been made for allocating the costs of production to the gas and the oil:

▪ On the basis of relative sales value.
▪ On the basis of relative heat content, a physical unit measured in British thermal units (BTUs). Each barrel of oil contains about 6 times as many BTUs as each mcf. of natural gas.

INSTRUCTIONS

1. Compute the total cost and the cost per unit to be allocated to gas and to oil under each of the proposed methods. Round off the unit costs to four decimal places.
2. Briefly compare the effects on costs of the two bases.
3. What factors should a cost accountant consider in choosing a basis?

PROBLEM 19–2A

Allocate joint costs on the basis of physical units, relative sales value, and adjusted relative sales value. (Objs. 1, 2, 3, 5). The Illinois Chemical Company uses a manufacturing process that produces two major products, Malovin and Namotex. In the first department, the raw materials are mixed and treated. In the second department, some raw materials are added, the mix is further processed, and the two products are then separated. Cost and production data for the second department for the month of June 19X9 are as follows:

	Quantity	Cost
Materials Transferred In From Prior Department	125,000 kg	$32,000
Materials Added in This Department	30,000 kg	3,000
Labor Added in This Department		1,800
Manufacturing Overhead Added in This Department		1,200
Finished Products Transferred Out		
Malovin	100,000 kg	
Namotex	50,000 kg	
Units Lost in Production (evaporation)	5,000 kg	

There was no beginning or ending work in process inventory. Malovin has a sales price of $.36 per kilogram, and Namotex has a sales price of $.32 per kilogram. Estimated selling and administrative expenses are Malovin, $.09 per kilogram, and Namotex, $.02 per kilogram.

INSTRUCTIONS

1. Prepare schedules showing the allocation of each element of manufacturing cost to each kilogram of Malovin and each kilogram of Namotex, using the following assumptions. (Round off the unit costs to the nearest one-tenth of a cent.)
   a. Costs are allocated to the joint products on a per-kilogram basis.
   b. Costs are allocated to the two products on the basis of relative sales value.
   c. Costs are allocated to each product on the basis of adjusted sales value (the sales price less applicable selling and administrative expenses).
2. Prepare a cost of production report for the second department for the month of June 19X9, assuming that costs are allocated on the basis of relative sales value.
3. Prepare condensed income statements showing the profit that would be reported on each product under each of the three allocation methods.

PROBLEM 19–3A **Allocate joint costs on the basis of relative sales value and adjusted relative sales value. (Objs. 2, 3).** The Utah Corporation has a single manufacturing process that results in two products. Chemtalic, a powder, has a sales price of $4 per pound. Magic Mix, a liquid, has a sales price of $10 per gallon. During December 19X9, total manufacturing costs in the final department were $98,000. Production for the month consisted of 30,000 pounds of Chemtalic and 12,000 gallons of Magic Mix. Because of its volatile nature, Magic Mix must be carefully packed in a special container. The costs of packing and selling Magic Mix are $3.50 per gallon. The costs of packing and selling Chemtalic are $.50 per pound.

INSTRUCTIONS 1. Compute the cost to be allocated to each unit of each product for December 19X9, under the following assumptions:
   a. The relative sales value method is used to allocate costs.
   b. The adjusted relative sales value method is used to allocate costs.
2. Briefly compare the effects of the two methods of allocating costs.

PROBLEM 19–4A   **Allocate joint costs on the basis of physical units and relative sales value; compute the profit or loss per pound; and evaluate allocation methods. (Objs. 1, 2, 6).** Two products result from production activities in the Separation Department of the Heraklion Company. Each pound of raw material placed into production in the department results in $\frac{1}{4}$ pound of Xano and $\frac{3}{4}$ pound of Citrotex. Xano sells for $1.20 per pound, and Citrotex sells for $2.50 per pound. Data for June 19X9 are given below. There was no beginning or ending work in process inventory.

Total raw materials placed in production in the department	104,000 pounds
Manufacturing costs incurred in the department	
Raw materials	$166,400
Labor and overhead	20,800

INSTRUCTIONS 1. Compute the cost allocated to each pound of Xano and to each pound of Citrotex if joint costs are allocated on the basis of physical units (pounds).
2. Compute the cost allocated to each pound of Xano and to each pound of Citrotex if joint costs are allocated on the basis of relative sales value.
3. Compute the gross profit or loss on Xano and on Citrotex based on the computations in Instructions 1 and 2.
4. Which of the cost allocation methods used above is preferable? Explain.

ALTERNATE PROBLEMS

PROBLEM 19–1B **Allocate joint costs on the basis of physical units and relative sales value. (Objs. 1, 2).** The Regional Petroleum Company owns a well that produces both crude oil and natural gas. During the year 19X9 the well produced 6,000 barrels of oil, which were sold at $18 per barrel, and 100,000 thousand cubic feet (mcf.) of natural gas, which were sold at $1.75 per mcf. Total costs of producing the oil and the gas were $143,000. Two proposals have been made for allocating the costs of production to gas and oil.

■ On the basis of relative sales value.
■ On the basis of relative heat content, measured in British thermal units (BTUs). Each barrel of oil contains about 6 times as many BTUs as each mcf. of natural gas.

INSTRUCTIONS

1. Compute the total cost and the cost per unit to be allocated to gas and to oil under each of the proposed methods. Round off the unit costs to four decimal places.
2. Briefly compare the effects on costs of the two bases.
3. What factors should a cost accountant consider in choosing a basis?

PROBLEM 19–2B **Allocate joint costs on the basis of physical units, relative sales value, and adjusted relative sales value. (Objs. 1, 2, 3).** Clower Materials Company uses a manufacturing process that produces two major products, Fluridine and Valodine. In the first department, the raw materials are mixed and treated. In the second department, some raw materials are added, the mix is further processed, and the two products are then separated. Cost and production data for the second department for the month of August 19X9 are as follows:

	Quantity	Cost
Materials Transferred in From Prior Department	120,000 gal	$360,000
Materials Added in This Department	30,000 gal	45,000
Labor Added in This Department		12,000
Manufacturing Overhead Added in This Department		18,000
Finished Products Transferred Out		
Fluridine	80,000 gal	
Valodine	50,000 gal	
Units Lost in Production (evaporation)	20,000 gal	

There was no beginning or ending work in process inventory. Floridan has a sales price of $7 per gallon, and Valodine has a sales price of $6 per gallon. It is estimated that selling and administrative expenses are $2.40 per gallon for Floridan and $.80 per gallon for Valodine.

INSTRUCTIONS

1. Prepare schedules showing the allocation of each element of manufacturing cost to each gallon of Fluridine and each gallon of Valodine, using the assumptions listed below. (Round off the unit costs to the nearest one-tenth of a cent.)
   a. Costs are allocated to the joint products on a per-gallon basis.
   b. Costs are allocated to the two products on the basis of relative sales value.

c. Costs are allocated to each product on the basis of adjusted relative sales value (the sales price less applicable selling and administrative expenses).

2. Prepare a cost of production report for the second department for the month of August 19X9 assuming that costs are allocated on the basis of relative sales value.

3. Prepare condensed income statements showing the profit that would be reported on each product under each of the three allocation methods.

PROBLEM 19–3B

Allocate joint costs on the basis of relative sales value and adjusted relative sales value. (Objs. 1, 2, 3). The Sea Hawk Company has a single manufacturing process that results in two products. Salonide, a salt, has a sales price of $1.80 per kilogram, and Sorex, a liquid, has a sales price of $5.40 per liter. During May 19X9, total manufacturing costs in the final department were $70,800. Production for the month was 20,000 kilograms of Salonide and 15,000 liters of Sorex. Additional costs to process Sorex are estimated to be $.50 per liter.

INSTRUCTIONS

1. Compute the cost to be allocated to each unit of each product for May 19X9, under the following assumptions:
   a. The relative sales value method is used to allocate costs.
   b. The adjusted relative sales value method is used to allocate costs.

2. Briefly compare the effects of the two methods of allocating costs.

PROBLEM 19–4B

Allocate joint costs on basis of physical units and relative sales value; compute the profit or loss per unit. (Objs. 1, 2, 6). The manufacturing process in the Cooking Department of the Economy Paint Company produces two products. Each gallon of raw material placed into production in the department results in 3 quarts of Super Coat and 1 quart of Basic Coat. Super Coat has a sales price of $4 per quart, and Basic Coat has a sales price of $2.25 per quart. Data for July 19X9 are given below. There was no beginning or ending work in process inventory.

Total raw materials placed in production in the department	40,000 gallons
Manufacturing costs incurred in the department	
Materials	$350,000
Labor and overhead	85,000

INSTRUCTIONS

1. Compute the cost allocated to each quart of Super Coat and the cost allocated to each quart of Basic Coat if joint costs are allocated on the basis of physical units (quarts).

2. Compute the cost allocated to each quart of Super Coat and to each quart of Basic Coat if joint costs are allocated on the basis of relative sale value.

3. Compute the gross profit or loss on Super Coat and on Basic Coat based on the computations in Instructions 1 and 2.
4. Which of the cost allocation methods used above is preferable? Explain.

MANAGERIAL DECISION CASES

Case 19–1. The following data relate to the manufacturing process of Malibu Industries, which produces two joint products:

Joint Costs

Materials	$120,000
Labor	60,000
Overhead	40,000

Production

Thelodine	6,000 pounds. Sales price, $42 per pound; additional costs to package and sell, $7 per pound.
Santosen	4,000 pounds. Sales price, $40 per pound; additional costs to package and sell, $4 per pound.

The production manager has proposed that management consider a small change in the manufacturing process. If the material is cooked slightly longer, the ratio of production for the two products can be changed to 50 percent each. However, as a result of the increased cooking time, there would be a shrinkage of 3 percent in volume, and additional labor costs of $1,400 per month would be incurred. There would be no change in the sales or the selling cost per unit.

Prepare an analysis of the current profitability and the future profitability if the proposed manufacturing change were to be made. What course of action would you recommend that management take?

Case 19–2. Renaldo Corporation produces two medicinal compounds from a joint process. The manufacturing process can be varied slightly to produce different proportions of its two joint products, Gastro Ease and Digesto, at no additional cost. Digesto must be further processed at a cost of $.30 per pound of finished product after separation. Total capacity of the Cooking Department is 10,000 pounds per month. The company can sell up to 8,000 pounds of Gastro Ease each month at $10 per pound. It can also sell up to 4,000 pounds of Digesto for $11.50 per pound. However, because of the manufacturing process used for Digesto after separation, it takes 1.25 pounds of the product at the point of separation to manufacture 1 pound of Digesto. For example, if the company decides to manufacture 4,000 pounds of Digesto, it will require an output of 5,000 pounds of the joint product from the Cooking Department. Joint costs for 10,000 pounds of departmental output are shown on page 475.

Materials	$40,000
Labor	9,000
Overhead	15,000

1. If the company decides to continue producing both Gastro Ease and Digesto, what will be the gross profit on each product, assuming that the physical units method of allocation is used and the maximum amount of Digesto is produced?
2. If the company decides to produce both products but to produce the maximum amount of Gastro Ease, what will the gross profit be, assuming that the physical units method of allocation is used?
3. If the company decides to produce Gastro Ease only, what will the gross profit be?
4. Based on gross profit alone, which alternative should the company select?
5. What factors other than gross profit should be considered in deciding whether to continue producing Digesto?

Process Cost Accounting

In this practice set you will apply the techniques and principles of process cost accounting to record and summarize the flow of costs connected with the Newtek Chemical Corporation for the month of January 19X9. In completing the project, you will make postings to the work in process accounts to record materials used, labor costs incurred, and manufacturing overhead costs. You will also compute equivalent production and complete the cost of production reports for producing departments. Then you will make entries to record the transfers of costs between departments, the recovery of a by-product, and the transfers of finished products from the final work in process inventory accounts to finished goods. However, in the interest of time you will not be required to make many of the routine entries to record costs, which you have learned to do in prior chapters. The practice set is designed to reinforce your knowledge of the essential elements of process cost accounting without the time-consuming work of detailed bookkeeping that would be required to record and post entries for individual transactions.

NEWTEK CHEMICAL CORPORATION

Newtek Chemical Corporation manufactures three main products that are sold to other chemical specialty companies and to hospitals. The continuous production operation starts in the Combining Department, where chemicals are mixed and subjected to electrical processing. Some of the mixture is transferred to the Butylprocessing Department, and the remainder to the Isotreatment Department. In the Butylprocessing Department, materials are added and the mixture is further processed. Two finished products, Butotek and HiButyl, are obtained and, on completion, are transferred to a refrigerated storeroom. The chemicals transferred from the Combining Department to the Isotreatment Department also receive further processing. In the process, a by-product is removed, and the main product, Isotone, is completed and transferred to the refrigerated storeroom.

The manufacturing flow is summarized by the diagram on page 477.

NEWTEK'S COST ACCOUNTING SYSTEM

The firm's process cost accounting system includes the usual journals and ledgers. All forms required to complete this practice set can be found in the *Study Guide and Working Papers*. If you are not using the *Study Guide and Working Papers*, you will have to record all such data on blank forms.

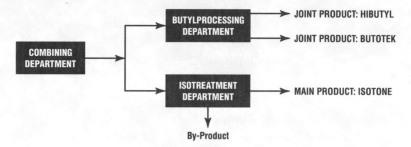

JOURNALS

Special journals have been omitted from this problem for the sake of simplicity. Cost data is supplied for each department as required.

GENERAL LEDGER

Newtek's chart of accounts includes the following accounts related to the flow of manufacturing costs. The January 1 balance for each account is given.

121	Raw Materials	-0-
123	Work in Process—Combining Department	$ 13,600 Dr.
124	Work in Process—Isotreatment Department	58,240 Dr.
125	Work in Process—Butylprocessing Department	22,400 Dr.
126	Finished Goods	143,200 Dr.
127	Inventory of By-Product	992 Dr.
500	Factory Payroll Clearing	-0-
501	Manufacturing Overhead Control	-0-

General ledger account forms are provided in the *Study Guide and Working Papers*. The January 1 balances have been entered. General ledger accounts for accounts 121, 500, and 501 are not provided, so you are not required to post to these accounts.

SUBSIDIARY LEDGERS

Three subsidiary cost ledgers are used in normal operations:

Materials Ledger
Departmental Overhead Analysis Sheets
Finished Goods Ledger

The first two ledgers are not provided because they are not required for the solution to this practice set. The finished goods ledger provided in the *Study Guide and Working Papers* contains separate accounts for Isotone, Butotek, and HiButyl. The January 1 balances, shown below, have been entered

Product	Balance Units	Price	Amount
Butotek	2,700	$16.00	$43,200
HiButyl	4,000	10.12	40,480
Isotone	3,000	19.84	59,520

The cost data accumulated for each department are given in summary form.

COMBINING DEPARTMENT

Prior period and current costs for the Combining Department are as follows:

Beginning Work in Process	
Materials	$ 4,000
Labor	5,120
Overhead	4,480
Balance of Accounts, Jan. 1	$14,600
Current Month	
Materials	$136,800
Labor	200,800
Overhead	276,320
Total Current Month's Costs	$613,920

BUTYLPROCESSING DEPARTMENT

The beginning inventory of the Butylprocessing Department includes costs in the prior department, as shown.

Beginning Work in Process	
Costs in Prior Department	$32,800
Costs in Current Department	
Materials	2,400
Labor	8,640
Overhead	14,400
Balance of Accounts, Jan. 1	$58,240
Current Month	
Materials	$ 55,200
Labor	154,560
Overhead	254,400
Total Current Month's Costs	$464,160

ISOTREATMENT DEPARTMENT

The Isotreatment Department's cost data also include prior elements.

Beginning Work in Process	$13,600
Costs in Prior Department	
Materials	3,200
Labor	2,400
Overhead	3,200
Balance of Accounts, Jan. 1	$22,400
Current Month	
Materials	$ 30,800
Labor	40,800
Overhead	51,680
Total Current Month's Costs	$123,280

PRODUCTION DATA

Data regarding the departmental operations during January are reported by the department managers. The monthly departmental production reports are shown below.

COMBINING DEPARTMENT
Monthly Production Report
January 19X9

Work in Process—Beginning	2,000 units
(All materials have been added; 25% of labor and overhead have been added.)	
Started in Production—Current Month	80,000 units
Completed and Transferred Out	
To Butylprocessing	48,000 units
To Isotreatment	28,000 units
Work in Process—Ending	4,000 units
(All materials have been added; 50% of labor and overhead have been added.)	
Lost in Production	2,000 units

BUTYLPROCESSING DEPARTMENT
Monthly Production Report
January 19X9

Work in Process—Beginning	4,000 units
(All materials have been added; 75% of labor and overhead have been added.)	
Transferred In From Combining Department	48,000 units
Finished Goods Transferred Out	
Butotek	28,000 units
HiButyl	18,000 units
Work in Process—Ending	4,000 units
(50% of materials have been added; 50% of labor and overhead have been added.)	
Lost in Production	2,000 units

ISOTREATMENT DEPARTMENT
Monthly Production Report
January 19X9

Work in Process—Beginning	2,000 units
(All materials have been added; 50% of labor and overhead have been added.)	
Transferred In From Combining Department	28,000 units
Increase in Number of Units Due to Added Materials	7,000 units
Main Product Completed and Transferred Out	34,000 units
Work in Process—Ending	3,000 units
(All materials have been added; $33\frac{1}{3}$% of labor and overhead have been added.)	
Lost in Production	2,000 units

In this practice set you will complete the following typical steps in the firm's cost accounting cycle. These steps represent the most important aspects of process cost accounting.

1. Charge the costs of materials used, direct labor, and manufacturing overhead to the producing departments.
2. Compute the equivalent production for each department.
3. Prepare a cost of production report for each department (carry the unit costs to four decimal places and round to three).
4. Transfer the costs from one process to another.
5. Transfer the value of any finished products to the Finished Goods account.
6. Transfer the value of any by-product to the Inventory of By-Product account. As you proceed, observe the specific instructions given.

CHARGING COSTS TO PRODUCTION

Each current cost element is to be charged to production by a general journal voucher entry. (The amounts are included in the cost data for each department.)

1. Record the entries on the general journal vouchers. Use the following voucher numbers: 1-1 for materials used, 1-2 for direct labor, and 1-3 for manufacturing overhead.
2. Post each entry to the general ledger accounts provided. (Be sure that you have entered the January 1, 19X9, balances given on pages 477 and 478, before posting to the accounts.)

DEPARTMENTAL PROCEDURES

Perform the departmental costing procedures as outlined below.

Combining Department. Complete the following steps to summarize and record the cost flow of this first department.

1. Compute the equivalent production using the average cost method for handling inventories.
2. Prepare a cost of production report.
3. Prepare a general journal voucher (1-4) to transfer costs out of the Combining Department to the Isotreatment Department and to the Butylprocessing Department. Then post this entry to the ledger accounts.

Butylprocessing Department. Complete the costing procedures outlined, giving careful attention to special directions.

1. Compute the equivalent production data using the average cost method.
2. Prepare a cost of production report. Show an adjustment for lost units on the report. Allocate joint production costs between the two finished products on the basis of the relative sales value of the products. Butotek sells for $36 per unit, and HiButyl sells

for $28 per unit. Show in a footnote to the report how you computed the joint cost allocation.

3. Prepare a general journal voucher (1-5) to transfer costs out of the Work in Process—Isotreatment Department account and into the Finished Goods account. Then post this entry to the general ledger accounts and to the two finished goods subsidiary ledger accounts affected. (Be sure that you have entered the January 1, 19X9, balances given on page 477 before posting to the accounts.)

Isotreatment Department. Complete the required cost procedures, including the recording of the by-product, as indicated.

1. Compute the equivalent units of production. Since the ending inventories are sometimes quite high, the company uses the first in, first out (FIFO) method of costing production in the department.

2. Prepare a cost of production report. Show an adjustment for the increase in units under Costs in Prior Department on the report, assuming that all materials are added in this department at the beginning of the departmental processing. Use the reversal cost method for assigning common costs to the by-product. This by-product material is collected and stored in bins. Periodically it is sent to a subcontractor who processes it for $1.36 per pound and returns it to the Newtek Chemical Corporation for resale. Newtek sells the by-product for $4.80 per pound after it has been treated. The company's normal gross margin on sales is 45 percent of the sales price. Show in a note to the cost of production report (Note B) your calculation of the amount to be assigned to the by-product. Because the total amount is small, the portion of the common costs assigned to the by-product is shown as a reduction in the costs of the units started and completed in the current month.

3. Prepare general journal vouchers to record the completion of the main product (1-6) and the recovery of the by-product (1-7). Post the entries to the appropriate general ledger and subsidiary ledger accounts.

PART THREE

Cost Accounting as a Management Tool

The Analysis of Cost Behavior

I n Parts 1 and 2 of this book you have seen how cost accounting is used to accumulate data about the costs of constructing, manufacturing, and selling goods or services. Cost accounting is also used in other ways. It helps management to plan future operations and to control and evaluate results, and it provides the basic data necessary for making managerial decisions.

OBJECTIVES

1. Explain the relationship between total costs and costs per unit for variable and fixed costs.
2. Estimate the costs that should be incurred when the number of hours worked, the fixed costs, and the variable costs per hour are known.
3. Classify costs as variable, fixed, or semivariable.
4. Analyze cost behavior using the scattergraph method for estimating variable and fixed components.
5. Analyze cost behavior using the high-low points method for estimating variable and fixed components.
6. Analyze cost behavior using the least squares method for estimating variable and fixed components.
7. Explain the engineering analysis and direct estimate methods of estimating variable and fixed components.

NEW TERMS

Cost behavior (p. 485)
Direct estimate method (p. 495)
Engineering analysis method (p. 489)
Fixed costs (p. 485)
High-low points method (p. 492)
Least squares method (p. 493)
Line of best fit (p. 493)
Scattergraph method (p. 491)
Semivariable costs (p. 487)
Stair-step costs (p. 488)
Variable costs (p. 485)

COST BEHAVIOR

One of the most basic concepts of cost accounting is cost behavior. **Cost behavior,** sometimes called *variability,* is the manner in which costs change as the volume (units of output, direct labor hours, or some other factor) changes. An understanding of cost behavior is essential to anyone who wishes to use accounting as a tool for planning, controlling, and evaluating operations. In general, costs can be classified as fixed, variable, or semivariable. A fourth category—stair-step—is also used by some accountants. Other accountants treat stair-step costs as a type of semivariable costs. Each of these important classifications will now be discussed.

Variable Costs

Variable costs are those costs that vary in direct proportion to changes in volume or level of activity. Direct materials, direct labor, and, in some instances, indirect materials are examples of variable costs. Direct materials costs vary in proportion to the number of units produced. Direct labor costs vary directly with the number of direct labor hours worked and tend to vary in proportion to the number of units produced. Indirect materials may vary with the number of units produced or the number of direct labor hours worked. If the direct materials cost for manufacturing one unit is $100, the direct materials cost for producing ten units is generally expected to be $1,000. If the indirect materials cost is $.80 per direct labor hour, and 27,000 hours are budgeted for the period, the total estimated indirect materials cost is $21,600 (27,000 × $.80 for each direct labor hour). If 33,000 direct labor hours are worked, the total indirect materials cost should be $26,400 (33,000 hours × $.80 per hour). *In this chapter, we assume that direct labor hours is the appropriate basis for measuring volume or activity level; this is true of most budgeting systems.*

Assuming that the cost of indirect materials is a purely variable cost, its behavior can be plotted on a graph showing the relationship between volume, expressed in terms of direct labor hours, and indirect materials cost. A graph reflecting the behavior of variable costs as volume changes is given on page 486. This graph shows what total indirect materials costs are expected to be at different activity levels, based on the assumption that indirect materials costs are purely variable and are $.80 per direct labor hour. Remember that although the *total* of a variable cost changes in direct proportion to a measure of volume, such as number of direct labor hours, the variable cost *per unit* of measurement is constant.

Fixed Costs

Fixed costs are costs that do not change in *total* amount as changes in volume of output or activity occur. The salary of the plant manager, for example, is the same in a given period regardless of changes in the level of production.

Depreciation of machinery and equipment is a very common fixed cost, assuming that the straight-line method for computing depreciation is used. If an asset cost $360,000 and has a life of ten

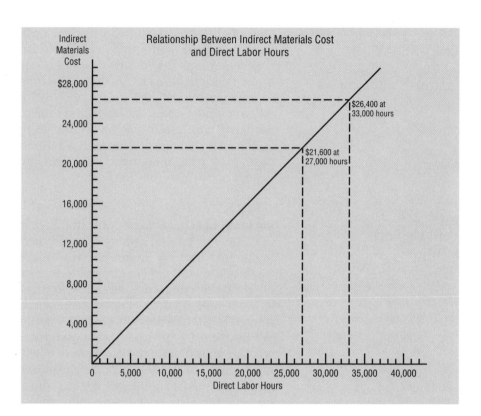

years, depreciation will be $36,000 per year if the straight-line depreciation method is used; it is irrelevant whether the level of activity is 27,000 direct labor hours or 33,000 direct labor hours. The depreciation will still be $36,000 per year. Obviously, however, the fixed cost *per unit* decreases as volume increases. If depreciation is $36,000 per year and 24,000 hours of direct labor are worked, the depreciation is $1.50 per hour. On the other hand, if only 12,000 hours are worked, the depreciation per hour increases to $3.

The relationship between total depreciation cost and volume (expressed in terms of direct labor hours) is shown in the following graph.

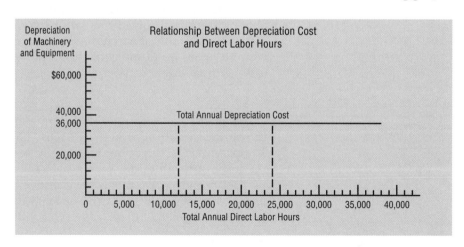

Semivariable Costs

It is obviously an easy task to estimate purely variable costs and purely fixed costs that are expected to occur at any given level of output. However, not all costs are purely fixed or purely variable. Some costs are semivariable.

Semivariable costs are those costs that vary in some degree with volume but not in direct proportion to it. Semivariable costs consist of a basic fixed element that is immune to changes in activity or volume and a variable element that reflects changes in activity or volume.

The cost of electric power is usually semivariable since it is necessary to have light, heat, and cooling in a factory whether or not goods are being produced. The portion of electric power cost that is needed to provide these basic service is the fixed element. Electric power is also required to operate machinery used in production, and the total amount varies with hours of operation. This portion of the electric power cost is the variable element.

If the electric power cost for a department is estimated to be $1,200 a year (fixed) plus $.40 per direct labor (variable), total costs at 27,000 hours are estimated to be $12,000 [(27,000 hours × $.40) + $1,200]. A graph illustrating the relationship between electric power cost and direct labor hours is shown below. This graph has two solid lines. The solid horizontal line represents fixed costs ($1,200), and the solid diagonal line represents total costs. Broken lines are used to indicate

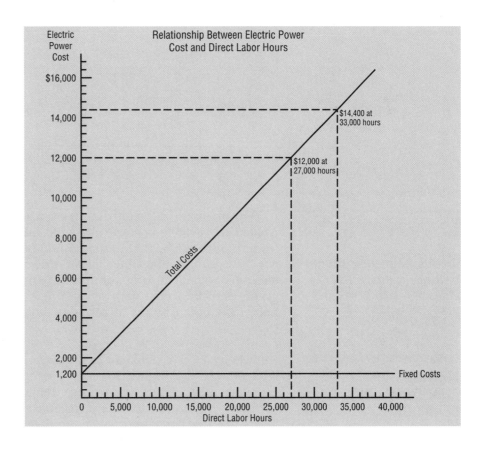

the total electric power cost at various levels of activity, for example, $14,400 at 33,000 hours.

Other examples of semivariable costs are indirect labor, repairs and maintenance, payroll taxes, and miscellaneous manufacturing overhead.

Stair-Step Costs

Stair-step costs are costs that are basically fixed within a narrow range but show abrupt and distinct increases when there are volume increases. This type of cost behavior is characteristic of many managerial salary costs and inspection labor costs. For example, only one inspector (with an annual salary of $24,000) may be required if production is not more than 5,000 direct labor hours. A second inspector (also earning $24,000 per year) must be added if production exceeds 5,000 direct labor hours but is less than 10,000 direct labor hours. In a similar fashion, an additional inspector earning $24,000 annually is needed for each additional 5,000 direct labor hours. The behavior of a stair-step cost is represented in the graph below.

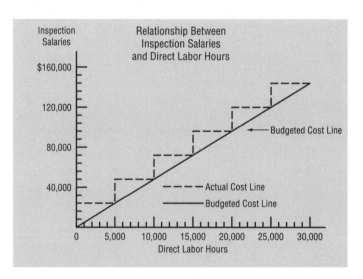

For planning and control purposes, stair-step costs are sometimes treated as variable costs. A diagonal line representing the budget allowance is usually fitted to the bottom of the stair-step pattern. In this way, the budget allowance never exceeds the amount that actually should be spent at any volume of activity. The diagonal line in the graph depicts a cost with a variable rate of $4.80 per direct labor hour ($24,000 ÷ 5,000 direct labor hours).

At this point you should be able to work Exercises 20–1 to 20–6 and 20–8.

METHODS OF ANALYZING COST BEHAVIOR

Knowledge of cost behavior is a fundamental part of product costing, controlling costs, and decision making. As we have already seen, some costs are purely fixed, some are purely variable, and others are semivariable. How are the fixed and variable elements of a cost determined? There are two basic approaches to determining cost behavior. One is

SELF-REVIEW

1. What happens to variable costs per unit as production volume increases?
2. What happens to total variable costs as production volume increases?
3. What happens to total fixed costs as production volume decreases?
4. What happens to fixed costs per unit as production volume decreases?
5. What is a semivariable cost?
6. What happens to total semivariable costs as production volume increases?
7. What are stair-step costs?

Answers to Self-Review

1. Variable costs per unit remain constant when production volume increases. Variable costs per unit are the same whether the volume increases, decreases, or remains constant.
2. Total variable costs increase in direct proportion to production volume.
3. Total fixed costs remain constant as production volume increases. Total fixed costs remain the same whether the volume increases, decreases, or remains the same.
4. As volume decreases, the fixed cost per unit increases. The same amount of cost must be spread over a small number of units. Conversely, as volume increases, the fixed cost per unit decreases.
5. A semivariable cost is one that varies to some degree with volume but not in direct proportion to it.
6. Total semivariable costs increase as production volume increases.
7. Stair-step costs are basically fixed within a narrow range but show an abrupt and distinct increase when volume is increased to another clearly defined point. A graph of these costs takes on the shape of stair steps.

the analysis, based on engineering studies, of what cost behavior should be. The other is the analysis of accounting and statistical records to project what cost behavior will be in the future, based on what it has been in the past.

Engineering Analysis of Costs

The **engineering analysis method** uses engineering specifications and analyses to determine what costs should be. The method is commonly used in analyzing direct materials and direct labor costs. Detailed engineering specifications are normally available to show precisely what materials are required in manufacturing a product. With known prices for materials, it is possible to determine with a high degree of accuracy how much the cost of materials should be at any production volume.

Engineering specifications may also be used to determine the amount of time that should be required for each step in the production process. Time and motion studies that analyze how workers should perform their tasks in the production process are often used to establish labor standards. With known wage rates, labor costs per direct labor hour and per unit of production can be budgeted with confidence.

Engineering studies also may be useful in analyzing manufacturing overhead costs. This is especially so when specialized equipment is a major element of cost. In this case, a significant part of the overhead is likely to be determined by the design of the equipment. For example, power costs, repairs and maintenance, and indirect materials used may depend largely on the type and size of equipment used. Also, time and motion studies may be used in analyzing indirect labor costs, such as the costs of storeroom personnel.

Analysis of Past Cost Behavior

Although the engineering approach is widely used in analyzing materials and labor costs and is used in estimating many overhead costs, some companies do not have qualified personnel to conduct engineering studies and do not wish to incur the high cost of hiring outside consultants. Instead, an analysis of past cost data is normally the starting point for these companies in making projections into the future.

There are many techniques for analyzing past cost-volume relationships. Some of these are highly technical, involving complex mathematical formulas. These statistical techniques require the development of precise formulas to express cost behavior. Only one of these, the method of least squares, is examined in this chapter. (Other statistical techniques are beyond the scope of this book.) Computer software programs for complex statistical techniques are widely available and are often used by accountants in analyzing cost behavior.

Some commonly used techniques for analyzing cost-volume relationships are less complex and are designed to give only a close approximation of cost behavior, which is sufficient for preparing a budget. Three widely used nontechnical approximation methods are the scattergraph method, the high-low points method, and the direct estimate method.

We will now explain and illustrate these commonly used techniques. For the purpose of this discussion, we will examine the relationship between electric power costs and the direct labor hours worked in the National Case Company for the period November 19X8 through October 19X9. The accountant has accumulated the figures to use in analyzing cost behavior. These data are shown in the following table:

Month	Direct Labor Hours	Electric Power Cost
November	2,140	$ 956
December	2,680	1,172
January	3,004	1,304
February	1,890	856
March	2,360	1,044
April	1,940	876
May	2,880	1,252
June	2,520	1,108
July	3,080	1,332

August	2,850	1,240
September	2,960	1,284
October	3,160	1,364

Scattergraph Method. In the **scattergraph method,** production and cost data for representative prior months (usually the 12 months or 24 months before the date of the computation) are plotted as points on a graph. (Most spreadsheet and database software packages provide graphing capabilities.) If the points seem to form a clear pattern showing a high degree of correlation between volume and costs, a line is drawn to fit the trend of the points. For example, the electric power costs and the direct labor costs in the Assembly Department of the National Case Company for the 12-month period from November 19X8 through October 19X9 are plotted in the graph below. Since it is clear that the points fall into a pattern, a line is drawn to fit the trend of the points, as shown. Different accountants might, of course, draw slightly different lines to fit the points.

The plotted line intersects the vertical axis at $100 when the volume is zero. This represents the fixed portion of the monthly electricity cost and is not dependent on the level of activity. The variable element is computed from the cost of a month for which the plotted line lies directly on the cost line. For example, the total electric power cost for the month of July was $1,332, and 3,080 direct labor hours

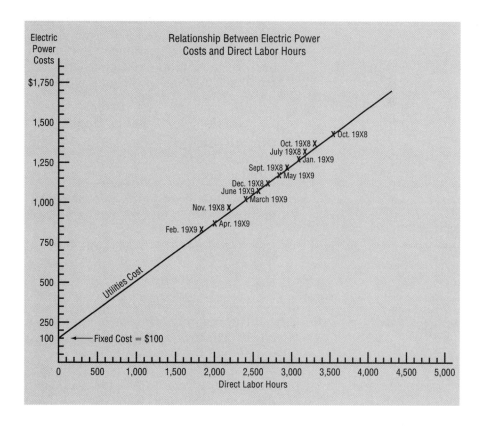

were used. The fixed amount ($100) is deducted from the total electric power cost for the month to compute the total variable electric power cost for the month. The total variable cost of $1,232 is then divided by the number of direct labor hours (3,080) to obtain the cost per direct labor hour, $.40.

Total Electric Power Costs	$1,332
Deduct Fixed Costs	100
Total Variable Cost	$1,232

$$\frac{\text{Total Variable Cost}}{\text{Total Direct Labor Hours}} = \text{Variable Rate per Direct Labor Hour}$$

$$\frac{\$1,232}{3,080 \text{ hr}} = \$.40 \text{ per Direct Labor Hour}$$

The same computations applied to the months of November and February will yield the same rounded rate. Thus the semivariable cost rate for electric power amounts to $100 per month (or $1,200 per year) plus $.40 per direct labor hour.

The scattergraph method is particularly useful when data are available for several prior periods and when the trend of the points is clearly evident. If the points on a scattergraph do not fit a reasonably clear pattern, it will be difficult to draw a line to fit the trend. Thus the scattergraph method may be inappropriate.

High-Low Points Methods. In the **high-low points method,** the cost and production data for the months of highest and lowest volume of production are determined. The differences are then computed. On the previous graph, October and February are the high and low months. The difference between these months is computed as follows:

Month	Direct Labor Hours	Electric Power Cost
October (High)	3,160	$1,364
February (Low)	1,890	856
Differences	1,270	$ 508

The difference in the electric power cost divided by the difference in direct labor hours yields the variable rate per hour of $.40.

$$\frac{\text{Difference in Cost}}{\text{Difference in Hours}} = \text{Variable Rate per Direct Labor Hour}$$

$$\frac{\$508}{1,270 \text{ hr}} = \$.40 \text{ per Direct Labor Hour}$$

The major advantage of the high-low points method is its simplicity. There is always a danger in using only the data for the high month and the low month, however, because the behavior of costs for other months may be inconsistent with these two months. It may be more appropriate to use the average of the two highest months and the average of the two lowest months in the calculation. Another ap-

At this point you should be able to work Exercises 20–7, 20–9, and 20–10 and Problems 20–2A to 20–4B.

proach is to use the second-highest and second-lowest months and compare the results of this computation with those obtained using the high and low months. If the two sets of results are about the same, the high-low points computations will be used. If the two calculations are very different, a more technical approach may be necessary.

Least Squares Method. When there are erratic relationships between the volume of activity and a cost item, it may be difficult to draw a line to fit the points on a scattergraph. In such circumstances the high-low points method may also give incorrect results. Thus it may be desirable or necessary to use a more precise and complex statistical method. One relatively simple statistical technique that is often used for determining the fixed and variable components of a cost is the **least squares method.** This is also sometimes referred to as *simple regression analysis.* This method determines mathematically a **line of best fit** through a set of plotted points in much the same way that a line is fitted to a set of points in a scattergraph. However, using the least squares method does not require that the points actually be plotted. Instead, a mathematical formula is developed for the line, and fixed and variable elements are computed from the formula.

When a line is drawn through a set of points at its most representative location, the sum of the deviations of the points from the line is at a minimum. With the least squares method, the line is computed so that the sum of the *squares* of the deviations is at a minimum. (There are mathematical reasons why the squares of the deviations are used rather than the actual deviations. Those reasons are not important to the student of accounting.)

The least squares method is demonstrated on page 494, using the data given on pages 490–491 for the electric power cost in the Assembly Department of the National Case Company for the months of November 19X8 through September 19X9. The steps in the process are as described below and as illustrated in the table below.

1. Compute the average monthly direct labor hours. To do this, add the direct labor hours for each month and divide the total by 12 months. The figures are entered in Column B in the table below (31,464 ÷ 12 = 2,622 hours per month).
2. Compute the average monthly electric power cost. To do this, determine the total electric power cost for all months and then divide the total by 12. The figures are shown in Column D ($13,788 ÷ 12 = $1,149 per month).
3. Compute the difference between (a) the actual labor hours each month and (b) the average monthly labor hours computed in Step 1. The difference for each month is entered in Column C.
4. Compute the difference between (a) the actual electric power cost for each month and (b) the average monthly electric power cost computed in Step 2. The difference for each month is entered in Column E.
5. The difference between monthly direct labor hours and average monthly labor hours computed in Step 3 is squared. Each square

LEAST SQUARES METHOD OF DETERMINING VARIABLE AND FIXED COSTS

A	B	C	D	E	F	G
Month	Direct Labor Hours	Deviation From Average Direct Labor Hours	Electric Power Cost	Deviation From Average Cost	Direct Labor Hours Deviation Squared (Column C Squared)	Column C Times Column E
November	2,140	(482)	$ 956	$(193)	232,324	$ 93,026
December	2,680	58	1,172	23	3,364	1,334
January	3,004	382	1,304	155	145,924	59,210
February	1,890	(732)	856	(293)	535,824	214,476
March	2,360	(262)	1,044	(105)	68,644	27,510
April	1,940	(682)	876	(273)	465,124	186,186
May	2,880	258	1,252	103	66,564	26,574
June	2,520	(102)	1,108	(41)	10,404	4,182
July	3,080	458	1,332	183	209,764	83,814
August	2,850	228	1,240	91	51,984	20,748
September	2,960	338	1,284	135	114,244	45,630
October	3,160	538	1,364	215	289,444	115,670
Totals	31,464		$13,788		2,193,608	$878,360
Average	2,622		$ 1,149			

Variable Costs = $\dfrac{\$878,360}{2,193,608 \text{ hours}}$ = $.400417941 per hour

is entered in Column F. These squares are then added, and the total (2,193,608) is entered.

6. The difference between each month's labor hours and the average monthly labor hours (previously entered in Column C) is multiplied by the difference between that month's electric power cost and the average monthly electric power cost (previously entered in Column E). The products are entered in Column G. The products are then added, and the total (878,360) is entered.

7. The total of Column G (878,360) is divided by the total of Column E (2,193,608). The quotient (.400417941) represents the variable rate per hour for electric power.

8. The fixed electric power cost per month can now be computed.
   a. The average electric power cost per month is $1,149.
   b. The variable portion of the average electric power cost is $1,049.90. This is the average direct labor hours (2,622) multiplied by the variable rate of $.400417941 per hour, computed in Step 7.

At this point you should be able to work Problems 20–5A and 20–5B.

   c. The difference between the total average electric power cost ($1,149) and the variable portion of the average electric power cost ($1,049.90) represents the fixed portion ($99.10) of the cost.

Life Made Easier—Computer Programs

Before the advent of the mainframe computer and, later, the desktop PC, the cost accumulation procedures and various mathematical computations required to analyze cost behavior, to make allocations, and to determine unit costs made the use of sophisticated cost-determination methodologies almost not feasible. For example, in this chapter you have seen that the method of least squares analysis of cost behavior is a far more precise and accurate procedure for determining fixed and variable cost elements than is the high-low points method or the scattergraph method, but to make all the manual calculations necessary to use the method made it impractical to use. The need to make almost countless measurements, especially in activities providing services, exacerbated the problem. The need for many computations also made it difficult for management to apply what-if procedures in making decisions. If management asked the accountant, "What would be the effect on costs and profits if we could increase prices by 5 percent, and cut volume by 3 percent?" the accountant would have to take time to make the calculations. If management repeated the question, substituting new figures, the accountant would be faced with hours of work. Furthermore, in many cases good operating decisions depended on the ability to measure detailed operating data, but measurement devices were cumbersome and often inaccurate.

The development of high-speed processors, hard drives with enormous storage capacity, high-capacity memory, and a multitude of sophisticated application programs, especially spreadsheet programs, have almost eliminated the computational problems. In the twinkling of an eye, the computer can make the calculations that once took a full day to carry out, and what-if calculations can be made almost instantaneously. Sensitive electronic devices can now measure almost every physical element at any point in the production process on a continuous basis, feed the information into computers, and convert the input within seconds into information that can be used to assist in controlling operations and reporting to management. Spreadsheet and statistical analysis packages now routinely contain programs for making analyses of many kinds, and custom programs can be easily and inexpensively developed to obtain other types of analyses. For instance, most commonly used spreadsheet packages (for example, Excel and Lotus), along with commonly used statistical packages (for example, SPSS and SAS), now contain regression analysis programs based on the least squares technique. (Some programs also contain even more sophisticated analyses.) There is no longer a need for the cost accountant to reject the best approach to solving any accounting problem on the basis that the calculations are too difficult and tedious.

Direct Estimate Method. A direct estimate is used when data on past performance are unavailable, when historical cost records are unreliable or incomplete, or when operating changes make existing data no longer applicable. With the **direct estimate method,** responsible operating managers use whatever data are available, plus their knowledge of plans and methods and their experience, to reach a conclusion as to what costs should be.

SELECTING THE METHOD OF ANALYSIS

The scattergraph method is appropriate when there are several points to be observed and when the plotted points representing costs clearly fall into a pattern. However, if there are only a few volume levels for which costs are known, it may be difficult to fit a line to the points. In this case, the high-low points method may be preferable. When

SELF-REVIEW

1. Name five methods for analyzing cost behavior discussed in this chapter.
2. Explain briefly how to estimate fixed and variable cost components using the high-low points method.
3. Under what conditions can the scattergraph method be used to estimate the fixed and variable components of a cost?
4. In what circumstances is the engineering analysis method of estimating the fixed and variable components of a cost likely to be more useful than other methods?
5. Which two methods of estimating the fixed and variable components of a cost may be described as developing a line of best fit? Explain.
6. How are the engineering analysis and direct estimate methods similar? How do they differ?

Answers to Self-Review

1. Five methods discussed in this chapter for analyzing cost behavior are engineering analysis, high-low points, scattergraph, least squares, and direst estimate methods.
2. With the high-low points method, the cost and production data for the periods of highest and lowest volume of production are determined. The difference between each is computed. The difference in cost is divided by the difference in volume to arrive at a variable cost per unit of volume. The fixed cost component is the excess of total cost for one of the periods over the variable costs. The variable cost for the period is the volume of production multiplied by the variable cost per unit.
3. The scattergraph method is useful when data are available for several prior periods and the trends of the points are clearly evident.
4. Engineering analysis of costs is likely to be most useful when equipment is involved and there are engineering specifications showing material and labor requirements. Also, equipment design and operating specifications dictate to a large extent overhead costs such as repairs, maintenance, power consumption, and indirect materials requirements.
5. The least squares method and the scattergraph method are both based on the premise that a line can be drawn that most nearly depicts the relationships between production volumes and total costs.
6. The engineering analysis method and the direst estimate method are similar in that they both depend on the knowledge that individuals have about the production process and operating conditions. They differ in that the engineering analysis method depends largely on the engineering specifications, technical analyses, time and motion studies, and other studies, whereas the direct estimate method is based largely on the experience of the estimators.

many factors are involved or costs do not clearly fit a pattern on the scattergraph, the direct estimation procedure may be the most logical approach to determining cost behavior. In more complex cases, the method of least squares or even more sophisticated statistical methods using computer programs may be necessary to satisfactorily separate the fixed and variable costs. The engineering approach may be especially appropriate when equipment and facilities costs make up a large part of total costs.

It is important to note the limitations of the nontechnical methods for analyzing cost behavior discussed in this chapter. Unless the cost-volume relationship shows a high degree of correlation, it will be impossible to fit a cost line to the points on the scattergraph. Likewise, the high and low points will not be representative of the cost-volume relationship. The direct estimate method, as its name implies, is fundamentally imprecise. However, the nontechnical methods usually yield results that are meaningful at a practical level.

PRINCIPLES AND PROCEDURES SUMMARY

- A knowledge of cost behavior—how total costs and unit costs vary with changes in production volume—is important to the cost accountant, especially in planning and in controlling costs. That knowledge provides the basis for estimating what costs should be under different operating conditions and production volumes.
- Costs are classified as fixed, variable, or semivariable.
    - Fixed costs remain constant in total, even though production volume increases or decreases. As volume increases, fixed costs per unit decrease.
    - Variable costs vary in total in direct proportion to the production volume. They remain constant per unit of production.
    - Semivariable costs vary in total, but not in direct proportion, according to changes in volume. They consist of a fixed component and a variable component.
- In order to plan and control semivariable costs, it is necessary to measure the variable and fixed components. Several techniques are commonly used to determine the variable and fixed components, among them:
    - The engineering analysis method, based on engineering specifications and equipment design.
    - The high-low points method, based on the difference in costs observed for the high and for the low production in past months.
    - The scattergraph method, which involves plotting production and cost data for several prior periods and then attempting to fit a line that seems to fit closely the pattern of cost and production data.
    - The least squares method, which is a technical and precise statistical technique for determining a line of best fit to a set of production and cost points.

- In most situations, the nontechnical methods yield results that are meaningful at a practical level.
- Variable cost information and fixed cost information make it possible to estimate what costs should be at any production level. These relationships are at the heart of manufacturing and operating budgets and are the basis for performance analyses and cost control systems.

MANAGERIAL IMPLICATIONS

- Although product cost accounting provides information that is useful to management in comparing product costs from period to period and sometimes in setting selling prices and making other decisions, a knowledge of how costs behave is even more useful in planning and controlling costs. Management decisions are based largely on the knowledge of how costs behave. In other words, cost accounting is a management tool.
- To plan future operations and control future costs, management must know what costs have been and how costs are affected by changes in production volumes.
- If the cost accountant is to provide management with useful cost information, he or she must be able to analyze costs into fixed and variable components so that management can be informed about the potential effects on costs and profits of different courses of action.
- In analyzing costs, the accountant must know more than the mathematics involved. In addition to being able to make the calculations, the accountant must know which techniques to use to analyze costs in a given situation and how to choose representative data. For example, the accountant must be able to recognize that data for some months may be completely unrepresentative of data for other months.

REVIEW QUESTIONS

1. Identify the basic cost behavior patterns and indicate how total costs change depending on each pattern as the activity level changes.
2. Explain how variable costs change as the activity level decreases.
3. How do fixed costs change in total and on a per-unit basis as production increases?
4. What are semivariable costs? Give four examples.
5. Are direct materials costs fixed costs or variable costs? Explain.
6. Give the steps to be followed if the high-low points method is to be used to analyze cost variability.
7. If the high-low points method is to be used to analyze cost behavior, what is the most important criterion that the accountant should keep in mind?

8. Explain stair-step costs and give an example.
9. What is meant by *engineering analysis of costs*? What costs are commonly analyzed by this method? Why are these costs particularly adaptable to engineering analysis?
10. Describe the scattergraph method of analyzing costs.
11. Explain the approach that the least squares method uses in analyzing semivariable costs.
12. What has been historically the greatest disadvantage to using the method of least squares? Why is this no longer a great disadvantage?
13. What is the direct estimate method of analyzing cost behavior? When is it used?
14. In a factory using high technology, do you think that a greater portion or a lesser portion of its manufacturing costs would be considered as fixed costs in comparison to a factory in which most of the work is done by hand? Explain.
15. Which of the following costs do you think is more likely to be a variable cost? A fixed cost? A semivariable cost?
    a. Repairs to factory equipment
    b. A royalty paid by a manufacturing company to a patent owner for using the patent to make a product.
    c. Payments made to lease factory equipment used in the manufacturing process
    d. Factory payroll taxes
    e. Electric power costs
    f. Direct materials
    g. *Ad valorem* taxes paid on factory equipment
    h. Insurance on factory equipment

MANAGERIAL DISCUSSION QUESTIONS

1. For planning and control purposes, how are stair-step costs generally treated? Why are they treated in this manner?
2. As cost accountant of Central States Manufacturing Company, you are developing a system for budgeting manufacturing costs. You have analyzed cost and production data for the past year. You have decided to use the high-low points method for determining the variable and fixed components of equipment repair costs and have examined the cost behavior for each month of the past year. You have observed, however, that even though the month of November of the past year was the lowest month of production, the repair costs for that month were among the highest of the year. What, if anything, do you propose to do to modify the usual procedure used in the high-low points method?
3. Explain why a distinction between fixed costs and variable costs is important to management when a factory is operating at less than full capacity.

4. The president of a corporation claims that depreciation is a variable cost because the depreciation cost per unit of output decreases as the volume of output increases. Comment on this.

5. How would a distinction between fixed and variable costs help management in forecasting cash needs for the business?

6. The president of Macro Microelectronics Company has expressed concern to the corporation's controller over the fact that the controller has been using the scattergraph method for estimating fixed and variable costs. The president believes that the method is not reliable enough. What is your reply?

7. Explain why an understanding of past cost behavior is important in the budgeting process.

8. As cost accountant for your company, you have suggested that the firm install a budgeting system. You explain to management that you wish to separate each factory overhead item into its fixed and variable components. The factory manager argues that this is not possible. To back up his position, he gives you the following example: If production is increased by 1,000 direct labor hours, inspection costs will remain constant, but for every 3,000 additional hours above that level, inspection costs will increase by $5,000 per month. How will you treat this cost in your analysis?

9. You have been asked by the controller of your company to analyze manufacturing costs for the past year in order to arrive at the variable and fixed components. In what circumstances would you choose each of the following activity bases as the unit of activity?
   a. Machine hours
   b. Direct labor hours
   c. Direct materials costs
   d. Direct labor costs

10. For several years the Elliott Company's cost accountant has analyzed the company's semivariable manufacturing costs by breaking them into fixed and variable components. During the past year, the company's production declined by more than 25 percent but the variable portions of some costs decreased by only 10 to 15 percent. Management has asked, "What is wrong?" What are the most likely reasons for this behavior?

11. Yesterday, the president of the company in which you are cost accountant held a meeting of managers. She expressed some concern that variable costs were increasing because volume was going down. She gave as an example the fact that depreciation costs per unit of product had increased from $4.34 per unit to $4.89 per unit, largely because of a decrease of about 10 percent in the volume of the product. She did, however, express her appreciation for the fact that some fixed costs, most notably materials costs, had increased very little. Materials costs had been $15 per unit during the past year, and during the past month, they had been held to $15.10 per unit, despite lower volume. What is your reaction to the president's remarks?

EXERCISES

EXERCISE 20–1 **Explain unit cost and total cost relationships. (Obj. 1).** At the Shelby Company, indirect materials are purely variable costs, varying in proportion to direct labor hours worked at the rate of $.80 per direct labor hour.
a. Compute the total indirect materials cost for each of the following four levels of activity:
(1) 16,212 direct labor hours
(2) 18,714 direct labor hours
(3) 20,800 direct labor hours
(4) 28,714 direct labor hours
b. What is the effect of increases in direct labor hours on the total cost of indirect materials?

EXERCISE 20–2 **Explain unit cost and total cost relationships. (Obj. 1).** At the Open Door Company, factory supervision is a fixed cost of $10,000 per month.
a. Compute the supervision cost per direct labor hour at each of the following monthly activity levels:
(1) 10,000 hours
(2) 11,000 hours
(3) 12,500 hours
(4) 14,285 hours
b. What is the effect of increases in direct labor hours on the fixed cost per unit?

EXERCISE 20–3 **Explain unit cost and total cost relationships. (Obj. 1).** The depreciation cost for the Dunn Company is $20,000 per month.
a. What should the depreciation cost per direct labor hour be if 4,000 hours are worked?
b. What should the depreciation cost per direct labor hour be if 4,500 hours are worked?
c. Is depreciation a fixed cost or a variable cost? Explain.

EXERCISE 20–4 **Estimate costs. (Obj. 2).** Fixed electric power costs in San Saba Production Company are estimated to be $1,360 per month and variable electric power costs are estimated to be $.40 per direct labor hour. What would be the total expected electric power for each of the following levels of direct labor activity?
a. 4,820 direct labor hours
b. 5,900 direct labor hours

EXERCISE 20–5 **Estimate costs. (Obj. 2).** The cost accountant of San Diego Manufacturers has estimated the fixed costs for factory indirect labor to be $14,200 per month and the variable indirect labor cost to be $10 per direct labor hour. What would be the total expected indirect labor costs for each of the following levels of direct labor activity?
a. 4,100 direct labor hours
b. 4,800 direct labor hours

EXERCISE 20–6   **Classify costs.**   **(Obj. 3).**   Indicate whether each of the following costs is likely to be fixed, variable, or semivariable, based on physical units of output:
a. Direct materials
b. Direct labor
c. Payroll taxes
d. Salaries of factory departmental managers
e. Insurance on factory building
f. Depreciation
g. Indirect materials
h. Indirect labor
i. Warehouse rental

EXERCISE 20–7   **Use the high-low points method.**   **(Obj. 5).**   The monthly managerial costs of the London Company's factory for each month of 19X9 have been analyzed. The month in which the greatest number of direct labor hours were worked was March, with 10,000 hours. The managerial costs for that month totaled $80,000. In July, the month of fewest direct labor hours, 6,800 hours were worked, and managerial costs were $64,000. Use the high-low points method to do the following:
a. Compute the variable cost per direct labor hour.
b. Compute the fixed cost per month.

EXERCISE 20–8   **Classify costs as variable, fixed, or semivariable.**   **(Obj. 3).**   The Offshore Company's accountant has accumulated cost figures at various activity levels. The following data show the activity levels and the direct management costs for six months:

Direct Labor Hours	Direct Management Costs
13,360	$82,000
15,960	94,000
11,200	60,000
10,000	60,000
14,620	82,000
15,220	94,000

a. What term can best be used to describe this cost behavior?
b. Explain this cost behavior.

DATA FOR EXERCISES 9 AND 10
The Gaines Company's records show the following data for the four quarters of 19X9.

Quarter	Direct Labor Hours	Indirect Labor	Indirect Materials
First	10,200	$26,080	$1,520
Second	14,600	27,894	1,960
Third	12,800	27,120	1,780
Fourth	13,000	27,200	1,800

EXERCISE 20–9   **Use the high-low points method.**   **(Obj. 5).**   Compute the fixed and variable components of the indirect labor cost for Gaines Company, using the high-low points method.

EXERCISE 20–10 **Use the high-low points method.** **(Obj. 5).** Compute the fixed and variable components of the indirect materials cost for Gaines Company, using the high-low points method.

PROBLEMS

PROBLEM 20–1A **Use the scattergraph and high-low points methods.** **(Objs. 4, 5).** The cost accountant of the Great Central Corporation has compiled the following information about the direct labor hours and the indirect labor costs for each month of 19X9:

Month	Direct Labor Hours	Indirect Labor Costs
January	4,680	$6,276
February	4,070	5,910
March	3,610	5,600
April	3,950	5,765
May	4,200	5,940
June	4,480	6,120
July	5,010	6,465
August	4,840	6,300
September	4,720	6,304
October	4,600	6,320
November	5,090	6,614
December	4,800	6,360

INSTRUCTIONS Plot these data on a scattergraph. Fit the points with a line and estimate the fixed costs from the graph.

PROBLEM 20–2A **Use the high-low points method.** **(Obj. 5).** The Atlanta Company recorded the following data about direct labor hours and indirect materials costs for the year ended May 31, 19X9:

Month	Direct Labor Hours	Indirect Materials Costs
June	16,800	$ 9,668
July	15,175	9,025
August	14,700	8,850
September	12,040	7,816
October	14,250	8,700
November	16,000	9,400
December	17,300	9,920
January	18,900	10,560
February	17,950	10,180
March	17,675	10,070
April	15,050	9,020
May	16,200	9,480
Total	192,040	$112,709

INSTRUCTIONS Compute the variable rate per direct labor hour, using the high-low points method. Show your computations. Carry the answer to 4 decimal places and round to 3 decimal places.

PROBLEM 20–3A

Use the high-low points method. **(Obj. 5).** Direct labor hours and indirect labor costs for each quarter of 19X9 for the Sharif Company are shown below.

	Direct Labor Hours	Indirect Labor Costs
First Quarter	30,800	$127,800
Second Quarter	36,000	146,000
Third Quarter	42,000	167,000
Fourth Quarter	38,400	154,400

INSTRUCTIONS

Using the high-low points method, compute the variable rate per direct labor hour and the fixed cost per quarter for indirect labor costs. Show your computations.

PROBLEM 20–4A

Use the high-low points method; estimate costs. **(Objs. 2, 5).** The following data involve the direct labor hours worked and the cost of supplies for eight months of 19X8 in the Forming Department of the Big Town Company.

	Direct Labor Hours	Supplies Cost
January	1,080	$1,432
February	1,200	1,480
March	1.290	1,516
April	1,400	1,562
May	1,450	1,580
June	1,300	1,521
July	1,020	1,402
August	1,100	1,440

INSTRUCTIONS

1. Using the high-low points method, compute the variable rate per direct labor hour and the fixed cost per month. Show your computations.
2. In January 19X9, 1,370 direct labor hours were worked in the Forming Department. Compute the expected cost of supplies for the month.
3. In January 19X9, the cost of supplies in the Forming Department was $1,550. Does this indicate that the cost of supplies was well controlled? Explain.

PROBLEM 20–5A

Use the high-low points method and the method of least squares. **(Objs. 5, 6).** The direct labor hours and indirect materials and supplies of the Abernathy Company for six months during 19X9 are shown below.

Month	Direct Labor Hours	Indirect Materials and Supplies
July	6,550	$ 9,240
August	8,100	10,910

September	8,600	11,475
October	8,820	11,702
November	7,340	10,085
December	6,500	9,150

INSTRUCTIONS

1. Using the high-low points method, compute the variable rate per direct labor hour and the fixed cost per month for indirect materials and supplies. (Round the variable costs to the nearest tenth of a cent per hour and the fixed costs to the nearest whole dollar per month.)
2. Using the method of least squares, compute the variable rate per direct labor hour and the fixed cost per month for indirect materials and supplies. (Round the variable costs to the nearest tenth of a cent per hour and the fixed costs to the nearest whole dollar per month.)

ALTERNATE PROBLEMS

PROBLEM 20–1B

Use the scattergraph and high-low points methods. (Objs. 4, 5). The cost accountant of the Meux Corporation has compiled the following information about the direct labor hours and the indirect labor costs for each month of 19X9:

Month	Direct Labor Hours	Indirect Labor Costs
January	29,400	$17,700
February	28,500	17,400
March	32,000	18,800
April	30,350	18,050
May	32,400	18,960
June	30,100	18,040
July	34,600	19,840
August	35,900	20,360
September	37,800	21,120
October	35,350	20,140
November	33,600	19,375
December	24,080	15,632

INSTRUCTIONS

Plot these data on a scattergraph. Fit the points with a line and estimate the fixed costs from the graph.

PROBLEM 20–2B

Use the high-low points method. (Obj. 5). The Far West Company's direct labor hours and indirect materials costs for the year ended March 31, 19X9, were as follows:

Month	Direct Labor Hours	Indirect Materials Costs
April	25,700	$ 8,120
May	28,950	8,780
June	32,800	10,520

July	37,450	11,540
August	38,600	11,720
September	41,900	12,740
October	42,875	13,200
November	42,000	13,112
December	38,100	12,040
January	36,785	11,580
February	35,420	11,360
March	30,180	9,640
Total	430,760	$134,352

INSTRUCTIONS   Compute the variable rate per direct labor hour using the high-low points method. Show your computations. Carry the answer to 4 decimal places and round to 3 decimal places.

PROBLEM 20–3B   **Use the high-low points method.   (Obj. 5).**   Direct labor hours and payroll taxes and fringe benefits for each quarter of 19X9 for the Pilot Point Company are shown below.

	Direct Labor Hours	Payroll Taxes and Fringe Benefits
First Quarter	60,000	$208,000
Second Quarter	68,000	224,000
Third Quarter	57,000	202,000
Fourth Quarter	64,000	216,000

INSTRUCTIONS   Using the high-low points method, compute the variable rate per direct labor hour and the fixed cost per quarter for payroll taxes and fringe benefits. Show your computations.

PROBLEM 20–4B   **Use the high-low points method; estimate costs.   (Objs. 2, 5).**   The following data involve the direct labor hours worked and indirect labor costs for the Soldering Department of the Brownwood Company for each quarter of 19X8.

	Direct Labor Hours	Indirect Labor Costs
First Quarter	9,200	$22,200
Second Quarter	12,100	25,100
Third Quarter	10,400	23,160
Fourth Quarter	10,700	23,780

INSTRUCTIONS   1. Using the high-low points method, compute the variable rate per direct labor hour and the fixed cost per month for indirect labor. Show your computations.
   2. In the first quarter of 19X9, 12,800 direct labor hours were worked in the Soldering Department. Compute the expected indirect labor costs for the quarter.
   3. In the first quarter of 19X9, the indirect labor costs in the Soldering Department were $27,100. Does this show that indirect labor costs were well controlled? Explain.

PROBLEM 20–5B **Use the high-low points method and the method of least squares. (Objs. 5, 6).** The direct labor hours and the utility costs of Pedro Products Company for six months during 19X9 are shown below.

Month	Direct Labor Hours	Utility Costs
January	4,800	$6,960
February	3,900	5,900
March	4,600	6,680
April	5,100	7,400
May	4,900	7,040
June	4,320	6,370

INSTRUCTIONS

1. Using the high-low points method, compute the variable rate per direct labor hour and the fixed cost per month for utility costs.
2. Using the method of least squares, compute the variable rate per direct labor hour and the fixed cost per month for utility costs. (Round the variable costs to the nearest tenth of a cent per hour and the fixed costs to the nearest whole dollar per month.)

MANAGERIAL DECISION CASES

Case 20-1. The Aztec Company is developing a budgeting program for its manufacturing operations. Figures for each month in the past year, 19X9, have been assembled, to help in analyzing indirect labor costs.

Month	Direct Labor Hours	Indirect Materials and Supplies
January	2,900	$4,180
February	2,300	4,260
March	2,800	4,300
April	3,100	4,420
May	3,000	4,720
June	3,600	4,680
July	3,400	5,060
August	2,700	4,300
September	2,820	4,110
October	2,825	4,135
November	2,900	4,116
December	2,300	4,360

1. What does this pattern of cost behavior suggest about the control of indirect labor costs in the factory?
2. Using the high-low points method, compute the fixed element and the variable element of indirect labor costs.
3. Is the high-low points method satisfactory for budgeting indirect labor in this example? Explain.

Case 20-2. The Sandova Manufacturing Company uses a budgeting system in its manufacturing operations. The company's management wishes to apply some of these budgetary techniques to its other operations and has chosen the Billing Department as the first department for which a budgetary control system will be applied. This department prepares and mails statements to customers on a monthly basis. Each bill shows details such as beginning balance, purchases, returns, and payments. The first step is to determine the fixed and variable costs in the department.

1. Suggest two activity bases that might be used in measuring variability.
2. Assume that the activity base to be used is the number of billings per month. An analysis of data for the past six months shows the following:

Month	Number of Billings	Total Cost
January	4,200	$8,531
February	4,100	8,455
March	3,600	8,160
April	4,750	8,842
May	5,380	9,228
June	5,200	9,118

Management has asked you to determine the variable cost for each bill sent and the estimated monthly fixed costs of the department. Prepare the analysis.

3. Based on an analysis of billings in the past year, it is anticipated that activity in July will be high, at an estimated 5,460 billings, but that in August billings will drop to 4,250. What is the estimated total billing cost in each of these two months?
4. Suppose that the actual costs for billing operations in August totaled $8,780. Does this suggest that billing costs were well controlled during the month? Explain.

Budgeting

The cost data provided by a job order or process cost accounting system help management make decisions and improve the efficiency of operations. However, these decisions and improvements can be made only after the cost data are available at the completion of the specific job or operation. Although past experience is a helpful guide in planning, management needs a more formal and reliable method of anticipating future conditions, planning operations, and evaluating performance. A budget provides the most efficient means for planning and controlling future activities.

OBJECTIVES

1. Develop a sales budget.
2. Prepare production, materials, labor, and overhead budgets and combine them into a manufacturing costs budget.
3. Develop a flexible overhead budget for planning and control purposes.
4. Prepare an operating expenses budget.
5. Prepare a budgeted income statement.
6. Use the flexible budget as a management tool in controlling costs.

NEW TERMS

Budget (p. 510)
Budgetary control system (p. 510)
Control (p. 510)
Controllable costs (p. 518)
Cost standard (p. 514)
Fixed budget (p. 513)
Flexible budget (p. 514)
Management by exception (p. 523)
Manufacturing costs budget or cost of goods manufactured budget (p. 513)
Master budget (p. 510)
Materials budget (p. 515)
Materials purchases budget (p. 515)
Materials usage budget (p. 515)
Noncontrollable costs (p. 518)
Operating budget (p. 510)
Performance report (p. 523)
Planning (p. 510)
Production budget (p. 512)
Sales budget (p. 510)

BUDGETARY CONTROL

A **budget** is a business's financial plan for a specific period. It is also the foundation of a firm's financial control system. Once financial goals are established, the budget is used to check and control operations using a budgetary control system. A **budgetary control system** is a system for comparing actual results with budgeted goals. Variations between actual results and planned results are investigated and analyzed. Action is taken to correct these variations while operations continue.

The budgetary control system covers all phases of business activity: sales, production, administration, and finance. In a large company, many individuals participate in developing the budget. The responsibility for coordinating the budget is delegated to a budget committee under the supervision of a budget director, who usually reports to the controller. In a small company, frequently the accountant serves as budget director. The budget director suggests procedures for budget preparation and gives assistance and information to those responsible for preparing preliminary budgets for their departments. The budget director also reviews the departmental budgets to make certain that they are compatible and will achieve the common goals. The budget director then assembles the final departmental budgets and prepares the master budget.

The **master budget** encompasses the entire financial plan of the company. It consists of individual budgets for sales, production, manufacturing costs, operating expenses, cash receipts and payments, and capital assets, and a set of projected financial statements for the budgetary period. The master budget is often called the **operating budget** because it provides the basic plan for operations during the period.

The operating budget is a tool that makes planning and control easier. **Planning** involves identifying objectives and determining the steps needed to achieve these objectives. **Control** refers to the means by which management is assured that all parts of the company function properly and that the objectives identified in the planning stage are attained.

The development of the master budget of the National Case Company for the year 19X9 will be discussed in detail in this chapter. The firm manufactures metal cases covered with a special hard, noncorrosive plastic. These cases are used by jewelry distributors, jewelry retailers, department stores, and others to hold jewelry and precious stones while they are not being displayed in counters or in show cases.

THE SALES BUDGET

The **sales budget** is a written plan containing detailed estimates of products or groups of products expected to be sold during the budget period. The sales budget is the key to the overall company budget because the anticipated sales volume determines the amount of goods produced; the labor, equipment, and capital required; and the nature and amount of various selling, administrative, and financial expenses. Sales estimates are based on past performance and on the forecast of business conditions for the coming period. The accounting department, sales management, and salespeople all have a role in developing the sales budget.

Analysis of Past Performance

As sales are made, sales data are accumulated by products, territories, customers, and other categories. These data are studied in detail or summarized for planning purposes. The following territorial sales summary of the National Case Company is for the year 19X8.

	NATIONAL CASE COMPANY Analysis of Sales Year Ended December 31, 19X8 (Figures show number of cases sold)				
	DISCOUNT CHAINS	JEWELRY MERCHANTS	WHOLESALE DISTRIBUTORS	OTHERS	TOTAL SALES
Western Region					
Los Angeles District	6,200	2,800	200	1,500	10,700
Seattle District	3,200	5,700	700	800	10,400
Denver District	1,600	3,200	-0-	1,100	5,900
Total	11,000	11,700	900	3,400	27,000
Southeastern Region					
Atlanta District	8,700	1,300	6,200	900	17,100
Miami District	4,300	600	4,800	300	10,000
Charleston District	1,600	800	1,000	500	3,900
Total	14,600	2,700	12,000	1,700	31,000
Total	25,600	14,400	12,900	5,100	58,000

The sales manager's staff analyzes all available data about past performance to evaluate the sales force's efforts and to set new plans and goals. The new plans may call for introducing new products and services and entering new markets. The new goals usually include increases in sales revenue.

Forecast of Business Conditions

General economic conditions and specific factors relating to a firm and its industry must also be considered in determining sales prospects. Every company knows that certain economic indexes are major indicators and measures of its sales prospects. For example, one firm may find that its sales vary with changes in the volume of automobile production. Another firm's sales may vary with the number of computers sold in the nation. The sales of another firm may have a high correlation with the national income. Similarly, sales of automobiles are greatly affected by interest rates, and sales of specific styles of automobiles are affected by gasoline prices. Many large companies hire professional economists to make economic analyses and forecasts for them.

Other factors may also affect sales prospects. For example, a manufacturer of home building products would be very interested in the local marriage rate, the birth rate, the availability of rental housing, the movement of new families to the suburbs, and interest rates. Another important factor in sales forecasting is the nature of the individual

At this point you should be able to work Exercise 21–1 and Problems 21–1A and 21–1B.

product. New uses for the product bring about wider sales possibilities. Changing habits, competitive items, and substitutes may lessen sales prospects.

The sales managers of the National Case Company have considered the economic and other factors relevant to their future prospects in arriving at the sales budget for 19X9 (Schedule A), shown below.

					Schedule A
NATIONAL CASE COMPANY					
Sales Budget					
Year Ended December 31, 19X9					
(Figures show number of cases to be sold)					
	DISCOUNT CHAINS	**JEWELRY MERCHANTS**	**WHOLESALE DISTRIBUTORS**	**OTHER**	**TOTAL SALES**
Western Region					
Los Angeles District	6,200	2,700	400	1,900	11,200
Seattle District	3,400	5,800	700	900	10,800
Denver District	1,800	3,200	100	1,400	6,500
Total	11,400	11,700	1,200	4,200	28,500
Southeastern Region					
Atlanta District	9,000	1,600	6,200	1,000	17,800
Miami District	4,800	800	4,800	400	10,800
Charleston District	1,800	800	1,400	900	4,900
Total	15,600	3,200	12,400	2,300	33,500
Total in Units	27,000	14,900	13,600	6,500	62,000
Total, in Dollars at $64 Per Case	$1,728,000	$953,600	$870,400	$416,000	$3,968,000

THE PRODUCTION BUDGET

After the sales budget has been determined, a production budget can be prepared for the production of units to meet the requirements of the sales budget. The **production budget** is a written plan containing detailed information about the quantities of each product to be produced during the budget period. The actual number of units to be completed is computed from the following data: the units to be sold, the desired size of the ending inventory, and the units in the beginning inventory.

The sales budget of the National Case Company, shown in Schedule A, projects sales of 62,000 cases in 19X9. Assume that an ending inventory of 12,000 is desired on December 31, 19X9, and that the beginning inventory on January 1, 19X9, is 14,000. This means that 60,000 cases must be produced during the year to meet the sales objective. The other 2,000 cases are made available by a planned reduction in the inventory. The production budget (Schedule B) on page 513 is computed by adding the estimated sales to the desired ending inventory and subtracting the beginning stock on hand ([62,000 + 12,000] − 14,000 = 60,000).

NATIONAL CASE COMPANY	Schedule B
Production Budget	
Year Ending December 31, 19X9	

	Number of Cases
Budgeted Sales for Year	62,000
Budgeted Ending Inventory of Finished Goods, Dec. 31	12,000
Total Budgeted Requirements	74,000
Deduct Finished Goods Inventory, Jan. 1	14,000
Budgeted Production	60,000*

*Works in process inventories expected to remain constant.

The task of producing 60,000 cases in 19X9 requires the scheduling of productive capacity in accordance with circumstances and company policies. The production could be distributed evenly throughout the year at the rate of 5,000 cases a month, or the operations might be concentrated into a few months of intensive effort. A level rate of production usually results in a more stable and experienced work force and fuller use of plant capacity. There is less need for overtime operations, and a smaller investment in plant and equipment is required.

The accumulation of inventories, especially in seasonal industries, may cause storage and warehousing problems. Interest rates, insurance, and other costs of carrying and storing inventories will increase. The additional funds tied up in the inventories may be sizable and costly. The inventories may even deteriorate or become obsolete. As you learned in Chapter 5, some companies use just-in-time inventory control to hold inventories of finished products, work in process, and raw materials to a minimum level.

Most companies seek a balance between completely stable production and highly seasonal production. This involves balancing the storage, financing, warehousing, and handling costs associated with stable output against idle facility costs, labor supply problems, overtime pay, and similar factors associated with a highly seasonal production. The National Case Company follows a policy of level production throughout the year since its sales are not seasonal.

MANUFACTURING COSTS BUDGET

Once the estimated production is determined, the cost of materials, labor, and manufacturing overhead at that production level must be computed. These costs are presented in the **manufacturing costs budget,** also called the **cost of goods manufactured budget.** The manufacturing budget is prepared for the level of production planned for the period. A budget for a single level of activity is referred to as a **fixed budget.**

Although a fixed budget is adequate for planning purposes, it is not satisfactory for cost control purposes. For cost control purposes,

SELF-REVIEW

1. What is included in the master budget?
2. Why is the master budget sometimes called the *operating budget?*
3. What factors are considered in developing a sales budget?
4. What factors determine how many units of a product are to be manufactured?
5. What is meant by the term *control* as it is used in cost accounting?

Answers to Self-Review

1. The master budget is an overall budget for the company. It includes individual budgets for sales, production, manufacturing costs, operating expenses, cash receipts and payments, and capital assets. It also includes projected financial statements for the budget period.
2. The master budget is sometimes called the *operating budget* because it provides a basic plan for operations during the period.
3. Major factors considered in developing the sales budget are economic forecasts, past sales, and changes in products.
4. The factors that determine the number of units to be produced are expected sales, the beginning inventory and the desired ending inventory level.
5. *Control* refers to the means by which management is assured that all parts of the company function properly and that objectives are obtained.

manufacturing costs cannot be budgeted for only one production level because production may differ from what was originally planned. Changes in anticipated (budgeted) sales volume during the year are generally reflected in changes in levels of production.

A **flexible budget** shows costs expected to be incurred at various levels of output. It permits ready computation of costs for any attained volume of activity or output. For budgetary control purposes, the actual costs incurred at the level of production reached can be compared with the budgeted or estimated costs at that level. These data can be used to judge performance and to fix responsibility for differences between actual and budgeted costs.

The flexible budget takes both fixed and variable manufacturing costs into account. The analysis of costs by breaking them into their fixed and variable components, discussed in the previous chapter, is a vital part of budgeting for both planning and control purposes. Each variable manufacturing cost element is budgeted as an amount per unit of product, per direct labor hour, or other activity indicator, and each fixed cost element is budgeted at a single amount per period. Since budgets are, at best, skilled estimates, budgeted amounts are rounded off to the nearest dollar. Many companies round off budgeted figures to the nearest hundred or even to the nearest thousand dollars, depending on the company's size.

The preparation of a manufacturing costs budget is made easier by the use of cost standards. A **cost standard** is the cost of materials, labor, or other cost element that should be used for each unit of product under efficient operating conditions. The standards for materials

NATIONAL CASE COMPANY   **Schedule C**
Schedule of Direct Costs
Year Ending December 31, 19X9

DIRECT MATERIALS

MATERIAL	QUANTITY	COST PER UNIT	COST PER CASE
DM-1	3 feet	$4.00 per foot	$12.00
LF-6	4 sets	.40 per set	1.60
MS-1	12 sets	.10 per set	1.20
PV-2	$\frac{2}{25}$ quart	$8.00 per quart	.64
Total Materials Cost per Case			$15.44

DIRECT LABOR

DEPARTMENT	HOURS PER UNIT	RATE PER HOUR	COSTS PER CASE
Assembly	.5	$12.00	$ 6.00
Finishing	.7	14.00	9.80
Total Labor Cost per Case			$15.80

and labor are presented in a schedule of direct costs (Schedule C), as shown above. In Chapter 22, standards will be examined in detail.

The Materials Budget

The **materials budget** is a schedule showing the number of units of each material to be used and to be purchased during the budget period. The materials budget for the National Case Company (Schedule D) consists of two parts, the materials usage budget and the materials purchase budget, as shown on page 516.

The **materials usage budget,** Schedule D-1, shows the materials expected to be used during the year. Since the materials are variable costs, the quantity required for production is computed by multiplying the budgeted production (Schedule B: 60,000 cases) by the quantity of materials required for each completed unit (Schedule C: 3 feet per case for DM-1). The cost of materials used in production is the quantity required extended at the cost per unit. For material DM-1, this amount is $720,000 (Schedule D-1: 180,000 feet at $4).

Note that you can quickly compute the total cost of materials required for the period. Multiplying the quantity of cases to be produced (Schedule B) by the cost of the direct materials for each case (Schedule C) gives a total of $926,400 this budget year (60,000 cases at $15.44 per case).

The **materials purchases budget,** Schedule D-2, shows the materials purchase requirements in units. These are determined by adjusting the production requirements according to anticipated changes in raw materials inventories. The resulting unit figure is extended at the

NATIONAL CASE COMPANY   **Schedule D**
Materials Budget
Year Ending December 31, 19X9

SCHEDULE D-1: MATERIALS USAGE BUDGET

Total Quantity Required	180,000	240,000	720,000	4,800
Price per Unit (Schedule C)	$ 4	$ .40	$ .10	$ 8
Budgeted Cost of Materials Required	$720,000	$ 96,000	$ 72,000	$ 38,400
Total				$926,400

SCHEDULE D-2: MATERIALS PURCHASES BUDGET

	Material Number			
	DM-1 (IN FEET)	**LF-6 (IN SETS)**	**MS-1 (IN SETS)**	**PV-2 (IN QUARTS)**
Quantity Required per Case	3	4	12	$\frac{2}{25}$
Total Quantity Required for 60,000 Cases (Schedule B)	180,000	240,000	720,000	4,800
Budgeted Ending Inventory of Raw Materials, Dec. 31	11,000	16,000	40,000	800
Total Budgeted Requirements	191,000	256,000	760,000	5,600
Beginning Inventory of Raw Materials, Jan. 1	10,000	16,000	50,000	300
Total Budgeted Purchases	181,000	240,000	710,000	5,300
Price per Unit (Schedule C)	$ 4.00	$ .40	$ .10	$ 8
Cost of Purchases	$724,000	$ 96,000	$ 71,000	$ 42,400
Total				$933,400

estimated price per unit. For example, an increase in inventories of 1,000 feet of material DM-1 results in purchase requirements for 181,000 feet. At $4 per foot, estimated purchases of DM-1 total $724,000 for the year.

A schedule of monthly production is essential for efficient purchasing. Factors affecting the schedule include storage problems, quantity discounts, time required to receive materials from suppliers, and costs of carrying inventory. A balance between different types of materials must be carefully maintained so that the proper amount of each type will be available as needed. The materials budget is, of course, extremely important in determining future cash requirements.

At this point you should be able to work Exercises 21–2 to 21–4 and Problems 21–2A and 21–2B.

Direct Labor Budget

The direct labor budget (Schedule E), shown on the next page, is an estimate of the total direct labor hours and direct labor cost required to complete the expected production during the budgetary period. It is generally assumed that direct labor is a completely variable cost. However, as manufacturing processes become more automated, direct labor

DEPARTMENT	SCHEDULED PRODUCTION (SCHEDULE B)	HOURS PER UNIT (SCHEDULE C)	TOTAL ESTIMATED HOURS	RATE PER HOUR (SCHEDULE C)	TOTAL COST
Assembly	60,000	0.5	30,000	$12.00	$360,000
Finishing	60,000	0.7	42,000	14.00	588,000
Total					$948,000

NATIONAL CASE COMPANY   **Schedule E**
Direct Labor Budget
Year Ending December 31, 19X9

costs may tend to take on semivariable characteristics. The direct labor hours are estimated by multiplying the total hours in each department required to produce one case (Schedule C) by the total number of cases to be produced (Schedule B). The result is multiplied by the dollar rate per hour (Schedule C) to obtain the total direct labor cost.

As with materials, the total direct labor cost for the period may be computed easily by multiplying the scheduled production (Schedule B) by the direct labor cost per case (Schedule E) for a total of $948,000 (60,000 cases at $15.80 per case).

It is usually possible to estimate with a fair degree of accuracy the number of direct labor hours required to manufacture a product. The estimate is customarily based on data from past experience or on established labor standards. A level production rate will obviously simplify the job of estimating the number of direct hours because no major allowances need be made for training inexperienced extra workers during peak periods or for carrying an oversized work force during lean periods.

The Manufacturing Overhead Budget

The manufacturing overhead costs are usually more difficult to budget than either direct materials or direct labor. Both labor and materials are generally considered to be variable costs and vary directly with the volume of output. Manufacturing overhead costs are less consistent. Some of these costs, such as certain indirect materials, are treated as variable costs. These tend to vary in direct proportion to the volume of production. (Volume of production for budgeting and control purposes usually refers to the number of direct labor hours.) Other manufacturing overhead costs, such as depreciation and managers' salaries, are fixed. These tend to remain constant during the period regardless of the level of activity. Still other overhead costs, such as utilities and payroll taxes, are semivariable. These vary to some degree with changes in volume or level of activity but not in direct proportion.

The manufacturing overhead budget for the company is developed by preparing a flexible budget for each department. Usually the flexible budget shows expected costs at volumes ranging from 80 to 120 percent of expected volume at intervals of 5 percent, such as 80, 85,

90, and 95 percent. Ths range is used because rarely does a company operate at less than 80 percent or more than 120 percent of its normal capacity. Using 5 percent intervals makes it easy to quickly compare actual results with the budget at very near the actual level of output.

Schedule E, page 517, showed that normal expected production amounts to 30,000 direct labor hours in the Assembly Department. The simplified manufacturing overhead budget for the Assembly Department (Schedule F), shown below, includes costs at 90, 100, and 110 percent of capacity (normal expected production).

Note that all overhead costs have been classified as fixed or variable. They also have been identified as controllable or noncontrollable at the department level. **Controllable costs** are those over which the activity manager or supervisor has some degree of control. **Noncontrollable costs** are those over which the activity manager or supervisor has almost no control. This is consistent with the use of the flexible budget as a tool for cost control. This classification of costs will make it easier to compare budgeted and actual performance in order to evaluate managerial efficiency.

In this example, the fixed and variable cost estimates have, for the sake of simplicity, been assumed to be the same as those calculated

NATIONAL CASE COMPANY   **Schedule F**
Assembly Department
Yearly Flexible Overhead Budget
Year Ending December 31, 19X9

			Total Budgeted Costs at		
	VARIABLE COST ELEMENT PER HOUR	**FIXED COST ELEMENT**	**90% OF CAPACITY (27,000 HOURS)**	**100% OF CAPACITY (30,000 HOURS)**	**110% OF CAPACITY (33,000 HOURS)**
Controllable Costs					
Indirect Materials	$ .80		$ 21,600	$ 24,000	$ 26,400
Indirect Labor	1.60	$36,000	79,200	84,000	88,800
Payroll Taxes and Fringe Benefits	1.36	3,600	40,320	44,400	48,480
Electric Power	.40	1,200	12,000	13,200	14,400
Other Overhead	.12	3,600	6,840	7,200	7,560
Total Controllable Costs	$4.28	$44,400	$159,960	$172,800	$185,640
Noncontrollable Costs					
Depreciation—Machinery and Equipment	-0-	$36,000	$ 36,000	$ 36,000	$ 36,000
Depreciation—Buildings	-0-	-0-	-0-	-0-	-0-
Property Taxes	-0-	4,800	4,800	4,800	4,800
Property Insurance	-0-	480	480	480	480
Total Noncontrollable Costs	-0-	$41,280	$ 41,280	$ 41,280	$ 41,280
Total Budgeted Costs	$4.28	$85,680	$201,240	$214,080	$226,920

in Chapter 20 for the period beginning November 1, 19X8, and ending October 31, 19X9. In practice, these amounts would be adjusted for inflation and other cost changes when the budget is prepared.

The variable cost items are those that vary directly in total with the number of direct labor hours worked. For example, the costs of indirect materials in the Assembly Department are budgeted at $.80 per direct labor hour. Based on the expected production in that department for 19X9, the total indirect materials costs for the department are budgeted at $24,000 ($.80 per hour × 30,000 hours).

As you have learned, the fixed cost items are those that remain constant regardless of the volume of production. For example, depreciation of the machinery and equipment in the Assembly Department is budgeted at $36,000 for the year. This total amount remains constant even if the actual volume is something other than 30,000 direct labor hours.

Some cost items are shown in both the Variable Costs and the Fixed Costs sections of the budget because they are partly fixed and partly variable. These are the semivariable costs. For example, the electric power costs of the Assembly Department are shown in the Variable Costs section as being $.40 per hour. Based on the expected volume of 30,000 direct labor hours, the total variable electric power costs in the department are expected to be $12,000. At the same time, certain basic electric power costs will be incurred even if there is no production. These fixed electric power costs in the Assembly Department are shown as $1,200 per year. Thus the total budgeted electric power costs in the Assembly Department are $13,200 ($12,000 variable plus $1,200 fixed).

The data from the flexible budgets prepared for each department (such as Schedule F) are used to put together the departmental manufacturing overhead budget (Schedule G). The departmental manufacturing overhead budget (Schedule G) for the National Case Company shows data for the two producing departments as well as for the service department. This combined schedule provides a handy resource for comparing the cost data in the three departments and the breakdown of variable and fixed elements.

The cost per unit manufactured is shown at the bottom of the manufacturing costs budget. The materials and labor costs per case are from Schedule C. The manufacturing overhead cost per unit is calculated by dividing the total manufacturing overhead cost by the number of cases produced.

Combining the Manufacturing Budgets

The manufacturing costs budget (Schedule H), shown on page 520, is prepared from the budgets of the three manufacturing cost elements. In this example, the work in process inventories have been omitted because, based on past experience, they are expected to remain unchanged. This is a commonly made assumption in preparing manufacturing budgets since work in process inventories are usually only a small part of the total costs to be accounted for and any change in them is not important.

NATIONAL CASE COMPANY   **Schedule G**
Departmental Manufacturing Overhead Budget
Year Ending December 31, 19X9

| | Assembly Department* | | Finishing Department† | | Factory Services Department‡ | | TOTAL |
	PER HOUR	TOTAL	PER HOUR	TOTAL	PER HOUR	TOTAL	TOTAL COST
Variable Costs							
Indirect Materials	$ .80	$ 24,000	$ .48	$ 20,160	$ .60	$43,200	$87,360
Indirect Labor	1.60	48,000	2.00	84,000	.80	57,600	180,600
Payroll Taxes and Fringe							
Benefits	1.36	40,800	1.48	62,160	.08	5,760	108,720
Electric Power	.40	12,000	.24	10,080	.16	11,520	33,600
Other Controllable Overhead	.12	3,600	.04	1,680	.12	8,640	13,920
Total Variable Costs	$4.28	$128,400	$4.24	$178,080	$1.76	$126,720	$433,200
Fixed Costs							
Depreciation—Machinery							
and Equipment		$ 36,000		$ 5,040		$ 11,520	$ 52,560
Depreciation—Buildings		-0-		-0-		17,280	17,280
Property Taxes		4,800		840		4,320	9,960
Property Insurance		480		168		1,440	2,088
Indirect Labor and Supervision		36,000		33,600		86,400	156,000
Payroll Taxes and Fringe							
Benefits		3,600		3,360		8,640	15,600
Utilities		1,200		672		2,880	4,752
Repairs and Maintenance		3,600		840		4,320	8,760
Total Fixed Costs		$ 85,680		$ 44,520		$136,800	$267,000
Total Manufacturing Overhead		$214,080		$222,600		$263,520	$700,200

*Based on 30,000 direct labor hours.
†Based on 42,000 direct labor hours.
‡Based on total of 72,000 direct labor hours in two producing departments.

NATIONAL CASE COMPANY   **Schedule H**
Manufacturing Costs Budget
Year Ending December 31, 19X9

Materials Used (Schedule D-2)	$	926,400
Direct Labor (Schedule E)		948,000
Total Manufacturing Overhead Costs (Schedule G)		700,200
Cost of Goods Manufactured (To Exhibit 1)		$2,574,600
Cost per Unit Manufactured		
Materials (Schedule C)	$	15.44
Direct Labor (Schedule C)		15.80
Manufacturing Overhead Costs		
($700,200 ÷ 60,000 cases)		11.67
Total Manufacturing Cost per Case		
($2,574,600 ÷ 60,000 cases)	$	42.91

SELF-REVIEW

1. What is the manufacturing costs budget? Name the detailed budgets that support the manufacturing costs budget.
2. How is the monthly production budget used in planning purchases?
3. What is the relationship between the materials purchases budget and the materials usage budget?
4. How is the overhead flexible budget used in preparing the manufacturing budget?
5. Why are work in process inventories sometimes omitted in preparing the manufacturing costs budget?

Answers to Self-Review

1. The manufacturing costs budget is the budget for manufacturing costs at the production level planned. Detailed individual budgets are prepared for materials, labor, and manufacturing overhead.
2. The monthly production budget, along with information about the beginning inventory, the time required to receive materials, and other information, is the basis for planning purchases of raw materials.
3. The materials usage budget, along with information about beginning and ending materials inventories, determines the materials purchases budget.
4. The overhead flexible budget shows how overhead costs should behave at different levels of activity. Once the production level has been established, the overhead costs that enter into the manufacturing budget can be estimated by using the flexible budget.
5. Work in process inventories are sometimes omitted because it is assumed that there will be little variation between the beginning and ending inventories. Also, in some cases the work in process inventory is relatively unimportant.

OPERATING EXPENSES BUDGET

Detailed budgets are normally prepared for the selling and administrative expenses anticipated as a result of the estimated sales and production operations. Since we are mainly interested in production costs at this time, only a summary of budgeted operating expenses is shown in Schedule 1, on page 522.

BUDGETED INCOME STATEMENT

Data from the supporting budgets (Schedules A, H, and I) are combined to prepare a budgeted income statement for the National Case Company for 19X9 (Exhibit 1). The finished goods inventories are priced at the cost per unit manufactured (Schedule H). The January 1 inventory is $600,740. This represents 14,000 cases (Schedule B) at $42.91 per case. The December 31 inventory equals 12,000 cases (Schedule B) at $42.91 per case.

OTHER BUDGET SCHEDULES

The budget director then proceeds to complete and assemble the other schedules in the master budget, including the schedule of budgeted cash receipts and payments, the budget of asset acquisitions and retirements, and the budgeted balance sheet for December 31, 19X9.

NATIONAL CASE COMPANY Schedule I
Operating Expenses Budget
Year Ending December 31, 19X9

Operating Expenses
  Selling Expenses

Sales Salaries and Commissions	$450,000	
Payroll Taxes and Fringe Benefits	50,000	
Delivery Expense	80,000	
Advertising Expense	30,000	
Travel Expense	40,000	
Total Selling Expenses		$650,000

Administrative and General Expenses

Officers' Salaries	$120,000	
Office Salaries	80,000	
Payroll Taxes and Fringe Benefits	30,000	
Office Supplies and Postage Expense	14,000	
Bad Debts Expense	14,000	
Miscellaneous Expenses	20,000	
Total Administrative and General Expenses		278,000
Total Operating Expenses (To Exhibit 1)		$928,000

NATIONAL CASE COMPANY Exhibit 1
Budgeted Income Statement
Year Ending December 31, 19X9

Revenue

Sales (Schedule A)		$3,968,000

Cost of Goods Sold

Finished Goods Inventory, Jan. 1	$ 600,740	
Add Cost of Goods Manufactured (Schedule H)	2,574,600	
Total Goods Available for Sale	$3,175,340	
Deduct Finished Goods Inventory, Dec. 31	514,920	
Cost of Goods Sold		2,660,420
Gross Profit on Sales		$1,307,580
Operating Expenses (Schedule I)		928,000
Net Income Before Income Taxes		$ 379,580
Provision for Income Taxes		120,000
Net Income After Income Taxes		$ 259,580

Since these items are not immediately related to product cost accounting, they will not be discussed here.

USING THE FLEXIBLE BUDGET AS A MANAGEMENT TOOL

Budgets are commonly used as a control device. Actual results are compared with budgeted amounts, and any important variations are investigated. The use of a flexible budget makes it possible to estimate what the overhead costs should be for any volume actually attained so that the comparison between actual costs and budgeted costs will be meaningful.

For example, assume that the Assembly Department actually worked 2,350 direct labor hours during January 19X9 and that the total electric power cost for the department was $1,104. How well has the manager controlled this cost element? Let us compare the actual cost with the amount that the flexible budget (Schedule F) shows should be the maximum electric power cost for the month.

Budgeted Cost for Month Based on 2,350 Hours

Fixed Cost for Month (yearly cost, $1,200 ÷ 12 months)	$ 100
Variable Costs (2,350 hours × $.40 per hour)	940
Total Budgeted Electric Power Cost Based on 2,350 Hours	$1,040
Actual Costs Incurred During Month	1,104
Unfavorable Budget Variance (overspent budget)	$ 64

The computation shows that the department spent $64 more on electric power than the budget allowance for the month. This amount may be large enough to require further analysis, or it may be that the amount is considered unimportant. At any rate, the difference between goals and performance is clearly shown. This concept of focusing on the things that are not according to plan is part of the general philosophy of **management by exception.** (Note, however, that this computation does not show how much the cost should have been for the number of cases produced, as opposed to the number of hours worked. In order to have this type of information, it is necessary to set manufacturing overhead standards, which are discussed in Chapter 23.)

PERIODIC PERFORMANCE REPORT

Variations between budget allowances and actual results should be pinpointed as quickly as possible so that corrective action can be taken right away. Monthly (or even weekly or daily) **performance reports,** comparing actual and budgeted amounts, are prepared. At the end of January 19X9, the National Case Company's cost accountant prepares a monthly overhead performance report (Exhibit 2), as shown on page 524.

The report shows that 4,700 cases were produced and 2,350 direct labor hours were spent in the work of manufacturing these cases. The fixed costs and the variable costs per hour shown in the flexible budget are used to compute the allowed costs for 2,350 hours. Each actual cost is then compared with the budget allowance. The difference

| | NATIONAL CASE COMPANY | | | | | | Exhibit 2 |

NATIONAL CASE COMPANY
Monthly Overhead Performance Report
Exhibit 2

Department: Assembly Month: January, 19X9
Volume for Month: 4,700 units Direct Labor Hours: 2,350

COST	VARIABLE RATE PER HOUR	Total Budget* for Actual Volume (Hours) VARIABLE	FIXED	TOTAL	ACTUAL*	OVER OR (UNDER) BUDGET	COMMENTS
Controllable							
Indirect Materials	$ .80	$1,880		$1,880	$1,984	$104	
Indirect Labor	1.60	3,760	$3,000	6,760	6,588	(172)	
Payroll Taxes and Fringe Benefits	1.36	3,196	300	3,496	3,496	-0-	
Electric Power	.40	940	100	1,040	1,104	64	
Other Controllable Overhead	.12	282	300	582	896	314	Press No. 1
Total		$10,058	$3,700	$13,758	$14,068	$310	
Noncontrollable							
Depreciation—Machinery and Equipment		-0-	$3,000	$ 3,000	$ 3,000	$-0-	
Depreciation—Buildings		-0-	-0-	-0-	-0-	-0-	
Property Taxes		-0-	400	400	400	-0-	
Property Insurance		-0-	40	40	40	-0-	
Total		$ -0-	$3,440	$ 3,440	$ 3,440	$-0-	
Total Departmental Overhead		$10,058	$7,140	$17,198	$17,508	$310	

*Figures rounded to nearest whole dollar.

BUSINESS HORIZON

Considering the "Relevant Range"

The scattergraph method, the high-low points method, and the method of least squares ("regression analysis") all result in an estimate of fixed costs based on historical data reflecting past operations. The data points (points reflecting actual costs at actual volumes) generally reflect costs within the "relevant range of activity"—the range of volume within which activity was actually carried out during the periods observed and which is used in the calculation of fixed and variable cost components. Management is usually concerned with this volume range and the range of volume anticipated during the coming period(s) for which a budget is being prepared. This means that the fixed cost component and the variable cost per unit component are reasonably reliable if the budgeted volume is within, or near, the range of measurements used in making the calculation. However, if the anticipated range of activity is far below or far above the activity range on which the estimated fixed and variable costs are based, the calculations may be wrong. It is quite possible, for example, that if the volume level became zero (no activity), the fixed costs might be either greater than or less than the estimate of fixed costs computed for the relevant range of activity. The accountant must be alert to recognize that decisions and estimates about activity levels outside the relevant range may require special studies and analyses to determine the anticipated behavior of costs for those levels.

is shown in the Over or (Under) Budget column. This column is the heart of the report, and any expenditures that exceed the budget receive immediate attention if they are important. Although the $104 and $64 overbudget costs are small in dollar amounts, they may require investigation because they represent deviations of 5 or 6 percent ($104 ÷ $1,984 and $64 ÷ $1,104).

One column of the report is for explanatory comments. For instance, the notation "Press No. 1" shows that the unusually high repair and maintenance cost of $896 was due to a breakdown in that press.

The report may be supplied to the department head in duplicate. He or she may then be asked to supply explanations, retain a copy, and forward the original to a superior for review. If very serious variances come to light, management might request weekly reports until the condition has been corrected.

At this point you should be able to work Exercises 21–6 to 21–10 and Problems 21–5A and 21–5B.

OTHER BUDGETARY CONSIDERATIONS

The departmental budgets in this chapter have included only direct departmental overhead costs—those that can be assigned directly to the individual department. Service costs have not been allocated. The concern in this chapter has been with planning and cost control. The service department has a separate budget for control purposes.

SELF-REVIEW

1. In addition to the manufacturing budget, what other budget schedules become part of the master budget?
2. How are budgets used as a control device?
3. Why is the flexible budget used in controlling costs?
4. What is an overhead performance report?
5. How are the costs of service departments, such as an electric generating plant, handled in budget reports?

Answers to Self-Review

1. In addition to the manufacturing budget, the operating expenses budget and the budgeted financial statements become part of the master budget.
2. Budgets are used as a control device by permitting a comparison between actual results with budgeted amounts. Important variations are investigated. The use of flexible budgets allows a comparison between actual costs and what costs should be for the actual production level.
3. The flexible budget is used in controlling costs because it shows what costs should be for the actual production level attained.
4. An overhead performance report is an analysis of what each overhead cost for the period should be, based on the flexible budget, for the production level attained and what the cost actually was. The difference between the two figures for each overhead cost is also shown.
5. Service departments have separate budgets. If the cost of service is directly tied to the activities of a production department on a measurable basis, the department may be charged with a standard rate of usage.

However, if the cost of a service is directly tied to the activities of a producing department on a measurable basis, the producing department may be charged with standard rates per unit of service. For example, if a factory has its own generating plant for electricity, it is customary to charge the producing departments a standard rate per kilowatt-hour of electricity used. The head of each producing department is thus made responsible for the electricity used.

PRINCIPLES AND PROCEDURES SUMMARY

- A budget provides the means for planning and controlling activities. It is the firm's financial control system.
- Preparation of the budget is the responsibility of the budget director, who suggests procedures for budget preparation and gives assistance to those responsible for preparing preliminary budgets for their departments.
- The master budget encompasses the entire financial plan of the company and includes the sales and production budgets, manufacturing costs budget, operating expenses budget, cash receipts and payments budget, and projected financial statements.
- The sales budget is the starting point in the budgeting process. Sales figures are derived from past experience, the economic outlook, and specific company plans for products.
- A production budget reflecting quantities of products to be produced is the next step after the sales budget in preparing a master budget.
- The manufacturing costs budget is a budget for materials, labors, and overhead.
- A flexible budget helps in planning costs. It shows what costs should be for each level of activity.
- The operating expenses budget contains detailed budgets for selling and administrative expenses.
- Budgeted cash receipts and cash disbursements, along with the budgeted balance sheet and income statement, round out the master budget.
- The flexible budget is a key element in controlling costs. Periodic performance reports permit budget allowances and actual results to be pinpointed quickly so that corrective action can be taken right away.
- By comparing what costs should be, according to the flexible budget, with actual costs, management can quickly see areas where costs are not being controlled. Focusing on problem areas is referred to as *management by exception.*

MANAGERIAL IMPLICATIONS

- No aspect of cost accounting is more important to management than the budgeting process.
- The planning budget shows the expected results of management planning on the financial statements. It provides the basis for mak-

ing certain that facilities, personnel, and materials are available when needed. It also provides information about needs for long-term and short-term financing.

■ The budget also provides a yardstick against which to measure actual performance each month.

■ The flexible budget is especially useful in evaluating performance and controlling costs because it can be used to estimate what costs should be at the actual level of output achieved during the year. By comparing actual costs with the flexible budget, management is provided with a good measure of how well costs are being controlled and can take immediate steps to correct areas in which costs are not being controlled properly.

■ For budgeting purposes, the level of output is often expressed in terms of direct labor hours.

REVIEW QUESTIONS

1. Explain what the term *budget* means.
2. What are the purposes of budgeting?
3. Explain what a master budget is.
4. What is the role of the accountant in the budgeting process?
5. What is the role of the budget director in the budgeting process?
6. Why is the sales budget important in the budgeting manufacturing costs?
7. Is economic forecasting important in the budgeting process? Explain.
8. What is the production budget?
9. What factors are used in computing the number of units of a product to be manufactured during the period?
10. What is a flexible budget?
11. How are costs in a flexible budget arrived at?
12. Explain two ways in which a flexible budget is used.
13. What costs are included in the manufacturing costs budget?
14. How would a firm go about setting the budget for direct labor?
15. What information is included in a performance report?
16. How often should a performance report be prepared? Explain.
17. List the major budget schedules that become a part of the master budget.

MANAGERIAL DISCUSSION QUESTIONS

1. What types of economic reports or forecasts would be of special interest in preparing budgets for each of the following?
   a. A manufacturer of automobiles
   b. A home builder
   c. A commercial bank
   d. A community college

2. The management of the company for which you are employed has asked you to explain the steps that would be necessary in setting up a master budget. Respond.

3. You have an appointment with the president of your company to explain how a budget can help in planning. What will you say to her?

4. You are helping to set up a budgeting system in the company for which you work. Should the managers of the factory's operating departments have a role in developing their own budgets? Explain your answer.

5. Explain to your supervisor how a formal budgeting system can help the company's planning.

6. Why would a flexible budget be more useful than a fixed budget in controlling costs and evaluating performance?

7. Why would a manager's performance be different if the manager were allowed to participate in the budgeting process than it would be if top management were to develop the budget without the manager's participation?

8. The actual indirect labor costs of a department in September 19X9 were $104,600. The flexible budget for the level of activity worked called for indirect labor costs of $96,400. With which personnel would management want to discuss this type of overrun?

EXERCISES

EXERCISE 21–1   **Prepare a sales budget.   (Obj. 1).**   In 19X9 the sales of Protek, a product of Ohio Manufacturers, were 612,000 units at an average price of $5.92 per unit. It is anticipated that the number of units sold in 19X9 will decrease 4 percent and the average selling price per unit will increase 5 percent. What will be the company's budgeted sales of Protek for 19X9?

EXERCISE 21–2   **Prepare a production budget.   (Obj. 2).**   The December 31, 19X8, inventory of Syntho, a product manufactured by Household Products, is 82,000 units. The company wants to have an ending inventory on December 31, 19X9, equal to 8 percent of the budgeted sales in 19X9. What will be the budgeted production for 19X9 if the budgeted sales are 800,000 units?

EXERCISE 21–3   **Compute the budgeted materials cost per unit.   (Obj. 2).**   Use the following information about the materials in Alchem, a medicinal product, to prepare a schedule of materials cost per unit of product:

Compound X: 8 ounces for each pound of Alchem; cost per pound, $1.54.

Filler: 4 ounces for each pound of Alchem; cost per pound, $.40.

Compound Y: 4 ounces for each pound of Alchem; cost per pound, $.80.

Packaging: 1 package per pound of Alchem; cost per package, $.20.

EXERCISE 21–4   **Prepare a materials purchases budget. (Obj. 2).** Low Cost Manufacturing Company has projected its sales of Perfecto smoker grills to be 10,000 units during the year 19X9. At the beginning of 19X9, the company will have 1,200 smoker grills in stock, but the controller and purchasing manager have decided that the number of units in the finished goods inventory, as well as the number of units in the raw materials inventory, must be decreased by 25 percent by the end of 19X9.

One of the parts required for each grill is a smoking pot. At the start of 19X9, the company expects to have 1,000 smoking pots in its raw materials inventory. The recorded cost of the 1,000 units is $48 each. During 19X9, it is anticipated that the cost of raw materials will rise by 3.5 percent per unit.

a. How many pots will be required for production in 19X9?

b. How many pots will be purchased in 19X9?

c. What will be the total budgeted cost of the pots to be purchased in 19X9?

EXERCISE 21–5   **Prepare a direct labor budget. (Obj. 2).** The production budget for the Southeast Company, Inc., calls for manufacturing 90,200 units of product during 19X9. Each unit is expected to require $2\frac{1}{4}$ hours of labor in the Mixing Department at a rate of $10.20 per hour and $1\frac{1}{4}$ hours of labor in the Cooking Department at a rate of $7.50 per hour. Prepare the direct labor budget for the company for 19X9.

EXERCISE 21–6   **Prepare a flexible overhead budget. (Obj. 3).** For 19X9, the overhead budget of the Extrusion Department of the Beasley Company includes the following three elements among the costs:

Indirect materials: $.50 per direct labor hour for variable costs plus $33,000 for fixed costs

Salaries of factory manager and factory clerical personnel: $128,000

Payroll taxes and fringe benefits: $4.40 per direct labor hour for variable costs plus $40,000 for fixed costs

Assume that the normal capacity is 60,000 direct labor hours. Determine the department's budget for these three items at 80, 90, 100, 110, and 120 percent of normal capacity.

EXERCISE 21–7   **Prepare a flexible overhead budget. (Obj. 3).** The monthly overhead costs of the Cleaning Department of Bear Creek Corporation have been analyzed as follows:

	Variable (per direct labor hour)	**Fixed** (per month)
Supervision	—	$4,600
Other indirect labor	$ .80	2,400
Utilities	.30	800
Depreciation	—	1,000
Payroll taxes	1.07	630
Other taxes	—	100
Fringe benefits	.88	1,400
Supplies	.18	200

Assume that the department works 6,000 hours during July 19X9. Prepare a budget for overhead for the month, showing the expected total for each cost element and the total for the department.

EXERCISE 21–8 **Prepare an operating expenses budget. (Obj. 4).** Deep South Company has projected its sales for 19X9 to be $1,200,000. Selling expenses are projected as follows:

Salaries of sales manager and other sales office personnel	$118,000
Advertising expense	$24,000, plus 2% of sales
Commissions of two salespersons	10% of sales (guarantee of $3,500 each per month)
Shipping and delivery costs	$20,000, plus 5% of sales
Miscellaneous	$2,000, plus 3% of sales

Prepare a selling expense budget for 19X9.

EXERCISE 21–9 **Prepare a monthly overhead performance report. (Obj. 6).** A portion of the flexible budget for overhead of the Erection Department of Riners Company for 19X9 is shown.

	Variable	TOTAL BUDGETED COST AT			
Item	Cost Element Per Hour	Fixed Cost Element	90% of Capacity	100% of Capacity	110% of Capacity
Indirect Labor	$.80	$36,000	$108,000	$116,000	$124,000
Power	.40	1,200	33,200	41,200	45,200

Capacity is 120,000 direct labor hours. Production is expected to be equal during each month of the year. In July, a total of 8,400 hours were worked. Indirect labor costs were $11,200 and power costs were $3,700.

Compute the budgeted amount for these two elements of cost based on the actual volume achieved in the month, and compute the amount by which actual costs were over (or under) this budgeted amount.

EXERCISE 21–10 **Prepare a monthly performance report; develop a flexible overhead budget. (Objs. 3, 6).** The monthly fixed cost element of indirect labor in the Forming Department of Taylor Company is $12,000, and the variable cost element is $2.20 per direct labor hour. During May 19X9, production was 4,200 direct labor hours. Indirect labor costs were $20,780.

a. Compute the amount of budget variance for indirect labor for the month.

b. What would be the expected indirect labor costs for each of the following levels of activity?

(1) 5,100 direct labor hours

(2) 5,340 direct labor hours

PROBLEMS

PROBLEM 21–1A

Prepare a sales budget. (Obj. 1). The regional sales of the Bicycle Parts Company for the year 19X9 have been forecast as follows:

Area	Sales
Orlando	$12,000,000
Miami	6,000,000
Jacksonville	4,500,000

The company sells three products. An analysis of past sales records indicates the following normal regional distribution of sales by product.

Area	Wheels	Seats	Chains
Orlando	40%	40%	20%
Miami	50%	20%	30%
Jacksonville	40%	30%	30%

Additional analysis shows the following distribution of sales for the first quarter and by quarters thereafter:

	FIRST QUARTER			Second	Third	Fourth
Area	Jan.	Feb.	Mar.	Quarter	Quarter	Quarter
Orlando	6%	6%	10%	30%	25%	23%
Miami	8%	10%	12%	28%	22%	20%
Jacksonville	6%	8%	12%	30%	24%	20%

INSTRUCTIONS

Prepare a total sales budget (in thousands of dollars) for the year 19X9. Show details by area and by product for each quarter and each month of the first quarter.

PROBLEM 21–2A

Prepare production and materials budget. (Obj. 2). The Mantle Frame Company manufactures a single product. Each unit requires the following raw materials.

Item	Quantity	Unit Cost	Total
Backing Units	2	$3.40	$6.80
Fasteners	3	.80	2.40
Plastic Frames	1	6.00	6.00

The beginning inventories on January 1, 19X9, are expected to be as follows:

Raw Materials
   Backing Units, 7,000 at $3.40 each
   Fasteners, 10,500 at $.80 each
   Plastic Frames, 3,500 at $6.00 each
Finished Goods, 4,000 units
Work in Process, 2,000 units (all materials added)

Sales forecast for the month of January 19X9 are 4,000 units; for February, 3,500 units; and for March, 3,000 units. Enough units should be on hand in the finished goods inventory at the end of each month to meet expected sales for the following month. The raw materials on hand should be equal to the following month's production requirements. Work in process remains almost constant.

INSTRUCTIONS

1. Prepare a production budget for the month of January 19X9.
2. Prepare a materials budget for January.

PROBLEM 21–3A

Prepare a direct labor budget; prepare a flexible overhead budget. (Objs. 2, 3). Beta Corporation manufactures a single product requiring 4 hours of labor for each unit of product. Direct labor costs are budgeted at $8 per hour. The budgeted output (normal capacity) for 19X9 is 20,000 units. Overhead cost data are as follows.

	Variable Cost Element per Hour	Fixed Cost Element per Year
Indirect Labor	$1.10	$48,000
Payroll Taxes and Fringe Benefits	1.82	9,600
Indirect Materials	.20	1,000
Power	.10	3,000
Depreciation	—	12,000
Taxes and Insurance	—	6,420
Repairs	.06	3,850

INSTRUCTIONS

1. Prepare the direct labor budget for the year.
2. Prepare a yearly flexible overhead budget at 90, 100, and 110 percent of capacity. Depreciation and taxes and insurance are non-controllable costs.

PROBLEM 21–4A

Prepare a budgeted income statement. (Obj. 5). The following information has been assembled by Peanuts Corporation relating to its 19X9 budget.

Budgeted sales (10,000 hours, 20,000 units), $1,000,000
Manufacturing costs:
   Direct materials, $18 per unit
   Direct labor, $15 per hour
   Manufacturing overhead:
     Fixed, $60,000
     Variable, $6.00 per hour
   Selling and administrative expenses:
     Fixed, $70,000
     Variable, 6% of sales

The inventories on January 1, 19X9, and the desired inventories on December 31, 19X9 are:

	Jan. 1, 19X9	Dec. 31, 19X9
Raw Materials (2,000 units)	$36,000	$34,200
Work in Process	$14,000	$14,000
Finished Goods	2,000 units	1,500 units

INSTRUCTIONS

1. Prepare a budgeted statement of cost of goods manufactured for 19X9.
2. Prepare a budgeted income statement for 19X9.

PROBLEM 21–5A **Prepare a monthly overhead performance report.** **(Obj. 6).** The monthly flexible manufacturing overhead budget for the Separation Department of Benevides Products Corporation follows:

	Variable Cost Element per Hour	Fixed Cost Element	9,000	9,500	10,000	10,500	11,000
			DIRECT LABOR HOURS				
Indirect Labor	$ .30	$2,000	$ 4,700	$ 4,850	$ 5,000	$ 5,150	$ 5,300
Payroll Taxes and Fringe Benefits	1.20	1,000	11,800	12,400	13,000	13,600	14,200
Indirect Materials	.10	100	1,000	1,050	1,100	1,150	1,200
Power and Water	.20	30	1,830	1,930	2,030	2,130	2,230
Depreciation	—	600	600	600	600	600	600
Taxes and Insurance	—	400	400	400	400	400	400
Repairs	.04	115	475	495	515	535	555

During the month of May 19X9, the departmental volume was 9,100 direct labor hours. Actual costs for the month were as follows:

Indirect Labor	$ 4,820
Payroll Taxes and Fringe Benefits	10,970
Indirect Materials	1,040
Power and Water	1,812
Depreciation	600
Taxes and Insurance	400
Repairs	530

INSTRUCTIONS

1. Complete the monthly departmental overhead performance report. Depreciation and taxes and insurance are noncontrollable.
2. Compare budgeted costs for the actual volume attained with actual costs for the month.
3. Which of the costs appear to be well controlled?
4. Which of the costs appear to be out of line?
5. Give some possible explanations for the lack of control over the items that appear to be significantly out of line.

ALTERNATE PROBLEMS

PROBLEM 21–1B **Prepare a sales budget.** **(Obj. 1).** District sales of the Do-It-Yourself Company for the year 19X9 have been forecast as follows:

District	Sales
Tucson	$9,000,000
Minneapolis	6,000,000
St. Louis	3,000,000

The company sells three products. An analysis of past sales records indicates the following normal district distribution of sales by product.

District	Siding	Roofing	Wallboard
Tucson	20%	50%	30%
Minneapolis	25%	45%	30%
St. Louis	30%	50%	20%

Additional analysis shows the following distribution of sales for the first quarter and by quarters thereafter:

	FIRST QUARTER			Second Quarter	Third Quarter	Fourth Quarter
District	Jan.	Feb.	Mar.			
Tucson	4%	6%	10%	30%	30%	20%
Minneapolis	4%	7%	10%	30%	30%	19%
St. Louis	5%	8%	10%	25%	28%	24%

INSTRUCTIONS Prepare a total sales budget (in thousands of dollars) for the year 19X9. Show details by district and by product for each quarter and each month of the first quarter.

PROBLEM 21–2B **Prepare production and materials budget. (Obj. 2).** The Toy Barrel Company manufactures a single product. Each unit requires the following raw materials.

Item	Quantity	Unit Cost	Total
Frames	1	$4.00	$4.00
Panels	4	1.50	6.00
Assembly Units	1	2.85	2.85

The beginning inventories on January 1, 19X9, are expected to be as follows:

Raw Materials
   Frames, 2,200 at $4.00 each
   Panels, 8,800 at $1.50 each
   Assembly Units, 2,200 at $2.85 each
Finished Goods, 3,000 units
Work in Process, 2,000 units (all materials added)

Sales forecast for the month of January 19X9 are 3,000 units; for February, 2,200 units; and for March, 1,600 units. Enough units should be on hand in the finished goods inventory at the end of each month to meet expected sales for the following month. The raw materials on hand should be equal to the following month's production requirements. Work in process remains almost constant.

INSTRUCTIONS 1. Prepare a production budget for the month of January 19X9.
2. Prepare a materials budget for January.

PROBLEM 21–3B **Prepare a direct labor budget; prepare a flexible overhead budget. (Objs. 2, 3).** Amro Company manufactures a single product requiring a half hour of labor for each unit of product. Direct labor costs are budgeted at $10 per hour. The budgeted output (normal capacity) for 19X9 is 60,000 units. Overhead cost data are as follows.

	Variable Cost Element per Hour	Fixed Cost Element per Year
Indirect Labor	.80	$36,000
Payroll Taxes and Fringe Benefits	$1.16	$ 7,500
Indirect Materials	.08	1,600
Power	.16	3,600
Depreciation	—	10,000
Taxes and Insurance	—	3,500
Repairs	.08	2,000

INSTRUCTIONS

1. Prepare the direct labor budget for the year.
2. Prepare a yearly flexible overhead budget at 90, 100, and 110 percent of capacity. Depreciation and taxes and insurance are non-controllable costs.

PROBLEM 21–4B

Prepare a budgeted income statement. (Obj. 5). The chief accountant of San Diego Products Company has accumulated the following information relating to the company's 19X9 budget.

Budgeted sales (14,000 hours, 28,000 units), $1,400,000
Manufacturing costs:
   Direct materials, $15 per unit
   Direct labor, $18 per hour
   Manufacturing overhead:
     Fixed, $80,000
     Variable, $8.00 per hour
   Selling and administrative expenses:
     Fixed, $80,000
     Variable, 8% of sales

The inventories on January 1, 19X9, and the desired inventories on December 31, 19X9, are:

	Jan. 1, 19X9	Dec. 31, 19X9
Raw Materials (5,000 units)	$75,000	$60,000
Work in Process	$24,000	$24,000
Finished Goods	1,400 units	1,800 units

INSTRUCTIONS

1. Prepare a budgeted statement of cost of goods manufactured for 19X9.
2. Prepare a budgeted income statement for 19X9.

PROBLEM 21–5B

Prepare a monthly overhead performance report. (Obj. 6). The monthly flexible manufacturing overhead budget for the Merging Department of the Orange Products Company is given below.

	Variable Cost Element per Hour	Fixed Cost Element	Direct Labor Hours				
			9,000	9,500	10,000	10,500	11,000
Indirect Labor	$.40	$1,000	$4,600	$4,800	$5,000	$5,200	$5,400
Payroll Taxes and Fringe Benefits	.62	160	5,740	6,050	6,360	6,670	6,980
Indirect Materials	.08	100	820	860	900	940	980
Power and Water	.04	110	470	490	510	530	550

Depreciation	—	920	920	920	920	920	920
Taxes and Insurance	—	185	185	185	185	185	400
Repairs	.03	50	320	335	350	365	380

During the month of August 19X9, the departmental volume was 10,650 direct labor hours. Actual costs for the month were as follows:

Indirect Labor	$5,405
Payroll Taxes and Fringe Benefits	6,740
Indirect Materials	942
Power and Water	548
Depreciation	920
Taxes and Insurance	185
Repairs	373

INSTRUCTIONS

1. Complete the monthly departmental overhead performance report. Depreciation and taxes and insurance are noncontrollable costs.
2. Compare budgeted costs for the actual volume attained with actual costs for the month.
3. Which of the costs appear to be well controlled?
4. Which of the costs appear to be out of line?
5. Give some possible explanations for the lack of control over the items that appear to be significantly out of line.

MANAGERIAL DECISION CASE

Space Corporation installed a new budgeting system in 19X9. The budget was based on carefully prepared sales forecasts and production schedules. It was anticipated that during the year 120,000 units of its product would be manufactured, spread equally over each month and requiring 960,000 direct labor hours. The overhead budget was based on careful analysis of fixed and variable costs.

In July 19X9, the president, your client, asked you for advice (you are an accountant). He was disturbed because the actual costs for June were over the budgeted amounts. The controller's report showed the yearly and monthly budgeted amounts and the actual results for June as follows.

Cost Item	Yearly			Monthly Budget	Actual for May
	Variable	Fixed	Total		
Indirect Materials	$ 960,000	$ 40,000	$1,000,000	$ 83,333	$ 96,200
Indirect Labor	290,000	160,000	450,000	37,500	29,200
Payroll Taxes and Fringe Benefits	1,658,000	32,000	1,690,000	140,833	141,200
Utilities	96,000	60,000	156,000	13,000	13,800
Repairs and Maintenance	96,000	30,000	126,000	10,500	14,700
Miscellaneous	48,000	50,000	98,000	8,167	8,666
Depreciation		72,000	72,000	6,000	7,000
Property Taxes and Insurance		80,000	80,000	6,667	7,200
	$3,148,000	$524,000	$3,672,000	$306,000	$317,966

You ask several questions and find, among other things, that production during the month was 11,250 units, requiring 90,000 direct labor hours.

1. Explain to your client how a flexible budget would be a better tool for evaluating the performance of the production manager.
2. Prepare a monthly overhead performance report. Evaluate the cost control exercised by the production manager based on this report by analyzing each item in the report.

C H A P T E R

22

Standard Costs: Materials and Labor

You learned in Chapter 21 that a budget is a projection of future costs and revenues that is used for both planning and control purposes. One very important way in which budgeting techniques are used in manufacturing operations is in developing standard costs. **Standard manufacturing costs** are predetermined measures of the cost of each manufacturing element (materials, labor, and overhead) under specified, efficient operating conditions. These costs are expressed in terms of standard quantity and standard cost per unit of product. In a standard cost system, the emphasis is on what costs should be. Most well-managed manufacturing companies use standard costs in evaluating the efficiency and performance of managers and production departments.

OBJECTIVES

1. Explain and illustrate the use of a standard manufacturing cost system for planning and control purposes.
2. Determine standard materials costs and standard labor costs per unit of product.
3. Compute materials quantity and materials price variances and identify them as being favorable or unfavorable.
4. Prepare journal entries to charge materials into production and record variances.
5. Compute labor efficiency and labor rate variances and identify them as being favorable or unfavorable.
6. Prepare journal entries to charge labor costs into production and record variances.

NEW TERMS

Labor efficiency variance, labor time variance, labor usage variance, or labor quantity variance (p. 549)
Labor rate variance or labor price variance (p. 550)
Materials price standard (p. 543)
Materials price variance (p. 545)
Materials quantity standard (p. 542)
Materials quantity variance or materials usage variance (p. 545)
Normal or attainable standards (p. 540)
Standard cost of a material for period (p. 543)
Standard cost sheet (p. 539)
Standard manufacturing costs (p. 538)
Theoretical or ideal standards (p. 540)
Variance (p. 542)

USING STANDARD COSTS

Standard costs for each unit of product are typically presented on a standard cost sheet such as Exhibit 1. A **standard cost sheet** is a form on which the standard cost of labor, materials, and overhead for each unit of product, along with supporting details, are shown. The supporting details include standard quantities of each type of material and labor, the price per unit of each type of materials, the hourly rate for each type of labor, and the overhead cost per hour of labor, along with the cost for materials, labor, and overhead per unit of finished product. In this chapter, you will learn how the standard costs for materials and labor are developed and how they are used. In Chapter 23, standard costs for manufacturing overhead will be discussed.

Uses of Standard Costs

Standard cost data can be used in numerous ways in addition to budgeting. The following are some typical uses:

- Reducing recordkeeping expenses by keeping records in terms of predetermined standard costs rather than varying historical costs that would require time-consuming computations.

NATIONAL CASE COMPANY Standard Cost Sheet Jewelry Case JC-14 For Year 19X9			**Exhibit 1**
	QUANTITY	**UNIT COSTS**	**STANDARD COST PER CASE**
Materials			
DM-1	3 ft	$4.00 per ft	$12.000
DM-8	4 sets	.40 per set	1.600
DM-4	12 sets	.10 per set	1.200
DM-5	$\frac{2}{25}$ qt	$8.00 per quart	.640
Total Materials Cost per Case			$15.440
Labor			
Assembly Department	.5 hr	$12.00 per hr	$ 6.000
Finishing Department	.7 hr	14.00 per hr	9.800
Total Labor Cost per Case			$15.800
Overhead			
Assembly Department			
Variable Costs	.5 hr	$ 6.040 per hr	$ 3.020
Fixed Costs	.5 hr	4.376 per hr	2.188
Total for Assembly Department	.5 hr	$10.486	$ 5.208
Finishing Department			
Variable Costs	.7 hr	$ 6.000 per hr	$ 4.200
Fixed Costs	.7 hr	3.231 per hr	2.262
Total for Finishing Department		$ 9.231	$ 6.462
Total Overhead Cost per Case			$11.670
Total Standard Cost per Case			$42.910

■ Measuring inventory and cost of goods sold in preparing financial statements. (The use of standard costs eliminates complex calculations for inventories and cost of goods sold.)
■ Evaluating various operations by comparing actual and standard costs.
■ Aiding in decision making, for example, in setting prices and evaluating alternatives.

Standard costs are often the best estimate of differential costs and incremental costs used in decision cost analysis. (Decision cost analysis will be discussed in Chapter 25.)

Setting Standards

The usefulness of standard costs depends on how realistic they are. Some companies rely almost entirely on past average costs in setting their standards. Other companies start with historical costs and adjust them for anticipated changes such as price increases or decreases for materials and rate changes for labor. A proper approach would be to use both historical costs and anticipated changes in prices in making the estimate. It is also important to obtain input from people within the company, such as the cost accountant, the industrial engineer, the purchasing manager, the personnel manager, the sales manager, and the production manager, who can provide relevant information.

One procedure for determining standards involves analyzing engineering specifications in the light of past experience, projections of future events, and company policy. For example, engineering specifications may indicate that 8 pounds of raw material are required for each completed unit. Yet past experience shows that an average of 9 pounds per unit is used. Management may believe that if spoilage and inefficiencies are kept to an acceptable level, $8\frac{1}{2}$ pounds would be a realistic standard quantity per unit.

In setting standards, management must choose a level of operating efficiency with which to work. **Theoretical standards** (sometimes called **ideal standards**) are goals that could be attained only under perfect operating conditions. **Normal standards** (sometimes called **attainable standards**) are standards based on a realistic, though demanding, view of efficiency.

Theoretical Standards. Theoretical standards represent goals that could be attained only by achieving perfection. They make no provision for lost or idle time, breakdowns, and other factors that reduce efficiency. Since they can seldom be met, theoretical standards have a psychological disadvantage. Responsible supervisors often develop the attitude "Why try when we aren't expected to meet these goals anyway?" As a result, theoretical standards are seldom used.

Normal Standards. Normal standards represent goals that can be met under reasonably efficient operating conditions because they provide for idle time, breakdowns, and common operating problems. In

SELF-REVIEW

1. What are standard manufacturing costs?
2. What is a standard cost sheet?
3. What are theoretical standards?
4. What are normal standards?
5. Should theoretical standards or normal standards be used to set goals? Explain your answer.

Answers to Self-Review

1. Standard manufacturing costs are predetermined measures of the cost of each manufacturing element under specified, efficient operating conditions.
2. A standard cost sheet is a form on which the standard quantities of each type of material and labor, the price per unit for each type of materials, and the hourly rate for each type of labor are shown.
3. Theoretical standards are goals that could be attained only under perfect operating conditions.
4. Normal standards are goals that can be met under reasonably efficient operating conditions.
5. Normal standards should generally be used because they succeed in encouraging efficiency while keeping goals reasonable enough to be met.

using normal standards, management must succeed in encouraging top efficiency while keeping goals reasonable enough to be met. Most standard cost systems are based on normal standards.

IMPLEMENTING A STANDARD COST SYSTEM

To develop and use a standard cost system, the accountant must do the following:

- Establish standards for each cost element (materials, labor, and overhead).
- Record actual costs incurred during the period.
- Determine the standard costs for the number of units produced during the period.
- Compute variances by comparing the actual costs of the units produced and the standard costs of those units.
- Break down the variance for each element into its component parts in order to determine the cause of the variance.
- Record production costs and variances.

The National Case Company decides to use a standard cost accounting system. Management has approved the standards shown on the standard cost sheet (Exhibit 1) on page 539. The cost accountant will follow the procedures listed above in accounting for the costs of materials and labor for January 19X9.

Materials Costs

Under the National Case Company's standard cost system, materials standards are set and the materials are accounted for as follows.

Failure to Meet Product Standards Costly to Producers

Manufacturers must establish and maintain manufacturing standards that ensure high product quality, protect consumers, and result in user satisfaction if they are to be successful and profitable. The manufacturing control process must ensure that both quality and quantity of the product are adequate. Even the best-managed companies, however, may have difficulty in controlling quality during the production process or in manufacturing enough units to meet demand during a period. Even worse, product problems often do not come to light until after the product has been sold to consumers. Problems that result in injury to users, or even death, frequently cost producers millions of dollars. This is why high standards are important whether a standard cost system or some other system of cost accounting is used. Almost daily, there are news reports about products that are alleged to have caused death or serious injury to consumers, and frequently these stories result from lawsuits brought by the injured parties against the manufacturer and distributors of the product. Also, there are frequent stories about manufacturers who have lost customers because of their inability to produce high-quality products in adequate quantities to meet customers' needs. In a single day in September 1997, the financial press (including *The Wall Street Journal* on September 4, 1997) reported costly product problems with a large and well-respected company, Clorox Company.

Clorox Company was reported to have recalled and halted production of Quicksilver, a product to be used in cleaning automobile wheels. The product was reported to contain small quantities of two poisonous substances and was implicated in the death of a child in August 1997. The company announced removal of the product from the shelves of approximately 16,000 retail dealers and also asked consumers to contact the company to obtain information on how to properly dispose of the product.

Establishing Standards. Quantity and price standards are set for each type of material used and are recorded on the standard cost sheet shown in Exhibit 1 on page 539.

Materials Quantity Standards. A **materials quantity standard** is the amount of material that should be consumed in manufacturing a unit of product. The engineers who design a product are responsible for determining how much material is needed for each unit. Detailed specifications, engineering studies, blueprints, and similar technical data show exactly what is needed. Sometimes test runs or analyses of past experience are used in developing quantity standards. Materials spoilage or waste that is a necessary part of the manufacturing process must be considered in setting the quantity standards. Then a variance between the actual quantity and the standard quantity will show only excessive spoilage. (A **variance** is simply the difference between the standard amount of an item and the actual amount of that item.) Production managers should help set the materials quantity standards, since they must get the work done within these standards.

Materials Price Standards. A **materials price standard** is the price that should be paid for a unit of raw material. Price standards are based on the prices that the firm expects to pay for materials during the coming period. If there is no reliable data on possible price changes, the prices at the time standards are set may be used. The purchasing agent is responsible for finding suppliers and taking advantage of competitive bidding. It is also the purchasing agent's job to buy in economical quantities and to make sure that both cost needs and quality needs are met. Purchasing agents should help to set price standards since they must explain price variances. During periods of inflation, it is customary to assume a price increase based on the company's recent history.

Recording Actual Costs

Actual costs incurred for raw materials purchases during the period are recorded in exactly the same way that you have learned in previous chapters. Purchases are recorded in the voucher register and posted to the Raw Materials account at the end of the month. The effect of the posting, in general journal form, is shown below.

19X9			
Jan. 31	Raw Materials	121	XXX.XX	
	Vouchers Payable	201		XXX.XX
	Recorded purchases of raw materials during the month.			

Although there is no change in the way in which raw materials purchases are recorded when a standard cost accounting system is used, the procedures for recording the costs of materials placed in production are much different. The actual journal entry to record materials placed in production is explained on page 546. However, before that entry is made, it is necessary to compute the standard materials costs of the month's production and to determine variances between actual costs and standard costs. Those steps are examined below.

Determining Standard Materials Costs of Production During the Period. The **total standard cost of a raw material for a period** the units of production during the period is found by multiplying (1) the total standard quantity of the raw material required to manufacture the number of units of production during the period by (2) the standard price per unit of raw materials. For example, Exhibit 2 shows that 3 feet of material DM-1 is required to manufacture one of National Case Company's jewelry cases (JC-14). Since 4,500 cases were produced during January 19X9, a total of 13,500 feet of material DM-1 were allowed ("standard quantity") for the month's case production (3 feet × 4,500 = 13,500). Each foot of material DM-1 had a standard cost of $4. Therefore, the total standard cost of material DM-1 for the month was $54,000 ($4 × 13,500).

NATIONAL CASE COMPANY   **Exhibit 2**
Summary of Materials Costs
Month Ended January 31, 19X9

PRODUCTION: 4,500 CASES

		Standard				**Actual**		
	QUANTITY	**TOTAL QUANTITY**	**UNIT**	**TOTAL**	**TOTAL QUANTITY**	**UNIT**	**TOTAL**	**TOTAL**
MATERIALS	**PER CASE**	**REQUIRED**	**COST**	**COST**	**USED**	**COST**	**COST**	**VARIANCE**
DM-1	3 ft	13,500	$4.00	$54,000	10,000 / 3,800	$4.00 / 4.08	$40,000 / 15,504	$1,504U
DM-8	4 sets	18,000	.40	7,200	16,000 / 2,200	.40 / .36	6,400 / 792	8F
DM-4	12 sets	54,000	.10	5,400	54,000	.10	5,400	-0-
DM-5	$\frac{2}{25}$ gal	360	8.00	2,880	360	8.00	2,880	-0-
Total				$69,480			$70,976	$1,496U

The standard materials costs for the month's production will be the sum of the standard costs of the individual items of material. The total standard materials cost for the 4,500 cases produced by National during the month of January is $69,480, as shown in column 5 of Exhibit 2.

Computing Variances. The total materials variance for January is the difference between the standard cost of $69,480 allowed for 4,500 cases and the actual costs of materials used, $70,096 (shown in column 8 of Exhibit 2). Since the actual costs exceed the standard cost by $1,496 ($70,095 − $69,480), the total materials variance is said to be unfavorable.

Although the accountant and management are interested in the total materials variance, they need detailed information about the variance for each individual material if the information is to be of use in controlling costs. The total materials variance for each type of material is the difference between the standard cost for the number of units produced during the period and the actual cost of that material used during the period. These calculations are shown in the last column of Exhibit 2. Notice that there is an unfavorable variance of $1,504 for material DM-1, with a small offsetting favorable variance of $8 for material DM-8. Favorable variances are indicated by the letter F, and unfavorable variances are indicated by the letter U.

Two factors could account for the total materials variance:

■ There may be a difference between the standard quantity called for and the actual quantity of materials used (a materials quantity or usage variance).

■ There may be a difference between the standard cost per unit and the actual cost per unit of materials used (a materials price or cost variance).

Materials Quantity Variance. The amount of a **materials quantity variance** or **materials usage variance** is computed by comparing the cost of the standard quantity of materials at the standard price per unit with the cost of the actual quantity of materials at the standard price per unit. This calculation simply tells us how much additional cost there would have been from using too many units of the material if the cost per unit of material had been the standard cost per unit. If the quantity actually used is less than standard, the calculation indicates how much would have been saved if the actual price per unit of raw material had been the standard price. If the actual quantity used exceeds the standard quantity, there is an *unfavorable* materials quantity, or usage variance. On the other hand, if the actual quantity is less than the standard quantity, there is a *favorable* materials quantity or usage variance. Exhibit 2 shows both an unfavorable variance and a favorable variance. The variances are computed as follows:

Materials Quantity Variance = (Standard Quantity × Standard Price)
  − (Actual Quantity × Standard Price)

For Material DM-1, the quantity variance is unfavorable.

13,500 standard units × $4 standard price per unit	$54,000
13,800 standard units × $4 standard price per unit	55,200
Materials Quantity Variance (300 units × $4)	$ 1,200U

For Material DM-8, the quantity variance is unfavorable.

18,000 standard units × $.40 standard price per unit	$7,200
18,200 actual units × $.40 standard price per unit	7,280
Materials Quantity Variance (200 × $.40)	$ 80U

Materials Price Variance. A **materials price variance** results when the actual price per unit differs from the standard price per unit. It is computed by taking the difference between the cost of the actual quantity used at the standard unit price and the cost of the actual quantity of materials used at the actual unit price. If the actual price per unit exceeds the standard price per unit, there is an unfavorable (U) variance. The variance is computed as follows:

Materials Price Variance = (Actual Quantity × Standard Price)
  − (Actual Quantity × Actual Price)

For Material DM-1, the price variance is unfavorable (U).

13,800 actual units × $4 standard price per unit		$55,200
10,000 actual units × $4 actual price per unit	$40,000	
3,800 actual units × $4.08 actual price per unit	15,504	55,504
Materials Price Variance		$ 304U

For Material DM-8, the price variance is favorable (F).

18,200 actual units × $.40 standard price per unit		$7,280
16,000 actual units × $.40 actual price per unit	$6,400	
2,200 actual units × $.36 actual price per unit	792	7,192
Materials Price Variance		$ 88F

Note that there are no variances for Materials DM-4 and DM-5. The standard quantity equals the actual quantity used for both. The standard price also equals the actual price for both types of materials. (See Exhibit 2.)

The results of the materials quantity and price variance computations are presented in the materials variances summary. (See Exhibit 3.) The materials quantity variance plus the materials price variance equals the total variance for each type of materials and for the period.

	NATIONAL CASE COMPANY **Materials Variances Summary** **Month Ended January 31, 19X9**		**Exhibit 3**
MATERIALS	**QUANTITY VARIANCE**	**PRICE VARIANCE**	**TOTAL VARIANCE**
DM-1	$1,200U	$304U	$1,504U
DM-8	80U	88F	8F
Total	$1,280U	$216U	$1,496U

Recording Production Costs and Variances for Materials

Using the data from the summary of materials costs (Exhibit 2) and the materials variances summary (Exhibit 3), the accountant journalizes the production costs and variances for the period. The Work in Process account is charged with the total standard cost for the period, $69,480. The Raw Materials account is credited for the actual cost of materials used, $70,976. These two amounts are obtained from Exhibit 2. Any difference represents the materials variances shown in Exhibit 3. Unfavorable variances are recorded as debits. Favorable variances are recorded as credits. Since both the materials quantity variance, $1,280, and the materials price variance, $216, were unfavorable, they are shown as debits. The complete entry is given below in general journal form.

19X9				
Jan. 31	Work in Process (Standard Cost)	122	69,480	
	Materials Quantity Variance	508	1,280	
	Materials Price Variance	509	216	
	Raw Materials (Actual Cost)	121		70,976
	Charged Work in Process with standard cost of materials, recorded actual cost of materials removed from inventory, and recorded materials variances.			

Recording Materials Variances as They Occur. The preceding variances were recorded only when the manufacturing costs were changed to work in process at the end of the month. However, some accountants believe that any variance in the price of materials should be recorded at the time the materials are purchased. This way, maximum

SELF-REVIEW

1. What is a materials quantity standard?
2. What is a materials price standard?
3. How are materials quantity standards determined?
4. What two variances account for the difference between actual materials cost and standard materials cost for a period?
5. Explain how to calculate the materials price variance.
6. Explain how to calculate the materials quantity variance.

Answers to Self-Review

1. A materials quantity standard is the amount of material that should be consumed in producing a unit of product.
2. A materials price standard is the price that should be paid for a unit of raw material.
3. Materials quantity standards are based on engineering specification, studies, blueprints, test runs, and experience.
4. The difference between the actual cost of a material put into production and its standard cost is explained by the materials quantity variance and the materials price variance.
5. The materials price variance is computed by comparing the actual cost of materials consumed with what the materials used would have cost if the price of the materials had been at standard cost per unit.
6. The materials quantity variance is computed by comparing the standard materials costs for the units of production during the period with the amount that the actual quantity of materials consumed would have cost if the cost per unit of raw material had been the standard price per unit.

control can be exercised at the time a variance occurs. This practice also allows the raw materials inventories to be carried at standard cost, with only quantities shown in the materials ledger. When materials are placed in production, their standard cost is debited to the Work in Process account and credited to the Raw Materials account. Because this procedure is not used frequently, it is not illustrated in this text.

LABOR COSTS

The procedure used to account for labor costs in a standard cost system is similar to that used for materials.

Establishing Standards

Both quantity (time) and rate (price) standards are established for direct labor and entered on the standard cost sheet, as shown in Exhibit 1, on page 539.

Labor Quantity Standards. Standards for direct labor quantity are based on human behavior, performance, and judgment. They are a good deal less exact than materials standards, which can be based on design specifications. Time and motion studies analyzing each step in the production process may be used in setting time standards. Production and time records that reflect past operating results are also useful. An analysis of the experience and skills of the available work force is essential.

Labor Rate Standards. Labor rate information is obtained from the personnel department and from labor union contracts. Standard labor rates are usually based on current rates being paid or scheduled to be paid. Often there will be no labor rate variances. However, labor rates may change during the period. Also, personnel doing the same job may be paid at different rates, or personnel earning different rates may be shifted from job to job or from department to department. Similarly, personnel with seniority may retire and new personnel earning a lower (or a higher) rate may be employed. In all these cases, labor rate variances may occur.

At this point you should be able to work Exercises 22–1 to 22–5 and Problems 22–1A and 22–1B.

As shown in Exhibit 1 (page 539), the Assembly Department has a labor quantity or labor time standard of .5 hour per case and a price or rate standard of $12 per direct labor hour. The standard labor cost per case in the Assembly Department is $6 ($12 × .5).

Exhibit 1 shows only one direct labor rate for each department. Separate standards are often set for each labor operation within a department if different personnel are used. For instance, trainees may have a lower standard rate than experienced workers have.

Recording Actual Costs

At the time labor costs are incurred, they are initially charged to the Factory Payroll Clearing account in exactly the same way they are recorded when a process cost accounting system is used. During the month of January 19X9, labor costs incurred by National Case Company are recorded as shown in the summary entry that follows:

19X9			
Jan. 31	Factory Payroll Clearing	500	72,680
	Salaries and Wages Payable (and other liability accounts)	XXX	72,680
	Recorded actual direct labor costs during the month.		

As you will see later, however, the procedure for charging labor costs into work in process are substantially different when standard cost accounting is used.

Determining Standard Labor Costs for the Period

The standard labor costs for the period are calculated using the actual production figure and the cost data from the standard cost sheet (Exhibit 1). A summary of labor costs for the National Case Company for January 19X9 is shown in Exhibit 4. In this summary, the total

	Standard				**Actual**			
DEPARTMENT	**HOURS PER CASE**	**TOTAL HOURS**	**RATE PER HOUR**	**TOTAL COST**	**HOURS**	**RATE PER HOUR**	**TOTAL COST**	**TOTAL VARIANCE**
Assembly	.5	2,250	$12.00	$27,000	2,350	$12.40	$29,140	$2,140U
Finishing	.7	3,150	14.00	44,100	3,110	14.00	43,540	560F
Total				$71,100			$72,680	$1,580U

NATIONAL CASE COMPANY
Summary of Labor Costs
Month Ended January 31, 19X9
Production: 4,500 Cases

Exhibit 4

standard labor hours in the Assembly Department are shown as 2,250 (4,500 cases at .5 hour per case). The standard cost of labor in the Assembly Department during January is $27,000 (2,250 hours at $12 per hour). The total standard labor cost for the month is $71,100 (4,500 cases at $15.80 per case).

Computing Variances

The total labor variance for each department is the difference between the total standard labor cost of production for the period and the total actual labor cost incurred. The actual costs are shown in the summary of labor costs (Exhibit 4). Since the actual labor costs, $72,680, exceed the standard labor costs, $71,100, there is a total unfavorable labor variance of $1,580 for January.

The total labor variance shown in the summary is analyzed by type and by department. As with materials, two types of labor variances are computed for each department. The labor efficiency variance is comparable to the materials quantity variance. The labor rate variance is similar to the materials price variance.

Labor Efficiency Variances. The **labor efficiency variance,** also called **labor time variance, labor usage variance,** or **labor quantity variance,** compares the cost of *actual* hours worked (based on the standard rate per hour) with the cost of standard hours *allowed* for the number of units produced (based on the standard rate per hour). This variance measures the effectiveness of labor. The production manager is usually responsible for the efficiency variance. If the actual hours exceed the standard hours, there is an unfavorable labor efficiency variance. The variance is computed as follows:

Labor Efficiency Variance = (Standard Quantity × Standard Rate) − (Actual Quantity × Standard Rate)

For the Assembly Department, the labor efficiency variance for January 19X9 is unfavorable.

2,250 standard hours × $12 standard rate per hour	$27,000
2,350 actual hours × $12 standard rate per hour	28,200
Labor Efficiency Variance (100 hours × $12 per hour)	$ 1,200U

For the Finishing Department, the labor efficiency variance is favorable.

3,150 standard hours × $14 standard rate per hour	$44,100
3,110 actual hours × $14 standard rate per hour	43,540
Labor Efficiency Variance (40 hours × $14 per hour)	$ 560F

Labor Rate Variance. The **labor rate variance** (also called the **labor price variance**) occurs when the actual labor rate per hour differs from the standard labor rate per hour. The variance is unfavorable if the actual rate exceeds the standard rate and is favorable if the actual rate is lower than the standard rate. Labor rates are frequently set by a contract with a labor union or by the personnel department. In this sense, the labor rate variance is outside the control of the production manager. However, the choice of personnel within the department may affect the labor rate. The labor rate variance is computed as follows:

Labor Rate Variance = (Actual Quantity × Standard Rate) −
(Actual Quantity × Actual Rate)

No labor rate variance occurred in the Finishing Department since the actual rate was the same as the standard rate (Exhibit 4).

For the Assembly Department, the labor rate variance is unfavorable.

2,350 actual hours × $12 standard rate per hour	$28,200
2,350 actual hours × $12.40 actual rate per hour	29,140
Labor Rate Variance (2,350 hours × $.40 per hour)	$ 940U

The labor efficiency and rate variances are summarized in Exhibit 5. The sum of the labor efficiency variance and the labor rate variance equals the total variance for each department and for the period.

NATIONAL CASE COMPANY   **Exhibit 5**
Labor Variances Summary
Month Ended January 31, 19X9

DEPARTMENT	LABOR EFFICIENCY VARIANCE	LABOR RATE VARIANCE	TOTAL VARIANCE
Assembly	$1,200U	$940U	$1,240U
Finishing	560F	-0-	560F
Total	$ 640U	$940U	$1,580U

Recording Production Costs and Variances

The data from the summary of labor costs (Exhibit 4) and the labor variances summary (Exhibit 5) are used to journalize labor costs for the period. Work in Process is debited for the total standard labor cost of $71,100. Factory Payroll Clearing is credited for the actual

SELF-REVIEW

1. Explain how the labor efficiency variance is computed.
2. Explain how the labor rate variance is computed.
3. At what point are the labor efficiency and labor rate variances recorded?
4. Are favorable labor variances recorded as debits or as credits?
5. Should the production manager have a role in setting labor time standards?

Answers to Self-Review

1. The labor efficiency variance is computed by comparing the standard cost of the standard hours set for the units produced with the standard cost of the actual hours used.
2. The labor rate variance is computed by comparing the standard rate at the standard hours with the actual rate at the standard hours.
3. The labor efficiency and labor rate variances are recorded at the end of the month at the time labor costs are removed from Factory Payroll Clearing account and charged to Work in Process.
4. Favorable labor variances are recorded as credits because the debit to Work in Process for standard cost is greater than the credit to the Factory Payroll Clearing account for actual costs.
5. Factory production managers should have a major role in setting standards because they are the ones who must meet the standards. If they are committed to the standards, they are likely to make every effort to ensure that the standards are met.

costs of $72,680. Any difference is accounted for by the labor variances shown in the labor variances summary (Exhibit 5). Unfavorable variances are recorded as debits. Favorable variances are recorded as credits. Since both labor variances are unfavorable, they are shown as debits. The complete entry is shown below in general journal form.

At this point you should be able to work Exercises 22–6 and 22–7 and Problems 22–2A to 22–3B.

19X9				
Jan. 31	Work in Process (Standard Cost)	122	71,100	
	Labor Efficiency Variance	510	640	
	Labor Rate Variance	511	940	
	Factory Payroll Clearing (Actual Cost)	500		72,680
	Charged Work in Process with standard cost of direct labor, removed actual labor cost from Factory Payroll Clearing, and recorded labor variances.			

PRINCIPLES AND PROCEDURES SUMMARY

■ Many manufacturing companies establish manufacturing cost standards to aid in controlling costs and measuring efficiency.
■ Standard manufacturing costs are predetermined measures of the cost of each manufacturing element.

- Two approaches may be used to setting standard costs:
  - Theoretical standards are based on goals that can be met only under perfect operating conditions.
  - Normal standards are based on goals that can be met under reasonably efficient working conditions. Most companies use normal standards.
- Materials quantity standards are based on engineering and design specifications, tempered by experience.
- Materials price standards are based on expectations about future costs, relying heavily on current cost documents and on expected changes.
- A standard cost for each material going into a product is developed.
- The standard cost for a material for the current period's production is found by multiplying the standard cost per unit by the standard number of units allowed for production during the period.
- The total standard cost of the current period's production is the sum of the standard cost amounts for the individual materials.
- There are two types of variance between standard materials costs for the period and actual materials costs:
  - The materials price variance represents the difference between actual prices of materials for the quantity used during the period and the standard unit prices of the materials for the quantity used during the period.
  - The materials quantity variance represents the difference between standard prices of materials for the standard quantity allowed during the period and the standard prices for the actual quantity of materials used during the year.
- Standard labor quantities are set by engineering specifications, time and motion studies, experience, and other factors.
- Standard labor rates are set by union contracts, company policy, an analysis of existing wage rates, and similar factors.
- The difference between the actual labor costs during the period and the standard labor costs during the period is analyzed in much the same way as material costs are analyzed:
  - The labor efficiency variance measures the amount by which labor costs were increased or decreased from the standard allowed, assuming that standard rates had prevailed. The labor efficiency variance is similar to the materials quantity variance.
  - The labor rate variance is similar to the materials price variance and measures the amount by which actual labor costs were greater or less than standard because wage rates for the actual hours worked were more than or less than standard rates.
- When materials and labor costs are charged to work in process, the variances are recorded. Favorable variances are credited to the variance accounts, and unfavorable variances are debited to the variance accounts.

MANAGERIAL IMPLICATIONS

- The establishment of standard costs is very important to management. It forces all parties involved to study the manufacturing processes, including materials and labor requirements.
- Standard costs provide a yardstick against which actual costs can be measured. Deviations of actual costs from standard costs alerts management to potential problem areas.
- Of particular importance to management is the computation of materials price and materials quantity variances. Analyzing overall materials cost variances in this manner helps to pinpoint responsibility for deviations from standard.
  - Generally, materials price variances are the responsibility of the purchasing department.
  - Materials usage or quantity variances are usually the responsibility of the production manager.
  - Responsibility is not automatically assigned. For example, excess materials usage may have resulted from the purchase of poor-quality raw materials; thus an excess of actual materials over standard may not be the fault of the production manager but of the purchasing department.
- Similarly, the division of the total labor variance into rate variances and efficiency variances will help to determine why actual labor costs are more than or less than standard.
  - Labor rate variances may be the responsibility of the personnel department. However, the production manager may use a mix of personnel, require overtime, and so on that results in rate variances.
  - Labor efficiency variances are generally the responsibility of the production manager, but the ability of the personnel department to acquire good employees, problems with defective materials that lead to excess hours, and similar factors must be considered.

REVIEW QUESTIONS

1. How does a theoretical standard differ from a normal standard?
2. What causes a materials price variance?
3. What does an unfavorable materials quantity variance suggest?
4. How is the variance for a raw material item during the period computed?
5. In general, who is responsible for materials price variances?
6. At what point in the accounting cycle are materials variances recorded?
7. When labor efficiency variances are unfavorable, which manager is likely to be called on to explain the problem?

8. Give two other terms that might be used for *labor efficiency variance*.
9. Explain how a labor efficiency variance is similar to a materials quantity variance.
10. Suggest four reasons that might explain an unfavorable materials quantity variance.

MANAGERIAL DISCUSSION QUESTIONS

1. The management of the Penoke Company has suggested that the company adopt a standard cost accounting system to get better control over operations. The controller is opposed to this idea because he thinks that the process cost accounting system is more suited to the company's operations, in which there are three manufacturing processes. What is your opinion? Explain.
2. What are some advantages to management of using a standard cost system?
3. The management of the Dole Corporation is developing standard costs. The vice president of finance has heard of theoretical standards and thinks that they should be used because they provide closer control over costs. Do you agree or disagree? Explain.
4. Assume that you are a cost accountant at the Winspear Company. Briefly explain to management the reasons why variances between actual and standard costs of materials may exist.
5. Which level of management is usually responsible for labor rate variances? Explain.
6. As a production manager, would you be likely to have more control over materials price variances or materials quantity variances? Explain.
7. The accountant for the Jobe Corporation has noticed that, historically, when there have been favorable labor rate variances, there have been unfavorable labor efficiency variances. What factors may explain this situation?
8. During the month of August, the overall labor efficiency variance was favorable. The production manager suggests that it is not, therefore, necessary to compute the labor efficiency for different types of labor. What is your opinion?

EXERCISES

EXERCISE 22–1 **Compute standard materials cost per unit of product.   (Obj. 2).** Zelmos is a product manufactured by Zelna Company. The company is establishing standard costs for the product, which requires two raw materials. A review of production records shows that although engineering standards call for 3 pounds of raw material 28A for each unit of Zelmos produced, almost invariably an average of 3.1 pounds is required for each unit produced during a month. Zelna has a contract with the supplier of material 28A to supply the raw material for $6 per pound for the next 12 months. Engineering specifications also call for 3 pounds of the other ingredient, raw material 34AK. Actual usage of raw material 34AK has ranged from 2.98 pounds to 3.01 pounds per unit of Zelmos. During the past year, material 34AK cost $1.04 per unit, but is expected to increase to an average of $1.07 per pound during the coming year. Compute the standard cost of each raw material per unit of Zelmos for the coming year.

EXERCISE 22–2 **Compute materials quantity and price variances. (Obj. 3).** The Sanger Company manufactures a product using a special type of alloy. Each unit of product should require $2\frac{1}{2}$ feet of alloy. The standard cost of the alloy is $1.75 per foot. During February 19X9, 28,260 units of product were manufactured, requiring 71,310 feet of alloy at a total cost of $122,653.20. Compute the materials quantity variance and the materials price variance for the month. Show whether the variances are favorable or unfavorable.

EXERCISE 22–3 **Prepare a journal entry to charge materials into production and record variances. (Obj. 4).** The standard cost of raw materials use in the Injection Department in January was $120,000 (10,000 units at $12 per unit). Actual materials placed in process were 10,040 units, which cost $11.75 each. Give the general journal entry to charge the materials to Work in Process and record variances.

EXERCISE 22–4 **Compute materials quantity and price variances; record variances. (Objs. 3, 4).** The standard materials cost of producing 1 pound of Hard Coat is as follows:

$8\frac{1}{2}$ ounces of resin at 12 cents per ounce	$1.02
$8\frac{1}{2}$ ounces of Long Last Mix at 30 cents per ounce	2.55
Total	$3.57

During April 19X9, 4,000 pounds of Hard Coat were produced. The actual materials costs were as follows:

32,480 ounces of resin at $12\frac{1}{2}$ cents per ounce	$ 4,060.00
32,160 ounces of Long Last Mix at $30\frac{1}{2}$ cents per ounce	9,808.80
Total	$13,868.80

a. Compute the materials price variances and the materials quantity variances for April 19X9. Show whether the variances are favorable or unfavorable.

b. Give the entries in general journal form to record the materials placed in work in process and the related variances.

EXERCISE 22–5 **Compute labor rate and labor efficiency variances. (Obj. 5).** The standard labor cost for a unit of product is 3 hours of labor at $14.40 per hour. Compute the labor rate variance and the labor efficiency variance for the month of May 19X9, when 2,000 units were produced in each of the following assumed cases. Show whether the variances are favorable or unfavorable.

a. 5,800 hours of labor were required at a total cost of $84,100.

b. 5,800 hours of labor were required at a total cost of $83,520.
c. 6,108 hours of labor were required at a total cost of $87,955.20.
d. 6,108 hours of labor were required at a total cost of $89,543.28.

EXERCISE 22-6 **Compute labor efficiency and labor rate variances; record variances. (Objs. 5,6).** The standard cost sheet calls for 1 hour and 45 minutes of labor in the Assembly Department for each boom box manufactured by the Minneapolis Sound Company. The standard labor cost is $14.40 per hour. During December 19X9, a total of 220 boom boxes were assembled, requiring 382 hours at a cost of $5,615.40.
a. Compute the labor efficiency variance and the labor rate variance for the month. Show whether each variance is favorable or unfavorable.
b. Give entries in general journal form to charge the standard labor cost to Work in Process and to record the labor variances for the month.

EXERCISE 22-7 **Compute labor rate and efficiency variances; record variances. (Objs. 5, 6).** In the Costing Department of the Apache Furniture Company, each desk manufactured requires 30 minutes of sanding labor and 45 minutes of painting labor. The standard wage rate for sanding personnel is $8 per hour, and the standard wage rate for painting personnel is $12 per hour. During May 19X9, 320 desks were manufactured. The sanding labor required was 158 hours at a total cost of $1,264, and the painting labor required was 246 hours at a total cost of $2,007.36.
a. Compute the labor rate variances and the labor efficiency variances for the month. Show whether the variances are favorable or unfavorable.
b. Give the entry in general journal form to charge the standard labor cost to Work in Process and to record the labor variances.

PROBLEMS

PROBLEM 22-1A

Compute materials quantity variances, materials price variances, and total materials variance; prepare the entry to charge material costs to Work in Process and record variances. (Objs. 3, 4). The Out Back Company manufactures a product called New Wonder, which requires three raw materials. Production is in batches of 1,040 pounds of raw materials that yield only 1,000 pounds of finished product. (Some evaporation of the base materials occurs, but the amount of evaporation varies slightly from batch to batch.) Standard costs are used as a control device. The standard materials costs for each batch of New Wonder are as follows:

Material	Quantity	Standard Cost per Pound	Standard Cost per Batch
Inert base	840 lb	$ .40	$ 336.00
Acid	160 lb	1.20	192.00
Activator	40 lb	20.50	820.00
Total	1,040 lb		$1,348.00

The output is packaged in 50-pound bags. During the month of August 19X9, 300 bags of New Wonder were produced. There was no beginning or ending work in process inventory. The materials actually used during August were as follows:

	Quantity	Cost per Gallon
Inert base	12,840 lb	$ .42
Acid	2,390 lb	1.12
Activator	612 lb	20.20

INSTRUCTIONS   Show whether the variances are favorable (F) or unfavorable (U).

1. Prepare a summary of materials costs for the month.
2. Compute the quantity and price variances for each of the materials.
3. Prepare a materials variances summary for the month.
4. Give the general journal entry on August 31, 19X9, to charge the standard materials costs to production and to record the price and quantity variances.

PROBLEM 22–2A   **Compute labor efficiency and labor rate variances; charge labor costs into production and record variances.   (Objs. 5, 6).**   In the Mounting Department of the Ebeneezer Motor Company, two classes of direct labor are used in the manufacturing process. Standard labor costs have been established for each unit of the product as follows:

Labor Class	Standard Hours	Standard Rate per Hour
Class 1	$\frac{1}{4}$ hr	$10.40
Class 2	2 hr	9.60

During the month of December 19X9, a total of 8,508 units were produced. The actual labor costs, by class, were as follows:

Labor Class	Hours	Cost
Class 1	2,148	$ 23,628.00
Class 2	16,536	$158,745.60

INSTRUCTIONS   Show whether the variances are favorable (F) or unfavorable (U).

1. Prepare a summary of labor costs for the month.
2. Compute the efficiency and rate variances for each class of labor.
3. Prepare a labor variances summary for the month.
4. Give the general entry on December 31, 19X9, to charge the standard labor cost to Work in Process, to remove the actual cost of labor used from the Factory Payroll Clearing account, and to record the labor efficiency and labor rate variances. Use Work in Process—Mounting Department 124.

PROBLEM 22–3A   **Compute materials quantity variances, materials price variances, labor efficiency variances, and labor rate variances; prepare the entry to charge costs into production and record variances.   (Objs. 3, 4, 5, 6).**   The Outer Space Company manufactures a product that is processed through two departments, the Cutting Department and the Curing Department. All materials are added in the Cutting Department. Certain data concerning standard costs that have been established for materials and labor are given below:

Raw Materials (per unit of product)

Sheet Metal No. 14: 20 sq ft at 60 cents per sq ft	$12.00
Coating: 7 lb at 72 cents per lb	5.04
Standard Materials Costs per Unit (10 sq ft)	$17.04

Direct Labor (per unit of product)

Cutting Dept.: $\frac{1}{4}$ hr at $9.60 per hr	$ 2.40
Curing Dept.: 4 minutes at $12 per hr	.80
Standard Direct Labor Costs per Unit	$ 3.20

During the month of July 19X9, 10,000 units (200,000 square feet) of the product were manufactured. Actual costs of materials and labor were as shown below.

Raw Materials (per unit of product)

Sheet Metal No. 14: 201,000 sq ft at 58.8 cents per sq ft	$118,188.00
Coating: 69,485 lb at 61 cents per lb	49,334.35
Total Actual Materials Costs	$167,522.35

Direct Labor

Cutting Dept.: 2,580 hr at $9.80 per hr	$ 25,284.00
Curing Dept.: 658 hr at $12.30 per hr	8,093.40
Total Actual Direct Labor Costs	$ 33,377.40

INSTRUCTIONS

1. Compute the quantity and price variances for each of the two raw materials.
2. Prepare a materials variances summary.
3. Compute the labor efficiency and rate variances for each department.
4. Prepare a labor variances summary.
5. Give the entries in general journal form on July 31, 19X9, to do the following:
   a. Charge the standard costs of materials to production, record the actual costs of the raw materials used, and record the materials variances using separate accounts for materials quantity variances and materials price variances. Use Work in Process—Cutting Department 124.
   b. Charge the standard costs of direct labor to production, remove the actual labor costs from Factory Payroll Clearing, and record the labor variances using separate accounts for labor efficiency and labor rate variances. Use Work in Process—Cutting Department 124 and Work in Process—Curing Department 125.

ALTERNATE PROBLEMS

PROBLEM 22–1B

Compute materials quantity variances and materials price variances; charge materials into production and record variances. (Objs. 3, 4). The Rainbow Lime Products Company manufactures a product called Senelco, which requires three raw materials. Production is in batches of 2,000 pounds of materials. Waste (which is thrown away) sometimes occurs. Standard costs are used as a control device.

The standard materials costs for each of Senelco have been established as given below.

Material	Quantity	Standard Cost per Pound	Standard Cost per Batch
Plastic base	1,800 lb	.60	$1,080
Tint	100 lb	.80	80
Hardener	100 lb	1.00	100
Total	2,000 lb		$1,260

The output is packaged in containers of 25 pounds each. During the month of October 19X9, 2,400 containers of Senelco were produced. There was no beginning or ending work in process inventory. The materials actually used during October were as follows:

	Quantity	Total Cost
Plastic base	55,296 lb	$33,764
Tint	3,072 lb	2,368
Hardener	3,012 lb	3,124

INSTRUCTIONS Carry the unit costs to five decimal places and round to four places. Show whether the variances are favorable (F) or unfavorable (U).

1. Prepare a summary of materials costs for the month.
2. Compute the quantity and price variances for each of the materials.
3. Prepare a materials variances summary for the month.
4. Give the general journal entry on October 31, 19X9, to charge the standard materials costs to production and to record the price and quantity variances.

PROBLEM 22–2B **Compute labor efficiency variances and labor rate variances; prepare the entry to charge labor costs to production and record variances. (Objs. 5,6).** In the Forming Department of the Mason Products Company, two classes of direct labor are used in the manufacturing process. Standard labor costs have been established for each unit of the product as follows:

Labor Class	Standard Hours	Standard Rate per Hour
Class DL-A	$\frac{1}{2}$ hr	$11.20
Class DL-C	1 hr	12.00

During the month of September 19X9, a total of 2,020 units were produced. The actual labor costs, by class, were as follows:

Labor Class	Hours	Cost
Class DL-A	1,053	$11,793.60
Class DL-C	2,005	24,862.00

INSTRUCTIONS In each answer, show whether the variances are favorable (F) or unfavorable (U).

1. Prepare a summary of labor costs for the month.
2. Compute the efficiency and rate variances for each class of labor.
3. Prepare a labor variances summary for the month.

4. Give the general journal entry on September 30, 19X9, to charge the standard labor cost to production, to remove the actual cost of the labor used from the Factory Payroll Clearing account, and to record the labor efficiency and labor rate variances. Use Work in Process—Forming Department 122.

PROBLEM 22–3B

Compute materials quantity variances, materials price variances, labor efficiency variances, and labor rate variances; charge materials and labor into production and record variances. (Objs. 3, 4, 5, 6). The Centennial Company manufactures a product that is processed through two departments, Preparation and Completion. All materials are added in the Preparation Department (the first department). Some data on standard costs that have been established for materials and labor are shown below.

Raw Materials

Base units: 4 units at $21 each	$84.00
Assembly sets: 4 sets at 60 cents each	2.40
Standard Materials Costs per Unit	$86.40

Direct Labor

Preparation Dept.: $\frac{1}{6}$ hr at $9.60 per hr	$ 1.60
Completion Dept.: $\frac{1}{4}$ hr at $8 per hr	2.00
Standard Direct Labor Costs per Unit	$ 3.60

During the month of July 19X9, 4,500 units of the product were manufactured. The actual costs of materials and labor were as follows:

Raw Materials

Base units: 18,100 at $21.20 each	$383,720.00
Assembly sets: 18,050 at 55 cents each	9,927.50
Total Actual Materials Costs	$393,647.50

Direct Labor

Preparation Dept.: 752 hr at $9.60 per hr	$ 7,219.20
Completion Dept.: 1,100 hr at $7.80 per hr	8,580.00
Total Actual Direct Labor Costs	$ 15,799.20

INSTRUCTIONS

1. Compute the quantity and price variances for each of the two raw materials.
2. Prepare a materials variances summary.
3. Compute the labor efficiency and rate variances for each department.
4. Prepare a labor variances summary.
5. Give the general journal entries on July 31, 19X9, to do the following:
   a. Charge the standard costs of materials to production, record the actual costs of the raw materials used, and record the materials variances using separate accounts for materials quantity variances and materials price variances. Use Work in Process—Preparation Department 123.
   b. Charge the standard costs of direct labor to production, remove the actual labor costs from Factory Payroll Clearing, and record the labor variances using separate accounts for labor efficiency and labor rate variances. Use Work in Process—Completion Department 124.

Manufacturing Overhead Standard Costs. Completing the Accounting Cycle for Standard Costs

Manufacturing overhead costs are harder to control than labor and materials. Manufacturing overhead consists of numerous cost items, few of which are directly related to an individual unit of product. The standard for manufacturing overhead per completed unit of product, unlike standards for direct materials and labor, is not an engineered standard (one based on engineering studies and time and motion studies). Instead, it is largely the result of an allocation process.

OBJECTIVES

1. Determine standard overhead cost per unit of product and total standard overhead for the period.
2. Compute total variance between standard overhead for the units produced during the period and the actual cost incurred.
3. Use the two-variance analysis method to analyze the total overhead variance for the period.
4. Use the three-variance analysis method to analyze the total overhead variance for the period.
5. Use the four-variance analysis method to analyze the total overhead variance for the period.
6. Apply manufacturing overhead to Work in Process and record overhead variances.
7. Transfer standard costs of products from Work in Process to Finished Goods and record cost of goods sold under the standard cost system.
8. Properly dispose of standard cost variances.
9. Prepare an income statement using standard costing.

NEW TERMS

Budget variance or controllable variance (p. 568)
Efficiency variance (p. 572)
Fixed overhead spending variance (p. 574)
Four-variance analysis method (p. 574)
Normal capacity (p. 562)
Spending variance (p. 572)
Three-variance analysis method (p. 572)
Two-variance analysis method (p. 568)
Variable overhead spending variance (p. 574)
Variance analysis (p. 568)
Volume variance or capacity variance (p. 568)

AN OVERVIEW OF STANDARD MANUFACTURING OVERHEAD COSTS

The standard manufacturing overhead cost per unit of product is determined at the start of the year. The standard cost per unit is based on the budgeted overhead allowed for the volume of activity chosen for determining the standard cost. Some companies use the expected actual production for the year in computing standard overhead cost per unit. Other companies base the standard on **normal capacity** for a period of from two to five years. Under this concept, the budget on which standard costs is based represents the average expected utilization of plant and labor for more than one year in order to even out the variations in costs resulting from swings in market demand.

The overhead rate is based on some measure of activity that bears the closest relationship to cost changes as volume changes. Typically, direct labor hours is used as the activity measure, although some companies use direct labor costs or machine hours. Assuming that direct labor hours is the activity measure, the overhead rate per direct labor hour is determined by dividing the overhead budgeted for the expected volume, or the normal volume, by the number of direct labor hours budgeted at that level. The standard overhead cost for a unit of product is determined by multiplying the overhead rate per direct labor hour by the number of hours allowed for each unit of that product. The total standard overhead for the period, which is the amount applied to Work in Process, may be determined either by multiplying the standard overhead per unit of product by the units of production or by multiplying the standard overhead per direct labor hour by the standard hours allowed for the units of production during the period. The two calculations yield identical results. NOTE: *In this chapter, we will assume that a new standard cost is computed each year on the basis of standard direct labor hours for the units budgeted to be produced during the year.*

Actual costs incurred during the period are recorded in the Manufacturing Overhead Control account in the normal manner you have learned. Then, at the end of the period, standard overhead costs for the units of production during the period are charged to Work in Process. Actual costs are compared with standard costs for the period's production, and differences that exist between the total standard overhead and the total actual overhead are analyzed through variance analysis and properly disposed of.

SETTING UP A STANDARD COST SYSTEM FOR OVERHEAD

Setting up and using a standard cost system for manufacturing overhead is done in the same way as for materials and labor. The specific steps listed below follow the description given in the preceding paragraph:

■ Establish standard overhead costs per unit of product.
■ Record the actual costs incurred during the period.
■ Determine the standard costs for the units produced during the period.

- Compute the total overhead variance by comparing the actual costs incurred during the period with the standard costs of the units produced during this period.
- Break down the total variance into its component parts.
- Record the standard costs of the work done during the period and the variances from the standard costs.
- Transfer the standard cost of units produced during the period from Work in Process to Finished Goods Inventory.

Each of these steps is analyzed below. The steps were followed by the National Case Company in accounting for manufacturing overhead costs during January 19X9, as demonstrated in the remainder of this chapter.

ESTABLISHING STANDARD OVERHEAD COSTS PER UNIT OF PRODUCT

Manufacturing overhead standards are established by using estimated costs and a selected basis for application. National Case Company charges overhead into production on the basis of the number of standard direct labor hours allowed for the production during the period. A rate per direct labor hour for 19X9 is found by dividing the budgeted overhead for the expected volume in 19X9 by the number of standard direct labor hours at that volume. (Remember that some companies use "normal" volume, reflecting the expected average volume over a two- or three-year period, rather than the expected actual volume for a single year.) The rate per completed unit of product is the standard overhead rate per hour multiplied by the standard direct labor hours per unit.

The development of National Case Company's manufacturing overhead budget for 19X9 was explained in Chapter 21. The manufacturing overhead budget for each producing and service department for the year 19X9 is summarized below.

	Assembly Department	Finishing Department	Factory Services Department	Total Cost
Variable Costs	$128,400	$178,080	$126,720	$433,200
Fixed Costs	85,680	44,520	136,800	267,000
Total	$214,080	$222,600	$263,520	$700,200

Overhead costs are charged into Work in Process from producing departments only. Service department costs must therefore be allocated to the producing departments by the techniques presented in Chapters 8 and 13. When standard costs are used, service department fixed costs and variable costs are often allocated on different bases. For example, the variable costs of the Factory Services Department of the National Case Company are allocated to the producing departments on the basis of direct labor hours. The fixed costs are allocated on the basis of floor space occupied. These allocations are shown on page 564.

	Basis	Assembly Department	Finishing Department	Total Cost
Variable Costs	Direct Labor Hours	$52,800*	$ 73,920*	$126,720
Fixed Costs	Floor Space Occupied	45,600†	91,200†	136,800
Total		$98,400	$165,120	$263,520

*Based on 30,000 hours for the Assembly Department and 42,000 hours for the Finishing Department.
†Based on 3,000 square feet for the Assembly Department and 6,000 square feet for the Finishing Department.

The allocated variable and fixed costs of the service department are added to the variable and fixed costs of the individual producing departments, as shown in the calculation below.

	Assembly Department	Finishing Department
Variable Costs		
Department Variable Costs	$128,400	$178,080
Allocated Service Department Costs	52,800	73,920
Total Variable Costs	$181,200	$252,000
Fixed Costs		
Departmental Fixed Costs	$ 85,680	$ 44,520
Allocated Service Department Costs	45,600	91,200
Total Fixed Costs	$131,280	$135,720
Total Costs	$312,480	$387,720

The total estimated overhead cost of each producing department, including allocated service department costs, is divided by the budgeted normal labor hours in each producing department. This gives the standard overhead rates per hour, as shown below. Note that separate variable and fixed rates are calculated to aid in analyzing differences between the standard overhead cost of each month and the actual overhead costs of the month.

	Total Cost	Total Hours	Standard Rates per Hour
Assembly Department			
Variable Costs	$181,200 ÷	30,000 =	$ 6.040
Fixed Costs	131,280 ÷	30,000 =	4.376
Total			$10.416
Finishing Department			
Variable Costs	$252,000 ÷	42,000 =	$ 6.000
Fixed Costs	135,720 ÷	42,000 =	3.231
Total			$ 9.231

The standard overhead rate per unit is computed by multiplying the standard rate per hour by the standard hours per unit, as shown on the next page.

These rates are then entered on the standard cost sheet. The standard cost sheet (Exhibit 1) for National Case Company is shown on page 565. This is the same standard cost sheet that you studied in Chapter 22 (page 539).

	STANDARD OVERHEAD PER CASE	
	Variable	Fixed
Assembly Department		
Variable Costs (.5 hr × $6.04 per hr)	$3.020	
Fixed Costs (.5 hr × $4.376 per hr)		$2.188
Finishing Department		
Variable Costs (.7 hr × $6 per hr)	4.200	
Fixed Costs (.7 hr × $3.231 per hr)		2.262
Total	$7.220	$4.450

Summary

Variable	$ 7.220
Fixed	4.450
Total	$11.670

NATIONAL CASE COMPANY   Exhibit 1
Standard Cost Sheet
Jewelry Case JC-14
For Year 19X9

	QUANTITY	UNIT COSTS	TOTAL COST PER CASE
Materials			
DM-1	3 ft	$4.00 per ft	$12.000
DM-8	4 sets	.40 per set	1.600
DM-4	12 sets	.10 per set	1.200
DM-5	$\frac{2}{25}$ quart	$8.00 per quart	.640
Total Materials Cost per Case			$15.440
Labor			
Assembly Department	.5 hr	$12.00 per hr	$ 6.000
Finishing Department	.7 hr	14.00 per hr	9.800
Total Labor Cost per Case			$15.800
Overhead			
Assembly Department			
Variable Costs	.5 hr	$ 6.040 per hr	$ 3.020
Fixed Costs	.5 hr	4.376 per hr	2.188
Total for Assembly Department		$10.416	$ 5.208
Finishing Department			
Variable Costs	.7 hr	$ 6.000 per hr	$ 4.200
Fixed Costs	.7 hr	3.231 per hr	2.262
Total for Finishing Department		$ 9.231	$ 6.462
Total Overhead Cost per Case			$11.670
Total Standard Cost per Case			$42.910

RECORDING ACTUAL COSTS

Actual manufacturing overhead costs are accounted for in two steps. The first step is to record in the Manufacturing Overhead Control account the actual costs incurred. The second step is to allocate the service department costs to the producing departments. Then it is easier to compare the actual manufacturing overhead costs with the standard costs charged to production.

Actual overhead costs incurred are recorded in the same manner as presented in Chapters 8 and 13. A summary entry for January is shown here.

19X9				
Jan. 31	Manufacturing Overhead Control	501	55,230.40	
	Various Payable (Prepaid Expenses, etc.)	XXX		55,230.40
	Record actual overhead costs during the month.			

The schedule of actual overhead costs (Exhibit 2) shows these costs classified by the department in which they were incurred.

NATIONAL CASE COMPANY Schedule of Actual Overhead Costs Month Ended January 31, 19X9				Exhibit 2
	ASSEMBLY DEPARTMENT (2,350 HR)	FINISHING DEPARTMENT (3,110 HR)	FACTORY SERVICES DEPARTMENT	TOTAL
Variable Costs	$10,060.00	$13,310.80	$ 9,609.60	$32,980.40
Fixed Costs	7,140.00	3,710.00	11,400.00	22,250.00
Total	$17,200.00	$17,020.80	$21,009.60	$55,230.40

The Factory Services Department costs for January, $21,009.60, must be allocated to the producing departments. The allocation is made using the following schedule, Exhibit 3. (Allocated costs are usually rounded to the nearest whole dollar.) In this schedule, variable costs are allocated on the basis of direct labor hours, and fixed costs are allocated on the basis of floor space occupied. The allocated costs are entered in the summary of manufacturing overhead costs (page 567).

DETERMINING STANDARD COSTS FOR PERIOD

Direct labor hours are used to apply manufacturing overhead to production. Thus the standard cost applied during the period is the standard hours allowed multiplied by the standard overhead rate per hour. The standard hours allowed is the product of the standard hours per completed unit and the number of units produced during the period. The standard hours in the Assembly Department totaled 2,250 (4,500 cases × .5 hour per case). The standard cost of manufacturing overhead in this department is $23,436 (2,250 hours × $10.416 per hour).

NATIONAL CASE COMPANY   **Exhibit 3**
Schedule of Allocation of Service Department Costs
Month Ended January 31, 19X9

	ASSEMBLY DEPARTMENT	FINISHING DEPARTMENT	TOTAL COST
Variable Costs			
Departmental Variable Costs	$10,060.00	$13,310.80	$23,370.80
Allocation of Service Dept. Costs*	4,136.00	5,473.60	9,609.60
Total Variable Costs	$14,196.00	$18,784.40	$32,980.40
Fixed Costs			
Departmental Fixed Costs	$ 7,140.00	$ 3,710.00	$10,850.00
Allocation of Service Dept. Costs†	3,800.00	7,600.00	11,400.00
Total Fixed Costs	$10,940.00	$11,310.00	$22,250.00
Total Costs	$25,136.00	$30,094.40	$55,230.40

*Based on 2,350 hours for the Assembly Department and 3,110 for the Finishing Department.
†Based on 3,000 square feet for the Assembly Department and 6,000 square feet for the Finishing Department.

NATIONAL CASE COMPANY   **Exhibit 4**
Summary of Manufacturing Overhead Costs
Month Ended January 31, 19X9
Actual Production 4,500 Cases

DEPARTMENT	Standard				Actual		
	HOURS PER TRAY	TOTAL HOURS	RATE PER HOUR	TOTAL COST	TOTAL HOURS	TOTAL COST	TOTAL VARIANCE
Assembly	.5	2,250	$10.416	$23,436.00	2,350	$25,136.00	$1,700.00U
Finishing	.7	3,150	9.231	29,077.65	3,110	30,094.40	1,016.75U
Total				$52,513.65		$55,230.40	$2,716.75U

Similarly, the standard overhead in the Finishing Department for the month is $29,077.65 (3,150 standard hours × $9.231 per hour). The total standard overhead cost for the month is thus $52,513.65. This figure is $1.35 less than the total standard cost of $52,515 obtained by multiplying the standard cost of $11.670 per case, shown on the standard cost sheet on page 565, by the 4,500 cases produced during the month. This difference is due to rounding and can be ignored. (In this chapter we have used standard costs per hour and standard hours per unit of product to determine the total standard cost per unit because, as you will see later, this procedure facilitates the analysis of variances.)

The standard manufacturing overhead costs for January and the actual costs for the month are presented in Exhibit 4.

MEASURING AND ANALYZING THE TOTAL OVERHEAD VARIANCE

The total manufacturing overhead variance in each department is the difference between the standard costs of production (the total standard hours allowed for the units produced multiplied by the standard overhead rate per hour, or the standard cost per unit of product multiplied by the number of units produced) and the actual costs incurred. In January, the total variance is $1,700 in the Assembly Department and $1,016.75 in the Finishing Department, as shown in Exhibit 4.

It is very important for management in its efforts to control costs to know why the actual costs incurred during the period differed from the standard costs for the work. To provide this information, the accountant uses **variance analysis,** which analyzes the total variance in each department and divides it into its component parts. This analysis may be done by using a two-variance analysis method, a three-variance analysis method, or a four-variance analysis method, depending on the degree of sophistication desired.

The Two-Variance Analysis Method

In the **two-variance analysis method,** the total variance for a department is separated into the budget variance and the volume variance.

- The **budget variance** (or **controllable variance**) in each department is the difference between (1) the actual costs incurred and (2) the overhead in the flexible budget for the standard hours allowed for the units produced.
- The **volume variance** (or **capacity variance**) results from the fact that the number of direct labor hours for which overhead was charged to production differs from the number of hours on which the original budget used to compute the standard overhead rate was based. This variance is computed by comparing (1) the standard cost of the units produced during the period (the standard cost per hour multiplied by the standard hours allowed for the units produced) and (2) the flexible budget for the standard hours allowed for the units produced.

Note that the two types of variances are found by comparing *actual* costs for the period with the budget allowance for the standard hours allowed for units produced during the period and *standard* costs for the period with the same budget allowance.

An analysis of the $1,700 unfavorable overhead variance in the Assembly Department, using the two-variance method, shows an unfavorable budget variance of $606 and an unfavorable volume variance of $1,094. For the Finishing Department, an analysis of the $1,016.75 unfavorable overhead variance shows a favorable budget variance of $115.60 and an unfavorable volume variance of $1,132.35. The analysis procedure is described below. We will first explain the budget variance in each department; then we will explain the volume variances.

Budget Variance. As previously pointed out, the overhead budget variance is computed by comparing (1) the actual costs incurred and

(2) the overhead allowed in the flexible budget for the standard hours for the number of units produced.

Budgeted Costs. The budgeted overhead for the standard hours allowed for the number of units produced consists of two parts:

- **Variable costs.** The total variable cost allowed for the number of units produced is computed by multiplying (1) the standard direct labor hours allowed for the number of units produced by (2) the standard variable overhead rate per hour. Calculating the variable costs allowed in the Assembly Department and the Finishing Department of National Case Company will be illustrated in the next section.
- **Fixed costs.** The fixed costs budgeted for the period are usually known or can easily be determined. Typically the fixed costs for a month are assumed to be one-twelfth of the annual costs unless there are anticipated changes in fixed costs during the budget year.

Actual Costs. The actual overhead costs are taken from the Summary of Manufacturing Overhead Costs (Exhibit 4).

- **Assembly Department.** The total flexible budget in the Assembly Department for 4,500 units is $24,530, which is computed as follows:

Variable costs:
(2,250 standard hours × $6.04 per hour)	$13,590.00
Fixed costs	
($\frac{1}{12}$ × annual fixed costs of $131,280)	10,940.00
Total	$24,530.00

The manufacturing overhead budget variance in the Assembly Department is thus an unfavorable variance of $606.

Actual costs (from Exhibit 4)	$25,136.00
Budgeted costs for standard hours (computed above)	24,530.00
Manufacturing overhead budget variance	$ 606.00U

If the budgeted fixed manufacturing overhead and the actual fixed overhead are equal, the budget variance results from a difference between the variable costs budgeted and the variable costs incurred. Since most variable costs are controllable at the departmental level, the manufacturing overhead budget variance is often called the *controllable variance.* However, if fixed costs incurred are different from those budgeted, that difference will also be reflected in the budget variance. (As discussed later in the section "The Three-Variance Analysis Method," the budget variance can be further analyzed into a "spending variance" and an "efficiency variance.")

- **Finishing Department.** In the Finishing Department, the budgeted fixed costs are $11,310 per month, which is one-twelfth of the budgeted annual costs of $135,720. The budgeted variable costs in the department are $6 per hour. The total of the budgeted costs for the 3,150 standard hours allowed is $30,210, computed as follows:

Variable costs	
(3,150 standard hours × $6 per hour)	$18,900.00
Fixed costs	
($\frac{1}{12}$ × annual fixed costs of $135,720)	11,310.00
Total	$30,210.00

The manufacturing overhead budget variance in the Finishing Department is thus a favorable variance of $115.60:

Actual costs (from Exhibit 4)	$30,094.40
Budgeted costs for standard hours (computed above)	30,210.00
Manufacturing overhead budget variance	$ 115.60F

Volume Variance. In almost every case, the standard hours allowed for units actually produced during the current period will differ from the number of hours originally budgeted in setting the standard overhead rates because production will not be exactly equal to that assumed when setting the standard overhead cost per hour or per unit. As a result, the fixed overhead charged to production (based on standard hours) will rarely be the same amount as that allowed in the budget for the output of the period. (Under the two-variance method, the resulting difference is called the *volume variance*.)

■ *Assembly Department.* For the Assembly Department, the volume variance is unfavorable, as shown here:

Standard costs charged to production		
(2,250 standard hours × $10.416		
per hour)		$23,436.00
Budgeted costs for production attained		
Variable costs (2,250 hours × $6.04		
per hour)	$13,590.00	
Fixed costs ($\frac{1}{12}$ × $131,280)	10,940.00	24,530.00
Manufacturing overhead volume variance		$ 1,094.00U

The unfavorable volume variance in the Assembly Department arises because the fixed overhead rate of $4,376 included in the total overhead rate of $10.416 (page 565) was based on the assumption that 2,500 hours would be worked during the month, although only the 2,250 hours allowed for the 4,500 units produced were actually charged to production. Fixed costs remained the same, however. Thus $1,094 (250 hours × $4.376) of fixed costs were underapplied.

■ *Finishing Department.* For the Finishing Department, the volume variance is also unfavorable.

Standard costs charged to production		
(3,150 standard hours × $9.231 per hour)		$29,077.65
Budgeted allowance for standard hours for		
production attained		
Variable costs (3,150 hours × $6 per hour)	$18,900.00	
Fixed costs ($\frac{1}{12}$ × $135,720)	11,310.00	30,210.00
Manufacturing overhead volume variance		$ 1,132.35U

Summarizing the Budget and Volume Variances. A review of the variance analysis in the Assembly Department shows the following:

Actual costs	$25,136.00
Budget allowance based on standard hours for units produced	24,530.00
Standard costs	23,436.00

$606.00U
Budget Variance

$1,094U
Volume Variance

The variance analysis for the Finishing Department can be summarized as shown below.

At this point you should be able to work Exercises 23–1 to 23–3 and Problems 23–1A and 23–1B.

Actual costs	$30,094.40
Budget allowance based on standard hours for units produced	30,210.00
Standard costs	20,077.65

$115.60U
Budget Variance

$1,132.35U
Volume Variance

SELF-REVIEW

1. Explain briefly how the budget variance is computed under the two-variance analysis method.
2. Explain briefly how the volume variance is computed under the two-variance analysis method.
3. Which of the variances computed under the two-variance analysis method is most likely to be controllable? Why?
4. If the budget variance and volume variance are added, what amount should the sum agree with?
5. Why is it almost certain that there will be a volume variance each month?

Answers to Self-Review

1. The budget variance is computed by comparing actual overhead costs incurred during the period with the budget allowance for the standard number of hours allowed for the units produced.
2. The volume variance is computed by comparing standard overhead for the production for the period with the budgeted costs for the number of units produced.
3. The budget variance is likely to be controllable. Usually, fixed costs will be very near the budgeted amount. As a result, the budget variance is likely to reflect the success of the manager in controlling variable costs. The volume variance, on the other hand, reflects the fact that fixed costs are being charged into production on the basis of the planning budget volume, expressed in hours. If the standard hours for the work done vary from the hours used in setting standards, a volume variance will exist.
4. The sum of the volume variance and budget variance should be equal to the total variance between actual cost and standard costs of the work done.
5. When the units of product produced during a period differ from the production anticipated when the standard cost per unit was set, there will be a volume variance. Since there is almost always a difference in those hours, there is almost always a volume variance.

The Three-Variance Analysis Method

Although the budget variance computed earlier is a measure of cost control in that it shows the variance between actual costs and the budgeted costs for the number of units produced during the period, many companies want a more detailed explanation of why this difference exists. The budget variance can be divided into the spending variance and the efficiency variance. The **spending variance** compares what *should have been* spent for the *actual hours worked* with the *actual* costs for those hours. The **efficiency variance** companies the *budgeted costs* for the *standard hours* worked with the budgeted costs for the *actual* hours worked. Thus a **three-variance analysis method** results in a volume variance (computed in the same way as under the two-variance method), a spending variance, and an efficiency variance. The spending variance and efficiency variance replace the budget variance of the two-variance analysis.

The $1,700 total unfavorable variance in the Assembly Department was determined under the two-variance method to consist of a $606 unfavorable budget variance and a $1,094 unfavorable volume variance. Under the three-variance method of analysis, the volume variance will continue to be an unfavorable variance of $1,094. However, the budget variance of $606 is made up of a $2 unfavorable spending variance and a $604 unfavorable efficiency variance. Similarly, in the two-variance method discussed on pages 568 to 571, the $1,016.75 total unfavorable overhead variance in the Finishing Department was shown to consist of a $115.60 favorable budget variance and a $1,132.35 unfavorable volume variance. A further analysis of the $115.60 budget variance shows that it consists of a $124.40 unfavorable spending variance and a $240.00 favorable efficiency variance. The calculations of these amounts are explained below.

Spending Variance. As noted above, the spending variance compares what *should have been spent* for the actual hours worked with the *actual costs* for those hours.

▪ *Assembly Department.* For the Assembly Department, the spending variance of $2 is computed as follows:

Budget for actual hours worked		
Variable costs (2,350 actual hours ×		
$6.04 per hour)	$14,194.00	
Fixed costs ($\frac{1}{12}$ × annual costs of $131,280)	10,940.00	
Total budget for actual hours		$25,134.00
Actual costs (from Exhibit 4, page 567)		25,136.00
Manufacturing overhead spending variance		$ 2.00U

▪ *Finishing Department.* For the Finishing Department, the analysis shows an unfavorable spending variance of $124.40.

Budget for actual hours worked	
Variable cost (3,100 actual hours × $6	
per hour)	$18,660.00
Fixed costs ($\frac{1}{12}$ × annual costs of $135,720)	11,310.00

Total budget for actual hours	$29,970.00
Actual costs (from Exhibit 4, page 567)	30,094.40
Manufacturing overhead spending variance	$ 124.40U

Efficiency Variance. The efficiency variance compares the *budgeted costs* for the *standard hours allowed* for the current production with the budgeted costs for the *actual hours worked*. Since the fixed costs budgeted at any number of hours is the same, only the variable costs need to be considered in computing the efficiency variance.

■ ***Assembly Department.*** For the Assembly Department, the efficiency variance is $604.

Budget based on standard hours		
Variable costs (2,250 standard hours ×		
$6.04 per hour)	$13,590.00	
Fixed costs ($\frac{1}{12}$ × annual costs of $131,280)	10,940.00	
Total budget for standard hours		$24,530.00
Budget based on actual hours (from above)		25,134.00
Manufacturing overhead efficiency variance		$ 604.00U

■ ***Finishing Department.*** The efficiency variance in the Finishing Department may be computed as follows (using only variable costs in the calculation):

Budgeted variable overhead for standard hours	
(3,150 standard hours × $6 per hour)	$18,900.00
Budgeted variable overhead for actual hours (3,110	
hours × $6 per hour)	18,660.00
Manufacturing overhead efficiency variance	$ 240.00F

Summarizing the Volume, Spending, and Efficiency Variances. Under the three-variance method, the total unfavorable overhead variance of $1,700 in the Assembly Department can be summarized as follows:

Standard costs	$23,436.00	$1,094.00U
		Volume Variance
Budget for standard hours	24,530.00	$604.00U
		Efficiency Variance
Budget for actual hours	25,134.00	$2.00U
		Spending Variance
Actual costs	25,136.00	

The figures for the Finishing Department are as shown.

Standard costs	$29,077.65	$1,132.35U
		Volume Variance
Budget for standard hours	30,210.00	$240.00F
		Efficiency Variance
Budget for actual hours	29,970.00	$124.40U
		Spending Variance
Actual costs	30,094.40	

The manufacturing overhead variances for the month of January that were determined by both the three-variance analysis and the two-variance analyses are summarized in Exhibit 5. As you have seen, the spending variance, plus the efficiency variance, both computed under the three-variance method, equals the budget variance computed under the two-variance analysis. The total variance equals the budget variance plus the volume variance under the two-variance analysis. Similarly, under the three-variance analysis, the efficiency variance, plus the spending variance, plus the volume variance, equals the total variance.

At this point you should be able to work Exercise 23–4 and Problems 23–2A and 23–2B.

NATIONAL CASE COMPANY					Exhibit 5
Manufacturing Overhead Variances Summary					
Two-Variance and Three-Variance Analysis					
Month Ended January 31, 19X9					
DEPARTMENT	**SPENDING VARIANCE**	**EFFICIENCY VARIANCE**	**BUDGET VARIANCE**	**VOLUME VARIANCE**	**TOTAL VARIANCE**
Assembly	$ 2.00U	$604.00U	$606.00U	$1,094.00U	$1,700.00U
Finishing	124.40	240.00F	115.60F	1,132.35U	1,016.75U
Total	$126.40U	$364.00U	$490.40U	$2,226.35U	$2,716.75U

The Four-Variance Analysis Method

The **four-variance analysis method** is a refinement of three-variance analysis. Under this method, the spending variance computed in the three-way analysis is further separated into two component parts. As you have just learned, the spending variance under the three-variance analysis is the difference between the *actual overhead costs incurred* during the period and the overhead budget for the actual hours worked. The two components of the total spending variance are the variance resulting because *variable costs* differed from the budget allowance and the variance resulting because actual *fixed overhead* differed from the budget allowance. Consequently, under four-variance analysis the total spending variance of the three-variance method is divided into:

1. The **variable overhead spending variance,** which is the difference between the actual variable overhead costs incurred and the budget allowance for variable overhead based on the *actual hours worked.*
2. The **fixed overhead spending variance,** which is the difference between the *actual fixed costs* incurred and the budgeted fixed overhead for the *actual hours worked.* (Since fixed costs are, by definition, the same for any number of hours worked, within the relevant range of activity, we generally define the fixed overhead spending variance as the difference between actual fixed costs and *budgeted fixed costs.*)

SELF-REVIEW

1. Compare the components of the three-variance analysis and the two-variance analysis.
2. Explain the efficiency variance computed under the three-variance analysis.
3. Which costs (variable costs or fixed costs) give rise to the efficiency variance? Explain.
4. Which of the variances computed under the three-variance method (the spending variance, the efficiency variance, or the volume variance) is likely to be more controllable by the manager of the producing department? Why?
5. Which of the variances would be least likely to be affected by a change in fixed costs during the reporting period? Explain.

Answers to Self-Review

1. The volume variance under both the two-variance and the three-variance analysis methods is the same. Under the three-variance method, the budget variance computed under the two-variance method is analyzed in two different parts: the spending variance and the efficiency variance.
2. The efficiency variance compares the budget allowance for standard hours allowed with the budget allowance for actual hours worked. It explains how much actual costs would have differed from standard costs if variable costs per hour had been as called for in the budget.
3. The efficiency variance reflects variable costs. The budget for fixed costs would be the same for both actual hours and standard hours.
4. The departmental manager is responsible for both the efficiency variance and the spending variance. The first variance reflects the cost variance resulting from taking too many or too few hours to perform the work, compared to standard. The spending variance reflects how much spending was more than or less than the budget based on actual hours worked.
5. Neither the efficiency variance nor the volume variance will be affected by a change in fixed costs during the period. Neither of these variances is dependent on actual costs.

The other two variances under the four-variance analysis are exactly the same as under the three-variance analysis. The volume variance is the difference between (1) standard overhead costs charged into production and (2) the budgeted overhead based on the standard hours allowed. The efficiency variance continues to be the difference between (1) the overhead budget based on standard hours and (2) the overhead budget based on actual hours.

Let us now compute the variable overhead spending variances and the fixed overhead spending variances for the National Case Company.

Assembly Department. The total spending variance computed under the three-variance analysis of the Assembly Department's operations for 19X9 was computed as being only $2 unfavorable. Here is how we compute the two component parts of that variance:

■ *Variable Overhead Spending Variance.* As you learned in the preceding discussion, the variable overhead spending variance is computed as follows:

Actual variable overhead costs incurred (Exhibit 3, page 567)	$13,994
Budgeted variable overhead for actual hours (2,350 hours × $6.04)	14,194
Variable overhead spending variance	$ 200F

The favorable variable overhead spending variance suggests that the manager of the Assembly Department has done a good job of controlling variable overhead during the month.

■ *Fixed Overhead Spending Variance.* The fixed overhead spending variance in the Assembly Department is an unfavorable variance of $202, computed as follows:

Actual fixed overhead costs incurred (Exhibit 3, page 567)	$11,142
Fixed cost budget	10,940
Fixed cost spending variance	$ 202U

You can readily grasp the importance of the additional information provided by the four-variance analysis. The total spending variance of $2 seemed completely insignificant. Although the two component parts of the variance—an unfavorable variance of $202 and $200—are not major amounts, you can see that two component variances might easily offset one another, making potentially significant control problems. Frequently, the production department manager is responsible for variable cost variances because the manager can generally control that variance. However, the production department often has little control over fixed overhead. Depreciation, taxes, insurance, and similar costs are beyond the control of producing department personnel.

Finishing Department. The two spending variances of the Finishing Department are determined in a like manner.

■ *Variable Overhead Spending Variance.* As you learned in the preceding discussion, the variable overhead spending variance is computed as follows:

Actual variable overhead costs incurred (Exhibit 3, page 567)	$19,124.40
Budgeted variable overhead for actual hours (3,110 hours × $6)	18,660.00
Variable overhead spending variance	464.40U

The unfavorable variable overhead spending variance may warrant further analysis to determine the specific causes. Note that in the three-variance analysis, this unfavorable variance was substantially reduced by an offsetting favorable fixed overhead spending variance.

▪ ***Fixed Overhead Spending Variance.*** The fixed overhead spending variance in the Assembly Department is a favorable variance of $340, computed as shown.

Actual fixed overhead costs incurred (Exhibit 3, page 567)	$10,970
Fixed cost budget	11,310
Fixed cost spending variance	$ 340F

A favorable fixed cost spending variance results most commonly because items such as insurance and taxes that were estimated when the budget was prepared were actually more or less than budgeted when the definite amount of cost became known. Also, changes in personnel costs, such as the addition of managers or factory clerical personnel, may change the fixed cost structure.

Summary of Variances Under Four-Variance Method.   Here is a summary of the variances for the Assembly Department, using the four-variance analysis method. The total departmental overhead variance of $1,700 (shown in Exhibit 5, page 574) is composed of the four following elements:

Volume variance (difference between standard costs charged into production and the budget allowance for standard hours, page 570)	$1,094.00U
Efficiency variance (difference between budget based on standard hours and budget based on actual hours, page 573)	604.00U
Variable overhead spending variance (difference between budget allowance for variable overhead based on actual hours and actual variable overhead, page 576)	200.00F
Fixed overhead spending variance (difference between budget allowance for fixed overhead based on actual hours and actual fixed overhead, page 576)	202.00U
Total Assembly Department overhead variance	$1,700.00U

At this point you should be able to work Exercise 23–5 and Problems 23–3A and 23–3B.

APPLYING OVERHEAD AND RECORDING OVERHEAD VARIANCES

We have seen in Chapter 22 that the National Case Company charges Work in Process with the standard costs of direct materials and direct labor. The same procedure is followed for manufacturing overhead. Manufacturing overhead is applied on the basis of standard cost for the number of units produced during the period (or on the basis of the standard rate per hour multiplied by the standard number of hours for the units produced during the period). Assuming that the two-variance analysis method is used, the summary of overhead variances (Exhibit 5, page 574) and the summary of actual and standard costs of the units of production (Exhibit 4, page 567) provide the information for the general journal entry to charge standard overhead costs to Work in Process and to record the overhead variances for the two overhead variances for the month. That entry is:

SELF-REVIEW

1. Compare the three-variance analysis method and the four-variance analysis method.
2. In what way is the four-variance analysis method superior to the three-variance analysis method? Explain.
3. Is the producing department manager more likely to be responsible for the fixed overhead spending variance or the variable overhead spending variance? Explain.
4. What are the primary causes of the variable overhead spending variance?

Answers to Self-Review

1. Under the four-variance method, the spending variance computed under the three-variance method is divided into two components: the variable overhead spending variance and the fixed overhead spending variance. The volume variance and the efficiency variance are the same under both analysis methods.
2. Under the three-variance method, favorable variances in either fixed overhead or variable overhead may offset unfavorable overhead in the other type of cost. Under the four-variance analysis method, however, separate computations are made for the two types of costs, so that a better picture of cost control is presented.
3. Generally, the departmental manager is more likely to be held responsible for variable overhead spending variances. The amounts spent for fixed overhead often are beyond the control of the production department manager. However, generally the manager is in a position to exercise some control over variable overhead cost levels for any number of hours worked.
4. The major reason for variable overhead spending variances centers around the lack of cost control as the number of hours worked changes.

19X9			
Jan. 31	Work in Process (Standard Cost)	53,513.65	
	Manufacturing Overhead Budget Variance	490.40	
	Manufacturing Overhead Volume Variance	2,226.35	
	Manufacturing Overhead Control		
	(Actual Cost)		55,230.40
	Changed Work in Process with standard		
	costs, closed Manufacturing Overhead Control,		
	and recorded overhead variances for month.		

Recording Transfer of Finished Goods and Sale of Products

Under a standard cost system, units of production completed during the period are valued at their standard cost when transferred from Work in Process to Finished Goods. Thus the 4,500 cases completed in January at a standard cost of $42.91 each are transferred by means of the following general journal entry (ignoring account numbers):

BUSINESS
HORIZON

The Cost Accounting Standards Board

Historically, the federal government has used two methods for paying contractors for equipment and facilities:

1. Fixed price contracts, under which the supplier is paid an agreed-upon amount for the products or services being acquired. Usually, but not always, the price is the result of competitive bids. This system is used when there are competitive products in existence or when there is an established price for the item being purchased.

2. Cost-plus contracts, under which the price is based on actual allowable costs, plus a fixed fee. These contracts are commonly used for products or facilities that do not currently exist and must be planned and constructed to meet the government's specifications. For example, the military forces may enter into a contract with an airplane manufacturer to design, develop, and construct a new bomber. The parties may agree on an estimate of the cost of the project. However, the design, development, and construction may take many years to complete and the estimate may prove to be grossly incorrect.

In the 1970s the government established the Cost Accounting Standards Board (CASB) to development guidelines for cost determination under government contracts, but in 1980 the CASB ceased operations because Congress refused to appropriate more money for the organization. In 1988 the CASB was reestablished within the Office of Federal Procurement Policy and was given the authority to develop and issue cost accounting standards and interpretations of the standards in order to achieve uniformity and consistency in the cost accounting principles used to measure, assign, and allocate costs to government contracts. The CASB has developed almost twenty cost accounting standards. Although these standards are not required to be used, except for government contracts, they have had a strong influence on cost accounting standards for general usage. Some of the cost accounting standards dealing with allocation procedures have been especially important. Here are some of the more important standards:

- CAS 402 Consistency of Allocating Costs Incurred for the Same Purpose
- CAS 403 Allocation of Home Office Costs to Segments
- CAS 410 Allocation of Business Unit General and Administrative Expenses to Final Cost Objectives
- CAS 418 Allocation of Direct and Indirect Costs

19X9			
Jan. 31	Finished Goods (Standard Cost)	193,095.00	
	Work in Process (Standard Cost)		193,095.00
	Removed standard cost of 4,500 cases at $42.91 each from Work in Process and transferred cost to Finished Goods.		

Finally, when products are sold, the transfer from Finished Goods to Cost of Goods Sold is also priced at standard cost. If 4,800 cases were sold during the month, the transfer would be recorded as follows (ignoring account numbers):

19X9			
Jan. 31	Cost of Goods Sold (Standard Cost)	205,968.00	
	Finished Goods (Standard Cost)		205,968.00
	Recorded cost of sales of 4,800 cases with standard cost of $42.91 each.		

DISPOSITION OF STANDARD COST VARIANCES

There is no unanimous agreement on the proper handling of standard cost variances. Various procedures currently used for disposing of the variance accounts are outlined below.

- The variances are prorated each month among Cost of Goods Sold, Finished Goods, and Work in Process. This restores the accounts to actual cost.
- The variances are allowed to accumulate each month until the end of the year, when the variance accounts are either prorated or closed into Cost of Goods Sold.
- The variances are allowed to accumulate each month until the end of the year, when the variance is closed to Cost of Goods Sold and is shown as an adjustment of Cost of Goods Sold in the income statement. (This is the most commonly used procedure and the one used by the National Case Company.)
- The variance accounts are closed into Cost of Goods Sold at the end of each month.
- The variances are closed into the Income and Expense Summary account at the end of each month and are shown as other income or other expense on the income statement.

For amounts that are immaterial, probably the most common practice is to accumulate variances during the year and then close them into Cost of Goods Sold at the end of the year. The second most common procedure, used when the amounts are large, is to allocate the variances among Cost of Goods Sold, Finished Goods, and Work in Process. Very few companies treat variances as other income or other expense, and few close the variance accounts monthly.

Showing Variances in the Income Statement

When variances are treated as an adjustment to cost of goods sold in the income statement, individual variances may be shown, or all variances may be combined and shown as a single figure entitled *Manufacturing Cost Variances From standard,* or some similar title. The condensed income statement on the next page shows in detail the individual variances between actual costs and standard costs for materials, labor, and overhead.

NATIONAL CASE COMPANY
Condensed Income Statement
Month Ended January 31, 19X9

Sales			$307,200.00
Cost of Goods Sold (at Standard Cost)		$205,968.00	
Add Materials Quantity Variance	$1,280.00		
Materials Price Variance	216.00		
Labor Efficiency Variance	640.00		
Labor Rate Variance	940.00		
Mfg. Overhead Volume Variance	2,226.35		
Mfg. Overhead Budget Variance	490.40	5,792.75	
Cost of Goods Sold—Adjusted			211,760.75
Gross Profit on Sales			$ 95,439.25
Operating Expenses			72,776.00
Net Income Before Income Taxes			$ 22,663.25
Provision for Income Taxes			3,400.00
Net Income After Income Taxes			$ 19,263.25

SELF-REVIEW

1. Under a standard cost accounting system, how are the amounts of manufacturing overhead charged to the Work in Process accounts determined?
2. What are the two most common ways to account for standard cost variances?
3. Which method is most commonly used to dispose of standard cost variances at year-end? Why is this method most commonly used?
4. When products are transferred from the final producing department to the Finished Goods account, how is the cost at which the products are transferred determined?
5. If standard cost variances are closed into Cost of Goods Sold, how are the variances shown in the income statement?

Answers to Self-Review

1. The amount of overhead costs charged to Work in Process under a standard cost accounting system is the standard overhead cost per unit of product multiplied by the equivalent units of production for the period.
2. The two most common ways to dispose of standard cost variances are:
   a. Variances are allowed to accumulate each month until year-end, when the variance accounts are closed into Cost of Goods Sold.
   b. Variances are allowed to accumulate each month until year-end, when the variance accounts are allocated between Finished Goods, Cost of Goods Sold, and Work in Process.
3. The most common way to dispose of standard cost variances is to allow them to accumulate during the month and to close them into Cost of Goods Sold at the end of the year. The method is used because it is simple and avoids arbitrary allocations.

At this point you should be able to complete Exercises 23–6 to 23–9 and Problems 23–4A to 23–5B.

4. Under the standard cost accounting system, the products are transferred to Finished Goods as recorded standard cost.
5. If variances are treated as part of Cost of Goods Sold, they are shown on the income statement as an addition to or deduction from the standard cost of goods sold.

PRINCIPLES AND PROCEDURES SUMMARY

■ Direct labor hours is the usual basis for applying manufacturing overhead in a standard cost accounting system.
■ The standard overhead cost per hour is computed by dividing the total overhead budgeted for the year (either normal production or expected actual production) by the standard hours allowed for the budgeted production.
■ Overhead costs are recorded and allocated between producing departments in the same way under a standard cost system as under other systems.
■ At the end of the accounting period, the difference between the actual overhead costs incurred in each department and the standard overhead costs for the work done in each department is computed. This is the total overhead variance for the department.
■ The total overhead variance figure does not provide adequate information to aid management in controlling costs. As a result, the accountant analyzes the total variance, isolating the individual component parts of the variance through variance analysis.
■ The accountant may use a two-variance analysis, a three-variance analysis, or a four-variance analysis. A four-variance analysis provides greater information than a three-variance analysis. Similarly, a three-variance analysis is superior to a two-variance analysis.
■ At the end of each month, the Work in Process account is charged for standard costs of units produced during the period, and favorable and unfavorable variances are recorded.
■ Favorable and unfavorable variances are usually accumulated during the year and are disposed of at the end of the year.
■ At the end of the year, most accountants close overhead variance accounts into Cost of Goods Sold. However, some accountants allocate the variances between Cost of Goods Sold, Finished Goods, and Work in Process.

MANAGERIAL IMPLICATIONS

■ Manufacturing overhead costs are more difficult to control than are labor and materials costs. As a result, the development of standard costs for overhead and the analysis of variances between actual costs and standard costs are of special importance in controlling costs.

■ Management is keenly interested in the total variance between actual overhead costs in a department during a period and standard overhead costs for the period. However, knowing the total variance between actual and standard costs is not adequate for controlling costs and measuring the performance of responsible personnel. Breaking down the total variance into its component parts permits the determination of why costs are out of line and the pinpointing of responsibility for deviations from standard.

■ The most rudimentary analysis is the two-variance analysis, in which a volume variance and budget variance are computed. The two-variance analysis does not provide adequate information for determining who is responsible for differences between actual costs and standard costs. The two-variance analysis determines the part of the variance resulting from the fact that the volume on which standard cost per unit or per hour was computed differs from the actual volume (the volume variance) and the part of the variance resulting from the fact that actual costs differed from the budget allowance based on standard hours allowed (the budget variance).

■ The three-variance method separates the budget variance into two component parts: the spending variance and the efficiency variance. The efficiency variance is a measure of the cost differential resulting from the fact that the units produced required more or fewer hours than standard. The spending variance measures how well the responsible manager controlled costs for the number of hours actually required to produce the units during the period.

■ The four-variance analysis further refines the variance process. It determines separately how much of the spending variance (under the three-variance method) results from control of fixed costs and how much results from control of variable costs. The four-variance method provides the greatest amount of information to aid management in controlling costs and measuring efficiency.

REVIEW QUESTIONS

1. Explain how the standard overhead cost for a period is determined.
2. What basis is used for charging overhead costs into Work in Process when a standard cost accounting system is used?
3. Are standard costs easier or more difficult to establish for overhead than for direct labor? Explain.
4. How is the total manufacturing overhead variance computed?
5. Explain the two variances computed under a two-variance method.
6. What causes the volume variance computed under the two-variance method?
7. Which variances computed under the three-variance method make up the budget variance computed under the two-variance method?
8. What is the main reason why an overhead efficiency variance arises?

9. What is the major cause of variable overhead spending variances?
10. Compare the components of the two-variance analysis method with those of the four-variance analysis method.
11. Under what circumstances, if any, can fixed overhead spending rise?
12. If a debit account is used to record an overhead variance, is the variance favorable or is it unfavorable?
13. Is it possible to have overhead variances even though costs are perfectly controlled? Explain.
14. What entry is made to transfer the cost of completed products from Work in Process to Finished Goods under a standard cost system?
15. What is the most common treatment given to overapplied and underapplied overhead balances at the end of the year?

MANAGERIAL DISCUSSION QUESTIONS

1. Is the budget variance or the volume variance more likely to be the responsibility of the producing department manager? Explain.
2. Is management likely to be more interested in the total overhead variance or in the individual components of the variance? Why?
3. The manager of the Cooking Department in your business has come to you, the cost accountant, to complain about the overhead variances you have reported for his department. He is particularly upset about the variable overhead spending variance because electric rates have increased drastically during the year and his department is a heavy consumer of power. Does his complaint have merit? What do you suggest doing about it, if anything?
4. During June 19X9, the Apollo Corporation had a substantial unfavorable manufacturing overhead volume variance. As a result, the company's production manager asked the controller to explain the variance. What factors are likely to be included in the controller's explanation?
5. As cost accountant, you have followed the practice of allocating overhead variances between Work in Process, Finished Goods, and Cost of Goods Sold. The controller has questioned this practice. She points out that for the year just ended the allocation of a large amount of unfavorable variances had led to an inventory cost that had to be "written down" because generally accepted accounting principles require that in published reports inventory should be valued at the lower of cost or market. The allocation of unfavorable variances led to an inventory cost that was greater than market. What is your reaction to this problem?
6. You have computed variances under the four-variance analysis method and have reported sizable volume variances, variable overhead spending variances, and fixed overhead spending variances. The president of your company has asked you which operating manager is primarily responsible for each of the variances. Write a brief statement providing answers to the president's question.

7. Your company uses the four-variance analysis approach to analyzing overhead variances. You have studied the variances for each of the past four years and found that in the months of July and August there have been large variable overhead spending variances. What are some possible causes of this variance pattern that you might wish to check into?

8. Your company uses the four-variance analysis method. The president of the company has asked you, as cost accountant, to compare the variable overhead spending variance with the materials price variance and the labor rate variance. Give a brief response to this question.

EXERCISES

EXERCISE 23–1   **Compute standard overhead cost per unit. (Obj. 1).**   D.C. Corporation uses direct labor hours as a basis for charging standard overhead to Work in Process. The standard overhead rate for 19X9 is based on a budget of 40,000 hours to produce 80,000 units. The budget at that level called for fixed overhead of $600,000 and variable overhead of $800,000. During the month of January, 7,000 units were produced. Fixed overhead was $50,000, and variable overhead was $7,220.
a. Determine the standard overhead cost per direct labor hour.
b. Compute the standard overhead cost per unit of product.

EXERCISE 23–2   **Compute standard overhead cost per unit; compute total standard overhead for units produced during period. (Obj. 1).**   Newark Corporation uses direct labor hours as a basis for charging standard overhead to Work in Process. The standard overhead rate for 19X9 is based on a budget of 80,000 hours to produce 160,000 units. The budget at that level called for fixed overhead of $1,200,000 and variable overhead of $1,600,000. During the month of January, 14,000 units were produced. Fixed overhead was $51,000, and variable overhead was $7,140.
a. Determine the standard overhead cost per direct labor hour.
b. Compute the standard overhead cost per unit of product.
c. Compute the standard cost of the units completed in January.

EXERCISE 23–3   **Compute standard overhead cost per unit; compute total standard overhead for units produced; compute total overhead variance; use the two-variance method to analyze total variance. (Obj. 1, 2, 3).**   Boise Corporation bases overhead charges on a standard cost per direct labor hour. The standard overhead rate is based on the budget at 10,000 hours to produce 5,000 units. The budget at that level called for fixed overhead of $100,000 and variable overhead of $80,000. During the year, 5,200 units were produced. Fixed overhead was $100,000 and variable overhead was $85,200.
a. Determine the standard overhead cost per unit.

b. What is the standard overhead cost of the units produced during the year?

c. Compute the total overhead variance for the year.

d. Using the two-variance method, compute the budget variance for the year.

e. Using the two-variance method, compute the volume variance for the year.

EXERCISE 23–4   **Compute standard overhead cost per unit; compute total standard overhead cost for year's production; compute total overhead variance; use the three-variance method to analyze total overhead variance.   (Objs. 1, 2, 4).**   Toledo Corporation has established standard overhead costs for the year 19X9 based on the following budget data:

Budgeted Production	2,000 units
Budgeted Direct Labor Hours	20,000 hours
Budgeted Fixed Costs	$240,000
Budgeted Variable Costs	$400,000

Information for January 19X9 is as follows:

Production	150 units
Direct Labor Hours	1,680 hours
Total Overhead Costs (Fixed as Budgeted)	$ 52,800

a. Compute the standard overhead cost per unit of product.

b. Compute the total standard overhead cost for production during January.

c. Compute the total overhead variance for January.

d. Use the three-variance method to analyze the total overhead variance for January.

EXERCISE 23–5   **Compute the standard overhead cost per unit; compute the total standard overhead cost for units produced during the period; compute the total variance for period; use the four-variance method to analyze manufacturing overhead variance.   (Objs. 1, 2, 5).**   St. Clair Company uses the standard cost accounting system. Standard overhead costs are based on the following information for 19X9.

Budgeted Production	48,000 units
Budgeted Direct Labor Hours	96,000 hours
Budgeted Fixed Costs	$240,000
Budgeted Variable Costs	$480,000

Data for June 19X9 are as follows:

Total Production	3,800 units
Budgeted Direct Labor Hours	7,450 hours
Fixed Costs Incurred	$21,300
Variable Costs Incurred	$36,900

a. Compute the standard overhead cost per unit of product.

b. Compute the total standard overhead cost for the units produced in June.

c. Compute the total overhead variance for June.

d. Using the four-variance analysis method, analyze the total overhead variance for 19X9.

EXERCISE 23–6　**Apply manufacturing overhead to Work in Process and record overhead variances. (Obj. 6).** Selected data for the Halifax Corporation for May 19X9 are as follows:

Standard cost of work	$82,000
Actual overhead costs incurred	$79,000
Favorable volume variance	$ 2,400
Favorable spending variance	800
Unfavorable efficiency variance	200

Give the general journal entry to apply standard overhead to Work in Process and record overhead variances for the month.

EXERCISE 23–7　**Record standard cost of goods transferred to Finished Goods and of cost of goods sold. (Obj. 7).** Stamford Company uses a standard cost system. The total standard cost per unit for materials, labor, and overhead is $120.50. During June 19X9, a total of 2,000 units were completed and transferred to Finished Goods. During the month 1,800 units were sold for $200 each. Give the general journal entries to record the cost of units transferred to finished goods and the cost of units sold during the month.

EXERCISE 23–8　**Properly dispose of overhead variance accounts. (Obj. 8).** Cleveland Corporation accumulates overhead variances during the year. At the end of the year all variances are closed out to Cost of Goods Sold. On December 31, 19X9, the variance accounts had the following balances:

Overhead Volume Variance	$2,300 favorable
Overhead Spending Variance	$1,600 unfavorable
Overhead Efficiency Variance	$1,100 unfavorable

Give the compound general journal entry to close the variance accounts.

EXERCISE 23–9　**Use three-variance analysis to analyze manufacturing overhead variance. Prepare partial income statement using standard costing. (Objs. 4, 9).** Selected accounts from the adjusted general ledger accounts of Columbus Corporation on December 31, 19X9, are as follows:

Sales	$287,000
Cost of Goods Sold (at Standard Cost)	$175,000
Materials Quantity Variance	880 Unfavorable
Materials Price Variance	316 Favorable
Labor Efficiency Variance	640 Unfavorable
Labor Rate Variance	840 Favorable
Manufacturing Overhead Volume Variance	1,800 Unfavorable
Manufacturing Overhead Budget Variance	490 Unfavorable

Prepare a partial income statement (through Gross Profit on Sales) for the year 19X9.

EXERCISE 23–10   Compute standard overhead cost for period; compute total overhead variance for period; use three-variance analysis to analyze
total overhead variance. (Objs. 2, 3, 4).

Data for Exercise 10.

Number of units produced at normal volume	5,000 units
Number of direct labor hours at normal volume	25,000 hours
Fixed overhead budgeted	$100,000
Variable overhead budgeted (25,000 hours at $3 per hour)	75,000
Total budgeted costs at normal capacity	175,000
Standard overhead per unit ($175,000 ÷ 5,000 units)	35

During June 19X9, 600 units were produced requiring 3,010 hours
of labor. The total costs were $17,062, consisting of:

Fixed costs	$ 8,333
Variable costs	8,729
Total	$17,062

a. Compute the standard overhead costs of the 600 units produced.
b. Determine the total overhead variance for the month. Is it favorable
   or unfavorable?
c. Analyze the total overhead variance into three component parts.
   Indicate whether each is favorable or unfavorable.

PROBLEMS

PROBLEM 23–1A

**Compute overhead cost per unit of product; compute total over-
head for a month's production; compute total overhead variance;
analyze total overhead variance, using the two-variance analysis
method. (Objs. 1, 2, 3).**   Grand Rapids Corporation uses a standard cost system. The manufacturing overhead rate is based on a normal yearly volume of 100,000 units, requiring 20,000 direct labor
hours, and on normal budgeted costs at that volume as shown below:

Fixed Costs	$200,000
Variable Costs	400,000
Total	$600,000

During the month of May 19X9, the company produced 8,200 units
of its product, requiring 1,700 direct labor hours. Actual manufacturing overhead costs for the month included fixed costs of $16,667
and variable costs of $33,260.

INSTRUCTIONS   1. Compute the standard overhead cost per unit of product.
2. Compute the total standard overhead cost for the month of May.
3. Compute the total variance between the actual and standard overhead costs for the month of May. Round off amounts to the nearest
   dollar. Indicate whether the variance is favorable (F) or unfavorable (U).

4. Divide the variance into its parts using the two-variance method. Indicate whether each variance is favorable or unfavorable.

PROBLEM 23–2A   **Compute materials and labor variance; compute standard cost for period; compute total overhead variance for month; use the three-variance analysis method to analyze total overhead for month. (Objs. 2, 3, 4).**   The Charleston Company manufactures one product. Its standard costs under efficient operating conditions are as follows:

Material, 10 gal at $4 per gallon	$40.00
Direct Labor, 3 hr at $12 per hr	36.00
Manufacturing Overhead, 3 hr at $6 per hr	18.00
Total Standard Costs per Unit	$94.00

The manufacturing overhead rate is based on a normal yearly volume of 360,000 direct labor hours. The fixed overhead totals $720,000 per year. Production and cost figures for the month of May 19X9 are as follows:

Units of Product Manufactured	10,500 units
Raw Materials Used	106,000 gal
Direct Labor Hours Worked	31,320 hr
Cost per Gallon of Raw Materials	$4.04
Direct Labor Rate per Hour	$12.16
Manufacturing Overhead Costs Incurred	184,400.00

INSTRUCTIONS   1. Compute the total materials variance. Compute the materials quantity variance and materials price variance. Show whether each variance is favorable or unfavorable.
2. Compute the total direct labor variance. Compute the labor rate variance and labor time or efficiency variance. Show whether each variance is favorable or unfavorable.
3. Compute the total standard manufacturing overhead cost for the month.
4. Compute the total manufacturing overhead variance for the month.
5. Analyze the total variance for May, using the three-variance analysis method. Indicate whether each variance is favorable or unfavorable.
6. Which manager in the company is most likely to be responsible for each of the variances that you have determined?

PROBLEM 23–3A   **Compute standard overhead cost per unit of product; compute total standard overhead cost of units produced during period; determine total overhead cost variance; use the four-variance method to analyze the total overhead cost variance for the period.   (Objs. 1, 2, 3, 5).**   Yonkers Company uses the four-variance method for analyzing the overhead variance. The 19X9 planning budget, on which cost standards were based, included the following data relating to overhead:

Budgeted Production	120,000 units
Direct Labor Hours	30,000 hours
Variable Overhead Costs ($40 per Direct Labor Hour)	$1,200,000
Fixed Overhead	$900,000

Actual data for the month of May 19X9 are as follows:

Units Produced	10,240 units
Direct Labor Hours Worked	2,600 hours
Variable Overhead Costs Incurred	$102,080
Fixed Overhead Costs Incurred	76,400

INSTRUCTIONS

1. Determine the standard overhead cost per unit of product.
2. Compute the total standard overhead cost for the month of May 19X9.
3. Compute the total overhead variance for the month of May 19X9.
4. Use the four-variance analysis method to analyze the total overhead variance for May.
5. Using the four-variance analysis that you have just completed, and making only one calculation, complete a three-variance analysis.

PROBLEM 23–4A **Compute standard overhead cost per unit of product; compute total standard overhead for work done; compute total overhead variance; use the four-variance method to analyze total variance; give journal entries to apply overhead to Work in Process and record the overhead variances. (Objs. 1, 2, 5, 6).** The Little Rock Corporation's standard overhead rate is $24 per direct labor hour. The overhead rate is based on budgeted fixed costs of $400,000 and budgeted variable costs of $200,000. Each unit requires 15 minutes of direct labor. During the year, 127,000 units were produced, requiring 32,000 direct labor hours, with actual total overhead cost of $761,800. The total overhead cost included $418,000 of fixed costs.

INSTRUCTIONS

1. Compute the standard overhead cost per unit of product.
2. Compute the standard overhead cost charged to Work in Process during the year.
3. Compute the total overhead variance for the year and show whether it is favorable or unfavorable.
4. Analyze the total overhead variance, using the four-variance analysis method. Indicate whether the variance is favorable or unfavorable.
5. Using the four variances computed in Instruction 4, give the general journal entry to apply manufacturing overhead to Work in Process and record the variances.

PROBLEM 23–5A **Apply manufacturing overhead to Work in Process and record overhead variances; transfer cost of completed products to finished goods; record cost of goods sold; prepare a partial income statement. (Objs. 6, 7, 9).** The actual costs, standard costs, and variances applicable to work performed in the Finishing Department of the Buffalo Company during July 19X9 are given below.

	Actual Costs	Standard Costs	Variances
Materials	$294,600	$293,800	Price: $1,820 favorable
			Quantity: $2,620 unfavorable
Labor	162,000	162,300	Rate: $500 unfavorable
			Efficiency: $800 favorable

Manufacturing
Overhead   93,250   92,600   Volume: $900 unfavorable
                                       Efficiency: $710 favorable
                                       Spending: $460 unfavorable

During the month, a total of 910 units with a standard cost of $548.70 each were completed and transferred to finished goods, and 876 units were sold for $900 each.

INSTRUCTIONS

1. Give general journal entries dated July 31, 19X9, to record the following. (Eliminate explanations.)
   a. Charge the raw materials to production and record the materials variances.
   b. Charge the labor to production and record the labor variances.
   c. Charge the manufacturing overhead to production and record the overhead variances.
   d. Transfer the completed units to finished goods.
   e. Record sales and cost of units sold.
   f. Close all variance accounts into Cost of Goods Sold.
2. Prepare a partial income statement (through Gross Profit on Sales) for July 19X9, assuming that all variances are treated each month as adjustments to Cost of Goods Sold for that month.

ALTERNATE PROBLEMS

PROBLEM 23–1B   **Compute overhead cost per unit of product; compute total overhead for a month's production; compute total overhead variance; analyze total overhead variance, using the two-variance analysis method. (Objs. 1, 2, 3).** The Durrance Manufacturing Company uses a standard cost system. The manufacturing overhead standard rate is based on direct labor hours, assuming a normal yearly volume of 40,000 units, requiring 20,000 direct labor hours, and on normal budgeted costs shown below for that volume.

Fixed Costs	$120,000
Variable Costs	80,000
Total	$200,000

During the month of June 19X9, the company produced 3,400 units of its product, requiring 1,645 direct labor hours. Actual manufacturing overhead costs for the month included fixed costs of $10,000 and variable costs of $6,720.

INSTRUCTIONS

1. Compute the standard overhead cost per unit of product.
2. Compute the total standard overhead cost for the month of June.
3. Compute the total variance between the actual and standard overhead costs for the month of June. Round off amounts to the nearest dollar. Indicate whether the variance is favorable (F) or unfavorable (U).
4. Divide the variance into its parts using the two-variance method. Indicate whether each variance is favorable or unfavorable.

PROBLEM 23–2B **Compute materials and labor variance; compute standard cost for period; compute total overhead variance for month; use the three-variance analysis method to analyze total overhead for month. (Objs. 1, 2, 4).** The El Paso Corporation manufactures one product. Its standard costs under efficient operating conditions are budgeted as follows:

Material, 12 lb at $.80	$ 9.60
Direct Labor, 1 hr at $12 per hr	12.00
Manufacturing Overhead, 1 hr at $8 per hr	8.00
Total Standard Costs per Unit	$29.60

The manufacturing overhead rate is based on a normal yearly volume of 200,000 direct labor hours. The fixed overhead costs total $480,000 per year. Production and cost figures for the month of July 19X9 are as follows:

Units of Product Manufactured	15,000 units
Raw Materials Used	182,300 lb
Direct Labor Hours Worked	15,400 hr
Cost per Pound of Raw Materials	$.76
Labor Rate per Hour	$12.40
Manufacturing Overhead Costs Incurred	$132,400

INSTRUCTIONS
1. Compute the total materials variance. Compute the materials quantity variance and materials price variance. Show whether each variance is favorable or unfavorable.
2. Compute the total direct labor variance. Compute the labor rate variance and labor time or efficiency variance. Show whether each variance is favorable or unfavorable.
3. Compute the total standard manufacturing overhead cost for the month.
4. Compute the total manufacturing overhead variance for the month.
5. Analyze the total variance for July, using the three-variance analysis method. Indicate whether each variance is favorable or unfavorable.
6. Which manager in the company is most likely to be responsible for each of the variances that you have determined?

PROBLEM 23–3B **Compute standard overhead cost per unit of product; compute total standard overhead cost of units produced during period; determine total overhead cost variance; use the four-variance method to analyze the total overhead cost variance for the period. (Objs. 1, 2, 4, 5).** Fort Lauderdale Company uses the four-variance method for analyzing the overhead variance. The 19X9 planning budget, on which cost standard was based, included the following data relating to overhead:

Budgeted Production for Period	30,000 units
Direct Labor Hours	60,000 hours
Variable Overhead Costs ($10 per Direct	
Labor Hour)	$600,000
Fixed Overhead	$900,000

Actual data for the month of June 19X9 are as follows:

Units Produced	2,240 units
Direct Labor Hours Worked	4,800 hours
Variable Overhead Costs Incurred	$49,200
Fixed Overhead Costs Incurred	$76,400

INSTRUCTIONS

1. Determine the standard overhead cost per unit of product.
2. Compute the total standard overhead cost for the month of June 19X9.
3. Compute the total overhead variance for the month of June 19X9.
4. Use the four-variance analysis method to analyze the total overhead variance for June.
5. Using the four-variance analysis that you have just completed, and making only one calculation, complete a three-variance analysis.

PROBLEM 23–4B

Compute standard overhead cost per unit of product; compute total standard overhead for work done; compute total overhead variance; use the four-variance method to analyze total variance; give journal entries to apply overhead to Work in Process and record the overhead variances. (Objs. 1, 2, 5, 6). Victoria Company's standard overhead rate is $10 per direct labor hour, based on expected production of 50,000 units of its product during the year. The overhead rate is based on budgeted fixed costs of $800,000 and budgeted variable costs of $200,000. Each unit requires 2 direct labor hours to complete. During the year, 60,000 units were produced, requiring 122,000 hours of direct labor. The actual total overhead was $1,087,000. Fixed costs were as budgeted.

INSTRUCTIONS

1. Compute the standard overhead cost per unit of product.
2. Compute the standard overhead cost charged to Work in Process during the year.
3. Compute the total overhead variance for the year and show whether it is favorable or unfavorable.
4. Analyze the total overhead variance, using the four-variance analysis method. Indicate whether the variance is favorable or unfavorable.
5. Using the four variances computed in Instruction 4, give the general journal entry to apply manufacturing overhead to Work in Process and to record the variances.

PROBLEM 23–5B

Apply manufacturing overhead to Work in Process and record overhead variances; transfer cost of completed products to finished goods; record cost of goods sold; prepare a partial income statement. (Objs. 6, 7, 9). The actual costs, standard costs, and variances applicable to work performed in the Completion Department of the Aspen Company during July 19X9 are given below.

	Actual Costs	Standard Costs	Variances
Materials	$147,300	$146,900	Price: $910 favorable
			Quantity: $1,310 unfavorable
Labor	81,000	81,150	Rate: $250 unfavorable
			Efficiency: $400 favorable

Manufacturing Overhead	46,625	46,300	Volume: $450 unfavorable Efficiency: $355 favorable Spending: $230 unfavorable

During the month, a total of 455 units with a standard cost of $274.35 each were completed and transferred to finished goods.

INSTRUCTIONS

1. Give general journal entries dated July 31, 19X9, to record the following. (Eliminate explanations.)
   a. Charge the raw materials to production and record the materials variances.
   b. Charge the labor to production and record the labor variances.
   c. Charge the manufacturing overhead to production and record the overhead variances.
   d. Transfer the completed units to finished goods.
   e. Record sales and cost of units sold.
   f. Close all variance accounts into Cost of Goods Sold.
2. Prepare a partial income statement (through Gross Profit on Sales) for July 19X9, assuming that all variances are treated each month as adjustments to Cost of Goods Sold for that month.

MINI-PRACTICE SET 3
Budgeting and Standard Costs

In this project you will apply the techniques and principles of budgeting and standard costs to the operations of Speedway Toys, Inc. You will prepare budgets for the year ended December 31, 19X9, determine standard costs per hour and per unit of product, and compute variances for the month of January 19X9.

THE COMPANY'S OPERATIONS

Speedway Toys, Inc., manufactures a battery-powered toy car that is sold in toy stores and department stores. In the firm's manufacturing process, highly skilled employees operate molding machines that form semiliquid plastic into car bodies. Assembly personnel insert a battery-driven motor assembly, which the firm purchases from a subcontractor, into the molded car body. Then the assembly personnel add wheels and axles (also purchased from a subcontractor) and decorative trim to complete the car.

PREPARATION OF BUDGETS

SALES BUDGET

The sales manager and her staff have analyzed sales records and other data and forecast that 61,000 cars will be sold in 19X9. Standard costs are to be based on this volume of production, which should require 30,000 direct labor hours.

PRODUCTION BUDGET

Speedway Toys, Inc., expects to begin 19X9 with an inventory of 7,000 completed toy cars. The company would like to reduce its finished goods inventory of toy cars at the end of 19X9 by 1,000 cars, to 6,000.

STANDARDS FOR DIRECT MATERIALS AND DIRECT LABOR

Speedway Toys, Inc., has established the following standards for direct materials and direct labor, which should be attainable under normal circumstances. Later you will be instructed to compute the standard cost per hour of direct labor and per unit of product. Data related to direct materials follow:

Material	Quantity	Cost per Unit	Cost per Car
Plastic	1.5 lb per car	$3.40 per lb	$ 5.10
Motor assembly	1 motor per car	6.50 per motor	6.50
Wheels and axles	1 set per car	.40 per set	.40
			$12.00

NOTE: Paint and stickers for decorative trim are considered part of indirect materials.

Data related to direct labor follow:

Job Title	Hours per Car	Rate per Car	Cost per Car
Molders	.2	$15.00	$3.00
Assemblers	.3	18.00	5.40
	.5		$8.40

MATERIALS BUDGET

Beginning inventories of raw materials on January 1, 19X9, are expected to be as follows:

Material	Amount
Plastic	5,500 lb
Motors	4,000 motors
Wheels and axles	2,500 sets

Speedway Toys, Inc., would like to have enough raw materials on hand at the end of the year to equal the following percentages of the 19X9 budgeted requirements:

Material	Percentage of 19X9 Budget
Plastic	5%
Motors	10%
Wheels and axles	1%

MANUFACTURING OVERHEAD BUDGET

The following information related to variable and fixed manufacturing overhead costs for 19X9 has been assembled. Later you will be directed to complete the manufacturing overhead budget and compute the standard overhead cost per hour and per unit.

SPEEDWAY TOYS, INC. Analysis of Fixed and Variable Overhead Costs Year Ended December 31, 19X9	VARIABLE OVERHEAD PER HOUR	FIXED OVERHEAD
Controllable Costs		
Indirect Materials	$ .04	—
Indirect Labor	2.00	$ 60,000
Payroll Taxes and Fringe Benefits	2.80	9,000
Utilities	.32	12,000
Repairs and Miscellaneous	.34	9,600
Noncontrollable Costs		
Depreciation	—	42,000
Insurance	—	12,000
Total Manufacturing Overhead	$5.50	$144,600

BUDGETING PROCEDURES TO BE COMPLETED

To contribute to the budgeting of Speedway Toys, Inc., you are to prepare the following budgets for the year ended December 31, 19X9. Remember that the sales budget has already been prepared. (All the forms required to complete the budgeting procedures are found in the *Study Guide and Working Papers*. If you are not using the *Study Guide and Working Papers,* you may prepare your answers on analysis paper or on lined paper.)

INSTRUCTIONS

A-1. Prepare a production budget based on expected production for 19X9.

A-2. Prepare a materials budget based on expected production for 19X9.

A-3. Prepare a direct labor budget based on expected production for 19X9.

A-4. Prepare a monthly flexible overhead budget at 90, 100, and 110 percent of capacity. *Capacity* is considered to be the 30,000 direct labor hours required to manufacture the 60,000 cars projected for 19X9.

A-5. Prepare a manufacturing costs budget. (Include costs per car.)

A-6. Using the budget overhead for 19X9 computed at 100 percent of capacity (in Instruction A-4), compute the standard cost per direct labor hour and the standard cost per unit of product for 19X9.

STANDARD COST ACCOUNTING PROCEDURES TO BE COMPLETED

During January 19X9, Speedway Toys, Inc., manufactured 4,800 toy cars. The costs of materials, labor, and overhead were as follows:

Material	Amount
Plastic	7,050 lb at $3.60 per lb
Motors	4,975 motors at $6.24 per motor
Wheels and axles	4,880 sets at $.425 per set

Direct Labor	Hours	Rate
Molders	930 hr	$15.20 per hr
Assemblers	1,510 hr	$18.40 per hr

Overhead	Amount
Variable	$13,120
Fixed	12,050

You are to prepare the following for the month of January 19X9. For all variances computed, show whether they are favorable or unfavorable. (If you are not using the *Study Guide and Working Papers,* you may prepare your answers on analysis paper or on lined paper.)

B-1. Prepare a summary of materials costs.

B-2. Prepare a summary of labor costs.

B-3. Compute the quantity and price variances for each material.

B-4. Compute the efficiency and rate variances for each type of labor.

B-5. Compute the total manufacturing overhead variance. Analyze the total overhead variance, using the three-variance analysis method.

B-6. Prepare entries in general journal form to record each of the following. (Omit explanations.)

    a. Charge the raw materials to production and record the materials variances.

    b. Charge the labor to production and record the labor variances.

    c. Charge the manufacturing overhead to production and record the overhead variances.

    d. Transfer the completed units to finished goods.

MANAGERIAL DECISIONS

From the data given on pages 595 to 597 and the work you have done, answer the following questions about the operations of Speedway Toys, Inc. (Write your answers to these questions on the rules paper provided in the *Study Guide and Working Papers* or on separate sheets.)

1. What factors might cause Speedway Toys, Inc., to revise its sales budget for the year?

2. What factors might have influenced the management of Speedway Toys, Inc., to set the level of the ending inventory for plastic, motors, and wheels and axles at 5, 10, and 1 percent budgeted requirements for the year?

3. a. Assume that production in February was 5,500 cars.

    (1) What would be the total budgeted variable overhead cost?

    (2) What would be the total budgeted fixed overhead cost?

    (3) What would be the total budgeted overhead cost?

   b. Assume that production in March was 5,250 cars.

    (1) What would be the total budgeted cost for indirect materials?

    (2) What would be the total budgeted cost for utilities?

    (3) What would be the total budgeted cost for insurance?

4. If Speedway Toys, Inc., wanted to make a gross profit of 40 percent for the year, what selling price would it set for the toy cars?

5. The president of Speedway Toys, Inc., thinks that the standard costs should be based on theoretical standards instead of normal standards as a way to motivate employees to reach a higher level of performance. What do you think about this plan?

6. Explain how the variances that you have computed for Speedway Toys, Inc., might be handled on the financial statements.

7. Answer the following questions about the materials variances:

    a. Give some possible causes for each materials variance that you computed.

    b. Which person in the company is probably responsible for each of these variances?

8. Answer the following questions about the labor variances:
   a. Give some possible causes for each labor variance that you computed.
   b. Which person in the company is probably responsible for each of these variances?
9. Answer the following questions about the manufacturing overhead variances:
   a. Give some possible causes for each overhead variance that you computed.
   b. Which person in the company is probably responsible for each of these variances?
10. The financial vice president states that he has heard of a four-variance method for analyzing overhead variances and asks you what it is and how much each variance would have been if that analysis method had been used. Respond to his question.

C H A P T E R

24

Cost-Volume-Profit Analysis

In this chapter you will learn about **cost-volume-profit analysis,** which is an analysis of how profits change as costs change in response to changes in production or sales volumes. The cost accounting systems you have studied up to this point have used a concept known as **absorption costing** under which all manufacturing costs, both direct and indirect, are assigned to the cost of goods manufactured. These costs are then offset against the revenue for the period in which the goods are sold. Absorption costing does not readily reflect cost-volume-profit relationships.

DIRECT COSTING

This chapter will also cover a concept for determining the cost of goods manufactured—**direct costing**—under which only those costs that are so closely associated with the product that they vary proportionately with the volume of production are assigned as product costs. Because of this relationship to variable costs, direct costing is sometimes called **variable costing.** Under direct costing, fixed manufacturing costs, along with all selling, general, and administrative costs, are classified as period costs. **Period costs** are costs that are identified with time intervals (the month or the year) rather than with units of goods or services. Under direct costing, all period costs, including fixed manufacturing overhead, are charged directly to expense in the period in which they are incurred or are consumed. Fixed manufacturing costs are generally the costs of providing the facilities and conditions for production, rather than the result of the level of actual production activity. For example, depreciation, property taxes, property insurance, factory supervision, and a part of utilities are typical fixed costs necessary for carrying on production. In direct costing, the only costs charged to the product are the manufacturing costs that result directly from the production of units of product during this period. These costs consist of direct materials, direct labor, and variable manufacturing overhead, and under direct costing they make up the cost of product manufactured and are deferred or inventoried until the product is sold. On the other hand, fixed costs must be incurred during each period regardless of whether products are sold or are kept in inventory, and under full costing these costs are charged to expense rather than to work in process.

Direct costing is not acceptable under generally accepted accounting principles (GAAP) because, under GAAP, an appropriate amount of all manufacturing costs, including fixed costs, must be charged to the units manufactured. However, direct costing is often used by management in making operating decisions. Frequently, income statements and balance sheets based on direct costing are prepared and compared to those based on absorption costing.

A COMPARISON OF ABSORPTION COSTING AND DIRECT COSTING

A comparison of absorption costing and direct costing makes it easier to evaluate and understand the two concepts. The manufacturing costs of Sun Times Jeans Company, which began operations on January 2, 19X8, will provide the basis for the comparison. The company manufactures one style of jeans and uses standard costing to account for its manufacturing activities. Based on a normal production volume of 10,000 units, a standard cost sheet was prepared and is summarized in Exhibit 1.

Each pair of jeans has a sales price of $50. Fixed selling and administrative expenses are estimated at $50,000 for the year. Variable selling and administrative expenses are estimated at $4 per unit sold. The budgeted income statement based on standard absorption costing for the year 19X8 is shown in Exhibit 2.

SUN TIMES JEANS   Exhibit 1
Standard Cost Sheet

Materials		$10.00
Labor		7.50
Manufacturing Overhead		
Variable Costs	$ 2.50	
Fixed Costs ($150,000/yr ÷ 10,000 units/yr)	15.00	17.50
Standard Manufacturing Cost per Unit		$35.00

SUN TIMES JEANS   Exhibit 2
Budgeted Income Statement
Year Ending December 31, 19X8

Sales (10,000 units at $50 each)			$500,000.00
Cost of Sales			
Materials (10,000 units at $10 each)		$100,000.00	
Labor (10,000 units at $7.50 each)		75,000.00	
Manufacturing Overhead			
Fixed	$150,000.00		
Variable (10,000 units at $2.50 each)	25,000.00	175,000.00	350,000.00
Gross Margin on Sales			$150,000.00
Selling and Administrative Expenses			
Fixed		$ 45,000.00	
Variable (10,000 units at $4 each)		40,000.00	85,000.00
Estimated Net Income			$ 65,000.00

During the year 19X8, 10,000 units were produced, but only 6,000 units were sold, and the following actual costs were incurred:

Materials	$100,000
Labor	75,000
Manufacturing Overhead	
Fixed	150,000
Variable	25,000
Selling and Administrative	
Fixed	45,000
Variable	24,000

The company had no beginning inventory of finished goods on January 2, 19X8.

Absorption Costing Approach

Based on the data for 19X8 above, an income statement using absorption costing is prepared, as shown in Exhibit 3. Note that under absorption costing, net income of $21,000 is reported for the year.

SUN TIMES JEANS Income Statement (Absorption Costing) Year Ended December 31, 19X8		**Exhibit 3**
Sales (6,000 units at $50 each)		$300,000
Cost of Sales		
Materials (10,000 units at $10 each)	$100,000	
Labor (10,000 units at $7.50 each)	75,000	
Manufacturing Overhead (10,000 units at $17.50 each)	175,000	
Total Cost of Goods Manufactured	$350,000	
Less Ending Inventory, December 31 (4,000 units at $35 each)	140,000	210,000
Gross Profit on Sales		$ 90,000
Selling and Administrative Expenses		
Fixed	$ 45,000	
Variable (6,000 units at $4 each)	24,000	69,000
Net Income		$ 21,000

During the year 19X9, production was cut to 6,500 units but sales rose to 9,500 units. Actual costs for 19X9 were:

Materials	$ 65,000
Labor	48,750
Manufacturing Overhead	
Fixed	150,000
Variable	16,250
Selling and Administrative Expenses	
Fixed	45,000
Variable	38,000

There is an unfavorable manufacturing overhead volume variance of $52,500 since not all fixed costs were charged into production, as shown in the following computation.

Actual fixed manufacturing costs	$150,000
Applied fixed costs (6,500 units at $15 per unit)	97,500
Unfavorable variance (underapplied overhead)	$ 52,500

Under absorption costing, this unfavorable variance would be added to the cost of goods sold during the period. Similarly, a favorable variance would reduce cost of goods sold during the period.

The income statement for 19X9, based on absorption costing, is shown in Exhibit 4.

One of the problems of using absorption costing is shown clearly by the income statement. Sales rose from 6,000 units in 19X8 to 9,500 units in 19X9. Yet net income declined from $21,000 to $7,000. Certainly, the cost accountant must be prepared to explain such seemingly contradictory results. However, the impact of changes in sales and

SUN TIMES JEANS			Exhibit 4
Income Statement			
(Absorption Costing)			
Year Ended December 31, 19X9			
Sales (9,500 at $50 each)			$475,000
Cost of Sales			
Beginning Inventory, January 1		$140,000	
Materials (6,500 units at $10 each)	$ 65,000		
Labor (6,500 units at $7.50 each)	48,750		
Manufacturing Overhead (6,500 units at $17.50 each)	113,750	227,500	
Total Cost of Goods Manufactured		$367,500	
Less Ending Inventory, December 31 (1,000 units at $35 each)		35,000	
Cost of Sales at Standard		$332,500	
Add Unfavorable Overhead Volume Variance		52,500	385,000
Gross Margin on Sales			$ 90,000
Selling and Administrative Expenses			
Fixed		$ 45,000	
Variable		38,000	83,000
Net Income			$ 7,000

production volume under absorption costing are difficult to explain to management.

Direct Costing Approach

Under the direct costing approach, only variable costs are treated as part of cost of goods manufactured. The cost of goods sold, which will, of course, include only variable costs, is deducted from sales to arrive at the contribution margin. The **contribution margin** is the amount available to cover fixed manufacturing costs and other expenses and to produce a profit.

Using the data from the Sun Times Jeans Company, the income statements for 19X8 (Exhibit 5, page 605) and 19X9 (Exhibit 6, page 605) are prepared using direct costing.

In 19X8 a difference of $60,000 exists between the net income of $21,000 reported under absorption costing (Exhibit 3) and the net loss of $39,000 reported under direct costing (Exhibit 5). The $60,000 reflects the fixed costs associated with the 4,000 unsold units (4,000 × $15 = $60,000), which, under absorption costing, are carried forward as an asset to be charged against revenue only in a later period when the units are sold. Under direct costing, the fixed costs are considered to be period costs and are matched against revenue in the year the costs are incurred. No part of fixed costs is included in the finished goods inventory or the work in process inventory under direct costing.

The income statement for Sun Times Jeans for 19X9, using direct costing, is shown in Exhibit 6.

SUN TIMES JEANS
Income Statement
(Direct Costing)
Year Ended December 31, 19X8

Exhibit 5

Sales (6,000 units at $50 each)		$300,000
Variable Costs		
Manufacturing Costs		
Materials (10,000 units at $10 each)	$100,000	
Labor (10,000 units at $7.50 each)	75,000	
Manufacturing Overhead (10,000 units at $2.50 each)	25,000	
Total Variable Manufacturing Costs	$200,000	
Less Ending Inventory, December 31		
(4,000 units at $20 each)	80,000	
Net Variable Manufacturing Costs	$120,000	
Selling and Administrative Expenses		
(6,000 units at $4 each)	24,000	144,000
Contribution Margin		$156,000
Fixed Costs		
Manufacturing Costs	$150,000	
Selling and Administrative Expenses	45,000	195,000
Net Loss		$(39,000)

SUN TIMES JEANS
Income Statement
(Direct Costing)
Year Ended December 31, 19X9

Exhibit 6

Sales (9,500 at $50 each)			$475,000
Variable Costs			
Manufacturing Costs			
Beginning Inventory, January 1		$ 80,000	
Materials (6,500 units at $10 each)	$65,000		
Labor (6,500 units at $7.50 each)	48,750		
Manufacturing Overhead (6,500 units at $2.50 each)	16,250	130,000	
Total Variable Manufacturing Costs		$210,000	
Less Ending Inventory, December 31 (1,000 units at			
$20 each)		20,000	
Net Variable Manufacturing Costs		$190,000	
Selling and Administrative Expenses			
(9,500 units at $4 each)		38,000	228,000
Contribution Margin			$247,000
Fixed Costs			
Manufacturing Costs		$150,000	
Selling and Administrative Expenses		45,000	195,000
Net Income			$ 52,000

The preceding income statements reflect one major advantage of direct costing. Direct costing more clearly reflects the impact of volume on costs and profits than does absorption costing. When the Sun Times Jeans Company's sales increased by 58 percent in 19X9, its net income under direct costing reflected the increase. The Sun Times Jeans Company went from a net loss of $39,000 in 19X8 (Exhibit 5) to a net income of $52,000 in 19X9 (Exhibit 6). However, under absorption costing, when sales increased from 19X8 to 19X9, the net income dropped from $21,000 (Exhibit 3) to $7,000 (Exhibit 4).

If production is greater than sales, so that inventories increase, the net income under absorption costing will be greater than under direct costing. This is because under absorption costing some of the fixed costs incurred during the year will be deferred and included in the finished goods inventory. However, under direct costing all fixed costs are charged to expense in the year they are incurred. Therefore, an increase in inventory results in a lower net income under direct costing than under absorption costing.

Sometimes, but rarely, production and sales are equal. This means that there is no change in inventories. When this happens, direct costing and absorption costing report the same net income.

As pointed out earlier, direct costing is not used for preparing published financial reports because it does not conform to GAAP. However, many accountants think that direct costing is better than absorption costing for making managerial decisions within a company. Under direct costing, the net income or net loss is directly related to sales volume. The net income or net loss is not affected by variations in inventory levels or by production changes. Furthermore, direct costing emphasizes the full impact of fixed costs on net income since these costs are not deferred but are charged to expense when they are incurred. For the same reason, no arbitrary allocations of fixed overhead are required.

For various reasons, management requires a knowledge of cost behavior under various operating conditions and at different levels of output. Also, costs must be classified into their fixed and variable components in most analyses performed for planning and control purposes. Under direct costing, the data are available in this form in the accounting records. This is a basic advantage for management if direct costing is used. Thus, management is willing to incur extra costs to accumulate direct cost data.

At this point you should be able to work Exercises 24–1 to 24–6 and Problems 24–1A to 24–1B.

The use of direct costing increases the meaningfulness of overall financial reporting for manufacturing activities. Many accountants, however, believe that the prime benefit of direct costing is the use of the data in profitability, break-even, and decision cost analyses.

COST-VOLUME-PROFIT ANALYSIS

The importance of the relationship between the volume of activity and the costs incurred has been stressed throughout this book. Direct costing, which was discussed earlier in this chapter, emphasizes the relationship between costs, volume, and profits. Management's use of cost-volume-profit (C-V-P) relationships goes far beyond direct cost-

SELF-REVIEW

1. What is meant by the statement that under direct costing fixed manufacturing costs are treated as period costs?
2. Why is direct costing sometimes called *variable costing*?
3. If in a given year the number of units of product manufactured exceeds the number of units sold, is the reported net income likely to be larger under absorption costing or under direct costing? Explain.
4. What is the contribution margin reported when the direct costing method is used?
5. Is direct costing acceptable for financial reporting under generally accepted accounting principles (GAAP)? If not, why not?

Answers to Self-Review

1. This statement means that all fixed manufacturing costs are charged to expense in the year in which they are incurred or used.
2. Direct costing is sometimes called *variable costing* because only variable manufacturing costs become part of the cost of goods manufactured.
3. If the number of units manufactured in a period exceeds the number of units sold, the reported net income will be greater under absorption costing than under direct costing. This is because under absorption costing some of the fixed manufacturing costs (those applicable to the unsold units) are deferred until a future period when the units are sold. Under direct costing, the fixed costs are charged to expense in the period in which they are incurred or used.
4. The contribution margin is the excess of sales revenues over the cost of good manufactured, which under direct costing includes only variable manufacturing costs. It is the margin available to pay fixed manufacturing costs and other expenses and earn a profit.
5. Direct costing is not accepted under generally accepted accounting principles (GAAP) because some of the manufacturing costs (fixed costs) are not treated as applicable to units manufactured during the period.

ing, however. The analysis of C-V-P data helps to provide the answers to questions such as the following:

1. What sales volume is required in order for the business to break even (to have neither a profit nor a loss)?
2. What sales volume would be necessary to produce a given amount of profit for the period?
3. What would be the impact of a specific change in gross profit per unit or of a specific change in the gross profit percentage?
4. What would be the profit at a specified sales volume?

A few examples of the use of C-V-P analysis in answering such questions are given in the following pages.

Computing the Break-Even Point

In cost-volume-profit analysis, all costs—manufacturing, selling, and administrative—are separated into their fixed and variable components. The contribution margin, that is, the excess of sales over the total of all variable costs, is then computed. The contribution margin shows the amount that is available to pay fixed costs and to earn a profit. The use of this technique is computing the **break-even point**— the sales volume at which there is neither profit nor loss—can best be explained with a simple example.

Maria Sylvester, the operator of a convenience store, has an opportunity to install a vending machine that will dispense sandwiches. The machine has a fixed rental of $80 per month and fixed operating costs of $20 per month. She can purchase the packaged sandwiches for $1 each, including all taxes. She plans to sell them from the machine at $1.50 each. Before deciding on whether to rent the machine, she needs to know how many sandwiches she must sell each month to break even and then to estimate whether she can sell at least that number. Several approaches can be used in computing the break-even sales volume.

A common approach to computing the break-even sales volume uses the contribution margin for each unit of product. The contribution margin for each unit is the excess of selling price over variable costs (both manufacturing costs and operating expenses) per unit. In Maria Sylvester's situation, the contribution margin is 50 cents (selling price of $1.50, less variable costs of $1) per sandwich. In other words, from the sale of each sandwich for $1.50, only 50 cents will be available for paying fixed costs and earning a profit. At break-even volume, there is no profit; so at the break-even volume the number of sandwiches that must be sold is the quantity (at 50 cents per sandwich) at which the contribution margin will just pay the fixed costs of $100 per month. The break-even point is 200 sandwiches, calculated as follows:

Break-Even Sales in Units per Period

$$= \frac{\text{Fixed Costs per Period}}{\text{Contribution Margin per Sandwich}}$$

$$= \frac{\$100 \text{ per month}}{\$.50 \text{ per sandwich}}$$

$$= 200 \text{ sandwiches}$$

The break-even point, expressed in dollars, may be computed easily by using the contribution margin ratio. The **contribution margin ratio** is found by dividing the contribution margin per unit of product sold by the sales price per unit. The ratio is commonly expressed as a percentage of the sales price. In this example, the contribution margin ratio is $33\frac{1}{3}$ percent. The contribution margin ratio is then divided into the fixed costs for the period to determine the break-even dollar sales volume.

$$\text{Contribution Margin Ratio} = \frac{\text{Contribution Margin per Sandwich}}{\text{Sales Price per Sandwich}}$$

$$= \frac{\$.50 \text{ per Sandwich}}{\$1.50 \text{ per Sandwich}} = 33\frac{1}{3} \text{ percent}$$

This ratio shows that $33\frac{1}{3}$ percent of every sales dollar is available for paying fixed costs and earning a profit. Since there is no profit at the break-even point, the contribution margin at that point equals the fixed costs. The break-even volume of $300 per month is computed as follows:

$$\text{Break-Even Sales in Dollars} = \frac{\text{Fixed Costs per Period}}{\text{Contribution Margin Ratio}}$$

$$= \frac{\$100 \text{ per month}}{.33\frac{1}{3}} = \$300 \text{ per month}$$

The break-even point expressed in sales dollars can also be computed by multiplying the number of units required to break even by the sales price per unit:

$$\text{Break-even point (in dollars)} = 200 \text{ sandwiches} \times \$1.50$$

$$= \$300 \text{ per month}$$

Estimating Profits at Different Sales Volumes

One way in which management commonly uses C-V-P analysis is to estimate the profit or loss that would be earned at different sales volumes, assuming that no change in selling price, variable costs per unit, or total fixed costs will occur. Once the contribution margin has been determined, it is an easy matter to estimate profit (or loss) at any level of sales.

For example, suppose that Maria Sylvester, for whose business the break-even point was computed above to be 300 sandwiches a month, estimates that she will sell an average of 1,000 sandwiches each month. The estimated profit will be $400 per month, computed by multiplying the contribution margin per unit by the projected sales and then subtracting the fixed costs.

$$\text{Profit} = (\text{Unit Sales} \times \text{Contribution Margin per Unit})$$
$$- \text{Fixed Cost per Period}$$

$$= (1,000 \text{ sandwiches} \times \$.50 \text{ per sandwich}) - \$100 \text{ per month}$$

$$= \$500 - \$100 = \$400 \text{ per month}$$

Estimating the Sales Volume Necessary to Earn a Desired Profit

The break-even approach is also used to estimate sales required to make a specific desired profit. For example, Maria Sylvester might ask what sales volume is needed to make a profit of $50 a month.

Sales in Dollars for Specific Profit

$$= \frac{\text{Fixed Costs per Period} + \text{Profit per Period}}{\text{Contribution Margin Ratio}}$$

$$= \frac{\$100 \text{ per month} + \$50 \text{ per month}}{.33\frac{1}{3}}$$

$$= \$450 \text{ per month}$$

The sales volume expressed in units required for a specific profit level is as follows:

Sales in Units for Specific Profit
$$= \frac{\text{Fixed Costs per Period} + \text{Profit per Period}}{\text{Contribution Margin per Unit}}$$

Thus, 300 sandwiches a month must be sold in order to earn $50:

$$\text{Sales in Units} = \frac{\$100 \text{ per month} + \$50 \text{ per month}}{\$.50 \text{ per sandwich}}$$

$$= 300 \text{ sandwiches per month}$$

SELF-REVIEW

1. How is the contribution margin per unit of product computed?
2. If the contribution margin per unit of product is known, how can it be used to compute the break-even point, expressed in units of product?
3. How is the contribution margin ratio for a unit of product determined?
4. If the contribution margin ratio is known, how can it be used in computing the break-even dollar sales volume?
5. Assume that you know the contribution margin ratio and the total fixed costs. How would you compute the sales volume, expressed in dollars, to earn a profit of $500,000?

Answers to Self-Review

1. The contribution margin per unit of product can be computed by subtracting all variable costs (both manufacturing costs and selling costs) from the selling price per unit.
2. The break-even point, expressed in units of product, can be determined by dividing the total fixed costs for the period by the contribution margin per unit.
3. The contribution margin ratio is the excess of selling price of each unit of product over the variable manufacturing and selling costs per unit, divided by the sales price per unit.
4. The break-even dollars sales volume can be computed by dividing the fixed costs for the period by the contribution margin ratio.
5. The sales volume necessary to earn a specified profit can be determined by dividing the total of fixed costs and the desired profit by the contribution margin ratio.

Break-Even Chart

A **break-even chart,** a graph that shows the total sales and total costs at any sales volume (expressed either in units or in dollar volume), provides a convenient means of estimating profit or loss at any sales volume. The following illustration shows the relation between volume, costs, and profits for Maria Sylvester's sandwich venture when volume is expressed in number of sandwiches.

The vertical scale of the break-even chart shows both the revenue from the sales of sandwiches and the total costs. The number of sand-

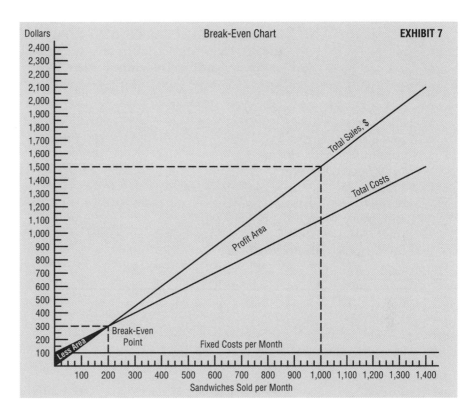

wiches sold per month is given on the horizontal scale. The chart shows that the total revenue (sales) line and the total cost line cross at the break-even point of 200 sandwiches per month. The estimated profit that would be earned at any volume of sales can be easily determined. For example, the chart shows that if the monthly sales are 1,000 sandwiches, the total sales revenue will be $1,500 and the total costs will be $1,100, resulting in a profit of $500.

Applying Break-Even Analysis in a More Complex Situation

The break-even analysis can be applied to a much more complex business than the one that has been illustrated—Maria Sylvester's proposed vending machine for sandwiches. All that is required is that the accountant be able to separate all costs into their variable and fixed components. For example, the accountant for Europa Manufacturing Company, which makes a variety of products, has analyzed and classified the costs of both manufacturing and nonmanufacturing operations and has prepared a budget based on the company's expected sales of $7,936,000 for 19X9.

The contribution margin ratio can now be computed. First, the contribution margin—the excess of sales volume over total variable costs—is computed. This shows that at the budgeted sales level, $1,926,960 ($7,936,000 − $6,009,040) will be available to cover fixed costs and earn a profit. The contribution margin ratio is therefore 24.3 percent (rounded to the nearest one-tenth of a percent).

EUROPA MANUFACTURING COMPANY   **Exhibit 8**
Budget Showing Variable and Fixed Costs
Year Ending December 31, 19X9

Sales			$7,936,000
Costs			
Variable Costs			
Manufacturing Costs	$4,769,040		
Nonmanufacturing Costs	1,240,000		
Total Variable Costs		$6,009,040	
Fixed Costs			
Manufacturing Costs	$ 534,000		
Nonmanufacturing Costs	656,000		
Total Fixed Costs		1,190,000	
Total Variable and Fixed Costs			7,199,040
Budgeted Profit			$ 736,960

$$\text{Contribution Margin Ratio} = \frac{\text{Contribution Margin}}{\text{Sales}}$$

$$= \frac{\$1,926,960}{\$7,936,000} = 24.3 \text{ percent}$$

Since at the break-even point the contribution margin will exactly equal fixed costs and since the contribution margin is 24.3 percent of sales, the break-even sales, expressed in dollars, can be computed as $4,897,000 (rounded to the nearest thousand dollars).

$$\text{Sales at Break-Even Point} = \frac{\text{Fixed Costs per Period}}{\text{Contribution Margin Ratio}}$$

$$= \frac{\$1,190,000}{.243} = \$4,897,000$$

The break-even chart for Europa Manufacturing Company is shown below. Sales, expressed in millions of dollars, are shown on the horizontal axis, and sales and total costs, both expressed in millions of dollars, are shown on the vertical axis. (When a company sells many products, it is not practical to express the sales volume in terms of units of product.) The intersection of the sales line and the total cost line shows that the break-even point is $4,897,000. Notice the rapid increase in dollar profits as volume increases past the break-even point.

A break-even point for a complex business with many products usually means that the contribution margins on all products are the same or that the relative sales volume of products with different contribution margins will stay constant as the sales volume increases or decreases.

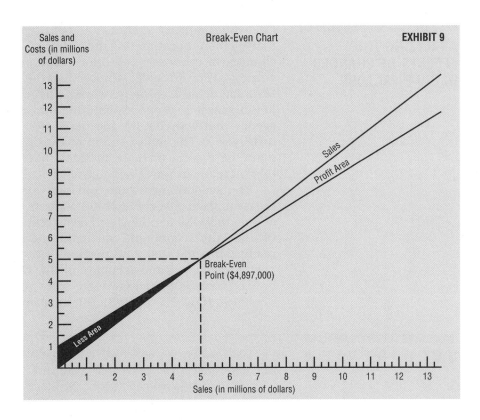

EXHIBIT 9

Break-Even Chart

Sales and Costs (in millions of dollars)

Sales

Profit Area

Break-Even Point ($4,897,000)

Less Area

Sales (in millions of dollars)

BUSINESS HORIZON

Production Volume Means Difference Between Profit and Loss

In establishing its business plans, an organization makes assumptions about the volume of product to be produced and sold. In many industries today, a very large part of manufacturing costs consists of fixed overhead—especially costs relating to depreciation, repairs, maintenance, and operation of expensive, sophisticated equipment. As the number of units produced and sold increases, the cost per unit decreases. Conversely, if the number of units produced and sold decreases, the cost per unit increases. Sometimes, even if all other factors remain constant, a decrease in volume below the volume on which plans were based may result in transforming what was expected to be a profit into a loss for the period.

The problem of increased costs resulting from a decrease in production volume appears to be at least part of the reason why Advanced Micro Devices (AMD) reported an unexpected net loss for the third quarter of 1997, rather than the profit it had anticipated. As reported in *The Wall Street Journal* (September 4, 1997) and in other newspapers, AMD had production problems in manufacturing a new microprocessing chip, the K6. The company had expected to produce between 1.2 and 1.5 million K6 chips in that quarter. The company made a revised forecast in early September 1997, anticipating that only about 1 million of the chips would be produced. The result was that the company forecast that it would have a net loss rather than the profit of $.31 per share of common stock that had been anticipated.

ANALYZING THE EFFECTS OF CHANGES IN C-V-P FACTORS

Cost-volume-profit analysis and break-even analysis are often used by management in estimating the effects on profits that would result from changes in economic conditions, operating conditions, or marketing strategies. For example, suppose that the marketing manager of Europa Manufacturing Company, whose budget and break-even chart were just discussed, proposes entering into a contract with an advertising agency that will cost an additional $64,000 per year for a period of three years. The management of Europa asks the accountant to estimate the annual increase in sales that would be necessary to justify this increase in advertising costs.

The accountant would consider this contract to represent an increase in fixed costs of $64,000 per year. Assuming no change in prices and no increase in other fixed costs resulting from an increase in sales volume, the accountant can make the estimate quickly. She has already estimated that 24.3 percent of each sales dollar is available for paying fixed costs and earning a profit. Thus, if the increase of $64,000 in fixed costs is to be recovered, sales volume must increase by about $263,400 ($64,000 ÷ .243). If management believes that sales cannot

SELF-REVIEW

1. What is a break-even chart? Name the lines that are shown on the chart.
2. Suppose that you are analyzing profitability for a business that manufactures and sells many different products. What information would you need to obtain in order to compute the contribution margin ratio?
3. What assumptions would you need to make if you were computing the break-even point for a company that manufactures and sells many different products?
4. Suppose that your employer is considering hiring an additional sales manager at a cost of $70,000 per year. Assuming no change in variable costs, what is the most important factor to consider in making the decision?
5. What, in your opinion, is the key element necessary in order to use C-V-P relationships to help reach management decisions?

Answers to Self-Review

1. A break-even chart shows the expected profit or loss at any sales volume, where the volume is expressed in quantity or in dollar volume.
2. In order to compute the contribution margin ratio, you would need to determine the ratio of variable costs to sales, which would involve determining the variable costs for the period.
3. If a company sells many products, it is necessary to assume that the contribution margin on all products are the same or that the relative sales volume of products with different contribution margins will remain constant.
4. The major question is the increase in sales volume that can be expected as a result of hiring the manager. Since variable costs are not reduced and fixed costs are increased, the only way to justify the hiring is through additional sales.
5. The key element in using C-V-P relationships is being able to determine total fixed costs and the variable cost ratio.

At this point you should be able to work Exercises 24–7 to 24–14 and Problems 24–3A to 24–6B.

be increased by at least that amount, the contract should not be entered into.

It is obvious that many factors must be considered in making management decisions. For example, in the above case, factors such as whether additional fixed costs will be necessary to maintain the required sales growth are important considerations. In addition, even though the contract is only for a three-year period, it is likely that at least part of the higher level of sales obtained by the advertising may be kept even after the advertising is ended because of the goodwill and loyalty of the new customers who were attracted by the advertising campaign. Although consideration of such factors may change the decision, the ability to use C-V-P analysis greatly simplifies the task of arriving at a decision. In Chapter 25 you will learn how a knowledge of the relationships between costs, volume, and profits can be used to help management make other important decisions.

PRINCIPLES AND PROCEDURES SUMMARY

- In direct costing, only variable manufacturing costs are considered to be product costs and are used in determining the cost of goods manufactured. For this reason, direct costing is often referred to as *variable costing*.
- In direct costing, fixed costs are classified as period costs and are charged against revenue in the period in which they are incurred or used.
- The direct costing method clearly reflects the impact of volume on costs and profits because fixed costs are not carried forward in inventories as they are in absorption costing.
- Under absorption costing, the deferral of fixed costs in the finished goods inventory distorts the relationship of profit (through cost of goods sold) when the quantity of goods sold during a period differs from the quantity of goods produced during the period.
- In an income statement prepared under the direct costing method, the cost of goods sold (which includes only variable manufacturing costs) and the variable operating expenses are deducted from sales revenue to compute the contribution margin. Then all fixed costs, including fixed manufacturing overhead, are deducted from the contribution margin to arrive at the net profit or loss for the period.
- Direct costing is only one way in which the relationship between costs, volume, and profit (C-V-P) is used by management.
- The contribution margin, reflecting the excess of sales over variable costs, may be used to quickly calculate such factors as (1) the break-even point, (2) an estimate of the profit that would result at any sales volume, and (3) an estimate of the amount of sales that would be necessary to earn any desired amount of profit.
- A break-even chart, which contains graphs showing the sales volume and the total cost at each sales volume, is a tool that makes it easy to estimate the profit or loss at any sales volume.

MANAGERIAL IMPLICATIONS

■ There is probably no accounting technique that is of more importance and benefit to management than cost-volume-profit analysis.

■ Direct costing is a commonly used tool that emphasizes the impact of production and sales volumes on profits. The profit or loss computed under the direct costing concept will vary along with changes in sales volume.

■ Under direct costing, the contribution margin is an important element. Contribution margin is the excess of sales over all variable costs, including variable manufacturing costs in cost of goods sold and variable selling and administrative expenses. The contribution margin is the amount available to pay direct costs and earn a profit.

■ By using the contribution margin approach, the accountant can easily estimate what the profit or loss would be at different sales volumes, expressed either in units sold or in dollars of sales.

■ Similarly, the contribution margin makes it easy to estimate the sales volume that would be necessary to break even. The ability to know the break-even point is of special importance in deciding whether to take on new product lines.

■ The accountant often prepares a break-even chart, which contains graphs showing the total costs as sales volume increases. This tool enables the accountant and others to quickly estimate the profit or loss at different sales volumes.

■ It is obviously important that changes in fixed costs, variable costs, and sales volumes resulting from every important management decision be considered before the decision is made.

REVIEW QUESTIONS

1. How does the cost of goods manufactured under absorption costing differ from that under direct costing?
2. If the ending inventory of finished goods increases during a year, would the net income reported under direct costing be greater than or less than it would be under absorption costing?
3. How does an income statement prepared under direct costing differ in format from one prepared under absorption costing?
4. Would it be possible to show a profit for a year using absorption costing while showing a loss under direct costing? Explain.
5. If production volume equals sales volume, would the income under absorption costing be more than or less than it would be under direct costing?
6. Does direct costing assume that all factory costs are directly related to the product? Explain.
7. Under direct costing, how are fixed manufacturing overhead costs treated?
8. Is direct costing widely used in published financial reports?

9. Which method, direct costing or absorption costing, more directly reflects the impact of volume on costs and profits? Explain.
10. Assuming that more units are sold than are produced, would reported net income be larger under absorption costing or under direct costing? Why?
11. Under direct costing, how is profit affected by variations in the inventory of finished goods?
12. Under direct costing, what costs enter into the cost of finished goods?
13. What is meant by the term *contribution margin?*
14. What is meant by the term *break-even point?*
15. Why does the cost line in a break-even chart not start at zero cost?
16. Why is it sometimes not feasible to have the horizontal axis in a break-even chart expressed in units of products sold?
17. Why is a constant product mix sometimes assumed in computing the break-even point in sales?

MANAGERIAL DISCUSSION QUESTIONS

1. What are the advantages to management of using a direct costing approach instead of an absorption costing approach?
2. You have told management that one of the advantages of direct costing is that it concentrates attention on the contribution margin. Management asks how contribution margin can be used in management control and decision making. Give some examples of how it can be used.
3. You have suggested that your company use direct costing to provide additional information for management decisions. Your company president is confused because the illustrative income statement you prepared shows cost of goods sold, reflecting variable manufacturing costs, variable selling, and general and administrative expenses under the same heading on the statement. Explain why this is done.
4. Of what benefit to management is a break-even chart?
5. Explain how management can use the break-even approach to estimate quickly the sales volume needed to make a specific desired profit.
6. A company has computed its break-even point. A proposal has been made to increase fixed costs by $80,000 per year. This would result in a decrease in variable costs of $2.40 per unit. Explain how the accountant would go about determining the impact of this proposal on the break-even point.
7. Your friend is accounting manager for a manufacturing company. He has suggested that C-V-P relationships provide the "definitive and final" answer in evaluating the effects of management decisions on profits. What is your response? Explain.

EXERCISES

DATA FOR EXERCISES 24–1 to 24–3

Harbison Company has the following standard costs per unit for its one product:

Materials		$ 40
Labor		16
Manufacturing Overhead		
Variable	$16	
Fixed	32	48
Total		$104

The fixed cost of $32 per unit is based on producing 10,000 units and fixed overhead costs of $320,000. The sales price is $160 per unit. Selling and administrative expenses consist of $8 variable cost per unit and fixed costs of $200,000 per year. During 19X9, 10,000 units were produced and sold.

EXERCISE 24–1   **Prepare an income statement based on absorption costing.   (Obj. 1).**   Prepare an income statement for Harbison Company for 19X9 based on absorption costing.

EXERCISE 24–2   **Compute contribution margin.   (Obj. 2).**   Compute Harbison's contribution margin per unit of product for 19X9 under direct costing.

EXERCISE 24–3   **Prepare an income statement based on direct costing.   (Obj. 3).**   Prepare an income statement for Harbison Company for 19X9 based on direct costing.

DATA FOR EXERCISES 24–4 and 24–5

Use the same data given for Exercises 24–1 to 24–3. Assume, however, that in 19X9 Harbison Company produced 10,800 units and sold 10,000 units.

EXERCISE 24–4   **Prepare an income statement using absorption costing.   (Obj. 1).**   Prepare an income statement for 19X9, based on absorption costing. (Overhead is applied to Work in Process on the basis of direct labor hours.)

EXERCISE 24–5   **Prepare an income statement using direct costing.   (Obj. 3).**   Prepare an income statement for 19X9, based on direct costing.

EXERCISE 24–6   **Prepare an income statement using absorption costing, prepare an income statement using direct costing, and compare the two statements.   (Objs. 1, 3, 4).**   Highland Company produces a single product. During 19X9, 22,000 units were produced and 25,000 units were sold. The following cost and selling price information is given.

Selling price	$40 per unit
Materials and labor	$12 per unit
Fixed manufacturing overhead (based on normal production of 20,000 units and annual cost of $200,000)	$10 per unit

Variable overhead $2 per unit
Selling and administrative costs (all fixed) $200,000 for year
There was no beginning inventory of work in process.

Under the cost accounting system used by the company, overhead is applied on the basis of $12 per unit of product. Underapplied or over-applied overhead is charged to cost of goods sold. The following costs were incurred during the year:

Materials and labor $264,000
Variable overhead $ 44,000
Fixed manufacturing overhead $200,000
Selling and administrative expenses $200,000

The beginning inventory of 6,000 units of product had a cost of $24 per unit under absorption costing. Under direct costing the beginning inventory cost would have been $14 per unit. FIFO costing is used.
a. Prepare an income statement for 19X9, based on absorption costing.
b. Prepare an income statement for 19X9, based on direct costing.
c. Prepare an analysis explaining the difference, if any, between net income reported under the two costing approaches.

EXERCISE 24–7 **Compute the break-even point. (Obj. 5).** George Company man-ufactures a product that sells for $124 per unit. The variable manu-facturing costs are $60 per unit; the variable selling and administra-tive expenses are $20 per unit. The fixed manufacturing costs are $192,000 per year; the fixed selling and administrative expenses are $308,000 per year. Compute the number of units that must be sold each year for the company to break even.

EXERCISE 24–8 **Estimate profit or loss at specific sales volume. (Obj. 6).** A com-pany's contribution margin ratio is 60 percent. Its fixed costs are $360,000 per year. What would be the company's anticipated profit or loss for the current year if the sales volume is expected to be $600,000? What would be the anticipated profit or loss if the sales volume is expected to be $1,000,000 for the year?

EXERCISE 24–9 **Determine sales volume to earn desired profit. (Obj. 6).** A com-pany's contribution margin ratio is 40 percent. Its fixed costs are $280,000 per year. What sales volume would be necessary if the com-pany's goal is to earn $400,000 for the year?

DATA FOR EXERCISES 24–10 to 24–13

Henry, a student at Haynes County Community College, has just started a part-time business of constructing and selling birdhouses. He plans to charge an average of $40 for each birdhouse. He estimates that his variable costs for materials, labor, and supplies will be $15 for each birdhouse. His fixed costs are estimated to be $300 per month, including manufacturing overhead and operating expenses.

EXERCISE 24–10 **Compile contribution margin; compute the break-even point. (Objs. 2, 5).** Compute the contribution margin per birdhouse and use that amount to compute the break-even volume expressed in number of birdhouses.

EXERCISE 24–11   **Compute total contribution margin. (Obj. 2).** If sales total 50 birdhouses during the month of April, what will be the total contribution margin? Show computations.

EXERCISE 24–12   **Forecasting profit at specified sales volume. (Obj. 6).** If Henry constructs and sells 50 birdhouses a month, what will be his estimated net income?

EXERCISE 24–13   **Forecasting volume necessary to earn desired profit. (Obj. 6).** If Henry's goal is to earn $400 per month, how many birdhouses will he have to construct and sell each month?

EXERCISE 24–14   **Analyze effects of changes in operations on profit. (Obj. 8).** A company's contribution margin is 48 percent. A proposal has been made to install certain equipment that would result in an increase of $50,000 per year in fixed costs but would increase the contribution margin (through a decrease in variable costs) to 54 percent. Existing fixed costs are $260,000 per year. What increase in sales volume would be necessary in order to justify purchasing the equipment?

PROBLEMS

PROBLEM 24–1A   **Prepare income statements using absorption and direct costing; compute contribution margin; compare results of two methods. (Objs. 1, 2, 3, 4).**   The Chickadee Company manufactures one product. The company uses standard costing. During the year 19X9, the normal volume of 10,000 units was produced, and 7,500 units were sold for $200 each. There was no beginning inventory of finished goods on January 1, 19X9. The following data are provided for the year 19X9.

	Costs Budgeted		Costs Incurred	
Materials ($39 per unit)		$390,000		$390,000
Labor ($49 per unit)		490,000		490,000
Manufacturing Overhead				
Fixed	$500,000		$500,000	
Variable ($9 per unit)	90,000	590,000	90,000	590,000
Rate per unit ($590,000 ÷				
10,000 units)		59		
Selling and Administrative				
Expenses				
Fixed	$198,000		$198,000	
Variable ($12.50 per unit sold)	125,000	323,000	93,750	291,750

INSTRUCTIONS   1. Prepare an income statement for the year 19X9 using standard absorption costing.
2. Compute the contribution margin under per-unit under direct costing.
3. Prepare an income statement for the year 19X9 using direct costing.
4. Prepare a reconciliation of net income under absorption costing and direct costing.

PROBLEM 24–2A

Prepare income statements using absorption and direct costing; compare results of two methods; compute contribution margin. (Objs. 1, 2, 3, 4). During the year 19X9 the Bronx Company produced 13,500 units. It sold 15,000 units at $200 each. The beginning inventory was 2,500 units. The company uses FIFO costing for finished goods. The costs incurred were as follows:

Materials (13,500 units at $39 per unit)		$526,500
Labor (13,500 units at $49 per unit)		661,500
Manufacturing Overhead (all charged to Work in Process)		
Fixed (13,500 units at $37.037 per unit)	$500,000	
Variable (13,500 units at $9 per unit)	121,500	621,500
Selling and Administrative Expenses		
Fixed	$198,000	
Variable (15,000 units at $12.50 per unit)	187,500	385,500

The company uses process cost accounting, and all manufacturing costs were charged to Work in Process.

INSTRUCTIONS

1. Prepare an income statement for the year 19X9 using absorption costing. The beginning inventory cost was $367,500. (Per-unit costs were materials, $39; labor, $49; fixed overhead, $50; variable overhead, $9.)
2. Compute the contribution margin per unit under direct costing.
3. Prepare an income statement for the year 19X9 using direct costing. The beginning inventory was $242,500.
4. Prepare a reconciliation of the net income under direct costing and absorption costing.

PROBLEM 24–3A

Compute break-even point; estimate net income or net loss; prepare a break-even chart. (Objs. 5, 6, 7). The Azores Manufacturing Company produces one product, which is sold at a fixed price of $20 per unit. The yearly fixed costs of the company total $640,000. During the year 19X9, the company sold 500,000 units and reported a net income of $160,000.

INSTRUCTIONS

1. Compute the company's break-even sales in units and in dollars.
2. Prepare a simple break-even chart.
3. Compute the sales in units needed for the company to earn a net income of $300,000.

PROBLEM 24–4A

Compute break-even point; estimate profitability as various sales volume; prepare a break-even chart. (Objs. 5, 6, 7). The Today Manufacturing Company produces one product, which is sold at a fixed price of $30 per unit. For the year 19X8, the company operated at full capacity and a total of 40,000 units were produced and sold. The company's fixed costs totaled $120,000, and the variable costs for the year were $960,000.

INSTRUCTIONS

1. Compute the company's break-even sales in units and in dollars.
2. Prepare a simple break-even chart.

3. How many units must be sold to make a net income of $60,000?
4. Assume that the company has forecast a net loss of $24,000 in 19X9. If all the other data given are correct, how many units are forecast to be sold in 19X9?

PROBLEM 24–5A

Compute break-even point; analyze effects of operating changes. (Objs. 5, 8). Serrento Company manufactures a variety of small electric kitchen appliances, such as mixers, coffee pots, blenders, bean pots, and timers. At the end of the year 19X9 the company's management became concerned about the lack of profitability. The company's accountant decided to attempt to get a better grasp of the profitability of products. He divided the products into two categories based on similar characteristics. Here are certain data about the two product groups and the company's operations.

	Group 1	Group 2	Total
Sales	$4,000,000	$6,000,000	$10,000,000
Manufacturing costs			
Materials	1,000,000	3,000,000	4,000,000
Labor	1,800,000	1,000,000	2,800,000
Manufacturing Overhead			
Variable			
Group 1 (20% of labor)	360,000		360,000
Group 2 (25% of labor)		250,000	250,000
Fixed			400,000
Selling and Administrative			
Expenses			
Variable			
Group 1 (10% of sales)	400,000		400,000
Group 2 (6% of sales)		360,000	360,000
Fixed			300,000

The company has unused capacity. The sales manager thinks that if the company spent an additional $200,000 per year on advertising, it could increase the sales of Group 1 products by 10 percent and the sales of Group 2 products by 4 percent.

INSTRUCTIONS

1. Compute the company's current break-even point.
2. The company's management has set a goal of earning a net profit of $1,000,000 before income taxes. If no changes are made in its operations, what total sales volume would be necessary to attain this goal?
3. What would be the total profit if the sales manager's recommendation to increase advertising costs were followed, assuming that his estimates are correct?
4. Should the recommendation be accepted?

PROBLEM 24–6A

Compute break-even point; analyze effects of operating changes. (Objs. 5, 8). Certain data related to the operations of the Charleston Corporation are given below.

	Per Unit
Selling price	$75.00
Variable manufacturing costs	25.00
Variable selling and administrative expenses	22.50
Fixed manufacturing costs (based on 150,000 units)	10.00
Fixed selling and administrative expenses (based on 150,000 units)	10.00

INSTRUCTIONS

1. Compute the projected annual break-even sales in units.
2. Assume that the selling price increases by 15 percent, variable manufacturing costs decrease by 1 percent, variable selling and administrative expenses increase by 5 percent, and total fixed costs increase to $3,600,000. How many units must be sold to produce a profit of $120,000?

ALTERNATE PROBLEMS

PROBLEM 24–1B

Prepare income statements using absorption and direct costing; compute contribution margin; compare results of two methods. (Objs. 1, 2, 3, 4). The Jolly Manufacturing Company makes one product. The company uses standard costing. During the year 19X9, the normal volume of 4,000 units was produced, and 3,000 units were sold for $210 each. Assume that there was no beginning inventory on January 1, 19X9. The following data are provided for the year 19X9.

	Costs Budgeted		Costs Incurred	
Materials ($40 per unit)		$160,000		$160,000
Labor ($50 per unit)		200,000		200,000
Manufacturing Overhead				
Fixed	$200,000		$200,000	
Variable ($10 per unit)	40,000	240,000	40,000	240,000
Rate per unit ($240,000 ÷				
4,000 units)		60		
Selling and Administrative				
Expenses				
Fixed	$ 80,000		$ 80,000	
Variable ($12 per unit sold)	48,000	128,000	36,000	116,000

INSTRUCTIONS

1. Prepare an income statement for the year 19X9 using standard absorption costing.
2. Compute the contribution margin under per-unit direct costing.
3. Prepare an income statement for the year 19X9 using direct costing.
4. Prepare a reconciliation of net income under direct costing and absorption costing.

PROBLEM 24–2B

Prepare income statements using absorption and direct costing; compare results of two methods; compute contribution margin. (Objs. 1, 2, 3, 4). During the year 19X9, the Topeka Manufacturing

Company produced 5,400 units and sold 6,000 units at $200 each. The beginning inventory was 1,000 units. The company uses FIFO costing for finished goods. The costs incurred were as follows:

Materials (5,400 units at $40 per unit)		$216,000
Labor (5,400 units at $50 per unit)		270,000
Manufacturing Overhead (all charged to Work in Process)		
Fixed	$200,000	
Variable (5,400 units at $20 per unit)	108,000	308,000
Selling and Administrative Expenses		
Fixed	$180,000	
Variable (6,000 units at $12 per unit)	72,000	252,000

INSTRUCTIONS

1. Prepare an income statement for the year 19X9 using absorption costing. The beginning finished goods inventory was $160,000. Unit costs of beginning inventory were materials, $40; labor, $50; fixed overhead, $50; variable overhead, $20.
2. Compute the contribution margin under direct costing.
3. Prepare an income statement for the year 19X9 using direct costing. The beginning inventory was $110,000. Variable costs were the same as those given in Instruction 2.
4. Prepare a reconciliation of the net income under direct costing and absorption costing.

PROBLEM 24–3B

Compute break-even point; estimate net income or net loss at various sales volumes; prepare break-even chart. (Objs. 5, 6, 7). The Memphis Manufacturing Company produces one product, which is sold at a price of $60 per unit. The yearly fixed costs of the company total $240,000. During the year 19X9, the company produced and sold 12,000 units and reported a net income of $48,000.

INSTRUCTIONS

1. Compute the company's break-even sales in units and in dollars.
2. Prepare a simple break-even chart.
3. Compute the sales in units needed for the company to earn a net income of $80,000.

PROBLEM 24–4B

Compute break-even point; estimate profitability at various sales volume; prepare a break-even chart. (Objs. 4, 5, 6, 7). The Oregon Corporation produces one product, which is sold at a fixed price of $10 per unit. For the year 19X8, the company operated at full capacity and a total of 100,000 units were produced and sold. The company's fixed costs totaled $300,000, and the variable costs for the year were $500,000.

INSTRUCTIONS

1. Compute the company's break-even sales in units and in dollars.
2. Prepare a simple break-even chart.
3. How many units must be sold to make a net income of $140,000?
4. Assume that the company has forecast a net loss of $20,000 in 19X9. If all the other data given are correct, how many units are forecast to be sold in 19X9?

PROBLEM 24–5B

Compute break-even point; analyze effects of operating changes. (Objs. 5, 8). Grayfriars Company manufactures two styles of reclining chairs. Management is unhappy with the company's operating results. The president has proposed that the Perfect Recliner be restyled. The production manager believes that this would increase both labor costs and variable manufacturing overhead of that style by 5 percent per chair. The sales manager proposes that the sales price of the chair be increased by 4 percent. It is anticipated that these changes will increase the number of Perfect Recliners sold by 8 percent but will reduce by 2 percent the number of Super Recliners sold. Here are certain data about the two types of chairs and the company's operations.

	Perfect Recliner	Super Recliner	Total
Sales	$4,000,000	$6,000,000	$10,000,000
Manufacturing costs			
Materials	1,800,000	2,700,000	4,500,000
Labor	1,200,000	2,000,000	3,200,000
Manufacturing Overhead			
Variable (20% of labor)	240,000	400,000	640,000
Fixed			400,000
Selling and Administrative Expenses			
Variable (10% of sales)	400,000	600,000	1,000,000
Fixed			200,000

INSTRUCTIONS

1. Compute the company's current break-even point.
2. Assuming that the company's goal is to earn a profit before taxes of $400,000 per year, what sales volume would be necessary under the current pricing and cost structure, assuming no change in the ratio of the two types of chairs sold?
3. What would be the estimated total profit if the recommendations are carried out?
4. Should the recommendations be adopted? Why?

PROBLEM 24–6B

Compute break-even point; analyze effects of operating changes. (Objs. 5, 8). Certain data related to the operations of the Alfa Corporation are given below.

	Per Unit
Selling price	$20.00
Variable manufacturing costs	4.00
Variable selling and administrative expenses	8.00
Fixed manufacturing costs (based on 100,000 units)	1.00
Fixed selling and administrative expenses (based on 100,000 units)	2.60

INSTRUCTIONS

1. Compute the projected annual break-even sales in units.
2. Assume that the selling price increases by 20 percent, variable manufacturing costs increase by 10 percent, variable selling and administrative expenses remain the same, and total fixed costs increase to $416,000. How many units must be sold to produce a profit equal to 10 percent of sales?

MANAGERIAL DECISION CASES

Case 24–1. A manufacturer of boom boxes sells 10,000 units per year at a selling price of $180 per unit. At the end of the current year, a new labor contract is being negotiated. The proposed contract calls for an increase of 12 percent in direct labor rates, and an increase of $10,000 per year in fixed manufacturing costs would also result. Data about current operations are as follows:

	Per Unit
Sales price	$180
Variable costs	
Materials	30
Labor (including taxes and fringe benefits)	60
Factory overhead, selling expenses, and administrative expenses	40
Fixed manufacturing costs (based on a volume of 10,000 units per year)	20
Fixed selling and administrative expenses (based on a volume of 10,000 units per year)	10

Management has asked you, the accountant, for assistance in estimating the results of several strategies that are being considered to offset the effects of the wage increase. You are to provide this assistance by answering the following questions:

1. If prices are unchanged, what volume of sales will be necessary to break even?
2. What sales price per unit will be necessary to keep profits at the present level if the number of units sold remains at 10,000 per year and the proposed labor contract takes effect?
3. If the selling price is increased by $10 per unit and there is a resulting decline of 2 percent in the number of units sold, what amount of profit should be anticipated, considering the proposed labor agreement?
4. What other factors should management consider in deciding on a course of action?

Case 24–2. Gibson Beauty Supplies distributes health and beauty aids to retail stores, beauty salons, and barber shops. Early in 19X9, the company decided to develop and market its own line of shampoos and hair conditioners. It contracted with another firm to manufacture and package the products. After several months, the management of Gibson became concerned over the profitability of the new line. An analysis of operations is shown below.

	Fixed Costs per Month	Percent of Selling Price per Bottle (Variable Costs)
Average cost of materials		30
Average cost of containers and packaging		10

Average freight in		2
Average delivery costs		
(all variable)		6
Sales commissions		10
Advertising		
Variable		5
Fixed	$1,000	
Warehousing		
Variable		3
Fixed	2,000	
Other		
Variable		2
Fixed	2,400	

Last month, sales were only $10,000. Several managers have suggested that this line of products should be discontinued.

1. What sales volume would be necessary for the company to break even on this line of products, assuming that the expense data given are reliable?
2. What sales volume would be necessary to earn a net profit of 5 percent of sales?
3. List the most important questions that should be asked by management to arrive at a decision about whether or not to discontinue this line of products.

C H A P T E R
25

Analysis of Manufacturing Costs for Decision Making

One of the basic functions of management is decision making. Often decision making means selecting a course of action from among a set of alternatives. There are always at least two possible courses of action—otherwise there would be no decision. Frequently one course of action is to do nothing. Cost analysis is an important element in choosing the best of the alternatives available.

OBJECTIVES

1. Explain the steps in management's decision-making process.
2. Make a decision on whether to add or discontinue a product.
3. Make a decision on whether to buy a part or to manufacture it.
4. Make a decision on whether to further process a product.
5. Make a decision on granting special prices for products.

NEW TERMS

Controllable costs (p. 630)
Differential cost (p. 630)
Differential revenues (p. 631)
Incremental cost (p. 630)
Noncontrollable costs (p. 630)
Nonmeasurable data (p. 631)
Opportunity costs (p. 630)
Relevant costs (p. 629)
Sunk cost (p. 630)

DECISION MAKING

In the decision process, management requires as much measurable data, properly analyzed, as is possible to handle. It is the accountant's job to gather the data and present it to management in a coherent, precise, and informative manner. The accountant analyzes the data in a manner that will make effective and efficient decision making easier.

The decision process may be summarized as follows:

- Defining the problem
- Identifying workable alternatives
- Determining the relevant cost and revenue data
- Evaluating the data
- Considering any other nonmeasurable data
- Making a decision

DEFINING THE PROBLEM AND IDENTIFYING ALTERNATIVES

In many situations that involve decision making based on an analysis of manufacturing costs, the problem can easily be identified and often results in a yes or no decision. Sometimes, however, when management is attempting to analyze a situation to determine the problem, facts may be uncovered that disclose other problems or several alternative solutions to the problem.

For example, cost data may show that the cost of manufacturing a specific part of a finished product has been increasing and that some corrective action must be taken. An analysis may suggest that a machine used in manufacturing the part has become so old that repair and maintenance costs are high and that production is often halted so that repairs can be made. In analyzing the apparent problem of aged machinery, other problem areas may be revealed—manufacturing specifications may be beyond the capabilities of the machine; defective raw materials may have been used, resulting in damage to the equipment; personnel may not have been properly trained; or many other inefficiencies or unsatisfactory manufacturing conditions may exist.

The alternatives seem to be either to repair the existing machine or to replace it with a new one. However, there may be other solutions. For example, it may be desirable to purchase the part made by that machine from an outside supplier or subcontractor, rather than to continue to manufacture the part within the factory. Or, it might be possible to replace this part with a different part, either manufactured by the company or purchased from an outsider. It is obvious that the analysis of manufacturing costs is only one element in arriving at a solution to the problem.

DETERMINING RELEVANT COST AND REVENUE DATA

The most basic requirement of costs for decision-making purposes is relevancy. Not all costs are relevant to the decision at hand. **Relevant costs** are those costs that will be used in arriving at a decision about the problem at hand. For planning purposes, relevant costs are future or expected costs. Historical costs are irrelevant except to the extent that they serve as a basis for estimating future outlays, including income tax effects. Further, only those costs that will change as a result of a decision are relevant. For control purposes, relevant costs are those pertinent to the operation being evaluated.

If a decision must be made to replace a machine, the book value of the existing machine is a historical cost and therefore is irrelevant. The cost of the new machine, however, is relevant. If a decision must be made to close a warehouse, the salaries of the warehouse personnel are relevant if these workers will be terminated when the warehouse closes. The nonrefundable prepaid rent on the warehouse for the remainder of the year is irrelevant since it has been paid and cannot be recovered.

A historical cost that has been incurred and thus is irrelevant for decision-making purposes is called a **sunk cost.** The prepaid rent and the cost of the existing machine discussed above are both sunk costs.

Controllability of Costs

Another concept involved in the analysis of cost data is controllability. Costs may be classified as controllable or noncontrollable. In reality, all costs are controllable at one level or another within a company. The classification pinpoints controllability at a particular level of management. **Controllable costs** at a specific level are those costs that can be authorized at that level. **Noncontrollable costs** at a particular level are costs that were authorized at some other level. For example, a department manager probably has control over the supplies used in the department but has no control over the plant depreciation allocated to the department.

Opportunity Costs

Not all costs used in decision making appear in the accounting records. **Opportunity costs** are earnings or potential benefits forgone because a certain course of action is taken. For example, assume that a decision is to be made between purchasing additional equipment and investing in top-grade bonds or stocks. The opportunity cost of a decision to purchase the equipment equals the estimated interest or dividends lost on the bonds or stocks when the funds are used for the purchase of equipment.

Differential Costs and Incremental Costs

In decision making, management always compares two or more alternatives. Even in deciding on the purchase of a machine when only one bid has been received from possible suppliers, management has two alternatives: to accept or to reject the bid. A **differential cost** is the difference in cost between one alternative and another. For example, the difference in cost between using a hand-operated process and an automated press would be a differential cost. Although the term **incremental cost** is often used interchangeably with differential cost, incremental cost actually means only an *increase* in cost from one alternative to another. For example, if it costs $2,000 to produce 20 units and $2,800 to produce 30 units, the incremental cost of producing the additional 10 units is $800.

Differential Revenues

Many decisions based on the analysis of financial data involve not only differential costs but also differential revenues. **Differential revenues** is the term used to describe the difference in revenues that will result from choosing one course of action over another. Most changes in pricing and most decisions to discontinue a product or a department or to add a new product involve analyzing not only the effects on costs resulting from the proposed action, but also the effects on revenues. If both of these factors can be estimated, the effects on profit can also be estimated.

EVALUATING DATA AND CONSIDERING NONMEASURABLE DATA

The analysis of manufacturing costs, if properly planned and carried out, will generally provide a sound basis on which to arrive at a decision. The analysis typically produces a quantitative guide for making a decision. If the facts on which the analysis is based are incorrect or irrelevant, the analysis may be useless. Thus, it is essential that correct and relevant data be used and that management know how to evaluate the results of the analysis.

Since the analysis of financial data is essentially numerical analysis, it cannot be the sole factor considered in arriving at business decisions. **Nonmeasurable data** is information that cannot be quantified. Factors such as customer relations, employee morale, supplier relations, and other areas of a business's activities must also be considered. The impact of these factors is hard to quantify and is often subjective. Nevertheless, although the analysis of financial data provides a sound basis for making decisions, nonmeasurable data must be considered as well.

MAKING A DECISION

Once financial data have been analyzed and the nonmeasurable factors have been considered, a rational decision can be reached. In a well-run business, procedures will be established to evaluate at a later time whether the correct decision was made. That, too, involves analysis of financial data.

COMMON DECISIONS IN A COST ACCOUNTING ENVIRONMENT

When data are evaluated, the concepts of relevant costs and differential costs, discussed above, and the contribution approach (discussed in Chapter 24) are used. Management must evaluate the potential profitability of each alternative and the difference in profitability between two or more choices. There are many decisions that must be made by management, all using financial data. Typical situations that affect current operations have been chosen for illustration in this chapter.

- Adding or dropping a product
- Making or buying a part
- Processing or selling a product
- Specially pricing a product

SELF-REVIEW

1. What is the role of the accountant in management's decision making?
2. Why is the concept of relevant costs so important in decision making?
3. What is a sunk cost? What is the general role of sunk costs in decision making?
4. What are differential revenues? Differential costs?
5. What is nonmeasurable data? Why must nonmeasurable data be considered in decision making?

Answers to Self-Review

1. The role of the accountant in management decision making is to gather the data and present it to management in a coherent, precise, and informative manner.
2. Relevant costs are those costs that will be used in arriving at a decision about the problem at hand. Other costs have no bearing on the decision.
3. A sunk cost is a historical cost that has been incurred. It is irrelevant to decision making.
4. Differential revenues are the difference in revenues that will result from choosing one course of action over another. Differential costs are the difference in cost between one alternative and another.
5. Nonmeasurable data is information that cannot be quantified. Nonmeasurable data must be considered because it reflects possible events and situations that might occur as a result of a decision, even though the results cannot be reduced to monetary terms.

In Chapter 27, you will learn how to make decisions involving capital investments—the acquisition of plant and equipment that will last over a period of several years.

Adding or Dropping a Product

San Diego Manufacturers makes three products. After reviewing the income statement for the past year, shown in Exhibit 1, management is thinking about discontinuing one of its products, Product C.

The steps in the decision process are as follows.

Defining the Problem. The problem is to decide whether the manufacture of Product C should be discontinued. A new loss of $4,700 was computed for that product during the year.

Identifying Workable Alternatives. The two alternatives being considered are to continue manufacturing Product C or to drop the product.

Determining Relevant Cost and Revenue Data. Relevant data can be found by the use of the contribution approach. Exhibit 2 presents the income statement prepared under the direct costing approach. This

SAN DIEGO MANUFACTURERS Income Statement (Absorption Costing) Year Ended December 31, 19X9				Exhibit 1
	PRODUCT A	**PRODUCT B**	**PRODUCT C**	**TOTAL**
Sales	$10,000	$18,000	$22,000	$50,000
Cost of Goods Sold	4,750	6,600	22,500	33,850
Gross Margin	$ 5,250	$11,400	$ (500)	$16,150
Operating Expenses	2,000	2,700	4,200	8,900
New Income (or Loss)	$ 3,250	$ 8,700	$ (4,700)	$ 7,250
Related Data:				
Units Sold	1,000	1,200	2,000	
Sales Price per Unit	$ 10.00	$ 15.00	$ 11.00	
Variable Manufacturing Cost per Unit	2.50	3.00	8.00	
Variable Operating Expenses per Unit	1.50	1.00	1.20	
Fixed Manufacturing Costs	2,250.00	3,000.00	6,500.00	
Fixed Operating Expenses	500.00	1,500.00	1,800.00	

income statement shows that Product C has a contribution margin of $3,600.

Evaluating the Data. Since Product C contributes $3,600 toward covering fixed costs and making a profit, dropping Product C will reduce the company's net income by $3,600 if all fixed costs that have been allocated to Product C continue. Exhibit 3 shows the effects that the

SAN DIEGO MANUFACTURERS Income Statement (Direct Costing) Year Ended December 31, 19X9				Exhibit 2
	PRODUCT A	**PRODUCT B**	**PRODUCT C**	**TOTAL**
Sales	$10,000	$18,000	$22,000	$50,000
Variable Costs				
Manufacturing	$ 2,500	$ 3,600	$16,000	$22,100
Operating	1,500	1,200	2,400	5,100
Total Variable Costs	$ 4,000	$ 4,800	$18,400	$27,200
Contribution Margin	$ 6,000	$13,200	$ 3,600	$22,800
Fixed Costs				
Manufacturing	$ 2,250	$ 3,000	$ 6,500	$11,750
Operating	500	1,500	1,800	3,800
Total Fixed Costs	$ 2,750	$ 4,500	$ 8,300	$15,550
Net Income or (Loss)	$ 3,250	$ 8,700	$ (4,700)	$ 7,250

	SAN DIEGO MANUFACTURERS		Exhibit 3

SAN DIEGO MANUFACTURERS   Exhibit 3
Income Statement
(Direct Costing)
Year Ended December 31, 19X9
(Eliminating Product C)

	PRODUCT A	PRODUCT B	TOTAL
Sales	$10,000	$18,000	$28,000
Variable Costs			
Manufacturing	$ 2,500	$ 3,600	$ 6,100
Operating	1,500	1,200	2,700
Total Variable Costs	$ 4,000	$ 4,800	$ 8,800
Contribution Margin	$ 6,000	$13,200	$19,200
Fixed Costs*			
Manufacturing	$ 5,036	$ 6,714	$11,750
Operating	950	2,850	3,800
Total Fixed Costs	$ 5,986	$ 9,564	$15,550
Net Income	$ 14	$ 3,636	$ 3,650

*Allocated on the basis of original departmental fixed costs.

elimination of Product C would have on the income statement. Note that the company's total net income is reduced to $3,650. When Product C was included, the total net income was $7,250 (see Exhibit 2). The smaller net income of 3,650 results from the absence of Product C's contribution margin ($7,250 − $3,600).

At this point you should be able to work Exercises 25–1 to 25–3 and Problems 25–1A to 25–2B.

Considering Nonmeasurable Data and Making a Decision.   Although other relevant factors should be considered, the quantitative (measurable) analysis shows that Product C should not be dropped.

Deciding Whether to Further Process a Product

Frequently, products can be sold in various stages of completion. For example, a furniture manufacturer may in some cases sell the furniture in unfinished condition or may elect to finish the furniture by sanding and varnishing it. Another example is a meat processing company that may elect to sell the meat in its original condition or may process it into sausages and other food products. In the oil refining industry, the production of kerosene, gasoline, jet fuel, and so on depends on the amount of processing. In Chapter 18 you learned that by-products are sometimes processed after their removal to increase their value. Also, you learned that by-products would be processed further only if the increase in value exceeded the cost of the additional processing. This basis principle applies to all decisions to process a product further or to sell it at its current stage of production.

For example, assume that Eastern Chemical Company produces a chemical product that is sold to other chemical manufacturers for use as a raw material. Eastern has the facilities to perform a further

SELF-REVIEW

1. What is generally the best approach in deciding whether a product should be dropped? Why?
2. Suggest some nonquantifiable factors that might be considered in making a decision to drop a product.
3. Why is capacity utilization a factor to consider in deciding whether to make or buy a part?
4. Do you think the decision to make or buy a part should be based on a per-unit analysis or on an analysis showing the total impact on costs and/or profit for the year?

Answers to Self-Review

1. The direct costing approach is generally appropriate in deciding whether a product should be dropped, especially if fixed costs will not change as a result of the decision. This approach shows the contribution margin to the net income, if any, of the product being considered.
2. Among nonquantifiable factors to consider are the potential impact on sales of other products, potential loss of customers, customer ill will, and supplier relationships.
3. Capacity utilization is important because there must be adequate capacity to make the part in question. If capacity is almost fully utilized, a decision to make the part might result in an inability to manufacture the product in the quantities needed. Also, it might result in having to purchase some of the parts that are to be manufactured; this could result in higher costs.
4. Either approach (per-unit, or for the year in total) is satisfactory as the basis for analysis. Generally, it is easier to use a per-unit calculation.

processing step before sale to customers. Market research has indicated that the company would still be able to sell all its output if it performed the additional processing. The company has adequate facilities, so there would be no additional capital outlay.

The accountant and a management committee have studied the processing necessary and have presented the following information:

Current and projected number of units produced per year, 500,000
Current selling price per unit, $2
Estimated selling price per unit after further processing, $3
Current manufacturing costs per unit:
  Variable costs, $.90
  Fixed costs ($200,000 per year), $.40
Present selling and administrative costs per unit:
  Variable expenses, $.20
  Fixed costs ($150,000 per year), $.30
Additional costs if product is further processed:
  Variable costs per unit:
    Manufacturing costs, $.50
    Selling and administrative expenses, $.10

Fixed costs:
   Manufacturing overhead per year, $50,000
   Selling and administrative expenses per year, $100,000
Costs that would be eliminated if product is further processed:
   Variable selling expenses per unit, $.05
   Fixed selling expenses (per year), $20,000

Defining the Problem.   The problem is whether or not to undertake additional processing of the product.

Identifying Workable Alternatives.   The alternatives are to undertake additional processing of its product in order to increase its sales value or to continue to sell the product at its current stage of production. A third possibility might be to further process a part of the product and continue to sell the remainder at its current stage of production. The management group has explored the third possibility and determined that this would not be a feasible option because it would be necessary to hire additional workers and supervisors if any part of the product were processed further; this would result in a duplication of functions and costs.

Determining the Relevant Cost and Revenue Data.   The relevant data in making this decision is the differential revenue and the differential costs—in other words, the differential income (including loss) from undertaking the additional processing.

Evaluating the Data

The relevant data provided by the accountant and management can be analyzed on either a per-unit basis or a total revenue and total cost basis. Since fixed costs are involved in the decision, it is easier to use the total approach. The relevant information is shown below in income statement format.

| | Total | | |
	Present Production	Proposed Process	Difference
Revenue (500,000 units)	$1,000,000	$1,500,000	$500,000
Costs			
Variable manufacturing costs	450,000	700,000	250,000
Variable selling and adm. expenses	100,000	125,000	25,000
Total variable costs	550,000	825,000	275,000
Contribution margin	$ 450,000	$ 675,000	$225,000
Fixed manufacturing costs	200,000	250,000	50,000
Fixed selling and administrative expenses	150,000	230,000	80,000
Total fixed costs	$ 350,000	$ 480,000	$130,000
Net income	$ 100,000	$ 195,000	$ 95,000

This analysis shows that if the projections and estimates of the accountant and management committee are correct, further processing the product before sale should increase income by $95,000 per year.

Considering Any Other Nonmeasurable Data. There appears to be no nonmeasurable data to be considered. The management group has already considered the question of whether the product can be sold in its further processed state. There is no reason to think that there are potential problems arising from environmental hazard or governmental regulation and restrictions.

Making a Decision. Based on the information provided and the analysis made, management should decide to further process the product before resale, because doing this would increase annual net income by $95,000, almost doubling the current net income.

Deciding Whether to Sell Products on Special Order at a Reduced Price

The concepts used in evaluating make or buy alternatives also apply to special pricing decisions. Assume that the Manchester Company is operating at a volume below full capacity and has an opportunity for a one-time sale of additional products but at a price less than its normal selling price. The sale will increase the firm's profits if the price is greater than the variable costs per unit.

Management must be careful to ensure that a sale at a special price or under other special conditions will not hurt its existing sales. Special product pricing is not satisfactory as a long-range pricing strategy since all costs, including fixed costs, must eventually be covered if a profit is to be made.

Every year the Manchester Company manufactures 32,000 bicycle accessories called Super Brakes in the Machining Department. The total standard cost per unit is $12.50, as shown in Exhibit 7, and Super Brakes regularly sell for $20 each. A Malaysian company offers to buy 4,000 Super Brakes at $10 per unit and pay all freight charges from the factory. Management at first rejects the offer, but the company's cost accountant advises management to reconsider on the basis of the analysis shown in Exhibit 7.

MANCHESTER COMPANY		Exhibit 7
Standard Cost Sheet		
Materials		$ 3.50
Labor ($\frac{1}{2}$ hr at $8.00 per hr)		4.00
Manufacturing Overhead		
Variable ($\frac{1}{2}$ hr at $4 per hr)	$2.00	
Fixed ($60,000 ÷ 20,000 hr)	3.00	5.00
Total Standard Cost per Unit		$12.50

Defining the Problem. Should the company accept an offer of $10 per unit for a product that has total standard cost per unit of $12.50?

Identifying Workable Alternatives. The two alternatives are to accept or to reject the offer.

Determining Relevant Cost and Revenue Data. The relevant revenue is $10 per unit, and the relevant cost is $9.50 per unit. The relevant cost is the total of the variable costs per unit ($3.50 + $4.00 + $2.00 = $9.50), as shown in Exhibit 8.

MANCHESTER COMPANY		Exhibit 8
Special Product Pricing Analysis		
(By Unit)		
Revenue per Unit		$10.00
Differential Cost per Unit		
Materials	$3.50	
Labor	4.00	
Variable Manufacturing Overhead	2.00	9.50
Contribution Margin per Unit		$ .50

Evaluating the Data. As in make or buy decisions, either a per-unit or a total annual impact basis can be used. Exhibit 8 shows that on a per-unit basis, a $.50 margin results from the sale.

The contribution margin of $.50 per unit on the special order would increase the firm's net income for the period by $2,000 (4,000 units × $.50). The results on an annual basis are presented in Exhibit 9.

	MANCHESTER COMPANY		Exhibit 9
	Special Product Pricing Analysis		
	SPECIAL ORDER REJECTED	**DIFFERENCE**	**SPECIAL ORDER ACCEPTED**
Sales (Annual)			
Regular Sources (32,000 at $20 each)	$640,000		$640,000
Special Order (4,000 at $10 each)	—	$ 40,000	40,000
Total Sales	$640,000	$ 40,000	$680,000
Variable Manufacturing Costs			
Materials (at $3.50 per unit)	$112,000	(14,000)	$126,000
Labor (at $4.00 per unit)	128,000	(16,000)	144,000
Manufacturing Overhead			
(at $2.00 per unit)	$ 64,000	(8,000)	72,000
Total Variable Costs	$304,000		$342,000
Contribution Margin	$336,000		$338,000
Less Fixed Costs	60,000		60,000
Net Income	$276,000	$ 2,000	$278,000

"Outsourcing" Decisions

From almost the beginning of modern business society, individual businesses have used the services of other businesses and individuals. When outside services have been used, it has generally been because it has been necessary to so, or because it costs less to do so.

Some services, such as telephone and electricity, and repairs to highly technical and specialized equipment can be obtained only from outsiders. In other cases, it might be possible for a company's own personnel to perform a service, but it is more practical to use an outside provider. For example, repairs to buildings and equipment are often fairly simple and routine, but the infrequency of repair needs does not justify the hiring of full-time employees to perform repair and maintenance work. Also, it may not be feasible to have employees take time from their regular duties to take care of repair and maintenance. Thus it is frequently less costly and more expedient for a business to call on providers of services than to use company personnel. The outside supplier may be a specialist whose personnel are highly skilled and do their work more efficiently than the company's personnel could do. The outside supplier may also have the most modern equipment available and know the latest techniques for performing the service. On the other hand, the development of computers and other electronic equipment has made it possible for employees to perform services that only a few years ago had to be entrusted to an outside supplier—desktop publishing is an example.

Since the late 1980s, well-run companies have become aware of the potential cost savings that may result from using outside sources to perform services, and the term *outsourcing* has become common in the business world. Even services that a few short years ago were considered so confidential and private that companies that would not even consider turning them over to an outsider are now being outsourced—preparation of payrolls and filing of tax returns related to payrolls are examples. The same is true of services that were viewed as being so closely related to routine operations that they had to be performed by company personnel (for example, accounting functions).

The decision to outsource a service is almost identical to the decision to purchase a part used in manufacturing a product from an outsider rather than manufacturing the part in the company's own factory. The analysis involves comparing the cost of performing the service and the cost of using an outside provider. But there are frequently noncost factors to consider in choosing a provider of services. In some cases, the question of how quickly service can be obtained from an outsider is critical. In other cases, there must be assurance that information provided to the service supplier is confidential—for example, data provided to an outsider about payrolls and accounting information.

The business section of your local newspaper or financial publications such as *The Wall Street Journal* will provide you with many illustrations of factors that lead companies to outsource (or not outsource) services. For example, in late August 1997 the financial press reported on the tentative decision of US Airways to outsource its information technology operations, previously performed by 875 of its own workers, to Sabre Group Holdings at a cost of "several hundred million dollars annually" but nonetheless resulting in "substantial savings" to US Airways. The company said that it expected the move to reduce costs and streamline such operations as aircraft scheduling and passenger check-in. The decision was especially interesting because, at the time, AMR Corporation, the parent company of American Airlines, a competitor of US Airways, owned 82 percent of the stock of Sabre Group. Obviously, a major "nonaccounting" consideration in the outsourcing decision was confidentiality of data. The president of US Airways, noting this problem, said: "Clearly, significant firewalls will be erected" to product the company's data. (Source: *The Wall Street Journal*, August 29, 1997.)

Considering Nonmeasurable Data. In special pricing decisions, there are two very important nonmeasurable factors. First, and most important, federal and state laws prohibit discriminatory pricing. Management should discuss this matter with legal counsel if there is any doubt about whether the pricing under the circumstances is legal. Second, if regular customers learn about the favorable pricing, they are likely to be very unhappy unless the company can justify the difference in price being charged. Because the customer is a foreign purchaser, it is unlikely that the special price is illegal and it is unlikely that existing domestic customers would object if they knew about the special price.

Making a Decision. Although acceptance of the special order would increase profit by $2,000, this is a somewhat marginal increase. Nevertheless, there appears to be little risk involved, so the company probably should accept the order.

SELF-REVIEW

1. What is the basic requirement that must be met before a company elects to further process a product that it can sell at an intermediate state of completion?
2. A company would have to add new equipment and facilities in order to further process a product that could be sold without that processing. What impact will this fact have on the decision to further process?
3. What special nonmeasurable factors must be taken into account when a company is considering selling its regular products on a special order at a price less than its normal price?
4. When a company must decide whether to accept an order at a special price, what are the pertinent measurable factors to be considered?

Answers to Self-Review

1. The basic requirement is that the increase in selling price must exceed the increase in costs. In other words, there must be a projected increase in net income.
2. If new equipment and facilities must be added, the company may feel "locked in" if it makes a decision to process further. If no new assets are required, the company generally can discontinue the further processing. If the equipment cost is high, the company may hesitate to make the decision to further process the product.
3. Two special nonmeasurable considerations are federal and state laws regulating discrimination between customers and the fact that other customers may become unhappy if they find that the company is selling goods to others at lower prices.
4. As in all managerial decisions, the key factors in making a decision to accept a special order are the differential revenues and differential costs.

At this point you should be able to complete Exercises 25–4 to 25–8 and Problems 25–3A to 25–5B.

PRINCIPLES AND PROCEDURES SUMMARY

- A major function of management is decision making. The cost accountant plays a vital role in gathering and analyzing data to assist management in this process.
- The decision process involves six basic steps:
  - Defining the problem
  - Identifying workable alternatives
  - Determining the relevant cost and revenue data
  - Evaluating the data
  - Considering any other nonmeasurable data
  - Making a decision
- The use of relevant costs and differential costs, together with the contribution approach, makes evaluating data easier and more accurate.
- Typical decisions requiring analysis of financial data that must be made by management are buying machinery, adding or dropping products, making or buying parts, deciding whether to further process a product or to sell it in its current stage of completion, and special pricing of products.
- In all these decisions, management must consider not only measurable factors of differential revenues and differential costs but also unmeasurable factors. For example, federal and state laws restrict offering different prices to different customers. In all cases, the impact of the decision on relationships with existing customers and the impact on other products sold by the company must be evaluated.

MANAGERIAL IMPLICATIONS

- In carrying out the role of assisting management in making operation decisions, the accountant must understand what accounting data is available and how it can be used in making the decisions.
- The accountant is the person primarily responsible for providing relevant accounting data.
- The relevant accounting data in making a decision are differential revenues and differential costs resulting from the decision.
- In such decisions as discontinuing or adding a product, processing a product further or selling it in its current stage of completion, manufacturing a part or buying the part from an outside source, and accepting or rejecting offers from customers to purchase the company's products under special terms accounting data is always of great importance.
- Although cost and revenue information is important in decision making, management must give proper consideration to noncost factors. Sometimes these factors are more important than differential revenues and differential costs in arriving at the proper decision.

REVIEW QUESTIONS

1. Define relevant costs.
2. What is a sunk cost? Give an example.
3. What are opportunity costs? Give an example.
4. Distinguish between differential costs and incremental costs.
5. What is meant by differential revenues?
6. When management is making a business decision, are sunk costs more important than incremental costs? Explain.
7. Why must nonmeasurable factors be considered in decision making?
8. Explain this statement: "There are always at least two alternatives."
9. What role does the accountant play in the decision-making process?
10. In deciding whether a new labor-saving machine should be purchased, what type of cost data is relevant?
11. In deciding whether to process a product further or to sell it in its current stage of completion, what are the relevant items of data?
12. Suggest some reasons why a company might decide to manufacture a part even though it might be cheaper to buy the part from an outside vendor.
13. Is absorption costing or direct costing more useful in making managerial decisions? Why?
14. When absorption costing is used, why might it be profitable to continue to manufacture a product line that is shown in the accounting records as being sold at a loss?

15. If a manufacturing plant is not operating at full capacity, why might a company decide to manufacture a part that is currently being purchased from an outside supplier?
16. Suggest some nonmeasurable factors that management must consider in deciding whether to accept a special order for the company's product at a price less than the normal price.

MANAGERIAL DISCUSSION QUESTIONS

1. Assume that the management of a firm where you are employed as an accountant has asked you to list the steps that should be used in making decisions from a set of alternatives. Prepare a list.
2. What type of information does management need in making a decision about whether to add or drop a product line?
3. BibBoy Toy Company manufactures wagons for distribution through discount outlets, catalog sales companies, and other outlets. One wagon part is purchased from an outside firm for $6 per unit. The company uses 22,000 of these items each year. The production manager states that the company could manufacture the part for less than $6 per unit. As accountant, explain the computations you would make in advising management whether it should continue to buy the part or manufacture it.
4. The Mohican Company has substantial capacity that is not being used in current manufacturing operations. Management is considering making bids on government supply contracts. What type of information would be useful in setting bid prices for these special jobs or products?
5. One of Myfair Company's joint products, ATEX, is sold after being processed in the Doubling Department. The other product, BETATEX, is further processed in the Acidizing Department. ATEX could also be processed in the Acidizing Department and sold to a different class of customers. Explain how you would go about deciding whether to further process ATEX, using measurable factors. Then suggest nonmeasurable factors that should be considered in reaching a decision.
6. Certain managers in the company by which you are employed have discussed for several weeks a proposal by the production manager that scrap materials resulting from the manufacturing process be processed further and sold. They have asked you to help them make the decision. What information will you need to give them sound advice?
7. Better Engines Inc. is in the process of acquiring a new factory building. The building is larger than is needed at the current level of production, but it is anticipated that the excess space will be needed within three or four years to accommodate expected growth in manufacturing. The director of operations has suggested that the company use the available space to manufacture an engine

part now being bought from an outside supplier and continue to manufacture the part until the building space is needed for the production and assembly line. What information would you need to accumulate in order to provide an accounting analysis of the proposal?

EXERCISES

EXERCISE 25–1 **Explain the steps in management's decision-making process. (Obj. 1).**   What are the six steps in making a managerial decision? Which of these steps is most likely to involve the accountant?

EXERCISE 25–2 **Make a decision about whether to discontinue manufacturing a product.   (Obj. 2).**   A company has analyzed its four products and has reported net income for three of the three products it manufactures. However, one product, large motors, shows a loss of $120,000. An analysis of the information reveals the following:

Direct variable manufacturing costs	$ 900,000
Allocated fixed manufacturing costs	200,000
Variable selling and administrative costs	50,000
Allocated fixed selling and administrative costs	$1,250,000
Net sales	$1,130,000
Net loss on big motors	$ (120,000)

All big motors are made to customers' special order, and there is no beginning or ending inventory.
a. Based on just the information given how much would the company's net income increase or decrease if it discontinued manufacturing big motors?
b. Based on just the information given, should the company discontinue manufacturing and selling big motors?
c. Suggest some additional data that would be important in making the decision.

EXERCISE 25–3 **Make a decision about whether to discontinue manufacturing a product.   (Obj. 2).**   The Denver Company manufactures three toys. An income statement for 19X9 that is based on absorption costing shows the following information for one product, Big Red Fire Trucks.

Sales (6,000 units at $40 each)	$240,000
Cost of goods sold	225,000
Gross margin on sales	$ 15,000
Operating expenses	45,000
Net loss on Big Fire Trucks	$ (30,000)

In addition, the following information relating to the income statement for Big Red Fire Trucks is given.

Variable manufacturing costs, $30 per unit
Fixed manufacturing costs, $45,000

Of the fixed manufacturing costs, $20,000 is directly related to the production of Big Red Fire Trucks and would be eliminated if Big Red Fire Trucks were discontinued

Variable operating expenses per unit, $5

Fixed operating expenses, $15,000 (none of the fixed operating expenses would be eliminated by discontinuing Big Red Fire Trucks)

a. Based only on the above information, should the company discontinue manufacturing Big Red Fire Trucks?
b. What other factors should be considered?

EXERCISE 25–4 **Decide whether to manufacture or buy a part. (Obj. 4).** The Astor Company is manufacturing a part that it uses in its finished product. Standard costs of the part are as follows:

Costs per Unit

Materials	$6.00
Labor	2.00
Overhead:	
Variable	2.40
Fixed	5.00

One department of the company makes 80,000 units of the part each year. The fixed overhead rate is based on fixed overhead costs allocated to this department. About $160,000 of the fixed overhead would be eliminated if the part were not manufactured. The company has an opportunity to purchase the part from an outside supplier for $14 per unit.

a. Should the company continue to manufacture the part, or should it accept the outside offer?
b. Assume the same facts as above, except that the part can be purchased from an outside supplier for $10.30 per unit. Should the company continue to manufacture the part, or should it accept the outside offer?
c. Assume the same basic facts given above, except that the part can be purchased from an outside supplier for $12.50. Should the company continue to manufacture the part, or should it accept the outside offer?

EXERCISE 25–5 **Decide whether to manufacture or buy a part. (Obj. 4).** A manufacturer of copying machines has been purchasing a part for $35 each, including delivery costs. One part is required for each copier. The factory has unused capacity that could be used in the manufacturing process. The vice president of production has recommended that the part not be manufactured and has presented the following cost data to support her recommendation.

Estimated cost of manufacturing part:

Direct materials	$16
Direct labor ($\frac{1}{2}$ hour)	5

Factory overhead ($\frac{1}{2}$ hour at $30)	15
Total estimated cost per unit	$36*

*The overhead rate of $30 per hour is based on estimated variable overhead of $20 per labor hour, which would be incurred on the part, and fixed overhead of $10 per hour, which is the rate of fixed overhead currently being charged to products based on normal volume of 100,000 hours per year.

a. Ignoring all other factors except those given, compute the relevant cost to manufacture this part.

b. Assuming that the company uses 2,000 of these parts per year, what would be the savings or increased costs if the company were to manufacture the parts instead of purchasing them?

EXERCISE 25–6　**Make a decision to process a product further or to sell it at its current stage of production.　(Obj. 4).**　Jackson Company manufactures 40,000 units of a product that can be sold at the end of operations in the Cooking Department for $10 per unit, or it can be processed further in the Refining Department and sold for $15 per unit. The Finishing Department will have unused capacity during the next two years. The assistant cost accountant has made an analysis of costs that would be charged to each unit of product in the Finishing Department if additional processing were undertaken. Here is a summary of that analysis.

Additional materials costs	$3.20
Additional labor costs	1.04
Additional variable manufacturing overhead	.60
Allocated portion of Finishing Department fixed costs	.40
Total additional costs	$5.24

Selling and administrative costs are estimated to be the same for both products.

a. What would be the difference in the company's net income if the product is transferred and completed in the Finishing Department instead of being sold at the end of production in the Cooking Department?

b. Suggest some factors (other than those given above) that management should consider in making the decision.

EXERCISE 25–7　**Decide whether to grant a special price on a product.　(Obj. 5).**　The standard costs for the Little Baby Doll manufactured by State Doll Company are:

Materials		$10.00
Labor (1 hr at $6/hr)		6.00
Manufacturing Overhead		
Variable (1 hr at $4/hr)	$4.00	
Fixed ($30,000 ÷ 5,000 hr)	6.00	10.00
Total		$26.00

The normal selling price of the doll is $35. The company is operating at only about 60 percent capacity. A foreign retail toy store has offered to buy 2,000 dolls at a price of $18.50 per doll. Additional selling and administrative expenses applicable to the special order would be $.50 per doll.

a. Should the order be accepted? Show all calculations.

b. Assume the same facts as above, except that the foreign store's order is $22.50 per unit. Should the order be accepted? Show all calculations.

c. Assume the same basic facts given above, except that the foreign store's order is $23.50 per unit, and additional selling and administrative expenses are $1 per unit. Should the order be accepted? Show all calculations.

EXERCISE 25–8   **Decide whether to grant a special price on an order. (Obj. 5).** Sparky Electronics manufactures handheld calculators. Average production has been 12,000 calculators per month, but the company has the capacity to manufacture 16,000 per month. It has received a proposal to provide National Mart, a large discount chain, with 2,500 calculators per month for $10.50 each. Current production costs per calculator are:

Materials	$6.00
Labor (20 min at $9/hr)	3.00
Overhead:	
Variable	.50
Fixed (based on budgeted fixed overhead of $12,000	
per month and 4,000 hours of labor)	1.00
Total production cost per calculator	$10.50

Under the contract terms, Sparky would be required to pack the calculators in a special box and deliver them to National Mart's central warehouse. It is estimated that these costs would be $.60 per calculator.

a. Calculate the increase or decrease in the company's profit that would result from accepting the order.

b. What other factors should management consider in deciding whether to accept the offer?

PROBLEMS

PROBLEM 25–1A   **Make a decision to add or drop a product. (Obj. 2).** The income statement for the Samedan Products Company appears below. Management is concerned over the loss on Product 3.

Materials and labor are variable costs. Manufacturing overhead is applied at the rate of 50 percent of the direct labor cost. Variable overhead is 10 percent of the direct labor cost. Fixed overhead totals $29,000 per month. Variable operating expenses are 20 percent of the sales dollars. Fixed operating expenses total $45,000. The first overhead costs and operating expenses are expected to continue if Product 3 is dropped.

SAMEDAN PRODUCTS COMPANY **Income Statement** **(Absorption Costing)** **Year Ended December 31, 19X9**				
	PRODUCT 1	**PRODUCT 2**	**PRODUCT 3**	**TOTAL**
Sales	$225,000	$62,500	$37,500	$325,000
Cost of Goods Sold				
Materials	$ 37,500	$ 7,500	$ 5,000	$ 50,000
Labor	50,000	12,500	10,000	72,500
Manufacturing Overhead	25,000	6,250	5,000	36,250
Total Cost of Goods Sold	$112,500	$26,250	$20,000	$158,750
Gross Margin	$112,500	$36,250	$17,500	$166,250
Operating Expenses	62,500	25,000	22,500	110,000
Net Income (or Loss)	$ 50,000	$11,250	$ (5,000)	$ 56,250

INSTRUCTIONS

1. Prepare an income statement using direct costing to show the effects of retaining Product 3.
2. Prepare an income statement using direct costing to show the effects of dropping Product 3.
3. Explain what decision should be made and why.

PROBLEM 25–2A   **Make a decision to add or drop a product.** **(Obj. 2).** Terry Towels Company is contemplating discontinuing its line of beach towels. An income statement for the past year shows a loss of $24,000 on the line, computed as follows:

Sales	$205,000
Cost of Goods Sold	130,000
Gross Profit	75,000
Selling and Administrative Expenses	99,000
Net Loss	$ (24,000)

The cost of goods sold includes overhead of $30,000, including fixed overhead of $10,000. The selling and administrative expenses include $33,000 of fixed expenses that will not be affected by the discontinuation of the beach towels.

1. What is the contribution margin, if any, on beach towels?
2. What would be the effects on profit or loss if beach towels are discontinued?
3. What other factors should be considered in deciding whether to discontinue the beach towels?

PROBLEM 25–3A   **Make a decision to manufacture or buy a part.** **(Obj. 4).** The Gritti Company is currently manufacturing a part used in its major product, clothes dryers. An outside supplier has offered to provide the part for $55 per unit. Cost data relating to production of the part for the past year, when 3,000 units were manufactured, are given here. Fixed costs are allocated on the basis of direct labor hours.

Materials	$79,500
Direct Labor	84,000
Indirect Labor	1,000
Other Variable Costs	3,000
Miscellaneous Fixed Costs	7,500

If the part is purchased from the outside supplier, the equipment can be used in producing other items that are in demand. A shipping cost of $1.24 per unit will be incurred if the part is purchased.

INSTRUCTIONS

1. Prepare a make or buy analysis comparing the unit costs of manufacturing the part with the unit costs of purchasing it. Round off to the nearest cent.
2. Recommend a course of action to management.

PROBLEM 25–4A

Make a decision to manufacture or buy a part. (Obj. 4). HyPro Desk Company, which manufactures wooden office equipment, utilizes only 60 percent of its capacity. The plant manager has proposed that the company manufacture a desk part that it now purchases. This could be done with existing equipment and facilities. The part being purchased costs $42 per desk for the 4,500 desks manufactured each year. One of the accounting clerks has pointed out that the estimated cost to manufacture the part is $46 per desk, computed as follows:

Materials	$22
Labor (1 hr)	9
Overhead applied (1 hr at $15/hr)	15

The variable overhead is $6 per hour, and the fixed overhead is $9 per hour. Fixed costs would be increased by $13,500 per year if the part were manufactured by the company.

INSTRUCTIONS

1. Ignoring other factors, what will be the annual effect on the company's net income if it chooses to manufacture the part?
2. What other factors should management consider in making this decision?
3. Should the company manufacture the part, or continue to purchase it from outside sources?

PROBLEM 25–5A

Make a decision about whether to process a product further or to sell it in its current state. (Obj. 4). Mountain Top Company produces two products from the same production process. The joint production costs of the two products were $303,000 during 19X9. Joint costs are allocated between the two products on the basis of physical volume. A total of 200,000 units of Product A were produced during 19X9, and 300,000 units of Product B were produced. The production manager has recommended that either Product A or Product B receive additional processing after separation. The accountant has supplied the following data that seem to be relevant in making the decision and has undertaken to determine what the results would have been in 19X9 if Product A had been further processed.

Product	Units Produced	Sales Value	Variable Costs Allocated	Fixed Costs Allocated
A	200,000	$200,000	$ 70,000	$31,000
B	300,000	330,000	140,000	62,000
Totals	500,000	$530,000	$210,000	$93,000

To further process Product A would require no additional fixed costs. Variable costs of further processing Product A are estimated to be $.40 per unit. The increase in selling price is estimated as $.25 per unit.

To further process Product B would not require additional capital investment but would require additional fixed costs of $60,000 per year for supervision and overhead. Additional variable costs for Product B would be $.10 per unit. The increase in selling for Product B is estimated to be $.40 per unit.

INSTRUCTIONS

1. Based on the figures for 19X9, should either product be processed further? If so, which? What would be the impact on profit for the company if your recommendation were followed?
2. List other factors that management should consider in making the decision.
3. Would your answer to Instruction 1 be different if joint costs were allocated on the basis of relative sales value? Explain.

PROBLEM 25–6A

Make a decision about special pricing. (Obj. 5). The Lopez Company produces a part used in automobiles. Annual production is 200,000 units, each of which regularly sells for $100. The standard costs are shown below. Nonmanufacturing costs are $10 per unit for variable costs and $12.50 per unit for fixed costs.

Materials		$20.00
Labor (2 hr × $8.75/hr)		17.50
Manufacturing Overhead		
Variable (1 hr × $7.50/hr)	$ 7.50	
Fixed (1 hr × $16/hr)	16.00	23.50
Total Standard Cost per Unit		$61.00

A foreign manufacturer needs 20,000 units and offers $60 per unit plus shipping costs. None of these units would be sold in the Lopez Company's normal market.

INSTRUCTIONS

1. Prepare an analysis to determine whether the company should accept the special order.
2. Ignoring all other factors, what is the lowest price that Lopez could accept for the special order and still earn any profit?

ALTERNATE PROBLEMS

PROBLEM 25–1B

Make a decision to add or drop a product. (Obj. 2). The income statement for the Home Products Company is shown below. Management is concerned over the loss on Product P.

Materials and labor are variable costs. Manufacturing overhead is applied at 50 percent of the direct labor cost. Variable overhead is 10

HOME PRODUCTS COMPANY
Income Statement
(Absorption Costing)
Year Ended December 31, 19X9

	PRODUCT N	PRODUCT O	PRODUCT P	TOTAL
Sales	$90,000	$25,000	$15,000	$130,000
Cost of Goods Sold				
Materials	$15,000	$ 3,000	$ 2,000	$ 20,000
Labor	20,000	5,000	4,000	29,000
Manufacturing Overhead	10,000	2,500	2,000	14,500
Cost of Goods Sold	$45,000	$10,500	$ 8,000	$ 63,500
Gross Margin on Sales	$45,000	$14,500	$ 7,000	$ 66,500
Operating Expenses	25,000	10,000	9,000	44,000
Net Income (or Loss)	$20,000	$ 4,500	$ (2,000)	$ 22,500

percent of the direct labor cost. Fixed overhead totals $11,600 per year. Variable operating expenses are 20 percent of the sales dollars. Fixed operating expenses total $18,000. The fixed overhead costs and operating expenses are expected to continue if Product P is dropped.

INSTRUCTIONS

1. Prepare an income statement using direct costing to show the effects of retaining Product P.
2. Prepare an income statement using direct costing to the effects of dropping Product P.
3. Explain what decision should be made and why.

PROBLEM 25–2B

Make a decision to add or drop a product. (Obj. 2). The accountant for Toy Time Company, a manufacturer of several toys, has prepared an income statement for each product for the year just ended. She is concerned that one product, Go-Go Cars, has, according to the accountant's calculation, had a loss of $40,000 for the year, computed as follows:

Sales	$240,000
Cost of Goods Sold	180,000
Gross Profit	60,000
Selling and Administrative Expenses	100,000
Net Loss	$ (40,000)

On seeing the statement, the company's vice president of production suggests that the line of Go-Go Cars be immediately discontinued. On questioning from the president, the accountant explains that the cost of goods sold figure includes overhead of $40,000, including fixed overhead of $24,000. The selling and administrative expenses include $24,000 of fixed expenses that would not be affected by the discontinuation of Go-Go Cars.

INSTRUCTIONS

1. Compute the contribution margin, if any, on beach towels.
2. What would be the effects on profit or loss if Go-Go Cars are discontinued?

3. What other factors should be considered in deciding whether to discontinue Go-Go Cars?

PROBLEM 25–3B

Make a decision to manufacture or buy a part. **(Obj. 4).** The Lindale Products Company is currently manufacturing a part used in its main product, lawn mowers. An outside supplier has offered to provide the part for $22 per unit. Cost data relating to production of the part for the past year, when 12,000 units were manufactured, follow. Fixed costs are allocated on the basis of direct labor hours.

Materials	$127,200
Direct Labor	134,400
Indirect Labor	1,600
Variable Overhead	4,800
Fixed Overhead	12,000

If the part is purchased from the outside supplier, the equipment can be used in producing other items that are in demand. A shipping cost of $.25 per unit is incurred if the part is purchased.

INSTRUCTIONS

1. Prepare a make or buy analysis comparing the unit costs of manufacturing the part with the unit costs of purchasing it. Round off to the nearest cent.
2. Recommend a course of action to management.

PROBLEM 25–4B

Make a decision to manufacture or buy a part. **(Obj. 4).** Perfect Vision TV Company manufactures television receivers for use in hotels and businesses. Only about 65 percent of the company's capacity is utilized. The chief engineer has proposed that the company assemble a component of the receivers that it now buys as a unit. This could be done with existing equipment and facilities. The part being purchased costs $35 per unit for the 5,000 receivers manufactured each year. The accountant has estimated, using the company's cost accounting system, that the cost to manufacture the unit would be $40, computed as follows:

Materials	$20.50
Labor ($\frac{3}{4}$ hour)	7.50
Overhead applied ($\frac{3}{4}$ hour at $16/hr)	12.00
Total	$40.00

The variable overhead is $6 per hour, and the fixed overhead is $10 per hour. Fixed costs would be increased by $13,500 per year if the unit were manufactured by the company.

INSTRUCTIONS

1. Ignoring other factors, what will be the annual effect on the company's net income if it chooses to manufacture the unit?
2. What other factors should management consider in making this decision?
3. Would your answer to Instruction 1 be different if joint costs were allocated to products on the basis of relative sales values? Explain.

PROBLEM 25–5B

Make a decision about whether to process a product further or to sell it in its current state. **(Obj. 4).** New Tech Chemical Company produces two products from the same production process. The joint production costs of the two products were $420,000 during 19X9. Joint costs are allocated between the two products on the basis of physical volume. A total of 400,000 units of Product A were produced during 19X9, and 200,000 units of Product B were produced. A production and pricing team of the company's executives and employees has suggested that Products A and B receive additional processing after separation. The following information was provided to the team. The group has asked you, the accountant, to determine what the results would have been in 19X9 if the two products had been further processed.

Product	Units Produced	Sales Value	Variable Costs Allocated	Fixed Costs Allocated
A	400,000	$345,000	$160,000	$120,000
B	200,000	185,000	80,000	60,000
Totals	600,000	$530,000	$240,000	$180,000

To further process Product A would require no additional fixed costs. Variable costs of further processing Product A are estimated to be $.50 per unit. The increase in selling price is estimated as $.45 per unit.

To further process Product B would not require additional capital investment but would require additional fixed costs of $60,000 per year for supervision and overhead. Additional variable costs for Product B would be $.15 per unit. The increase in selling price for Product B is estimated to be $.40 per unit.

INSTRUCTIONS

1. Based on the figures for 19X9, should either product be processed further? If so, which? What would be the impact on profit for the company if your recommendation were followed?
2. List other factors that management should consider in making the decision.
3. Would your answer to Instruction 1 be different if joint costs were allocated to products on the basis of relative sales value? Explain.

PROBLEM 25–6B   **Make a decision about special pricing.   (Obj. 5).**   The Alcoe Company produces an electrical relay used in home air-conditioning units. Annual production totals 100,000 units, each of which regularly sells for $40. The standard costs are shown below. Nonmanufacturing costs are $4 per unit for variable costs and $5 per unit for fixed costs.

Materials		$ 8.00
Labor (2 hr × $3.50/hr)		7.00
Manufacturing Overhead		
Variable (1 hr × $3/hr)	$3.00	
Fixed (1 hr × $6.40/hr)	6.40	9.40
Total Standard Cost per Unit		$24.40

A foreign air-conditioning manufacturer needs 10,000 units and offers $24 per unit plus shipping costs. The sales manager is opposed to accepting the $24 price. She says: "I know the product will not be sold in the United States, where it would compete with our regularly priced goods, but we will lose $.40 on every unit. We will be using some of our idle capacity, but taking a loss like this doesn't make sense." The cost accountant replies that it is a good deal and the company should accept the offer.

INSTRUCTIONS

1. Prepare an analysis to determine whether the special offer should be accepted.
2. Ignoring all factors except the costs presented, what is the minimum selling price at which the company could accept the special order and make any profit?

MANAGERIAL DECISION CASE

The cost accountant at the Top Hat Company has prepared an analysis of the profitability of each of the firm's four products. That analysis is presented below. All fixed costs are allocated costs.

	Totals	Product A	Product B	Product C	Product D
Sales	$62,600	$10,000	$18,000	$12,600	$22,000
Cost of Goods Sold	44,274	4,750	7,056	13,968	18,500
Gross Profit on Sales	$18,326	$ 5,250	$10,944	$ (1,368)	$ 3,500
Operating Expenses	12,012	1,990	2,976	2,826	4,220
Net Income	$ 6,314	$ 3,260	$ 7,968	$ (4,194)	$ (720)
Units Sold		1,000	1,200	1,800	2,000
Sales Price per Unit		$10.00	$15.00	$ 7.00	$11.00
Variable Cost of Goods Sold per Unit		$ 2.50	$ 3.00	$ 6.50	$ 6.00
Variable Operating Expenses per Unit		$ 1.17	$ 1.25	$ 1.00	$ 1.20

Several suggestions have been made about changing the product mix in order to reduce or eliminate the loss on Products C and D. The company's management has asked you to prepare an analysis of the effects on the company's net income before taxes of each of the following proposals. (In each case, consider only the product changes stated in the proposal. The activity of other products remains unchanged.)

Proposal 1. Discontinue Product C.
Proposal 2. Increase the sales price of Product C to $8. This will probably result in a decrease in the number of units sold to 1,500.
Proposal 3. Use that part of the plant in which Product C is made to produce a new product, T. The total variable costs and expenses per unit of Product T are estimated at $8.05, and it is estimated that 1,600 units can be produced and sold at $9.50 each.
Proposal 4. Use part of the plant in which Product A is made to produce additional Product D. Reduce the production of Product A to 500 units, to be sold at $12 each. Increase the production of Product D to 2,500 units, to be sold at $10.50 each.

Cost Accounting for Distribution Activities and Service Businesses

In previous chapters of this book, emphasis has been placed on manufacturing costs. In direct costing and in specific decision cases, nonmanufacturing costs, separated into fixed and variable components, also have been included in various analyses. Up to this point, however, we have directed little attention to specific nonmanufacturing cost elements. In this chapter, special emphasis will be given to the analysis and control of costs related to distribution functions and service businesses.

USING COST ACCOUNTING IN NONMANUFACTURING ACTIVITIES

Distribution functions may be defined as all of those activities that take place after the point of production to get goods sold and delivered to ultimate consumers. Thus the term embraces the sales and delivery activities of a manufacturing company, wholesale establishments, retailers, and other entities in getting products into the hands of consumers. **Service businesses** are organizations that offer and provide services rather than physical products. Attorneys, public accounting firms, physicians, business consultants, financial advisers, hospitals, educational institutions, Internet providers, and various types of repair shops are examples of service businesses.

The application of cost accounting concepts and procedures to nonmanufacturing activities offers additional challenges to accountants. Historically, cost accounting has focused on manufacturing operations. Cost accounting systems such as job order costing, process costing, and standard costing, along with budgeting and other cost control techniques, have been developed that superbly meet the needs of manufacturing businesses. In recent years, service activities and distribution functions have gained increased importance, whereas manufacturing has declined in relative importance in the American economy. As a result, cost accountants have been called on to use their skills in developing cost accounting and control techniques for service businesses and distribution operations. In this chapter, we will discuss some of the common approaches to applying cost accounting techniques in planning and controlling nonmanufacturing activities.

First, we shall examine the use of cost accounting techniques in planning and controlling distribution costs. Distribution costs are incurred not only in businesses whose major activities are the purchase, resale, and distribution of products, such as the operation of wholesale outlets and retail stores, but they are also incurred by manufacturing companies in marketing the products they have manufactured. Then, we shall examine similar uses of cost accounting techniques in planning and controlling costs of activities in businesses that provide services, rather than products.

DISTRIBUTION COST ANALYSIS AND CONTROL

It is more difficult to standardize, measure, predict, and control some distribution costs than manufacturing costs because some distribution activities are less standardized and less repetitive than manufacturing operations. Sometimes it may be almost impossible to determine directly the relationship between distribution costs incurred and the benefits resulting from those costs. Some costs incurred in distribution activities are expected to provide benefits only in the current period—for example, a bonus paid a salesperson for attaining a specific sales volume. Other costs are expected to provide benefits in future periods; however, both the benefits and the future periods affected may be indefinite and difficult to measure and the amount spent during the current period may depend almost entirely on the desire of management. A good example is the cost of an advertising campaign to promote a new product. It may be years after advertising costs have been incurred before the results will be known, and even then the benefit of most advertising expenditures can never be measured with precision.

In addition, some nonmanufacturing activities, especially selling activities, are difficult to standardize. Each salesperson has his or her own approach to selling. Different customers may require different sales efforts and approaches. The approach used in selling some products may need to be different from the approach used for other products. As a result, too often in distribution activities, emphasis is placed on increasing sales volume, with inadequate attention given to planning and controlling related costs. If a firm's producing departments operate efficiently, but selling and warehousing activities are inefficient, profits may be substantially reduced. This makes it even more important for the accountant to recognize the need to analyze, plan, and control nonmanufacturing costs.

There is no standard approach to planning and controlling distribution activities. Since the operating functions and techniques vary from company to company and even within a company, the accountant must be alert to opportunities for planning and control and must be able to develop analytical techniques appropriate to the circumstances. In this chapter, some common techniques are explained and illustrated. The ideas discussed here are merely examples of the types of techniques that might be used. Adequate planning and control of distribution costs depend on the accountant's ability to select the proper analytical techniques, apply them, and skillfully interpret the results.

ANALYZING DISTRIBUTION COSTS

Control of distribution costs may appear to be difficult because these costs may not relate closely to a measurable activity and because some activities are difficult to standardize. Three major procedures are used for controlling costs and measuring the performance of sales and distribution activities. These procedures are:

- Percentage-of-sales analysis
- Comparison of actual revenues and costs with those in the planning budget or with those in the flexible budget
- Analysis of sales and individual costs using measurable activity factors

Percentage-of-Sales Analysis

One way to measure the efficiency of distribution activities is to express each expense as a percentage of sales. For example, it is customary in analyzing financial statements to express sales salaries as a percentage of net sales. One company's income statement may show that sales salaries are 8 percent of net sales, whereas a similar company's report may show that sales salaries are 10 percent of net sales. The lower percentage could mean that the first company has better control of sales salaries. However, further investigation will be necessary to determine whether this is so. It may be that different services are provided by the sales staffs, that gross profit percentages are different, or that other factors differ. Percentage-of-sales analysis is used frequently for comparing different companies or comparing different segments of a single company. Percentage-of-sales analysis is also used to compare the same calculations between years for the same company.

In analyzing operations, management and accountants almost always make comparisons of financial statement items over several fiscal periods. For example, if a company's advertising expense was 4 percent of sales one year and 2 percent the following year, it might indicate that advertising expenditures were used more efficiently in the second year. On the other hand, it might suggest that too little was spent on advertising in the second year—or that too much was spent in the first year.

It is also extremely helpful to make percentage-of-sales analyses of operations by segments of a distribution business. The variety of segments for which costs can be classified and analyzed is almost endless. Almost any organizational segment, activity, or function can be selected as the focal point of analysis. It is possible to determine the contribution to profit of each region, territory, area, district, individual branch, or store, or even of each salesperson, product, or customer. These analyses help to pinpoint costs that may be out of line in one or more segments of the business and to better understand the profitability of each segment. Such analyses may instill a spirit of competition that will cause employees in different segments of the business to work harder to improve profitability. The following example illustrates the typical use of percentage-of-sales analysis for segments of a business.

GBS Suppliers, a distributor of cosmetics and other personal care products, operates 78 stores throughout the western portion of the United States. The company's home office is in Tulsa, and it has three regions—Plains, Mountain, and Coastal—each with a regional manager. The stores sell a line of "professional products" to beauty salons and barber shops and sell other product lines to individual customers for use in the home. The products are grouped into five categories: cosmetics, hair products, skin-care products, appliances such as hair dryers, and accessories such as combs, brushes, and scissors. Beauty salons and barber shops pay a lower price than do retail customers. In order to plan and control the operations of the 78 stores, the company analyzes profitability in many ways. The smaller the unit of activity chosen for measurement, the more difficult it becomes to measure profit with precision and the less reliable the results become, because there are fewer costs that can be traced directly to the unit for which profit is being measured. Thus some companies may measure net profit for the larger segments such as each region and each retail store but determine only gross profit for individual product lines. In analyzing operations and assessing cost control, GBS expresses every item on each region's income statement as a percentage of that region's net sales. The same procedure is used for each item on each store's income statement.

Analysis by Region. For GBS, the profitability of each region is relatively easy to measure because most expenses (except interest, central warehousing, and general and administrative overhead of the corporate offices) can be identified directly with a specific region. The income statements of the three regions for 19X9 are given below.

GBS SUPPLIERS
Income Statement by Region
Year Ended December 31, 19X9

ITEM	PLAINS REGION AMOUNT	%	MOUNTAIN REGION AMOUNT	%	COASTAL REGION AMOUNT	%
Sales	$5,018,000	100.20	$7,527,000	100.20	$7,025,000	100.18
Less Sales Returns and Allowances	10,100	.20	15,300	.20	12,600	.18
Net Sales	$5,007,900	100.00	$7,511,700	100.00	$7,012,400	100.00
Cost of Goods Sold	2,616,000	52.24	3,900,000	51.92	3,640,000	51.91
Gross Profit on Sales	$2,391,900	47.76	$3,611,700	48.08	$3,372,400	48.09
Regional Operating Expenses:						
Store Salaries	$ 734,000	14.66	$ 849,000	11.30	$ 918,400	13.10
Administrative Salaries	80,000	1.60	90,000	1.20	91,000	1.30
Payroll Benefits and Taxes	193,400	3.86	229,400	3.05	245,600	3.50
Rent	315,000	6.29	402,000	5.35	420,000	5.99
Utilities	77,800	1.55	127,000	1.69	112,000	1.60
Telephone	35,000	.70	42,500	.57	47,300	.67
Maintenance and Repairs	26,200	.52	31,600	.42	39,800	.57
Advertising	60,000	1.20	66,000	.88	86,800	1.24
Supplies	18,000	.36	26,500	.35	23,000	.33
Credit Card Fees	5,200	.10	8,400	.11	7,900	.11
Postage	4,100	.08	6,700	.09	5,400	.08
Travel and Entertainment	3,000	.06	3,600	.05	3,700	.05
Taxes and Insurance	20,400	.41	34,000	1.00	70,500	1.01
Depreciation	49,600	.99	75,300	.45	20,700	.30
Miscellaneous	5,100	.10	7,800	.10	9,000	.13
Total Direct Expenses	$1,626,800	32.48	$1,999,800	26.62*	$2,101,100	29.96*
Net Income Before Indirect Expenses	$ 765,100	15.28	$1,611,900	21.46	$1,271,300	18.13
Indirect Expenses:						
Interest	$ 40,000	.80	$ 60,000	.80	$ 56,000	.80
Warehouse	78,500	1.57	117,000	1.56	109,200	1.56
General and Administrative	50,200	1.00	75,300	1.00	70,300	1.00
Total Indirect Expenses	$ 168,700	3.37	$ 252,300	3.36	$ 235,500	3.36
Net Income Before Income Taxes	$ 596,400	11.91	$1,359,600	18.10	$1,035,800	14.77
Allocated Income Taxes	239,000	4.77	543,800	7.24	414,000	5.90
Net Income After Income Taxes	$ 357,400	7.14	$ 815,800	10.86	$ 621,800	8.87

*Adjusted for rounding.

The accountant and management carefully examine the percentage of sales for each item on the income statements for each region. The percentage figures are compared with the corresponding figures for the previous period. In addition, percentage figures for each region are compared with the corresponding figures for other regions and with the total of all regions. Variations are analyzed to determine their causes. This type of analysis is useful in controlling costs and evaluating operations.

On the regional income statements illustrated for GBS, all expenses are classified as either direct operating expenses or indirect expenses. Since the direct operating expenses (which include all expenses except those related to financing, the costs of the central warehouse, and the corporation's general and administrative expenses) must be borne by the region's operations, no distinction between controllable expenses and noncontrollable expenses appears on the regional income statements. Unlike GBS, some companies subclassify the regional expenses into controllable and noncontrollable expenditures because, like managers of individual stores, regional managers may have no control over many fixed costs.

A comparison of percentages of sales for individual items on a region-by-region basis may provide information that will be useful to management in detecting problem areas and in controlling costs. For example, management would be keenly interested in investigating the reasons why Store Salaries, Administrative Salaries, Rent, and Advertising expenses for the Plains Region 1 appear to be out of line with these expenses for the other two regions. Similarly, management would probably investigate the relatively low expenditures for Store Salaries, Administrative Salaries, and Advertising for the Mountain Region to determine whether the other regions could get these costs in line with those of the Mountain Region.

Analysis by Store. Obviously the management of GBS is interested in the profitability of each store and in analyzing the differences in profit between the stores. This information is vital in making decisions such as compensation of managers or whether a store should be closed. To illustrate the statements prepared for each store's operations, the income statements of two stores, Store 28 and Store 36, are shown on page 661. Note that these statements contain only the costs directly identified with each store.

The first classification of operating expenses shown in this statement is Controllable Expenses (those expenses over which the store manager has a substantial degree of control). These expenses include variable costs and semivariable costs. The second classification of expenses is Noncontrollable Expenses, over which the store manager generally has little control. Note that the classification Noncontrollable Expenses in the income statements of GBS represents fixed expenses. This statement does not include the allocated expenses of the home office or the district manager's office, because store managers usually have little control over allocated expenses. Only those expenses that can be traced directly to individual stores are included on the income

GBS SUPPLIERS
Income Statements—Stores 28 and 36
Year Ended December 31, 19X9

ITEM	STORE 28 AMOUNT	STORE 28 PERCENT	STORE 36 AMOUNT	STORE 36 PERCENT
Sales	$252,345	100.14	$299,955	100.27
Sales Returns and Allowances	345	.14	800	.27
Net Sales	$252,000	100.00	$299,155	100.00
Cost of Goods Sold	131,084	52.02	147,155	49.19
Gross Profit on Sales	$120,916	47.98	$152,000	50.81
Operating Expenses				
Controllable Expenses:				
Store Salaries	$ 30,723	12.19	$ 25,413	8.49
Payroll Taxes	2,542	1.01	1,715	.57
Employee Insurance	1,329	.53	1,173	.39
Workers' Compensation				
Insurance	396	.16	280	.09
Pension and Retirement	3,072	1.22	2,541	.85
Utilities	3,639	1.44	1,798	.60
Telephone	1,567	.62	859	.29
Maintenance and Repairs	1,168	.46	1,403	.47
Advertising	2,700	1.07	2,300	.77
Supplies	681	.27	533	.18
Credit Card Fees	357	.14	277	.09
Postage	204	.08	131	.04
Travel and Entertainment	282	.11	420	.14
Bad Debts	258	.10	60	.02
Cash Short or (Over)	(456)	(.18)	127	.04
Miscellaneous	967	.38	800	.27
Total Controllable Expenses	$ 49,429	19.61*	$ 39,830	13.31*
Noncontrollable Expenses:				
Rent	$ 14,923	5.92	11,573	3.87
Depreciation	2,334	.93	651	.22
Casualty Insurance	610	.24	720	.24
Property Taxes	912	.36	361	.12
Total Noncontrollable Expenses	$ 18,779	7.45	$ 13,305	4.45
Total Operating Expenses	$ 68,208	27.06	$ 53,135	17.76
Contribution of Store	$ 52,708	20.92	$ 98,865	33.05

*Adjusted for rounding.

statement for each GBS store. The management of GBS thinks that a store's **contribution,** the excess of net sales over controllable expenses, is the best measure of an individual store's performance. In some companies, however, a part (or even all) of the indirect expenses may be allocated to individual stores, and operating performance measured by the profit that remains after deducting all the store's expenses, including allocated indirect expenses. This procedure, which requires allocation (sometimes somewhat arbitrary allocation) of indirect costs, may be used on the theory that every segment should be responsible for a part of the indirect expenses and that a segment does not truly produce a profit until its share of the indirect costs is covered.

Operating Analyses

Earlier in this chapter it was suggested that the accountant must be alert to the development and use of analytical procedures that will help in controlling distribution costs and increasing profits. Percentage-of-sales analysis is only one tool. Another useful technique is to analyze the activities that underlie the items on the income statement. Many types of analyses can be made for almost every revenue and expense item. A few illustrations will suggest the types of analyses that might prove useful.

Analyses of Sales Data. Obviously the amount of sales is of crucial importance to a business, both in controlling costs and in planning future activities. Studies of the characteristics of a company's sales, its customers, its products, and its sales procedures provide the accountant with information to help management increase profit. Typical analyses are discussed below. These examples are representative of the types of analyses that may be made, but the analyses shown are far from exhaustive.

Sales per Square Foot of Floor Space Occupied. Computing the sales per square foot of floor space used for selling activities (sales for the period divided by the square feet of floor space) may help to answer such questions as whether there is too much floor space for the existing sales volume and for potential sales volume.

A comparison of sales per square foot of floor space occupied by each business segment, such as for each retail store run by GBS, might reveal that some stores are making better use of their space than are others. For example, if any analysis of operations of Store 22 showed sales of $287 per square foot of floor space in 19X9, but the average for all stores is only $220, management would be keenly interested in analyzing why Store 22 appears to have used its space so much more efficiently. On the other hand, if Store 8 had sales of only $184 per square foot during the year, management would certainly take steps to investigate this poor performance. The operations of all stores can be studied to determine how stores that use space poorly can increase their sales per square foot.

Average Sales per Order and Average Sales per Invoice. Small orders are costly. Sales efforts, handling costs, billing costs, and other costs may be almost as great for a small order as for a large one. Clearly, large orders are desirable. Special efforts should be made to increase the size of each order for customers with low average sales per invoice.

Analysis of Total Sales Made to Each Customer During the Period. A business may classify its customers on the basis of the total sales

SELF-REVIEW

1. Why is it sometimes more difficult to analyze, plan, and control distribution expenses than manufacturing costs?
2. Are there likely to be more discretionary costs in a manufacturing operation or in a distribution operation? Explain.
3. A distribution company has several retail stores. For 19X9 sales salaries were 18 percent of net sales in Store 4, whereas in Store 19 sales salaries were only 14.4 percent of sales. On the surface, which store appears to be better at controlling costs? What factors would you investigate in trying to determine the extent to which sales salaries are being better controlled in one of the stores?
4. Why is contribution, rather than net profit, often used to compare the efficiency of two segments of a business, such as two stores in a chain of stores?
5. What argument can be given that cost control at the segment level should be measured by the final net profit of the segment, after considering all fixed expenses and all allocated indirect expenses?

Answers to Self-Review

1. Manufacturing operations tend to be more standardized than distribution activities, even though many distribution activities can be standardized. For example, different customers may require different sales techniques, and different products may also require different sales efforts. Some distribution costs are more discretionary than are manufacturing costs. Generally, if goods are to be manufactured, all necessary costs must be incurred. However, some distribution costs, such as advertising, may be varied in total or even postponed altogether during a particular year.
2. All manufacturing costs must be incurred if goods are to be produced. It is not possible for management to decide to reduce most expenditures in manufacturing operations or even to substantially vary the manufacturing costs necessary to produce a specified volume of goods. However, some distribution costs, for example advertising, for a period may be reduced, increased, or completely eliminated.
3. On the surface, sales salaries appear to be much better controlled in Store 19. However, it would be necessary to examine the types of goods being sold in each store to compare the sales efforts needed. Also, it would be necessary to see whether the store has matured, so that less sales effort is required. In addition, advertising costs must be compared and local wage rates compared with those where Store 4 is located.
4. The store manager should have responsibility for variable costs in his or her segment. The manager may or may not have control over fixed costs. Certainly, the segment manager may have little control over costs that have been allocated from the home office.
5. The argument is sometimes made that each segment of a business not only must meet its own direct expenses but also must pay its share of fixed expenses and allocated costs before it is truly profitable.

made to each during a period. For example, GBS classifies each customer on the basis of sales for the year according to the following schedule.

Sales for Past Year

$10,000 or over
    5,000 to $9,999
    4,000 to 4,999
    2,000 to 3,999
      500 to 1,999
Less than   500

This analysis may lead to further examination of the cost of serving customers who make small annual purchases. Such questions as the following will lead to further analysis of operations:

- Is the gross profit on small sales adequate to cover the costs of servicing these customers?
- Should a service charge be levied against small sales invoices?
- Should some small accounts be dropped?
- What can be done to increase the purchases of each customer?
- Should price differentials between large and small customers be increased?
- Does each customer who makes small purchases represent growth potential?
- Should sales representatives continue to call on small customers in remote areas?

Analysis of Sales by Product Classes. Some products show lower gross profit rates than others or require greater selling efforts or higher delivery costs. Some product lines may have the potential for future growth, and other product lines may be "dying." Typical questions to ask in such analyses include the following:

- Should certain product lines with a low gross profit be dropped?
- What are the unusual costs related to each product line?
- Which product lines have high turnover, and which product lines have low turnover? (This may reflect the relative cost of carrying inventories.)
- What are the space requirements for storing each product line?

Obviously, answering questions about sales, such as those listed above, will require a detailed analysis of sales records, inventory records, warehouse reports, and many other types of records that cover a wide range of operations.

The sales analyses discussed in this section are merely examples of the methods that can be used to examine distribution activities and measure their efficiency. Remember that the accountant must constantly be alert to the operations of the business where he or she is employed in order to develop effective cost control procedures.

Analysis of Activities Causing Expenses. Many of the analyses of sales described above lead directly into an investigation of expenses and cost behavior. Every expense item on the income statement represents a potential area of research and analysis. Some expense items are inherently larger than others, and some may be easier to control than others. Thus, the accountant must carefully study the cost structure of the business in order to determine where the effort to analyze expenses can achieve the greatest benefits. Sales salaries and commissions almost always form a large part of distribution expenses; therefore, it is usually worthwhile to analyze this item. Some analyses, in addition to those already discussed, that can be made to shed light on the degree to which sales salaries and commissions are being controlled include the following:

- Percentage of total sales salaries and commissions to total net sales
- Percentage of sales salaries and commissions for each salesperson to that person's net sales
- Average sales per day, per week, per month, or per year for each salesperson
- Sales returns and allowances of each salesperson as a percent of that person's net sales
- Average number of customer calls as compared to the number of sales made by each salesperson for the period

The analyses of sales salaries and commissions listed above are only representative of the many meaningful and useful analyses that can be made in which specific costs are related to specific activities. The following list shows some of the other quantifiable relationships that can be used in measuring the efficiency of distribution activities:

- Sales representatives' salaries: number of calls made, number of miles traveled, or sales volume
- Sales representatives' travel expenses: miles traveled or number of calls
- Delivery expense: number of items delivered, number of miles traveled by truck, or weight delivered
- Warehouse expense: weight or number of units handled
- Billing costs: number of invoice lines or number of invoices handled

The alert cost accountant will be quick to recognize activity measurements that can be used in cost control and in determining bases for estimating the variability of costs.

At this point you should be able to work Exercises 26–1 to 26–4 and Problems 26–1A to 26–2B.

BUDGETS FOR DISTRIBUTION COSTS

Both planning budget techniques, in which a budget is prepared at only the expected level of activity, and flexible budget techniques, in which a budget may be determined for any level of activity, are used in planning and controlling distribution activities. Because the techniques used in preparing both types of budgets for distribution costs are so similar to those used for manufacturing activities, we will present only an overview of distribution cost budgeting.

The Planning Budget

In manufacturing operations, variable costs depend on the production level; fixed costs exist because of managerial decisions, even though those decisions may be based on management's estimation of production level. For example, direct labor, direct material, and variable overhead costs all change directly according to the volume of output, whereas fixed costs such as depreciation, taxes, and insurance exist because of managerial decisions to produce some predetermined range of volume of products. Other fixed costs, such as salaries of factory managers and storeroom personnel, are created by the decision to carry on an anticipated level of production. In distribution activities, too, some costs vary according to the volume of activity and others are fixed.

However, some distribution costs bear little relation to existing facilities or to volume; instead, these expenses are **discretionary costs**—that is, they are costs that can be changed easily by a decision of management. For example, advertising expenses may not vary directly according to sales and are not unavoidably fixed in amount. In fact, advertising expenses may vary in inverse relation to production or sales—as sales fall, advertising is likely to be increased in an effort to boost sales. The amount spent will depend on the decisions made by management. Those responsible for decisions estimate the need for advertising and make plans for obtaining the desired coverage.

Nevertheless, the approaches and techniques used to budget costs of manufacturing operations, discussed in Chapter 21, can be adapted easily to distribution activities. For instance, management salaries and sales salaries can be forecast using past experience, anticipated changes in salary rates, and expected personnel requirements. Sales representatives' commissions can be budgeted from the knowledge of commission rates and budgeted sales volumes. The travel costs of sales representatives can be based on past experience, sales forecasts, known rates for travel expenses, and travel plans. Since most of the bases on which variable costs are estimated are tied to sales volume, many companies simply use sales volume as the basis for determining variability. Once fixed costs and variable cost rates have been determined using the techniques you learned in Chapter 21, the planning budget can be assembled.

The Flexible Budget

Flexible budgets may be used to control the costs of distribution in much the same way they are used to control manufacturing costs, especially when distribution activities can be reduced to repetitive operations that can be easily measured on some uniform and consistent basis. When flexible budgets are prepared for distribution activities, it is common to express cost variability on the basis of gross sales or, more frequently, net sales.

GBS requires monthly, quarterly, and yearly budgets for each store. The flexible budget for Store 28 for 19X9 is shown below. In this budget, variability is expressed as a percentage of net sales. The concepts used in this budget are exactly the same as those used in manufacturing operations, discussed in Chapter 20.

For example, estimated Pension and Retirement Expense consists of $2,000 of fixed costs and variable costs equal to one-half of 1 percent of net sales. The flexible budget for Store 28 calls for total

GBS SUPPLIES
Flexible Budget—Store 28
Year Ending December 31, 19X9

ITEM	COST FORMULA FIXED PORTION	COST FORMULA VARIABLE PORTION (% OF SALES)	SALES VOLUME			
Sales			$200,000	$225,000	$250,000	$275,000
Cost of Goods Sold		50.00	$100,000	$112,500	$125,000	$137,500
Gross Profit on Sales		50.00	$100,000	$112,500	$125,000	$137,500
Operating Expenses						
Controllable Expenses:						
Store Salaries	$20,000	5.00	$ 30,000	$ 31,250	$ 32,500	$ 33,750
Payroll Taxes	1,600	.40	2,400	2,500	2,600	2,700
Employee Insurance	1,200	.10	1,400	1,425	1,450	1,475
Workers' Compensation Insurance	220	.08	380	400	420	440
Pension and Retirement	2,000	.50	3,000	3,125	3,250	3,375
Utilities	3,600		3,600	3,600	3,600	3,600
Telephone	1,500		1,500	1,500	1,500	1,500
Maintenance and Repairs	600	.20	1,000	1,050	1,100	1,150
Advertising	2,700		2,700	2,700	2,700	2,700
Supplies	200	.20	600	650	700	750
Credit Card Fees		.20	400	450	500	550
Postage	240	.20	240	240	240	240
Travel and Entertainment	100	.10	300	325	350	375
Bad Debts		.10	200	225	250	275
Miscellaneous		.30	600	675	750	825
Total Controllable Expenses	$33,960	7.18	$ 48,320	$ 50,115	$ 51,910	$ 53,705
Noncontrollable Expenses:						
Rent	$14,923		$ 14,923	$ 14,923	$ 14,923	$ 14,923
Depreciation	2,334		2,334	2,334	2,334	2,334
Casualty Insurance	600		600	600	600	600
Property Taxes	900		900	900	900	900
Total Noncontrollable Expenses	$18,757		$ 18,757	$ 18,757	$ 18,757	$ 18,757
Total Operating Expenses	$52,717	7.18	$ 67,077	$ 68,872	$ 70,667	$ 72,462
Contribution of Store			$ 32,923	$ 43,628	$ 54,333	$ 65,038

Pension and Retirement Expense at sales volumes of $200,000, $225,000, $250,000, and $275,000 as follows:

	Sales Volume			
	$200,000	**$225,000**	**$250,000**	**$275,000**
Fixed costs	$ 2,000	$ 2,000	$ 2,000	$ 2,000
Variable costs				
.005 × $200,000	1,000			
.005 × $225,000		1,125		
.005 × $250,000			1,250	
.005 × $275,000				1,375
Total Pension and Retirement	$ 3,000	$ 3,125	$ 3,250	$ 3,375

In distribution activities, as in manufacturing, a key step in using the flexible budget as a cost control tool is the prompt and regular comparison of actual costs with the budget allowance for the volume attained. For example, Store 28 had sales of $252,000 in 19X9. A comparison of actual results with the flexible budget based on sales of $252,000 is shown on page 669.

The comparison of actual costs with the flexible budget shown on page 669 is for the entire year 19X9. However, making this comparison only on an annual basis would be ineffective in controlling costs because action could not be taken promptly to correct problems. Instead, monthly comparisons of budgeted amounts and actual results are made so that important variances can be investigated at the earliest possible moment. The management of GBS would have taken steps to investigate and correct certain deviations that appear in the comparison. For example, the gross profit on sales is substantially below the amount shown in the flexible budget for sales at this level. There may be logical reasons for this budget variance. For instance, the portion of sales made to beauty salons (which has a lower gross profit than the sales made to retail customers) may be greater than expected when the flexible budget was set up. In any event, a thorough investigation of this variance would be in order. Similarly, the reasons for the variance in store salaries, although favorable, should be determined.

The income statement of Store 36 shows a substantial amount of "cash over," which suggests shortcomings in either the procedures for handling cash or the accounting records.

Break-Even Analysis for Distribution Business

The break-even technique that you learned in Chapter 24 is a familiar tool that is of great value in analyzing distribution activities, especially in making decisions about the operations of sales divisions or segments. For example, if the management of GBS Suppliers prepared a break-even chart for Store 28 at the same time that it prepared the flexible budget given on page 669, the chart would appear as shown on page 670.

GBS SUPPLIERS
Comparisons of Actual Results with Flexible Budget—Store 28
Year Ending December 31, 19X9

	FLEXIBLE BUDGET FOR SALES OF $252,000	ACTUAL	VARIANCE OVER (UNDER)
Sales	$252,000	$252,000	
Cost of Goods Sold	126,000	131,084	$ 5,084
Gross Profit on Sales	$126,000	$120,916	$(5,084)
Operating Expenses			
Controllable Expenses:			
Store Salaries	$ 32,600	$ 30,723	$(1,877)
Payroll Taxes	2,608	2,542	(66)
Employee Insurance	1,452	1,329	(123)
Workers' Compensation			
Insurance	422	396	(26)
Pension and Retirement	3,260	3,072	(188)
Utilities	3,600	3,639	39
Telephone	1,500	1,567	67
Maintenance and Repairs	1,104	1,168	64
Advertising	2,700	2,700	0
Supplies	704	681	(23)
Credit Card Fees	504	357	(147)
Postage	240	204	(36)
Travel and Entertainment	352	282	(70)
Bad Debts	252	258	6
Cash Short or (Over)	-0-	(456)	(456)
Miscellaneous	756	967	211
Total Controllable Expenses	$ 52,054	$ 49,429	$(2,625)
Noncontrollable Expenses:			
Rent	$ 14,923	$ 24,923	$ -0-
Depreciation	2,334	2,334	-0-
Casualty Insurance	600	610	10
Property Taxes	900	912	12
Total Noncontrollable Expenses	$ 18,757	$ 18,779	$ 22
Total Operating Expenses	$ 70,811	$ 68,208	$(2,603)
Contribution of Store	$ 55,189	$ 52,708	$(2,481)

The break-even point for Store 28 can be easily determined, using the information from the flexible budget. The total variable costs are 57.18 percent of sales:

	Percent
Cost of Goods Sold	50.00
Variable Operating Expenses	7.18
Total	57.18

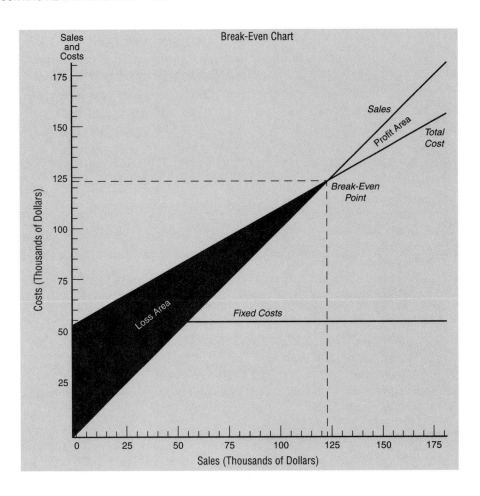

Therefore, the contribution margin is 42.82 percent (100 percent − 57.18 percent). As you learned in Chapter 24, at the break-even point the contribution margin exactly equals fixed costs, shown in the flexible budget on page 667 to be $52,717. If no profit or loss is earned, the fixed costs will equal 42.82 percent of sales. The break-even point in sales is computed to be $123,113:

At break-even, 42.82% of sales = $52,717
Break-even sales   = $52,717 ÷ .4282 = $123,113

At this point you should be able to work Exercises 26–5 to 26–8 and Problems 26–3A to 26–4B.

Setting and Using Standard Costs for Distribution Activities

As you have already learned, many distribution activities are repetitive and are similar to manufacturing operations. The accountant, working with management, can establish and apply standard costs for these activities. For example, suppose that a distribution company has analyzed the operations of its Packing and Shipping Department. The information analyzed, plus the results of a study by a time and motion expert, has indicated that the average time to pack and prepare for shipment 25 pounds of merchandise should be approximately 15 minutes. (Four boxes should be packed each hour.) In preparing the budget for the year 19X9, the following data is used. These figures do not include transportation costs, which can be ignored for the purpose of the illustration.

Total fixed costs for the year including fixed labor costs, $24,000
Variable costs, other than labor, $1 per 25-pound box of merchandise
Labor costs, including payroll taxes and employee benefits, for hourly employees involved in packaging and preparation activities, $15 per hour
Expected amount of merchandise to be packed and shipped during the year, 192,000 pounds
Time required to properly pack one box, 15 minutes (four boxes should be packed for each hour of labor)

The standard cost for packaging and shipping each 25-pound box of product is $7.875, computed as follows:

Number of boxes to be packed, (192,000 lb at 25 lb per box)		7,680 boxes
Standard time required to pack 7,680 boxes, (7,680 boxes at 4 boxes per hr)		1,920 hours
Fixed cost for year		$24,000
Variable costs for year:		
Labor (1,920 hours × $15 per hr)	$28,800	
Other ($1 per box × 7,680 boxes)	7,680	
Total variable costs		36,480
Total Budgeted costs		$60,480
Standard cost of packing and shipping each 25-lb box ($60,480 ÷ 7,680 boxes)		$ 7,875

The standard cost of $7.875 per box consists of the following elements:

Fixed costs ($24,000 ÷ 7,680)	$3.125
Labor costs ($15 per hr ÷ 4 boxes per hr)	3.750
Other	1.000
Total packing and shipping costs per box	$7.875

The standard cost established for this distribution activity can be used in exactly the same way as standard costs are used in manufacturing. For example, suppose that fixed costs were spread equally through each month of the year and that, in March 19X9, 720 boxes were packed and shipped. Costs for the month were:

Fixed costs ($24,000 ÷ 12)	$2,000
Labor and fringe benefits (200 hr × $15.56 per hr)	3,112
Other variable costs	720
Packaging and shipping costs	$5,832

Packing and shipping costs per box ($5,832 ÷ 720 boxes), $8.10 per box

Obviously, management will be concerned about the difference between the standard cost of the 720 boxes packed and the actual cost.

Actual cost $5,832

Standard cost (720 boxes × $7.875 per box)   5,670

Variance $ 162U

The variance can be easily analyzed. Since other variable costs were as budgeted, the variances are found in the fixed costs and the labor costs.

Fixed Costs

Fixed costs can be treated in the same manner as overhead. Applying variance analysis, we can determine any volume variance and any budget variance. There is no budget variance in fixed costs because the actual fixed costs incurred, $2,500, exactly equaled the fixed costs budgeted, $2,500. However, there is a $250 favorable volume variance, computed in the usual way.

Fixed costs budgeted for the production obtained $2,000

Standard fixed costs for production attained

   (720 boxes × $3.125 per box)   2,250

Volume variance $ 250F

There is a $444 unfavorable labor variance:

Actual labor costs $3,144

Standard labor costs (720 boxes × $3.750 per box)   2,700

Total labor variance $ 444U

Using the labor variance analysis method that you learned in Chapter 22, the time or efficiency variance and the labor rate variance can be computed.

The time variance is $300 unfavorable:

Standard hours × standard rate (standard cost) $2,700

Actual hours × standard rate (200 hr × $15 per hr)   3,000

Labor time variance $ 300U

The labor rate variance is $144 unfavorable:

Actual hours × actual rate (actual cost) $3,144

Actual hours × standard rate (200 hr × $15 per hr)   3,000

Labor rate variance $ 144U

At this point you should be able to work Exercises 26–9 and 26–10 and Problems 26–7A and 26–7B.

The total unfavorable labor variance of $444 is thus explained as a $300 unfavorable time variance and a $144 unfavorable labor rate variance. Management would certainly investigate the reason for these variances. It is possible that because production exceeded the number of boxes packed and shipped in the month exceeded the average monthly volume, workers were required to work overtime, resulting in a rate variance. Similarly, part-time workers, who were less efficient, may have led to the rather large labor time variance. Other possible reasons would, of course, be considered and investigated.

SELF-REVIEW

1. Can a flexible budget be prepared for distribution functions? Is so, what basis would be used for measuring variability?
2. Why are comparisons between budgeted amounts and actual costs made on a monthly basis rather than annually?
3. If the percentage of cost of goods sold to sales is known, the percentage of variable operating expenses to sales is known, and fixed costs are known, how can the break-even point be easily calculated?
4. What is the major difference between the calculation of the break-even point for a manufacturing concern and for a merchandising concern?

Answers to Self-Review

1. Flexible budgets can be prepared for distribution activities. Typically, sales are used as the basis for measuring variability.
2. Comparisons between budgeted amounts and actual amounts are done on a monthly basis so that immediate action can be taken when there are significant variances. Waiting until the end of the year to make the comparisons and then taking action would delay, if not defeat, the intended purpose of the analysis.
3. The break-even point is computed by dividing fixed costs by the sum of the percentage of cost of goods sold to sales and the percentage of variable expenses to sales.
4. In a manufacturing concern, the break-even point is determined by dividing the percentage of all variable costs (materials, labor, variable overhead, and variable operating expenses) of sales into the fixed costs. In a merchandising operation, cost of goods sold is substituted for materials, labor, and overhead.

COST ACCOUNTING FOR SERVICE BUSINESSES

The service sector of the economy has grown dramatically since the late 1970s, whereas the manufacturing sector has declined in relative importance. The growth of the service sector is a result of technological changes as well as of the increasing affluence and leisure time of society. Technology has increased the output per labor hour in manufacturing and agriculture, so that a much smaller portion of the labor force is required for those activities. Technology has also led to new products and services. The computer industry and the telecommunications industry are but two service areas that have resulted from the technological revolution, and they have quickly become essential elements of the world's economy.

Technology and increased affluence have also led to rapid growth in other purely service-oriented businesses. For example, the number of firms providing a wide variety of financial services, such as commercial banks, investment banking firms, brokerage firms, financial management companies, credit card companies, and insurance companies, has greatly expanded. Health care facilities, educational institutions, governmental agencies, legal and accounting firms, transportation companies, travel agencies, and financial services institutions are examples of rapidly growing business sectors that provide services rather than manufacture products or buy and sell products. Firms providing "rented" or temporary employees and part-time businesses operated from the home via the Internet and computer hookups are other examples of nonmanufacturing businesses that have proliferated recently.

Accounting fills an important need in service businesses. The requirements of management and other interested parties, such as creditors and stockholders, for general financial information are met by the basic financial reports such as the income statement, the balance sheet, and the funds flow statement. However, when management needs to make business decisions, for example, in setting prices or deciding whether to add or drop product lines, to purchase new equipment, to discontinue a business segment or to extend special prices, the general financial statements are inadequate. Similarly, general financial statements are inadequate for budgetary purposes and for controlling costs.

Cost accounting techniques can be used to provide information that helps in the decision-making process. The concepts and practices of cost accounting for manufacturing businesses, which were discussed in previous chapters of this book, may be applied to service firms as well. Historically, however, cost accounting has been far more widely used in manufacturing operations than in service activities. This is because costs are more easily identified with the physical units of goods manufactured than they are with services provided. Also, in manufacturing operations, one of the chief purposes of cost accounting has been to determine the cost of inventories. In service businesses, there are no inventories. Finally, in businesses offering services rather than physical products, it is often difficult to relate costs to specific activities. In the remainder of this chapter, we will examine how cost accounting techniques can be used in service businesses. It should be kept in mind that there are great differences between the activities and organizational structures of various types of service operations. For example, a hospital, an educational institution, and a law firm are run very differently, but all three are service operations. Thus, the application of cost accounting techniques to service activities in a specific situation may be unique. Nevertheless, the basic principles are the same.

Accumulating Costs

In manufacturing activities, costs are accumulated by jobs or by departments and are then assigned to individual units of product. In service businesses, the center for cost measurement and cost control—and thus for cost accumulation—is also usually the department. Departments are established and organized to provide specific services or perform specific functions. The department manager is responsible for the efficient operations of the department. Thus, if efficiency and effectiveness are to be measured, costs must be accumulated on

BUSINESS
HORIZON

Price Controls in Regulated Industries

Historically, prices charged in certain public service industries, such as electric power, telephone and telegraph, natural gas distribution, railroads, and trucking companies operating in interstate commerce, have been subject to price controls. In many cases, rates charged for services have been fixed by federal, state, or local government agencies, and in other cases, rates set by the company supplying the services have had to be approved by those government agencies. Such regulations have been developed because the industries have become monopolistic. For example, in the past it was not feasible to have more than one electric company providing services in a city because each supplier would need its own generating plants and electric distribution systems. Not only would this lead to tremendous expenditures for facilities, but it would not be feasible to have, for example, four different sets of power lines and poles in each street. The result was that one company was given a franchise in an area, and only that company could supply power in the area. Since there was no competition, a provider of service could, if not controlled, charge any amount it wished for its services, and one would expect that prices would be exorbitant. Thus, government was given the power to set or regulate prices.

The traditional approach to setting and controlling prices was cost-based. The regulated company was permitted to recover its costs, plus an appropriate return on investment. Frequently, there have been arguments about what costs should be recoverable, and it has often been alleged that public utilities did not worry about controlling costs because they were usually entitled to recover the costs incurred. The result was that prices charged were sometimes greater than would be necessary if costs were carefully controlled.

In recent years, there has been a widespread move to "deregulate" public utilities. Almost every state is, under urging from the federal government, moving toward deregulating electric, natural gas, and other utilities. Under this concept, the electric company that owns power lines is required to rent those lines to other electric companies that want to use them. Small, cheap, efficient generators have been developed that produce power at much less cost per kilowatt-hour than older, massive, inefficient plants. It has become possible for the new entrants to sell their power at a much lower rate than that charged by the original utility that built the plant and constructed the distribution lines. Thus one of the major questions is how much the company that owns the lines should be allowed to charge the companies using its lines. Another cost allocation problem!

Yet another important question, going beyond accounting calculations, is what utility companies perceive to be a matter of equity. Consider, for example, electric utility companies. Those companies built massive generating plants on the assumption that they would be permitted to charge enough for the power generated and distributed to recover costs, plus the allowed profit. The capital investment decision analyses were based on the assumption of indefinite monopolistic operating conditions, with the attendant price controls allowing recovery of costs, plus a "reasonable return on

BUSINESS HORIZON

Price Controls in Regulated Industries
(continued)

investment." Permitting other companies with newer, low-cost generating plants to sell electricity to the existing company's customers, using the existing company's distribution lines, would, in the opinion of the existing companies, be unfair. They further argue that the newer companies can pick and choose their customers, selling primarily to large-volume industrial and commercial users, which are the most profitable customers of the existing company. The result would be, they argue, that rates charged smaller customers, especially home owners, would increase. During the next few years you will probably read more about this controversy in the business pages of your local newspaper.

a departmental basis. In addition, appropriate accumulation of costs is necessary so that prices of services may be determined on a logical and timely basis. Some departments are set up solely to provide services to other departments in the firm. These service departments do not earn income directly; instead, they incur costs as they provide services to other departments that do earn income in the firm. Thus, they are often referred to as *cost centers*. **Cost centers** are organizational or functional units for which costs are accumulated. For example, in a commercial bank the building services department provides space, lighting, heat, air conditioning, power, cleaning, and similar services for all the other departments in the bank. The data processing department, the accounting department, the security department, and the mailroom also provide services for the entire bank.

Service departments are designed to provide efficient services at the lowest possible cost. The type of service departments required by a firm depends on the nature of the firm's activities and on its organizational structure.

In every service business, there are departments or other organizational units that provide services directly to customers or clients and earn income. These departments may all be considered sales departments. Since they deal directly with customers and earn income, they are called *profit centers*. **Profit centers** are accounting units to which both revenues and costs are assigned. In a commercial bank, the commercial loan department, consumer loan department, trust department, depositor services department, and credit card department are examples of profit centers. In a public accounting firm, the profit centers might be the tax department, the auditing department, the management services department, and the write-up department (a department that maintains accounting records for clients). In most service businesses, there is a need to determine the profitability of each profit center in order to maximize overall profit and control operations.

In addition, many service companies use what is essentially job order cost accounting to determine costs (and ultimately profit) on specific jobs or contracts. For example, a legal firm almost invariably accumulates costs related to a specific lawsuit or engagement. Some of the costs accumulated for a job may be billed directly to clients. Others may be passed on directly but have to be absorbed by the firm. When the engagement is finished, profit or loss on the job is measured by comparing total billings for the job with the expenses incurred. Job order costing is also used by accounting firms, engineering firms, computer services organizations, repair service organizations, and many others.

If cost accounting techniques are to be used by a service business, procedures must be developed for properly accumulating and classifying costs and revenues. In addition, procedures must be developed for measuring, recording, and reporting the level of activity. Since there are no physical products being manufactured, the service business must find other reasonable measures of effort and accomplishment. For example, within one department, the number of personal visits from customers, the number of telephone calls received from customers, the number of hours worked by employees, and the number of forms completed may be important in measuring activity and in estimating and controlling costs.

Analyzing Costs

In order to prepare budgets, control costs, and evaluate performance, costs must be divided into their fixed and variable components. The process for analyzing cost behavior in a service business is almost identical to that described in Chapter 20 for a manufacturing business. In some cases, the level of activity or volume may be expressed in terms of direct labor hours. In other cases, the activity base may be expressed in some other unit of activity appropriate for the department. For example, in a bank's new deposits department the activity measured may be the number of accounts opened during the period. Similarly, in a hospital, the activity for a nursing floor might be the total number of "room-nights" occupied by patients on the floor. The activity measured in an academic department of a college might be the number of credit hours taught in the department.

Preparing Operating and Flexible Budgets

The operating budget and flexible budgets for a service business are prepared in the same way as for a manufacturing company. A detailed expense budget and profit and loss statement are prepared for each cost center. The departmental budgets are combined into the firm's operating budget. The operating budget, which becomes part of the master budget, reflects the activity level and the resulting revenues and costs expected for the budget period.

For example, suppose that an accounting firm has three profit centers: its auditing, tax, and management consulting departments. The revenue budget for the period is based on an analysis of the revenues from services provided during the previous period and on an estimate of the growth or decline in revenues that will be earned from this service in the future period. An analysis of the number of clients, types of clients, types or services used by each client, and number of professional staff hours required for each client in the past period is the starting point for planning. Adjustments for changes in the rates charged, new services to be provided to existing clients, the addition of new clients, and similar factors are used to modify the figures for the prior year's operations and arrive at the revenue budget for the new period. Based on an analysis of cost behavior in previous periods, and on adjustments for changes in salaries and benefits, for changes in economic conditions such as inflation, and for other anticipated changes, the expense budget can be prepared. The procedures for estimating total fixed costs and total variable costs are identical to those described in Chapter 20 for manufacturing operations.

Although the operating budget offers a basis for planning operations, it does not provide a satisfactory tool for controlling costs. Instead, a service business needs a flexible budget similar to the flexible budget for a manufacturing business, which was explained in Chapter 21. Variable costs that will be incurred during the period depend on the level of activity. If the actual level differs from the activity level used in preparing the operating budget, costs (and profits) will differ from those projected in the operating budget. For example, if the tax department or a public accounting firm prepares an operating budget based on the assumption that it will bill clients for 20,000 hours of professional labor during the year, the budget is valid only if that number of hours is actually used. If 22,000 hours are required, management will want to know the budget allowance for each cost element at a level of 22,000 hours.

In order to be able to measure what costs should be at the actual level of activity, a flexible budget is prepared. The variable costs in the flexible budget are found by multiplying the variable cost per unit of activity for each cost element by the number of units of activity assumed. Again, the procedure followed is almost identical to that used in a manufacturing business.

Using Budgeting Techniques in Making Operating Decisions

Flexible budgeting techniques can be very useful in service business when operating decisions are being made, especially when individual customers or service contracts are involved. For example, consider the case of Business Seminars, Inc., which offers seminars through the United States covering specific business topics in accounting, finance, marketing, management, computer information systems, and contract law. The organization, which has offices in Chicago, offers approximately 200 seminars each year throughout the United States. A seminar in time management has been proposed in Seattle. It is estimated that approximately 20 participants will attend the seminar and will pay a registration fee of $200 per person. The organization hires independent professional people to conduct the seminars. The standard instructor pay is $1,000 per day, and if the seminar is for only one day and is held more than 800 miles from the instructor's home, one-half day's pay, or $500, is provided for travel time. The instructor lives in Houston, Texas. Other costs related to the seminar are:

SELF-REVIEW

1. Why is it generally desirable to have large sales per invoice and large sales per customer?
2. How does a profit center differ from a cost center?
3. What are some factors that have contributed to a great rise in the number of service-type businesses in recent years?
4. Is it possible to use a single base for all types of service businesses in measuring cost variability, preparing flexible budgets, analyzing costs, and so on? Explain.

Answers to Self-Review

1. Many costs related to a sales invoice or to a single sale tend to be fixed. For example, the cost of preparing an invoice for $25 is probably little different from preparing an invoice for $5,000. Similarly, costs such as shipping department costs do not vary directly with the total value or quantity of goods shipped. A large portion of the costs related to shipping are fixed for each shipment made.
2. A profit center represents a unit of the business that has both revenues and expenses, and a cost center has only expenses—no revenues.
3. The growth in the number of service-type industries has resulted in part from the fact that technology has dramatically increased the manufacturing output per hour of labor. Technology has also given rise to a tremendous number of consumer products requiring services. For example, the increases in speed of transportation has spawned huge travel businesses. Communications advancements have particularly given rise to new service organizations. Families with two wage earners have increased the demand for restaurants, laundries, house-cleaning services, and nurseries and preschool facilities.
4. Each type of service business may have some attribute or activity measure that is appropriate for measuring and controlling costs and making budget analyses. It may be necessary and desirable to use a number of different bases for analyzing and controlling costs within a single business. For example, some costs in a hospital might be related to the number of "patient-nights" that rooms were used. On the other hand, costs of the outpatient unit may be best expressed in terms of the number of patients receiving services.

Limousine to and from airport, $22 each way	$ 44.00
Air fare	440.00
Taxi to and from airport	40.00
Hotel, including tax	118.00
Meals	44.00
Telephone	5.00
Tips	5.00

Advertising (cost of preparing and mailing flyer), $2,000
Instructional materials, $20 per participant

Costs of shipping materials, $4 per participant
Lunch for participants, $21 per participant
Coffee breaks, $12 per participant
Projector and screen in hotel, $100
Telephone and postage directly chargeable to seminar, $40

General overhead of the organization is estimated to be 30% of revenues.

A question has been raised as to whether it would be profitable to conduct the seminar. To answer this question, the same techniques that you have learned in previous chapters are used. The principal tool in making the decision is preparation of a budget, which is shown below:

PROPOSED SEATTLE SEMINAR
BUDGET FOR 20 PARTICIPANTS

Revenues (20 × $200)		$ 4,000
Fixed costs:		
Instructor's fee	$1,500	
Instructor's travel and transportation (limo, airline, taxi, hotel, meals, telephone, tips)	696	
Advertising	2,000	
Projector and screen	100	
Telephone and postage	40	
Total fixed costs	$4,336	
Variable costs:		
Instructional materials (20 × $20)	$ 400	
Costs of shipping materials (20 × $4)	80	
Lunches (20 × $21)	420	
Coffee breaks (20 × $5)	120	
Total variable costs	$1,020	
Total costs (other than overhead)		5,356
Estimated loss on seminar (before overhead)		$(1,356)

It is clear that, based on the projections, it would be inadvisable to attempt to conduct the seminar. Not only does the proposed seminar cover no overhead costs, it does not even cover the direct costs resulting from the program. This type of analysis leads management and the accountant to discuss possible courses of actions. Some of the things that might be investigated are obvious:

■ Is there a potential instructor in Seattle who could be hired, eliminating travel costs?
■ Would it be possible to charge more than $200 for the seminar? If so, what amount, and what would be the estimated attendance?
■ Would charging less than $200 increase attendance enough to produce a profit?

- Would it be possible for the instructor to conduct more than one seminar while in Seattle, thus spreading advertising costs and spreading travel costs?
- Is there a potential market for more than 20 participants at the price of $200? If so, how much would have to be spent for advertising to attract enough participants to make the seminar profitable?
- What is the break-even point based on current expenses and revenues per participant?

Obviously, there are other questions reflecting possible solutions that should be investigated before the idea is discarded. Most of the proposed solutions will likely be actions that will result in spreading the instructor's travel costs and advertising costs to other seminars that might be offered or that will involve "tinkering" with the proposed price.

Using Standard Costs

In many service businesses, standard costs are developed for use in controlling costs and in making such decisions as the prices to charge for services. The procedure for developing and applying standard costs are similar to those used in manufacturing businesses. Fixed costs and variable costs (based on a high, but attainable, level of efficiency) are estimated for either the expected or the normal activity level. The standard cost per unit of activity is found by dividing the budgeted costs by the number of activity units budgeted. At the end of the period, the total standard cost (the number of units of activity multiplied by the standard cost per unit of activity) is compared with the total actual cost, and the variance is computed. The variance is then analyzed into its component parts.

It is possible to separate the variances in some items in the same way that you learned in earlier chapters to determine the quantity and price components of variances in materials and labor in manufacturing operations. For example, suppose that in a dry cleaning firm, a standard time of 10 minutes has been developed for pressing men's trousers and the standard labor rate is $9 per hour for pressers. Thus, the standard labor cost of pressing a pair of trousers is $1.50 (10 ÷ 60 × $9). During the month of September 19X9 a total of 3,624 pairs of trousers were pressed, requiring 616 hours of pressing labor at a total cost of $5,698 ($9.25 per hour). The standard labor time for 3,624 pairs of trousers is 604 hours (3,624 × 10 ÷ 60), and the standard cost for the 3,624 pairs of trousers is $5,436 (3,624 × $1.50). Since the actual cost of $5,698 exceeded the standard cost of $5,436 by $262, management wants to know why the $262 variance exists. Using the variance analysis techniques discussed in Chapter 21, an unfavorable labor efficiency variance of $108 and an unfavorable labor rate variance of $300 can be computed.

You will remember from Chapter 22 that the labor efficiency variance is found by comparing the budget allowance for *actual* hours worked with the budget allowance for *standard* hours allowed for the work done. The labor efficiency variance for pants pressed during the month of September 19X9 is $108 unfavorable:

Actual hours (616) × standard rate ($9)	$5,544
Standard hours (604) × standard rate ($9)	5,436
Efficiency variance	$ 108U

You will also recall from Chapter 22 that the labor rate variance is measured by comparing the actual labor costs with what the labor costs would have been for the actual work if the standard rate has been paid. The labor rate variance for September is computed as $154 unfavorable:

Actual hours (616) × standard rate ($9)	$5,544
Actual hours (616) × actual rate ($9.25)	5,698
Rate variance	$ 154U

Thus, the total variance in pressing wages for the month, $262, is seen to be composed of an unfavorable efficiency variance of $108 and an unfavorable rate variance of $154. This information is useful to management in getting costs back under control.

SELF-REVIEW

1. Can flexible budget techniques be used to aid in controlling costs in a service business? Explain.
2. In making a business decision, what consideration must be given to fixed costs?
3. Explain how standard costs can be used in a service business.
4. If standard costs are used in a service business, can the variance between actual costs and standard costs be analyzed into component parts? Explain.

Answers to Self-Review

1. Yes, flexible budget techniques can be used in controlling many costs in a service business. This is true for costs that exhibit a degree of variability with some specific activity measure or costs, such as fixed costs, that are predetermined.
2. For individual decisions, fixed costs can sometimes be ignored because they will exist no matter what decision is made. However, management must keep in mind that fixed costs represent cash outlays or assets consumed, and for the business as a whole these costs must be covered by an excess of revenues over variable costs.
3. Standard costs can be established for any activity for which there is a measurable activity and for which a relationship between costs and the activity can be established. Standard costs are especially helpful in comparing the actual costs with the standard costs of a specific job or contract.
4. The variance between standard costs and actual costs for certain types of costs can be readily computed. For example, in many service concerns it is fairly easy, using the techniques used in manufacturing cost analysis, to determine a labor time variance and a labor rate variance. However, if a cost cannot be readily related to some measurable factor, it may be difficult or impossible to divide the total variance into component parts.

At this point you should be able to work Exercises 26–11 and 26–12 and Problems 26–7A and 26–7B.

PRINCIPLES AND PROCEDURES SUMMARY

- Nonmanufacturing costs have received less attention in cost accounting than have manufacturing costs. With the growing importance of the service sector of the economy, however, since the late 1980s accountants have given far more attention to applying cost accounting concepts to distribution activities and to businesses that render services.
- Many of the techniques used in accounting for manufacturing can be adapted to distribution functions and service businesses.
- The basic concepts of planning, including budgeting, are easily applied to distribution and service activities.
- Such cost control tools as the flexible budget may be used to control distribution costs and other costs in service organizations.
- It is common in distribution activities to prepare income statements for various segments of the business and to prepare vertical analyses, expressing each item as a percentage of net sales to assist in analyzing the controlling costs.
- Analyses of sales activities are especially important because they lead to decisions that could increase the company's profitability. Various measures of the relationship between sales volume and sales activities aid in improving efficiency of distribution functions.
- Flexible budgeting concepts and techniques can readily be applied to many nonmanufacturing activities.
- The concepts of flexible budgeting, break-even analysis, and cost-volume-profit analyses are especially applicable to service concerns and are useful in making operating decisions.
- Standard costs can be established for activities that have some readily measurable activity that has a relation to costs. Variances can be determined and analyzed into component parts.

MANAGERIAL IMPLICATIONS

- Cost accounting principles and procedures are useful to management in planning and controlling not only manufacturing operations but also distribution activities and service businesses.
- Distribution functions are all the activities involved in getting goods sold and delivered to customers.
- Service businesses are businesses such as accounting and law firms that provide services rather than physical products.
- It is more difficult to measure, standardize, and control some distribution costs than it is to measure, standardize, and control manufacturing costs. The accountant must be able to adapt procedures and principles used in accounting for manufacturing operations to the special problems of distribution functions and service businesses.
- Techniques such as percentage-of-sales analysis, comparisons of actual costs with the planning budget and flexible budget, and comparisons of costs and of ratios with those of prior periods can be

used to provide management with data that it can use in operating the business profitably.

■ In distribution activities, the accountant can select activity bases that are meaningful and then analyze costs related to those activity basis—for example, the cost of loading each 100 pounds of product into a truck or the cost of delivering each 100 pounds of merchandise.

■ The key to developing useful techniques for analyzing distribution activities is to be alert and recognize activities that affect costs and then to analyze the unit cost of those activities.

■ Analyses are made for segments of the business as well as for the business as a whole.

■ The concepts and techniques used to prepare budgets, including flexible budgets, for manufacturing operations can also be adapted and applied to both distribution activities and service businesses.

■ Standard costs can be developed for many activities in distribution functions and in service businesses.

■ Other techniques, such as break-even analysis, are especially useful in assisting the management of service organizations.

REVIEW QUESTIONS

1. What are distribution costs?
2. Why is it more difficult to budget some distribution costs than to budget manufacturing costs?
3. What is a percentage-of-sales analysis?
4. Would percentage-of-sales analysis be more useful and reliable when applied to a large segment of a business (for example, a district) or to a smaller segment (for example, the menswear department in a department store)? Why?
5. What is the difference between controllable distribution expenses and noncontrollable distribution expenses?
6. List some possible bases for determining cost variability for each of the following.
   a. Warehouse activities
   b. Billing
   c. Deliveries by truck
7. Why is the flexible budget for a retail store normally based on levels of sales volume?
8. In some companies, advertising is a variable expense for a given year, whereas in other companies, advertising is considered a fixed expense for a given year. Explain why this is possible.
9. Name some cost accounting techniques used in manufacturing businesses that may be applied in the analysis and control of distribution costs.
10. Explain how each of the following calculations is made and how each might be useful in analyzing and controlling distribution costs:
    a. Sales per square foot of floor space

    b. Average sales per salesperson's call

    c. Average number of sales calls per day

    d. Average amount of sales per order

11. What would be the major problem in attempting to measure profit for each group of customers?

12. What are discretionary costs? Give two examples.

13. How often should comparison of actual results with the flexible budget be made? Why?

14. What is the feature that distinguishes a service business from a manufacturing or distribution business?

15. How does a cost center differ from a profit center?

16. What is meant by the comment that many service companies employ what is in effect a job order cost accounting system?

17. Can standard cost analysis be applied in service companies? Explain.

MANAGERIAL DISCUSSION QUESTIONS

1. How does a contribution margin approach help management evaluate the performance of one segment of a distribution business?

2. If a segment has no positive contribution margin, what options should management examine?

3. Disks and Such has made a percentage-of-sales analysis for each of its nine stores. For eight stores, the rent expense is 5.7 percent of net sales, but in one store the rent expense is 9.2 percent of net sales. As controller of the company, you want to know why the rent expense is so high for the one store. What are some possible reasons?

4. The Carlton Company has analyzed its customers by the volume of annual sales. The company has found that the average annual sales to a customer are $12,320. However, annual sales to 3 percent of the customers are under $500 each. What steps should the Carlton Company consider taking with these customers?

5. The Big Sky Company, a wholesale distributor, has recorded an operating loss for each of the past three years. A percentage-of-sales analysis shows that its gross profit is 21.6 percent. The average gross profit rate for the industry is 24.8 percent. What questions should be asked by management about the firm's gross profit rate?

6. The Wide Net Company operates over 100 retail stores. Net income after income taxes is computed for each store. Included in the computation are allocated home office expenses, allocated interest expense, and allocated federal income taxes. Since the store managers are paid a bonus based on the amount of net income, they have protested the inclusion of allocated expenses in the calculation. Comment on this objection.

7. The Capital Corporation employs eight outside sales representatives. In preparing a flexible budget, the accountant based the

sales representatives' travel costs on sales volume. Comment on the use of this basis for budgeting travel costs.

8. The president of KMA corporation has suggested that all district managers be paid a commission based on the profit after controllable expenses. The vice president of sales argues that the commission for district managers should be based on net sales. What is your suggestion? Why?

9. The Philadelphia Hardware Company handles over 2,000 products. The firm is considering whether to drop certain product lines. An analysis of the inventory records shows that 200 products make up less than 1 percent of the total inventory. What other information would be needed to reach a decision in which, if any, products should be discontinued?

10. What use is made of a flexible budget in a service business?

11. You are business manager for a partnership of attorneys. You have analyzed past records and discover that the number of hours spent by support staff (legal assistants, intern law students, and junior staff members) for whom direct billing is not made on any one legal engagement will usually be about 80 percent of the hours spent by attorneys whose time can be billed directly to the clients. You have been asked to develop a plan for charging clients so that the costs of the support people will be included in the charges. Suggest how you might carry out this request; that is, describe a billing system that meets the request.

EXERCISES

EXERCISE 26–1

Prepare a percentage-of-sales analysis to measure efficiency. (Obj. 1). Acton Manufacturing Company operates three retail outlets. During January 19X9, the sales, sales salaries, and electric power costs of the three stores were:

	Store 1	Store 2	Store 3
Net sales	$62,000	$51,000	$48,000
Salaries	9,300	8,600	10,080
Electric power costs	496	774	720

a. Analyze the salaries and electric power costs of each store as a percentage of sales in that store.

b. Ignoring all other factors, compare the efficiency of the three stores with regard to salaries and electric power costs.

c. What additional questions would you ask in trying to evaluate the relative efficiency of the three stores with regard to these two items?

EXERCISE 26–2

Analyze data related to sales activities. (Obj. 2). The Nash Company has analyzed the records of its field sales representatives. Data for two of these employees for the month of September 19X9 are given on page 687.

	Marx	**Hope**
Number of sales calls made	80	80
Net sales	$240,000	$192,000
Number of sales invoices	240	192
Number of customers in area	120	120

Compute the following of each salesperson:
a. Average sales per sales invoice
b. Number of invoices per sales call
c. Average sales per sales call made
d. Percent of potential customers called on during month
e. Average sales per potential customer for month

EXERCISE 26–3 **Analyze data related to sales activities; make operating analyses to aid in increasing efficiency of sales; prepare an expense analysis to aid in controlling costs of distribution. (Objs. 1, 2).** Selected information for the month of May 19X9 for two stores owned by the Halifax Children's Clothing Company is given below.

	Store 1	**Store 2**
Net sales	$128,000	$120,000
Sales salaries and commissions	8,800	7,200
Number of sales transactions	4,205	3,225
Square feet of floor space	1,200	1,600
Number of salespersons	4	3

a. For each store, compute the following:
  (1) Sales volume per square foot of floor space
  (2) Average sales amount per sales transaction
  (3) Average monthly sales per salesperson
  (4) Average number of sales transactions per month per salesperson
  (5) Sales salaries and commissions as a percent of sales
b. Compare these five computations for the two stores.

EXERCISE 26–4 **Analyze sales and expense data to aid in increasing profitability. (Objs. 2, 3).** The Clinton Company has analyzed the sales for each of its salespeople. Data relating to the customers of Alicia Kilmosky are shown below.

Monthly Sales	**Number of Customers**	**Gross Profit Rate (%)**
$1,000 to $1,444	3	26
700 to 999	22	27
500 to 699	20	28
300 to 499	18	29
200 to 299	15	30
Under $200 (average, $120)	12	30

Costs for a salesperson to call on a customer are estimated to be $10 per call plus 2 percent of the sales volume of the order received. Costs for handling an order are estimated to be $3, plus 2 percent of sales.

a. Compute the estimated average contribution or average loss on each order that is under $200.

b. Compute the estimated average contribution or average loss on each order that is between $700 and $999, assuming that the average of such orders is $800.

EXERCISE 26–5 **Prepare a budget for distribution expenses. (Obj. 4).** The Vanacek Company has four sales divisions. It allocates all general office expenses to these divisions. Fixed expenses of $24,000 per month are allocated equally to the divisions. All other expenses are allocated on the basis of sales. For the month of December 19X9, budgeted sales were $800,000 for Division A; $1,000,000 for Division B; $1,200,000 for Division C; and $900,000 for Division D. The total general office expenses for the month of December were budgeted as $39,600.

How much of the budgeted general office expenses would be allocated to each division for the month of December?

EXERCISE 26–6 **Prepare a flexible budget for distribution activities. (Obj. 4).** The Primo Company has average sales per delivery of $200. The Delivery Department's monthly fixed costs are $4,000, and its variable costs are $25 per delivery. Compute the company's budget for delivery expenses at the following sales volumes:
a. $100,000
b. $125,000
c. $160,000

EXERCISE 26–7 **Prepare a flexible budget for distribution activities. (Obj. 4).** The Guynes Company has several stores, all in rented buildings. In preparing the flexible budgets for the stores, the accountant finds that most lease contracts for the stores are similar to the one for Store 84. For Store 84, the monthly rental is 6 percent of net sales for the month, but in no case is the monthly rental to be less than $1,500 per month. What would be the amount of rent at each of the following monthly sales levels?
a. $18,000
b. $24,000
c. $31,000

EXERCISE 26–8 **Prepare a break-even analysis for distribution activity. (Obj. 5).** The Fresh One Retail Fruit Company's gross profit rate is 40 percent of net sales, its variable expenses are 28 percent of net sales, and its monthly fixed costs are $12,000.
a. Compute the company's monthly break-even sales volume.
b. What will the estimated profit or loss be if the sales volume is $68,000 for a month?

EXERCISE 26–9 **Setting standard costs for distribution activities. (Obj. 6).** The accountant for the Genova Company is seeking to develop standard costs for as many of its distribution activities as possible. What activity basis might be used for setting standards for each of the following costs for the company?

a. Deliveries by truck
b. Travel of sales representatives
c. Shipping goods to customers

EXERCISE 26–10

Compute standard cost variances for distribution activities. (Obj. 6). Middleton Company has established a standard labor cost of $1.175 per invoice for its billing activities. This standard cost was based on a detailed study of activities needed to prepare and mail invoices. The standard cost was computed as follows:

Fixed labor costs for the year	$18,000
Variable labor costs:	
6 minutes per invoice at standard labor cost of	
$8 per hour × budgeted volume of 48,000 invoices	38,400
Total labor costs for billing	$56,400

During July 19X9, a total of 3,750 invoices were prepared and mailed, requiring 392 hours of variable labor. Total labor costs were $4,636.40, including fixed labor costs of $1,500.

a. Compute the total labor cost variance for the billing activities for July.
b. Compute the volume variance and budget variance for fixed labor costs.
c. Compute the time variance and the rate variance for variable labor costs.

EXERCISE 26–11

Prepare a flexible budget for a service business. (Obj. 7). The chief accountant for First Gas Utility is attempting to develop a flexible budget for the company's customer service department. One division of that department is the cashiering function, which exists because some customers bring their payments to the company's office each month. The company employs four cashiers. The costs of the cash receipts function and the number of persons serviced for each of four months, June through September, are given below.

Month	Number of Customers	Operating Costs
June	5,280	$6,584
July	5,700	6,710
August	6,000	6,800
September	4,920	6,476

a. Based on this information, what is the amount of fixed costs of the cashiering function?
b. What would be the budget allowance for 4,500 customers?

EXERCISE 26–12

Use standard costs for a service business. (Obj. 8). Portugal Engineering Company has developed standard costs for its electrical installations department. The company bids on electrical installation jobs. Its standard cost per hour for engineers is $40. The company's bid on an installation project for National Chemical Company, for which it estimated that the job would require, 5,000 hours, was accepted.

The job actually required 4,600 hours, and the total engineering salaries and wages were $195,500.

a. What is the total variance between actual and standard engineering salaries and wages?

b. Compute the engineering salaries and wages rate variance.

c. Compute the engineering salaries and wages time variance.

PROBLEMS

PROBLEM 26–1A

Prepare a percentage-of-sales analysis. (Obj. 1). Gift Outlets, Inc. operates three small gift stores. A monthly income statement is prepared for each store. This statement shows both the direct operating expenses of the stores and the allocated indirect expenses. The income statements of the three stores for March 19X9 are shown below.

	Store 1	Store 2	Store 3
Net Sales	$120,000	$160,000	$88,000
Cost of Goods Sold	62,000	91,000	45,000
Gross Profit on Sales	$ 58,000	$ 69,000	$43,000
Direct Expenses:			
Salaries and Commissions	$ 24,000	$ 28,400	$24,400
Payroll Benefits and Taxes	6,000	7,000	5,100
Delivery Fees	1,300	1,480	1,200
Advertising	2,240	2,360	2,240
Credit Card Fees	1,660	2,200	1,140
Supplies	1,240	1,320	1,160
Rent	2,100	2,200	1,600
Utilities	560	950	625
Repairs and Maintenance	300	160	325
Property Taxes	250	320	250
Depreciation	2,000	2,000	1,140
Miscellaneous	1,400	1,600	1,130
Total Direct Expenses	$ 43,050	$ 49,990	$40,310
Contribution After Direct Expenses	$ 14,950	$ 19,010	$ 2,690
Indirect Expenses:			
Purchasing	$ 2,400	$ 3,200	$ 1,780
General and Administrative	4,800	6,400	3,920
Interest	800	1,000	800
Total Indirect Expenses	$ 8,000	$ 10,600	$ 6,500
Net Income (or Loss) for Month	$ 6,950	$ 8,410	($ 3,810)

INSTRUCTIONS

1. For each store, prepare an analysis expressing each item on the income statement as a percent of net sales. Round the percents to 1 decimal place.

2. Compare the percentages for the three stores. Note the significant differences and make any comments about the differences that you believe are appropriate.

3. What types of questions would management ask about each of the differences listed in Instruction 2?

PROBLEM 26–2A

Make operating analyses to aid in increasing efficiency of sales; prepare an expense analysis to aid in controlling costs of distribution. (Objs. 1, 2). Selected information for the month of June 19X9 for two stores owned by the Gentleman's Tie Company is given below.

	Store 18	Store 22
Net Sales	$128,000	$120,000
Rent Expense	2,400	2,480
Sales Salaries and Commissions	8,800	7,200
Number of sales transactions	4,205	3,225
Square feet of floor space	1,200	1,600
Number of salespersons	4	3

INSTRUCTIONS

1. For each store, compute the following:
   a. Sales volume per square foot of floor space
   b. Average sales amount per sales transaction
   c. Average monthly sales per salesperson
   d. Average number of sales transactions per month per salesperson
   e. Rent expense as a percent of sales
   f. Rent expense per square foot of floor space
   g. Sales salaries and commissions as a percent of sales
   h. Sales salaries and commissions per salesperson
2. Compare these eight computations for the two stores. Comment on the relative utilization of space and personnel by the two stores and on relative profitability.

PROBLEM 26–3A

Prepare a monthly flexible budget for distribution activities. (Obj. 4). The South Mississippi Company has a gross profit of 45 percent of net sales. After analyzing its operating expenses, the firm determined that its fixed monthly expenses and its variable expenses (expressed as a percent of net sales) are as shown below.

	Fixed Expenses (Monthly)	Variable Expenses (Percent of Net Sales)
Sales Salaries	$4,000	2.0
Warehouse Salaries	1,200	-0-
Office Salaries	2,600	-0-
Payroll Taxes	880	0.2
Advertising	600	-0-
Delivery	1,200	1.0
Supplies	100	0.5
Depreciation	500	-0-
Rent	2,500	-0-
Utilities	450	-0-
Repairs and Maintenance	100	-0-
Property Taxes	150	-0-
Miscellaneous	300	1.0

INSTRUCTIONS

Prepare a monthly flexible budget for the company at sales levels of $30,000, $40,000, and $50,000.

PROBLEM 26–4A **Prepare a break-even analysis for a distribution business.** **(Obj. 5).** Use the data given for the South Mississippi Company in Problem 26-3A to carry out the following instructions.

INSTRUCTIONS
1. Compute the monthly sales volume at the break-even point for the South Mississippi Company.
2. Prepare a monthly break-even chart.
3. What sales volume would be required to earn a net income of $10,000 for the month?
4. The sales manager of the South Mississippi Company estimates that if the average sales price of merchandise were to be decreased by 4 percent, the number of units sold could be increased by 10 percent.
   a. What effect would this have on the break-even point?
   b. What would be the new break-even point?

PROBLEM 26–5A **Compute standard cost variances for distribution activities; measure and analyze variances.** **(Obj. 6).** Wilberforce Company has established a standard cost of $2 per hundred pounds (cwt.) of merchandise received in its merchandise receiving section. The standard cost was based on a detailed study of the activities in unloading merchandise, opening it, and storing it in the appropriate location in the storeroom. A summary of the standard cost for handling each cwt. follows:

Fixed costs (including fixed labor costs)	$ 48,000
Variable costs:	
Variable labor (including taxes and fringe benefits):	
5 minutes per cwt. at standard cost of	
$12 per hour × budgeted volume of 60,000 cwt.	60,000
Other variable costs (5,000 hours × $2.40 per hour)	12,000
Total cost	$120,000

Standard cost per cwt. ($120,000 ÷ 60,000 cwt.), $2
Standard cost per labor hour, $24

During March 19X9, a total of 4,800 cwt. of merchandise was handled, requiring 390 hours of labor. The total cost of variable labor, taxes, and fringe benefits was $4,758. Fixed costs were $4,000, and other variable costs were $936.

INSTRUCTIONS
1. Compute the total cost variance for the merchandise receiving section for March.
2. Compute the total labor variance for March.
3. Analyze the labor variance into a time variance and a rate variance.
4. Compute the total variance for Other variable costs. Analyze this variance into two component parts:
   a. An efficiency variance
   b. A spending variance

PROBLEM 26–6A **Prepare a flexible budget and a break-even analysis for a service business.** **(Obj. 7).** Top Line Consultants, Inc., is a business consulting firm. During the year 19X9, the firm earned a net income of

$136,000. This amount was more than the net income projected in the firm's operating budget. Management believes that this difference is largely due to the fact that 6,200 billable hours were worked, whereas the budget was for 6,000 billable hours. (*Billable hours* are the hours for which clients are charged. Some hours worked by the firm's staff are not billable because the staff members are not involved in a consulting job for a client.) The firm's managing partner has asked you to prepare a comparison of the actual results and the results that would have been anticipated in a flexible budget based on 6,200 billable hours, the actual number of billable hours for the year.

	Income Statement (Actual)	Operating Budget
Billable Hours	6,200	6,000
Revenues From Charges to Clients	$705,000	$660,000
Fixed Professional Salaries	$210,000	$200,000
Variable Professional Salaries	108,000	120,000
Other Fixed Expenses	100,000	100,000
Other Variable Expenses	151,000	134,000
Total Expenses	$569,000	$554,000
Net Income for Year	$136,000	$106,000

INSTRUCTIONS

1. Prepare a three-column statement showing the actual income statement figures, the flexible budget based on actual billable hours, and the variance between each item.
2. Analyze the variance between actual amounts and amounts based on actual billable hours for each revenue and expense. Make whatever comments you think are appropriate about each variance.
3. Compute the firm's break-even point.

PROBLEM 26–7A

Develop and apply standard cost analysis in a service company. (Obj. 7). Fashion Tailors operates an alteration service for the men's clothing departments of several local department stores and employs several alterations tailors. Its four tailors alter trousers. When jackets are received for alterations, they are sent to another company that performs the alterations. Fashion has become concerned about cost control and has asked you to develop a system of cost control using standard costing. Your research of the company's operations indicates that it usually takes about 15 minutes to alter either the waistband or the legs of trousers. Based on the examination and adjustments for known or expected cost changes, you have established the following standard monthly data:

Fixed overhead per month	$1,512.00
Variable overhead per hour of labor	1.00
Labor rate per hour (including taxes)	8.10
Number of trousers altered	2,016
Total labor hours	504

In March 19X9, the first month in which your standard cost system was installed, actual results were:

Fixed overhead costs incurred	$1,500.00
Variable overhead costs	580.00
Labor costs	3,864.00
Number of trousers altered	1,824
Labor hours	480

INSTRUCTIONS Round all answers to the nearest whole dollar.

1. Compute the standard labor cost per pair of trousers altered.
2. Compute the total labor variance for the month of March.
3. Compute the labor rate variance and time variance.
4. Compute the total variable overhead variance.
5. Compute the variable overhead spending and efficiency variances.

ALTERNATE PROBLEMS

PROBLEM 26–1B **Prepare a percentage-of-sales analysis. (Obj. 1).** College Sound Stores, operates two retail stores selling CDs, tapes, and other electronic sound supplies. The company delivers large orders. A monthly income statement is prepared for each store. This statement reflects both the direct operating expenses of the stores and the allocated indirect expenses. The income statements for May 19X9 are shown below.

	Store 1	Store 2
Net Sales	$120,000	$185,000
Cost of Goods Sold	75,000	123,600
Gross Profit on Sales	$ 45,000	$ 71,400
Direct Expenses:		
Salaries and Commissions	$ 12,000	$ 14,800
Payroll Taxes and Benefits	1,800	2,175
Delivery Fees	3,000	2,400
Advertising	900	870
Credit Card Fees	840	930
Supplies	1,050	1,350
Rent	5,400	6,300
Utilities	1,050	1,440
Repairs and Maintenance	660	270
Property Taxes	600	630
Depreciation	1,800	2,250
Auto and Truck	1,500	2,400
Miscellaneous	2,400	3,000
Total Direct Expenses	$ 33,000	$ 38,415
Contribution After Direct Expenses	$ 12,000	$ 32,985
Indirect Expenses		
Purchasing	$ 1,800	$ 2,400

General and Administrative	7,200	7,800
Interest	2,400	3,000
Total Indirect Expenses	$ 8,400	$ 13,200
Net Income for Month	$ 600	$ 19,785

INSTRUCTIONS

1. Prepare an analysis for each store expressing each item on the income statement as a percent of net sales. Round the percents to 1 decimal place.
2. Compare the percentages for the two stores. Note the significant differences and make any comments about the differences that you believe are appropriate.
3. What types of questions would management ask about each of the differences listed in Instruction 2?

PROBLEM 26-2B

Make operating analyses to aid in increasing efficiency of sales; prepare an expense analysis to aid in controlling costs of distribution. (Objs. 2, 3). Selected information for the month of June 19X9 for two shirt stores owned by the Delta Shirt Company is given below.

	Store 4	Store 12
Net Sales	$84,000	$117,600
Rent Expense	2,880	3,304
Sales Salaries and Commissions	7,200	5,799
Number of sales transactions	2,400	2,800
Square feet of floor space	1,600	2,100
Number of salespersons	4	3

INSTRUCTIONS

1. For each store, compute the following:
   a. Sales volume per square foot of floor space
   b. Average sales amount per sales transaction
   c. Average monthly sales per salesperson
   d. Average number of sales transactions per month per salesperson
   e. Rent expense as a percent of sales
   f. Rent expense per square foot of floor space
   g. Sales salaries and commissions as a percent of sales
   h. Sales salaries and commissions per salesperson
2. Compare these eight computations for the two stores. Comment on the relative utilization of space and personnel by the two stores and on relative profitability.

PROBLEM 26-3B

Prepare a monthly flexible budget for distribution activities. (Obj. 4). Sports Wear Express has a gross profit of 30 percent of net sales. The firm has analyzed its fixed expenses and its variable expenses (expressed as a percent of net sales) as shown below.

	Fixed Expenses (Monthly)	**Variable Expenses (Percent of Net Sales)**
Sales Salaries	$14,000	1.5
Delivery Salaries	5,200	2.0
Other Salaries	6,800	-0-

Payroll Taxes	2,000	.2
Advertising	1,200	-0-
Supplies	300	.1
Depreciation	600	-0-
Rent	3,000	-0-
Utilities	700	-0-
Repairs and Maintenance	200	-0-
Property Taxes	300	-0-
Auto and Truck	600	.5
Miscellaneous	820	1.2

INSTRUCTIONS Prepare a monthly flexible budget for the company at sales levels of $100,000, $150,000, and $180,000.

PROBLEM 26–4B **Prepare a break-even analysis for a distribution business. (Obj. 5).** Use the data given for Sports Wear Express in Problem 26-3B to carry out the following instructions.

1. Compute the monthly sales volume at the break-even point for Sports Wear Express.
2. Prepare a monthly break-even chart.
3. What sales volume would be required to earn a net income of $10,000 for the month?
4. The sales manager of Sports Wear Express estimates that if the average sales price of merchandise were to be decreased by 2 percent, the number of units sold could be increased by 8 percent.
   a. What effect would this have on the break-even point?
   b. What would be the new break-even point?

PROBLEM 26–5B **Compute standard cost variances for distribution activities; measure and analyze variances. (Obj. 6).** The Fourth of July Company has established a standard cost of $3.44 per hundred pounds (cwt.) of product shipped by its shipping department. The standard cost was based on a detailed study of the activities of unloading merchandise, opening it, and storing it in the appropriate location in the storeroom. A summary of the standard cost for handling each cwt. follows:

Fixed costs (including fixed labor costs)	$ 36,000
Variable costs:	
Variable labor (including taxes and fringe benefits):	
8 minutes per cwt. at standard cost of	
$15 per hour × budgeted volume of 45,000 cwt.	90,000
Other variable costs (6,000 hours × $4.80 per hour)	28,800
Total cost	$154,800

Cost per cwt. ($154,800 ÷ 45,000 cwt.), $3.44
Cost per labor hour, $154,800 ÷ (45,000 cwt. ÷ 7.5 cwt. per hr), $25.80

During March 19X9, a total of 4,500 cwt. of merchandise was handled, requiring 620 hours of labor. The total cost of variable labor, taxes, and fringe benefits was $8,866. Fixed costs were $3,000, and other variable costs were $3,038.

INSTRUCTIONS

1. Compute the total cost variance for the shipping department for March.
2. Compute the total labor variance for March.
3. Analyze the labor variance into a time variance and a rate variance.
4. Compute the total variance for Other variable costs. Analyze this variance into two component parts: an efficiency variance and a spending variance.

PROBLEM 26–6B

Prepare a flexible budget and a break-even analysis for a service business. (Obj. 7). Robinson and Associates is a public accounting firm. Its auditing department earned a net income (contribution) of $603,000 during 19X9. This amount was less than the net income predicted in the firm's operating budget (shown below) even though the number of billable hours for the year exceeded the budgeted number. (*Billable hour* are the hours for which clients are charged. Some hours worked by the firm's staff are not billable because the staff members are not involved in an audit job for a client.) The department's managing partner has asked you to prepare a comparison of the actual results and the results that would have been anticipated in a flexible budget based on 48,000 billable hours, the actual number of billable hours for the year.

	Income Statement (Actual)	Operating Budget
Billable Hours	48,000	42,000
Revenues from Charges to Clients	$3,000,000	$2,730,000
Fixed Professional Salaries	$ 520,000	$ 500,000
Variable Professional Salaries	1,070,000	900,000
Other Fixed Expenses	420,000	420,000
Other Variable Expenses	387,000	273,000
Total Departmental Expenses	$2,397,000	$2,093,000
Departmental Contributions	$ 603,000	$ 637,000

INSTRUCTIONS

1. Prepare a three-column statement showing the actual income statement figures, the flexible budget based on actual billable hours, and the variance between each item.
2. Analyze the variance between actual amounts and amounts based on actual billable hours for each revenue and expense. Make whatever comments you think are appropriate about each variance.
3. Compute the firm's break-even point.

PROBLEM 26–7B

Develop and apply standard cost analysis in a service company. (Obj. 7). Speed Delivery Services operates a small parcel delivery service in Memphis, Tennessee. You have been asked to develop standard costs for the operation. Clients may telephone or fax Speed Delivery Services to arrange for individual deliveries, but the company also operates routine daily deliveries for many clients. The company has become concerned about cost control and has asked you to develop a system of cost control using standard costing. Your research indicates that all parcels are approximately the same size and weight and that size and weight have negligible effects on costs. Your research also indicates that most deliveries require about the same amount of time, usually about 45 minutes, and that drivers typically take 15 minutes to get from one delivery to the next. You have decided to develop standard costs based on average monthly costs of the past 12 months, adjusted for known and projected cost changes. Based on the examination and adjustments, you have established the following monthly data:

Fixed overhead per month	$8,000.00
Variable overhead per hour of labor	3.00
Labor rate per hour (including taxes)	8.00
Number of deliveries made	4,000
Total labor hours (labor costs are variable)	4,000

In January 19X9, the first month in which your standard cost system was installed, actual results were:

Fixed overhead costs incurred	$ 8,200.00
Variable overhead costs	10,600.00
Labor costs	29,322.00
Labor hours	3,620
Number of deliveries made	3,600

INSTRUCTIONS

1. Compute the standard delivery cost per delivery.
2. Compute that total labor variance for the month of January.
3. Compute the labor rate variance and time variance.
4. Compute the total variable overhead variance.
5. Compute the variable overhead spending and efficiency variances.

MANAGERIAL DECISION CASES

Case 26–1. The Best by Mail Company is a mail-order house. During the year it sends catalogs to several hundred thousand customers who order the company's specialty products. The Best by Mail Company pays delivery costs on all products sold. Consumers may either send a cash payment (by personal check) with their orders (in which case they are entitled to take a discount of 4 percent of the sales price), or they may use credit cards for charges. The company pays an average of 3 percent of the sales amount to credit card companies on all card purchases. Approximately 50 percent of all orders are accompanied by a cash payment.

The company's profits have declined in recent years. The controller argues that one reason for the decrease in profits is that there has been a large growth in the number of customers ordering small quantities of merchandise. Over 20,000 orders of less than $10 each have been received in each of the past two years. These small orders represent about 20 percent of the total number of invoices for the year and about 8 percent of the total dollar volume of sales. The controller has suggested that one of three steps be taken:

1. Accept no order for less than $10.
2. Add a handling charge of $1 to all orders for less than $10.
3. Require a cash payment on all orders and eliminate the discount for cash payments.

The controller also submitted the following information, on which he based his recommendations:

Cost of order and invoice forms for each shipment	$ .20
Labor costs to process orders and invoices (15 min)	1.50
Accounts receivable processing (6 min)	.60
Postage for billing	.20
Other billing costs	.30
Minimum cost to remove merchandise from shelves, package items, and prepare them for shipment	1.00
Supplies for shipment	.30
Minimum postage for shipment	.55
Gross profit rate	50 percent

1. Assuming that 20,000 small orders are involved and that the average of each order is $8, estimate the effect on the firm's profit of each of the controller's suggested courses of action. (Make your estimates as accurate as you can from the available information.)
2. What other factors must be considered in making a decision?
3. What is your recommended course of action? Why?

Case 26–2. The MedCenter Group operates a general hospital but rents space and beds to separate entities for specialized areas such as pediatrics, maternity, and psychiatry. The medical center charges each separate entity for common services to its patients such as meals and laundry and for administrative services such as billing and collections. All uncollectible accounts are charged directly to the entity. Space and bed rentals are fixed for the year.

During the entire year ended June 30, 19X8, the Pediatrics Department at the MedCenter hospital charged each patient an average of $480 per day, had a capacity of 60 beds, operated 24 hours per day for 365 days, and had revenue of $9,104,000.

Expenses charged by the medical center to the Pediatrics Department for the year ended June 30, 19X8, were as follows:

	Amount Allocated on Basis of	
	Patient Days	**Bed Capacity**
Dietary	$ 343,616	
Janitorial		$ 102,400
Laundry	224,000	
Laboratory, other than direct charges to patients	382,400	
Pharmacy	270,400	

Repairs and maintenance	41,600	57,120
General administrative services		1,054,080
Rent		2,202,560
Billing and Collections	320,000	
Uncollectible accounts expense	376,000	
Other	144,384	207,840
	$2,102,400	$3,624,000

The only personnel directly employed by the Pediatrics Department are supervising nurses, nurses, and aides. The medical center has minimum personnel requirements based on total annual patient days. These requirements, beginning at the minimum expected level of operation, follow:

Annual Patient Days	Aides	Nurses	Supervising Nurses
10,000–14,000	21	11	4
14,001–17,000	22	12	4
17,001–23,725	22	13	4
23,726–25,550	25	14	5
25,551–37,375	26	14	5
27,376–29,200	29	16	6

The staffing levels represent full-time equivalents, and it should be assumed that the Pediatrics Department always employs only the minimum number of required full-time equivalent personnel.

Annual salaries (including payroll taxes and fringe benefits) for each class of employee follow: supervising nurses, $72,000; nurses, $52,000; and aides, $20,000. Salary expense for the year ended June 30, 19X8, for supervising nurses, nurses, and aides was $288,000, $676,000, and $440,000, respectively.

The Pediatrics Department operated at 100 percent capacity during 111 days for the year. It is estimated that during 90 of these capacity days, the demand averaged 17 patients more than capacity and even went as high as 20 patients more on some days. The medical center has an additional 20 beds available for rent for the year ending June 30, 19X9.

INSTRUCTIONS

1. Calculate the *minimum* number of patient days required for the Pediatrics Department to break even for the year ending June 30, 19X9, if the additional 20 beds are not rented. Patient demand is unknown, but assume that revenue per patient day, cost per patient day, cost per bed, and employee salary rates will remain the same as for the year ended June 30, 19X8.

2. Assuming that patient demand, revenue per patient day, cost per patient day, cost per bed, and employee salary rates for the year ending June 30, 19X9, remain the same as for the year ended June 30, 19X8, should the Pediatrics Department rent the additional 20 beds? Show the annual gain or loss from the additional beds.

Decision Making—Capital Investment Decisions

In Chapter 25 you learned the important factors to be considered in choosing cost information to be used in making operating decisions. The operating decisions you studied in that chapter related to product costs and sales. Among the decisions you studied were: (1) to add or discontinue a product, (2) to purchase or manufacture a part, (3) to process a product further, and (4) to accept a special order for a product at a reduced price. In all those situations in Chapter 25, it was assumed that no additional equipment or other assets would have to be acquired and that none would have to be replaced. In this chapter, you will learn the fundamentals of making long-term decisions involving the investment of funds in capital assets. **Capital assets** are productive assets such as machinery, equipment, buildings, and land that have a life of more than one year. The costs incurred to purchase capital assets are referred to as **capital expenditures.** The analysis of proposed capital expenditures is an extension of the decision-making process you learned in Chapter 25. The capital expenditures budget is a necessary part of a company's master budget.

OBJECTIVES

1. Evaluate capital expenditure proposals using the accounting rate of return on investment method.
2. Evaluate capital expenditure proposals using the payback period method.
3. Use a "present value of $1" table to compute the present value of a future cash flow.
4. Compute the present value of a proposed capital expenditure using a "present value of $1" table.
5. Compute the present value of a proposed capital expenditure using a "present value of an annuity of $1" table, where appropriate.
6. Compute the net present value of a capital expenditure.
7. Evaluate capital expenditure proposals using the discounted benefit-cost index.
8. Estimate the time-adjusted rate of return (discounted rate of return) from future cash flows from a proposed capital expenditure.
9. Properly consider the impact of income taxes in evaluating capital investment proposals.

NEW TERMS

Accounting rate of return on investment (p. 705)
Capital assets (p. 701)
Capital expenditures (p. 701)
Discounted benefit-cost index (p. 721)
Interpolation (p. 722)
Modified accelerated cost-recovery system (MACRS) (p. 708)
Net present value (p. 720)
Payback period (p. 713)
Present value of a future amount (p. 713)
Present value of an annuity (p. 720)
Present value of future cash flows (p. 716)
Tax shield (p. 725)
Time-adjusted rate of return method or discounted rate of return method (p. 721)

THE NATURE OF CAPITAL EXPENDITURES

Capital expenditures for machinery, equipment, buildings, and land involve long-range commitments of funds to acquire assets to produce future benefits. Capital expenditures usually involve large cash outlays at the time the asset is acquired. The outlays may be financed from working capital generated by operations, through funds obtained by issuing capital stock, or by taking on long-term obligations such as mortgages and other loans. Acquisitions of capital assets represent long-term commitments because working capital is restored only gradually as the asset acquired is used to create revenue or reduce costs over a period of years.

Because capital expenditures are long-term commitments, it is difficult to reverse the decision once a capital outlay has been authorized. Usually it is difficult or impractical for the business to sell its capital assets at will. The capital outlay becomes a sunk cost that can be recovered only through use of the asset over a long period of time. Extreme care must therefore be taken to avoid incorrect capital asset acquisition decisions.

In making decisions to invest in long-term assets, there are two major considerations—the effect on profitability and the effect on cash flow. Obviously, profitability and cash flows are closely related. In the long run, the total profit from a capital asset acquisition should equal the total net cash flows resulting from acquiring and using the asset. However, the timing of some of the important factors affecting net income (revenues and expenses) and the factors affecting cash flows (cash outflows and cash inflows) differs. For example, the expenditure for an asset affects net income in the following ways:

1. The asset acquisition has no impact on net income at the time of acquisition.
2. In subsequent years, the asset's acquisition cost is charged to expense through depreciation.
3. Because depreciation is deducted for tax purposes, taxable income is reduced by the depreciation charge. This reduces income taxes, which results in higher after-tax net income.

On the other hand, the asset purchase has the following impact on cash flows:

1. The expenditure for the asset's acquisition is a cash outflow in the year the expenditure is made.
2. Depreciation for accounting purposes is not a cash expenditure and has no direct effect on cash flows.
3. Depreciation is deductible for tax purposes. Depreciation deducted on the tax return reduces taxable income. This reduces income taxes, which results in higher net cash inflows. (Note that this is the same as the impact on accounting net income.)

In estimating the profit to be obtained from a capital expenditure and the cash inflows and outflows related to the asset, predictions must be made for several years in advance. Revenue that may be produced and expenses that may be incurred as the result of the capital expenditure must therefore be considered in long-range terms. However, the outlay at the time the asset is acquired is an expenditure "today," and there is usually little uncertainty about the amount.

CAPITAL EXPENDITURE ANALYSIS

Several factors should be considered, and guidelines established, for evaluating capital expenditure proposals.

- Proposed outlays should be classified according to the nature of the project, with certain classifications having prior claim for available investment funds.
- Guidelines should be developed to reflect management's goals as to minimum cash flows from a project, maximum time for recovery of invested funds, and minimum profitability requirements.
- Proposed expenditures should be analyzed and ranked, with the amount of funds available for capital outlays setting a limit on total expenditures.

Let us take a closer look at these guidelines and how they affect investment decisions.

Classification of Capital Expenditures

To evaluate proposed outlays more effectively, management customarily requires that proposals be classified according to their nature. One such classification system follows:

Type 1: Projects to meet legal or safety requirements. These have top priority because they are unavoidable if the company is to avoid penalties and even to stay in business.

Type 2: Projects to replace equipment. These are often necessary to sustain operations.

Type 3: Projects to expand facilities.

Type 4: Projects to improve existing products or to add new products.

These categories are not mutually exclusive; some projects may belong in more than one group. For example, local or state laws requiring pollution controls may make it necessary to replace old equipment that emits fumes. The replacement of this equipment is both a Type 1 and a Type 2 project. Similarly, the replacement of a machine with one of higher capacity would be both a Type 2 and a Type 3 project. The classification system, however, provides a basis for setting guidelines.

Profitability and Cash Flow Guidelines

Minimum profitability guidelines also vary with the type of project. The more speculative the nature of the project, the higher the minimum acceptable return will be to allow for the risk involved. In the case of proposals to meet legal or safety requirements, profitability may not be a consideration. In such cases, comparisons of alternative means of meeting specified requirements concentrate on minimizing costs.

Other factors affect the minimum return expected on a project. If available funds are to be used, the opportunity cost concept described in Chapter 25 is used. In this case, the opportunity cost would be the alternative use of the funds. As a minimum, the return on the proposed expenditure should be greater than the interest that could be earned by investing the funds in risk-free government securities. Returns on investment are frequently computed on the basis of both profitability and the rate of return reflecting cash flows resulting from the investment, both of which are discussed subsequently in this chapter.

Recovery Guidelines

Management may specify the maximum period of time it expects for the cash flows from an asset to recover the asset's cost. Generally, a shorter recovery period is preferable to a longer one. For example, if the net cash flow from one project will provide for cost recovery in 3 years, whereas it will take 15 years for the net cash flow from another project to recover costs, the second project will have an adverse affect on the company's liquidity for a longer period. The period of time required to recover costs will clearly vary with the type of investment. For example, it will take much longer to recover funds from an investment in a new steel plant than it will to generate cash flows to recover the cost of a personal computer.

Availability of Funds

Proposed capital outlays are normally presented and evaluated at the time the annual budget is being prepared. However, emergencies, such as equipment breakdowns and fire losses, may result in capital expenditure proposals at other times during the year.

As part of the annual budget process, management may identify a specific sum of money available for capital outlays during the coming year. A ranking of proposals is made from which management selects the projects to be funded. When management decides to authorize proposals in excess of currently available funds or when unforeseen events result in new proposals occurring during the year, the method of financing these expenditures must be carefully decided. The effects of the financing method on the short-term and long-term financial condition of the business must be considered.

CAPITAL EXPENDITURE EVALUATION TECHNIQUES

Various techniques are used, either separately or together, in the evaluation process. Each technique provides a measure of some aspect of the proposal. This measure may be compared with previously established guidelines as well as with alternative proposals. Evaluation techniques may be placed in one of two broad categories: (1) techniques centering on expected profitability of the proposed project or (2) techniques centering on expected net cash flows from the project. Over the life of a project, the ultimate total profit and the ultimate net cash flows will be the same. As we will see, however, the profit or loss for any specific month or year may be greatly different from the net

SELF-REVIEW

1. What are capital assets?
2. Why do proposed investments that are necessary to meet legal or safety requirements have top priority among capital investment proposals?
3. How does the effect on net profit of a cash outlay to acquire a capital asset differ from its effect on cash flows?
4. In general, would management prefer an investment that requires a short or a long period before the investment is recovered from cash flows? Why?

Answers to Self-Review

1. Capital assets are productive assets such as machinery, equipment, buildings, and land that have a life of more than one year.
2. If capital expenditures related to safety or legal requirements are not made, the business may be closed or subjected to fines and penalties.
3. The purchase price of a new asset represents an immediate cash outlay affecting current cash flow. However, the cost of a new asset affects net income during the life of the asset through depreciation charges.
4. In general, management prefers a shorter payback period because there is less risk in short-term ventures than in long-term ventures. Also, there is less impact on a company's liquidity from assets that will have a quick payout because a short payout period means that the amounts tied up in capital assets will be converted into working capital more quickly.

cash flow that month. A commonly used evaluation technique involving profitability is the accounting rate of return computation. Among the more widely used methods based on cash flows are the payback period, the time-adjusted rate of return on investment, the net present value, and the discounted benefit-cost index method. Each of these methods is defined and explained in this chapter.

EVALUATION TECHNIQUES FOCUSING ON PROFITABILITY

Capital asset acquisitions are almost always evaluated on the basis of profitability. Typically, the **accounting rate of return on investment** analysis, which measures the average rate (percentage) of profit (net income) on the investment over the asset's life, is the measure of profitability chosen. Management seeks the highest possible rate of profit on funds to be invested. This rate may be computed in one of two ways. The additional net income produced by the capital outlay may be divided either by the original investment or by the average investment over the life of the asset. Although the total amount of the original investment is used more often, some accountants prefer to use the average investment. Their reasoning is that the original outlay is recovered during the life of the project. This means that not all the original cost is invested throughout the life of the project. As a result, using the original outlay results in an understatement of the effective rate of return. However, if a company consistently uses one (or both) approach(es), the method will serve as a guide to comparing alternative investment opportunities.

The average investment would theoretically be computed by adding the initial outlay and the book value (undepreciated cost) at the end of each year and dividing this total by the number of figures used in the addition. For example, if an asset with a depreciable life of four years and no salvage value was purchased for $100,000, the average investment would be computed as follows, assuming that the straight-line method is used in computing depreciation:

Initial investment	$100,000
Book value—end of Year 1	75,000
Book value—end of Year 2	50,000
Book value—end of Year 3	25,000
Book value—end of Year 4	-0-
Total	$250,000

$$\text{Average Investment} = \frac{\$250,000}{5} = \$50,000$$

If the asset in the above example had an estimated salvage value of $20,000 at the end of 4 years, the annual straight-line depreciation would be $20,000 [($100,000 − $20,000) ÷ 4] and the average investment would be $60,000, computed as follows:

Initial investment	$100,000
Book value—end of Year 1	80,000
Book value—end of Year 2	60,000
Book value—end of Year 3	40,000
Book value—end of Year 4	20,000
Total	$300,000

$$\text{Average Investment} = \frac{\$300,000}{5} = \$60,000$$

When straight-line depreciation is used, the average investment can be computed much more simply by using only two figures, the initial investment and the book value at the end of the asset's useful life (the anticipated salvage value). In the above illustration, the average investment could be computed as follows:

$$\text{Average Investment} = \frac{\text{Initial Investment} + \text{Estimated Salvage}}{2}$$

$$= \frac{\$100,000 + \$20,000}{2} = \frac{\$120,000}{2} = \$60,000$$

However, if a depreciation method other than the straight-line method is used, the calculation of average investment will require the use of year-end book values, as previously illustrated.

The accounting rate of return is computed according to the following formula:

Accounting Rate of Return on Investment

$$= \frac{\text{Additional Annual Net Income}}{\text{Investment}}$$

Note that the additional annual net income before taxes can be computed by subtracting the annual depreciation from the annual cash inflow or cash savings expected to be realized from the new asset. The increase in annual income after taxes would be the annual net income before taxes reduced by the increase in annual income taxes expected as a result of acquiring and using the new asset. Income taxes are as much a part of the cost of an asset's operation as are other costs and should be considered in the investment decision. These concepts are examined in this chapter.

An Application of the Accounting Rate of Return Analysis— Investment in Additional Equipment

To illustrate the accounting rate of return approach to evaluating a capital investment proposal, let us examine a simple, but common, decision faced by Rodriquez Manufacturers. Rodriquez is considering whether to buy a machine that will improve labor productivity. This machine is not a replacement for an existing machine but is an additional piece of equipment. The machine has a 10-year useful life with no anticipated salvage value. The following cost and revenue data are provided for the two alternatives faced: (1) to not buy the machine and (2) to buy the machine.

	If Machine Is Not Bought	If Machine Is Bought
Annual sales	8,000 units	8,000 units
Sales price per unit	$ 20.00	$ 20.00
Cost of machine		$15,000.00
Manufacturing cost data:		
Materials cost per unit	$ 8.00	$ 8.00
Labor cost per unit	6.00	5.50
Variable overhead cost per unit	2.00	2.00
Fixed overhead cost per year	$12,000.00	$13,500.00*
Federal and state income taxes, combined rate	40%	40%

*Includes yearly depreciation of $1,500 on the new machine.

If a contribution approach is used, the net income under each alternative is as shown below. (This illustration assumes that net income for tax purposes is identical to net income for accounting purposes.)

NOTE: In this chapter we will assume that straight-line depreciation is used for both financial accounting purposes and income tax purposes. Furthermore, we will assume that in the first full year of an asset's useful life, the owner will be entitled to deduct a full year of depreciation on the asset in computing income taxes. Both these assumptions are made in order to simplify the discussion of capital expenditure analysis. In fact, currently taxpayers are given the option

	IF MACHINE IS NOT BOUGHT	DIFFERENCE	IF MACHINE IS BOUGHT
RODRIQUEZ MANUFACTURERS			
Analysis of Proposed Purchase of Machine			
Sales (Annual)	$160,000		$160,000
Variable Costs			
Materials	$ 64,000		$ 64,000
Labor	48,000	$ 4,000	44,000
Manufacturing Overhead	16,000		16,000
Total Variable Costs	$128,000		$124,000
Contribution Margin	$ 32,000		$ 36,000
Fixed Costs	12,000	(1,500)	13,500
Net Income Before Taxes	$ 20,000	$ 2,500	$ 22,500
Income Taxes	8,000	(1,000)	9,000
Net Income After Taxes	$ 12,000	$ 1,500	$ 13,500

to use the **modified accelerated cost-recovery system (MACRS)** in charging off the cost of new items of plant and equipment for tax purposes. MACRS permits a much more rapid charge-off of an asset's cost than does straight-line depreciation, so most taxpayers use the MACRS computation. In addition, if a taxpayer chooses to use the straight-line depreciation method, only one-half of one year's depreciation is deductible during the tax year of the asset's acquisition. On average, assets will be acquired at midyear, and the taxpayer will be allowed one-half of one year's depreciation in that tax year (the first half year of the asset's physical life) and a deduction in the second tax year for depreciation on the asset during the second half of its first physical year of life. In practice, a cost accountant preparing capital expenditure analyses would seek the help of a tax expert in making estimates of future taxes related to the asset. The goal of this chapter is not to analyze the tax law but to apply the tax estimate in making the capital expenditure decision; making the above assumptions permits us to focus on the expenditure decision, rather than on the tax computation.

Based on the above analysis, Rodriquez might decide to purchase the new machine. However, further analysis is needed to make the decision. A basic question is: What is the rate of return on the investment in the equipment?

The proposed purchase of machinery by Rodriquez Manufacturers can be evaluated by the accounting rate of return on investment method. The calculation can be based on the initial investment in the asset or on the average investment over the life of the asset.

Computing Accounting Rate of Return on Initial Investment. If the rate of return based on the *initial* investment is chosen as the measure of profitability, the additional annual net income of $1,500, after taxes, is divided by the initial investment of $15,000. The result is an annual rate of return of 10 percent on the initial investment.

Rate of Return on Initial Investment

$$= \frac{\text{Annual Cash Savings} - \text{Depreciation of Asset} - \text{Income Taxes}}{\text{Investment}}$$

$$= \frac{\$4,000 - \$1,500 - \$1,000}{\$15,000} = 10 \text{ percent}$$

However, if the initial investment is used in computing the accounting rate of return, the percentage of return can be considered to be understated because a portion of the cost is recovered through operations each year as the asset's cost is charged to expense through depreciation. As a result, the rate of return on average investment is often computed instead of, or in addition to, the return on initial investment. The *average investment* can be defined as the average book value (original cost minus accumulated depreciation) over the life of the asset.

Computing Accounting Rate of Return on Average Investment. If the accounting rate of return on investment is based on the average investment, the rate of return for the new machine being considered for purchase by Rodriquez Manufacturers will be increased to 20 percent. The increase in annual after-tax profit remains the same as in the previous example, $1,500. In this case, straight-line depreciation is being used and there is no salvage value so, as explained on page 707, the average investment can be computed simply by adding the initial book value ($15,000) of the investment and the ending book value ($0) together ($15,000 + $0 = $15,000) and dividing the total by 2. Thus, the average investment is $7,500.

Rate of Return on Average Investment

$$= \frac{\text{Additional Annual Net Income After Taxes}}{\text{Average Investment}}$$

$$= \frac{\$1,500}{\$7,500} = 20 \text{ percent}$$

The annual after-tax profit resulting from the project is 20 percent of the average unrecovered investment in the asset, as compared to 10 percent of the initial investment.

Another Application of the Accounting Rate of Return Analysis— Replacing Existing Equipment

The decision process for replacing existing equipment is much like that for buying new machinery. It is important to understand, however, that when a decision is made about whether to replace existing equipment, the original cost of the equipment and its book value are *not considered* when the accounting rate of return analysis is used. Both amounts represent sunk costs. Whether the existing equipment is replaced or not, its book value is charged off against revenue. The only difference is whether the book value is charged off immediately or over a period of years. If the equipment is not replaced, the book value is charged off over future periods as depreciation. If the equipment is replaced, the book value is charged off immediately. Note again that the total amount of book value will be reflected in long-run profit and loss will be the same under either decision. (However, as you will learn later, the time at which any undepreciated cost is charged off for income tax purposes will affect the years in which income taxes are affected.)

To illustrate this analysis, assume that Rodriquez Manufacturers bought for $15,000 the new machinery discussed above. Five years later, an equipment supplier tells the company that a new development has made the machine obsolete. A more efficient new model, with a list price of $12,500, a five-year estimated useful life, and with no salvage value, is available. The new machine should reduce labor costs per unit from $5.50 to $5. It should also reduce variable manufacturing overhead from $2 to $1.75 per unit. No trade-in allowance is provided for the old equipment, and it has no resale value. Production and sales are still estimated to be 8,000 units per year.

In making the decision whether to replace or not replace the machine, the results of the two alternatives over the next five years (the remaining useful life of the new equipment) are examined. The five-year replacement analysis below, based on direct costing, shows total net income. After-tax income, of $67,500 over the five years if the old

RODRIQUEZ MANUFACTURERS
Equipment Replacement Analysis
(5-Year Income)

	RETAINING EXISTING EQUIPMENT	DIFFERENCE	REPLACING EQUIPMENT
Sales	$800,000		$800,000
Variable Manufacturing Costs			
Materials	$320,000		$320,000
Labor	220,000	$20,000	200,000
Manufacturing Overhead	80,000	10,000	70,000
Total Variable Costs	$620,000		$590,000
Contribution Margin	$180,000		$210,000
Less: Fixed Costs	$ 67,500	(5,000)	$ 72,500*
Loss on Disposal of Existing Equipment		$ (7,500)	7,500
Total	$ 67,500	$17,500	$ 80,000
Net Income Before Taxes	$112,500	$17,500	$130,000
Income Taxes	45,000	7,000	52,000
Net Income After Taxes	$ 67,500	$10,500	$ 78,000

*New fixed costs computed as follows:

Old fixed costs (5 years)	$67,500
Less depreciation on old asset (5 years)	(7,500)
Add depreciation on new asset	12,500
New total fixed costs for 5 years	$72,500

equipment is retained, are compared with after-tax net income of $78,000 if the equipment is replaced. The analysis shows an increase in net income of $10,500 over the five-year period, or $2,100 per year (shown in the annual replacement analysis illustrated, using direct costing). These two statements indicate that the replacement should be made.

Even though the analysis above indicates that the new equipment should be acquired to replace the old, further analysis is called for. The accountant for Rodriquez Manufacturers computes the accounting rate of return from the new investment and compares this return with the returns from alternative investments. Again, the rate of return may be computed on the initial investment or on the average investment.

Computing Accounting Rate of Return on Initial Investment. The average net increase in after-tax income of $2,100 that would be realized from replacing the old equipment can be computed by dividing the total after-tax savings over a period of five years ($10,500) by five years ($10,500 ÷ 5 years = $2,100 per year). The annual net savings can be calculated also, by subtracting the depreciation on the new equipment from the annual variable cost reductions in labor and overhead, and deducting the related income tax increase, as shown below.

RODRIQUEZ MANUFACTURERS **Equipment Replacement Analysis** **(Annual Savings)**	
Variable Cost Reductions	
Labor ($5.50 − $5.00) per Unit	$ .05
Manufacturing Overhead ($2.00 − $1.75) per Unit	.25
Total Variable Costs per Unit	$ .75
Total Units	8,000
Total Variable Cost Reduction	$6,000
Less Annual Depreciation on New Equipment	
($12,500 ÷ 5)	2,500
Net Annual Pre-Tax Savings from Replacement	$3,500
Less Additional Annual Income Taxes (40%)	1,400
Net Increase in Annual After-Tax Net Income	$2,100

The annual accounting method rate of return on initial investment is 16.8 percent. As in the case of a decision to purchase additional equipment, the accounting rate of return on initial investment is determined by dividing the annual savings (increase in income, after taxes) of $2,100 by the initial investment of $12,500.

Rate of Return on Initial Investment

$$= \frac{\text{Additional Annual Net Income}}{\text{Initial Investment}}$$

$$= \frac{\$2,100}{\$12,500} = 16.8 \text{ percent}$$

At this point you should be able to work Exercises 27–1 to 27–3 and Problems 27–1A to 27–2B.

Computing Accounting Rate of Return on Average Investment. The average investment in the replacement machine can again be calculated easily because there is no salvage value and straight-line depreciation is being used. The average investment during the asset's five-year life is its cost of $12,500 divided by 2, or $6,250. The accounting rate of return on average investment is therefore the increase in average annual after-tax profit, $2,100, divided by the average investment, $6,250, yielding a rate of 33.6 percent.

SELF-REVIEW

1. In the accounting rate of return on investment approach to evaluating a proposal to invest in new equipment, how is the cost of the new asset used in the calculation?
2. In computing the accounting rate of return on average investment, how is average investment determined?
3. Should income taxes be considered in measuring the accounting rate of return on investment? Explain.
4. If an asset is expected to have a salvage value at the end of its economic usefulness, how is the salvage value treated in computing return on average investment?
5. A company is analyzing two capital expenditure proposals to decide which opportunity to invest in and, among other analyses, is using the accounting rate of return on investment as a basis for comparing the two projects. Should the company use the initial investment in the assets or the average investment in the assets in making the calculation? Explain.

Answers to Self-Review

1. In the accounting rate of return on investment approach, the cost of the asset is used in the calculation through future depreciation expense charges. Also, the asset's cost can be depreciated for tax purposes, reducing income taxes each year and resulting in a higher after-tax net income.
2. Average investment is computed by adding the initial cost of the asset and the asset's net book value as of the end of each year. The sum is then divided by the number of items included in the total.
3. Income taxes should be deducted in computing the net income used in the calculation of accounting return on investment. For this purpose, income taxes are an expense like any other expense.
4. Average investment is computed by adding the asset's initial cost and its book value at the end of each year and dividing the total by the number of items in the computation. If a proposed investment is expected to have a salvage value at the end of its useful life, the salvage value becomes a part of the total of the value to be divided by the number of items included.
5. The company should make both computations. The relative rankings will be the same unless salvage values enter into the computation. In that case, assets with high salvage values will show relatively lower returns on average investment than on initial investment.

EVALUATION TECHNIQUES FOCUSING ON CASH FLOWS

The ultimate objective of any investment is to increase a company's net cash flows. As a result, most companies use one or more analysis techniques involving net cash flow when evaluating capital investment decisions. Cash flow analyses fit into one of two classifications:

- ▪ Computing the **payback period**—the number of years that it will take net cash flows to recover the initial investment in the asset.
- ▪ Computing the **present value of a future amount**—the amount that an investor would invest today in order to earn a specified rate of return from receiving the expected stream of annual net cash flows. This calculation can be used in several ways.

Both of these techniques are used by almost every company in evaluating proposed capital expenditures.

The Payback Period

A commonly used guideline for evaluating proposed capital expenditures is the number of years required to recover the investment out of the cash flows expected to be realized from the project. In other words, the payback period is the length of time it should take for the cash earnings or savings from the project to return the amount of the initial outlay. This period is computed by dividing the initial outlay by the annual cash earnings or savings.

$$\text{Payback Period} = \frac{\text{Investment}}{\text{Annual After-Tax Cash Earnings or Savings}}$$

Obviously, a short payback period, which means rapid recovery of an investment, is generally better than a longer payback period for the same type of investment.

The payback period method has several advantages. It is easy to calculate. It serves as a screening device to eliminate proposals requiring long recovery periods. Also, it provides some indication of profitability. This method is widely used. Most commonly, it is applied along with other techniques.

A major limitation to this method is that it ignores the economic life of the project. Thus it does not provide a clear indication of profitability. Sole reliance on the payback method could be disastrous. For example, assume that the payback period for Project A is 7 years and the payback period for Project B is 10 years. If Project A had an economic life of 5 years and Project B had an economic life of 15 years, the initial investment in Project A would never be recovered because the asset would be worn out in 5 years, even though the cost would be only five-sevenths recovered at that time. Even though the payback period of Project B is longer, it is a far more desirable investment than is Project A. The failure to consider the time value of money is an additional important shortcoming of the payback period method.

Example of Payback Period—Purchase of Additional Asset. A simple example will illustrate the use of the payback period method. On page 707 you examined a case in which Rodriquez Manufacturers is

BUSINESS HORIZON

Using "Joint Ventures" and Alliances to Share Risks and Cut Costs

Increasingly, both large and small businesses are joining with their competitors, suppliers, or customers in cooperative ventures designed to improve efficiency and reduce both operating costs and capital investments. Various types of cooperative ventures have been developed. Two of the more common arrangements are joint ventures and alliances. Joint ventures have been used for decades in certain industries but have now spread to many industries. Alliances are relatively new but are growing daily in importance.

In one type of joint venture, two or more companies agree to join together in a specific venture. The joint venture may take the form of a separate partnership that carries on agreed-upon business activities in its own name, owns property in its own name, maintains its own accounts, and measures profit or loss at the venture level.

More commonly, the cooperative activity is a joint venture that is not a legal partnership and does not have its own identity. Both parties contribute cash or other assets to the project. Each party owns an undivided interest in the assets of the venture, and the venture does not hold assets in its own name. One of the parties is named as the manager (operator) and is responsible for carrying out day-to-day activities, although all the parties establish a management committee with representatives from each party setting policies and giving operating guidelines to the operator in accordance with the joint operating agreement. Budgets are prepared for the venture, and all parties must approve authorizations for expenditure when the amount proposed to be spent exceeds a specified sum. The operator pays the costs of acquiring assets and pays costs, billing the other parties for their share. Joint ventures are used extremely frequently in the oil and gas exploration and production business. For example, when several companies own mineral rights in the same reservoir, it is illogical for each company to drill oil wells, install costly equipment, and make other substantial capital expenditures to produce the contents of the same reservoir. In most cases the parties form a joint venture, the purpose of which is to drill and develop the reservoir and produce the contents in an orderly manner. Each party pays its share of costs and receives its share of revenues. When the reservoir is exhausted, the joint venture is terminated.

In recent years companies have formed even more restricted ventures called *alliances*. With alliances, the parties may agree to share each other's equipment, buildings, and other facilities, perform services, and even to use each other's name in the alliance. Normally, there is little or no investment in new facilities or equipment. One of the most important alliances was that proposed by American Airlines and British Airways in 1997 to combine their efforts in certain international flight markets. The two airlines would share the aircraft on those flights, with each airline providing certain ground services. As a result, a passenger could fly either American Airlines or British Airways on the same plane and receive frequent flyer mileage credit on either airline. The two airlines would reduce the number of total flights, thus reducing the need for aircraft and ground facilities and personnel. They would be required to surrender part of their departure slots in the London airports. Why would the two airlines do this? Obviously, the idea was to cut capital investment and operating costs drastically, thus increasing profit. The prospects are that similar alliances will be forged between companies in other capital-intensive industries in order to reduce capital investment and operating expenses.

considering the purchase of a machine for $15,000 that will result in annual pre-tax cash savings (reduced labor costs) of $4,000 during its 10-year life ($.50 per unit × 8,000 units per year). However, purchase of the asset will also affect income taxes each year, resulting in an increased cash outflow for taxes. Assuming that straight-line depreciation is used for tax purposes as well as for accounting purposes, the effect on income taxes will be as follows:

Additional Yearly Income Taxes

Annual labor savings	$4,000
Less additional depreciation	1,500
Increase in taxable income	2,500
Income tax rate	.40
Additional taxes	$1,000

Additional Yearly After-Tax Cash Flow

Annual labor savings	$4,000
Annual increase in income taxes	1,000
Net increase in cash flow	$3,000

$$\text{Payback Period} = \frac{\text{Investment}}{\text{Annual After-Tax Increase in Cash Flow}}$$

$$= \frac{\$15,000}{\$3,000} = 5 \text{ years}$$

When management compares the payback period of 5 years with the expected life of 10 years for the machine, it appears that the machine's cost will be recovered in the first one-half of the new asset's life (5 years ÷ 10 years) and will continue to generate after-tax cash flows of $3,000 per year one-half of its life after acquisition costs have been recovered.

Example of Payback Period—Replacement of Asset.   As a second example of the payback period, consider the proposed replacement of an old asset. You read that Rodriquez Manufacturers is considering the replacement of existing equipment with new equipment at a cost of $12,500. The pre-tax cash savings are estimated to be $6,000 per year (8,000 units × $.75 per unit). The old equipment, which has a book value of $7,500, has no salvage value and will be discarded. The question arises: "What is the payback period for the replacement asset?"

In this example, computation of the annual income tax is slightly more complicated than for the previous example, in which there was no existing asset to be disposed of. Since the original equipment is not being used as a trade-in and has no salvage value, the remaining tax basis of the asset can be deducted for tax purposes. Assuming that Rodriquez had used straight-line depreciation on its tax return, the tax basis would be the same as the book value, $7,500 ($15,000 − $7,500 accumulated depreciation = $7,500).

The charge-off of the $7,500 remaining tax basis will result in a tax saving of $3,000 in the year the new asset is purchased and the old asset abandoned.

Book value at date of abandonment	$7,500
Tax rate	.40
Tax benefit resulting from abandonment	$3,000

Because of the immediate tax saving resulting from abandonment of the old asset if the new replacement asset is purchased, the immediate additional capital expenditure resulting from the replacement will be only $9,500. Thus the payback period would be 2.38 years:

$$\text{Payback Period} = \frac{\text{Net Investment}}{\text{Annual After-Tax Increase in Cash Flow}}$$

$$= \frac{\$9,500}{\$4,000} = 2.38 \text{ years}$$

Both examples just given appear to be satisfactory investment opportunities. In both cases, however, the payback period must be compared with guidelines established by management. If these guidelines are met, the payback periods can be compared with the payback periods of other proposals. Additional methods of evaluation, such as the accounting rate of return on investment or the time-adjusted rate of return, discussed below, are normally used along with the payback period in making a capital investment decision.

At this point you should be able to work Exercises 27–4 and 27–5 and Problems 27–3A to 27–4B.

Using Present Value of Future Cash Flows Concepts in Capital Budgeting

The major drawback of the accounting rate of return on investment method is that it fails to consider the time value of money. A dollar received today is certainly more valuable than a dollar to be received a year from now. For example, if you invest $100 today at 10 percent interest, you receive $110 at the end of the year. Thus $110 to be received a year from now would justify an investment of only $100 today if the desired return on investment is 10 percent. We refer to the amount that would be invested today ($100 in this example) in order to receive a specified amount ($110 in this example) at a specified time (one year later in this example) and in order to earn a specified interest rate on the investment (10 percent in this example) as the **present value of future cash flows.** It is easy to see that the present value in this example is 90.909 percent of the future cash flow to be received ($100 present value ÷ $110 future cash flow). For simplicity, we say that the present value of 1, due one year from now, at a discount rate of 10 percent, is .909.

Computing Net Present Value of Future Cash Flows from a Capital Investment. We have seen that a capital investment is an investment in an asset that will last for more than one year and will generally lead to increased future cash flows either through additional revenues or through cost savings. Let us now see how the present value of future cash flows for periods more than one year would be computed. First, look at how amounts invested today accumulate if an investment earns 10 percent per year. Suppose you invested $100 today to earn interest at 10 percent per year and are to receive the proceeds two years from today. Here is how your investment would grow:

Year	Balance at Beginning of Year	Interest Earned	Balance at End of Year
1	$100	$10	$110
2	110	11	121

We can see that if you invest $100 today and earn interest at 10 percent, compounded annually, you will receive $121 at the end of year 2. Since $100 (today's investment) is 82.6 percent of $121, we can say that the present value of an amount to be received two years from today is .826 of the amount to be received two years from the date of investment if interest of 10 percent is to be earned.

Let's carry this one year further and assume that you invest $100 today that is to earn interest at 10 percent per year, compounded annually, and that you will receive the proceeds three years from now. Continuing the table above, we can see that the accumulation at the end of year 3 will be $133.10.

Year	Balance at Beginning of Year	Interest Earned	Balance at End of Year
1	$100.00	$10.00	$110.00
2	110.00	11.00	121.00
3	121.00	12.10	133.10

If the amount we have to invest today to receive $133.10 three years from now is $100, we can say that the present value factor is .751 ($100 ÷ $133.10).

Now, suppose that we are told that, three years from now, we will receive $14,100 and are asked how much we would have to invest today in order to have earned interest at 10 percent when the $14,100 is received. We can easily compute the investment because we have just seen that the present value factor for an amount to be received three years from now with an interest rate of 10 percent is .751. The amount that would have to invested is .751 × $14,100, or approximately $10,589. Fortunately, we don't have to make the calculations of present value factors manually because tables are available showing the "present value of $1 due at the end of the period" for almost unlimited numbers of periods. In addition, spreadsheet packages and many other programs contain present value functions. A limited present value table is shown on page 718. Refer to the table and note the column labeled "10%." Note that the "present value of $1" factors for amounts to be received at the end of the first three years are .909, .826, and .751, respectively. These figures agree with the above computations.

Since a capital project is expected to increase net cash flows over a period of years, the present value of a project is the sum of the present values of the cash inflows for each year of the life of the project. Read carefully the following two examples of computing the present

"PRESENT VALUE OF $1" TABLE
Present Value of $1 Received at End of Year

Years	1%	2%	4%	6%	8%	10%	12%	14%	15%	16%	18%	20%	22%	24%	25%	26%
1	0.990	0.980	0.962	0.943	0.926	0.909	0.893	0.877	0.870	0.862	0.847	0.833	0.820	0.806	0.800	0.794
2	0.980	0.961	0.925	0.890	0.857	0.826	0.797	0.769	0.756	0.743	0.718	0.694	0.672	0.650	0.640	0.630
3	0.971	0.942	0.889	0.840	0.794	0.751	0.712	0.675	0.658	0.641	0.609	0.579	0.551	0.524	0.512	0.500
4	0.961	0.924	0.855	0.792	0.735	0.683	0.636	0.592	0.572	0.552	0.516	0.482	0.451	0.423	0.410	0.397
5	0.951	0.906	0.822	0.747	0.681	0.621	0.567	0.519	0.497	0.476	0.437	0.402	0.370	0.341	0.328	0.315
6	0.942	0.888	0.790	0.705	0.630	0.564	0.507	0.456	0.432	0.410	0.370	0.335	0.303	0.275	0.262	0.250
7	0.933	0.871	0.760	0.665	0.583	0.513	0.452	0.400	0.376	0.354	0.314	0.279	0.249	0.222	0.210	0.198
8	0.923	0.853	0.731	0.627	0.540	0.467	0.404	0.351	0.327	0.305	0.266	0.233	0.204	0.179	0.168	0.157
9	0.914	0.837	0.703	0.592	0.500	0.424	0.361	0.308	0.284	0.263	0.225	0.194	0.167	0.144	0.134	0.125
10	0.905	0.820	0.676	0.558	0.463	0.386	0.322	0.270	0.247	0.227	0.191	0.162	0.137	0.116	0.107	0.099
11	0.896	0.804	0.650	0.527	0.429	0.350	0.287	0.237	0.215	0.195	0.162	0.135	0.112	0.094	0.086	0.079
12	0.887	0.788	0.625	0.497	0.397	0.319	0.257	0.208	0.187	0.168	0.137	0.112	0.092	0.076	0.069	0.062
13	0.879	0.773	0.601	0.469	0.368	0.290	0.229	0.182	0.163	0.145	0.116	0.093	0.075	0.061	0.055	0.050
14	0.870	0.758	0.577	0.442	0.340	0.263	0.205	0.160	0.141	0.125	0.099	0.078	0.062	0.049	0.044	0.039
15	0.861	0.743	0.555	0.417	0.315	0.239	0.183	0.140	0.123	0.108	0.084	0.065	0.051	0.040	0.035	0.031
16	0.853	0.728	0.534	0.394	0.292	0.218	0.163	0.123	0.107	0.093	0.071	0.054	0.042	0.032	0.028	0.025
17	0.844	0.714	0.513	0.371	0.270	0.198	0.146	0.108	0.093	0.080	0.060	0.045	0.034	0.026	0.023	0.020
18	0.836	0.700	0.494	0.350	0.250	0.180	0.130	0.095	0.081	0.069	0.051	0.038	0.028	0.021	0.018	0.016
19	0.828	0.686	0.475	0.331	0.232	0.164	0.116	0.083	0.070	0.060	0.043	0.031	0.023	0.017	0.014	0.012
20	0.820	0.673	0.456	0.312	0.215	0.149	0.104	0.073	0.061	0.051	0.037	0.026	0.019	0.014	0.012	0.010
21	0.811	0.660	0.439	0.294	0.199	0.135	0.093	0.064	0.053	0.044	0.031	0.022	0.015	0.011	0.009	0.008
22	0.803	0.647	0.422	0.278	0.184	0.123	0.083	0.056	0.046	0.038	0.026	0.018	0.013	0.009	0.007	0.006
23	0.795	0.634	0.406	0.262	0.170	0.112	0.074	0.049	0.040	0.033	0.022	0.015	0.010	0.007	0.006	0.005
24	0.788	0.622	0.390	0.247	0.158	0.102	0.066	0.043	0.035	0.028	0.019	0.013	0.008	0.006	0.005	0.004
25	0.780	0.610	0.375	0.233	0.146	0.092	0.059	0.038	0.030	0.024	0.016	0.010	0.007	0.005	0.004	0.003
26	0.772	0.598	0.361	0.220	0.135	0.084	0.053	0.033	0.026	0.021	0.014	0.009	0.006	0.004	0.003	0.002
27	0.764	0.586	0.347	0.207	0.125	0.076	0.047	0.029	0.023	0.018	0.011	0.007	0.005	0.003	0.002	0.002
28	0.757	0.574	0.333	0.196	0.116	0.069	0.042	0.026	0.020	0.016	0.010	0.006	0.004	0.002	0.002	0.002
29	0.749	0.563	0.321	0.185	0.107	0.063	0.037	0.022	0.017	0.014	0.008	0.005	0.003	0.002	0.002	0.001
30	0.742	0.552	0.308	0.174	0.099	0.057	0.033	0.020	0.015	0.012	0.007	0.004	0.003	0.002	0.001	0.001

value of a capital investment. In the first example, we will assume that the cash flows are not equal during each year of the asset's life. In the second example, we will assume that the cash flows during each year of the asset's life are equal.

Illustration of Present Value Computation When Annual Cash Flows Are Not Equal. To see how the present value method works, assume that Rose Corporation is considering purchasing an asset for $18,000. The asset is expected to yield the following stream of net cash flows over the five-year life of the asset involved:

Year 1	$6,000
Year 2	8,000
Year 3	6,000
Year 4	5,000
Year 5	4,000

Assume further that the company's desired rate of return is 14 percent. The basic capital budgeting question is: "What is the present value of this stream of future cash flows, using a discount rate of 14 percent?" The starting point in answering this question is to look at the "14%" column of the table on page 718, where you will find the present value factor to be applied to the amount received at the end of each future year in order to determine the present value of the stream of cash flows. These factors are applied to the relevant yearly cash flows, as shown below. The sums of the present value of the yearly cash inflows for the five-year period total $20,500. This amount is the present value of the project.

Year	Cash Flow	Present Value Factor (14%)	Present Value
1	6,000	.877	$ 5,262
2	8,000	.769	6,152
3	6,000	.675	4,050
4	5,000	.592	2,960
5	4,000	.519	2,076
Total present value of future cash inflows			$20,500

Illustration of Present Value Computation When Annual Cash Flows Are Equal. In the preceding example, the net present value for Rose Corporation's proposed capital expenditure was computed by using the "present value of $1" table. Note that in that example, the annual cash flows were not equal. Let us now return to the decision faced by Rodriquez Manufacturers when that company considered purchasing a new machine to replace an existing machine. The decision to be made was discussed on page 710. To review the problem briefly, a more efficient new machine, with a list of $12,500, a five-year estimated useful life, and with no salvage value, is available to replace an older machine with a new book value of $7,500. The new machine should reduce labor costs per unit from $5.50 to $5. It should also reduce variable manufacturing overhead from $2 to $1.75 per unit. The company's projected production and sales were 8,000 units per year. The company's increase in net cash flow each year is therefore expected to be $6,000 ($.75 per unit savings × 8,000 units per year) before income taxes. The increase in income taxes was computed to be $2,000 per year, so that the after-tax increase in cash flow is $4,000 per year:

Savings in labor costs per unit	$ .50
Savings in variable overhead costs per unit	.25
Total savings per unit	$ .75
Units per year	8,000
Total savings per year	$6,000
Less income tax increase	2,000
Net increase in cash flow after taxes	$4,000

The present value of the future cash inflows could be computed by using the "present value of $1" table to find the factor for each year to be applied to that year's net cash flow. Assuming that the return required by Rodriquez Manufacturers on a capital investment is 14 percent per year, the factors would be the same as those in the preceding example for Rose Corporation. As you have learned, the net present value would be the sum of the discounted annual cash flows

ANNUITY TABLE
Present Value of $1 Received or Paid Annually*

Years	2%	6%	10%	14%	16%	18%	20%	22%	24%	25%	30%	40%	50%
1	.980	.943	.909	.877	.862	.847	.833	.820	.806	.800	.769	.714	.667
2	1.942	1.833	1.736	1.647	1.605	1.566	1.528	1.492	1.457	1.440	1.361	1.224	1.111
3	2.884	2.673	2.487	2.322	2.246	2.174	2.106	2.042	1.981	1.952	1.816	1.589	1.407
4	3.808	3.465	3.170	2.914	2.798	2.690	2.589	2.494	2.404	2.362	2.166	1.849	1.605
5	4.713	4.212	3.791	3.433	3.274	3.127	2.991	2.864	2.745	2.689	2.436	2.035	1.737
6	5.601	4.917	4.355	3.889	3.685	3.498	3.326	3.167	3.020	2.951	2.643	2.168	1.824
7	6.472	5.582	4.868	4.288	4.039	3.812	3.605	3.416	3.242	3.161	2.802	2.263	1.883
8	7.325	6.210	5.335	4.639	4.344	4.078	3.837	3.619	3.421	3.329	2.925	2.331	1.992
9	8.163	6.802	5.759	4.946	4.607	4.303	4.031	3.786	3.566	3.463	3.019	2.379	1.948
10	8.983	7.360	6.145	5.216	4.833	4.494	4.192	3.923	3.682	3.571	3.092	2.414	1.965
11	9.787	7.887	6.495	5.453	5.029	4.656	4.327	4.035	3.776	3.656	3.147	2.438	1.977
12	10.575	8.384	6.814	5.660	5.197	4.793	4.439	4.127	3.851	3.725	3.190	2.456	1.985
13	11.348	8.853	7.103	5.842	5.342	4.910	4.533	4.203	3.912	3.780	3.223	2.468	1.990
14	12.106	9.295	7.367	6.002	5.468	5.008	4.611	4.265	3.962	3.824	3.249	2.477	1.993
15	12.849	9.712	7.606	6.142	5.575	5.092	4.675	4.315	4.001	3.859	3.268	2.484	1.995
16	13.578	10.106	7.824	6.265	5.669	5.162	4.730	4.357	4.033	3.887	3.283	2.489	1.997
17	14.292	10.477	8.022	6.373	5.749	5.222	4.775	4.391	4.059	3.910	3.295	2.492	1.998
18	14.992	10.828	8.201	6.467	5.818	5.273	4.812	4.419	4.080	3.928	3.304	2.494	1.999
19	15.678	11.158	8.365	6.550	5.877	5.316	4.844	4.442	4.097	3.942	3.311	2.496	1.999
20	16.351	11.470	8.514	6.623	5.929	5.353	4.870	4.460	4.110	3.954	3.316	2.497	1.999
21	17.011	11.764	8.649	6.687	5.973	5.384	4.891	4.476	4.121	3.963	3.320	2.498	2.000
22	17.658	12.042	8.772	6.743	6.011	5.410	4.909	4.488	4.130	3.970	3.323	2.498	2.000
23	18.292	12.303	8.883	6.792	6.044	5.432	4,925	4.499	4.137	3.976	3.325	2.499	2.000
24	18.914	12.550	8.985	6.835	6.073	5.451	4.937	4.507	4.143	3.981	3.327	2.499	2.000
25	19.523	12.783	9.077	6.873	6.097	5.467	4.948	4.514	4.147	3.985	3.329	2.499	2.000

*Partial table.

for the five-year life of the asset. Since the factor for each year would be applied to the same annual cash flows, a short-cut calculation would be to add the individual factors for the five years and multiply that total by the annual cash flow. Adding the factors for the first five years in the "present value of $1" table gives a total present value factor of 3.432. Fortunately, this addition is not necessary because a "present value of an annuity of $1 received or paid annually" contains the cumulative factors of the "present value of $1" table. The **present value of an annuity** is the amount that would be invested today in order to receive a specified number of identical cash payments, paid at specific intervals, and in order to earn a specified rate on the investment. A portion of an annuity table for annual payments is shown above. Look at the "14%" column, and you will find that the present value of an annuity of $1 received or paid annually for five years is 3.433. (There is a difference of .001 between the 3.433 factor shown in this table and the 3.432 total found by adding the first five factors in the 14% column of the "present value of $1" table because of rounding in the table.) The present value of annual net after-tax cash flows of $4,000 resulting from savings generated by the new machine is therefore $13,732 ($4,000 × 3.433).

Using Discounted Present Value Data. There are several ways in which the present value of future cash flows can be used by management. Obviously, if the present value of the future cash flows is less than the cost of the new asset, management will be unlikely to approve the expenditure unless that are unusual circumstances, such as safety problems or governmental requirements. If, on the other hand, the present value of future cash flows based on the company's required rate of return exceeds the investment required, management may approve the project.

Net Present Value Calculations. The amount by which the total present value of expected net future cash inflows exceeds the investment outlay is referred to as the **net present value.** For example, in the preceding example, we calculated the present value of future cash flows from the replacement machine being considered by Rodriquez Manufacturers to be $13,732. The machine purchase required new investment expenditures of $9,500, after considering the tax reduction resulting from abandoning the old machine. Thus the net present value of the machine, based on a discount rate of 14 percent, is $4,232.

Total present value of future cash inflows	$13,732
Initial investment in capital asset	9,500
Net present value	$ 8,598

The net present value is important to management. A proposed project with a high net present value would generally be preferable to one with a low net present value, and certainly preferable to one with a negative net present value. However, the dollar amount of present value does not indicate the proportionate relationship between the net present value and the project's cost. A net present value of $50,000 for a capital investment of $100,000 might be viewed differently by management than a net present value of $50,000 for a project costing $2,000,000.

Discounted Benefit-Cost Index. The **discounted benefit-cost index,** which is the ratio of the present value of a project to the initial amount of investment, provides management with the relative importance of the discounted cash flows to the asset's cost. For example, the replacement machinery being considered by Rodriquez Manufacturers has a present value of $13,732 and required a new cash expenditure of $9,500. The discounted benefit-cost index is therefore 144.5 percent:

Discounted Benefit-Cost Index

$$= \frac{\text{Present Value of Net After-Tax Cash Inflows}}{\text{Net Investment}}$$

$$= \frac{\$13,732}{\$9,500} = 144.5\%$$

At this point you should be able to work Exercises 27–6 to 27–11 and Problems 27–5A to 27–6B.

When management ranks investment proposals with different present values and costs, different lifetimes, and different cash flow patterns, the discounted benefit-cost ratio helps management decide which projects give the greatest return for each dollar invested.

Estimating Time-Adjusted Rate of Return on Investment. Frequently, the accountant has an estimate of the future cash flows related to a proposed asset acquisition and knows the capital expenditure necessary to acquire the asset but does not know the project's discount rate. In order to determine that discount rate, the **time-adjusted rate of return method** (sometimes called the *discounted rate of return method*), a procedure for computing the discount rate that, when applied to the annual cash flows, will yield a present value equal to the capital expenditure required. This can be easily computed when the estimated cash flows are equal each year.

To illustrate the time-adjusted rate of return method, let us again use a familiar project—the proposed acquisition by Rodriquez Manufacturers of a machine costing $12,500 that would increase net cash flows by $4,000 per year, after taxes, for a period of five years.

Earlier in this chapter, you learned that the present value of a future stream of cash inflows could be determined by using an annuity table showing the present value of $1 received or paid annually. To determine the present value, we used the following formula:

Present Value = Annual Cash Flow
  × Present Value Factor (for Years and Appropriate Discount Rate)

Note that the present value factor was dependent on the number of years and on the discount rate. In the earlier example, we knew the annual cash flow and the present value factor (based on knowledge of the number of years and the discount rate desired); the present value was the missing factor that had to be computed.

If we are trying to estimate the discounted rate of return, we must first determine the discount factor. This is an easy matter. We use the same formula:

Present Value = Annual Cash Flow × Discount Factor

but restate it as follows:

Discount Factor = Present Value ÷ Annual Cash Flow

In the case of the machine replacement decision to be made by Rodriquez, the present value can be viewed as the present value of the after-tax stream of cash flows, discounted at an unknown rate. Substituting the known elements, the equation can then be stated as:

Discount Factor = $9,500 ÷ $4,000

  = 2.083

Remember that the discount factor found in the annuity table is dependent on two elements—the number of years of payments and the discount rate chosen. In this example, we know that Rodriquez expects to receive cash flows for five years. Therefore, we must look in the annuity table in the "Years" column for the 5-year row. Then we can follow that row across the table until we find a factor close to 2.375. We find that the 2.375 factor falls between the factor for "30%" (where the factor is 2.436) and the factor for "40%" (where the factor is 2.035). We know, then, that the rate of return is between 30 and

40 percent per year. It is obvious that the rate is closer to 30 percent than it is to 40 percent. In practice, the table used would be more complete and contain a column for each percentage point, but we can use interpolation to arrive at a reasonably close estimate from this table. (**Interpolation** is the insertion of a number between two other numbers, based on an estimation or calculation of the value of the number being inserted.)

If the present value factor is 2.436, the discount rate is 30 percent, and if the present value factor is 2.035, the discount rate is 40 percent. Thus for a decrease of .401 in the present value factor, the rate of return increases by 10 percentage points. In other words, approximately each .04 increase in the present value factor reflects a decrease of 1 percentage point in the discount rate (.401 ÷ 10 = .040).

The present value factor computed for the proposed machine replacement by Rodriquez is 2.035. This factor is .353 less than the 2.436 factor shown in the table for a 30 percent discount rate.

Present value factor at 30% discount rate	2.436
Present value factor computed for machine	2.375
Difference	0.061

Since each .040 difference in the present value factor reflects a change of 1 percentage point in the discount rate, a difference of .061 in the present value factor represents a change in the discount rate of approximately 1.5 percentage points (.061 ÷ .040 = 1.53). Remember that a lower present value factor means a higher discount rate, so the discount rate is approximately 1.5 percentage points *higher* than 30 percent, or approximately 31.5 percent.

Remember that this is merely an approximation of the discount rate. A more precise calculation could be made by using a more detailed table, and a precise calculation could be made by using a spreadsheet or other computer program containing present value functions.

At this point you should be able to work Exercise 27–12 and Problems 27–7A and 27–7B.

THE ROLE OF INCOME TAXES IN CAPITAL INVESTMENT EVALUATION

In our discussion of capital budgeting we have emphasized that income taxes should be considered in evaluating proposed capital expenditures. Income taxes represent a future cash outlay, just as any other expense does, and management must consider this factor when evaluating capital expenditure proposals. Tax considerations are especially important when cash flow projections are being used to analyze proposed expenditures. The impact that taxes have on the decision vary widely from one situation to another. If the taxes payable are tied closely to cash flows before taxes, they are relatively unimportant in the decision to make or not make an investment. For example, if a company is contemplating investing in one of two alternative investments and in both cases income taxes follow cash flows closely, it is probably not a critical matter whether the two projects are compared on a pre-tax or post-tax basis. If an accounting rate of return is being used, the relative rates between the two projects should be approximately the same whether the calculations are pre-tax or post-tax. Of course, the rate of return for both projects will be less on an after-tax

SELF-REVIEW

1. How does the cash sales price of an asset that is being replaced by the purchase of a new asset affect the payback period?
2. (Use the "present value of $1 table" in answering this question.) Find the present value of $1, due 10 years from now, assuming a 10 percent rate of return. What factor is given in the table? What does that number mean?
3. Why can't the "present value of an annuity of $1" table be used to determine the present value of a future series of annual cash receipts if the annual amounts are not equal?
4. How is the discounted benefit-cost index computed? How is it used in capital budgeting?
5. What is meant by the time-adjusted rate of return?

Answers to Self-Review

1. The cash sales price of an asset that is being replaced reduces the amount of cash outflow for purchase of the new asset. Therefore, it reduces the payback period.
2. The present value factor for the "amount of $1" due 10 years from now, using a discount rate of 10 percent, is .389. This number means that the amount that would be invested to receive any given sum 10 years from now would be .389 times that future sum if the rate of return is to be 10 percent.
3. The present value factor of an "annuity of $1" table is the sum of the individual factors in the "present value of $1" table for the number of years of the annuity and at the discount rate specified. If the annuity table were used, there would be no single annuity amount to which the present value factor could be applied.
4. The discounted benefit-cost index is found by dividing the present value of the future cash flows by the capital expenditure to be made.
5. The time-adjusted rate of return is the discount rate that when applied to the annual cash flows will yield a present value equal to the capital expenditure required to acquire the asset.

basis than on a pre-tax basis. Frequently, evaluations of investment decisions are made on both a pre-tax and an after-tax basis. However, because of peculiarities in the tax laws, cash outflows for income taxes may have little relation to other cash flows. So, a good rule to follow in evaluating investment proposals on a basis using cash flows is to use the after-tax cash flow.

Common Factors That Affect Income Taxes, in Turn Affecting Cash Flows

We have seen that income taxes should be deducted in estimating annual cash flows. This requires an estimation of income taxes related to a capital project's income or loss for each year of the project's useful life. The starting point for the tax projections is usually the estimated cash flow before considering taxes. Here is an overview of some items that frequently cause difficulty in computing the cash flow items to be used—especially items involving income taxes.

Disposition of Old Assets. When old assets are sold, abandoned, or traded in as a result of the acquisition of the new assets, there may be immediate income tax results. In effect, the increase or decrease in income taxes paid at that time increases or decreases the cash outlay related to the acquisition.

Sale of Old Assets. When the acquisition of new assets will lead to the sale of old assets, the resulting gain or loss has no effect on the capital expenditure decision because the book value of the assets is a sunk cost. However, the cash received from sale of the old assets reduces the new investment. If there is a gain or loss for tax purposes, there will be a resulting increase or decrease in income taxes. In analyzing the proposed capital expenditure, the amount of the income tax that has to be paid on a gain on the sale should be treated as a reduction of the sales price, in effect increasing the initial expenditure. On the other hand, a tax reduction resulting from a loss on the sale should be treated as a reduction of the new investment.

Trade-In of Old Assets. For tax purposes, no gain or loss is generally recognized on the trade-in of old assets. Therefore, there is no tax effect. The book value of the old assets traded in will, however, become a part of the depreciable basis of the new assets. This will result in additional depreciation for tax purposes in later years, which in turn will reduce the income taxes payable in those years. The cash outflow for taxes in those later years will therefore be reduced.

Abandonment of Old Assets. If old assets are abandoned, any net salvage value would be treated as a reduction of initial investment in the new assets. The book value of the abandoned assets represents a sunk cost and therefore will not affect the decision. However, for tax purposes the remaining book value for tax purposes will be deductible as a tax loss, reducing the tax liability in the year of abandonment. This reduction in tax liability should be considered as a reduction of the initial investment in the new asset. This point was illustrated in the discussion of the decision by Rodriquez to replace an old machine that had no salvage.

Depreciation of New Assets—The Tax Shield. Depreciation does not result in a cash outflow; it represents an allocation of the asset's initial cost. In cash flow analysis, the initial investment is treated as a cash outflow in the year of the asset's purchase. However, depreciation provides a tax shield. A **tax shield** is a tax reduction resulting from the deduction of a noncash expenditure or loss. Since depreciation, to the extent of the asset's tax basis (usually initial cost) is deductible, it reduces income taxes by an amount equal to the amount of deductible depreciation, multiplied by the tax rate. This, too, has been illustrated in computing the present value of the after-tax cash flows in the decision by Rodriquez to purchase an additional asset and the decision to replace an old asset.

Depreciation Methods. For accounting purposes, depreciation is usually computed on a straight-line basis or on a unit-of-depreciation method. In the evaluation in this chapter, we have assumed that straight-line depreciation is used for both financial accounting and tax purposes. However, for income tax purposes, taxpayers are entitled to use special "speeded-up" depreciation methods. Limited amounts of asset costs can be deducted in the year assets are purchased. As mentioned earlier, taxpayers are also entitled to use MACRS for tax purposes. This system allows the taxpayer to charge off large amounts of depreciation in the first few years of an asset's life and allows the charging off all the asset's cost over a period that may be far shorter than the useful life of the asset. This means that in the first years of an asset's life, taxes are reduced. This will result in higher taxes in the later years of the asset's life. But because a dollar of cash inflow in this year (resulting from a dollar in tax saving in this year) is more valuable than a dollar of cash inflow in later years, the present value of the cash stream is increased by speeding up depreciation. In making forecasts of cash inflows from taxes, the company must give consideration to all such special tax rules.

At this point you should be able to work Exercise 27–13.

PRINCIPLES AND PROCEDURES SUMMARY

- Proper decisions related to capital expenditures (expenditures for property, plant, and equipment with a life of more than one year) are of vital importance to the business. Every company should establish guidelines for making capital investment decisions.
- These guidelines usually include assigning priorities for different classifications of expenditures, minimum profitability rates, requirements for cash flows and projected rates of return on investment, and the ranking of proposed expenditures.
- The accountant and others involved in capital planning utilize many techniques in analyzing proposed expenditures. These techniques center on measures of anticipated profit and on measures of anticipated cash flows from the investment.
- The measure of profitability used is normally the accounting rate of return on the investment. It is necessary to determine the annual profit, using normal accounting principles, and to express this profit as a percentage of investment in the asset. The rate of return may be measured on the initial investment or on the average investment during the asset's lifetime. The accountant should make certain that management understands this fact.
- In making an accounting rate of return analysis, emphasis is placed on additional net income that would result if the asset were to be acquired.
- In making rate-of-return analyses, the anticipated profit used should be the net income after income taxes.
- Several analyses related to cash flows are used in evaluating capital expenditure proposals. These include:
  - The payback period, which is an estimate of the number of years that will be required for the company to recover, from the cash flows generated by the asset, its investment in the project.

- The present value of future net cash flows generated from the asset, based on the discount rate established by the company.
- The estimated time-adjusted rate of return on the investment.
■ It is important for the accountant to understand the effects of income taxes on cash flows and on profitability.

MANAGERIAL IMPLICATIONS

■ Management should not approve proposed investments in assets until various analyses have been applied to evaluate expected profitability and cash flows from the proposed project.
■ Although the expected accounting rate of return, based on the initial or the average investment in the asset, is useful in evaluating proposed capital expenditures, analyses of cash flows from the project are more important.
■ The accounting rate of return does not consider the time value of money. It treats a profit to be earned 10 years in the future as being equally important as the same amount of profit to be earned in the current year.
■ Cash flow analyses recognize the difference in value of cash flows received in different time periods.
■ The accountant should use, at a minimum, the following techniques for evaluating the expected cash flows from a proposed capital expenditure:
  - The number of years expected to be required to recover the asset's cost from future cash flows generated from the asset's use (the payback period).
  - The present value of the expected future cash flows, based on the rate of return desired by the company.
  - The net present value of the asset.
  - The discounted benefit-cost ratio.
  - The estimated time-adjusted rate of return expected to be earned from investing in the asset.

REVIEW QUESTIONS

1. What is meant by the term *capital expenditures?*
2. Capital expenditures become sunk costs. Explain.
3. List various classifications of capital expenditures that might permit easier evaluation by management.
4. How, if at all, does the book value of assets being replaced affect the investment decision?
5. In what way do opportunity costs affect the decision to enlarge a facility through the purchase of new assets?
6. How is the accounting rate of return calculated? What basis or bases can be used for computing the rate?

7. What is meant by the payback period? How is the payback period computed?
8. In general, would management prefer a project with a short payback period or a long one? Why?
9. What is the major shortcoming of the payback period method?
10. What is meant by the time-adjusted rate of return? Why is it useful for evaluating investment opportunities?
11. How much would you have to invest today to receive $70,000 five years from now if there were no income taxes involved and you are to earn 15 percent compound interest?
12. Explain what the term *net present value* means.
13. How would you compute the discounted benefit-cost ratio?
14. Suppose that you know that you can invest $20,000 today and receive $6,000 per year for five years. Explain briefly how you would determine the approximate compound rate of return on your investment, using an annuity table.
15. Explain the relationship between a "present value of $1" table and a "present value of an annuity of $1" table.
16. Explain the relationship between the net present value of cash flows from a proposed investment and the discounted benefit-cost ratio.
17. How does the book value of an asset being abandoned and replaced by a new asset affect the cash flow for purposes of computing the time-adjusted rate of return on investment?
18. An existing asset is to be sold at an amount in excess of its tax basis, and a new replacement asset is to be purchased. Explain how the sale of the old asset would affect the cash flows used in computing the time-adjusted rate of return on the new asset.

MANAGERIAL DISCUSSION QUESTIONS

1. What type of guidelines might management set in analyzing and evaluating proposed capital outlays?
2. What impact does the availability of funds have on management's evaluation of capital investment opportunities?
3. Explain to management the strengths and weaknesses of the payback period method as a means for evaluating capital outlays.
4. The Dayton Company has traditionally used an unadjusted rate of return method for evaluating capital projects. A young accountant recently hired by the company suggests that it should use a time-adjusted rate of return. Explain what is meant by this, and give reasons to support the recommendation.
5. Assume that you work as an accountant at the Hadley Corporation. Management has asked you to recommend the capital outlay evaluation method that you think is most useful. Indicate the one that you recommend, giving reasons to support your answer.
6. The manager of your company states that in evaluating capital expenditure proposals, it does not matter whether one uses the accounting rate of return, the payback period, or the time-adjusted

rate of return methods because the ranking of the proposals will always be the same. Is he correct? Explain.

EXERCISES

EXERCISE 27–1 **Evaluate capital expenditure proposals using the accounting rate of return method. (Obj. 1).** An asset costing $100,000 will have an estimated net salvage value of $10,000 at the end of its 10-year life. It is expected to produce a net cash inflow, before taxes, of $20,000 per year. Straight-line depreciation will be used. The company's income tax rate is 30 percent.
a. Compute the after-tax accounting rate of return on the beginning investment.
b. Compute the after-tax accounting rate of return on the average investment.

EXERCISE 27–2 **Evaluate capital expenditure proposals using the accounting rate of return method. (Obj. 1).** The City Concrete Company is considering the purchase of an additional machine that will cost $120,000. It has an expected useful life of eight years and will have no salvage value. It is estimated that the machine will result in annual cash savings of $20,000. The company uses the straight-line method in computing depreciation. Its income tax rate is 35 percent.
a. Compute the after-tax accounting rate of return on the beginning investment.
b. Compute the after-tax accounting rate of return on the average investment.

EXERCISE 27–3 **Evaluate capital expenditure proposals using the accounting rate of return method. (Obj. 1).** Brookline Corporation is considering purchasing a new machine costing $100,000 to replace an existing machine, which has a book value of $20,000 and has no sales or trade-in value. The old machine has a remaining useful life of eight years. The new machine also has an estimated useful life of eight years and will have no net salvage value at the end of its lifetime. The new machine is expected to produce a net cash inflow, before taxes, of $16,000 per year. The company uses straight-line depreciation for both accounting and tax purposes. The company's income tax rate is 25 percent.
a. Compute the estimated *after-tax* average annual income tax that is applicable to the increased income during the new asset's life.
b. Compute the *after-tax* accounting rate of return on the beginning investment.
c. Compute the *after-tax* accounting rate of return on the average investment.

EXERCISE 27–4 **Evaluate capital expenditure proposals using payback period analysis (additional asset). (Obj. 2).** An asset costing $100,000 will have an estimated net salvage value of $10,000 at the end of its 10-year life. It is expected to produce a net cash inflow, before taxes, of $20,000 per year. Straight-line depreciation will be used. The company's income tax rate is 30 percent. Compute the payback period of the proposed expenditure.

EXERCISE 27-5 **Evaluate capital expenditure proposals using payback period analyses (additional asset). (Obj. 2).** Playtime Clothing Manufacturers is considering the purchase of an additional machine that will cost $120,000. It has an expected useful life of 10 years and will have no salvage value. It is estimated that purchasing the machine will result in annual cash savings of $20,000. The company uses the straight-line method in computing depreciation for both accounting and tax purposes. Its income tax rate is 35 percent. Compute the payback period for the proposed expenditure.

EXERCISE 27-6 **Compute the present value of a capital expenditure using the "present value of $1" table. (Obj. 4).** Clementine Corporation is considering making an investment that will provide a one-time return of $44,000 three years later. If the company wants to earn 10 percent compound interest on its investment, how much should it invest today?

EXERCISE 27-7 **Compute the net present value of a capital expenditure using the "present value of $1" table. (Obj. 4).** Peak Corporation has prepared a schedule of after-tax cash flows expected during an asset's three-year life. The amounts expected are $8,000 in the first year, $12,000 in the second year, and $22,000 in the third year. Using a discount rate of 12 percent, determine the present value of the stream of future cash flows.

EXERCISE 27-8 **Compute the present value of a proposed capital expenditure, using the "present value of an annuity of $1" table. (Obj. 5).** Domino Manufacturing Corporation has prepared a schedule showing expected after-tax net cash flows during each year of life of a proposed capital investment. The analysis shows that the cash flow each year for 10 years from the date of the acquisition of the asset should be $22,000. Assuming that the company has established a desired time-adjusted rate of return of 10 percent after taxes, what is the present value of the $22,000, discounted at 10 percent per year?

EXERCISE 27-9 **Compute the present value of a proposed capital expenditure, using the "present value of an annuity of $1" table. (Obj. 5).** A company has analyzed the expected cash flows from a capital investment and has estimated that the net cash flow after taxes should be $12,000 per year during the asset's 10-year life. The company's desired rate of return is 14 percent. What is the present value of the future cash stream expected from this asset using a 14 percent discounted rate?

EXERCISE 27-10 **Compute the net present value of a capital expenditure. (Obj. 6).** Beacon Light Manufacturing Company has computed the present value of expected after-tax cash flows from a proposed investment in a new machine to be $120,000, reflecting a discount rate of 15 percent. The purchase price of the asset is $78,000. Compute the net present value of the machine.

EXERCISE 27–11   **Compute a discounted benefit-cost index. (Obj. 7).** Midnight Blue Manufacturing Company has computed the present value of after-tax cash flows from a proposed investment in a new machine to be $240,000. The machine's cost is $180,000. Compute the discounted benefit-cost index.

EXERCISE 27–12   **Compute the estimated time-adjusted rate of return (discounted rate of return). (Obj. 8).** Mountain Spring Company is considering a proposal to buy an additional machine. The cost of the machine is $424,350. Annual after-tax cash flows are estimated to be $100,000. The machine has a life of 10 years. Estimate the adjusted rate of return on the proposed investment. (NOTE: You will need to use the annuity table on page 720 to solve this exercise.)

EXERCISE 27–13   **Consider the impact of income taxes in evaluating capital investment proposals. (Obj. 9).**

a. Lucerne Sweets Company is contemplating selling an old asset for $50,000 and purchasing a new one for $400,000. The old asset has a tax basis of $10,000. The company's tax rate is 30 percent. How, if at all, would the sale of the old asset affect the decision to purchase the new asset, assuming that present value of future after-tax cash flow is a major consideration in the decision?

b. Suppose that in a, above, the seller of the new equipment offered to give Lucerne Sweets a trade-in allowance of $70,000 for the old asset, so that Lucerne could purchase the new asset for $330,000. Under the income tax law, no gain or loss is recognized on the trade-in of an asset. The book value (for tax purposes) becomes part of the cost of the new asset. How, if at all, would the trade-in of the old asset affect the decision if the present value of future after-tax net cash flows is a major factor in the decision?

c. Assume the same facts as in a, above, except that the old machine had no value and was to be discarded. Salvage proceeds and removal costs are expected to be the same for the old asset. Present value of future net cash flows is a major factor in the decision. How, if at all, would abandonment of the old asset affect the decision?

PROBLEMS

PROBLEM 27–1A

Evaluate a capital expenditure (additional asset) proposal using the accounting rate of return method. (Obj. 1). The management of the Tornado Company has requested information about a proposal to invest $2,000,000 in a new plant. A study shows that the plant can produce an annual net income of $300,000 before depreciation and before taxes. The plant has an estimated useful life of 20 years with no salvage value. Straight-line depreciation will be used for both accounting and income tax purposes. The company's income tax rate is 25 percent.

INSTRUCTIONS   1. Compute the after-tax accounting rate of return on investment based on the initial investment.

2. Compute the after-tax accounting rate of return on investment based on the average investment.

PROBLEM 27–2A

Evaluate a capital expenditure (replacement asset) proposal using the accounting rate of return method. (Obj. 1). A proposal has been made by the production manager of the Crating Department at Software Inc. to replace a machine that has six more years of useful life with a more efficient model. Straight-line depreciation is used for both accounting and tax purposes. Relevant annual operating costs are shown below.

	Old Machine	**New Machine**
Labor	$72,500	$37,500
Maintenance	17,500	12,500
Power	10,000	13,750
Depreciation	6,250	13,750

The old machine cost $90,000 and has a book value of $37,500. The new machine costs $82,500 and has an estimated useful life of 6 years with no salvage value. The current salvage value of the old equipment is equal to the cost of its removal. The company's income tax rate is 30 percent.

INSTRUCTIONS

1. Compute the additional income tax that would be paid each year if the new asset is acquired.
2. Compute the after-tax accounting rate of return on investment based on the initial investment.
3. Compute the after-tax accounting rate of return on investment based on the average investment.

PROBLEM 27–3A

Evaluate a capital expenditure (additional equipment) proposal using the accounting rate of return method and the payback period method. (Objs. 1, 2). The Sunrise Products Company has an opportunity to expand its production by buying new equipment at a cost of $140,000. The equipment has an estimated useful life of five years, would be depreciated under the straight-line method for both accounting and tax purposes, and is expected to have no salvage value. The equipment would add $50,000 per year in net cash flow before taxes. The company's income tax rate is 30 percent.

INSTRUCTIONS

1. Compute the after-tax accounting rate of return on investment based on the average investment.
2. Compute the payback period.

PROBLEM 27–4A

Evaluate a capital expenditure (replacement asset) proposal using the accounting rate of return method and the payback period method. (Objs. 1, 2). Salem Industries is considering a proposal to replace a machine that has eight more years of useful life with a more efficient model. Straight-line depreciation is used for both accounting and tax purposes. Relevant annual operating costs are shown on the following page.

	Old Machine	New Machine
Labor	$70,000	$47,500
Maintenance	17,500	12,500
Power	10,000	13,000
Depreciation	6,000	12,000

The old machine cost $100,000 and has a book value of $48,000. The new machine costs $96,000 and has an estimated useful life of eight years with no salvage value. The current salvage value of the old equipment is equal to the cost of its removal. The company's income tax rate is 30 percent.

INSTRUCTIONS

1. Compute the additional income tax that would be paid each year if the new asset is acquired.
2. Compute the after-tax accounting rate of return on investment based on the average investment.
3. Compute the payback period of the proposed new asset.

PROBLEM 27–5A **Compute the present value of a proposed capital expenditure (additional asset), using the "present value of $1" table. (Obj. 4).** Global Inc. is analyzing a proposal to acquire an additional asset that will cost $2,000,000 and will be used for a period of four years. After that time, the asset will have no salvage value. Estimated increased cash flows, before income taxes, from the use of the asset are estimated to be:

Year 1	$600,000
Year 2	700,000
Year 3	900,000
Year 4	600,000

Straight-line depreciation is used for both accounting and tax purposes. The company's tax rate is 34 percent.

INSTRUCTIONS

Compute the present value of the asset's after-tax cash flows, using the corporation's minimum after-tax rate of return of 14 percent. (Use the "present value of $1" table on page 718.)

PROBLEM 27–6A **Compute the payback period, the present value, and the net present value of a proposed capital expenditure (replacement asset) using a "present value of an annuity of $1" table. (Objs. 5, 6, 7).** (Note that the same data were given for Problem 27–2A.) A proposal has been made by the production manager of the Crating Department at Software Inc. to replace a machine that has six more years of useful life with a more efficient model. Straight-line depreciation is used for both accounting and tax purposes. Relevant annual operating costs are shown below.

	Old Machine	New Machine
Labor	$72,500	$37,500
Maintenance	17,500	12,500
Power	10,000	13,750
Depreciation	6,250	13,750

The old machine cost $90,000 and has a book value of $37,500. The new machine costs $82,500 and has an estimated useful life of six years with no salvage value. The current salvage value of the old equipment is equal to the cost of its removal. The company's income tax rate is 30 percent.

INSTRUCTIONS
1. Compute the payback period of the investment.
2. Compute the present value of the proposed capital expenditure, using a "present value of an annuity of $1" table and a 16 percent discount rate.
3. Compute the net present value of the proposed capital expenditures, using the present value you computed in Instruction 2.

PROBLEM 27–7A **Compute the payback period, the present value of proposed capital expenditures, the net present value of capital expenditures, and the discounted benefit-cost index; estimate the discounted rate of return from future cash flows. (Objs. 2, 5, 6, 7, 8).** Information about three proposed capital expenditures being considered by Daybreak Corporation is given below.

	Proposal A	Proposal B	Proposal C
Investment Required	$300,000	$1,600,000	$1,600,000
Annual After-Tax Cash Flow	$ 50,000	$ 300,000	$ 385,000
Useful Life in Years	14	25	10

INSTRUCTIONS
1. Calculate the payback period for each proposal. Round your answer to 1 decimal place. Rank the proposals in order by payback period.
2. Compute the present value of each proposal, using the company's minimum time-adjusted rate of return of 16 percent.
3. Compute the net present value of each project. Rank the projects on the basis of net present value.
4. Compute the discounted benefit-cost ratio for each project. Rank the proposals in order, based on the discounted benefit-cost index.
5. Estimate the time-adjusted rate of return for each proposal. Round calculations to the nearest one-hundredth of 1 percent. Rank the proposals in order on the basis of the time-adjusted rate of return.

ALTERNATE PROBLEMS

PROBLEM 27–1B **Evaluate a capital expenditure (additional asset) proposal using the accounting rate of return method. (Obj. 1).** The management of the New China Company is considering investing $720,000 in a new machine. A study shows that the machine can produce an annual net income of $200,000 before depreciation and before taxes. The machine has an estimated useful life of eight years with no salvage value. Straight-line depreciation will be used for both accounting and income tax purposes. The company's income tax rate is 30 percent.

INSTRUCTIONS
1. Compute the after-tax accounting rate of return on investment based on the initial investment.

2. Compute the after-tax accounting rate of return on investment based on the average investment.

PROBLEM 27–2B

Evaluate a capital expenditure (replacement asset) proposal using the accounting rate of return method. (Obj. 1). A proposal has been made by the manager of the Finishing Department at New Designs Inc. to replace a machine that has eight more years of useful life with a more efficient model. Straight-line depreciation is used for both accounting and tax purposes. Relevant annual operating costs are shown below.

	Old Machine	New Machine
Labor	$29,000	$15,000
Maintenance	7,000	5,000
Power	4,000	5,500
Depreciation	2,500	5,000

The old machine cost $50,000 and has a book value of $20,000. The new machine costs $40,000 and has an estimated useful life of eight years with no salvage value. The current salvage value of the old equipment is equal to the cost of its removal. The company's tax rate is 25 percent.

INSTRUCTIONS

1. Compute the additional income tax that would be paid each year if the new asset is acquired.
2. Compute the after-tax accounting rate of return on investment based on the initial investment. Carry calculations to nearest one-tenth of a percent.
3. Compute the after-tax accounting rate of return on investment based on the average investment. Carry calculations to nearest one-tenth of a percent.

PROBLEM 27–3B

Evaluate a capital expenditure (additional equipment) proposal using the accounting rate of return method and payback period method. (Objs. 1, 2). The Eastern Products Company has an opportunity to expand its production by buying new equipment at a cost of $520,000. The equipment has an estimated useful life of six years, would be depreciated under the straight-line method for both accounting and tax purposes, and is expected to have no salvage value. The equipment would add $140,000 per year in net cash flow before taxes. The company's income tax rate is 30 percent.

INSTRUCTIONS

1. Compute the additional income tax that would be paid each year if the new asset is acquired. (Round to the nearest whole dollar.)
2. Compute the after-tax accounting rate of return on investment based on the average investment.
3. Compute the payback period.

PROBLEM 27–4B

Evaluate a capital expenditure (replacement asset) proposal using the accounting rate of return method and the payback period method. (Objs. 1, 2). Toledo Industries is considering a proposal to replace a machine that has eight more years of useful life with a more efficient model. Straight-line depreciation is used for both accounting and tax purposes. Relevant annual operating costs are shown below.

	Old Machine	New Machine
Labor	$82,000	$61,500
Maintenance	18,500	13,500
Power	12,000	14,000
Depreciation	7,500	12,500

The old machine cost $120,000 and has a book value of $60,000. The new machine costs $100,000 and has an estimated useful life of eight years with no salvage value. The current salvage value of the old equipment is equal to the cost of its removal. The company's income tax rate is 30 percent.

INSTRUCTIONS

1. Compute the additional income tax that would be paid each year if the new asset is acquired.
2. Compute the after-tax accounting rate of return on investment based on the average investment.
3. Compute the payback period of the proposed new asset.

PROBLEM 27–5B   **Compute the present value of a proposed capital expenditure (additional asset), using the "present value of $1" table.   (Obj. 4).** Dakota Inc. is analyzing a proposal to acquire an additional asset that will cost $600,000 and will be used for a period of five years. After that time, the asset will have no salvage value. Estimated increased cash flows, before income taxes, from the use of the asset, are estimated to be:

Year 1	$125,000
Year 2	250,000
Year 3	280,000
Year 4	280,000
Year 5	$125,000

Straight-line depreciation is used for both accounting and tax purposes. The company's tax rate is 30 percent.

INSTRUCTIONS   Compute the present value of the asset's after-tax cash flows, using the corporation's minimum after-tax rate of return of 16 percent. (Use the "present value of $1" table on page 720. Round computations to the nearest whole dollar.)

PROBLEM 27–6B   **Compute the payback period, the present value, and the net present value of a proposed capital expenditure (replacement asset) using a "present value of an annuity of $1" table.   (Objs. 2, 5, 6).**   (Note that the same data were given for Problem 27–2B.) A proposal has been made by the manager of the Finishing Department at New Designs Inc. to replace a machine that has eight more years of useful life with a more efficient model. Straight-line depreciation is used for both accounting and tax purposes. Relevant annual operating costs are shown on the following page.

	Old Machine	New Machine
Labor	$29,000	$15,000
Maintenance	7,000	5,000
Power	4,000	5,500
Depreciation	2,500	5,000

The old machine cost $50,000 and has a book value of $20,000. The new machine costs $40,000 and has an estimated useful life of eight years with no salvage value. The current salvage value of the old equipment is equal to the cost of its removal. The company's tax rate is 25 percent.

INSTRUCTIONS
1. Compute the payback period of the investment.
2. Compute the present value of the proposed capital expenditure, using a "present value of an annuity of $1" table and a discount rate of 10 percent.
3. Compute the net present value of the proposed capital expenditures, using the present value you computed in Instruction 2.

PROBLEM 27–7B **Compute the payback period, the present value of proposed capital expenditures, the net present value of capital expenditures, and the discounted benefit-cost index; estimate the discounted rate of return from future cash flows. (Objs. 2, 5, 6, 7, 8).** Thomasa Corporation is considering three proposed capital expenditures. Information about the proposals is given below.

	Proposal A	Proposal B	Proposal C
Investment Required	$250,000	$779,000	$924,000
Annual After-Tax Cash Flow	$ 48,000	$160,000	$154,000
Useful Life in Years	10	25	14

INSTRUCTIONS
1. Calculate the payback period for each proposal. Round your answer to 1 decimal place. Rank the proposals in order by payback period.
2. Compute the present value of each proposal, using the company's minimum time-adjusted rate of return of 14 percent.
3. Compute the net present value of each project. Rank the projects on the basis of net present value.
4. Compute the discounted benefit-cost ratio for each project. Rank the proposals in order, based on the discounted benefit-cost index.
5. Estimate the time-adjusted rate of return for each proposal. Round calculations to the nearest one-hundredth of 1 percent. Rank the proposals in order on the basis of the time-adjusted rate of return.

MANAGERIAL DECISION CASE

The Kuehn Company is considering the purchase of a machine at a cost of $800,000 to manufacture a new product. The machine has an estimated useful life of eight years and no salvage value. It is expected that the machine will produce from 80,000 to 100,000 units of the product per year and that all units will be sold at $10 each. Costs other than those related to the machine are as follows:

Per Unit

Materials	$5
Labor	1
Variable overhead	1

The machine would occupy space that now stands empty and has no intended use. Fixed costs allocated to the space are $12,000 per year. The following costs are related to the machine. (The company uses straight-line depreciation for both accounting and tax purposes.) The company's income tax rate is 30 percent.

Taxes (Property)	$ 8,000 per year
Insurance	8,000 per year
Repairs and maintenance	4,000 per year
Power	20 cents per unit produced
Miscellaneous	$ 4,000 per year

According to its policy, the company does not make capital investments that have a less than 12 percent per year time-adjusted rate of return.

INSTRUCTIONS Write a memorandum to management stating whether the company should purchase the machine and produce the new product. In reaching your decision, use the following analytical methods presented in this chapter. Show all calculations.

1. After-tax accounting rate of return on initial and average investment
2. Payback period
3. Present value of after-tax cash flows at 12 percent.
4. Net present value of future after-tax cash flows, using a 12 percent discount rate
5. Discounted benefit-cost analysis
6. Time-adjusted rate of return on investment

Glossary

Adjusted sales value basis (p. 454) The adjusted sales price is the ultimate selling price of the total units of the product, less the additional costs that must be incurred after split-off to complete the product (and less the estimated selling expenses if they vary widely between products.)

Abnormal lost units (p. 370) Units of product that are lost as the result of unusual conditions and not as a result of normal recurring events.

Abnormal spoilage (p. 370) Units of product that are spoiled in the manufacturing process as the result of unusual nonrecurring events. These units cannot be reworked into finished goods.

Absorption costing (p. 600) A cost accounting concept under which all manufacturing costs, both direct and indirect, are assigned to the cost of goods manufactured.

Accounting rate of return on investment (p. 709) The average rate (percentage) of profit as computed under accounting principles on a proposed investment.

Analysis of semimonthly factory payroll (p. 145) A schedule summarizing the labor costs incurred by employees who are on a fixed monthly salary. These costs are considered indirect labor.

Analysis of time tickets (p. 143) A schedule that summarizes for a specific time period the time tickets prepared by employees. The analysis shows the direct labor costs incurred on each job by department and the indirect labor for each department.

Assigned weights basis (p. 454) A basis for assigning joint costs to the products that involves the assigning of weights (usually expressed as percentages or a multiplying factor) to each unit of each product.

Average cost method for work in process (p. 343) Combines each element of cost in the beginning inventory of work in process with the cost incurred in the current period for that element.

Average cost per unit (p. 289) The average cost per unit of product transferred out of a department. It is found by dividing the total costs of units transferred by the number of units transferred.

Basis (p. 191) A factor that has a measurable relationship to overhead costs.

Bill of materials (p. 57) A form that lists all the materials required for a job and the date the materials will be needed.

Bin tag (p. 72) An informal record of the quantities of a material received, issued, and on hand which is attached to the material at its storage location.

Blind copy (p. 52) A copy of the purchase order that does not indicate the quantity of merchandise ordered. The blind copy is usually sent to the receiving clerk.

Break-even chart (p. 610) A chart containing two graphs. One shows the total sales volume and the other shows total costs at all sales volumes (expressed either in units or in dollar volume).

Break-even point (p. 608) That sales volume at which total sales exactly equals total cost, so that there is neither a profit nor a loss.

Budget (p. 10, 510) The overall financial plan for company's future activities.

Budget variance (p. 568) The difference between (a) the actual costs incurred and (b) the overhead in the flexible budget for the standard hours allowed for the units produced.

Budgetary control system (p. 510) A system for comparing actual results with budgeted goals.

By-product (p. 380, 428) A product of little value that is produced in conjunction with the production of a main product of relatively high value.

Capacity variance (p. 568) Another name sometimes used for volume variance (see volume variance).

Capital assets (p. 705) Productive assets such as machinery, equipment, buildings, and land that have a life of more than one year.

Capital expenditures (p. 705) Costs incurred to purchase capital assets.

Combined cost of production report (p. 354) A single report in which the cost of production report for each producing department is included.

Common costs (p. 428) Costs incurred in manufacturing two or more products up to the point of separation of the products (as used in Chapter 18).

Common physical unit allocation basis (p. 454) Joint costs are frequently allocated on the basis of some physical measure, such as gallons, pound or liters, that is common to the two products.

Completed jobs journal (p. 230). A special journal that is used to record jobs that are completed and have been transferred from work in process to finished goods.

Continuous or Cycle Inventory Method (p. 109) A method of determining the physical inventory count in which materials are counted on a continuous or revolving basis throughout the year.

Contribution (p. 661) The excess of net sales over controllable expenses.

Contribution margin (p. 604) The excess of sales over total of all variable costs—including variable costs in cost of goods sold, variable selling expenses and variable general and administrative expenses.

Contribution margin ratio (p. 608) It is the percentage of sales remaining out of each sales dollar after variable costs have been covered.

Control (p. 510) The means by which management is assured that all parts of the company function properly and that the objectives identified in the planning stage are attained.

Controllable costs (p. 518, 630) Costs over which the departmental manager or supervisor to whose department the costs are charged can exercise some degree of control.

Controllable variance (p. 568) The difference between (a) the actual costs incurred and (b) the overhead in the flexible budget for the standard hours allowed for the units produced.

Conversion cost (p. 8) The sum of direct labor and manufacturing overhead.

Co-products (p. 428) When two or more products, both of relatively high value, result from a manufacturing process. Co-products are usually referred to as *joint products.*

Cost accountant (p. 12) An accountant who specializes in analyzing the cost recording and reporting needs of a business.

Cost behavior (p. 485) The manner in which costs change as the volume (measured in units of output, direct labor hours, or some other factor) changes.

Cost centers (p. 676) Organizational or functional units for which costs are accumulated.

Cost of goods manufactured budget (p. 513) Usually called the *manufacturing costs budget,* this budget shows the costs budgeted for materials, labor, and manufacturing overhead for the production level anticipated.

Cost of production report (p. 296, 315) A monthly report for each department showing the quantity of products to be accounted for in that department, the quantity of products accounted for, the costs to be accounted for (costs in prior departments, materials, labor and overhead), and the costs actually accounted for (costs of products transferred out of the department and the costs related to products still in process at the end of the month).

Cost or market, whichever is lower, rule (p. 101) A method of valuing inventory in which inventory is valued at either its original cost or its replacement cost, whichever is lower.

Cost standard (p. 514) The costs that should be used under efficient operating conditions.

Cost-volume-profit analysis (p. 600) An analysis of how profits change as costs change in response to changes in production or sales volume.

Credit memorandum (p. 59) A form sent to the supplier indicating that more materials were received than had been ordered.

Cutoff date (p. 108) The date, usually the last day of the company's fiscal year, used to determine if materials costs have been assigned to the appropriate accounting period.

Debit memorandum (p. 58) Notice to a vendor of a deduction from an invoice for the cost of returned materials.

Defective units (p. 370) Units of product that are damaged in the manufacturing process but that can be reprocessed or reworked to make into good finished products.

Defective goods (p. 276) Units of production that fail to meet production standards but that can be brought up to standard with additional work.

Departmental overhead analysis sheet (p. 74) A subsidiary ledger account with columns to record the overhead costs chargeable to a department.

Departmental work in process accounts (p. 245) The work in process account maintained for costs incurred in each producing department.

Differential cost (p. 630) The difference in cost between one alternative and another.

Differential revenues (p. 631) The term used to describe the difference in revenues that will result from choosing one course of action over another.

Direct costing (p. 601) A system under which only those costs that are so closely associated with the product that they vary proportionally with the volume of production are assigned as product costs.

Direct estimate method (p. 495) A method by which operating managers use whatever data are available, plus their knowledge of plans and methods and their experience to reach a conclusion as to what fixed and variable costs should be.

Direct labor (p. 7) Costs attributable to factory employees who work directly on the product being manufactured.

Direct materials (p. 5) Items that go into a product and become a significant part of it.

Discounted benefit-cost index (p. 721) The ratio of the present value of a project to the amount of initial investment in the project.

Discounted rate of return (p. 721) This discount rate will yield a present value equal to the capital expenditure required to acquire the asset when applied to the annual cash flow. It is sometimes called the *time-adjusted rate of return.*

Discretionary costs (p. 666) Costs that can be changed at the discretion of management.

Distribution functions (p. 656) The activities after the point of production in getting goods sold and delivered to ultimate consumers.

Distribution memorandum (p. 169) A form that indicates how the total cost of an invoice is to be distributed to individual accounts.

Economic Order Quantity (EOQ) (p. 48) A formula that computes the most advantageous number of units to order.

Efficiency variance (p. 572) The difference between budgeted overhead for the *standard* hours allowed for the units produced and the budgeted costs for the **actual hours** worked.

Engineering analysis method (p. 489) A method that uses engineering specifications and analyses to determine what costs should be.

Equivalent expanded units (p. 382) The equivalent production in a department when the number of units has been increased in the production process. The total units, including the increase, are included in the computation of equivalent units.

Equivalent good units (p. 372) The equivalent production, disregarding spoiled or lost units of product.

Equivalent units of production (p. 316) The number of units of product that could have been completed had all costs of a production element (materials, labor or overhead) been used in starting and completing units of products, and there had been no ending inventory of work in process.

Federal Unemployment Insurance Tax (FUTA tax) (p. 150) A tax levied by the federal govern-

ment against employers to benefit unemployed workers.

Finished goods inventory account (p. 9) The account that shows the cost of products that have been completed and are ready for sale.

Finished goods ledger (p. 232) A subsidiary ledger consisting of stock ledger cards for each item that a company manufactures for stock. The total of the balances on all the stock ledger cards must equal the balance in the Finished Goods control account in the general ledger.

First in, first out (FIFO) method (p. 97, 401) A method of inventory valuation that assumes the oldest items are sold first.

First in, first out method for costing (p. 343) A method under which costs of goods started and finished this period are computed separately from units that were in beginning work in process. Costs of beginning inventory of work in process and additional costs incurred on those units are considered to be the costs of the first units transferred out. All other goods transferred out are costed at the average cost per equivalent unit for costs incurred during this period.

Fixed budget (p. 513) A budget based on a single level of expected sales and production.

Fixed costs (p. 170, 217 485) Manufacturing overhead costs that do not vary substantially with changes in volume.

Fixed overhead spending variance (p. 574) The difference between the **actual** fixed costs incurred and the budgeted fixed overhead for the **actual hours worked.**

Flexible budget (p. 514) A budget showing the costs expected to be incurred at various levels of output.

Four-variance analysis method (p. 574) A procedure that divides the total overhead variance for the period into a volume variance, an efficiency variance, a fixed overhead spending variance and a variable overhead spending variance.

Fringe benefits (p. 154) Compensation (other than wages) for employees including vacation and holiday pay and pension and insurance plan contributions.

High-low points method (p. 492) A method for estimating the fixed and variable costs of an activity.

Idle time (p. 142) Nonproductive work time of an employee. Usually charged to manufacturing overhead, but in some circumstances charged to specific jobs.

Incremental cost (p. 630) An increase in cost from one alternative to another.

Indirect labor (p. 7) Costs attributable to factory employees who support production but are not directly involved in the manufacture of a product.

Indirect materials (p. 7) Materials used in manufacturing a product that cannot easily be allocated to specific products. Also includes factory supplies.

Individual earnings record (p. 130) A record of each employee's earnings and deductions posted from the payroll register.

Interpolation (p. 726) The insertion of a number between two other numbers, based on an estimation or calculation of the value of the number being inserted.

Invoice (p. 53) Form received from the supplier indicating the type and quantity of materials ordered, unit price and total amount due, and the credit terms.

Job cost sheet (p. 74) A form on which all the costs—materials, direct labor, and overhead—charged to a specific job are recorded.

Job order cost system (p. 11) A cost accounting system in which costs are accumulated according to specific job orders.

Joint costs (p. 428) Costs incurred prior to the point of separation of the products that apply to two or more products resulting from a single manufacturing process.

Joint products (p. 428, 453) Two or more products, each of significant value, that are produced together and simultaneously in the production process before they are physically separated to become two clear and distinct products.

Just-in-Time (JIT) concept (p. 114) An inventory system in which raw materials are delivered just in time to be placed into production.

Labor efficiency variance (p. 549) A measure of the efficiency of labor. It is the difference between the cost of actual hours worked, based on the standard rate per hour, with the cost of standard hours allowed for the number of units produced, based on the standard rate per hour. (Also called *labor time variance* and *labor usage variance*.)

Labor price rate variance (p. 550) The labor rate variance compares the actual labor costs incurred with what the costs would have been for the hours actually worked if the rate per hour had been the standard rate.

Labor time variance (p. 549) Another name given *labor efficiency variance*. See definition of *labor efficiency variance*.

Labor usage variance (p. 549) Another name given to *labor efficiency variance*.

Last in, first out (LIFO) method (p. 97) A method of inventory valuation that assumes that the most recently purchased items are sold first.

Lead time (p. 48) The amount of time it takes for materials to be received from a supplier.

Least squares method (p. 493) A statistical method for estimating fixed and variable costs.

Line of best fit (p. 493) A straight line drawn through a series of points reflecting cost volume data for a number of periods. The line best represents the relationship between volume and cost at various volumes of output.

Lost units (p. 370) Units of product that either disappear in the manufacturing process (as the result of evaporation, condensation, etc.) or are spoiled in the manufacturing process to the extent that they cannot be converted into finished products.

Lost-unit cost (p. 377) It is the difference in the per-unit prior department unit cost if there had been no lost units and the per-unit cost prior-department costs were based on good units only.

Main product (p. 428) A product of relatively high value compared to other products produced as part of a single production process.

Management by exception (p. 523) A theory that management should focus its attention on things that are not going according to plan.

Manufacturing (p. 4) The process of converting raw materials into finished products by using labor and incurring additional costs, called overhead.

Manufacturing overhead (p. 7) All manufacturing costs that are not classified as direct materials or direct labor.

Manufacturing cost budget (p. 513) This budget shows the costs budgeted to be incurred for materials, labor, and manufacturing overhead for the production level anticipated.

Manufacturing overhead applied journal (p. 208) A special journal in which manufacturing overhead applied to individual jobs is recorded.

Market price (p. 101) The replacement cost/current cost of replacing an item of inventory. It is the price at which the materials could be bought at the inventory date.

Market value at point of separation method (p. 438) Under the normal market value at point of separation method, an amount equal to the estimated market value of the by-product at the point at which it is separated from the main product, is removed from the work in process account, and assigned to the by-product inventory.

Master budget (p. 510) A budget encompassing the entire financial plan of the company.

Materials budget (p. 515) A budget indicating the materials to be purchased and the materials to be used for the period.

Materials ledger (p. 53) Subsidiary ledger that contains a detailed record for each type of raw materials.

Materials ledger card (p. 53) A record maintained to show the receipts, issues, and balance on hand of a particular raw material.

Materials price standard (p. 543) The price that should be paid for a unit of materials.

Materials price variance (p. 545) The difference between the cost of the actual quantity of raw materials used at the standard unit price and the cost of the actual quantity of materials used at the actual unit price.

Materials purchases budget (p. 515) A budget showing the quantities and costs of materials that must be purchased during the period. It reflects materials to be used in production and materials inventory changes.

Materials quantity standard (p. 542) The amount of material that should be consumed in manufacturing a unit of product.

Materials quantity variance (p. 545) The difference between standard cost of the materials in production for the period and what the standard cost of materials for the materials actually used would have been.

Materials requisition (p. 72) A form prepared by the department head or job supervisor and sent to the storeroom indicating the materials needed for a particular job or a particular department.

Materials requisition journal (p. 74, 295) A special journal which is used to record materials returned to the storeroom as indicated on returned materials reports.

Materials usage budget (p. 515) A budget showing the quantities and costs of materials budgeted to be used in production during the period.

Materials usage variance (Chapter 22) Another name given to the materials quantity variance.

Medicare tax (p. 128) A tax levied on employees and employers to provide medical benefits for elderly persons.

Modified accelerated cost recovery system (MACRs) (p. 708) A depreciation system allowed under federal income tax laws. It permits large depreciation deductions in the early years of an asset's life and permits depreciating costs over a number of years that may be less than actual economic life.

Moving average method (p. 97) A method of inventory valuation using a moving average cost to value items issued and items in the ending inventory. A new average is computed after each new purchase is received.

Net present value (p. 720) The amount by which the total present value of expected net future cash inflows exceeds the investment outlay.

Noncontrollable costs (p. 518, 630) Costs that are not within the scope of influence or control of the manager or supervisor to whom the costs are charged.

Nonmeasurable data (p. 631) Data that cannot be quantified.

Normal capacity (p. 562) The average expected volume over a period of two to five future years.

Normal lost units (p. 370) Those quantities of product that result from recurring, normal events, activities, and conditions, and are expected as part of the regular manufacturing process. They can be predicted with reasonable accuracy.

Normal net profit method (p. 434) A value equal to the expected selling price, less (1) additional cost to process the by-product, (2) estimated selling and administrative expenses, and (3) a normal net profit margin, is assigned to the by-product and removed from the cost of the main product.

Normal spoiled units or **normal spoilage (p. 370)** Units of product that are spoiled and cannot be completed as finished products, resulting from normal processing conditions.

Normal standards (p. 540) Goals that can be met under reasonable efficient operating conditions.

Operating budget (p. 510) The budget that provides the basic plan for operations during the period. (Also known as the master budget.)

Opportunity costs (p. 630) Earnings or potential benefits foregone because a certain course of action is taken.

Overapplied overhead (p. 33, 210) A credit balance in the manufacturing overhead account. This balance means that more overhead was applied than was actually incurred.

Overhead application rate (p. 191) The ratio between total overhead costs and the basis.

Overtime compensation (p. 127) Additional compensation paid to employees for time worked in excess of 40 hours in any one work week, usually paid at the rate of one and one-half times the employee's regular rate.

Overtime premium (p. 127) The extra amount paid when an employee worked more than 40 hours in one work week.

Payback period (p. 713) The number of years that will be required for the after-tax net cash flows each year will be equal to the initial net investment.

Payroll register (p. 126) A record of payroll information for each employee for a particular pay period.

Performance report (p. 523) A report comparing actual results with budget allowances for the work done during the period with the actual costs for the period.

Period costs (p. 601) Costs that are deemed to be deductible against revenues in the period in which the costs are incurred. Period costs are not added to the cost of goods manufactured.

Planning (p. 510) Involves identifying objectives and determining the steps for achieving these objectives.

Present value of a future amount (p. 713) The amount that would be invested today in order to receive a specified amount at a specified time and in order to earn a specified interest rate on the investment.

Present value of an annuity (720) The amount that would be invested today in order to receive a specified number of identical cash payments, paid at specified intervals, and in order to earn a specified rate on the investment.

Prime cost (p. 8) The sum of direct materials and direct labor.

Process cost accounting (p. 288) A method of accounting in which costs are accumulated for each producing department or each process.

Process cost system (p. 11, 288) A cost accounting system in which costs are accumulated without regard to specific units of product.

Procurement (p. 22) The first step in the cost cycle in which materials, labor, and other services are obtained for use in the production of the company's products.

Production (p. 22) The step in the cost cycle in which materials, labor, and other services are used to make the company's products.

Production budget (p. 512) A budget showing the units budgeted to be produced during the period.

Production department (p. 24) A factory department that engages in work directly related to making the company's products.

Production report (p. 296) A monthly report summarizing the number of units of products started production, the number of units completed and transferred out, the number of units in process at the end of the month and the stage of completion of the units in process at the end of the month.

Profit centers (p. 676) Accounting units to which both revenues and costs are assigned.

Purchase order (p. 50) A form that represents authorization for the suppliers to ship specified materials to the company.

Purchase requisition (p. 50) A form sent to the purchasing agent or purchasing department requesting that certain materials be ordered.

Purchasing agent (p. 47) The person responsible for the purchasing of materials needed by the company.

Raw Materials Inventory account (p. 8) The account that shows the cost of raw materials and factory supplies that will be used in the manufacturing process.

Receiving report (p. 52) A form prepared by the receiving clerk indicating the type, quantity, and condition of materials received from a supplier.

Relative sales value allocation basis (p. 454) An allocation method that assigns joint costs to the joint products on the basis of the relative total sales values of the joint products produced during the period.

Relevant costs (p. 629) Costs that will be used in arriving at a decision in the problem at hand.

Return shipping order (p. 78) A form prepared by the purchasing unit and sent to the storeroom authorizing the return of materials to the supplier.

Returned materials journal (p. 77) A special journal that is used to record materials returned to the storeroom as indicated on returned materials reports.

Returned material report (p. 76) A form accompanying materials that have been issued and now are being returned to the storeroom.

Reorder point (p. 48) The minimum level of material that should be on hand as well as other factors determines when an order should be placed to purchase additional items.

Reversal cost method (p. 434) Another name given the *normal net profit method* for assigning an invnetory value to by-products.

Rework costs (p. 276) The costs required to bring defective goods up to standard.

Safety stock (p. 48) The minimum level of material that should be on hand to ensure that the company does not run out of the material.

Sales budget (p. 510) A written plan containing detailed estimates of products or groups of products expected to be sold during the budget period.

Sales journal (p. 233) A special journal that is used to record the sales of finished goods and the related cost of each sale.

Scattergraph method (p. 491) A method for estimating fixed and variable components of cost.

Schedule of departmental overhead costs (p. 171) A multi-column listing of total monthly overhead costs classified by department and by type of cost.

Schedule of monthly fixed overhead costs (p. 170) A multi-column listing of all fixed overhead charges for the month classified by department and by type of charge.

Scrap (p. 267) The residue of manufacturing processes.

Scrap report (p. 268) A report giving a description and quantity of scrap being moved from the factory to storage.

Seconds (p. 271) Goods with slight defects that are sold at a discount.

Selling (p. 22) The final step in the cost cycle, in which merchandise is sold and shipped to customers.

Semivariable costs (p. 487) Costs that vary in some degree with volume but not in direct proportion to it.

Service businesses (p. 676) Organizations that offer and provide services rather than physical products.

Service Department (p. 24) A factory department that provides support services to the production departments.

Social security tax (p. 127) A tax levied on employees and employers to provide retirement benefits.

Spending variance (p. 217, 572) A variance that compares the amount of actual overhead expenditures with the amount that should have been spent based on the number of hours worked.

Split-off point (p. 454) That point in the production process at which the joint products are separated and are no longer produced together in a manufacturing process.

Spoiled goods (p. 270) Goods that have been damaged in the manufacturing process and do not meet quality standards or specifications required for sale.

Spoiled goods report (p. 271) A report listing the quantity and dollar value of spoiled goods.

Spoiled units (p. 370) Units of product that have been damaged or improperly manufactured and do not meet quality standards.

Stair-step costs (p. 488) Costs that are basically fixed within a narrow range, but show abrupt and distinct increases when volume increases to certain levels.

Standard (p. 514) The amount of material, labor, or other cost element that is normally used under efficient operating conditions.

Standard cost sheet (p. 539) A form on which the standard cost of labor, materials, and overhead for each unit of product, along with supporting details are shown.

Standard manufacturing costs (p. 538) Predetermined measures of the expected cost of each manufacturing element under specified efficient operating conditions.

State Unemployment insurance tax (SUTA tax) (p. 151) A tax levied by a state government against employers to benefit unemployed workers.

Statement of cost of goods manufactured (p. 3) A financial statement used in a manufacturing business that shows details of how the cost of the goods manufactured during the fiscal period was calculated.

Summary of factory wages (p. 147) A monthly schedule that combines the data from the Analyses of Time Tickets and Analyses of Semimonthly Payroll prepared during the month.

Sunk cost (p. 630) A historical cost that has been incurred and thus is irrelevant for decision-making purposes.

Survey method (p. 454) Products are assigned weights based on the knowledge of engineers, production managers, cost accountants, and others.

Tax shield (p. 725) The tax reduction resulting from deduction of a non-cash expenditure of loss.

Theoretical standards (p. 540) Goals that could be attained only by achieving perfection.

Three-variance analysis method (p. 572) A procedure for analyzing the total overhead variance into a volume variance (computed in the same way as under the two-variance method), a spending variance, and an efficiency variance.

Time adjusted rate of return (p. 721) A procedure for computing the discount rate. It is sometimes called the *discounted rate of return*.

Time card (p. 126) A record of the time worked by an individual employee.

Timekeeping (p. 126) The procedure for keeping records of the time worked by each employee.

Time ticket (p. 141) An employee-generated record that reports the individual jobs worked on by the employee, the departments in which the work was done, the type of work performed, and the amount of time spent on each job and each task.

Two-variance analysis method (p. 568) A procedure that separates the total variance for a department into two components; the *budget variance* and the *volume variance.*

Underapplied overhead (p. 33, 210) Underapplied overhead occurs when less overhead is charged to production than was actually incurred. The departmental manufacturing overhead account will have a debit balance.

Variable costing (p. 601) A name commonly given to *direct costing* and under which only variable manufacturing costs are treated as product costs. All fixed costs are charged to expense in the period in which they are incurred or used.

Variable costs (p. 217, 485) Manufacturing costs that vary in total in direct proportion to changes in volume or level of activity. The costs per unit of output remains constant.

Variable overhead spending variance (p. 574) The difference between the **actual** variable overhead costs incurred and the budget allowance for variable overhead based on the actual hours worked.

Variance (p. 542) The difference between the standard amount of an item and the actual amount of that item.

Variance analysis (p. 568) The analysis of the total variance in each department that divides the total variance into its component parts.

Volume variance (p. 217, 568) (1) A variance that compares the amount of fixed overhead based on the actual hours worked with the amount of fixed overhead budgeted. (2) The difference between the standard cost of the units produced during the period (or the standard cost per hour multiplied by the standard hours allowed for the units produced) and the flexible budget for the standard hours allowed for units.

Voucher register (p. 54) A special journal in which unpaid vouchers are recorded. A voucher is recorded in this journal as a debit to Raw Materials and a credit to Vouchers Payable.

Warehousing (p. 22) The step in the cost cycle in which finished goods are moved from the factory to the warehouse for storage until they are sold.

Work in process inventory account (p. 8) The account that shows the cost of raw materials, direct labor, and manufacturing overhead assigned to products on which manufacturing has begun but has not been completed at the end of the fiscal period.

Index